Case Studies in Abnormal Psychology

Fourth Edition

Thomas F. Oltmanns
University of Virginia

John M. Neale
State University of New York at Stony Brook

Gerald C. Davison
University of Southern California

John Wiley & Sons, Inc.
New York   Chichester   Brisbane   Toronto   Singapore

ACQUISITIONS EDITOR: *Karen Dubno*
MARKETING MANAGER: *Catherine Faduska*
SENIOR PRODUCTION EDITOR: *Suzanne Magida*
COVER DESIGN: *Harold Nolan*
MANUFACTURING MANAGER: *Susan Stetzer*

This book was set in 10/12 Times Roman by Digitype and
printed and bound by Courier Stoughton. The cover was printed by NEBC

Recognizing the importance of preserving what has been written, it is a
policy of John Wiley & Sons, Inc. to have books of enduring value published
in the United States printed on acid-free paper, and we exert our best
efforts to that end.

The paper on this book was manufactured by a mill whose forest management programs include
sustained yield harvesting of its timberlands. Sustained yield harvesting principles ensure that
the number of trees cut each year does not exceed the amount of new growth.

Library of Congress Cataloging in Publication Data:

Oltmanns, Thomas F.
    Case studies in abnormal psychology / Thomas F. Oltmanns, John M.
Neale, Gerald C. Davison. — 4th ed.
        p.   cm.
    Includes bibliographical references.
    ISBN 0-471-00581-9 (pbk.)
    1. Psychology, Pathological—Case studies. 2. Psychiatry—Case
studies. I. Neale, John M., 1943–   . II. Davison, Gerald C.
III. Title.
RC465.047   1995
616.89'09—dc20   94-42723
                                                                                CIP

Printed in the United States of America

10 9 8 7 6 5

PREFACE

Most textbooks on abnormal psychology include short descriptions of actual clinical cases. However, these presentations are necessarily brief and too fragmented for students to gain a clear understanding of the idiographic complexities of a person's troubled life. They cannot describe the client's developmental history, the manner in which a therapist might conceptualize the problem, or the formulation and implementation of a treatment plan. In contrast to such brief descriptions, a detailed case study can serve as a mnemonic device that may enhance the student's ability to understand and recall abstract theoretical and research issues.

The purpose of this book is therefore threefold: (1) to provide detailed descriptions of a range of clinical problems, (2) to illustrate some of the ways in which these problems can be viewed and treated, and (3) to discuss some of the evidence that is available concerning the epidemiology and etiology of the disorders in question. The book is appropriate for both undergraduate and graduate courses in abnormal psychology. It may also be useful in courses in psychiatric social work or nursing and could be helpful to students enrolled in various practicum courses that teach how best to conceptualize mental health problems and plan treatment. It may be used on its own or as a supplement to a standard textbook in abnormal psychology, such as Davison and Neale's *Abnormal Psychology*, Sixth Edition (Wiley, 1994).

In selecting cases for inclusion in the book, we have sampled from a variety of problems, ranging from classic psychotic disorders (e.g., schizophrenia and bipolar mood disorder) to personality disorders (e.g., paranoia and psychopathy) to various disorders of childhood and aging (e.g., school phobia and depression in later adult life). We have deliberately focused on cases that illustrate particular problems that are of interest to students of abnormal psychology. We do not mean to imply, however, that all the cases fit neatly into specific diagnostic molds. In addition to describing "classic" behavioral symptoms (e.g., hallucinations, compulsive rituals, or specific fears), we have emphasized the social context in which these disorders appear as well as attendant problems that are significant in determining the person's overall adjustment, even though they may not be relevant from a diagnostic stand-point. For example, our case on hypertension considers issues in etiology and treatment when the person is African American. Several of the cases include a consideration of marital adjustment and parent–child relationships. Our coverage also extends to examples of multiple personality, transsexualism, and borderline personality. Each of these disorders represents an area that has received increased attention in the contemporary literature, and each has been the focus of theoretical controversy. Nevertheless, they are not typically covered in much detail by standard textbooks, and their inclusion should be helpful to most instructors. In this fourth edition, we have added new cases dealing with posttraumatic stress disorder (following rape) and anorexia nervosa. Both are problems with which college students may be particularly concerned.

Our cognitive-behavioral perspective is clearly evident in these discussions. Nevertheless, we have tried to present alternative conceptual positions. The cases can therefore be used to show students how a given problem can be reasonably viewed and treated from several different perspectives. Although most of the interventions described are behavioral (including rational restructuring and other cognitive techniques), we have also presented nonbehavioral approaches such as Gestalt therapy and biological treatments (e.g., antipsychotic medication, ECT, and psychosurgery) when they are relevant to the case. Whenever possible, we have provided information concerning the long-term results of treatment. In some cases, the outcome was not positive. We have tried to present an honest view of the limitations, as well as the potential benefits, of various treatment programs. Note also that two of the cases were not in treatment; we believe that it is important to point out that many people who have psychological disorders do not see therapists.

Each case study concludes with a discussion of current knowledge about etiology. Some of these discussions are necessarily more brief than others. More research has been done on schizophrenia, for example, than on bulimia or paranoid personality. We had two goals in mind for these discussions. First, we have tried to use the case material to illustrate the application of research to individual clients' problems. Second, we alert readers to important gaps in our knowledge of abnormal psychology, our abiding belief being that realizing what we do not know is as important as appreciating what we do know. All of these discussions have been revised in the fourth edition to include new ideas and empirical evidence that are changing the way that particular disorders are viewed and treated. We have also updated our discussions of diagnostic issues by including relevant criteria from the American Psychiatric Association's most recent version of the *Diagnostic and Statistical Manual of Mental Disorders* (*DSM-IV*, 1994).

All of the cases in this book are based on actual clinical experience, primarily our own but, in some instances, that of our colleagues and students. Various demographic characteristics (names, locations, and occupations) and some concrete clinical details have been changed to protect the anonymity of clients and their families. In some instances, the cases are composites of clinical problems with which we have dealt. Our intent is not to put forth claims of efficacy and utility for any particular conceptualization or intervention but, instead, to illustrate the ways clinicians think about their work and implement abstractions to help a client cope with life problems. The names used in the case studies are fictitious; any resemblance to actual persons is purely coincidental.

As in the first three editions of this book, we have not identified the authors of specific case studies. This procedure has been adopted and maintained in an effort to help preserve the clients' anonymity. Nevertheless, we remain grateful to Arthur Stone, who wrote one of the original cases, and to Ron Thompson and Kevin Leach, who provided extensive consultation on two other cases. We thank Elana Farace and Sarah Liebman for drafting the two cases that are new to this edition. We also acknowledge Sarah Liebman's valuable assistance in other preparations for the most recent revision.

We would also like to thank the following reviewers for their helpful and constructive comments: Ron Evans, Washburn University; Jan Hastrup, SUNY at Buffalo; Russell Jones, Virginia Polytechnic Institute and State University; Janet Morahan Martin, Bryant College; Richard McNally, Harvard University; Linda Musun Miller, University of Arkansas–Little Rock; Mark Pantle, Baylor University; Esther Rothblum, University of Vermont; Gary Sterner, Eastern Washington University; and John Wixted, University of California–San Diego.

Finally, we would like to express our sincere appreciation to the superb editorial staff at Wiley, especially Karen Dubno, the psychology editor, and Suzanne Magida, our production editor. Their conscientious efforts were essential to the completion of this revision.

Thomas F. Oltmanns
John M. Neale
Gerald C. Davison

CONTENTS

1 OBSESSIVE COMPULSIVE DISORDER

Karen Rusa was a 30-year-old married woman and the mother of four children. Although she had been having anxiety-related problems for a number of years, she had never sought professional help prior to this time. During the preceding three months, she had become increasingly depressed; her family physician finally suggested that she seek psychological services.

For the past several months Karen had been experiencing intrusive, repetitive thoughts that centered around her children's safety. She frequently found herself imagining that a serious accident had occurred; she was unable to put these thoughts out of her mind. On one such occasion she imagined that her son, Alan, had broken his leg playing football at school. There was no reason to believe that an accident had occurred, but Karen brooded about the possibility until she finally called the school to see if Alan was all right. Even after receiving reassurance that he had not been hurt, she described herself as being somewhat surprised when he later arrived home unharmed. Karen also noted that her daily routine was seriously hampered by an extensive series of counting rituals that she performed throughout each day. Specific numbers had come to have a special meaning to Karen; she found that her preoccupation with these numbers was interfering with her ability to perform everyday activities. One example was grocery shopping. Karen believed that if she selected the first item (e.g., a box of cereal) on the shelf, something terrible would happen to her oldest child. If she selected the second item, some unknown disaster would befall her second child, and so on for the four children. The children's ages were also important. The sixth item in a row, for example, was associated with her youngest child, who was six years old. Thus specific items had to be avoided to ensure the safety of her children. Obviously, the ritual required some concentration because the children's ages changed. Karen's preoccupation with numbers extended to other activities, most notably the pattern in which she smoked cigarettes and drank coffee. If she had one cigarette, she believed that she had to smoke at least four in a row or one of the children would be harmed in some way. If she drank one cup of coffee, she felt compelled to drink four. Karen acknowledged the irrationality of these rituals but, nevertheless, maintained that she felt much more comfortable when she observed them conscientiously. When she was occasionally in too great a hurry to observe the rituals, she experienced considerable anxiety, in the form of a subjective feeling of dread and apprehension. She described herself as tense, jumpy, and unable to relax during these periods. Her fears were most often confirmed because something unfortunate invariably happened to one of the children within a few days after each such "failure." The fact that minor accidents are likely to occur at a fairly high rate in any family of four children did not diminish Karen's conviction that she had been directly responsible because of her inability to observe the numerical rules.

In addition to her obsessive ideas and compulsive behaviors, Karen reported dissatisfaction with her marriage and problems in managing her children. Her husband, Tony, had been placed on complete physical disability 11 months prior to her first visit to the mental health center. Although he was only 32 years old, Tony suffered from a very serious heart condition that made even the most routine physical exertion potentially dangerous. Since leaving his job as a clerk at a plumbing supply store, he had spent most of his time at home. He enjoyed lying on the couch watching television and did so for most of his waking hours. He had convinced Karen that she should be responsible for all of the household chores and family errands. Her days were spent getting the children dressed, fed, and transported to school; cleaning; washing; shopping; and fetching potato chips, dip, and beer whenever Tony needed a snack. He argued, of course, that the stress of walking to the refrigerator would be unhealthy, although the merits of his reasoning—as well as his nutritional judgment—might easily have been questioned. The inequity of this situation was apparent to Karen, and extremely frustrating, yet she found herself unable to handle it effectively. She fantasized about abandoning the family, but she did not believe that she could follow through on this impulse.

The children were also clearly out of her control. Robert, age 6, and Alan, age 8, were very active and mischievous. Neither responded well to parental discipline, which was inconsistent at best. Both experienced behavioral problems at school, and Alan was being considered for placement in a special classroom for particularly disruptive children. On one occasion, Karen had been called to take Alan home early after he had kicked the school principal and told him to "go to hell." Alan's teacher described him as always being out of his seat and constantly pestering the other children during study periods. The boys were also prone to minor physical illnesses; it seemed to Karen that at least one of the boys was always sick with a cold or some kind of infection. The girls were also difficult to handle. Denise, age 9, and Jennifer, age 11, spent much of their time at home arguing with each other. Jennifer was moderately obese. Denise teased her mercilessly about her weight. After they had quarreled for some time, Jennifer would appeal tearfully to Karen, who would attempt to intervene on her behalf. Karen was becoming increasingly distressed by her inability to handle this confusing situation, and she was getting little, if any, help from Tony. During the past several weeks, she had been spending more and more time crying and hiding alone in her bedroom.

SOCIAL HISTORY

Karen was raised in New York City by Italian immigrant parents. She was the first of four children. Her family was deeply religious, and she was raised to be a devout Roman Catholic. She attended parochial schools from the first grade through high school and was a reasonably good student. Her memories of the severe practices of the church and school authorities were vivid. The formal rituals of the church played an important role in her life, as they did for the other members of her family. Beginning at a very early age, Karen was taught that she had to observe many specific guidelines that governed social behavior within the church (not eating meat on Fridays, going to confession regularly, and so forth). She was told that her strict adherence to these norms would ensure the safety of her immortal soul and, conversely, that transgressions would be severely punished.

The depth of her belief and the severity of its consequences can be seen in the following story, which Karen recalled during an early session. When she was eight years old, Karen and her classmates at school were to receive their first communion in the church. This is a particularly important and solemn occasion for Roman Catholics that signifies the child's advancement to adult status in the church community. Before the child is allowed to partake in communion, however, a complete confession must be made of *all* prior sins. Karen was told that she was to confess all of her sins, regardless of their severity or the time of their occurrence, to her priest, who would prescribe an appropriate penance for her sins. She remembered her parents' and teachers' warnings that if she failed to mention any of her sins, her soul would be banished to hell for eternity. This threat was still vivid in Karen's mind many years later. Despite the terror aroused by these circumstances, Karen intentionally failed to tell the priest about one of her sins; she had stolen a small picture book from her classroom and was now afraid either to return it or to tell anyone about the crime. She lived with intense guilt about this omission for several years and could remember having occasionally terrifying nightmares that centered around imagined punishments for not providing a complete confession. In subsequent years, Karen intensified her efforts to abide by even the most minute details of church regulations, but she continued to harbor the conviction that she could never atone for this mortal sin.

Karen remembered her parents as having been very strict disciplinarians. Her mother was apparently a cold, rigid person who had insisted on the maintenance of order and cleanliness in their household. Beyond her unerring adherence to religious rules and regulations, Karen's mother kept the family on a tight schedule with regard to meals and other routine activities. When the children deviated from these guidelines, they were severely punished. Karen's most positive recollections of interaction with her mother centered around their mutual participation in prescribed church functions. She did not remember her parents ever demonstrating affection for each other in front of their children.

Shortly after she graduated from high school, Karen married Tony. He was two years older than Karen and had been working as a stockboy at a department store. Their courtship was hurried. In retrospect, Karen wondered whether her interest in Tony had been motivated by a desire to escape from the confines of her parents' home.

Karen became pregnant two months after their marriage. During this pregnancy, she witnessed an unfortunate accident at her neighbor's apartment. While Karen was chatting with her friend, the woman's one-year-old daughter crawled off the porch and was run over by another child riding a bicycle. The girl was seriously injured and remained in the hospital for several weeks. Shortly after this accident, Karen began experiencing repetitive, intrusive thoughts about injuring herself. At unpredictable but frequent intervals throughout the day, she would find herself thinking about jumping out of windows, walking in front of cars, and other similar dangerous behaviors. These thoughts were, of course, frightening to her, but she could not prevent their occurrence. When one of the thoughts did come into her mind, she attempted to get rid of it by quickly repeating a short prayer that she had learned as a child and then asking God for forgiveness for having entertained such a sinful impulse. This procedure was moderately successful as a temporary source of distraction, but it did not prevent the reappearance of a similar intrusive thought several hours later. These thoughts of self-injury gradually disappeared after the birth of her first child, Jennifer.

When Jennifer was nine months old, Karen once again became pregnant. She and Tony decided to move to the suburbs, where they would be able to afford a house with a yard in which the children could play. Tony found a job as a clerk at a plumbing supply store. Karen stayed at home with Jennifer and tended to household responsibilities. Although she was proud of their new home, Karen became somewhat depressed during this period because she missed her old friends.

It was at this time that Karen began to be disillusioned with the church. Her distress centered around a number of reforms that had been introduced by Pope John XXIII and the Ecumenical Council. The Mass, for example, was no longer said in Latin, and nonclerical persons were allowed to administer various rites of the church. Similarly, church members were no longer admonished to give up meat on Fridays and other rituals were modified or completely eliminated. Most people found these changes refreshing, but Karen was horrified. The church's rituals had come to play a central role in her life. In deemphasizing the importance of traditional rituals, the church was depriving Karen of her principal means of controlling her own destiny. She was extremely uncomfortable with these new practices and soon stopped going to church all together.

Karen's situation showed little change throughout the next few years. By the time she was 25 years old, she had four children. She found this responsibility overwhelming and was generally unhappy most of the time. Her relationship with Tony had essentially reached a stalemate; they were not satisfied with their marriage, but they agreed to stay together for the children. Although they did not fight with each other openly, a sense of covert tension and estrangement pervaded their relationship. Tony refused to participate in what he considered to be unnecessarily rigid and complicated household regulations, particularly those dealing with the children's behavior. Karen had established very specific guidelines for meals, bedtime, and so on but found that she was unable to enforce these rules by herself. She remained distant from Tony and resisted most of his attempts to display physical affection. They did maintain a sexual relationship, but it lacked spontaneity and genuine warmth. Karen believed that sex was her marital responsibility, so she was willing to perform or acquiesce as necessary. Since the birth of their fourth child, Karen had been particularly anxious about becoming pregnant again. She refused to use any form of artificial birth control, which was, of course, contrary to the teachings of the church. Their sexual encounters were therefore carefully scheduled to avoid the days surrounding ovulation. This scheduling became increasingly complex until Karen finally settled on two four-day periods preceding and following menstruation during which she was willing to have intercourse with Tony. When they did engage in sexual activity, it came to follow a careful, routine sequence that was usually limited to the minimum physical stimulation necessary for Tony to achieve orgasm. On most occasions, Karen described herself as being tense and anxious at these times; she did not view herself as an active participant. She was not, however, totally inorgasmic; she did occasionally experience an orgasm during intercourse and was able to reach orgasm through self-stimulation. Masturbation made her feel quite guilty, and she did not discuss this activity with Tony. Thus, overall,

Karen was chronically unhappy and generally dissatisfied with her life, but she nevertheless clung to her miserable surroundings and established patterns of behaviors out of fear that any change would be for the worse.

This unhappy yet tolerable equilibrium was disturbed by Tony's deteriorating health. One day, while he was working at the store, he experienced sudden chest pains and numbness in his extremities. Recognizing these symptoms as serious in nature (he had had high blood pressure for years and was therefore well informed in this regard), Tony asked a friend to drive him to the hospital. His experience was diagnosed as a mild heart attack. Further testing revealed serious structural abnormalities in his heart. He was eventually discharged from the hospital, given a complete medical disability, and laid off from his job.

Karen became more and more depressed after Tony began staying home during the day. It was during this time that her fears about the children's safety became clearly unreasonable, and she started performing her counting rituals. Karen could not remember when she first began checking the order of items on a shelf or counting the number of cigarettes she smoked in sequence. She did realize that her situation was desperate because she felt that she had lost control of her own behavior and experienced considerable anxiety whenever she attempted to resist performing the rituals. At this point she finally decided to seek professional help.

CONCEPTUALIZATION AND TREATMENT

The ritualistic behavior was seen by the therapist as one part of Karen's overall difficult situation. The counting obsession represented Karen's attempt to reintroduce a sense of personal control over her own life. In this sense, the rituals were being performed instead of either the more socially acceptable religious activities that she had employed as a child or the more effective social skills that she had apparently never developed. For example, she was unassertive in her relationship with Tony and markedly ineffective in her interactions with the children. Treatment was therefore aimed at the development of interpersonal skills that would give Karen more control over her environment. It was hoped that as she was able to effect a more satisfactory relationship with her family, her increased competence would eliminate the necessity of turning to admittedly superstitious, ineffective attempts to achieve self-control.

During the course of their early sessions, it became evident to both Karen and her therapist that Karen was not behaving assertively, particularly with her husband. That is, she was unable to express openly either negative or positive feelings. Instead of standing up for her rights, she would meekly acquiesce to even his most unreasonable demands. At the same time, she would become extremely frustrated and angry with him and would look for subtle ways to "even the score." She was similarly unable to convey her appreciation to him on those (admittedly rare) occasions when he did please her.

Karen quickly recognized her deficiency in this regard but was nevertheless unable to alter her behavior spontaneously. She and the therapist therefore agreed to pursue a systematic program of assertion training. The initial sessions in this sequence were devoted to a careful assessment of the situations in which Karen was unassertive. She was asked to keep a daily notebook of such situations in which she noted the people involved, the nature of their interaction, and her perception of the situation, including what she thought would happen if she did behave assertively. Having identified typical problem situations, Karen and her therapist role-played several incidents as a way of introducing Karen to more appropriate responses. At first, the therapist played Karen's part and modeled appropriate behaviors for her. They then switched roles so that Karen could practice these new responses. After each role-playing sequence, the therapist provided Karen with feedback about the effectiveness of her behavior.

They also discussed some of Karen's irrational fears associated with assertion. These thoughts generally centered on her implicit belief that everyone should love her and that if she stood up for her own rights people would reject her. In many situations, these irrational self-statements were inhibiting the expression of assertive behaviors.

After Karen became proficient with such exercises in the therapy sessions, she was asked to start transferring her skills to life outside the clinic. Beginning with relatively easy assignments to ensure initial successful experiences, she was asked to perform more and more difficult assertion tasks between therapy sessions. These experiences then became the focus of future sessions until she had been successful in even the most difficult situations.

After assertion training had produced some positive results, the therapist began teaching Karen more effective child management skills. These were based primarily on procedures associated with instrumental learning. She was taught, for example, to ignore her daughters when they were quarreling and to reinforce them positively for playing together appropriately. Again, her efforts were initially channeled toward the behaviors that could be changed easily. The most difficult problems, such as getting the children to stop fighting at mealtimes, were left until Karen had mastered some of the general principles of child management.

In addition to these skill-training programs, the therapist also discussed Karen's concerns about religion. It was clear that the church was still very important to her and that she experienced considerable guilt and anxiety over her failure to attend services regularly. The fact that her children were not involved in church activities was also troubling to Karen. She worried that if any harm came to one of them, God would not protect them. For these reasons, Karen was encouraged to visit several priests at churches in her area in an effort to find one who was more conservative and thus more compatible with her own views. Although most of the local priests had moved toward contemporary practices in their own churches, they did refer her to an older priest at a church somewhat farther from her neighborhood who still adhered to several of the traditional rituals she had learned as a child. She made an appointment to visit this priest and was both pleased and relieved after their initial meeting. He was able to discuss with her some of the changes that had been made in the church. In some cases he was able to explain the rationale behind a particular change in a way that was acceptable to her. This process was, no doubt, facilitated by the fact that he shared many of her concerns about abandoning traditional practices. Karen felt much more comfortable with this priest than she did with the liberal pastor who was in charge of the church in her immediate neighborhood. Within weeks she was once again attending church regularly with her four children.

The combination of assertion training, parent education, and a renewed interest in church activities did lead to an important improvement in Karen's mood. After three months of treatment, she reported an increased sense of self-confidence and an improvement in her family life. There was also some reduction in her anxiety level. She continued to observe her numbers rituals, but they were somewhat less frequent and, when she did fail to perform the counting routines, she was not as distraught as she had been at the beginning of treatment.

At this point, the rituals were addressed directly through the combined use of flooding and response prevention. Flooding is a behavior therapy procedure in which the person is exposed to stimuli that provoke intense anxiety (either in imagination or in reality) for extended periods of time and without an opportunity to escape. This procedure was instituted as follows: Karen was asked to smoke a single cigarette at the beginning of the session. When she was finished with the cigarette, she would begin to feel anxious and worry about her oldest daughter. She was then instructed to resist the temptation to smoke another cigarette. Thus the response that she employed to neutralize her anxiety and to control the ruminations was prevented. The therapist believed that this type of prolonged exposure to the anxiety-provoking situation would lead to a reduction in Karen's anxiety. The procedure was carried out during four consecutive two-hour sessions. Karen was encouraged to practice the same response prevention procedure on her own between sessions. When she had mastered the cigarette-smoking problem, the procedure was extended progressively to other similar situations in which she had been concerned about numbers.

Treatment was terminated after 20 sessions. Karen was no longer depressed and had not engaged in her compulsive counting rituals for four weeks. The children were better behaved at home, and Karen had plans to institute further changes in this regard. Her relationship with Tony was somewhat improved. Although he had become quite upset initially when Karen began to assert herself, he became more cooperative when he saw an improvement in her adjustment. Karen's reduced anxiety also led to some initial improvements in their sexual relationship, although this problem was not addressed directly in treatment. These improvements were still evident at a follow-up interview six months after termination.

DISCUSSION

Obsessive Compulsive Disorder (OCD) is included in the *Diagnostic and Statistical Manual of Mental Disorders* (*DSM-IV* pp. 422–423) under the general heading of Anxiety Disorders. It is defined by the following criteria:

- **A.** Either obsessions or compulsions:
  Obsessions as defined by (1), (2), (3), and (4):
  1. Recurrent and persistent thoughts, impulses, or images that are experienced, at some time during the disturbance, as intrusive and inappropriate, and cause marked anxiety or distress
  2. The thoughts, impulses, or images are not simply excessive worries about real-life problems
  3. The person attempts to ignore or suppress such thoughts, impulses, or images, or to neutralize them with some other thought or action
  4. The person recognizes that the obsessional thoughts, impulses, or images are a product of his or her own mind
  Compulsions as defined by (1) and (2):
  1. Repetitive behaviors (e.g., handwashing, ordering, checking) or mental acts (e.g., praying, counting, repeating words silently) that the person feels driven to perform in response to an obsession, or according to rules that must be applied rigidly
  2. The behaviors or mental acts are aimed at preventing or reducing distress or preventing some dreaded event or situation; however, these behaviors or mental acts either are not connected in a realistic way with what they are designed to neutralize or prevent, or are clearly excessive
- **B.** At some point during the course of the disorder, the person has recognized that the obsessions or compulsions are excessive or unreasonable.
- **C.** The obsessions or compulsions cause marked distress, are time-consuming (take more than 1 hour a day), or significantly interfere with the person's normal routine, occupational functioning, or usual social activities or relationships.

Regardless of whether the repetitive element is a thought (obsession) or an overt response (compulsion), the central feature of the disorder is the subjective experience of a loss of *volition*.

Obsessions can be described in terms of both form and content. Akhtar, Wig, Varma, Pershad, and Varma (1975, pp. 343–44) outlined five typical forms of obsessional symptoms:

Obsessive doubt: An inclination not to believe that a task has been completed satisfactorily.

Obsessive thinking: A seemingly endless thought chain, usually one pertaining to future events.

Obsessive impulse: A powerful urge to carry out actions that may be trivial, socially disruptive, or even assaultive.

Obsessive fear: A fear of losing self-control and thus inadvertently committing a socially embarrassing act.

Obsessive image: The persistence before the mind's eye of something seen, usually recently.

The content of obsessive thoughts may also vary. Jenike, Baer, and Minichiello (1986) analyzed the obsessions of 100 patients and found that the most common themes were contamination, aggression, and need for symmetry. More than half of the patients in this sample reported more than one type of obsessive thought.

Compulsions represent ritualistic behavior patterns that are often performed in accordance with an obsessive thought. Whereas obsessions generally lead to an *increase* in subjective anxiety, compulsions generally *reduce* the person's anxiety or discomfort. Compulsive behavior, in fact, is designed to neutralize or to prevent discomfort or some dreaded event or situation. Roughly 75 percent of all patients with obsessive symptoms also exhibit compulsive behaviors (Akhtar et al., 1975). Most compulsive patients fall into one of two groups: "cleaners" and "checkers."[1] Cleaning and washing rituals are associated with fear of contact with contaminating objects. For example, a patient who is afraid of contamination by germs or bodily secretions may spend hours each day bathing or disinfecting his or her home. This ritualistic behavior restores the patient's sense of safety. Repetitive checking, on the other hand, is more often motivated by a fear of some catastrophic event. For example, a patient who experiences obsessive thoughts about gas explosions may engage in compulsive checking of the burners on a gas stove. The

---

[1]Some investigators have suggested that there may be important differences between these two subgroups in terms of their etiology and response to treatment (e.g., Rachman & Hodgson, 1980). Cleaning compulsions may be more likely to develop in families in which the parents are overprotective, whereas checking rituals, which are more often associated with doubts and indecisiveness, are more often encouraged by parents who are excessively critical.

absolute proportions of OCD patients who exhibit cleaning and checking rituals have varied from one study to the next (Barlow, 1988). Jenike et al. (1986) found that 79 percent of patients exhibited checking rituals, and 58 percent performed cleaning rituals.

Karen experienced obsessive thoughts and fears that centered around the health of her children. Her compulsive behaviors fall into a type of checking rituals known as repeating. "Repeaters" perform an action, often a particular magical number of times, in an effort to prevent disastrous events from happening.

Some other behaviors that take a repetitive form and are associated with either a decrease or increase in anxiety have also been considered "compulsive" in the popular media. These include problems such as gambling, drug addiction, and exhibitionism. There are, however, some important distinctions between these actions and truly compulsive behaviors (Rasmussen & Eisen, 1992; Tynes, White, & Steketee, 1990). First, addictive behaviors involve a pleasure-seeking component that is absent in compulsive behaviors. Second, the anxiety that is associated with the performance of criminal activities (e.g., stealing) is appropriate in light of social sanctions; obsessive compulsive patients experience anxiety that is inappropriate to the situation.

Obsessive Compulsive Disorder should be distinguished from Obsessive Compulsive Personality Disorder (OCPD). The latter does not involve specific ritualistic behaviors; it is intended to refer to a general *personality style.* People with an obsessive compulsive personality are preoccupied with orderliness and perfectionism as well as mental and interpersonal control (*DSM-IV*). They are inflexible and overly devoted to work to the point that they avoid leisure activities and ignore friendships. Although OCD and OCPD may appear in the same individual, an etiological relationship has not been established (Black et al., 1993). In fact, Dependent Personality Disorder and Avoidant Personality Disorder are more common than OCPD among patients who are being treated for OCD (Baer & Jenike, 1992).

The phobic disorders (i.e., agoraphobia, specific phobia, and social phobia) are similar to OCD because they involve severe anxiety and are characterized by behaviors that are designed to reduce that anxiety. Some obsessive compulsive patients also display phobic avoidance of situations associated with anxiety about dirt or contamination. There are, however, some important differences between OCD and the phobic disorders. For example, phobic patients do not show the same tendency toward superstitious or "magical" thinking that is often characteristic of obsessive compulsive patients, nor do they manifest compulsive symptoms. Also, for the phobic patient, the anxiety-inducing stimulus is unrelated to the content of any obsessions the patient may experience.

Obsessive thoughts should also be distinguished from delusional beliefs. Two criteria are important in this regard. First, obsessive patients are ambivalent about their thoughts; they realize the essential absurdity of their idea at the same time that they are preoccupied with the ideas. Second, and perhaps most important, is the struggle against the idea. Obsessive patients try, often desperately, to resist their obsessive ideas, whereas delusional patients do not.

Depression is a common complication of OCD. Two out of every three patients with OCD have experienced at least one episode of major depression at some point during their lives (Rasmussen & Eisen, 1992). The relationship between these phenomena is unclear. Sometimes compulsive symptoms appear before the onset of depression; in other cases this relationship is reversed. The successful treatment or alleviation of depressive symptoms does not invariably lead to a reduction in the frequency of compulsive behaviors, and vice versa (Foa, Kozak, Steketee, & McCarthy, 1992). Rachman (1976) suggested that the appearance of a depressed mood may act as a sensitizing event in the precipitation of compulsive symptoms. In other words, a person may initially be prone to ruminative thoughts but not find them particularly disturbing until after the onset of a serious mood disturbance such as agitated depression.

Although OCD was previously thought to be relatively rare, recent community studies suggest that milder forms of the disorder may affect between 1 percent and 3 percent of the general population (Karno & Golding, 1991). The disorder seems to be equally distributed between men and women. It is more common among those who are young, divorced or separated, and unemployed.

Kringlen (1970) reported the results of a 20-year follow-up of 91 patients who had been hospitalized with obsessive compulsive disorder. More than 80 percent of these patients had exhibited nervous symptoms as children. They had typically been raised in strict, puritanical homes. The average age of onset for compulsive symptoms in female patients was between 10 and 20 years, although most of the women did not seek professional help until some years later. Somewhat more than 50 percent of the patients showed an acute onset of symptoms following a specific stressful event. Marital problems were common among compulsive patients.

The prognosis for patients with OCD is mixed. In Kringlen's sample, which included only cases that were severe enough to warrant hospitalization, only 25 percent of the people were significantly improved 10 to 20 years after admission. The results of another long-term follow-up study were somewhat more positive. Berrios and Chiu (1989) studied the outcomes of 42 OCD patients several years after hospital discharge. Half of these people were improved at follow-up. In many cases, they still experienced some type of obsessive or compulsive symptoms, but there had been a marked reduction in the extent to which these symptoms interfered with the patients' ability to function. The difference between these studies may be the product of improvements in treatment methods. Behavioral procedures and medications that have been introduced since Kringlen's study was conducted may lead to better outcomes for many patients.

Karen was in many ways a typical OCD patient. She had, in fact, been raised in a strict, puritanical family setting. As a child, she was generally anxious and quite concerned with order and rituals. Since midadolescence, Karen had experienced difficulty with intrusive, repetitive ideas that she found distressing. These problems would come and go without apparent reason. She was also prone to serious depression.

Karen's family background is also consistent with the literature on OCD (e.g., Frost, Steketee, Cohn, & Griess, 1994; Pauls, 1992). There is a relatively high incidence of psychiatric anomalies—particularly obsessional traits, anxious personalities, and other affective disturbances—among the biological relatives of obsessive compulsive patients. One representative parent from a family study was described in the following way:

> The father of one obsessive compulsive young man was so upset by finding some dirt in the bathroom of the motel where he was staying, that he was unable to sleep in the bed provided, or even remain in the motel; since no alternative accommodations were available, he spent much of that night anxiously walking the town streets. The father did not regard himself as suffering from an exaggerated anxiety over dirt; in his view, the motel suffered from a distressing dirtiness which had deprived him of a night's sleep. He thought of himself as particular about cleanliness, but this seemed quite reasonable and natural to him, certainly not a feeling to be resisted. He did not hold any irrational beliefs about his insistence on cleanliness, nor did he convert his anxieties about dirt into rituals, as his son did (Hoover & Insel, 1984, p. 209).

It seems likely that the similarity between the behavior of many obsessive compulsive patients and their parents reflects the influence of both genetic and environmental variables (Black, Noyes, Goldstein, & Blum, 1992; Carey & Gottesman, 1981). In Karen's case, her mother's rigid, moralistic behavior may have had an important influence on the development of later symptoms. Karen's mother provided a salient model for her daughter's subsequent compulsive behavior. She also reinforced early tendencies toward such response patterns.

Theoretical Perspectives and Treatment Implications

According to traditional psychoanalytic theory, compulsive symptoms are the product of the ego's unconscious attempt to fend off anxiety associated with hostile impulses. Freud (1909/1925) argued that compulsive patients had experienced overly harsh toilet training and were therefore fixated in the anal-sadistic stage of development. Such individuals presumably suffer serious conflict over the expression of anger. Since these feelings are dangerous, or unacceptable to the ego, the anticipation of their expression is seen as anxiety provoking. This anxiety is dealt with primarily through the defense mechanism known as *reaction formation*, in which the original impulse (anger) is transformed into its antithesis (love or oversolicitude). This conceptual approach is not incompatible with Karen's situation. Her principal symptoms were compulsive rituals that were intended to protect her children from harm. But her feelings about her children were, in fact, ambivalent. It would not be unreasonable to assume that she was most often very angry with them, perhaps to the point that she might have considered doing them physical harm. Of course, this impulse would be anxiety provoking to the ego, which would convert it to its opposite form. Thus, instead of injuring the children, she would spend a good deal of her time every day performing irrational responses aimed at *protecting* them.

Some recognition was given to these considerations in the treatment that was employed. Karen's anger and frustration were identified as central features of her adjustment problems, but the therapeutic procedures went beyond the goal of insight-oriented treatment. Karen's recognition of her anger and hostility was not sufficient to effect change; specific training procedures were used to help her develop a repertoire of more adaptive responses.

Learning theorists (see Teasdale, 1974) would view Karen's problems in a distinctly different fashion. Within this general model, two factors would be given primary consideration. Both involve the principle of *negative reinforcement*,[2] which states that the probability of a response is increased if it leads to the termination of an aversive stimulus. Consider, for example, the net effect of Karen's rituals. Their performance ensured that she would be away from her home for extended periods of time. If she went to her neighbor's house for coffee, she would be gone for at least two hours before she could consume enough cups and smoke enough cigarettes to satisfy the rituals. Grocery shopping, which she did by herself, had also turned into a long, complicated process. Given that being at home with her family was mostly an aversive experience for Karen, her rituals might be seen as an operant response that was being maintained by negative reinforcement.[3]

A behavioral clinician would be most likely to point to the anxiety reduction associated with the performance of the rituals. Whenever Karen was engaged in an activity that reminded her of numbers and, consequently, her children, she became anxious. She was able to neutralize this anxiety tempo-

---

[2]Negative reinforcement should be distinguished from punishment, in which the *appearance* of an aversive stimulus is made contingent on the emission of a response, so the probability of the response is therefore *reduced.*

[3]This phenomenon would be labeled *secondary gain* by a psychoanalyst, who would give primary emphasis to the ego-defensive nature of the symptom.

rarily by counting the appropriate number of boxes, and so on. This ritual was therefore reinforced and maintained by the reduction of anxiety. This notion is similar to the psychoanalytic view in that the symptom is produced as a means of reducing tension. The two theories differ in that the behavioral view does not see her anxiety as being directly attributable to the unconscious urge to harm her children, nor does the behavioral view hold that the anxiety reduction is mediated by an unconsciously activated defense mechanism.

Some elements of the behavioral view were incorporated into the treatment procedure followed with Karen. In particular, by teaching her to be more assertive and to manage her children more effectively, the therapist was able to make her home life less aversive. She now experienced more pleasurable interactions with her children and her husband; and one important source of negative reinforcement for her rituals was removed. Unfortunately, this view of human behavior is fairly limited. In particular, it does not account for the importance of cognitive events. By focusing exclusively on environmental events, behaviorists may ignore important factors associated with the client's perceptions, beliefs, and attitudes. These variables also seemed to play an important role in Karen's problem.

Cognitive theorists (e.g., Mandler, 1975) have argued that the person's perception of control is an important variable in understanding anxiety. People tend to be less anxious when they can control their own behavior and the events in their environment. Barlow (1988) has proposed a model for the etiology of OCD in which perception of control plays an important part. His view begins with the recognition that most normal people experience intrusive thoughts from time to time, especially when they have been exposed to stress or negative mood states. Most intrusive thoughts do not become persistent or troublesome, but they may set the stage for the development of OCD if several factors fall into place at the same time. According to Barlow's (1988) model, people who develop OCD may be those who (1) exhibit exaggerated, negative emotional responses to stress, (2) are prone to believe that things are out of control, and (3) have learned that some thoughts are particularly dangerous or unacceptable. Alarmed by the intrusive appearance of forbidden thoughts, the person may struggle to avoid them, but cognitive events are difficult to control. In fact, active attempts at thought suppression often backfire and increase the severity of the problem (Wegner, 1989). This vicious negative feedback loop magnifies feelings of helplessness and loss of control and also serves to focus narrow attention on the content of unwanted thoughts. The person's anxiety level continues to escalate, and compulsive rituals are employed in an attempt to regain control over mental events as well as life experiences.

The relevance of this perspective to Karen's situation is clear. Her family situation had become very stressful in recent months, and she had experienced frequent intrusive thoughts related to her children's safety. Karen did not feel like she was in control of this situation. As a child, she had been taught that strict observation of the rituals of the church would guarantee her salvation. These rituals became the primary means for controlling her fate and ensuring her safety. As an adult, Karen found herself stripped of these control mechanisms. The church now maintained that salvation (or the protection of one's soul) depended more on faith than on the performance of specific overt responses. Thus, it may be that Karen's counting rituals represented a substitute for the religious practices she had learned as a child. She admitted that they were irrational and probably unnecessary, but they did make her feel at ease in much the same way that going to church had left her with a comforting feeling as a child.

Treatment was therefore aimed initially at reducing the level of stress and giving Karen alternative means of controlling her environment. These included assertion training and instruction in parenting skills. But these measures could only affect earthly matters. Considering her deeply ingrained religious beliefs, it was also judged necessary to help her reestablish contact with the church. After these procedures had achieved some modest success, it was possible to attack the counting rituals directly through the use of prolonged exposure and response prevention.

The therapy procedures that were employed depend on the assumption that stimuli that precede the performance of a ritual have come to be anxiety provoking. Extinction is presumably prevented by the performance of the compulsive ritual, which can be seen as an avoidance response. It follows, therefore, that if the compulsive response can be prevented for an extended period of time while the person is exposed to the initiating stimuli, the anxiety should extinguish. In Karen's case, this procedure began with a situation in which she had smoked a single cigarette. This event normally evoked increasing anxiety if she did not immediately smoke another cigarette. By encouraging Karen to resist lighting another cigarette, the therapist was able to help her overcome anxiety through an extinction process.

Some empirical data indicate that behavior therapy is effective in treating compulsive disorders (Rachman & Hodgson, 1980). The most effective procedure seems to be *in vivo* (i.e., in the natural environment), graduated, prolonged exposure coupled with response prevention. This technique was employed by Marks, Hodgson, and Rachman (1975) with 20 chronic cases of Obsessive Compulsive Disorder. Two years after the termination of treatment, 15 of the patients were still considered much improved. Although a control group was not included in this study, the poor prognosis generally associated with this kind of patient favors the conclusion that the treatment itself was responsible for the observed change. The results of subsequent controlled studies indicate that exposure coupled with response prevention is indeed an effective form of treatment for OCD patients (Foa, Steketee, & Ozarow, 1985).

In some cases, medication may also be beneficial, particularly in conjunction with behavior therapy. Several studies have demonstrated that tricyclic antidepressant medication may be helpful in treating patients with OCD (Goodman, McDougle, & Price, 1992). Many of these reports have been concerned with clomipramine, but it is not the only drug that has been found to be an effective treatment for OCD, and the actual mechanism of action for these drugs is unclear. Some investigators maintain that clomipramine produces a specific "anti-obsessional" effect (e.g., Leonard et al., 1989). Others have argued that the drugs' beneficial effect can probably be traced to the relief of depression that frequently accompanies compulsive symptoms (instead of affecting the compulsive symptoms directly). In any case, their administration may often be considered, especially when behavior therapy alone is ineffective and when the patient's mood is also dysphoric.

The newer generation of antidepressant drugs known as selective serotonin reuptake inhibitors (SSRIs), such as fluoxetine (Prozac), has also been used with OCD patients. Controlled studies indicate that these drugs are frequently effective in the treatment of OCD (e.g., Wood, Tollefson, & Birkett, 1993). The SSRIs are sometimes preferred to the tricyclic antidepressants because they have fewer side effects.

When both psychotherapy and medication fail, one other form of treatment may be considered — psychosurgery, which refers to techniques in which neural pathways in the brain are surgically altered in an effort to change the person's behavior. Although psychosurgery was originally intended to be used with psychotic patients, clinical research indicates that it may be most effective with depression and compulsive disorders (see Perse, 1988). One longitudinal study followed up on 26 patients who had received psychosurgery after failing to respond to all other forms of treatment. In comparison to similar OCD patients who had not received surgery, 10 of the 26 patients were obviously improved several years after the procedure was performed. Six others showed mild improvement, 6 were unchanged, and 4 had gotten worse (Hay et al., 1993). Positive results were also reported by Mitchell-Heggs, Kelly, and Richardson (1976). These investigators found that 24 out of 27 (89 percent) obsessive patients were improved 16 months after treatment; 7 of these 24 were considered completely symptom free, and an additional 11 were much improved. Since the mean duration of illness prior to surgery was 13 years for the patients in this study, the reported rates of improvement are probably not due to spontaneous remission.

These results cannot be ignored, but they should also be interpreted with considerable caution (Rachman, 1979). First, it is virtually impossible to conduct a double-blind[4] evaluation of psychosurgery. Second, surgical

---

[4]A double-blind procedure is used to reduce the biasing effects of the expectations of the patient and the therapist. In drug studies, patients and therapists can be kept "blind" to the patient's treatment status by assigning some patients to a placebo control group.

procedures have varied widely across studies, thus making general statements about psychosurgery questionable. Third, and perhaps most important, psychosurgery may produce general changes in the patient's intellectual and emotional capacities. These changes are both unpredictable and poorly understood. Thus most investigators agree that such radical procedures should only be considered when the patient's symptoms are chronic and severely disturbing and when other treatment programs have already been unsuccessful.

2 PANIC DISORDER WITH AGORAPHOBIA

Dennis Holt was 31 years old, divorced, and a successful insurance sales-man. He had experienced panic attacks on several occasions during the past 10 years, but he did not seek psychological treatment until shortly after the last incident. It happened while Dennis and his fiancée, Elaine, were doing their Christmas shopping at a local mall. Their first stop was a large department store where Elaine hoped to find a present for her mother. Dennis was in a good mood when they arrived at the store. Although he was usually uneasy in large crowds of people, he was also caught up in the holiday spirit and was looking forward to spending the bonus that he had recently received from his company. Ten minutes after they began shopping, Dennis suddenly felt very sick. His hands began to tremble uncontrollably, his vision became blurred, and his body felt weak all over. He experienced a tremendous pressure on his chest and began to gasp for breath, sensing that he was about to smother. These dramatic physical symptoms were accompanied by an overwhelming sensation of apprehension. He was terrified but did not known why. Without saying anything to Elaine, he whirled and dashed from the store, seeking refuge in their car, which was parked outside. Once there, he rolled down the windows to let in more air, lay down on the back seat, and closed his eyes. He continued to feel dizzy and short of breath for about 10 minutes more. Elaine did not find him for more than an hour because she had been browsing in an adjacent aisle and had not seen him flee from the store. When she noticed that he was gone, she looked for him in other stores before she realized that something was wrong and finally decided to check the car. This was the first panic attack that Dennis had experienced since he and Elaine had begun dating several months previously. After they returned to his apartment, he explained what had happened and his past history of attacks in somewhat greater detail; she persuaded him to seek professional help.

When Dennis arrived at the psychological clinic for his first appointment, he was neatly dressed in an expensive suit. He was five minutes early, so the receptionist asked him if he would like to take a seat in the large, comfortably furnished waiting room where several other clients were sitting. Politely indicating that he would prefer to stand, Dennis leaned casually against the corridor wall. Everything about his physical appearance—his posture, his neatly trimmed hair, his friendly smile—conveyed a sense of confidence and success. Nothing betrayed the real sense of dread with which he had struggled since he had promised Elaine that he would consult a psychologist. Was he, in fact, crazy? He wanted help, but he did not want anyone to think that he was emotionally unstable.

The first interview was not very productive. Dennis began by cracking jokes with the psychologist and attempted to engage in an endless sequence of witty small talk and verbal banter. In response to the psychologist's persistent but gentle queries, Dennis explained that he had promised his fiancée that he would seek some advice about his intermittent panic attacks. Nevertheless, he was reluctant to admit that he had any really serious problems, and he evaded many questions pertaining to his current adjustment. Dennis seemed intent on convincing the psychologist that he was not "just another nut." He continued to chat on a superficial level and, at one point, even began asking the psychologist whether he had adequate life insurance coverage.

In subsequent sessions it became clear that the panic attacks, which never occurred more than two or three times per year, were simply the most dramatic of Dennis's problems. He was also an extremely tense and anxious person between attacks. He frequently experienced severe headaches that sometimes lasted for several hours. These generally took the form of a steady, diffuse pain across his forehead; Dennis sometimes felt as if a tight band were stretched around the top of his head. The headaches were accompanied by an aching sensation in his neck and shoulders. Dennis also complained that he could not relax, noting that he suffered from chronic muscle tension and occasional insomnia. His job often required that he work late in the evening, visiting people in their homes after dinner. When he returned to his apartment, he was always "wound up" and on edge, unable to sleep. He had tried various distractions and popular remedies, but nothing worked. His attempt at transcendantal meditation had failed, and the expensive reclining chair with an electric vibrator seemed to add to his discomfort.

Dennis was very self-conscious. Although he was an attractive man and one of the most successful salespersons in his firm, he worried constantly about what others thought of him. This concern was obvious in his behavior both before and after sessions at the clinic. At the end of every session, he seemed to make a point of joking loudly so that anyone outside the psychologist's office would hear the laughter. He would then open the door, as he continued to chuckle, and say something like, "Well, Bill [the therapist's first name], that was a lot of fun. Let's get together again soon!" as he left the office. The most peculiar incident of this sort occurred prior to the fourth treatment session. Dennis had avoided the clinic waiting room on past visits, but this time it happened that he and his therapist met at a location that required them to walk through the waiting room together in order to reach the therapist's office. Thinking nothing of it, the therapist set off across the room in which several other clients were waiting, and Dennis quickly followed. When they reached the middle of the long room, Dennis suddenly clasped his right arm around the therapist's shoulders, smiled, and in a voice that was slightly too loud said, "Well, Bill, what's up? How can I help you today?" The therapist was taken completely by surprise but said nothing until they reached his office. Dennis quickly closed the door and leaned against the wall, holding his hand over his heart as he gulped for air. He was visibly shaken. Once he had caught his breath, he apologized profusely and explained that he did not know what had come over him. He said that he had always been afraid that the other people in the clinic, particularly the other clients, would realize that he was a client and therefore think that he was crazy. He had panicked as they walked across the waiting room and had been unable to resist the urge to divert attention from himself by seeming to be a therapist.

This preoccupation with social evaluation was also evident in Dennis's work. He became extremely tense whenever he was about to call on a prospective client. Between the point at which an appointment was arranged and his arrival at the person's home, Dennis worried constantly. Would they like him? Could he make the sale? His anxiety became most exaggerated as he drove his car to the person's home. In an effort to cope with this anxiety, Dennis had constructed a 45-minute recording that he played for himself on the cassette deck in his car. The tape contained a long pep talk, recorded in his own voice, in which he continually reassured and encouraged himself: "Go out there and charm 'em, Dennis. You're the best damn salesman this company's ever had! They're gonna be putty in your hands, big fella. Flash that smile and give 'em the old Holt handshake. They'll love you!" and on and on. Unfortunately, the net effect of the recording was probably to increase his tension. Despite this anxiety, he managed to perform effectively in the selling role, just as he was able to project an air of confidence in the clinic. But, on the inside, he was miserable. He worried constantly about his performance and what others thought of him. Every two or three months he would become convinced that he could no longer stand the tension and decide to quit his job. Then he would make a big sale or receive a bonus for exceeding his quota for that period and change his mind.

SOCIAL HISTORY

Dennis was an only child. His father was an accountant and his mother was an elementary-school teacher. No one else in his family had been treated for serious adjustment problems.

Dennis and his mother got along well, but his relationship with his father had always been difficult. His father was a demanding perfectionist who held very high, probably unrealistic, expectations for Dennis. When Dennis was in elementary school, his father always wanted him to be the best athlete and the best student in his class. Although Dennis was adequate in both of these areas, he did not excel in either. His father frequently expressed the hope that Dennis would become an aeronautical engineer when he grew up. Now that Dennis was working as an insurance salesman, his father never missed an opportunity to express his disapproval and disappointment. He was also unhappy about Dennis's previous divorce. Most times his parents came to visit, Dennis and his father ended up in an argument.

Dennis remembered being shy as a child. Nevertheless, he enjoyed the company of other children and always had a number of friends. When he reached adolescence, he was particularly timid around girls. In an effort to overcome his shyness, he joined the high-school drama club and played bit parts in several of its productions. This experience provided an easy avenue for meeting other students with whom he became friends. He also learned that he could speak in front of a group of people without making a fool of himself, but he continued to feel uncomfortable in public speaking and social situations.

After graduating from high school, Dennis attended a private liberal arts college for two years. Although he had been a reasonably good student in high school, he began to experience academic problems in college. He attributed his sporadic performance to test anxiety. In his own words, he "choked" on examinations. Shortly after he entered the classroom, the palms of his hands would began to perspire profusely. Then his breathing would become more rapid and shallow and his mouth would become very dry. He sometimes found himself glancing back and forth from his watch to the clock on the wall, worrying about the grade he would get and unable to concentrate on the test questions. On the worst occasions, his mind would go blank. Some of his instructors were sympathetic to the problem and allowed him to take extra time to finish examinations; others permitted him to turn in supplementary papers that were written out of class. Nevertheless, his grades began to suffer and by the end of his first year he was placed on academic probation.

During his second year in college, Dennis began to experience gastrointestinal problems. He had always seemed to have a sensitive stomach and avoided rich or fried foods that often led to excessive flatulence or nausea. Now the symptoms were getting worse. He suffered intermittently from constipation, cramping, and diarrhea. He would frequently go for three or four days without having a bowel movement. During these periods, he experienced considerable discomfort and occasional severe cramps in his lower abdominal tract. These problems persisted for several months until, at the urging of his roommate, Dennis finally made an appointment for a complete gastrointestinal examination at the local hospital. The physicians were unable to find any evidence of structural pathology and diagnosed Dennis's problems as "irritable colon." They gave him prescriptions for a laxative and tincture of belladonna, which suppresses motor and secretory activity in the gastrointestinal tract. These medications provided some relief, but Dennis continued to suffer from intermittent bowel problems.

Dennis had several girlfriends and dated regularly throughout high school and college. During his sophomore year in college, he developed a serious relationship with the younger sister of one of his closest friends. Mary was a freshman at the same school. She and Dennis shared some interests and enjoyed each other's company, so they spent a great deal of time together. At the end of the academic year, Dennis decided that he had had enough of college. He was bored with his classes and tired of the continual pressure from his parents to get better grades. An older friend of his had recently landed a well-paying job with an insurance firm, so Dennis decided that he would complete applications with a number of companies. Two of them invited him to interviews, and one eventually offered him a position in sales. The new job required that he relocate in a nearby state. For the first several months, he and Mary drove back and forth to visit each other on weekends. At the end of the fall semester, Mary decided that she would also drop out of school. She and Dennis began living together; they were married two years later.

Dennis and Mary were reasonably happy for the first three years. He was successful at his job, and she eventually became a certified realtor. As they were both promoted by their respective firms, they found themselves spending more and more time working and less and less time with each other. Their interests also began to diverge. When Mary had some time off or an evening free, she liked to go out to restaurants and parties. Dennis liked to stay home and watch television.

Dennis's first real panic attack occurred when he was 24 years old. He and Mary were at a dinner theater with three other couples, including Mary's boss and his wife. The evening had been planned for several weeks, in spite of Dennis's repeated objections. He was self-conscious about eating in public and did not care for Mary's colleagues; he had finally agreed to accompany her because it seemed that it would be important for her advancement in the firm.

He was also looking forward to seeing *A Chorus Line*, which would be performed after the meal was served. As the meal progressed, Dennis began to feel increasingly uncomfortable. He was particularly concerned that he might experience one of his gastrointestinal attacks during dinner and be forced to spend the rest of the evening in the men's restroom. He did not want to have to explain the problem to all of Mary's friends. In an attempt to prevent such an attack, he had taken antispasmodic medication for his stomach and was eating sparingly. Just as everyone else had finished eating dessert, Dennis began to experience a choking sensation in his throat and chest. He could not get his breath, and it seemed certain to him that he was going to faint on the spot. Unable to speak or move, he remained frozen in his seat in utter terror. The others quickly realized that something was wrong and, assuming that he had choked on some food, Mary began to pound on his back between the shoulder blades. There was now a sharp pain in his chest, and he began to experience heart palpitations. Dennis was finally able to wheeze that he thought he was having a heart attack. Two of the other men helped him up, and a waiter directed them to a lounge in the building where he was able to lie down. In less than 30 minutes, all of the symptoms had passed; Dennis and Mary were able to excuse themselves from the others and drive home.

Dennis was frightened by this experience, but he did not seek medical advice. He was convinced that he was in good physical condition and attributed the attack to something he had eaten or perhaps to an interaction between the food and medication. He did, however, become even more reluctant to go to restaurants with Mary and her friends. Interestingly, he continued to eat business lunches with his own colleagues without apparent discomfort.

The second panic attack occurred about six months later, while Dennis was driving alone in rush hour traffic. The symptoms were essentially the same; the sudden sensation of smothering, accompanied by an inexplicable, intense fear. Fortunately, Dennis was in the right lane of traffic when the sensation began. He was able to pull his car off the road and lie on the seat until the experience was over.

By this point, Dennis was convinced that he needed medical help. He made an appointment with a specialist in internal medicine who gave him a complete physical examination. There was no evidence of cardiovascular or gastrointestinal pathology. The physician told Dennis that the problem seemed to be with his nerves and gave him a prescription for diazepam (Valium), a minor tranquilizer often used in treating anxiety states. Dennis took five milligrams of Valium three times per day for four months. It did help him relax and, in combination with his other medication, seemed to improve his gastrointestinal distress. However, he did not like the side effects (such as drowsiness) or the feeling of being dependent on medication to control his anxiety. He saw the latter as a sign of weakness and eventually discontinued taking the Valium.

Mary asked Dennis for a divorce three years after they were married (two years after his first panic attack). It came as no surprise to Dennis; their relationship had deteriorated considerably. He had become even more reluctant to go out with her in the evening and on weekends, insisting that he needed to stay home and rest his nerves. He was very apprehensive in crowded public places and also careful about where and when he drove his car. He tried to avoid rush hour traffic. When he did drive in heavy traffic, he always stayed in the right lane, even if it was much slower, so that he could pull off the road if he had an attack. Long bridges also made him extremely uncomfortable because they did not afford an opportunity to pull over; he dreaded the possibility of being trapped on a bridge during one of his "spells." These fears did not prevent him from doing his work. He continued to force himself to meet new people, and he drove long distances every day. The most drastic impact was on his social life. These increased restrictions led to greater tension between Dennis and Mary. They had both become more and more irritable and seldom enjoyed being with each other. When she decided that she could no longer stand to live with him, he agreed to the divorce.

After Mary left, Dennis moved to an apartment in which he was still living when he entered treatment five years later. His chronic anxiety, occasional panic attacks, headaches, and gastrointestinal problems persisted relatively unchanged, although they varied in severity. He had a number of friends and managed to see them fairly frequently. He did, however, avoid situations that involved large crowds. He would not, for example, accompany his friends to a professional football game, but he did like to play golf, where he could be out in the fresh air with very few people and lots of open space around him. He met Elaine four years after the divorce. She was slightly older than he and much less active socially than Mary had been. They enjoyed spending quiet evenings watching television and occasionally got together with one or two other couples to play bridge. Although they planned to get married, neither Dennis nor Elaine wanted to rush into anything.

CONCEPTUALIZATION AND TREATMENT

When Dennis entered treatment, he expressed a desire to learn how to control his anxiety, particularly when it reached its most excessive proportions in the form of panic attacks. He did not feel comfortable taking medication because he considered it to be an artificial "crutch." On the other hand, he was also opposed to the idea of long-term psychotherapy aimed at uncovering deeply ingrained psychic conflict. He had read about behavioral approaches to the treatment of anxiety and was looking for a psychologist with whom he could follow such an approach and had, in fact, found such a person. His therapist viewed Dennis's problem as being largely attributable to a deficiency in particular behavioral and cognitive skills. They discussed this conceptual approach to anxiety. The therapist agreed to help Dennis identify problem areas and teach him more appropriate responses that might substitute for his current, maladaptive efforts to cope with his environment. The process of arriving at this agreement was accompanied by an obvious change in Dennis's behavior toward the therapist. He became much less defensive and dropped his annoying, superficial displays of bravado when he realized that the psychologist intended to function as a teacher, not a judge who would rule on his sanity or a detective who might probe for long-lost secrets.

After establishing a working relationship, the first major task was to determine the situations in which Dennis was most likely to become anxious. These fell into two general classes: situations in which he experienced panic attacks, and situations in which he became tense and anxious but did not experience a full attack. The most frequent anxiety-provoking situations were his visits to prospective clients' homes. It was interesting that he had never experienced a panic attack while in the presence of a client. One possible explanation for this phenomenon, and the one adopted by the therapist, was that Dennis was at least nominally in control of these situations, and he had well-rehearsed responses that might be used in almost any circumstances that might arise. Nevertheless, he was almost always uncomfortable during these presentations. The panic attacks had always occurred in crowded public places such as department stores and theaters and in traffic jams. These situations shared two common features. First, they were usually places that he had tried to avoid, such as the dinner theater in which his first attack occurred. Second, they were situations that he could not control; he could not make the traffic start moving, for example, and he could not make Elaine shop more quickly.

The therapist hypothesized that Dennis contributed to the onset of his own panic attacks. Presumably without awareness, he would maintain excessive muscle tension in his neck, shoulders, arms, and legs for extended periods of time while breathing in a shallow, rapid manner, thus leading to the experience of dizziness and exhaustion. Of course, when these physical sensations suddenly became apparent, Dennis did not have a ready explanation for their appearance. The emotional response of fear could therefore be seen as the inevitable product of a dramatic change in arousal that Dennis could not attribute to external stimuli. Given this hypothesis, it seemed that future panic attacks might be avoided by teaching Dennis to control, and be aware of, the muscle tension in various parts of his body and by helping him realize that he could precipitate the physical phenomena associated with a panic attack through his own muscular responses. These goals could be accomplished through a procedure known as progressive relaxation, originally developed by Jacobson (1938), in which he would be taught to relax specific muscle groups throughout his body.

Dennis's anxiety in work-related situations, on the other hand, did not seem to be the product of a deficiency in his overt response repertoire; he knew what to say and was obviously successful at it, as judged by his outstanding sales record. The therapist's hypothesis was that Dennis's perceptions and expectations — the things that he said to himself and other people — were at the root of this area of his problem. It became clear, for example, that Dennis believed that it would be a catastrophe if someone did not like him. He also insisted to himself that he had to be the *best* salesperson in this firm. These were most likely attitudes that had been instilled in Dennis by his father, who had continually emphasized his demand for perfection and whose affection seemed to hinge on its attainment. More adaptive self-statements would have to be substituted for these irrational demands before Dennis would feel more comfortable in social situations, particularly those that involved his work.

The therapist had agreed to help Dennis learn new, adaptive responses; he decided to begin with training in relaxation. His purpose at the outset was not to eliminate the occurrence of any more panic attacks. They were, of course, the most dramatic and perhaps the most difficult of Dennis's problems. But their infrequency also meant that even if Dennis learned to control them, he would not be able to notice any improvement in his adjustment for a very long time. Therefore the therapist's first goal was to select a simpler problem and an area in which Dennis could see rapid improvement, thus enhancing his motivation for further change efforts. The most suitable place to begin, therefore, was his inability to relax when he returned to his apartment after work.

Relaxation training was introduced to Dennis as an active coping skill that he could use to control muscular tension. Just as he had learned to be tense and anxious, he could now learn to relax. The therapist explained that he would begin by teaching Dennis how to use the procedure in the clinic setting. Dennis would then be expected to practice progressive relaxation at home on a daily basis for a period of several weeks. He was cautioned against expecting a sudden change in his anxiety level and told that, for most people, the development of relaxation skills takes considerable effort. He was also asked to purchase a small tape recorder to record the therapist's relaxation instructions. The tape would be used to guide his practice sessions at home.

Relaxation training began during the sixth treatment session. The lights in the room were dimmed and a small white-noise generator was turned on to minimize the distraction from noise in the hall and waiting room. A large comfortable reclining chair had been moved into the office for use in this exercise. The therapist began by asking Dennis to watch as he stretched out in the recliner and demonstrated the procedure, which involved the alternate tensing and relaxing of a sequence of major muscle groups. Then they exchanged places. Speaking in a low, soft voice, the therapist asked Dennis to close his eyes and move around in the chair until he could settle into a comfortable reclining position. He drew Dennis's attention to his pattern of breathing and asked him to take deep, slow breaths while imagining that he was inhaling feelings of relaxation and exhaling tension. When Dennis seemed to be comfortable, the therapist asked him to lift his forearms off the arms of the chair and tighten his hands into fists. He was instructed to hold that position for 5 seconds, noting the muscular tension, and then let go, releasing the tension and allow his hands to slip back onto the arms of the chair. The therapist asked Dennis to study the difference between the feeling of tension that he had just experienced and the relaxation that he now enjoyed. After a 10-second pause, the therapist asked Dennis to clench his fists again, hold that position for another 5 seconds while concentrating on the sensation of muscular tension, and then relax. This cycle was then repeated through a sequence of several other groups of muscles, including his upper arms, shoulders, neck, face, back, abdomen, legs, and feet. Throughout this process, the therapist continued to remind Dennis to breathe slowly and deeply. When all of the muscle groups had been completed, the therapist conducted a leisurely review, beginning with the hands and arms. Instead of tensing his muscles again, Dennis was asked simply to concentrate on each area of his body in sequence and relax away any tension that remained. This review was followed by a 30-second period in which Dennis was instructed simply to rest and enjoy the sensation of total relaxation that he had now accomplished. The therapist told Dennis that he would count backward slowly from five to one and that when he reached one Dennis should open his eyes and stretch, thus ending the exercise.

Dennis responded positively to relaxation training from the very beginning. He noted that he felt awkward and self-conscious at the beginning of the procedure but had quickly overcome his apprehension. Although he did not think that he had reached a state of complete relaxation, he did feel much more relaxed than he had when he arrived for the session; he indicated that he was looking forward to practicing the procedure during the coming week. He and the therapist then discussed the manner in which this practice would take place. The therapist asked Dennis to pick a regular time that he could set aside for the exercise, preferably the same time every day, and also a time in which he would not be so tired that he would fall asleep. Dennis decided on midmorning. He usually stayed at home to finish paperwork in the morning before going out to call on clients. His home office had a reclining chair that would be ideal for this purpose, and no one was likely to call or disturb him at that time of day. The therapist then explained a subjective rating scale that he could use to keep track of his progress. Using a 10-point scale, with 1 being complete relaxation ("similar to the quiet, drifting feeling that you have before you go to sleep") and 10 being maximum tension ("like you feel when you've already had a tough day and a potential client has just decided against buying a policy"), Dennis was asked to keep a written record of his subjective level of tension both before and after each practice session.

Dennis was faithful in completing his homework assignment. He practiced relaxation every morning except Sunday, when he slept in and delayed the exercise until early evening. His average self-rating of tension was about 6 or 7 before practice and 3 or 4 at the end of each session. He said that he enjoyed the exercise and stated that he was pleased finally to be learning a skill with which he could cope with his tension. His outlook was clearly hopeful but not overly optimistic. The therapist expressed confidence in Dennis's ability to overcome his anxiety, noting once again that relaxation had been demonstrated to be an effective procedure for this kind of problem and adding that Dennis's willingness to practice regularly outside of their weekly sessions was a good prognostic sign.

The next three sessions were mostly spent discussing Dennis's progress with his relaxation training. In order to provide additional practice and iron out any small difficulties in his technique, they still took time to practice relaxation during each session. By the end of the first month of training, Dennis was consistently able to reduce his subjective tension to a level of 1 or 2 at the end of each practice session. His only problem arose in trying to use the procedure during periods of very high tension. For example, during the second week of practice, he had tried unsuccessfully to use the exercise to eliminate a severe headache that had developed in the afternoon and persisted throughout the evening. The therapist pointed out that Dennis should not be discouraged because he had not reached a stage of proficiency that would allow him to deal with the most serious levels of stress. He also noted that the object of relaxation was primarily to teach Dennis to be aware of muscular tension before it had progressed to such an advanced level. Relaxation could therefore be seen as a kind of preventive procedure, not a way of coping with problems like headaches after they became severe.

After four weeks, the therapist asked Dennis to try practicing relaxation without the taped instructions and without following the tension-relaxation procedure. He was asked to find a comfortable reclining position and spend 15 to 20 minutes in relaxation. Instead of alternately tensing and relaxing specific muscle groups, he was instructed simply to concentrate on breathing slowly and "letting go." His daily records showed that he was soon able to achieve a comparable level of relaxation using this simplified procedure. He also noted that he had gradually become more aware of muscle tension, particularly in the muscles of his face, neck, and shoulders, as it developed throughout the day. When he became aware of these sensations, he tried to shrug his shoulders or roll his head back and forth on his shoulders and think about relaxing the muscles that were becoming uncomfortable. It was not surprising that he also found that he was experiencing fewer and less severe headaches than he had prior to treatment.

After Dennis was making satisfactory progress with relaxation, the therapist shifted the focus of their discussions to introduce a process known as *rational restructuring*.[1] He began with the observation that emotions, or feelings, are influenced by what people say to themselves. In other words it is not necessarily the objective situation with which we are confronted, but rather what we tell ourselves about the situation that determines our emotional response. For example, a woman who is fearful when speaking in front of a large group of people is not in physical danger. It is probably what that woman is telling herself about the audience ("They'll all think that I'm stupid," or "I'm sure none of them will like me") that leads to undue levels of anxiety. The therapist provided several similar examples and explained the general principles behind rational restructuring while carefully avoiding specific reference to Dennis's own experience. By following this gradual introduction, he was able to help Dennis understand the rationale for their future discussions and get him to agree that cognitive processes may mediate inappropriate emotional responses without triggering unnecessary defensive arguments (e.g., "I don't say those things to myself!").

Once Dennis agreed to the general assumptions behind rational restructuring, the therapist outlined a number of the common irrational beliefs that have been identified by Ellis (1962). These include the notions that people have to be *perfect* in *everything* they do and that people should be *loved* by *everyone* they know. As Ellis points out, these demands are impossible. If you make your happiness contingent on their fulfillment, you will inevitably make yourself miserable. It would be nice if everyone loved us. We might feel better if they did, but it is not a *disaster* if they do not. Dennis was intrigued by these notions and, throughout the discussion, often thought of examples of situations in which other people (such as his former wife, Mary) seemed to be making themselves unhappy by harboring such irrational beliefs. As they talked further, the therapist asked Dennis if he could think of examples in which he engaged in this kind of thinking. Initially, this was difficult. The therapist noted that we are often unaware of the irrational statements that we make to ourselves; they have been so deeply instilled and overlearned that they become essentially automatic responses. Confronted with an audience, the person with public speaking anxiety does not actually whisper, "I have to be perfect in everything I do, including public speaking, and it is imperative that they all think that I am witty and clever. If they do not, I am a miserable failure." The only subjective experience may be an immediate sensation of overwhelming fear. Nevertheless, that emotional response may be mediated by these beliefs. Furthermore, if that person could learn to make more rational statements (e.g., "I hope that I will do well and that many of the people will

---

[1]This procedure is also referred to as *rational emotive therapy* by its principal proponent, Albert Ellis.

enjoy my talk, but if they do not, it's not the end of the world"), anxiety could be controlled.

These discussions filled the next several sessions. Much of the time was spent taking specific experiences that had been anxiety provoking for Dennis and analyzing the self-statements that might have accompanied his response. Many of these centered around contacts with clients. The applicability of the rational restructuring approach to these situations was particularly evident given the tape recording that he had made to coach himself before appointments. The therapist pointed out that Dennis had been on the right track in this attempt to cope with his anxiety, but many of the statements in the tape created unrealistic, or irrational, expectations that probably exacerbated his problem. Instead of assuring himself that the client would like him because he was the best salesperson in the company, Dennis would have been better able to control his anxiety if he had been able to reduce the demands that he placed on himself and recognize that the success or failure of his career did not depend on the outcome of a single client contact.

Dennis gradually became proficient in noticing the irrational beliefs that led to his anxiety in various situations. At first, he could only dissect these situations in discussions with his therapist. The goal, of course, was to help him practice this skill until he could employ rational self-statements as a coping response before and during stressful experiences. In order to facilitate this process and provide for generalization of these new cognitive responses outside of the therapy sessions, the therapist asked Dennis to begin a kind of diary. Each night, he was to take a few minutes to write down a description of any situation in which he had become particularly anxious during the day. He was instructed to note the irrational statements that he must have been making in order to become anxious as well as complementary rational statements that would have been more appropriate. After keeping this record for four weeks, Dennis noted that he was beginning to be able to feel less anxious in social situations and during sales visits.

The final step in treatment was concerned with Dennis's avoidance of situations that had been previously associated with panic attacks. He had not experienced an attack in the three months since his first visit to the psychologist, probably because he had refused to accompany Elaine to any movies, restaurants, or department stores. He was now able to achieve a state of complete relaxation quickly and without the aid of the formal tension-relaxation procedure. The therapist therefore decided to begin a program of graduated, prolonged exposure. This would be accomplished *in vivo* (i.e., in the natural environment), by having Dennis purposefully enter situations that had previously led to feelings of apprehension and dread and then remain there until he had successfully demonstrated to himself that he would not have a panic attack. At the beginning of treatment, this procedure would have been likely to fail because Dennis did not believe that he could handle such situations. The therapist noted that he had now acquired new skills with which he would be able to cope with whatever anxiety, if any, he might experience. They intentionally began with a fairly easy situation and arranged for Elaine to accompany Dennis. He indicated that her presence would make him feel less vulnerable. His assignment for the week was to go to a specific department store, during the morning on a weekday when there would not be a large crowd present, and spend 15 minutes browsing in the men's department, which was located just inside the front entrance. When this task had been successfully accomplished, Dennis and the therapist designed a hierarchy of stressful situations to which he would expose himself in sequence and for increasing amounts of time. These began with more simple situations, such as the first one at the men's department, and continued on to those that had previously been most difficult for him. The latter included activities such as attending a play with Elaine and sitting in the middle of a center row (where he did not have easy access to an aisle or exit).

The treatment sessions were terminated after six months. Dennis had made considerable progress during that time. He had successfully mastered all of the situations in the prolonged-exposure hierarchy and had not experienced a panic attack since the one that provoked his entry into treatment. His general anxiety level was also considerably reduced. He continued to experience occasional tension headaches, particularly after especially busy days, but they were less frequent (perhaps two or three each month) and less severe than they had been in the past. His insomnia had disappeared completely. Whenever he did have trouble sleeping, he would utilize the formal tension-relaxation procedure. In this way he was able to eliminate muscular tension and simultaneously distract himself from whatever problems he was worrying about. Unfortunately, his gastrointestinal problems remained. He still suffered from intermittent constipation and diarrhea and continued to use medication to relieve these discomforts on an *ad hoc* basis.

DISCUSSION

Disorders in which anxiety is the most prominent symptom are quite common. During any given year, 17 percent of the people in the United States may suffer from at least one form of anxiety disorder, although only one out of four of these people receives treatment for the problem (Kessler et al., 1994). *DSM-IV* recognizes eight disorders that are characterized by anxiety and avoidance behaviors:

1. Panic Disorder (with or without Agoraphobia)
2. Agoraphobia without History of Panic Disorder
3. Specific Phobia

4. Social Phobia
5. Obsessive Compulsive Disorder
6. Posttraumatic Stress Disorder
7. Acute Stress Disorder
8. Generalized Anxiety Disorder

The *DSM-IV* description and organization of anxiety disorders pays special attention to the presence or absence of panic attacks. These extraordinarily frightening experiences, which seldom last more than a few minutes, are discrete periods of apprehension or fear, accompanied by sensations such as shortness of breath, palpitations, chest pains, choking or smothering sensations, dizziness, perspiring, and trembling or shaking. Some patients, like Dennis, experience only one or two attacks a year, whereas others may have them on a daily basis. Most cases of agoraphobia begin with the experience of panic attacks. The *DSM-IV* definition of a panic attack (p. 395) includes the following criteria: A discrete period of intense fear or discomfort, in which four (or more) of the following symptoms developed abruptly and reached a peak within 10 minutes:

1. Palpitations, pounding heart, or accelerated heart rate
2. Sweating
3. Trembling or shaking
4. Sensations of shortness of breath or smothering
5. Feeling of choking
6. Chest pain or discomfort
7. Nausea or abdominal distress
8. Feeling dizzy, unsteady, lightheaded, or faint
9. Derealization (feeling of unreality) or depersonalization (being detached from oneself)
10. Fear of losing control or going crazy
11. Fear of dying
12. Paresthesias (numbness or tingling sensations)
13. Chills or hot flushes

The *DSM-IV* criteria for Panic Disorder require that the person experience recurrent unexpected panic attacks. At least one of these attacks must be followed by a period of at least one month in which the person has worried about having further attacks or else changed his or her behavior as a result of the attacks.

In phobic disorders, the most important element is a persistent, irrational fear of a specific object or situation that the person goes out of his or her way to avoid. The distinction among agoraphobias, social phobias (e.g., fear of public speaking), and specific phobias (e.g., fear of small animals or fear of heights) is based on a system proposed by Marks (1970). Fears in these three categories can generally be distinguished on the basis of differences in symptomatology, age at onset, sex ratio, and treatment response (e.g., Persson & Nordlund, 1985).

Agoraphobia is defined as an exaggerated fear of being in situations or places from which escape might be difficult, or in which help, if needed, might be unavailable. It is among the most common and debilitating of the phobic disorders. In severe cases of agoraphobia, the person becomes entirely housebound—unable to venture outside for fear of experiencing intense anxiety. Agoraphobics frequently report fear of becoming physically ill, fainting, having a heart attack, or dying (Thorpe & Burns, 1983), particularly during a panic attack. These fears increase if the person's access to support (e.g., a companion) or an avenue of escape is blocked or impaired.

In contrast to the circumscribed fears seen in phobic disorders, Generalized Anxiety Disorder (GAD) is characterized by unrealistic and excessive worry and anxiety occurring more days than not for a period of at least six months. The person must exhibit three or more of the following six symptoms in association with these worries: restlessness or feeling keyed up or on edge, being easily fatigued, difficulty concentrating, irritability, muscle tension, and sleep disturbance (APA, 1994; Rapee, 1991).

Dennis met the criteria for both Panic Disorder with Agoraphobia and GAD. Although his panic attacks were not especially frequent, he was persistently afraid of having another. His behavior met the criteria for agoraphobia in that he was apprehensive about being in public places from which escape might be difficult. He had occasionally forced himself to enter such situations, but the constriction of his social activities had a very negative impact on his life. Dennis's fear was not so severe that he was entirely housebound, but he did avoid public places from which he was afraid he might not be able to escape.

Dennis also met *DSM-IV* criteria for GAD. His muscle tension was clearly evidenced by his inability to relax, his frequent tension headaches, and the constant fatigue from which he suffered. His irregular bowel movements and diarrhea were further signs of autonomic difficulties. He experienced continual apprehension and frequently had difficulty sleeping.

Data regarding the frequency of specific anxiety disorders in the community have been reported by investigators involved in a large-scale epidemiological study, known as the ECA study, concerned with the distribution of mental disorders in five American cities (Robins & Regier, 1991). Approximately six out of every one hundred people interviewed in a 12-month period reported some form of phobic disorder; some people fit more than one subcategory. Specific phobias were the most common (about 5 percent), followed by agoraphobia (about 3 percent), and social phobias (about 2 percent). Specific phobias and agoraphobia were more common among women than men, but gender differences were not found for the prevalence of social phobias (Boyd et al., 1990). Generalized Anxiety Disorder was also relatively common among people in this study, with a 12-month prevalence rate of 4 percent. Panic Disorder, on the other hand, was the least common form of anxiety disorder. Slightly more than 1 percent of the subjects in the ECA study qualified for a diagnosis of Panic Disorder during the 12-month period immediately prior to their interview (Weissman, 1990).

Depression and drug abuse are frequently associated with chronic anxiety disorders (Brown & Barlow, 1992; Chambless et al., 1987). At least half of all patients with one form of anxiety disorder have also experienced an episode of major depression at some point during their lives.

Alcoholism and barbiturate abuse are common results of attempts to use drugs to cope with chronic tension and generalized anxiety. In fact, some patients become addicted to minor tranquilizers such as Valium that have been prescribed by well-intentioned physicians. Fortunately, Dennis did not become dependent on the use of medication. Although Valium did make him feel more relaxed, he resisted its use because it made him feel even less in control of his own emotions.

Etiological Considerations

Several twin studies have found that genetic factors seem to be influential in the transmission of anxiety disorders, especially those that involve the experience of panic attacks (e.g., Carey & Gottesman, 1981; Kendler, Neale, Kessler, Heath, & Eaves, 1992a; Torgerson, 1983). A somewhat inconsistent picture has emerged with regard to the influence of genetic factors in the etiology of GAD (Kendler, Neale, Kessler, Heath, & Eaves, 1992b). The data indicate that GAD is somewhat less heritable than other forms of anxiety disorder. Studies of the distribution of various psychological disorders in families also suggest that the etiology of some forms of anxiety and depression may be related. First-degree relatives of patients diagnosed as having both major depression and panic disorder show markedly increased rates of depression, anxiety disorders, and alcoholism in comparison to relatives of normals and those of depressed patients without anxiety disorder (Weissman, 1985). Thus, biological factors appear to be important in the etiology of anxiety disorders, but environmental events are also influential.

Traditional psychological views of anxiety have been based on psychoanalytic and learning theories. Although there are obvious differences between these points of view, both theories treat anxiety as a signal of some expected negative event. Neither draws an important distinction between chronic anxiety and panic attacks. A psychoanalytically oriented therapist would have viewed Dennis's chronic anxiety as a symptom of unconscious conflict between the ego and previously punished id impulses (Compton, 1992). These impulses are usually presumed to be sexual or aggressive in nature and traceable to early childhood experiences. In an effort to avoid their imminent expression, which is signaled by the subjective experience of anxiety, the ego employs the defense mechanism known as *repression*. This theoretical position is so general that it could be applied to almost any case. It might have been argued, for example, that Dennis secretly harbored violent impulses toward his father, who criticized and belittled him. Since he was also afraid of his father (a classic assumption of psychoanalytic theory) and since he would be punished if he harmed his father, these impulses were anxiety provoking and therefore repressed. But when he entered situations in which he might be evaluated by other people, he was reminded of his father's criticism. The hostile impulses then became more intense, and his anxiety would increase proportionately. Alternatively, one might have argued that Dennis had not gotten over his sexual desire for his mother (another classic assumption) and that he was currently troubled by unconscious impulses to perform incestuous sexual acts. There was, however, no clear evidence to support either of these notions. Dennis did not hide his resentment of this father. They argued openly and frequently about every imaginable topic. Nor was there any evidence of sexual problems. Dennis and Elaine had intercourse regularly, and both were satisfied with this aspect of their relationship.

The conditioning model (e.g., Miller, 1948; Mowrer, 1947) would view Dennis's problem as a fear response that had been learned through the association of previously neutral stimuli (e.g., a crowded theater) with a painful or frightening stimulus. Once Dennis had learned to fear particular situations, his avoidance of them would presumably be reinforced by the reduction in anxiety that he experienced after he fled. There are a number of problems with this model (e.g., Costello, 1970; Seligman, 1971). One is that very few patients with anxiety disorders can remember having experienced a traumatic event (Solyom, Beck, Solyom, & Hugel, 1974). In Dennis's case, his first panic attack was certainly a terrifying experience, and the fear that he experienced may have become paired with the stimuli that were present when it occurred. This process might account for the maintenance of his tendency to avoid crowded public places, but it does not explain the original onset of his intense fear.

A traditional learning theory explanation would view Dennis's problem as a response that had developed in large part through the association of previously neutral stimuli with a frightening experience (e.g., Mowrer, 1947). It is assumed that stimuli that are emotionally neutral, such as those found in a crowded theater, come to be associated with intense fear through the process of classical conditioning. Once Dennis learned to fear particular situations, his avoidance of them would presumably be reinforced by the reduction in anxiety that he experienced after he fled. This theoretical perspective has been applied most extensively to the investigation and treatment of specific phobias (Marks, 1987) that are associated with obvious stimuli in the person's external environment. One problem with the model is the fact that relatively few people with anxiety disorders can remember having experienced a traumatic event (Solyom, Beck, Solyom, & Hugel, 1974).

The conditioning approach to fear responses has also been extended to explain the etiology of panic disorder, in which the person's attacks are not always triggered by external cues. Wolpe and Rowan (1988), for example, have argued that recurrent panic attacks are typically the result of classical conditioning. The person's first attack (the unconditioned response) is supposedly triggered by disturbing physiological sensations that accompany hyperventilation (the unconditioned stimulus) in the presence of a high level of prolonged anxiety. Endogenous stimuli that accompany a low intensity type of hyperventilation (the conditioned stimuli) then provoke further episodes of panic (the conditioned response). The assumption that the conditioned stimuli are *internal* allows this model to account for panic attacks that appear to be uncued by environmental stimuli.

Unfortunately, the attempt to incorporate internal stimuli into this type of classical conditioning model has resulted in some conceptual confusion. The physiological sensations that presumably cue the attack also define the attack itself. McNally (1990) has pointed out that, in Wolpe's model, the panic attack is viewed as both the unconditioned stimulus and the unconditioned response. In other words, it presumably triggers itself. The model would be more useful if these issues could be clarified and if the various internal and behavioral variables were defined more specifically.

Cognitive perspectives on anxiety disorders place primary emphasis on the way in which people interpret information from their environment. According to one view (Beck & Emery, 1985), maladaptive emotions such as chronic, generalized anxiety are the products of self-defeating cognitive schemata. Some people make themselves unnecessarily anxious by interpreting most events in a negative fashion. They view the world in a distorted manner that is biased against themselves. The negative thoughts and images that are triggered by environmental events lead to persistent feelings of threat and insecurity.

One influential cognitive theory of panic disorder has been proposed by Clark (1986), who argued that panic disorder is caused by the catastrophic misinterpretation of bodily sensations. An anxious mood presumably leads to a variety of physiological sensations that typically accompany negative emotional reactions (changes in heart rate and respiration rate, dizziness, etc.). This process is accompanied by a narrowing of the person's attention focus and increased awareness of bodily sensations. Next, the person misinterprets the bodily sensation as a catastrophic event. Support for Clark's theory comes from several research studies reporting that the subjective experience of body sensations is closely associated with maladaptive self-statements among patients with panic disorder (McNally, 1990).

Consider how this approach might explain one of Dennis's panic attacks. After he had his first attack, Dennis became highly vigilant, watching for the slightest indication that he was having another one. If he became short of breath, for whatever reason, he would interpret the experience as being a sign that he was about to have another attack. This reaction ensured continued operation of the feedback loop, with the misinterpretation enhancing Dennis's sense of threat, and so on until the process would spiral out of control. Thus, according to Clark's model, cognitive misinterpretation and biological reactions associated with the perception of threat are *both* necessary for a panic attack to occur.

A sharp contrast to the cognitive theory of panic disorder has been proposed by Klein (1981, 1993), whose explanation for the etiology of panic attacks and agoraphobia is based on an integration of biological and psychological factors. He maintains that the human brain contains a "suffocation monitor." When it detects a threat of suffocation, this monitor triggers distressing feelings associated with breathlessness that in turn provoke urgent efforts to escape to open surroundings. According to Klein's model, unexpected panic attacks represent a misfire of this system, or a *false suffocation alarm*. The threshold for this alarm can presumably be influenced by a number of variables. Biological factors include hormone levels. Social and psychological factors include stressful life events (such as maternal loss) and the development of separation anxiety during childhood, which seem to increase the rate of panic disorder when these children become adults.

According to Klein's theory, agoraphobic avoidance — anticipatory fear of having a panic attack — most often appears after a person has experienced a number of uncued panic attacks. The probability of developing agoraphobia is a function of the number and severity of these attacks. It is probably also influenced by the person's tendency toward worrying or anxious apprehension. This is the point, in Klein's model, at which psychological variables may play their most important role. The suffocation alarm itself is presumably a primitive (from an evolutionary point of view) biological mechanism that is not affected by cognitive processes.

Treatment

Klein's (1993) view of agoraphobia is based on several years of successful experience using antidepressant medication to treat patients with anxiety disorders. He has suggested that the beneficial effects that he has observed are mediated by the drugs' ability to raise, or normalize, the patients' alarm threshold, thereby preventing further spontaneous panic attacks. Some psychiatrists consider tricyclic antidepressants such as imipramine (Tofranil) to be the preferred medication for panic disorder (Agras, 1993; Noyes, 1991) because, in comparison to high-potency benzodiazepines such as alprazolam (Xanax), patients are less likely to become dependent on the drug, and they experience fewer problems when imipramine is withdrawn. Klein carefully points out that the use of medication must be supplemented by psychological treatment aimed at reducing the patients' expectations of future panic episodes. According to Klein, it doesn't matter whether the psychological treatment is behavioral or supportive in nature, as long as it allows patients to initiate contact with previously feared situations in the real world, thereby extinguishing anticipatory anxiety.

Anxiety disorders are also treated with minor tranquilizers from the class of drugs known as benzodiazepines, which includes diazepam (Valium) and alprazolam (Xanax). Dennis had taken Valium for a few months after his second panic attack. The benzodiazepines reduce many symptoms of anxiety, especially vigilance and subjective somatic sensations, such as increased muscle tension, palpitations, increased perspiration, and gastrointestinal distress. They have relatively less effect on the tendency to worry and ruminate. Alprazolam is considered by some psychiatrists to be the drug of choice for patients with panic disorder because it leads to more rapid clinical improvement than antidepressant medication and it has fewer side effects. Several placebo-controlled outcome studies indicate that alprazolam is an effective form of treatment for patients with panic disorders (e.g., Ballenger et al., 1988).

There are, of course, some side effects associated with the use of benzodiazepines. These include sedation accompanied by mild psychomotor impairment as well as problems in attention and memory. Dennis discontinued taking Valium because he was bothered by these side effects. The most serious adverse effect of benzodiazepines is their potential for addiction. Approximately 40 percent of people who use benzodiazepines for six months or more will exhibit symptoms of withdrawal if the medication is discontinued (Sussman & Chou, 1988). People who have previously abused other chemical substances, like alcohol, are at greatest risk for becoming dependent on benzodiazepines.

The therapist who treated Dennis combined the use of relaxation with a cognitive approach to his problems (e.g., Rapee & Barlow, 1988). He hypothesized that Dennis's perceptions of social events and the things that he said to himself about these events played an important role in the maintenance of his anxiety. The therapist helped Dennis recognize the general kinds of self-statements that were associated with his anxiety and then modeled more appropriate statements that he would be able to use to cope more effectively with stressful situations. The latter component of the process is particularly important. In addition to helping Dennis gain "insight" into his problem, the therapist taught him specific cognitive skills (adaptive self-statements) that had previously been absent from his repertoire of coping responses. If insight had been sufficient, Dennis would have experienced a decline in his anxiety level as soon as he recognized that he clung to several irrational beliefs, but he did not. Positive change was evident only after a prolonged period of practice employing rational self-statements, both in and out of therapy sessions.

It should also be noted that the therapist did not rely solely on the cognitive form of intervention. In addition to talking with Dennis about his problem, the therapist helped him learn specific behavioral responses (e.g., applied relaxation) and insisted that he confront various situations in the natural environment. This approach was founded on the realization that although cognitive variables may play an important role in the change process, the most effective treatment programs are performance based. This was clear in Dennis's case. His apprehension in crowded public places was not significantly reduced until he had actually mastered a series of such situations in the prolonged exposure procedure.

Controlled outcome studies indicate that cognitive-behavioral procedures are effective for the treatment of anxiety disorders (Borkovec & Costello, 1993; Chambless & Gillis, 1993). One report by Barlow, Craske, Cerny, and Klosko (1989) compared three forms of intervention for panic disorder patients. Clients were randomly assigned to one of the treatment groups or a waiting list control group. Clients were treated for 15 weeks in one of the following treatment conditions: (1) applied muscle relaxation, (2) exposure and cognitive restructuring, or (3) relaxation combined with exposure and cognitive restructuring. All three forms of treatment were found to be effective in terms of adjustment ratings made by clinicians and clients. Panic attacks were significantly reduced in all three groups and virtually eliminated in the groups that received exposure and cognitive restructuring; almost 90 percent of the clients in these groups were panic-free at the end of treatment. Follow-up data indicated that most of these positive effects were maintained for at least six months after the end of treatment. Overall, the results of this study suggest that cognitive-behavioral procedures are an effective form of intervention for patients with panic disorders.

3 POSTTRAUMATIC STRESS DISORDER: RAPE TRAUMA

Jocelyn Rowley, a 20-year-old single woman, was a sophomore at a midwestern university. She had always been a good student, but her grades had fallen recently; and she was having trouble studying. Her academic difficulties, coupled with some problems with relationships and with sleeping, had finally led Jocelyn to see a therapist for the first time. Although she was afraid of being alone, she had no interest in her current friends or boyfriend. She told the therapist that when she was doing everyday things like reading a book, she sometimes was overcome by vivid images of violent events in which she was the victim of a mugging or an assault. These symptoms had begun rather suddenly, and together they made her afraid that she was losing her mind.

Most of Jocelyn's symptoms had begun about two months before she visited the university's counseling service. Since then she had been having nightmares almost every night about unfamiliar men in dark clothing trying to harm her. She was not having trouble falling asleep, but she was trying to stay awake to avoid the nightmares. During the day, if someone walked up behind her and tapped her unexpectedly on the shoulder, she would be extremely startled, to the point that her friends became offended by her reactions. When she was studying, especially if she was reading her English textbook, images of physical brutality would intrude on her thoughts and distract her. She had a great deal of difficulty concentrating on her schoolwork.

Jocelyn also reported problems with interpersonal relationships. She and her boyfriend had argued frequently in recent weeks, even though she could not identify any specific problems in their relationship. "I just get so *angry* at him," she told the therapist. Her boyfriend had complained that she was not emotionally invested in the relationship. He had also accused her of cheating on him, which she denied. These problems were understandably causing her boyfriend to distance himself from her. Unfortunately, his reaction made Jocelyn feel abandoned.

Jocelyn was afraid to walk alone to the library at night. She could not bring herself to ask anyone to walk with her because she didn't know if she could feel safe with anyone. Her inability to study in the library intensified her academic problems. Jocelyn's roommates had begun to complain that she was unusually sensitive to their teasing. They noticed that she cried frequently and at unexpected times.

In the course of the first few therapy sessions, the psychologist asked a number of questions about Jocelyn's life just prior to entering therapy. Because the symptoms had such a rapid onset, the therapist was looking for a specific stressful event that might have caused her symptoms. During these first few sessions, Jocelyn reported that she had begun to feel more and more dissociated from herself. She would catch a glimpse of herself in the mirror and think "Is that me?" She would walk around in the midwestern winter with no gloves on and be relieved when her hands hurt from the cold, because "at least it's an indication that I'm alive."

After several sessions, Jocelyn eventually told her therapist that she had been raped by the teaching assistant in her English literature course. The rape occurred two months before she entered therapy. Jocelyn seemed surprised when the therapist was interested in the event, saying "Oh, well, that's already taken care of. It didn't really affect me much at all." The therapist explained that serious trauma such as rape rarely is resolved by itself, especially not quickly.

Jocelyn gradually revealed the story of the rape over the next few sessions. She had needed help writing an English paper, and her T.A. had invited her to his house one night so that he could tutor her. When she arrived at the house, which he shared with several male graduate students, he was busy working. He left her alone in his room to study her English textbook. When he returned, he approached her from behind while she was reading and grabbed her. The T.A. forced her onto his bed and raped her. Jocelyn said that she had not struggled or fought physically because she was terrified and stunned at what was happening to her. She had protested verbally, saying "No!" and "Don't do this to me!" several times, but he ignored her earnest objections. She had been afraid to yell loudly because there were only other men in the house, and she was not sure whether or not they would help her.

After the rape, the T.A. walked Jocelyn back to her dorm and warned her not to tell anyone. She agreed at the time, thinking that if she never told anyone what had happened, she could effectively erase the event and prevent it from having a negative effect on her life. She went up to her dorm room and took an hour-long hot shower, trying to scrub away the effects of the rape. While describing these events to the therapist, Jocelyn shook and her voice was breathy. She kept saying, "You believe me, don't you?"

For several days after the rape occurred, Jocelyn believed that she had been able to keep it from affecting her everyday life. The more she tried not to think about it, however, the more times it came to mind. She began to feel stupid and guilty for having gone to a T.A.'s house in the first place and because she had not been able to anticipate the rape. Jocelyn wondered whether her own behavior had contributed to the rape: Had she dressed in some way or said something that indicated a sexual invitation to him? She was ashamed that she was not strong enough to have prevented the rape or its negative consequences.

Jocelyn had initially believed that only one aspect of her life changed after the rape; she no longer attended discussion sections for her English course. Unfortunately, several other problems soon became evident. Her exaggerated startle response became more and more of a problem because her friends were puzzled by her intense reactions to their casual, friendly gestures. Frequent nightmares prevented her from getting any real sleep, and she was having trouble functioning academically. She had no further contact with her T.A. unless she saw him while walking across campus. When that happened, she would jump into a doorway to avoid him. She also began to withdraw from relationships with other people, especially her boyfriend. He responded to this retreat by pressuring her sexually. She no longer had any interest in sex and repeatedly rejected his physical advances. All of these problems finally made Jocelyn believe that she was losing control of her feelings, and she decided to seek professional help.

SOCIAL HISTORY

Jocelyn had grown up in a small midwestern town 100 miles away from the university. She was the oldest of three children. Both of her parents were successful in their professional occupations, and they were involved in the community and their children's schools. Her family was Protestant, but not very active in the church. Jocelyn had attended public schools and was mostly an A student. She was involved in several extracurricular activities, such as the school yearbook and science club. In high school she had some trouble making friends, both because she was shy and because it was considered "nerdy" to be an A student. It wasn't until she enrolled at the university that she was able to form a relatively large peer group.

Jocelyn's parents were strict about dating and curfews. She had not been interested in attending large parties or drinking when she was in high school.

She did have a boyfriend during her junior and senior years. They began dating when they were both 16 years old and became sexually involved a year later. That relationship had ended when they left their hometown to attend different colleges.

Jocelyn recalled that her high-school boyfriend had occasionally pressured her into having sex when she thought it was too risky, or when she was not interested. She denied having previously been a victim of sexual assault, although one incident that she described did sound abusive to the therapist: When she was about 13 years old, Jocelyn went to a summer music camp to play the trombone, an instrument not usually played by a female. One day after rehearsal, the boys in her section ganged up on her, teasing her that "Girls can't play trombones!" One boy began to wrestle with her, and in the melee placed a finger inside her shorts into her vagina. Jocelyn remembered yelling at him. The boy let her go, and then all the boys ran away. Jocelyn had never viewed that event as being assaultive until she thought about it in reference to being raped.

Jocelyn's adjustment to college had not been problematic; she made several friends, and most of her grades were good. She had never before sought psychological help. Jocelyn felt as if she had the world under control until she was raped by someone she knew.

CONCEPTUALIZATION AND TREATMENT

As Jocelyn began to address her anxiety symptoms, additional problems were caused by other people's reactions to the account of her rape. These difficulties kept the focus of treatment away from her primary anxiety symptoms. After telling her psychologist that she had been raped, Jocelyn began to tell other people in her life, including her boyfriend and her roommates. Her roommates were understandably frightened by what had happened to her, and they tried to divorce themselves from the possibility that it might happen to them. They did this by either accusing her of lying or pointing out differences between them: "I never would have gone to a T.A.'s house," or "You've slept with more people than me—he must have sensed that," or "You didn't *look* beat up—you must not have fought back hard enough."

Her boyfriend's unfortunate and self-centered reaction to the description of her rape quickly led to the end of their relationship. He sought help to cope with his own feelings about her rape by talking to some mutual friends. Jocelyn had specifically asked him not to discuss the attack with other people she knew. Jocelyn's general feelings of being out of control of her life were exacerbated by her apparent inability to contain the spread of gossip about her assault. One specific event, which would have been trivial under ordinary circumstances, led to a series of heated exchanges between Jocelyn and her boyfriend. He approached her from behind and playfully put his arms around her. When she jumped and screamed in fright, he tightened his grip, preventing her escape. After arguing about this incident a number of times, they decided not to see each other anymore.

The absence of meaningful support from her friends fueled Jocelyn's progressive withdrawal. Her anxiety symptoms became more pronounced, and she also became depressed. During this time, Jocelyn approached her English professor and told her that she had been sexually assaulted by the T.A. The professor recommended that Jocelyn report the attack to the appropriate campus office, but she refused. Jocelyn was not ready to report him to the university or press charges because she felt that she could not bear being in the same room with him for any reason. The professor assigned Jocelyn to a different T.A. so that she could continue to go to discussions. Unfortunately, the professor also sent a memo to Jocelyn's other professors telling them that Jocelyn had been assaulted and asking them to be lenient with her. When Jocelyn heard about this memo, she felt infantilized. It also contributed to her despair over her inability to control the spread of gossip about her rape.

Treatment during this time focused primarily on giving Jocelyn an opportunity to express her considerable anger and frustration about her situation. Jocelyn frequently railed to her therapist against the unfairness of the situation. For example, in order to deal with her fear of walking alone after dark, she was trying to find someone to walk with her. It seemed bitterly ironic, however, that she was seeking someone she knew to protect her from violence from strangers. It was, after all, someone she knew rather well who had raped her.

Jocelyn also felt a great deal of guilt over not having been able to prevent her assault. Perhaps she hadn't fought hard enough. Maybe she had unknowingly flirted with him. Did he assume that she knew he was inviting her to his house for sex? Was she was just a "dunce" for not having recognized that implicit invitation? She also felt very guilty about the effect of her situation on her boyfriend and roommates — she seemed to take personal responsibility for the fact that she had made them fearful and resentful.

In one session, the therapist pointed out that the intrusive images that Jocelyn now experienced while reading her English textbook might result from the fact that she had been reading that textbook when her attacker grabbed her from behind. Jocelyn was relieved to hear this explanation, because she had worried that she really was going crazy. This insight did not immediately diminish the frequency of her intrusive images, however, and she remained frustrated and depressed.

By this time Jocelyn's nightmares had become increasingly severe. The content of her dreams was more and more obviously rape related. The dream would begin with Jocelyn in a crowded parking lot. Then a shadowy male in dark clothing would approach her, tell her he wanted to rape her, and proceed to attack her. She remembered trying to fight off the attack in her dream, but her limbs felt as if they were in thick glue and her struggles were ineffective. The other people in the parking lot stood watching, clapping and cheering for her assailant. Jocelyn would wake up in the middle of the room, crouched as if awaiting attack. These experiences terrified Jocelyn, and they also frightened her roommates.

The therapist's treatment strategy moved to a focused, cognitive-behavioral intervention that had two main parts. The first part is to address the cognitive processes that prolong a maladaptive view of traumatic events. Specific procedures include self-monitoring of activities, graded task assignments (such as going out alone), and modification of maladaptive thoughts regarding the event (such as guilt and self-blame) (Foa & Rothbaum, 1990). This part of the treatment procedure had actually begun as soon as Jocelyn entered therapy. It was continued in parallel with the second part of the therapy, which is based on prolonged exposure.

In prolonged exposure, the victim reexperiences the original trauma in a safe situation in order to decrease slowly the emotional intensity associated with memory of the event. This step is based on the notion that repeated presentation of an aversive stimulus will lead to habituation (defined as the process by which a person's response to the same stimulus lessens with repeated presentations). Jocelyn had, of course, experienced many fleeting and terrifying images of the rape during the weeks after it happened. This form of "reliving" the traumatic experience is symptomatic of the disorder. It presumably does not lead to improvement in the person's condition because the experiences are too intensely frightening and too short-lived to allow negative emotions to be processed completely. In the therapy, Jocelyn was asked to relive the rape scene in her imagination. She described it aloud to the therapist in the present tense. The therapist helped Jocelyn repeat this sequence many times during each session. The sessions were recorded on audiotape, and Jocelyn was required to listen to the tape at least once every day.

As the end of the semester approached, Jocelyn found that she was increasingly able to resume her studies. This was an extremely important sign of improvement. Flunking out of school would have been the ultimate proof that the rape had permanently affected her life, and she struggled not to let that happen. She ended the semester by passing three of her four classes, including English. Therapy was terminated somewhat prematurely after 16 sessions (twice weekly for eight weeks) because the semester was ending and Jocelyn was going home for the summer. The psychologist could not convince Jocelyn to continue therapy during the summer, although she still suffered from occasional nightmares and other symptoms. Jocelyn refused to see a therapist in the summer because she would have to tell her parents, and she was not ready to do that.

A follow-up call to Jocelyn when she returned the following spring, after having taken a semester off, revealed that Jocelyn had finally told her parents about the rape. They were much more supportive than Jocelyn had anticipated. She had continued treatment with another therapist, and her symptoms had diminished slowly over time. She now had nightmares only on rare occasions, and they were usually triggered by a specific event, such as viewing a sexually violent movie or when someone physically restrained her in a joking manner. Jocelyn decided not to return to therapy at the university counseling services, saying that she was tired of being preoccupied by the rape. She believed that it was time for her to concentrate on her studies.

DISCUSSION

Koss, Gidycz, and Wisniewski (1987) administered their Sexual Experiences Survey to 6159 female college students from 32 institutions across the United States. They found a 27.5 percent prevalence rate for having been the victim of either attempted or completed rape. An additional 11.2 percent of the women reported that they had been subjected to sexual coercion, and 14.5 percent had been touched sexually against their will. An astounding 84 percent of the raped women knew their attacker. Rape, including acquaintance rape, is a prominent problem in society for which resources are only now becoming routinely available. One fairly frequent outcome of rape is Posttraumatic Stress Disorder (PTSD).

PTSD is included in the *Diagnostic and Statistical Manual of Mental Disorders* (*DSM-IV*; pp. 427–428) under the general heading of Anxiety Disorders. It is defined by the following criteria:

A. The person has been exposed to a traumatic event in which both of the following were present:
    1. The person experienced, witnessed, or was confronted with an event or events that involved actual or threatened death or serious injury, or a threat to the physical integrity of self or others
    2. The person's response involved intense fear, helplessness, or horror
B. The traumatic event is persistently reexperienced in one (or more) of the following ways:
    1. Recurrent and intrusive distressing recollections of the event, including images, thoughts, or perceptions
    2. Recurrent distressing dreams of the event
    3. Acting or feeling as if the traumatic event were recurring
    4. Intense psychological distress at exposure cues that symbolize or resemble an aspect of the traumatic event
    5. Physiological reactivity on exposure to cues that symbolize or resemble an aspect of the traumatic event

C.   Persistent avoidance of stimuli associated with the trauma and numbing of general responsiveness (not present before the trauma), as indicated by three (or more) of the following:
1.   Efforts to avoid thoughts, feelings, or conversation associated with the trauma
2.   Efforts to avoid activities, places, or people that arouse recollections of the trauma
3.   Inability to recall an important aspect of the trauma
4.   Markedly diminished interest or participation in significant activities
5.   Feeling of detachment or estrangement from others
6.   Restricted range of affect (such as being unable to have loving feelings)
7.   Sense of a foreshortened future (for example, does not expect to have a career, marriage, children, or a normal life span)
D.   Persistent symptoms of increased arousal (not present before the trauma), as indicated by two (or more) of the following:
1.   Difficulty falling or staying asleep
2.   Irritability or outbursts of anger
3.   Difficulty concentrating
4.   Hypervigilance
5.   Exaggerated startle response
E.   Duration of the disturbance is more than 1 month
F.   The disturbance causes clinically significant distress or impairment in social, occupational, or other important areas of functioning

The rape, and the fear surrounding it, was clearly responsible for provoking the symptoms that Jocelyn was experiencing. One of the key elements of PTSD is the recurrence or reexperience of stimuli associated with the event. Jocelyn experienced this symptom in the form of intrusive, violent images that came to mind whenever she opened her English textbook. Her recurrent nightmares were another symptom linked to reexperiencing the event. Whenever one of these images or dreams occurred, Jocelyn would become extremely fearful and distract herself (escape) as quickly as possible. This type of reexperiencing of the trauma should be distinguished from the procedures used in cognitive-behavioral treatment. The latter is designed to ensure *prolonged* exposure in the context of a safe and supportive environment, which allows the person's intense emotional response to diminish gradually.

Avoidance of rape-related stimuli has been shown to differentiate rape victims with PTSD from those rape victims who did not develop PTSD. Jocelyn's avoidance was manifested by withdrawal from her friends, her decision against reporting the rape, and perhaps in her decision against returning to therapy the following semester. Her feelings of dissociation, such as asking

"Is that me?" when looking into the mirror, were another sign of Jocelyn's avoidance. Foa, Feske, Murdock, Kozak, and McCarthy (1991) conducted a laboratory experiment that found that rape victims with PTSD took longer than those without PTSD to process threat-related words. This result supports the hypothesis that rape victims with PTSD experience the world differently from those who are not suffering from this disorder.

Jocelyn's increased arousal was consistent with the *DSM-IV* description of PTSD. Her exaggerated startle response, irritability in interpersonal relationships, difficulty studying, and sleep disturbance are all signs of the heightened arousal that is associated with this disorder. The length of time that had elapsed since the initial appearance of her symptoms and the obvious impact that these symptoms had on her adjustment also indicate that Jocelyn met the formal diagnostic criteria for PTSD.

The term *Posttraumatic Stress Disorder* was introduced to the formal diagnostic manual with the publication of the *DSM-III* in 1980. The concept of a severe and maladaptive reaction to a traumatic event was recognized many years earlier, but it was described in different terms. It was known as "traumatic neurosis of war" in *DSM-I* (APA, 1952). The disorder had been observed among soldiers returning from World War II. The category was dropped in the next edition of the diagnostic manual, *DSM-II* (APA, 1968), even though the phenomenon was well documented in combat veterans (Kinzie, 1989). *DSM-III* returned the concept to the manual and listed it with other types of anxiety disorders. This version of the manual expanded the range of possible stressors from a limited focus on combat experiences to the consideration of any traumatic event that was "outside the range of usual human experience" (*DSM-III-R,* p. 247). In other words, people who had been victims of a crime or survivors of a natural disaster might also develop the symptoms of PTSD.

Following the publication of *DSM-III*, clinicians reported that many victims of rape did indeed suffer from the symptoms of PTSD. There were problems, however, with the way in which the disorder was described in the diagnostic manual. For example, epidemiological studies began to indicate that rape was not "outside the range of usual human experience": Reports collected from adult women in the general community (Kilpatrick, Saunders, Veronen, Best, & Von, 1987) and female college students (Koss et al., 1987) found that rape is *not* an uncommon event. The *DSM-III* criteria also put the therapist in the position of having to make a judgment about the expected or usual impact of an environmental event (Penk et al., 1988). The authors of *DSM-IV* sought to correct these problems with the criteria for PTSD. The traumatic event is now described as one in which the person experienced a threat of death or serious injury and responded with intense fear. This description clearly includes rape as a traumatic event.

The classification of PTSD has been criticized on a number of grounds.

Some scientists suggest that PTSD may not be a mental disorder because it is a reaction to an event that would be distressing for almost anyone (O'Donohue & Elliott, 1992). Thus, perhaps PTSD should be separated from anxiety disorders and placed in an "etiologically based" category along with other disorders that follow traumatic events (Davidson & Foa, 1991, p. 347). This grouping would include adjustment disorders and enduring personality changes that may follow trauma. This approach is currently used in the International Classification of Diseases (*ICD-10*; World Health Organization, 1990).

Further questions about the classification of PTSD as an anxiety disorder involve the nature of its core symptoms. Some symptoms in PTSD do involve anxiety, such as recurrent, intrusive images, avoidance, hypervigilance, and startle responses. These are similar to the symptoms of Obsessive Compulsive Disorder, Phobic Disorder, and Generalized Anxiety Disorder. Davidson and Foa (1991) have also noted, however, that PTSD shares many symptoms with Dissociative Disorders such as amnesia, fugue, and multiple personality. These include flashbacks, memory impairment, and body dissociation. These classification issues will need to be addressed in future versions of the *DSM*.

It is difficult to estimate the true prevalence of PTSD from epidemiological studies because the disorder is precipitated by traumatic events. These events may be personal, affecting one person at a time, as in the case of rape, but they may also be events that affect a large number of people simultaneously. For example, if people in southern Florida had been interviewed soon after a severe event such as Hurricane Andrew in 1992, their prevalence for PTSD would be higher than in most other communities of the United States. The Epidemiologic Catchment Area (ECA) study asked questions about symptoms of PTSD in only 1 of the 5 cities that were included in the investigation (Helzer, Robins, & McEvoy, 1987). The researchers found that only 5 men and 13 women per 1000 had met the criteria for PTSD at some time in their lives.

Another problem in determining the prevalence rate of PTSD is the variability in the longitudinal course of the disorder. Rothbaum, Foa, Riggs, Murdock, and Walsh (1992) found that most victims (94 percent) fit the diagnostic criteria for PTSD immediately after the rape. The rate tapers off over time, with 65 percent of the victims fitting the criteria 1 month after the rape and 47 percent at 12 weeks postrape. Bownes, O'Gorman, and Sayers (1991) found that 70 percent of the rape victims in their study met the diagnostic criteria for PTSD 9 months after they had been raped. All of the victims in this study had reported their rape to the police. It is therefore difficult to generalize from these results to other studies because only a small percentage of rapes are reported to the police. One long-term study found that 16.7 percent of rape victims still met the criteria for PTSD an average of 17 years after they had been raped (Kilpatrick et al., 1987). This finding indicates that although the symptoms diminish over time for many people, some victims experience persistent and severe problems for a very long period of time.

Etiological Considerations

All victims of trauma do not develop PTSD. What determines whether or not a victim will develop PTSD following a traumatic event, such as rape? Clinical scientists have looked for prerape differences between victims who develop PTSD and those who do not. One common line of investigation is whether or not rape victims who developed PTSD had different premorbid personality characteristics or a different pattern of adjustment that may have contributed to developing PTSD. The evidence for this relationship is sketchy.

Resnick, Kilpatrick, Best, and Kramer (1992) found a relationship between precrime depression and the level of stress associated with the crime (e.g., an attack with life threat, actual injury, or completed rape) and the development of PTSD. If the victim had been depressed before the assault, and if the victim happened to be assaulted in a particularly severe manner, then she was much more likely to suffer from PTSD following the crime than were victims of lower stress crimes. With regard to demographic characteristics, there do not appear to be systematic differences between crime victims who develop PTSD and those who do not in terms of variables such as race, employment, education, and income.

Similar results were found in a related study of 294 crime victims (Kilpatrick et al., 1989). Features of the assault itself seem to influence whether or not victims develop PTSD. During the assault, life threat, physical injury, and completed rape together are the best predictors of crime-related PTSD. It is important to keep in mind that a perceived "life threat" may be present even in situations that are not overtly violent. In fact, Foa and Steketee (1989) found that the severity of the *perceived* life threat, rather than *actual* life threat, was the best predictor of whether a person would develop PTSD.

Rape is particularly traumatic in comparison to other crimes. Kilpatrick et al. (1989) noted that rape victims are much more likely to suffer from PTSD than victims of other crimes. What are the distinguishing features of rape that account for its devastating impact? In comparison to many other traumatic events, rape involves directed, focused, intentional harm that is associated with the most intimate interpersonal act (Koss & Burkhart, 1989).

Cognitive factors may also influence whether a rape victim will develop PTSD. Crime victims who perceive (perhaps with justification) that future negative events are uncontrollable are much more likely to have severe PTSD symptomatology than those victims who perceive some future control (Kushner, Riggs, Foa, & Miller, 1992). This indication is particularly important when viewed in light of the finding that 41 percent of the women who were raped reported that they expect to be raped again (Koss et al., 1987).

Risk for persistent problems following a traumatic event is also increased by avoidance of emotional feelings and rumination about the traumatic event. Victims who suppress their feelings of anger may have an increased risk of developing PTSD after a rape (Riggs, Dancu, Gershuny, Greenberg, & Foa, 1992). Intense anger may interfere with the modification of the traumatic memory (to make it more congruent with previous feelings of safety). Anger also inhibits fear, so the victim cannot habituate to the fear response.

Protective factors such as the person's level of social support may help to prevent or limit the development of PTSD and other psychological consequences of rape (Keane, 1985). Unfortunately, simply having a social support network may not be enough. The tendency of the victim to withdraw and avoid situations is an inherent part of the disorder (Kinzie, 1989). This avoidance may mean that victims do not take advantage of social support, even if it is available to them. This consideration may help to explain why not all studies have found that social support served as a protective factor (Popiel & Susskind, 1985).

Attitudes that society holds toward victims of sexual assault are also important in relation to social support. For example, some people apparently believe that certain women somehow deserved to be raped (Warshaw, 1988). These women undoubtedly receive less social support than other victims. People may also be more supportive after hearing the details of an assault that was clearly nonconsensual—one in which the victim violently fought back when attacked by a stranger—than when the circumstances surrounding the assault were more ambiguous (the woman's protests were verbal and not physical). Myths about rape, especially about acquaintance rape, may decrease the amount of social support received by victims of these crimes.

Theoretical Perspectives and Treatment Implications

A two-factor classical conditioning perspective has been used to explain the development of both combat-related (Keane, Zimering, & Caddell, 1985) and rape-induced (Kilpatrick, Veronen, & Resick, 1979) PTSD. In this model, rape is viewed as the unconditioned stimulus (UCS) that elicits an unconditioned response (UCR) of extreme fear, which has physiological, behavioral, and cognitive components. Stimuli that are paired with the UCS become conditioned stimuli (CS) and are able to evoke a conditioned response (CR) that is similar to the UCR.

This conceptual view of PTSD provided the framework for a comparison of several types of therapy with rape victims (Foa, Rothbaum, Riggs, & Murdock, 1991). The treatment that produced the best long-term outcome (at 3.5 months) employed prolonged exposure. This procedure started with initial sessions of information gathering. These were followed by 7 sessions devoted to reliving the rape scene in the client's imagination. Clients were instructed to relive the assault by imagining it and describing it to the therapist, as many times as possible during the 60-minute sessions. The sessions were tape-recorded and patients were instructed to listen to the tape at least one time a day. Patients were also required to participate in situations or events outside the therapy sessions that were deemed to be safe but would elicit the fear or avoidance response. An adapted form of this treatment was used in Jocelyn's therapy.

Traditional stimulus–response learning theories may account for fear and avoidance symptoms in rape victims, but they do not provide a compelling explanation for the other symptoms of the disorder. Foa and Steketee (1989) suggest that perceived threat, more than actual threat, is better able to predict many of the other symptoms. Some meaning or perception of the traumatic event may mediate the development of PTSD. Resick and Schnicke (1992) expanded this conceptual model, noting that prolonged exposure to the aversive stimulus can lead to habituation, but it does not affect cognitive misattributions, conflicts, or expectations. They recommend combining prolonged exposure therapy with cognitive therapy, which would address maladaptive ways of perceiving events in the person's environment.

Final Comments

We have used the term *victim* rather than *survivor* to describe a person who experienced a traumatic event. This choice was made primarily because *victim* is the term used in the scientific literature on PTSD. We also want to point out, however, that many rape victims prefer to think of themselves as survivors in order to enhance their sense of control over events in their environments. Further information and resources are also available in Robin Warshaw's book *I Never Called It Rape* (1988). Her descriptions are less technical than this case, and they may provide additional sources of support.

4 HYPERTENSION IN AN AFRICAN AMERICAN MAN

John Williams had been complaining to his wife of dizziness, fatigue, and occasional light-headedness that almost caused him to faint one day at the watercooler in the law office where he worked downtown. His boss had been after him for weeks to see a doctor, but John had stubbornly refused. He felt angry and frightened when suggestions were made that he see a physician — angry because he interpreted the suggestion as condescending on his boss's part, and frightened because he had an ineffable feeling that all was not right with him physically.

He was correct about the latter. His first clear knowledge of having hypertension, or high blood pressure, came during a visit to his dentist. Before taking X-rays of his mouth, the dental assistant, as had become routine in the office, wound the black blood pressure cuff around John's right arm, pumped it full of air until the blood stopped flowing, and then slowly released the valve, noting when the first and the last sounds of the pulse could be heard through the stethoscope pressed to the vein in his arm beneath the cuff. Alarmed at the reading — 165/110 — she took the pressure reading again after doing the X-rays and found it to be almost exactly the same. She tried to smile pleasantly and reassuringly to the powerfully built patient waiting for his teeth to be cleaned, but she found it hard to do, especially when she noticed a worried expression on his face.

He did not ask about the blood pressure reading until he was sitting across from the dentist's desk in the consulting room to discuss treatment plans. How have you been feeling lately, John was asked by the dentist he had known for the past 10 years. Have you been feeling tired, irritable? Any headaches? How has the work been going? Under a lot of pressure? John searched the man's face for some hint of what was going on, but he already sensed that he had high blood pressure. Finally, he just asked for the numbers and what they meant, thanked the dentist, and went home.

It took him 30 minutes to reach his condominium in the suburbs. As he turned the key, he wondered how, or whether, he would raise the issue with his wife. Although not a physician himself, he knew what the kind of high blood pressure he seemed to have might mean to a 40-year-old like himself, especially someone who was so driven to succeed professionally and financially. Certainly he would have to slow down, and perhaps also take some medication. But what else, he wondered.

SOCIAL HISTORY

John Williams was the only child of a well-to-do African American family in Atlanta. Born in 1939, he grew up in an upper-middle-class environment. His father was a successful attorney, and his mother was a music teacher in one of the local high schools. Life was sweet in his childhood, as John recalled during one of his therapy sessions with a clinical psychologist. He had many friends in the neighborhood. Even though they were all African American in the segregated part of the city that was his home, he seldom had the feeling of being excluded from anything important. More fortunate than most African Americans, whether in the South or the North, John knew no material wants and was taught during countless dinnertime conversations that there were plenty of opportunities for success available to a youngster like him; he had superior intelligence, an engaging wit, and a degree of ambition that matched that of his hard-working father.

In high school John excelled at everything he attempted. A "straight A" student, he was also a varsity athlete in three sports, dated the young women generally regarded by his peers to be the most desirable, and, in his senior year, was elected president of his class. This was the middle 1950s, well before the civil rights struggles and other social activist movements that led to some major legal and social changes in the country, especially in the South. The idea of leaving Georgia for college was tempting, but it created as much anxiety in John's mother as it brought anticipatory pride in his father. Mr. Williams wanted his son to have a college education with "class," as he put it. To be sure, there were first-rate black colleges to which he would apply, such as Howard University in Washington, D.C.; however, with the encouragement of his guidance counselor and the urging of his father, John also applied to several Ivy League schools. The excitement was considerable in April when the acceptance from Harvard arrived in the mail.

Even though Harvard was located in the "liberal" Northeast, racial discrimination had to be considered. Years later, John told the therapist, a white man with whom he had roomed confided to John that one month before school was to begin their freshman year, he had received a letter from the housing office indicating that they would like to have him room with an African American student, but that this assignment would be made only if the student had no objection. The student, a Jew from Brooklyn, New York, was outraged because he readily saw the discrimination and prejudice that lay behind the seemingly genteel and considerate inquiry. This incident, and others throughout the four years of friendship between the two young men, was a prototype for many discussions they would have about the pressures on members of minority groups who elected to try "to make it" in society, especially in the elite circles of a private, selective college.

John knew what a "house nigger" was, but it took the handwritten invitation slipped under his door one night to teach him about what he and Matt, his roommate, would call a "club nigger." Fraternities existed at Harvard, but they differed from their Greek-letter counterparts on other campuses in that they were not residential. All undergraduates were affiliated with a house, modeled after the "colleges" of Oxford and Cambridge, in which they lived and took all their meals. The clubs operated outside the house system and were by invitation only; some of them bore names of winged and sharp-toothed animals such as bats and wolves, others the more familiar Greek initials. It seemed to John that his being African American, or Negro, as he called himself then, would exclude him from these clubs, although he hated himself for even thinking about it. Thinking, he would tell himself, implied that he cared, and to care about the clubs was to accord them a legitimacy and importance he desperately resisted. As he stopped to pick up the engraved envelope, he could feel the blood pound in his ears.

When he looked back on things, this single moment crystallized much of the conflict John felt about his blackness in a white world. He and his race had come far from the days a fair-skinned youngster might hope to "pass" for white. As light as John's complexion was, and as little curliness was to be found in his hair—there was more than one white slave owner in his ancestry—he had grown up proud of the fact that he was African American and feeling that whatever barriers there might be in "making it" were of less importance than his self-respect and pride. But still, as he lingered over breakfast coffee with Matt the morning the invitation arrived, wasn't it "a gas" that one of the prestigious clubs wanted him as a member?

Not that he got any encouragement from Matt, who viewed his own candidacy for this sort of thing as unlikely an event as John had considered his own. Matt had an uneasy feeling about it all, but he kept it to himself, wondering, for one thing, whether it was just not sour grapes on his own part that this African American man was sought after when he, a Caucasian, was not.

John agonized all day over whether to attend the reception for newly solicited members. He was tempted to phone his parents, but what would he tell them, and how? Was there something to celebrate? Would his father smile quietly to himself as he heard the news, confirming his own good judgment in sending his son to one of the bastions of eastern elitism? Surely John was going to succeed — and in the white world, no less. In the end, John did not phone; he feared at one and the same time that his father would either congratulate him on the invitation or chide him for even considering it. No way to win on that score, he told himself. At some level he knew that it was his own conflict he was wrestling with, not his father's reaction.

The day of his initiation, John awoke with a screaming headache. He took three aspirins — a habit he had gotten into since coming to college — and told himself to stop worrying about the party that evening. Perhaps he need not have worried. The welcome he received seemed genuine. And yet he could not shake the feeling that his new "brothers" were being nicer to him than they were to the other initiates, too nice somehow. His wine glass was never empty, always filled by a brother who, it struck John, smiled a bit too ingratiatingly. In fact, it seemed to him that his new friends must have suffered from aching mouths, so broadly did they smile whenever they talked to him. He tried to reassure himself that the cordiality was real, and maybe it was. The problem, he knew, was that he did not really know, nor could he devise a practical way to find out.

His membership in the club turned out to be a boon to his social standing but an emotional disaster. Headaches and feelings of pressure in the brain were more regularly part of his existence than ever before. He hated himself for even being in the club, yet he prided himself on being the only African American member. He was furious at the fact that so few Jews were members and was also suspicious that there were no other African Americans, but he found the young men in the club congenial and enjoyable to spend time with, and he did experience a thrill whenever he donned the club necktie. His friends from the club were certainly no less bright than his other classmates, no less interested in abstract ideas and "deep" conversations over sherry after dinner. But the clubs were by nature exclusionary, and John was coming to realize that he might be seen as the quintessential Uncle Tom.

His anger at himself and at his brothers grew to an intensity that was frightening. To Matt, in whom he confided his doubts, fears, guilt, and rage, John seemed a tragic figure. There seemed to be no way for him to win. To express his concerns to his club brothers seemed out of the question. But not to do so, at least to one of them, had begun to make the thought of going to the handsome Georgian building for the evening a challenge, almost a dare. He dreaded the possibility of someone making a racist remark. How should he react? He had learned, since coming north, to let it pass, but the muscle tension that mounted in his body told him this was not the best thing for him to do. Once a club member used the word "niggardly," and he felt himself blush. How infantile to react that way, he told himself. And yet, maybe the word was used to taunt him. But how inane to think that. Sure, Uncle Tom, he concluded.

The four years of college passed quickly. As his family and friends expected, John did very well academically and also managed to earn a varsity letter in baseball. His admission to a first-rate law school was a foregone conclusion, although John's problem by this time was his uncertainty as to whether he had been admitted solely on his academic merits or whether the several prestigious schools, like the club, wanted him primarily for his color. And so the conflicts continued through law school. By this time they took the form of John's having to excel to what even his ambitious father regarded to be an unreasonable degree. John just had to prove he was good, indeed, that he was the best.

John became engaged to an African American woman from a prominent family, but the joys of the relationship were dulled by his relentless drive for excellence and perfection. One major change was that his problems with hypertension were now impossible to hide; she insisted that he have a complete physical examination, something he had consciously avoided since entering college. The reading was 130/85, something the doctor called "high normal," sufficient in magnitude to be worrisome in a young man. His fiancée was convinced that John's grim pursuit of straight As, law review, and all the rest were at fault. But she knew little as yet about the reasons that lay behind his near-obsessive push.

John graduated at the top of his class. It was now the middle 1960s, and the developing social turmoil surrounding Vietnam and the civil rights movement seemed to affect him deeply. On the one hand, he felt that he should be out on the barricades, but his studies and his new job at a top law firm took precedence. He tried to assuage his guilt by donating money to civil rights groups, but it did not seem to help. He had cast his lot with the white world, he told himself, and his wife and his own family back in Atlanta supported that decision. Middle- and upper-middle-class professional African Americans had their role to play, his father continually reminded him, and who could better play that role than John Williams? The sense he had that it was, indeed, a *role*, turned out to be important in the psychotherapy he began some weeks after the alarmingly high blood pressure reading in the dentist's office.

CONCEPTUALIZATION AND TREATMENT

The choice of a therapist is never an easy matter. For John it presented special difficulties. Though he lived near a large city, there were few African American psychiatrists or psychologists. As he had grown accustomed to doing in most other areas of his life, John decided to work with a white person, in this instance in a very special relationship. He was uncertain whether he could relate openly to a white. His only really close white friend was his old college roommate, Matt, and even then he recalled holding back on the expression of thoughts and emotions having to do with race. Would this same problem arise in a therapeutic relationship? In fact, was race even an issue?

"Well, what do you really want out of life?" asked Dr. Shaw, a distinguished and experienced clinical psychologist. "The same thing everyone else is after," was his reply. "But what is that?" queried the psychologist.

The first couple of sessions were like this: Dr. Shaw trying to get John to examine what he really wanted, and John sparring with him, fending off the probes with generalities about "all other people." In Shaw's mind, John Williams did not want to confront the conflicts of playing a role in the white professional world. He identified with being African American, Shaw believed, but he sensed a falseness about his life. Racial slurs went by without comment. He took pride in the fact that his wife wore her hair straight but, at the same time, castigated himself for feeling this way. He hid from his law office colleagues the fact that he was a member of several civil rights groups and that he considered Martin Luther King to have been somewhat too moderate. But what was *he* doing about it? King and others had risked personal safety in freedom marches, but John was terrified of being seen in one. What would the people in the firm think of him? Would they want a "radical" in the office?

Dr. Shaw thought to himself during these early sessions that he should pressure his client more, but he realized he was holding back in a way he would not with a white client. Was it his right to suggest to John that he was at the same time proud and ashamed of his racial heritage, that he despised himself for hiding his feelings? Indeed, was it his duty? But how could Shaw be certain, and wouldn't it be terrible if he intimated something to John that was off base? But that, too, was something he worried far less about with his white clients. No therapist is infallible. Yet somehow he believed that with John he had to be more certain about his interpretations.

Dr. Shaw routinely referred clients with medical or psychophysiological problems to an internist. This doctor prescribed some antihypertensive medication for John to take daily. But the physician's hope was that this relatively young patient would not come to rely on the drug. In an extended consultation, Shaw and his medical colleague agreed that John's high-pressure lifestyle was a major factor. What they could not agree on was what role the man's race played. Absence of similar problems in three generations of John's family did not support the assumption that the patient had inherited a predisposition for hypertension, although the two men agreed at the same time that, for whatever reason, John's particular response to stress was hypertension, more specifically essential hypertension, because physical causes had been ruled out through a complete medical checkup.

A crisis took place in the fifth and final session. For months afterward Dr.

Shaw wondered whether he had blundered so badly that his client was driven from therapy.

Dr. Shaw: John, I've been wondering about what you've told me about your college days.
John (a bit suspiciously): What aspect of them?
Dr. Shaw: Well, I guess I was thinking about the club. (Shaw noted to himself that he seldom said "I guess" in such circumstances. Stop pussyfooting, he told himself.)
John (feeling his ears becoming warm): Well, what about the club?
Dr. Shaw: Your feelings of being the only black.
John: Well, I felt really good about it. I used to daydream about what my high school friends would think.
Dr. Shaw: And what would they have thought?
John: They'd have envied me to the utmost. I mean, I must be doing something right to get into one of the Greeks.
Dr. Shaw: Yes, I know you were quite proud about it. . . . But I wonder if you had any other feelings about it.
John (definitely on edge, wary): What do you mean?
Dr. Shaw: Well, lots of times people are conflicted about things that are important to them. Like the nervous bridegroom on the wedding day. He's eager for the honeymoon, but he knows he's giving up something.
John: What do you think I was giving up?
Dr. Shaw: You feel you were giving up something by being in the club?
John: Come on, Doc, don't play games. You know damn well that *you* think I gave up something. What did I give up?
Dr. Shaw: John, if anything was given up, it was you who gave it up, not I. (That sounded too harsh, he told himself immediately, but maybe it was time to apply more pressure on him. Otherwise he may never move.)
John: I resent what you're implying.
Dr. Shaw: Okay, but can you explore it, just hypothetically?
John (suspicion mounting, almost a feeling of panic setting in): Okay, Shaw, let me think of what I gave up.

At this point there was a lengthy silence. John stared at his feet, Dr. Shaw at his notes, occasionally glancing up at John but not wanting to look at him too much. John began to dwell on the thoughts he had never shared with anyone, not even with his roommate, Matt. Oreo cookie, he called himself, black on the outside and white on the inside. Who needs the damned club? If they were serious about being democratic, I would not be the only African American. Just me, and oh, that Chinese kid, whose family just happened to own half of Hong Kong. Yuh, David and me, the two typical minority members. And they can congratulate themselves for being so damned liberal. And I can congratulate myself for making it in the door. But how would they have reacted if I had dated a white woman? Or worn my hair in an Afro? And put on a dashiki? Ha! How do you wear a club tie with a dashiki? Even the one overt sign of club membership conflicts with a dashiki! What am I doing with these mothers? How hypocritical can I be?[1]

Dr. Shaw: John, can you share some of your thoughts with me?
John: Doc, I can't do it. You're one of them.
Dr. Shaw: One of whom?
John: Doc, I can't talk to a white man about this. I can't talk to a black man about this. I'm too ashamed, too mixed up (beginning to sob). I can't handle this.
Dr. Shaw: This is hard for you, I know, John. But this is a place you can use to look at those feelings. Try to sort them out. Try to figure out what you really want. . . .
John (interrupting the psychologist): No! It's not for you to tell me what I should be doing. *I'm* the one who has to decide.

Long silence again.

Dr. Shaw: John?

John just stares at his feet, jaws clenched, that familiar tightness in his head. My blood pressure must be soaring, he told himself. I can't handle this. If I'm not careful I'll be a psychological success, but I'll die from a stroke. No, that's an exaggeration. Or is it? I'm bullshitting myself so much that I don't even know what I want, or think, or feel. . . .

Dr. Shaw: John, perhaps that's enough for today.
John (relieved): Yes, that's right. That's enough . . . for today.
Dr. Shaw: See you next week, same time.
John (knowing he would break the appointment): Yuh. Thanks. I'll see you next week.

DISCUSSION

It has been known for thousands of years that mental and emotional states can affect the functioning of the body. When a person is under strain, there are numerous physiological changes, such as increases in heart rate and in blood

---

[1]Dr. Shaw later learned something of what was going through John's mind during these lengthy silences.

pressure; these changes are usually temporary, diminishing when the stressor is removed. But in some individuals the changes persist; when this happens over a long period of time, a psychophysiological disorder can result.

Perhaps you have heard the expression "Oh, don't worry about that. It's only in your mind." A person suffering from asthma that has some psychogenic components is often seen as someone of weak will or someone with a physical malady that is somehow not genuine. To believe this is to overlook the simple and important fact that many medical illnesses are caused in part by psychological factors. A disease such as hypertension can be life threatening even when a person's emotions seem to be playing a major role in causing the sustained high blood pressure.

The classic psychophysiological disorders are grouped in terms of the organ system affected. Some of the major ones follow:

1. *Skin disorders:* Neurodermatitis and hyperhydrosis (dry skin).
2. *Respiratory disorders:* Bronchial asthma, hyperventilation (breathing very rapidly, often leading to fainting).
3. *Cardiovascular disorders:* Migraine headache and high blood pressure (hypertension).
4. *Gastrointestinal disorders:* Peptic ulcers, ulcerative colitis, heartburn.

Psychophysiological disorders are common in highly industrialized societies. One survey (Schwab, Fennell, & Warheit, 1974) found that over 40 percent of Americans had had headaches during the previous year and over 50 percent of Americans had suffered gastrointestinal symptoms such as constipation and diarrhea. Psychological factors are being increasingly recognized as playing an important role in all recognized bodily illnesses. In *DSM-IV*, a judgment is made of "psychological factors affecting medical condition," and these factors can include any of the Axis I (e.g., anxiety disorders) or Axis II (e.g., personality disorders) conditions. They also can include psychological factors that are not severe enough to qualify as mental disorders but that nonetheless are believed to play a role in a medical disorder, for example, a sedentary lifestyle.

Before we turn to hypertension, let us review briefly the major types of theories that have been advanced about psychophysiological disorders in general. Two basic questions must be addressed in any attempt to understand these problems: (1) Why do only some people exposed to stress develop psychophysiological disorders? (2) Given that stress does produce such a disorder, what determines which of them will arise? As with other psychopathologies, both biological and psychological theories have been proposed.

Biological Theories

The *somatic weakness theory* states that a particular organ—for genetic reasons or because of poor diet or earlier illnesses—can be weak and thus vulnerable to stress. For example, a congenitally weak respiratory system might predispose a person to developing asthma under stress.

According to the *specific-reaction theory*, people are genetically predisposed to react to stress with overreactions in particular autonomic systems. Thus one person has elevated blood pressure when stressed and another secretes an excess of stomach acid under similar circumstances. The first individual would be a candidate for hypertension, the second for ulcers.

A third kind of biological theory is couched in terms of evolution. Over millions of years, we have developed autonomic nervous systems that equip us to respond to danger with either fight or flight. In either event, the healthy body prepares itself by increasing the rate of breathing, diverting blood into the muscles, releasing sugar into the bloodstream, and the like. When the danger has passed, this burst of sympathetic nervous system activity subsides. Humankind has developed the dubious distinction, however, of being able to respond in this way to *psychological* dangers, not just to the life-threatening challenges that beset other animals. Indeed, we are able to stir up our autonomic nervous systems by our very thoughts and imaginings, thereby maintaining our bodies in a state of hyperarousal. It is as if we are runners in a 100-yard dash, crouched at the starting line, and tensely ready for the signal "go!" Only no signal comes, and we just stay there, expectant and highly aroused.

Psychological Theories

Psychoanalysts have for many years viewed psychophysiological disorders as symbolic manifestations of unresolved repressed conflicts. Franz Alexander (1950), for example, proposed that an ulcer can be formed if a person has repressed an unfulfilled childhood longing for parental love; by continually producing acid the stomach is preparing itself for food, equated symbolically with love. Analytic interpretations of hypertension implicate undischarged hostile impulses, and this line of work will be discussed more fully later.

Cognitive and behavioral factors also have been implicated in psychophysiological disorders. The previously mentioned theory based on evolution indicates that thoughts cause emotional arousal. Human beings can stir themselves up with regrets from the past and worries about the future. Our higher mental capacities, then, can subject our bodies to stress without the presence of actual physical dangers. And appraisal, one characteristic of our cognitive activity, is of special importance. One person can judge a particular situation as dangerous while another appraises it as challenging and interesting. The autonomic and motoric activity arising from these contrasting cognitions is different.

None of these theories enjoys unequivocal support; some views, such as the psychoanalytic one, are difficult to test. It would seem that a multifactorial point of view should be adopted in attempting to understand these puzzling disorders. Investigators will have to consider both physical diatheses, or predispositions, and highly specific psychological ways of reacting to stress. Thus one person might have a genetically determined tendency to react to emotional situations with elevated blood pressure and thus be at risk for hypertension; however, she will not develop this disorder if her life does not contain a certain amount of stress. Furthermore, the way she construes an event as stressful will be a function of her psychology; failing a test, for instance, might be something she has learned to disregard as threatening, while a cross look from her boyfriend may be considered a catastrophe. Someone else, on the other hand, might have a constitution that is fortunately not disposed to react in any abnormal way to stress; that is, his blood pressure declines rapidly once a stressor is removed. But his psychology might have him construe as very threatening an event such as failing an examination. He will therefore end up with some sort of emotional problem, such as an anxiety disorder, *but* his organ systems will not be affected as seriously as they might be if he were predisposed. The outcome will be that he will not develop a psychophysiological disorder but, instead, another kind of emotional problem.

Essential Hypertension

We are now ready to consider what is known or hypothesized about the problem from which John Williams suffers. High blood pressure is estimated to be involved in a great many deaths in the United States each year, and the problem is showing up in younger and younger age groups. Everyone has blood pressure, of course, because the heart pumps the blood throughout the body under pressure. If it remains at an elevated level—readings above 140/90 are regarded as high—a strain is placed on the cardiovascular system and, over a period of years, there is an increased risk of stroke or heart attack.

It is believed that 25 percent of the adult population of this country has high blood pressure (*World Almanac and Book of Facts*, 1993). High blood pressure is known as "the silent killer" because (1) over time it is dangerous to one's physical health, and (2) it can be present for years without the person knowing it unless a blood pressure reading is taken. Sometimes symptoms do develop, however, as we saw in John Williams's case: fatigue, nervousness, dizziness, heart palpitations, headaches, and, for some people, even a feeling of pressure in the head.

On a physiological level, hypertension is currently viewed as a heterogeneous condition brought on by many possible disturbances in the various systems of the body that are responsible for regulating blood pressure. The mechanisms relevant to the regulation of blood pressure are extremely complex. Increases in blood pressure can be due to increased cardiac output caused by heightened stimulation of the heart by the sympathetic nervous system, kidney malfunction, hormones, salt and water metabolism, as well as central nervous system mechanisms (Weiner, 1977). Many of these controlling physiological mechanisms could be affected by psychological stress, a topic to which we now turn.

We know from various research studies that stress increases blood pressure in the short term. Kasl and Cobb (1970), for example, found that people who knew that their jobs were to be terminated in two months had higher blood pressure during that period as well as two years following the loss of the job than control subjects whose employment remained constant. More directly relevant to John Williams is research by Hokanson and his colleagues (Hokanson & Burgess, 1962; Stone & Hokanson, 1969). In a laboratory setting, subjects were given a task but were then made angry by a confederate of the experimenter. Fifty percent of the subjects were given the opportunity to retaliate against their harasser, but the others were not. Results showed that being harassed in this way raised blood pressure, which is not surprising. Of greater interest was the fact that subjects who could take retaliatory action against the source of their frustration showed larger decreases in their elevated blood pressure than did control subjects, who were denied that opportunity. Applying these analogue findings to John Williams, we can hypothesize that his habit of inhibiting anger and his resentment of white people played a role in the development of his high blood pressure. An additional finding of Hokanson, however, provides an even more important possibility. Considering only the subjects who retaliated, blood pressure decreases were found only when they aggressed against a fellow college student, not when their harasser was presented to them as a visiting professor. Expressing resentment and anger to a high-status source of frustration, then, did not reduce blood pressure. In John's case, if he *had* asserted himself more, this might not have helped him *if* he perceived the people angering him as higher in status than himself. This is where issues of race enter, because the therapist would have had to discuss with John his underlying feelings about white people: whether he regarded them as superior, for example. One can appreciate how much more subtle and complex things become when moving from the laboratory study to a real-life case.

Some confirmatory data are closer to actual life circumstances. It is widely known that African Americans as a group have an especially high incidence of hypertension (Thomas & Dobbins, 1986). Is there a racial basis to this? Probably not. The causes may be found in social factors. Harburg et al. (1973) studied two areas of Detroit; one was a poor neighborhood with a high crime rate, much crowding, and many marital breakups; the other was a middle-class neighborhood. In both, black and white married men had their blood pressure taken several times in their homes, and they were also given a test that posed stressful situations to them and asked how they would respond. One test item, for example, had them imagine that they were seeking a place to rent and that the landlord refused them because of their race or religion. The response categories were: "(1) I'd get angry or mad and show it, (2) I'd get annoyed and show it, (3) I'd get annoyed, but would keep it in, (4) I'd get angry or mad, but would keep it in, (5) I wouldn't feel angry or annoyed" (p. 280).

Results showed that blood pressure was higher among African Americans than among whites. But African Americans living in the poor neighborhood had higher blood pressure than those living in the middle-class area. Thus, while race was one factor, of equal importance was social class and the accompanying stress that comes with living in marginal circumstances. It would seem that high blood pressure among African Americans has a great deal to do with the socially created stress under which they live. Furthermore, results from the stressful situation test indicated that for most subjects holding anger in was related to high blood pressure. Harburg's findings, a reanalysis of them by Gentry, Chesney, Hall, and Harburg (1981) and Gentry, Chesney, Gary, Hall, and Harburg (1982), and a replication by Dimsdale et al. (1986) focus on the role of unexpressed anger, or "anger-in," in the development and maintenance of high blood pressure. Other research (e.g., Spielberger, Johnson, Russell, Crane, & Worden, 1985) examined the relationship by correlating blood pressure in normals with scores on the Anger Expression Scale, a 20-item self-report inventory on which subjects respond by indicating how often they react in various ways when they are angry. For example, do they control their temper? Do they keep things in? Do they slam doors, or argue with others? In a study by Johnson (1984, reported in Spielberger et al., 1985), there were strong and positive correlations between blood pressure and the tendency to suppress anger. Suppressed anger, which activates the autonomic nervous system, may over time lead to fixed elevations in blood pressure, that is, high blood pressure. These findings on anger-in and hypertension have also been confirmed in other studies (e.g., Netter & Neuhauser-Mettermich, 1991; Sullivan, Procci et al., 1981; Sullivan, Schoentgen et al., 1981).

John Williams was not stressed by socioeconomic factors, but, like many people, he "succeeded" in increasing his life pressures by his constant striving for perfection, over and above the pressure probably created by the prejudice encountered in his frequent contacts with whites. His blood pressure was apparently increased as well by the tremendous conflicts he experienced as an African American man who was false to himself, who compromised his beliefs and his ideals in order to succeed in white society.

Remember that the studies discussed so far, except for Harburg's, have at least two major limitations. First, in no instance was true high blood pressure created, only temporary increases in blood pressure. Second, most of the research was analogue in nature; that is, the situations studied were not real life. We must always be mindful when we are extrapolating from "make-believe" to the real world. What we learn from laboratory studies provides fruitful leads and ways of thinking about problems, but matters are still far from proven.

Going back to our general discussion of theories of psychophysiological disorders, we suggested that a diathesis–stress view was the best one to employ. John Williams's life was full of emotionally stressful events. But it was a psychophysiological disorder that he developed, not any of the many other problems that people under duress are subject to, such as mood disorders or anxiety disorders. Furthermore, given that it was a psychophysiological problem, he had essential hypertension, not asthma, hives, or any of the other such disorders. Did he have a somatic weakness in his cardiovascular system, or was his system somehow predisposed to overreact to stress, as in the specific-reaction theory? We do not know in John's case. Evidence that should lead us to consider the possibility—although it is unclear what the treatment implications would be—is in research such as a study by Hodapp, Weyer, and Becker (1976). The blood pressure of hypertensives and normals was measured while resting, while viewing slides of landscapes, and while performing a demanding intellectual task (the stressor). All subjects showed blood pressure increases during the stress, but hypertensives maintained that increase even when the stressor was removed. It is as though some people's cardiovascular system is preset to be elevated and to maintain that elevation once it is stressed. Of course, this study and others like it cannot demonstrate a cause–effect relationship because the hypertensive patients were, in fact, already hypertensive! There are, however, longitudinal data consistent with the idea that heightened blood pressure reactivity may be an important diathesis. In one such longitudinal study, Wood et al. (1984) followed up with subjects who had had their blood pressure monitored during a stress task many years earlier. Those who had reacted strongly were five times more likely to be hypertensive. Further support for the importance of reactivity comes from high-risk research comparing individuals with and without a positive history for hypertension (e.g., Hastrup, Light, & Obrist, 1982). As anticipated, people with a positive family history showed greater blood pressure reactivity to stress. Coupled with other research showing the heritability of blood pressure reactivity (Matthews & Rakaczky, 1987) and the heritability of hypertension, blood pressure reactivity becomes a good candidate for a genetically transmitted diathesis. There is little doubt that essential hypertension is caused by an interplay between a diathesis and stress.

Issues of Race and Psychotherapy

Mention has already been made of how being African American might contribute to high blood pressure. John Williams's race also played a role in the therapy he terminated prematurely. Not adequately appreciated in the psychotherapy literature are the social conditions under which African Americans have been living in this country as well as the sometimes subtle, unconscious biases existing in the primarily white investigators who offer the generalizations (Comas-Diaz, 1992).

Complicating the matter still further is the difficulty a white therapist can experience with a black client. It is said that racism entails not only negative stereotypes (e.g., all African Americans are sexually promiscuous) but also positive ones (e.g., they have a natural talent for athletics). The therapist has no easy task to get past these prejudgments, or prejudices, to look at the African American client as he or she would regard a white client, to consider the person's psychological difficulties in useful ways, placing race in a context that will promote a fruitful assessment and intervention instead of impeding them.

These issues are to be seen in the case of John Williams. Should the therapist have encouraged a more assertive stance toward the prejudices that seemed to be oppressing him? Or should the therapist have promoted an adjustment to the situation, an attitude that he really had things good, that life is imperfect, and perhaps he should just find a way to make the best of it? Did John Williams really wish that he were white—a conclusion some whites come to when African Americans complain of obstacles in their paths to general social acceptance? Should John have declined that seductive invitation to the club at Harvard on the basis that a token African American was worse than no African American at all? Was his wish to be accepted by his white classmates an unhealthy one, or could it be seen as no less healthy than the wish a white initiate would have? Was John really "Uncle-Tomming" by joining the exclusive group while knowing that true acceptance would ultimately be denied him? Indeed, what evidence did he have that he was not "truly" accepted by his club members? If people were being nice to him, was it because he was African American and they were trying to demonstrate their liberalism and open-mindedness? How was he to know if a display of affection or approval arose from such motivations?

Dr. Shaw was more reluctant to push John than he would have been a white client. It has been suggested that some white therapists are oversympathetic toward their African American clients, lest they seem to be expressing racial prejudice (Adams, 1950; Greene, 1985). In psychoanalytic terms, Shaw was having *countertransference* problems with Williams; that is, concerns about his own racism and his efforts to overcome it were getting in the way of dealing with his client.

There is, moreover, a general issue in psychotherapy about how much pressure a therapist should place on a client. In one well-known study of group therapy (Yalom & Lieberman, 1971), casualties occurred most often when the group leader was confrontative and authoritative. Clearly clients can be hurt if their therapists demand more of them than they are capable of giving. On the other hand, the art of therapy requires that therapists encourage movement on the part of their clients that might not occur otherwise. After some hesitation, Dr. Shaw did apply such pressure, but he seemed to misread his client's readiness to explore his conflicts and lost the opportunity to work further with him. By most standards, Dr. Shaw failed with John Williams, even though he saw him for only five sessions.

The difficulties in establishing rapport should have been anticipated by Dr. Shaw. Clients in general may need time to feel comfortable with a therapist, to come to trust that this stranger has their best interests at heart and will be able to relate in a nonjudgmental way so that secrets of the heart can be shared. But John, like many African American clients, was suspicious and hostile because of the racial difference itself, as earlier research showed (Kennedy, 1952; Ridley, 1984; St. Clair, 1951). Will this white person truly be able to empathize with my suffering? Will he or she translate whatever personal prejudices exist into a lack of sympathy, or too much sympathy? Will he or she truly be able to appreciate the tensions I am under? How will he or she judge my desires to be accepted by whites for what I am, my fierce pride in being African American, especially as I succeed in a white world? Will he or she see me as copping out or decide that my inhibition of resentment is adaptive and healthy? Indeed, will and can the therapist help me explore within myself what *I* really want? Must I want only what other African Americans want in order to be a whole person?

The Psychological Treatment of Hypertension

What kinds of treatment show promise in dealing with essential hypertension? In the most general terms, therapists of various persuasions agree that anxiety must be reduced to lessen the sympathetic nervous system arousal that maintains the blood pressure at abnormally high levels. Although there are probably limits to how normal the client can become — over time structural changes occur in the cardiovascular system that render it chronically hyperaroused to some extent — therapy can justifiably be attempted to help the client cope better with pressures and anxiety and thereby reduce blood pressure to a degree.

A psychoanalytic worker employs techniques such as free association and interpretation in efforts to lift repressions so that the person can examine hitherto repressed conflicts. John might have learned as a young child that to be loved one had to achieve, even if that means denying oneself what one really wanted. Operating with the hypothesis that hypertension arises from hostile impulses pressing for discharge, an analyst might encourage the client to recognize and express anger. Hypertension as an illness lends itself well to the hydraulic metaphor of psychoanalysis; siphoning off undischarged energy is expected to reduce the pressure in the psychic apparatus.

Client-centered therapists would focus on John's denial of his inner self, his not marching to the beat of his own drum, his compromising his ideas and deeply felt beliefs in order to meet with favor and acceptance from others. Dr. Shaw was operating in this framework, but we have seen that he did not get further than suggesting to John that he might be acting against his own self. The transcript provided earlier shows the kind of empathic listening and reflection common in client-centered therapy. Note, however, that Dr. Shaw did not merely reflect back to John what he had just said. A useful distinction should be drawn between what one writer has termed *primary accurate empathy* and *advanced empathy* (Egan, 1975) or what we have elsewhere likened to interpretation (Davison & Neale, 1994). Primary empathy is seen in the following exchange.

John: Doc, I can't talk to a white man about this. I can't talk to a black man about this. I'm too ashamed, too mixed up (beginning to sob). I can't handle this.
Dr. Shaw: This is hard for you, I know, John. . . .

Dr. Shaw acknowledges that he appreciates how difficult it is for John to be talking about his private thoughts. The hope is that the relationship will be strengthened and that John will be encouraged to continue exploring his feelings. In another part of the session, however, Dr. Shaw goes beyond what John has expressed, restating to him what is implied, what he, Dr. Shaw, believes is going on with John. He makes an *inference* about what is troubling the client in the hope of helping John view himself in a new, better perspective, one that will generate movement, greater honesty with the self. (Dr. Shaw has asked John how he felt about being the only African American in his club at college.)

Dr. Shaw: [I'd like to know about] Your feelings of being the only black.
John: Well, I felt really good about it. . . . [My high school friends would've] envied me to the utmost. . . .
Dr. Shaw: Yes, I know you were quite proud about it. . . . But I wonder if you had any other feelings about it.

Advanced empathy can be confrontational, as it certainly was in this instance. Too confrontational, it turned out. From our perspective, Dr. Shaw was on target, but John was too frightened, too angry to consider the interpretation. Therapists, beginning with Freud, have been mindful of the importance of timing. Shaw erred, perhaps due to the impatience he felt with himself for dancing too gingerly around John's problems for fear of sounding like a bigoted white person, an insensitive therapist who does not truly understand the client's torment.

If John had consulted a behavior therapist, some of the things already mentioned might have happened because contemporary behavior therapists also believe that many clients can benefit from expression of feelings (they call it *assertion training*, not the discharge of repressed hostility) and from a clearer idea of what is motivating them (they call it *behavioral assessment*). However, behavior therapists tend to be more concrete and active in prescribing techniques for their client. For John, there might have been role playing in the consulting room to help him rehearse with the therapist ways of expressing resentment and disagreement with people. The therapist, however, would have had to make the ethical judgment of how "activist" John should be: Would an assertive response be called for at the very hint of a racial slur, even at the risk of alienating, say, one of the partners in John's law office? Or would the therapist suggest systematic desensitization to harden John to these racist comments so that they would bother him less and presumably elicit little if any overt response? These are weighty moral questions.

Relaxation training and meditation (e.g., Benson, 1975; Patel et al., 1985) have also been used extensively and with some success in efforts to control hypertension (DiTomasso, 1987). In a recent clinical trial conducted by De-Quattro and Davison (Lee et al., 1987), intensively practiced relaxation reduced blood pressure in a group of male borderline hypertensives more than did a treatment condition in which subjects received state-of-the-art medical advice and instructions concerning diet, weight loss, and other known risk factors (the relaxation subjects also received this information). Of interest was the additional finding that relaxation was especially effective among those men whose sympathetic arousal was high, supporting an earlier suggestion by Esler et al. (1977) that there is a subset of hypertensives who may be particularly appropriate for sympathetic dampening therapies like relaxation. From the same dataset also emerged the finding that anger and hostility as assessed by a cognitive assessment technique called Articulated Thoughts in Simulated Situations (Davison, Robins, & Johnson, 1983) was reduced significantly more by the relaxation than by the information-only treatment and that this reduction was correlated with drops in blood pressure: The less angry and hostile subjects became in their thinking, the more benefit in blood pressure reduction they achieved from the training in relaxation (Davison, Williams, Nezami, Bice, & DeQuattro, 1991).

There is great interest nowadays in biofeedback, a technique that uses a highly sensitive electronic apparatus to inform a person of bodily changes that are usually too subtle to be detected. John might have learned when his blood pressure had passed a certain level and then been reinforced for bringing it down below that level. Statistically significant changes have been achieved with both normals and hypertensives in laboratory settings (Blanchard, 1990), but what clinical success has been achieved may be due in part to relaxation per se (McGrady, Nadsady, & Schumann-Brzezinski, 1991). Attention to the person's driven lifestyle seems to be essential if anything like biofeedback is going to play a significant role in lowering blood pressure.

Other interventions are also used to help people reduce their blood pressure. Medications are frequently prescribed. Indeed, the responsible psychological practitioner consults and often works with a physician to coordinate nonmedical with medical therapy. Regular exercise as well as losing weight through sensible diet continue to be part of any comprehensive approach to controlling high blood pressure.

5 DISSOCIATIVE IDENTITY DISORDER: MULTIPLE PERSONALITY

The instructor in Paula's human sexuality course suggested that she talk to a psychologist. Several factors contributed to his concern. Although Paula was a good student, her behavior in class had been rather odd on occasion. She was generally bright and attentive, though somewhat anxious and reluctant to speak. Every now and then, it seemed as though she came to class "high." She participated actively in the discussions, but she did not seem to be familiar with the readings or previous lecture material. Her scores on the first two exams had been As, but she failed to appear for the third. When he asked her where she had been, Paula maintained with apparent sincerity that she couldn't recall. Finally, she had handed in an essay assignment that described in rather vague, but sufficiently believable, terms the abusive, incestuous relationship that her father had forced upon her from the age of five until well after she was married and had had her first child. All of this led her professor to believe that Paula needed help. Fortunately, she was inclined to agree with him because there were a number of things that were bothering her. She made an appointment to talk to Dr. Harpin, a clinical psychologist at the student health center.

Paula Stewart was 38 years old, divorced, and the mother of a son who was 18 years old and a daughter who was 15. She was about 90 pounds overweight, but in other ways her appearance was unremarkable. For the past five years, Paula had been taking courses at the university and working part-time at a variety of secretarial positions on campus. She and her daughter lived together in a small, rural community located about 20 miles from the university—the same town in which Paula had been born. Her son had moved away from home and joined the Marines after dropping out of high school. Paula's mother and father still lived in their home just down the street from Paula's.

Over a series of sessions, Dr. Harpin noticed that Paula's behavior was often erratic. Her moods vacillated frequently and quickly from anger and irritability to severe depression. When she was depressed, her movements became agitated and she experienced sleep difficulties. She threatened suicide frequently and had, on several occasions, made some attempts to harm herself. In addition to these emotional difficulties, Paula frequently complained of severe headaches, dizziness, and breathing problems. An unusual dermatological condition also appeared at frequent intervals. Her eyes would swell and tear, and her arms and chest would become marked with large red blotches that itched painfully. Paula believed that it was poison ivy, but no one had been able to find any of the plants around her home or in any other area where she might have been in contact with it. She was tense and anxious much of the time.

It also seemed that Paula abused alcohol, although the circumstances were not clear. This situation was a source of distress and considerable confusion for Paula. She had found empty beer cans and whiskey bottles in the back seat of her car, but she denied drinking alcoholic beverages of any kind. Once every two or three weeks, she would wake up in the morning with terrible headaches as though she were hungover. Dr. Harpin attributed her confusion and other memory problems to her alcohol consumption.

Paula's relationships with other people were unpredictable. She would explode with little provocation and often argued that no one understood how serious her problems were. On occasion, she threatened to kill other people, particularly her mother and an older man, Cal, who lived nearby. Paula complained that her mother interfered in her life. Their conflict often centered on the way in which Paula chose to raise her children. Paula's mother nagged, told her how to discipline them, and seemed to compete with Paula for their attention and respect. Paula's mother recognized that Paula had problems— as evidenced by her frequently asking Paula if she was "crazy"—but she did not sympathize with her daughter's plight or attempt, in any serious way, to help. She seemed inclined to believe that Paula fabricated most of her own problems.

Paula's relationship with Cal was puzzling to both of them. They had known each other since she was an adolescent. Although he was 15 years older than she and had been married to another woman for more than 20 years, Cal had persistently shown a romantic interest in Paula. He would frequently come to her house saying that she had called. More often than not, this made Paula furious. She maintained that she was not at all interested in him and would never encourage such behavior. At other times, however, she insisted that he was the only person who understood and cared for her. Paula's mother and daughter were also puzzled and disturbed by her stormy relationship with Cal and the inconsistent way in which she seemed to deal with him.

Paula's father was still alive, but she did not spend any time with him. In fact, he behaved as though she didn't exist. She was able to recall and discuss some aspects of the incestuous relationship her father had forced upon her in previous years, but her memory was sketchy and she was inclined to pursue the issue gingerly only on those occasions when she was not depressed.

Throughout the first year of treatment, Paula's memory problems became increasingly severe. The notes she wrote during classes were often incomplete, as though she had suddenly stopped listening in the middle of a number of lectures. She sometimes complained that she lost parts of days. On one occasion, for example, she told Dr. Harpin that she had gone home with a severe headache in the middle of the afternoon and then couldn't remember anything until she awakened the following morning. Another time she was eating lunch, only to find herself hours later driving her car. Her daughter asked her about a loud argument Paula had had with her mother on the phone, and she couldn't remember even talking to her mother that day. These unexplained experiences were extremely frustrating to Paula, but the therapist continued to believe that they were induced by alcohol.

One day, Dr. Harpin received a message from his secretary saying that a woman named Sherry had called. She had identified herself as a friend of Paula's and had said that she would like to discuss the case. Before responding directly to this request, Dr. Harpin decided to check with Paula to find out more about this friend and determine whether she would consent to this consultation. Paula denied knowing anyone named Sherry, so Dr. Harpin did not return the original call. It did strike him as odd, however, that someone knew that he was Paula's therapist.

Two weeks after receiving this call, Dr. Harpin decided to try to use hypnosis in an attempt to explore the frequent gaps in Paula's memory. They had used hypnosis on one previous occasion as an aid to the process of applied relaxation, and it was clear that Paula was easily hypnotized. Unfortunately, it didn't help with the memory problem; Paula couldn't remember anything else about the time she had lost.

Upon waking out of a trance, Paula complained of a splitting headache. Then she placed her hands tightly over her eyes and slowly rubbed her face for a minute or two. Lowering her hands, she gazed slowly about the room as though she were lost. Dr. Harpin was puzzled. "Do you know where you are?" he asked. She said she didn't know, so he asked if she knew who he was. Rather than providing a quick answer, she glanced around the room. She noticed his professional license hanging on the wall, read his name, and finally replied, "Yes. You're Dr. Harpin, the one who's working with Paula." This switch to her use of the third person struck Dr. Harpin as being very odd and roused further curiosity about her state of mind.

"How do you feel?"
"Okay."
"Do you still have a headache?"
"No, *I* don't have a headache."

The way she emphasized the word "I" was unusual, so Dr. Harpin said, "You make it sound like somebody else has a headache." He was completely unprepared for her response.

"Yes. Paula does."

Pausing for a moment to collect his wits, Dr. Harpin—who was simultaneously confused and fascinated by this startling exchange—decided to pursue the identity issue further.

"If Paula has a headache, but you don't, what's your name?"
"Why should I tell you? I don't think I can trust you."
"Why not? Don't you want to talk to me?"
"Why should I? You wouldn't talk to me when I called last week!"

Dr. Harpin finally remembered the call from Sherry, who had wanted to talk to him about Paula's case. He asked the woman, once again, what her name was, and she said, "Sherry." After they talked for a couple of minutes, Dr. Harpin said, "I'd like to talk to Paula now."

"Oh, she's boring."
"That doesn't matter. She's my client, and I want to talk to her to see how she feels."
"Will you talk to me again?"
"Yes."
"Why should I believe you. You wouldn't talk to me before."
"Now I know who you are. Please let me talk to Paula."

At that point, she closed her eyes and waited quietly for a few moments. When her eyes opened, Paula was back and her headache was gone, but she could not remember anything about the last half hour. Dr. Harpin was stunned and incredulous. Although he was aware of the literature on multiple personality and a few well-known cases, he could not believe what Paula had said.

When Paula appeared for their next appointment, she still could not remember anything that had happened and seemed just as she had before this remarkable incident. Dr. Harpin decided to attempt to discuss with Paula a traumatic incident that had happened a number of years ago. Paula had frequently mentioned a day when she was 15 years old. She couldn't remember the details, but it was clearly a source of considerable distress for her and seemed to involve her father and a neighbor, Henry.

Dr. Harpin asked Paula to describe what she could remember about the day: where they were living at the time, what time of year it was, who was home, and so on. Paula filled in the details slowly and as best she could. Her father had grabbed her, hit her across the face, and dragged her toward the bedroom. No matter how hard she tried, she couldn't remember anything else. Paula said that she was getting a headache. Dr. Harpin suggested that she lean back in the chair and breathe slowly. She paused for a moment and closed her eyes. In a few moments, she opened her eyes and said, "She can't remember. She wasn't there. I was!" Sherry was back.

Paula's appearance had changed suddenly. She had been very tense, clutching the arms of the chair and sitting upright. She also had had an annoying, hacking cough. Now she eased down in the chair, folded her arms, and crossed her legs in front of her. The cough was completely gone. Sherry explained why Paula couldn't remember the incident with her father. As Sherry put it, when Paula was dragged into the bedroom, she simply decided to take off, leaving Sherry to experience the pain and humiliation of the ensuing rape. Dr. Harpin translated this to mean that Paula had experienced a dissociative episode. The incident was so extremely traumatic that she had completely separated the experience and its memory from the rest of her consciousness.

After discussing the rape in some detail, Dr. Harpin decided to find out as much as he could about Sherry. She provided only sketchy information, admitting that she was in her thirties but denying that she had a last name. Sherry's attitude toward Paula was contemptuous. She was angry because Paula had so frequently left Sherry to experience painful sexual encounters. They discussed numerous incidents dating from Paula's adolescence to the present, but none of Sherry's memories traced back prior to the incident with Paula's father and Henry. Since that time, Sherry was apparently aware of everything that Paula had done. Paula, on the other hand, was completely oblivious to Sherry's existence.

Toward the end of this conversation, Dr. Harpin asked whether it was Sherry or Paula who had been responsible for the beer bottles Paula found in her car. Sherry said, "Oh, we did that." Intrigued by the plural pronoun, Dr. Harpin asked whom she meant to describe, and the patient said, "Oh, Janet and I."

"Who's Janet?"

"You don't want to talk to her. She's always angry. You know how adolescents are."

By this point, Dr. Harpin knew that Sherry found it easier than Paula to switch back and forth among these personalities, so he encouraged her to try. Sherry agreed, somewhat reluctantly, and soon there was another dramatic change in Paula's appearance. She fidgeted in her chair, pulled at her hair, and began to bounce her leg continuously. She was reluctant to talk, but adopted a coy, somewhat flirtatious manner. She claimed to be 15 years old.

Several sessions later, Sherry presented Dr. Harpin with a request. She said that she and Janet were extremely concerned about Caroline, who was presumably only five years old and had been crying a lot lately. Sherry and Janet wanted Dr. Harpin to talk to Caroline. He agreed to try. Sherry closed her eyes and effortlessly transformed her posture and mannerisms to those of a little girl. She pulled her legs up onto the chair and folded them under her body. Holding her hand in a fist clenched close to the side of her mouth almost as if she were sucking her thumb, she turned sideways in the chair and peered at Dr. Harpin bashfully out of the corner of her eye. She seemed to be rather frightened.

"Will you talk to me, Caroline?" Dr. Harpin began.

After an extended pause, Caroline asked, "What's your name? I don't know you." Her voice seemed higher and weaker than it had been moments before.

"I'm Dr. Harpin."
"Do you know my mommy and daddy?"
"No. But I'm a friend of Sherry's. She asked me to talk to you. Do you know Sherry?"
"Yes. She watches me. She takes care of me."
"Do you know Janet?"
"She's big. She has fun!"
"Do you know her very well?"
"Not really. She gets mad easy."
"Sherry told me that you've been feeling sad. Why is that?"
"I'm a bad girl."
"Why do you think you're bad?"
"Mommy told me I'm bad. That's why she has to punish me."
"I don't think you're a bad girl."
"Yes I am. If I'm not bad, why would they punish me?"
"What do they punish you for?"
"I don't know. They just do. They hurt me. Once I pinched my brother when he took my toy puppy. Then they took my puppy away, and they won't give it back! Grandpa gave it to me. He's good to me."

After talking to Caroline for several more minutes, Dr. Harpin decided he would learn more by discussing these issues with Sherry. Before ending his conversation with Caroline, he asked if he could talk to her again.

"Mommy and Daddy won't like it if they know I'm talking to you."
"I'm sure it will be okay. Sherry said it's all right. Now can I talk to her again?"
"I don't want to go back. It's dark."
"I'll still be right here."

At this point, Caroline closed her eyes and sat up. After rubbing her face with both hands, she looked at Dr. Harpin and said, "I think she likes you. She feels a little better now.

At their next session, Dr. Harpin asked Paula if she remembered ever having a stuffed puppy when she was a child. A fond smile of recognition followed several moments' reflection. She had indeed had such a toy. He asked if she knew what had happened to it. She insisted that she had no idea. It had been almost 30 years since she remembered seeing it, but she agreed to look around in the attic of her mother's house.

Much to everyone's surprise, Paula was able to find the puppy, which was known as Jingles because of the sound made by a small bell sewn into its tail. Unfortunately, it became the source of considerable aggravation for Paula. The first day she found it, she left it in the living room before she went to bed. When she woke up in the morning, Jingles was in bed with her. This happened two nights in a row. On the third night, she locked the puppy in her car, which was kept in the garage, and went to bed. Once again, the puppy was in bed with her when she woke up in the morning. She was annoyed and also a bit frightened by this strange turn of events. In subsequent sessions, Sherry provided the following explanation for what had happened. Caroline would wake up in the middle of the night crying, wanting to hold her stuffed animal. In an effort to console her, Sherry would then retrieve Jingles from the living room or garage. Of course, Paula would not remember what had happened. When she threatened to throw the puppy in the garbage, Dr. Harpin proposed another alternative. Why not bring Jingles to his office for safe keeping? That way, he knew, if Caroline wanted the animal, he would have it for her.

Thus far there were four names: Paula, Sherry, Janet, and Caroline. The clinical picture was as fascinating as it was unbelievable. Dr. Harpin felt that he needed help as much as his client. In his 15 years of clinical experience, he had never seen a case that resembled Paula's in any way. It fit closely with some of the published cases of multiple personality, but he had never really believed that this sort of thing happened, except in fiction. Surely it was the product of the therapist's imagination, or the client's manipulative strategy. He was groping for advice from colleagues and a plan for the treatment of this complex set of problems. His contacts with Paula continued to deal largely with day-to-day crises.

He asked Paula if she had read any of the well-known books dealing with multiple personality. She had not. Had she seen *The Three Faces of Eve* or *Sybil*? No. Since she was not familiar with other examples of this phenomenon, it seemed unlikely that she had simply invented the alternate personalities as a way of attracting attention or convincing others of the severity of her problems. In an attempt to help Paula—who was not aware of the alternates—understand the problems that she faced, Dr. Harpin asked her to read *Sybil*. She reacted with interest and disbelief. What did it have to do with her situation? She was still completely unable to remember those times when she spoke as if she were Sherry, Janet, or Caroline. There were, however, times when Sherry discussed the book with Dr. Harpin, and Janet was also reading it. To make matters more confusing, they all seemed to be reading at a different pace. Paula might be two-thirds of the way through the book, but Janet—an adolescent who did not read as quickly—was aware of only the first part of the book.

Dr. Harpin also used videotape to help Paula understand the problem. With her consent, he recorded her behavior during a sequence of three therapy sessions. She alternated among the various personalities several times during the course of these tapes. Paula was then asked to view the tapes and discuss her reactions to her own behavior. Again, she was surprised, interested, and puzzled, showing no signs of previous awareness of this behavior. She would often ask, "Did *I* say that?" or "Who am I? *What* am I?"

Another unusual set of circumstances led to the identification of still another personality, Heather. Paula had complained on numerous occasions that a loaded shotgun, which belonged to her father, kept appearing at her house. She had no use for guns, and their presence upset her, so she would take the gun back to her father's house. Several days later, she would find it again at her house. Her parents and daughter adamantly denied knowing anything about the gun. Recognizing that Paula was frequently unaware of things that she did as the other personalities, Dr. Harpin discussed the gun with Sherry and Janet. Both denied any knowledge of these incidents. Janet said, "I know you think it's me, but it's not!" Finally, Sherry suggested that it might be someone else. "You mean there might be others?" Dr. Harpin asked. Sherry acknowledged the possibility, but said that she was not aware of any others.

At the beginning of the next session, Dr. Harpin decided to use hypnosis in an effort to see if he could identify more alternates. While Paula was in the trance, he asked if anyone else, with whom he had not yet spoken, was able to hear what he was saying. This was when Heather emerged. She was presumably 23. It was she who had been bringing the gun to Paula's house, and it was she who had been calling Cal. Heather told Dr. Harpin that she was in love with Cal. If she couldn't marry him, she wanted to kill herself. This was the first alternate with whom Sherry did not have co-consciousness, and her existence explained several important inconsistencies in Paula's behavior and gaps in her memory.

Heather's affection for Cal illustrates another important characteristic of the multiple personality phenomenon. There were important, and occasionally radical, differences among Paula, Sherry, and the other alternates in terms of tastes and preferences as well as mannerisms and abilities. Heather loved Cal (couldn't live without him), but the others hated him. In fact, Paula's most remarkable reaction to videotapes of her own behavior centered around one conversation with Heather. Paula insisted that it was not she. "I would *never* say those things!" she said. Paula's attitude toward her parents was also at odds with those of some of the alternates, and this inconsistency undoubtedly explained some of the erratic shifts in her behavior and relationship with other people. Sherry didn't like Paula's children and was inconsiderate in her behavior toward them. She frequently promised them things to keep them quiet and then failed to honor her commitment. Heather and Paula played the piano and organ, but the others didn't. Sherry would go to class for Paula, but Janet would not, and so on.

SOCIAL HISTORY

Paula grew up in a small rural community. Her father owned a farm, where they lived until she was six years old. She had one brother, two years older than she. Her mother was an outspoken, dominant woman who maintained firm control of the family. Both parents were strict disciplinarians. They belonged to a fundamentalist Baptist church and were strongly opposed to drinking alcohol, playing cards, and dancing. The parents of Paula's mother lived on the neighboring farm. This grandfather was the only sympathetic adult figure throughout Paula's childhood. It was he who had given her the stuffed puppy, Jingles, which had become such an important source of comfort to her until her parents took it away. When Paula was upset, her grandfather was the only person who was able to console her and stop her crying (although she never dared to tell him about the things that her father forced her to do). When Paula was six years old, her father bought a small gasoline station in town. The Stewart family left their farm, and Paula was separated from her grandfather, who was able to visit only on weekends.

Paula's father was a shy, withdrawn, unaffectionate man who did not have many friends. For the first few years of her life, he ignored her completely. She desperately wanted his attention, but he was not interested in her at all. Then, when she was five years old, he suddenly began to demonstrate physical affection. He would hug and kiss her roughly, and when no one else was around, he would fondle her genitals. Paula didn't know how to respond.

His touches weren't pleasant or enjoyable, but she would accept whatever affection he was willing to provide.

When she was 11, Mr. Stewart caught Paula kissing in the barn with an adolescent boy who had been helping with the farm work. Her father became extremely angry. He told the boy never to talk to Paula again. That evening, Mr. Stewart came to Paula's room and explained harshly that if she needed to be loved, he would be the source of her affection. Then he forced her to have intercourse with him.

When she was 15, their sexual encounters started to become violent. The pretense of affection and love was obviously dissolved; he wanted to hurt her. In one incident, which Paula and Dr. Harpin had discussed repeatedly, her father dragged her into his bedroom by her hair and tied her to the bed. After slapping her repeatedly, he forced her to have intercourse with him while a neighbor, Henry, watched. Then Henry raped her. The incest and physical abuse continued until she was 20 years old.

Paula's mother was a strict disciplinarian who often punished her by putting her hands in scalding hot water or locking her in a dark closet for hours on end. Mrs. Stewart was not a sympathetic listener and did not realize—or seem to care—that her husband was abusing Paula sexually. If she did know, she may have been afraid to intervene. Mr. Stewart may also have abused his wife as well as his daughter, but Paula could not remember witnessing any violence between her parents.

Perhaps in an effort to tear herself away from this abusive family, Paula pursued relationships with other men at an early age. Many of these men were older than she, including teachers and neighbors. The longest relationship of this sort was with Cal, the owner of a small construction business and an elected county commissioner. Paula was 16 and Cal was 31 when they started seeing each other. Although he took advantage of Paula sexually, Cal was a more sympathetic character than her father or the neighbor, Henry. He did listen to her and seemed to care for her. On numerous occasions, Cal promised that he would marry her. For Paula, he was a "rescuer," someone who offered a way out of her pathological family situation. Unfortunately, he didn't come through. He married another woman but continued to pursue Paula's affection and sexual favors. She continued to oblige, in spite of the strong feelings of anger and betrayal that she harbored.

A few incidents that occurred while Paula was in high school were probably precursors of the memory problems and dissociative experiences that she later encountered as an adult. They suggest that the problem of alternate personalities began during adolescence, although it was not discovered until many years later. People sometimes told Paula about things that she had done, things that she could not remember doing. Most of these involved promiscuous behavior. Paula was particularly upset by a rumor that went around the school when she was a sophomore. Several other girls claimed that Paula had been seen in a county police car with three male officers. They were parked in a remote picnic area outside of town, and Paula presumably had intercourse with all of them. She couldn't remember a thing, but she also didn't know where she had been that night.

Another time, a photographer from a nearby city — in which the university was located — called to ask if she would be willing to pose for him again. Paula had no idea what he meant. Nevertheless, he offered her a small amount of money, so she agreed to meet him at his studio. When she arrived, it became clear that he expected her to pose in the nude. She was horrified to find that he already had some nude photographs of her that had been taken a few months earlier. In retrospect, it seems that Sherry had already begun acting independently.

After graduating from high school, Paula enrolled in the university's school of education. She didn't study and dropped out after one year, having decided that she did not want to be a teacher. She then worked at various odd jobs, including six months in training with an airline firm in New York, before moving to Pittsburgh, where she found a clerical job.

She met her husband, Roger, shortly after arriving in Pittsburgh. He was in the Air Force and still married to another woman when he and Paula began having an affair. When Paula became pregnant, Roger agreed to get a divorce, but he couldn't marry her until the divorce became final. Then he was transferred to Japan. Paula moved back to live with her parents until the baby was born. Her sister-in-law provided some support during her pregnancy, but her mother was primarily interested in scolding and chastising Paula for having a child out of wedlock. Several weeks after her son was born, Paula's father began to abuse her again. She also continued her affair with Cal.

Two years later, Roger returned from Japan to stay with Paula and her parents during a 45-day leave. It was a momentous visit; they were married, and Paula became pregnant once again. When his leave was over, Roger persuaded Paula to bring the baby and move with him to an Air Force base in California, where he was to receive further training before being reassigned overseas. One week after arriving in California, Paula decided that she could not stay married to Roger and did not want to leave the country, so she returned home to live with her parents.

In the next three years, she held five different jobs. She was either fired from each of these positions or left voluntarily after disagreements over her work assignments. Roger returned one more time on a 30-day leave. They did not get along at all and spent most of their time arguing about her parents and methods of disciplining their children. He left after only 12 days. They did not speak to each other afterwards, and he made no further attempt to contact Paula or visit the children.

Shortly after the birth of her daughter, Paula gained a considerable amount of weight. Prior to her second pregnancy, she had weighed 115 pounds. The week before the birth, she was up to 170 and four months later she weighed 195! She also developed a hysterical aphonia. She was completely unable to speak. She couldn't even whisper, in spite of the fact that her physician was unable to identify a physiological explanation for the condition. Six weeks later, her voice came back as quickly as it had disappeared.

CONCEPTUALIZATION AND TREATMENT

Dr. Harpin's initial diagnostic impression, before the emergence of the alternate personalities, was that Paula fit the *DSM-IV* criteria for both dysthymia (a long-lasting form of depression that is not sufficiently severe to meet the criteria for major depressive disorder) and borderline personality disorder. Throughout the first year of treatment, his approach to the problem was focused primarily on the management of frequent, specific crises. These included numerous transient suicidal threats, fights with her mother and daughter, confusion and anger over her relationship—or lack of a relationship—with Cal, difficulties in her school work and with professors teaching her classes, and a variety of incidents involving her employers. When immediate problems of this sort were not pressing, Paula usually wanted to talk about the way her father had abused her. Her focus was on both the anger and the guilt that she felt about these incidents. She wondered whether in some way she hadn't encouraged his sexual advances.

After the appearance of the alternate personalities, Dr. Harpin's initial hypothesis was that Paula was malingering, that is, feigning a dramatic set of symptoms in an effort to gain some benefit from him or her family. This explanation was attractive for several reasons, including his skepticism regarding the existence of a phenomenon such as multiple personality. Nevertheless, he eventually abandoned this view. One problem was the apparent absence of information that would have been necessary for Paula to fake this disorder. She had not read or seen any of the popular descriptions of multiple personality, and it was therefore unlikely that she would be able to create or imitate the problem in such a believable, detailed fashion. The other problem was the lack of a clear motive. She was not, for example, facing criminal charges that might be avoided by the existence of a severe form of mental illness. Nor was she able to avoid personal or family responsibilities by the onset of these conditions, because she continued to go to school, work, and take care of her daughter after the emergence of the alternates. The only thing she might stand to gain was increased attention from Dr. Harpin. It seemed unlikely that this would explain the problem, since he had already been spending an inordinate amount of time and energy on the case as a result of the previous suicidal gestures, and he had repeatedly conveyed to Paula his concern for her numerous problems.

It eventually became clear that Paula was experiencing a genuine disruption of consciousness that was generally precipitated by stressful experiences. Faced with an extremely threatening or unpleasant circumstance, Paula's response was often to dissociate — to entirely blot out (or repress) her awareness of that event. This pattern of cognitive activity could be traced to the violent abuse that she received from her father during adolescence. By her own description, when these events began, Paula would usually "leave" the situation and Sherry would be left to face her father. The turbulent nature of these years and the concentration of abuse during this time might account for the fact that the ages of most of the alternates seemed to cluster between 15 and 23. Over time, the extent of this fragmentation of conscious experience became more severe, and her control over changes in her patterns of awareness eroded progressively. Current stressful circumstances that precipitated alterations in consciousness — or changes in personality — included unusual demands on her time involving school and work; relationships with men, particularly Cal; and continued hostility between Paula and her parents.

One approach to the resolution of these dissociative episodes might involve the recall and exploration of previous traumatic experiences that seemed to be responsible for particular splits in Paula's consciousness. Perhaps the most salient of these episodes was the rape scene involving Paula's father and the neighbor, Henry. The existence of Sherry suggested that the split could be traced to about this period of time, and it was an incident that Sherry mentioned repeatedly. Previous psychoanalytic accounts of multiple personality, such as *The Three Faces of Eve,* suggest that the patient's disturbance in consciousness might improve if the repression of these memories can be lifted. Unfortunately, this approach did not seem to be useful in Paula's case. She and Dr. Harpin spent many hours discussing this incident — from the perspectives of both Paula and Sherry — but it only seemed to make things worse. Sherry cried and sobbed again and again. She screamed things that she had wanted to say to her father. Paula's recollection of the details of that day improved slightly. But the episode continued to be extremely distressing every time it was discussed, and there was no associated improvement with regard to Paula's control of the alternate personalities.

A different approach was needed. Dr. Harpin had two principal goals in mind during the next several months of treatment: to discourage further fragmentation of Paula's conscious experience and to facilitate the integration of information across the divisions of conscious experience. In other words, without encouraging or crystallizing the existence of separate personalities, Dr. Harpin wanted to help Paula recognize the nature of the problem and the way her behavior patterns changed in association with loss of memory for these incidents. This was done, in part, by having her read and discuss *Sybil* and allowing her to view videotapes of her own behavior. Dr. Harpin's hope was that the videotapes might jog Paula's memory and begin to break down the barriers that had been erected to prevent the exchange of information between the subdivisions of her conscious working memory.

Of course, the crisis management approach could never be completely abandoned. It seemed to Dr. Harpin that each time they were beginning to make progress toward integration of the various alternatives, Paula would provoke another disruptive incident. One Saturday, for example, Sherry called him from a neighboring state. She said that she just needed to get away, so she got into her car and drove, without any particular plan or destination in mind. The point was simply to get away and have a good time. Her goal, she said, was to drink as much as she could and have sex with as many men as possible. A letter that she sent Dr. Harpin two days later captured her feelings and also provided some insight regarding her motivation. She wrote:

> Now it's time to get down to some serious drinking and sex. It's funny. They think they're getting what they want, but I'm using them! *I'm* in charge. Men can't hurt me any more. From now on, I'm only going to let Paula be in control when she's at work. Maybe I'll turn things over to her when I'm in bed with a complete stranger. Who knows? Maybe I'll even take on her dad.

The suicidal gestures also continued and were occasionally more severe. One incident was particularly critical because all of the personalities became depressed at the same time. On this particular occasion, Dr. Harpin arranged an involuntary hospitalization to prevent Paula from taking her own life.

DISCUSSION

Multiple personality disorder (MPD)—which is called Dissociative Identity disorder in *DSM-IV*—is probably a rare phenomenon. Prior to 1980, fewer than two or three hundred cases had been reported in the professional literature (Fahy, 1988). This number is incredibly small compared to the millions of patients who suffer from disorders such as schizophrenia and depression at any point in time. Some investigators have suggested that MPD appears more frequently than previously assumed (e.g., Ross, 1991), but these claims have been disputed (e.g., Lauer, Black, & Keen, 1993; Merskey, 1992). Carefully collected, epidemiological data have not been presented to support the argument that MPD is a common form of psychopathology.

Multiple personality disorder has attracted considerable attention because a few dramatic cases have received widespread publicity through popular books and films. These include *The Three Faces of Eve* (Thigpen & Cleckley, 1957), *Sybil* (Schreiber, 1973), and *The Minds of Billy Milligan* (Keyes, 1981). Case studies such as these may represent our best source of information about the disorder. A few investigators have managed to identify samples of patients with MPD for the purpose of research (e.g., Boon & Draijer, 1993; Coons, Bowman, & Milstein, 1988; Putnam, Guroff, Silberman, Barban, & Post, 1986). Their descriptions have made significant contributions to the base of knowledge that is beginning to emerge regarding this enigmatic disorder.

Previous diagnostic systems typically considered multiple personality disorder to be a form of hysterical neurosis. This assumption was based, in part, on the frequent observation that these patients also exhibit symptoms of conversion hysteria (now referred to as Somatoform Disorders in *DSM-IV*, p. 487). Some examples of this association were evident in Paula's case. She experienced aphonia, an unexplained inability to speak, following the birth of her daughter and intermittently had problems with an unusual skin rash. It is now clear, however, that the rather extensive list of accessory problems exhibited by multiple personality patients extends well beyond those associated only with hysteria. Other symptoms that have been reported in several cases include auditory hallucinations and various manifestations of borderline personality.

DSM-IV lists the following diagnostic criteria for multiple personality disorder, which it renamed Dissociative Identity Disorder:

A. The presence of two or more distinct identities or personality states (each with its own relatively enduring pattern of perceiving, relating to, and thinking about the environment and self).
B. At least two of these identities or personality states recurrently take control of the person's behavior.
C. Inability to recall important personal information that is too extensive to be explained by ordinary forgetfulness.
D. The disorder is not due to the direct physiological effects of a substance (such as blackouts or chaotic behavior during alcohol intoxication).

The manual also notes that the transition between different personalities is usually sudden and often beyond volitional control.

Memory disturbances are perhaps the most important feature of this disorder. Most people behave differently, or may seem to be somewhat different people, as a function of the environmental stimuli with which they are confronted, but the changes are seldom as dramatic or complete as those seen in cases of multiple personality. Furthermore, very few people forget what they have done or who they are whenever they alter their pattern of behavior. In multiple personality disorder, the original personality is typically unaware of the existence of the alternates. It is not unusual for the person to express concern about large chunks of time that seem to be missing or unaccounted for. The alternate personalities may, or may not, be aware of each other or "co-conscious." At any given moment only one personality is controlling the person's behavior and interacting with the environment, but other personalities may simultaneously perceive, and subsequently remember, events that are taking place.

The boundaries of this diagnostic category are difficult to define. Some clinicians have argued that it should be considered broadly (e.g., Kluft, 1991), while others would prefer that the term be applied only to severe or classic cases (e.g., Freeland et al., 1993; Thigpen & Cleckley, 1984). Because the disorder is rare and clinicians are not routinely familiar with its manifestations, some patients have probably been misdiagnosed as suffering from other disorders, most notably schizophrenia and borderline personality disorder. Several diagnostic signs might alert a clinician to suspect that a patient may be experiencing multiple personality (Greaves, 1980). These include:

1. Reports of time distortions or time lapses.
2. Reports of being told of behavioral episodes by others that are not remembered by the patient.
3. Reports of notable changes in the patient's behavior by a reliable observer, during which time the patient may call him- or herself by different names or refer to him- or herself in the third person.
4. Elicitability of other personalities through hypnosis.
5. The use of the word "we" in the course of an interview in which the word seems to take on a collective meaning rather than an editorial "we."
6. The discovery of writing, drawings, or other productions or objects among the patient's personal belongings that he or she does not recognize and cannot account for.
7. A history of severe headaches, particularly when accompanied by blackouts, seizures, dreams, visions, or deep sleep.

Paula exhibited almost all of the signs included on this list. Time lapses and headaches were a frequent source of concern when she began treatment at the student health center. She had been told about incidents that she could not remember as far back as high school. Her children and at least one professor had noticed marked changes in her behavior that were not easily explained by environmental circumstances. It should be emphasized, of course, that none of these problems, alone or in combination, would be considered sufficient evidence to diagnose multiple personality disorder if the patient does not also meet other specific diagnostic criteria such as those listed in *DSM-IV*.

Etiological Considerations

A variety of hypotheses have been proposed to account for the development of multiple personality. One simple explanation is that the patient produces the symptoms voluntarily, or plays the role of multiple personality, in an effort to attract attention or avoid responsibility. A few widely publicized criminal trials in which the defendant claimed innocence by reason of insanity have indicated that the syndrome can be faked rather convincingly.[1]

The best known example involves the case of Kenneth Bianchi, also known as the Hillside Strangler. Several experienced clinicians interviewed Bianchi after he was arrested. With the aid of hypnosis, they discovered an alternate personality, Steve, who proudly claimed responsibility for several brutal rape-murders. The prosecution called Martin Orne, a psychiatrist at the University of Pennsylvania, as an expert witness to examine Bianchi. Orne raised serious questions about the case by indicating that the defendant was probably faking hypnosis during the interviews and by demonstrating that Bianchi's symptoms changed dramatically as a result of subtle suggestions (Orne, Dinges, & Orne, 1984). He proposed that the defendant was faking symptoms of multiple personality in an attempt to avoid the death penalty. The court found Orne's skepticism persuasive, and Bianchi was eventually convicted of murder. These circumstances are clearly rather extreme; very few patients have such an obvious motive for feigning a psychological disorder. The Bianchi case should not be taken to mean that all patients who exhibit signs of multiple personality are malingering or faking. Nevertheless, it does indicate that therapists should be cautious in evaluating the evidence for any diagnostic decision, particularly when the disorder is as difficult to define and evaluate as multiple personality.

A related social-psychological hypothesis holds that multiple personality disorder is a product of the therapist's influence on the client. This is not to say that the patient is faking the disorder, but rather that patients respond to cues that are provided during the course of treatment (e.g., Weissberg, 1993). Clinicians have frequently noted, for example, that patients with multiple personality disorder are easily hypnotized and the alternate personalities are often "discovered" during hypnosis, a process that is capable of inducing phenomena such as amnesia, one important symptom of dissociative disorders. According to this view, some therapists may provide their patients with information and suggestions about multiple personality, subtly and unconsciously encouraging them to behave in ways that are consistent with these expectations, and rewarding them with extra attention and care when they adopt the role. It is interesting to note in this regard that, despite the fact that the vast majority of clinicians work an entire career without seeing a single case of multiple personality, a small handful of therapists claim to have treated large numbers of multiple personality patients (Modestin, 1992). This radically disproportionate distribution of cases is consistent with the hypothesis that some clinicians find (and perhaps encourage the development of) symptoms in which they are particularly interested.

---

[1]See "The Ten Faces of Billy Milligan," *Newsweek*, December 18, 1978, p. 106, for a description of a case in which the defendant was acquitted by reason of insanity.

Some empirical support for this hypothesis was reported by Spanos, Weekes, and Bertrand (1985). In this experiment, college students were asked to play the role of an accused murderer (named Harry or Betty, depending on the subject's sex) who was being evaluated by a psychiatrist prior to a trial. They were asked to use whatever they knew about criminal behavior *as well as any cues that were provided in the context of the simulated diagnostic interview* to give a convincing performance. Subjects who were assigned to the "Bianchi Treatment," which was modeled directly after transcripts of interviews used in the Hillside Strangler case, were hypnotized and the person playing the psychiatrist read statement such as the following: "I've talked a bit to Harry (Betty) but I think perhaps there might be another part of Harry (Betty) that I haven't talked to, another part that maybe feels somewhat differently from the part that I've talked to. And I would like to communicate with that other part." Then addressing the "other part" directly, the psychiatrist asked, "Would you talk to me, Part, by saying 'I'm here'?" Sixteen people received the Bianchi Treatment, and 13 of these spontaneously adopted a name other than Harry or Betty. Ten of the 16 (and none of the control subjects) later displayed spontaneous amnesia for what they had said while they were hypnotized. This study shows that under special laboratory conditions, the demand characteristics of an interview setting can lead some people to exhibit unusual behaviors that are associated with multiple personality (amnesia and use of an alternate name). Generalizing from this situation to actual clinical interviews, it seems possible that the things a therapist says to a client and the way in which the client is addressed by the therapist can influence the client's behavior in important ways.

Are all patients with MPD simply trying to please their therapists or responding to subtle suggestions? The hypothesis probably accounts for some cases, but it does not provide a convincing explanation for many others. In many cases, important symptoms have been observed before the patient enters treatment. In Paula's case, the phone call from Sherry (which was the first clear-cut evidence of an independent alternate personality) occurred before the use of hypnosis. Furthermore, most therapists are not looking for multiple personality disorder. Dr. Harpin, for example, had never seen a case of this sort before treating Paula. He went out of his way to consider other explanations of her behavior before considering the diagnosis of multiple personality disorder. The suffering experienced by these patients as a function of their symptoms also makes it seem unlikely that they are doing it for attention.

If MPD is, in fact, a genuine psychological phenomenon involving a disturbance in consciousness and loss of volitional control, how can we account for its development? Two important clues seem to be present in most cases that have been reported: The patients are excellent hypnotic subjects, and many were victims of severe physical and sexual abuse during childhood (Boon & Draijer, 1993; Putnam, 1991). One parsimonious explanation, which is based on these observations and has been proposed by Bliss (1986), is that patients with multiple personalities are people who spontaneously use, and unintentionally abuse, self-hypnosis; they escape into trances to avoid extreme conflict or threat. Although this process is initially somewhat useful in protecting the principal personality from painful experiences, the individual loses control of the process and is unable to either stop it or recognize that it is happening.

The credibility of the self-hypnosis hypothesis view rests heavily on the analogy between hypnotic phenomena and the dissociative symptoms of multiple personality disorder. There are, in fact, numerous points of similarity, but there are also important differences (Gruenewald, 1984). Perhaps most important in this regard is the issue of control. In hypnosis, according to Gruenewald's view of the phenomenon, the person voluntarily complies with the hypnotist's suggestions and is capable of resuming normal attentional functions on cue. This central regulatory mechanism seems to be disrupted in dissociative disorders such as multiple personality. There are also differences between the amnesic phenomena associated with hypnosis and multiple personality disorder. Lapses in memory induced by hypnosis are typically transient and easily reversible, while those seen in dissociative disorders are stable and may be unresponsive to treatment. These considerations indicate that the self-hypnotic view is still open to serious question, but it is one reasonable hypothesis that fits with some therapists' clinical experience.

TREATMENT

Most efforts to treat patients with multiple personality disorder have focused on two principal strategies: stabilize the most functional or competent personality or integrate the disparate personalities into one. The former approach was employed initially by Thigpen and Cleckley (1957) in treating the patient described in *The Three Faces of Eve*. Follow-up reports on this case, which described the subsequent emergence of numerous additional personalities, include the difficulties and possible futility of this method.

Most experts agree that integration is presently the treatment of choice (Kluft, 1987; Smith, 1993). Dr. Harpin employed a number of techniques in trying to help Paula fuse the various alternates. The first step involves facilitating recognition by the patient of the existence of alternate personalities. One approach might be using videotapes of the alternate behavior in an effort to help the patient recognize radical changes that are otherwise unknown. It may also be important to help patients understand the general nature of the problem as it has appeared in others' lives so that they can gain perspective on their own dilemma. This was the goal that Dr. Harpin had in mind when he asked Paula to read *Sybil*. Fusion may eventually be accomplished if the main personality comes to share the memories and emotions of the alternates. Finally, the most important step involves learning to react to conflict and stress in an adaptive fashion rather than engaging in the avoidance behaviors associated with dissociative states.

While working toward the process of integration, it is also important that the therapist avoid further fragmentation of the patient's behavior or personality. Unfortunately, this is a difficult caveat to heed. The existence of independent personalities of such different tastes and styles is fascinating, and the therapist is easily tempted to explore and discuss every exotic detail of the patient's experience. Extended and persistent questioning of this sort may encourage additional dissociative experiences and impede integration. The use of separate names to describe and address alternate personalities may also serve to stabilize and condone their existence (Fahy, Abas, & Brown, 1989). Finally, although hypnosis can be a useful tool in attempting to facilitate the patient's recall of forgotten events, it can also lead to the emergence of additional personalities. None of these problems is easy to avoid. They all suggest that therapists who are confronted with patients exhibiting symptoms of multiple personality disorder must be extremely cautious in planning their interventions. They must attend to the unique features of the patient's dissociative experience without ignoring other potentially crucial aspects of the person's problem.

6 MAJOR DEPRESSIVE DISORDER

Janet called the mental health center to ask if someone could help her five-year-old son, Adam. He had been having trouble sleeping for the past several weeks, and Janet was becoming concerned about his health. Adam refused to go to sleep at his regular bedtime and also woke up at irregular intervals throughout the night. Whenever he woke up, Adam would come downstairs to be with Janet. Her initial reaction had been sympathetic; she would give him some water, talk to him, and rock him back to sleep. As the cycle came to repeat itself night after night, Janet's tolerance grew thin and she became more belligerent. She found herself engaged in repeated battles that usually ended when she agreed to let him sleep in her room. Janet felt guilty about giving in to a five-year-old's demands, but it seemed like the only way they would ever get any sleep. The family physician was unable to identify a physical explanation for Adam's problem; he suggested that Janet contact a psychologist. This advice led Janet to inquire about the mental health center's series of parent training groups.

Applicants for the groups were routinely screened during an individual intake interview. The therapist began by asking several questions about Janet and her family. Janet was 30 years old and had been divorced from her husband, David, for a little more than one year. Adam was the youngest of Janet's three children; Jennifer was 10 and Claire was 8. Janet had resumed her college education on a part-time basis when Adam was 2 years old. She had hoped to finish her bachelor's degree at the end of the next semester and enter law school in the fall. Unfortunately, she had withdrawn from classes one month prior to her appointment at the mental health center. Her current plans were indefinite. She spent almost all of her time at home with Adam.

Janet and the children lived in a large, comfortable house that she had received as part of the divorce settlement. Finances were a major concern to Janet, but she managed to make ends meet through the combination of student loans, a grant-in-aid from the university, and child-support payments from David. David lived in a nearby town with a younger woman whom he had married shortly after the divorce. He visited Janet and the children once or twice every month and took the children to spend weekends with him once a month.

Having collected the necessary background information, the therapist asked for a description of the circumstances surrounding the development of Adam's sleep difficulties and the factors that currently affected the problem. This discussion covered the sequence of a typical evening's events, beginning with dinner and progressing through the following morning. It was clear during this discussion that Janet felt completely overwhelmed by the situation. She was exasperated and felt that she was completely unable to control her son. At several points during the interview, Janet seemed to be on the verge of tears. Her eyes were watery, and her voice broke as they discussed her response to David's occasional visits. The therapist, therefore, suggested that they put off a further analysis of Adam's problems and spend some time discussing Janet's situation in a broader perspective.

In the subsequent conversation it became clear that Janet's mood had been depressed since her husband had asked for a divorce. She felt sad, discouraged, and lonely. This feeling seemed to become even more severe just prior to her withdrawal from classes at the university (one year after David's departure and two months before her first clinic appointment). When David left, she remembered feeling "down in the dumps," but she could usually cheer herself up by playing with the children or going for a walk. Now she was nearing desperation. She cried frequently and for long periods of time. Nothing seemed to cheer her up. She had lost interest in her friends, and the children seemed to be more of a burden than ever. Her depression was somewhat worse in the morning, when it seemed that she would never be able to make it through the day.

Janet was preoccupied by her divorce from David and admitted that she spent hours each day brooding about the events that led to their separation. These worries interfered considerably with her ability to concentrate and seemed directly related to her withdrawal from the university. She had found that she was totally unable to study the assigned reading or concentrate on a 45-minute lecture. Withdrawing from school had precipitated further problems. She was no longer eligible for student aid and would have to begin paying back her loans within a few months. In short, one worry led to another, and her attitude became increasingly pessimistic. Janet harbored considerable resentment toward David and his new wife, although she blamed herself for the divorce. Among other things, she believed that her return to school had placed additional strain on an already difficult situation, and she wondered whether she had acted selfishly. The therapist noted that Janet's reasoning often seemed somewhat vague and illogical. She argued that she had been a poor marital partner and cited several examples of her own misconduct. These included events that struck the therapist as being very common, if not entirely reasonable. She sometimes spent too much money on her clothes, complained too openly and too often about many of David's faults, failed to show interest in sports, and so on. Janet seemed to blow these events totally out of proportion until they appeared to her to be terrible sins. She also generalized from her marriage to other relationships in her life. If her first marriage had failed, how could she ever expect to develop a satisfactory relationship with another man? Furthermore, Janet had begun to question her value as a friend and parent. The collapse of her marriage seemed to affect the manner in which she viewed all of her social relationships.

The future looked bleak from her current perspective, but she had not given up all hope. Her interest in solving Adam's problem, for example, was an encouraging sign. Although she was not optimistic about the chances of success, she was willing to try to develop new skills that would help her become a more effective parent.

SOCIAL HISTORY

Janet's early childhood had been uneventful. Not having any siblings, she spent most of her time with adults, particularly her mother. She remembered her parents' relationship as being warm and pleasant. The family took frequent outings together and, despite the usual number of quarrels and disagreements, everyone seemed to enjoy being together.

When Janet was 10 years old, her mother died in an automobile accident. Janet could remember the events of that day with terrible clarity. When she arrived home from school, her mother's best friend was there to meet her. She explained that Janet's mother had been in an accident and that her father had gone to the hospital. He arrived home several hours later and told Janet that her mother had died. The following months were very difficult for Janet and her father. Janet's father was overcome with grief, but he managed to continue working and arranged for neighborhood friends to care for Janet when he was not home. Janet also managed to struggle through her normal schedule of activities. Her performance at school was not markedly affected, and she continued to play with her small circle of friends. She did remember, however, that she often spent long hours sitting in her mother's room gazing at old photographs and crying softly to herself. On one occasion, her father found her wearing some of her mother's clothes and makeup. His response seemed to be appropriate and sympathetic. They had a long talk about how much they both missed Janet's mother and how they could help each other through this difficult time. Shortly after this incident, Janet's father donated her mother's clothes to the Salvation Army.

Even prior to her mother's death, Janet had been reserved socially. She tended to have one or two special friends with whom she spent much of her time outside of school, but she felt awkward and self-conscious in larger groups of children. Although her friends were important to her and she enjoyed spending time with them, Janet usually waited for them to contact her. She did not initiate activities and hesitated to express her own preferences when they were trying to decide what to do. In retrospect, Janet attributed this lack of assertiveness to her fear that her friends would abandon her or ridicule her interests. She was also self-conscious about her weight. She was not really fat, but she tended to be a bit plump and was therefore afraid that the others would tease her if she drew attention to herself.

This friendship pattern persisted throughout high school and into her college years. She was interested in boys and dated intermittently until her junior year in high school, when she began to date one boy on a regular basis. Janet was certain that she was in love with him and soon lost all contact with the few girlfriends with whom she had been close. She and her boyfriend, John, spent all of their time together, both after school and on the weekends. Janet remembered that the other kids seemed to make fun of her relationship with John and admitted that it did seem silly from her current perspective. Whether they were alone or in a group, Janet always sat next to John, holding his hand and giggling at his dreary jokes. The others teased Janet and John about acting as if they were married. This criticism troubled Janet, even though she fully expected that she and John would be married shortly after they graduated from high school.

Her marriage plans did not work out, however. She and John broke up during Janet's first year in college. He announced suddenly that he wanted to date other women and that their relationship was over. Janet met David a few weeks afterward, and they were married the following summer. Janet later wondered whether she had rushed into her relationship with David primarily to avoid the vacuum created by John's sudden exit. Whatever her motivation might have been, her marriage was followed shortly by her first pregnancy, which precipitated her withdrawal from the university during her sophomore year. For the next seven years, Janet was occupied as a full-time mother and housekeeper.

When Adam was two years old and able to attend a day-care center, Janet decided to resume her college education. She and David had discussed her desire to complete her degree and pursue a profession on several occasions. He was less than excited about this prospect and preferred that Janet continue in her present role. She disagreed but admitted that the children were too young and they could not afford both tuition and day care. Now that Adam was older, the circumstances were finally in Janet's favor, and David agreed to take a more active role in various responsibilities that had previously been assumed by Janet alone. Adam was enrolled at a day-care center on a half-time basis, and Janet began taking two courses each semester.

Following Janet's return to school, her relationship with David became increasingly strained. They had even less time than usual to spend with each other. David found it difficult to adjust to his increased household responsibilities. Janet was no longer able to prepare meals for the family every night of the week, so David had to learn to cook. He also had to share the cleaning and drive the children to many of their lessons and social activities. A more balanced and stable relationship would have been able to withstand the stress associated with these changes, but Janet and David were unable to adjust. Instead of working to improve their communications, they bickered continuously. They found it impossible to negotiate a mutually acceptable exchange of responsibilities. The final blow came when David met another woman to whom he was attracted and who offered him an alternative to the escalating hostility with Janet. He asked for a divorce and moved to an apartment.

Janet was shaken by David's departure, in spite of the fact that they had not been happy together. Fortunately, she did have a few friends to whom she could turn for support. The most important one was a neighbor who had children of approximately the same ages as Janet's daughters. There were also two couples with whom she and David had socialized. They were all helpful for the first few weeks, but she quickly lost contact with the couples. It was awkward to get together as a threesome, and Janet had never been close enough with the women to preserve their relationships on an individual basis. That left the neighbor, Susan, as her sole adviser and confidante. Susan was the only person with whom Janet felt she could discuss her feelings openly. They spent hours talking about the recent events in Janet's life and her plans for the coming months.

For the next few months, Janet was able to continue her studies. With the children's help she managed the household chores and kept up with her work. She even found time for some brief social activities. She agreed to go out on two blind dates arranged by people with whom she and David had been friends. These were generally unpleasant encounters; one of her dates was boring and unattractive, and the other was obnoxiously aggressive. After the latter experience, she discontinued the minimal efforts she had made to develop new friendships. The process seemed too difficult and threatening. Janet referred to single-parent clubs as "meat markets" where people paired off for casual sexual encounters. She might have gotten acquainted with other people in her classes at the university, but she did not know how to initiate or maintain a conversation with her classmates.

As time wore on, Janet found herself brooding more and more about the divorce. She was gaining weight at the rate of three or four pounds a month. The first few pounds had been easy to ignore and were more a nuisance than anything else. But soon her clothes no longer fit, and the children began to comment on her appearance. To make matters worse, Claire developed a serious ear infection just prior to Janet's midterm exams. The added worry of Claire's health and her concern about missed classes and lost studying time contributed substantially to a decline in Janet's mood. She finally realized that she would have to withdraw from her classes to avoid receiving failing grades.

By this point, one month prior to her appointment at the mental health center, she had lost interest in most of her previous activities. Even casual reading had come to be a tedious chore. She did not have any hobbies because she never had enough time. She also found that her friend Susan was becoming markedly aloof. When Janet called, Susan seldom talked for more than a few minutes before finding an excuse to hang up. Their contacts gradually diminished to an occasional wave across the street or a quick, polite conversation when they picked up their children from school. It seemed that Susan had grown tired of Janet's company.

This was Janet's situation when she contacted the mental health center. Her mood was depressed and anxious. She was preoccupied with financial concerns and her lack of social relationships. Adam's sleeping problem, which had begun about one week after she withdrew from her classes, was the last straw. She felt that she could no longer control her difficult situation and recognized that she needed help.

CONCEPTUALIZATION AND TREATMENT

The therapist and Janet discussed her overall situation and agreed that Adam was only a small part of the problem. They decided to work together on an individual basis instead of having Janet join the parent training group.

Janet's depression was viewed as being directly related to interpersonal problems and deficits in her repertoire of social behaviors. The two most important examples involved her inability to establish and maintain new friendships and her lack of appropriate responses to the children's behavior. The therapist pointed out that her depressed mood would be likely to improve if she was able to solve some of the immediate problems in her life and engage in more pleasant activities. In other words, instead of concentrating on her patterns of thinking about the world or her perception of recent events, the therapist decided to help her learn to perform specific behaviors more effectively. His assumption was that new behaviors would be maintained by their own natural consequences.

As an initial step, the therapist asked Janet to list all of the activities that she enjoyed. This procedure was used both as a way of identifying pleasurable events that could be increased in frequency and as a way of shifting the focus of attention away from the unpleasant factors with which Janet was currently preoccupied. Most of the activities Janet mentioned were things that she had not done for several months or years. For example, prior to her return to school, her favorite pastime had been riding horses. She said that she would like to begin riding again, but she felt that it was prohibitively expensive and time consuming. With considerable prodding from the therapist, Janet also listed a few other activities. These included talking with a friend over a cup of coffee, listening to music late at night after the children were asleep, and going for walks in the woods behind her home. In some cases, Janet indicated that these activities used to be pleasant, but she did not think that they would be enjoyable at the present time.

Despite Janet's ambivalence, the therapist encouraged her to pick one activity that she would try at least twice before their next meeting. A short walk in the woods seemed like the most practical alternative, considering that Adam might interrupt listening to music and she did not want to call Susan. The therapist also asked Janet to call the campus riding club to inquire about their activities.

At the same time that the therapist encouraged Janet to increase her activity level, he also began to concentrate on an assessment of her skills in social interactions. For several sessions, they covered topics such as selecting situations in which Janet might be likely to meet people with whom she would be interested in developing a friendship, initiating a conversation, maintaining a conversation by asking the other person a series of consecutive questions, and other elementary issues. Having identified areas that were problematic for Janet, they discussed solutions and actually practiced, or role-played, various social interactions.

During the first few weeks of treatment, Janet's mood seemed to be improving. Perhaps most important was her luck in finding a part-time job at a local riding stable. She learned of the opening when she called to ask about the campus riding club. They were looking for someone who would feed and exercise the horses every morning. The wages were low, but she was allowed to ride as long as she wanted each day without charge. Furthermore, the schedule allowed her to finish before the girls returned from school. The money also helped her return Adam to the day-care center on a part-time basis. Janet reported that she still felt depressed when she was at home, but she loved to ride and it helped to know that she would go to work in the morning.

An unfortunate sequence of events led to a serious setback shortly after it seemed that Janet's mood was beginning to improve. Her financial aid had been discontinued, and she could no longer cover her monthly mortgage payments. Within several weeks, she received a notice from the bank threatening to foreclose her mortgage and sell her house. Her appearance was noticeably changed when she arrived for her next appointment. She was apathetic and lethargic. She cried through most of the session, and her outlook had grown distinctly more pessimistic. The therapist was particularly alarmed by an incident that Janet described as happening the previous day. She had been filling her car with gas when a mechanic at the service station mentioned that her muffler sounded like it was cracked. He told her that she should get it fixed right away because of the dangerous exhaust fumes. In his words, "that's a good way to kill yourself." The thought of suicide had not occurred to Janet prior to this comment, but she found that she could not get it out of her mind. She was frightened by the idea and tried to distract herself by watching television. The thoughts continued to intrude despite these efforts.

The therapist immediately discussed several changes in the treatment plan with Janet. He arranged for her to consult a psychiatrist, who prescribed imipramine (Tofranil), an antidepressant drug. She also agreed to increase the frequency of her appointments at the clinic to three times a week. These changes were primarily motivated by the onset of suicidal ideation. More drastic action, such as hospitalization or calling relatives for additional support, did not seem to be necessary because her thoughts were not particularly lethal. For example, she said that she did not want to die, even though she was thinking quite a lot about death. The idea frightened her, and she did not have a specific plan arranged by which she would accomplish her own death. Nevertheless, the obvious deterioration in her condition warranted a more intense treatment program.

The next month proved to be a difficult one for Janet, but she was able to persevere. Two or three weeks after she began taking the medication, her mood seemed to brighten. The suicidal ideation disappeared, she became more talkative, and she resumed most of her normal activities. The people who owned the riding stable were understanding and held Janet's new job for her until she was able to return. The financial crisis was solved, at least temporarily, when her father agreed to provide her with substantial assistance. In fact, he expressed surprise and some dismay that she had never asked him for help in the past or even told him that she was in financial trouble. The problem-solving and social skills program progressed well after Janet began taking medication. Within several weeks, she was able to reestablish her friendship with Susan. She was able to meet a few people at the riding stable, and her social network seemed to be widening.

After Janet's mood had improved, the issue of Adam's sleeping problem was addressed. The therapist explained that Janet needed to set firm limits on Adam's manipulative behavior. Her inconsistency in dealing with his demands, coupled with the attention that he received during the bedtime scene, could be thought of as leading to intermittent reinforcement of his inappropriate behavior. Janet and the therapist worked out a simple set of responses that she would follow whenever he got up and came downstairs. She would offer him a drink, take him back to his room, tuck him in bed, and leave immediately. Ten days after the procedure was implemented, Adam began sleeping through the night without interruption. This rapid success enhanced Janet's sense of control over her situation. Her enthusiasm led her to enroll in the parent training program for which she had originally applied. She continued to improve her relationship with her children.

Janet's individual therapy sessions were discontinued nine months after her first appointment. At that point, she was planning to return to school, was still working part-time at the riding stable, and had started to date one of the men she met at work. Her children were all healthy, and she had managed to keep their house. The antidepressant medication had been decreased to a small dosage for six months and was discontinued eight months after it was initiated.

DISCUSSION

A sad or dysphoric mood is obviously the most prominent feature of clinical depression. Depressed patients describe themselves as feeling discouraged, hopeless, and apathetic. This dejected emotional state is usually accompanied by a variety of unpleasant thoughts that may include suicidal ideation. Beck (1967) has described these cognitive features of depression as the *depressive triad:* a negative view of the self, the world, and the future. Depressed people see themselves as inadequate and unworthy. They are often filled with guilt and remorse over apparently ordinary and trivial events. These patients hold a similarly dim view of their environment. Everyday experiences and social interactions are interpreted in the most critical fashion. The future seems bleak and empty. In fact, some extremely depressed patients find it impossible to imagine any future at all.

Clinical depression is identified by changes in several important areas in the person's life. In addition to a prominent and relatively persistent dysphoric mood, *DSM-IV* (p. 327) lists several features for major depressive episodes. Specifically, at least five of the following symptoms must have been present for at least two weeks if the patient is to meet the criteria for this diagnostic category:

1. Depressed mood most of the day, nearly every day, as indicated either by subjective report (e.g., feels sad or empty) or observation made by others (e.g., appears tearful).

2. Markedly diminished interest or pleasure in all, or almost all, activities most of the day, nearly every day (as indicated either by subjective account or observation by others).
3. Significant weight loss when not dieting or weight gain (for example, a change of more than 5 percent of body weight in a month), or decrease or increase in appetite nearly every day.
4. Insomnia or hypersomnia (prolonged sleep) nearly every day.
5. Psychomotor agitation or retardation nearly every day (observable by others, not merely subjective feelings of restlessness or being slowed down).
6. Fatigue or loss of energy nearly every day.
7. Feelings of worthlessness or excessive or inappropriate guilt (which may be delusional) nearly every day (not merely self-reproach or guilt about being sick).
8. Diminished ability to think or concentrate, or indecisiveness, nearly every day (either by subjective account or as observed by others).
9. Recurrent thoughts of death (not just fear of dying), recurrent suicidal ideation without a specific plan, or a suicide attempt or a specific plan for committing suicide.

Janet clearly fit these criteria. Her mood had been markedly depressed since her separation from David. She had gained considerable weight — 25 pounds in nine months. Her concentration was severely impaired, as evidenced by her inability to study and her loss of interest in almost everything. Excessive and inappropriate guilt was clearly a prominent feature of her constant brooding about the divorce. Although she did not actually attempt to harm herself, she experienced a distressing period of ruminative suicidal ideation. Sleep impairment may also have been a problem, but it was difficult to evaluate in the context of Adam's behavior. Prior to her first visit at the clinic, Janet had been sleeping less than her usual number of hours per night, and she reported considerable fatigue. It was difficult to know whether she would have been able to sleep if Adam had not been so demanding of her attention throughout the night.

Most therapists agree that it is important to recognize the difference between clinical depression and other states of unhappiness and disappointment. Consider, for example, people who are mourning the loss of a friend or relative. *DSM-IV* suggests that a diagnosis of major depressive episode should be made only if bereavement persists for more than two months (assuming that the person meets the diagnostic criteria for this condition). Is this a qualitative or a quantitative distinction? Are patients who might be considered clinically depressed simply more unhappy than their peers, or are these phenomena completely distinct? This is one of the most interesting and difficult questions facing investigators in the field of mood disorders. The present diagnostic system handles the problem by including an intermediate category, dysthymia, that lies between major depressive disorder and normal mood.

This category includes patients who exhibit chronic depressed symptoms that are not of sufficient severity to meet the criteria for major mood disorder.

Etiological Considerations

Several psychological models have been proposed to account for the development of major depression. Some of these ideas have been generated as a result of clinical experience in the treatment of depressed patients. Others represent attempts to extrapolate theories and results from laboratory research with animals and normal human subjects to explain depressives' behavior. Each model focuses on somewhat different features of depressive disorders (e.g., interpersonal relations, inactivity, or self-deprecating thoughts), but most share an interest in the role of negative or stressful events in the precipitation of major depression.

Freud's explanation for the development of depression began with a comparison between depression and bereavement (Freud, 1917/1925).[1] The two conditions are similar. Both involve a dejected mood, a loss of interest in the outside world, and an inhibition of activity. One principal feature distinguishes between the person who is depressed and the person who is mourning: a disturbance of self-regard. Depressed people chastise themselves, saying that they are worthless, morally depraved, and worthy of punishment. Freud noted the disparity between such extreme negative views and the more benign opinions of other people who do not hold the depressed person in such contempt. In other words, the depressed person's view does not seem to be an accurate self-perception. Freud went on to argue that depressed people are not *really* complaining about themselves but are, in fact, expressing hostile feelings that pertain to someone else. Depression is therefore the manifestation of a process in which anger is turned inward and directed against the self instead of against its original object.

Why would some people direct hostility against themselves? Freud argued that the foundation for this problem is laid in early childhood. For various reasons, people who are prone to depression have formed dependent interpersonal relationships. This dependency fosters frustration and hostility. Because these negative feelings might threaten the relationship if they are expressed openly, they are denied awareness. Problems then arise when the relationship is ended, for whatever reason. The depressed person's ego presumably identifies with the lost loved one. The intense hostility that had been felt for that person is now turned against the self, or *introjected*. Following this model, treatment would consist of an attempt to make the client aware of these unconscious, hostile impulses. Their more direct expression would presumably eliminate the depression.

---

[1]Freud pointed out that his account was intended to apply to only a subset of depressed patients and that biological factors were probably more important in other cases.

At least one aspect of this model seems consistent with Janet's situation. She had, in fact, formed a series of intense, dependent relationships with men, beginning in high school. One might argue that her depression was precipitated by the loss incurred during her separation and divorce from David. She resented the separation deeply. Her guilt might be seen as a criticism of David's behavior. Other aspects of Janet's behavior, however, are inconsistent with Freud's model. Although Janet was critical of herself, she was also quite vocal in David's presence. They fought openly several times, both before and after the divorce, and he was fully aware of Janet's anger and resentment. It therefore seems unlikely that Janet's depression was a simple manifestation of misdirected hostility. It is also unlikely that her depression would be relieved by simply encouraging her to express her feelings more openly.

More recent attempts to explain the development of depression in psychological terms have borrowed and extended various aspects of Freud's psychoanalytic model. One important element involves his observation that depression is often precipitated by the loss of someone or something that is important to the person. Several investigations have been conducted to determine whether stressful life events play a causal role in the etiology of depression (see Monroe & Simons, 1991). One classic study by Brown and Harris (1978) received considerable attention because it led to the development of a model that might organize and begin to explain the relationship between various types of environmental conditions and the onset of depression.

Brown and Harris (1978) interviewed 114 women who were being treated for depression and a random sample of 458 women who were living in the community. The latter group was subsequently divided into those who exhibited clear symptoms of depression during the interview (76, or 17 percent of the sample) and those who did not. All of the women were asked about the occurrence of stressful events, particularly during the past year. Several interesting patterns emerged in the subsequent data analyses. First, Brown and Harris did find an increased incidence of stressful events among the depressed patients, but only with regard to a particular subset of such events — those that were severe and involved long-term consequences for the woman's well-being. Divorce and marital separation were prominent among these events. Sixty-one percent of the depressed patients had experienced such an event in the nine months preceding the onset of their symptoms; only 20 percent of the nondepressed women in the community sample had experienced an event of this nature in the nine months prior to their interview. Thus, the experience of a severe event with long-term consequences led to a pronounced increase in the probability of depression.

Brown and Harris referred to these events as "provoking agents." They also found other events or social circumstances that they called "vulnerability factors." These were not capable of precipitating depression on their own, but they did lead to a substantial increase in risk *given the experience of a stressful life event.* The vulnerability factors were (1) lack of an intimate, confiding relationship (generally with a spouse or boyfriend); (2) presence in the home of three or more children under the age of 14; (3) lack of full- or part-time employment; and (4) loss of the woman's mother before the age of 11. Consider, for example, the intimacy factor. Among the women who did experience a severe event and who also were involved in an intimate relationship, only 1 in 10 became depressed. The comparable figure among women who experienced a severe event in the absence of such a relationship was 1 in 3. The social support afforded by such a relationship is thus a powerful mediator between stress and the onset of depression, even if the absence of intimacy does not provoke depression by itself.

Subsequent investigations have extended these findings and identified additional factors that help to explain the relation between stressful life events and depression. The impact of a stressful event apparently depends on the meaning that the event has for the person. Severe events that occur in the context of ongoing difficulties (such as a chronically distressed marriage) and events that occur in areas of a woman's life to which she is particularly committed (such as a child's health or the development of a career) are most likely to lead to the onset of depression (Brown, Bifulco, & Harris, 1987).

The evidence regarding stressful life events and depression should not be accepted uncritically. For example, some investigators have been unable to replicate the pattern of vulnerability factors that was identified by Brown and Harris. The evidence regarding parental loss and the subsequent development of depression is equivocal at best. The separation of children from their parents (rather than parental death) may be associated with an elevated risk of adult depression, but the crucial factors may be the extent of family discord and quality of parenting (Tennant, 1988).

Furthermore, subsequent investigations have also found that the association between stressful life events and depression is bidirectional. Stress may cause depression, but depression also causes stress. In comparison to women who are not depressed and women with medical disorders, depressed women generate higher levels of stress, especially in interpersonal relationships such as marriage (Hammen, 1991). This result indicates the operation of a dynamic process. Stressors that are not related to the person's own behavior may precipitate the onset of a depressed mood. The depressed person may then engage in maladaptive ways of coping with the immediate situation, and these dysfunctional behaviors may lead to even higher levels of stress.

Several of the findings from the Brown and Harris study are consistent with Janet's situation. She had clearly experienced a high level of stress in the months preceding her first treatment. The divorce from David is one obvious example. Her difficulties with the children may be another instance. When Claire's illness eventually forced her to withdraw from the university, there were important long-term consequences for her graduation and subsequent plans to enter law school. It is also interesting that each of the vulnerability factors outlined by Brown and Harris was present in this case. Janet had, in fact, lost her mother at the age of 10. She was not involved in an intimate, confiding relationship, although her friendship with Susan may have been an important substitute until it dissolved. Her three children were all young and living at home. Following her withdrawal from classes, she was not involved in occupational activities outside of her home. These were probably important factors affecting the development of her depression.

Stressful life events are likely to precipitate depression, particularly in the absence of adequate social support (e.g., Bebbington et al., 1988). The manner in which these experiences combine to take their effect, however, is currently a matter of dispute and speculation. It is important to remember that most people experience stressful events at one time or another, but most people do not become seriously depressed. What factors make some people more psychologically vulnerable? Do people who are prone to depression respond differently than others to the problems of everyday life? Are they less likely than other people to establish or maintain a protective social support network? These questions have been addressed by other etiological models.

Like Freud, social learning theorists (e.g., Coyne, 1976; Lewinsohn, Haberman, Teri, & Hautzinger, 1985) have also emphasized the importance of interpersonal relationships and social skills (cf. narcissism and dependence) in the development and maintenance of depression. This model provides an interesting account of the way in which depressed people respond to stressful life events and the effect that these responses have on other people who constitute their social support systems. Other people respond empathically and are initially attentive when the depressed person cries or talks about depressing experiences, yet, the long-range result of this process is usually negative. The depressed person's few remaining friends eventually become tired of this behavior and begin to avoid further interactions. Whatever sources of social support may have been available are eventually driven away. One important factor in this regard is a lack of social skills. Depressed people may be ineffective in their interactions with other people. An important aspect of treatment would therefore be to identify specific skills in which the person is deficient and to teach the person more effective ways of interacting with others.

Several aspects of this model are consistent with the present case. After her separation from David, Janet had become isolated. Her long discussions with Susan had eventually soured their relationship and eliminated one of her last sources of social support. When Janet and her therapist discussed things that she might do to meet new friends, she seemed lost. The few attempts that she had made, such as her blind dates, had gone badly, and she did not know where else to begin.

Several research studies have demonstrated that depressed people do indeed have a negative impact on other people's moods and nonverbal behavior (Gotlib & Meltzer, 1987; Hokanson et al., 1989). Their social networks are also smaller and less supportive than those of people who are not depressed. They know fewer people, interact with them less often, and consider them to be less supportive (Gotlib & Lee, 1989). Family interactions are generally more negative and argumentative for people who are clinically depressed. Perhaps most important, these maladaptive patterns of interpersonal relationships are not uniquely associated with active episodes of major depression. The problems persist into periods of symptomatic remission (Gotlib & Hammen, 1992). These results are consistent with the hypothesis that the social behavior of depressed people is maladaptive and that depressed people may, perhaps unwittingly, play an active role in cutting themselves off from other people. Thus, depressed people may turn away sources of social support that might otherwise help them cope with stressful events. This kind of phenomenon seemed to be operating in Janet's relationship with Susan.

In addition to the social and behavioral aspects of depression, it is also important to consider the way in which depressed people perceive or interpret events in their environment. What do they think about themselves and things that happen in their world? More specifically, how do they explain the experience of negative events? Beck (1987) has proposed that certain negative cognitive patterns play a prominent role in people who are prone to the development of depression. The way in which depressed people process information about themselves and their environment is presumably distorted by the activation of self-defeating schemas[2] that prevent the recognition or assimilation of positive events.

The hopelessness theory of depression presents a similar view (Abramson, Metalsky, & Alloy, 1989).[3] According to this theory, the perceived occurrence of negative life events may lead to the development of hopelessness, which in turn causes the onset of symptoms of depression. Two cognitive elements define the state of hopelessness: (1) the expectation that highly desired outcomes will not occur or that highly aversive outcomes will occur, and (2) the belief that the person cannot do anything (is *helpless*) to change the likelihood that these events will occur.

The crucial link in this causal chain occurs between the perception of negative life events and the appearance of hopelessness. Why do some people become hopeless after such experiences while others do not? The theory holds

---

[2]*Schemas* are conceptual frameworks that people use to organize their knowledge of the world. A schema may also influence the way in which new information is processed and evaluated when it is received.

[3]This is the most recent revision of the helplessness model of depression that was originally proposed by Seligman (1975) and subsequently revised by Abramson, Seligman, and Teasdale (1978).

that the likelihood of developing hopelessness will depend on the person's inferences regarding three factors: the cause of the event, the consequences of the event, and the implications of the event with regard to the self. For example, hopeless depression is likely to occur if the person views a negative event as being important and also attributes the event to factors that are enduring (stable) and likely to affect many outcomes (global). The theory also recognizes that the perceived consequences of the negative event may be as important as inferred causes. If the person views the negative consequences of the event as important, persistent, and wide-ranging, depression will be more likely to develop than if the consequences are viewed as unimportant, short-lived, or limited in scope. The third and final consideration involves negative inferences about the self. Depression is a more likely outcome if the person interprets a negative event to mean that she or he is a less able, worthy, or desirable person.

Depressed people do express an inordinately high proportion of negative statements about themselves and how they relate to the world. Janet's verbal behavior provided several clear examples of the negative schemas that Beck has described, and her interpretation of the events leading up to and surrounding her divorce fit nicely with the hopelessness theory. She believed that the disintegration of her marriage was her own fault rather than David's; she argued that her failure in that relationship was characteristic of her interactions with all other men rather than specific to one person; and she maintained that she would never be able to change this pattern of behavior.

No one doubts that depressed people express negative thoughts. The difficult question, and one that is currently a matter of considerable controversy, is whether cognitive events play a central, formative role in the development of depression. Are they antecedents or consequences of emotional changes? Cognitive theorists have reported a considerable amount of empirical evidence in support of their position (e.g., Peterson & Seligman, 1984). On the other hand, critics have pointed to a number of problems with studies purporting to implicate cognitive events in the etiology of depression (Coyne, 1992). Longitudinal analyses have indicated that dysfunctional attitudes and tendencies toward cognitive distortion do not precede the onset of depression but seem to appear and recede in synchrony with dysphoric mood states (Lewinsohn, Hoberman, & Rosenbaum, 1988).

Treatment

Janet's treatment involved a combination of behavior therapy and antidepressant medication. Following the social learning/interpersonal model, her therapist focused on increasing Janet's level of participation in pleasant events and helped her learn new social skills. By encouraging activities such as riding, the therapist hoped to interrupt and reverse the ongoing, interactive process in which social isolation and inactivity led to increased depression, depression led to further withdrawal, and so on. Through the development of new response patterns, particularly those involving interpersonal communication and parenting skills, he hoped to enable Janet to deal more effectively with future stressful events. Increased social activity and more effective communication would also lead to a more supportive social network that might help reduce the impact of stressful events.

The therapy that Janet received was, in many respects, quite similar to another psychological approach to treating depression that is known as interpersonal psychotherapy, or IPT (Klerman, Weissman, Rounsaville, & Chevron, 1984). The focus of IPT is the connection between depressive symptoms and *current interpersonal problems.* Relatively little attention is paid to long-standing personality problems or developmental issues. The treatment takes a practical, problem-solving approach to resolving the sorts of daily conflicts in close relationships that can exacerbate and maintain depression. Deficits in social skills are addressed in an active and supportive fashion. The depressed person is also encouraged to pursue new activities that might take the place of relationships or occupational roles that have been lost. Therapy sessions often include nondirective discussions of social difficulties and unexpressed or unacknowledged negative emotions as well as role playing to practice specific social skills.

Antidepressant medication was introduced when the risk of suicide became apparent. Janet's suicidal ideation was not extremely lethal. She had not planned a particular method by which she might end her life, and she reported that the idea of harming herself was very frightening. The risk would have been much greater if she did have more specific plans and if she had really wanted to die. Nevertheless, her morbid ruminations marked a clear deterioration in her condition that called for more intensive treatment. Three general classes of drugs are useful in the treatment of depression: tricyclics (TCAs), monoamine oxidase (MAO) inhibitors, and selective serotonin reuptake inhibitors (SSRIs). Tricyclics are used more frequently than MAO inhibitors, particularly in the United States, because the latter are sometimes associated with more troublesome side effects, most notably cardiovascular problems. Both of these medications have been shown to be effective antidepressants in double-blind placebo-controlled studies (Paykel, 1988). Improvements in the patient's mood and other specific affective symptoms are typically evident after two to four weeks of drug treatment. Their continued administration also seems to reduce the probability of symptomatic relapse.

The third type of drug, selective serotonin reuptake inhibitors (SSRIs), was developed in the 1980s and now accounts for more than half of all prescriptions written for antidepressant medication (Silverstone, 1992; Thompson, 1993). Fluoxetine (Prozac) is an SSRI. The SSRIs inhibit the reuptake of serotonin into the presynaptic nerve ending and therefore increase the amount of serotonin available in the synaptic cleft. SSRIs have fewer side effects (such as weight gain, constipation, and drowsiness) than TCAs or MAO inhibitors; they are easier to take (one pill a day instead of experimenting for weeks to find the proper dosage); and they are less dangerous if the patient takes an overdose. This does not mean, of course, that they are without side effects of their own. Some patients experience nausea, headaches, fatigue, and restlessness, although these symptoms are usually mild and transient. Controlled outcome studies indicate that Prozac and other SSRIs are at least as effective as traditional forms of antidepressant medication (Stokes, 1993).

How do the effects of medication and psychotherapy compare in the treatment of depression? Research studies indicate that both forms of treatment can be effective. One ambitious outcome study known as the Treatment of Depression Collaborative Research Program compared the efficacy of two types of psychotherapy—cognitive and interpersonal therapy—with antidepressant medication over 16 weeks of treatment (Elkin et al., 1989). Unipolar depressed outpatients were randomly assigned to one of four treatment groups: interpersonal therapy, cognitive therapy, medication (a tricyclic antidepressant), or placebo plus "clinical management" (extensive support and encouragement).

The results of this study were generally quite positive over the short run. All three types of active treatment were superior to the placebo plus clinical management condition in terms of their ability to reduce depression and improve overall levels of functioning. Patients improved somewhat more rapidly if they were receiving medication, but the rate of improvement in both psychotherapy groups caught up to the drug condition by the end of treatment. Cognitive and interpersonal therapy were equivalent to antidepressant medication in terms of their ability to treat less severely disturbed patients. People who were more severely depressed responded best to medication. Furthermore, within the severely depressed patients, interpersonal therapy was more effective than cognitive therapy (Klein & Ross, 1993).

Follow-up evaluations conducted 18 months after the completion of treatment were less encouraging than the original outcome data, however. By that point, patients in the three active treatment groups were no longer functioning at a higher level than those who received only the placebo and clinical management. Less than 30 percent of the patients who were considered markedly improved at the end of treatment were still nondepressed at follow-up. This aspect of the study's results points to the need for continued efforts to improve currently available treatment methods.

One obvious disadvantage associated with both medication and psychotherapy is the extended delay involved in achieving therapeutic effects. In the face of a serious suicidal threat, for example, the therapist may not be able to wait several weeks for a change in the patient's adjustment. There are also many patients who do not respond positively to medication or psychosocial treatment approaches. Another form of intervention that may be tried with depressed patients, particularly if they exhibit profound motor retardation and have failed to respond positively to antidepressant medication, is electroconvulsive therapy (ECT). In the standard ECT procedure, a brief seizure is induced by passing an electrical current between two electrodes that have been placed over the patient's temples. A full course of treatment generally involves the induction of six to eight seizures spaced at 48-hour intervals. The procedure was first introduced as a treatment for schizophrenia, but it soon became apparent that it was most effective with depressed patients. Many studies have supported this conclusion (Abrams & Fink, 1984).

Much of the controversy surrounding ECT is based on misconceptions concerning the procedure and its effects (Fink, 1977). Although it is often referred to as "shock therapy," ECT does *not* involve the perception of an electrical current. In fact, a short-acting anesthetic is administered prior to the seizure so that the patient is not conscious when the current is applied. Many of the deleterious side effects of ECT have been eliminated by modifications in the treatment procedure, such as the use of muscle relaxants to avoid bone fractures during the seizure. The extent and severity of memory loss can be greatly reduced by the use of unilateral electrode placement. If both electrodes are placed over the nondominant hemisphere of the patient's brain, the patient can experience less verbal memory impairment, but the treatment may be less effective in terms of its antidepressant results (Royal College of Psychiatrists, 1989). Although the mechanism by which ECT produces its effect has not been established, this criticism could also be leveled against most forms of psychiatric medication. There is, of course, the serious question of permanent changes in brain structure and function. Some critics of ECT have argued that it produces irreversible neurological impairment (Friedberg, 1977). Proponents of ECT maintain that the evidence for this conclusion is inadequate (Crowe, 1984), but the possibility has not been ruled out. Nevertheless, most of the objections to the use of ECT are based on misconceptions. The evidence supporting its therapeutic efficacy seems to justify the continued use of ECT with some severely depressed patients who have not responded to less intrusive forms of treatment.

7 BIPOLAR MOOD DISORDER

By the time he was admitted to the hospital, George Lawler was talking a mile a minute. He harangued the other patients and ward staff, declaring that he was the coach of the U.S. Olympic track team and offering to hold tryouts for the other patients in the hospital. His movements were rapid and somewhat erratic as he paced the halls of the ward and explored every room. At the slightest provocation, he flew into a rage. When an attendant blocked his entrance to the nursing station, he threatened to report her to the president of the Olympic committee. He had not slept for three nights. His face was covered with a stubbly growth of beard, and his hair was scattered in various directions. His eyes were sunken and bloodshot, but they still gleamed with an intense excitement.

His life had taken a drastic change over the past two weeks. George was 35 years old, married, and the father of two young children. He worked at a small junior college where he taught physical education and coached both the men's and women's track teams. Until his breakdown, the teams had been having an outstanding season. They were undefeated in dual competition and heavy favorites to win the conference championship. The campus was following their accomplishments closely because it had been 12 years since one of the school teams had won a championship. In fact, track was the only sport in which the school had a winning record that season.

This was not the first time that George had experienced psychological problems. His first serious episode had occurred during his junior year in college. It did not seem to be triggered by any particular incident; in fact, things had been going well. George was majoring in physical education and playing defensive back on the university football team. He was in good academic standing and fairly popular with the other students. His scholarship removed many of the financial concerns that plagued other students. Nevertheless, during the spring semester, George found that he was losing interest in everything. It was not surprising that he did not look forward to classes or studying. He had never been an outstanding student. But he noticed that he no longer enjoyed going out with his friends. They said he seemed depressed all the time. George said he just did not care anymore. He began avoiding his girlfriend and, when they were together, he found fault with almost everything she did. Most of his time was spent in his apartment in front of the television. It did not seem to matter what program he watched because his concentration was seriously impaired. He kept the set on as a kind of distraction, not as entertainment. When he did not show up for spring football practice, the coach called him to his office for a long talk. George told his coach that he did not have the energy to play football. In fact, he did not feel he could make it through the easiest set of drills. He did not care about the team or about his future in sports. Recognizing that George's problem was more than a simple lack of motivation, the coach persuaded him to visit a friend of his—a psychiatrist at the student health clinic. George began taking antidepressant medication and attending individual counseling sessions. Within several weeks he was back to his normal level of functioning, and treatment was discontinued.

George had also experienced intervals of unusual ambition and energy. As a student, George had frequently spent several days cramming for exams at the end of a semester. Many of his friends took amphetamines to stay awake, but George seemed able to summon endless, internal reserves of energy. In retrospect, these periods seemed to be clear-cut hypomanic episodes but, at the time, they went relatively unnoticed. George's temporary tendency toward excess verbosity, his lack of need for sleep, and his ambitious goals did not seem pathological. In fact, these energetic intervals were quite productive, and his behavioral excesses were probably adaptive in the competitive university environment.

There had been two subsequent episodes of depression with symptoms that were similar to those of the first episode. The most recent incident had occurred eight months prior to his current hospitalization. It was September, two weeks after the start of the fall semester. George had been worried about his job and the team all summer. Who would replace his star sprinter, who had transferred to the state university? Would his high jumper get hurt during the football season? Could they improve on last year's winning record? Over the past month, these concerns had become constant and consuming. George was having trouble getting to sleep; he was also waking up in the middle of the night for no apparent reason. He felt tired all the time. His wife and children noticed that he was always brooding and seemed preoccupied. Then came the bad news. First, he was told by the athletic department that he would not get the increase in travel funds that he had expected. Then he learned that one of his assistant coaches was taking a leave of absence to finish working on her degree. Neither of these events would have a drastic effect on the upcoming season, but George took them to be disasters. His mood changed from one of tension and anxiety to severe depression. Over several days, George became more and more lethargic until he was almost completely unresponsive. His speech was slow and, when he did say more than a word or two, he spoke in a dull monotone. Refusing to get out of bed, he alternated between long hours of sleep and staring vacuously at the ceiling. He called the athletic director and quit his job, pointing to minor incidents as evidence of his own incompetence. He believed, for example, that the assistant coach had quit because of a brief argument that he had with her six months earlier. In fact, they had a positive relationship, and she had always planned to return to school at one time or another. She was leaving earlier than she had expected for personal reasons. George seemed to be blaming himself for everything. He apologized profusely to his wife and children for failing them as a husband and father. His despair seemed genuine. Suicide appeared to be the only reasonable solution. He threatened to end it all if his family would only leave him alone.

George's wife, Cheryl, called the psychiatrist who had treated him during his last episode (two years earlier) and arranged a special appointment. The psychiatrist decided to prescribe lithium carbonate, a drug that is used to treat manic episodes but that is also an effective antidepressant with bipolar patients (those who show both manic and depressed phases of disturbance). Although George had never been hospitalized for a manic episode, the psychiatrist suggested that his past history of "maniclike" behavior (increased energy, sleeplessness, inflated self-esteem, and so on) and his positive family history for bipolar mood disorder (his uncle Ralph) were both consistent with the diagnosis of bipolar disorder. The lithium seemed to be effective. Three weeks later, George was back at work. Maintenance doses of lithium were prescribed in an attempt to prevent future mood swings.

His first fully developed manic period began suddenly near the end of the next spring track season. The team was having a good year, and a few team members had turned in remarkable individual performances. Two days before the conference meet, Cheryl noticed that George was behaving strangely. There was a driven quality about his preparation for the meet. He was working much longer hours and demanding more from the athletes. When he was home, he talked endlessly about the team, bragging about its chances for national recognition, and planning intricate strategies for particularly important events. Cheryl was clearly worried about this change in George's behavior, but she attributed it to the pressures of his job and assured herself that he would return to normal when the season was over.

George was clearly losing control over his own behavior. The following incident, which occurred on the day of the conference meet, illustrates the dramatic quality of his disturbance. While the men's team was dressing in the locker room prior to taking the field, George paced rapidly up and down the aisles, gesturing emphatically and talking at length about specific events and the virtues of winning. When the men were all in uniform, George gathered them around his own locker. Without Cheryl's knowledge, he had removed a ceremonial sword from their fireplace mantel and brought it with him that morning. He drew the sword from his locker and leaped up on a bench in the midst of the men. Swinging the sword above his head, he began chanting the school fight song. The athletes joined in, and he lead them out onto the field screaming and shaking their fists in the air. A reporter for the school newspaper later described the incident as the most inspirational pre-game performance he had ever seen in a locker room. Without question, the team was driven to an exceptional emotional peak, and it did go on to win the meet by an embarrassing margin. In fact, George was later given the school's annual coaching award. His behavior prior to the meet was specifically cited as an example of his outstanding leadership qualities. Unfortunately, the action was also another manifestation of psychopathology and a signal of further problems that would soon follow.

George did not return home after the meet. He stayed in his office, working straight through the night in preparation for the regional meet. Cheryl was finally able to locate him by phoning his friend who worked in the office next door. She and his colleagues tried to persuade him to slow down, but he would not listen. The next morning George was approached by a reporter from the school newspaper. Here, George thought, was the perfect opportunity to expound on his ability as a coach and to publicize his exciting plans for future competition. The interview turned into a grandiose tirade, with George rambling uninterrupted for three hours. The reporter could neither interrupt nor extract himself from this unexpected and embarrassing situation.

The interview turned into a professional disaster for George. Among other things, George boasted that he was going to send the star high jumper from the women's team to the NCAA national meet in Oregon. He planned to go along as her chaperon and said that he would pay for their trip out of the proceeds of a recent community fund-raising drive. This announcement was startling in two regards. First, the money in question had been raised with the athletic department's assurance that it would be used to improve the college's track facilities and to sponsor running clinics for local youngsters. George did not have the authority to reroute the funds. His announcement was certain to anger the business leaders who had organized the drive. Second, the prospect of a married male coach chaperoning a female athlete, who also happened to be quite attractive, promised to raise a minor scandal. Recognizing the sensitive nature of these plans, the reporter asked George if he might want to reconsider his brash announcement. George replied—asking the reporter to quote him—that it was not every year that he had the opportunity to take a free trip with a pretty girl and he was not about to pass it up. He added that this might blossom into a genuine romance.

The article appeared, along with a picture of George, on the front page of the school paper the next morning. His disheveled appearance and outrageous remarks raised an instant furor in the athletic department and the school administration. The head of the department finally located George in his office making a series of long-distance calls. The director demanded an explanation and immediately found himself in the midst of an ear-shattering shouting match. George claimed that he had just been named head coach of the Olympic track team. He was now calling potential assistant coaches and athletes around the country to organize tryouts for the following month. Any interference, he claimed, would be attributed to foreign countries that were reluctant to compete against a team led by a coach with such a distinguished record. The department head realized that George was not kidding and that he could not reason with him. He returned to his own office and phoned Cheryl. When she arrived, they were unable to convince George that he needed help. They eventually realized that their only option was to call the police, who then took George to a psychiatric hospital. Following an intake evaluation, George was committed for three days of observation. Because he did not recognize the severity of his problems and refused to cooperate with his family and the hospital staff, it was necessary to follow an involuntary commitment procedure. The commitment order was signed by a judge on the following day, after a hospital psychiatrist testified in court that George might be dangerous to himself or others.

SOCIAL HISTORY

In most respects George's childhood was unremarkable. He grew up in a small, midwestern town where his father taught history and coached the high-school football team. He had one older brother and two younger sisters. All of the children were fair to average students and very athletic. George loved all sports and excelled at most: He was the quarterback of the high-school football team and a starting forward in basketball; in the spring he doubled as the first baseman on the baseball team and 400-meter specialist in track. When he accepted a football scholarship to the state university, everyone expected him to go on to play professional ball.

He was always popular with his peers. They looked to him for leadership, and he seemed to enjoy the role. He and his friends were mischievous but were never serious discipline problems. Although some of his friends began drinking alcohol during high school, George always refused to join them. He had seen the problems created by his father's drinking and did not want to follow the same path.

George's father was an alcoholic. He had been abstinent for 10 years, but the family could remember vividly how difficult the problem had been. When George was five years old, he began to notice that his parents argued quite a lot—when his father was home, that is. His mother was distraught over her husband's drinking. She pleaded with him, screamed, and frequently threatened to take the children and leave if he touched another drop. He would agree, then disappear overnight or lock himself in the bathroom to drink liquor he had hidden there. The principal of the high school and the school board finally became involved after receiving complaints about George's father being drunk in the classroom. Instead of losing his job, George's father agreed to a period of hospitalization at a nearby drug treatment center. He joined Alcoholics Anonymous and remained sober. Everyone agreed that the change in his behavior was remarkable.

George's uncle Ralph, his mother's brother, had also experienced serious adjustment problems. Ralph was several years older than George's mother, and the principal incidents occurred before George was born. George was therefore uncertain of the details, but he had been told that Ralph had been hospitalized twice following periods of rather wild behavior. A later search of hospital records confirmed that these had, in fact, been maniclike episodes. Although Ralph had been assigned a diagnosis of acute schizophrenic reaction, contemporary diagnostic criteria would certainly have required a diagnosis of manic disorder.

CONCEPTUALIZATION AND TREATMENT

When George was admitted to the hospital, he was clearly out of control. He was racing in high gear despite the fact that he had not slept for several days. He was nearing a state of physical exhaustion. The psychiatrist immediately prescribed a moderate dosage of haloperidol (Haldol), an antipsychotic drug that is also used to treat schizophrenic patients. George was supposed to have been taking lithium carbonate prior to the onset of the episode, but a check of his blood lithium level indicated that he had not been following the prescribed procedure. He was therefore started on a dose of 900 milligrams of lithium on the first day. This was increased to 1800 milligrams per day over the next two weeks. The hospital nursing staff took blood tests every third day to ensure that the blood lithium level did not exceed 1.4 milliequivalents per liter—the point at which toxic effects might be expected. After three weeks, the Haldol was discontinued and George continued to receive maintenance doses of lithium (2100 milligrams per day).

George and Cheryl were, once again, given specific instructions pertaining to the potential hazards of taking lithium. The importance of a proper diet, and particularly a normal level of salt intake, was stressed. They were also told about the early warning signs of lithium intoxication (e.g., nausea, gastrointestinal distress, muscular weakness) so that they could warn George's psychiatrist if the dosage needed to be reduced.

In addition, George was involved in a number of other therapeutic activities. He and the other patients on the ward met daily for sessions of group psychotherapy. There were also several recreational and occupational activities that could be chosen by the patients according to their own interests. Visits by family members and close friends were encouraged during the evening hours. When George's behavior improved, he was taken off restricted status and allowed to leave the ward for short periods of time.

George was discharged from the hospital after 27 days. His behavior had improved dramatically. The first few days in the hospital had been difficult for everyone concerned. He had been so excited that the entire ward routine had been disrupted. Mealtimes were utterly chaotic and, when the patients were supposed to go to sleep for the night, George shouted and ran around like a child going to his first slumber party. The physical exertion finally took its toll. He fell into a state of nearly complete exhaustion. After sleeping for the better part of three days, George's demeanor was somewhat more subdued. He had given up the grandiose notion about Olympic fame and seemed to be in better control of his speech and motor behavior. But he had not returned to normal. He was still given to rambling speeches and continued to flirt with the female staff members. His mood was unstable, fluctuating between comical amusement and quick irritation. In contrast to most of the other patients, George was gregarious and energetic. He organized group activities and saw himself as a hospital aide, not as a patient.

These residual symptoms dissipated gradually over the next two weeks. He was switched to voluntary status and now recognized the severity of his previous condition. In retrospect, the events that had struck him as exhilarating and amusing seemed like a nightmare. He said that his thoughts had been racing a mile a minute. He had been totally preoccupied with the conference meet and upcoming events. The locker room incident caused him considerable concern as he admitted the possibility that he could have seriously injured someone with the sword.

Following discharge from the hospital, George was kept on a maintenance dosage of lithium. He attended an outpatient clinic regularly for individual psychotherapy, and his blood levels of lithium were carefully monitored. George and Cheryl also began conjoint therapy sessions with a dual purpose in mind. They needed to work on improving their own relationship, and they also wanted to acquire more effective means of interacting with and controlling their children.

This aspect of the treatment program was unsuccessful. Cheryl had been seriously embarrassed by George's behavior during the manic episode. The cruelest blow came with the newspaper article in which George had announced his affection for another woman. This incident seemed to leave an insurmountable wall of tension between George and Cheryl even though they both made a serious effort to improve their relationship. Their therapist designed a contractual program in which they agreed to change specific behaviors identified by their partner as particularly problematic. For example, Cheryl had always been annoyed by George's absence from their evening meal. His track season was over, and she argued that he could easily arrange to be home by 6 P.M. for dinner if he cared for her and the children. George, on the other hand, complained that Cheryl never showed any interest in sports. They agreed to an exchange of the following format: George would be home from work by 6 P.M. every day during the week, and Cheryl would go to a baseball game with him once a month. Other agreements were reached involving problems such as Cheryl's long-distance telephone calls, George's leaving his clothes all over the house, and so on. A concurrent program of communication training was begun to improve their ability to listen, make requests, provide positive feedback, and to learn a variety of other important skills. The therapist noticed an improvement in their interactions during therapy sessions, but they continued to have periodic, heated fights at home. Cheryl finally decided that the situation was hopeless and, six months after George was discharged from the hospital, she filed for a divorce.

George was, of course, shaken by this development, but he managed to avoid becoming seriously depressed. His friends from work were an important source of social support, particularly during the first weeks after Cheryl and the children moved to another apartment. He also met more frequently with his therapist during this period and continued to take lithium carbonate.

DISCUSSION

Mood disorders are characterized by a serious, prolonged disturbance of mood. These disturbances may take the form of depression or elation. They are accompanied by a host of other problems, including changes in sleep patterns, appetite, and activity level. Several classification systems have been used to subdivide this broad category into more homogeneous groups. For example, a distinction has been drawn between psychotic and neurotic depression on the basis of the severity of the symptoms. Another system, known as the exogenous/endogenous distinction, relies on the presence or absence of an external event that may have triggered the change in the patient's mood. Most of these systems have now been abandoned. Some were difficult to use reliably. In other cases the distinction being drawn did not lead to meaningful treatment considerations. Consider, for example, the exogenous/endogenous distinction. It is often difficult to determine whether or not a stressful event actually occurred at the time that the patient began to feel depressed. The patient's memory may be blurred by subsequent emotional experiences, and friends may provide conflicting reports. Furthermore, even if everyone agrees that a particular event did occur, how can we determine whether it actually led to a change in the patient's mood? The loss of a job, for example, might be a *consequence* of the early signs of depression (e.g., loss of concentration, erratic sleeping patterns) and not a precipitant of the disorder.

The classification system that currently seems most useful and that is represented in *DSM-IV* draws a distinction between bipolar and unipolar mood disorders. In bipolar disorders the patient experiences periods of extreme elation known as manic episodes. These periods usually alternate with periods of normal mood and periods of severe depression to form a kind of unpredictable emotional cycle that some patients liken to a roller-coaster ride. Unipolar patients, on the other hand, experience serious depression without ever swinging to the opposite extreme. George had exhibited manic as well as depressive symptoms, so his problem would be diagnosed as a bipolar mood disorder.

DSM-IV (p. 332) lists the following criteria for manic episode:

A. A distinct period of abnormally and persistently elevated, expansive, or irritable mood lasting at least 1 week (or any duration if hospitalization is necessary).

B. During the period of mood disturbance, three (or more) of the following symptoms have persisted (four if the mood is only irritable) and have been present to a significant degree:
    1. Inflated self-esteem or grandiosity.
    2. Decreased need for sleep, for example, feeling rested after only three hours of sleep.
    3. More talkative than usual or pressure to keep talking.
    4. Flight of ideas or subjective experience that thoughts are racing.
    5. Distractibility, for example, attention too easily drawn to unimportant or irrelevant external stimuli.
    6. Increase in goal-directed activity (either socially, at work or school, or sexually) or psychomotor agitation.
    7. Excessive involvement in pleasurable activities that have a high potential for painful consequences, for example, the person engages in unrestrained buying sprees, sexual indiscretions, or foolish business investments.

C. The mood disturbance is sufficiently severe to cause marked impairment in occupational functioning or in usual social activities or relationships with others, or to necessitate hospitalization to prevent harm to self or others.

Bipolar mood disorders should be distinguished from schizophrenia as well as from unipolar mood disorders. Kraepelin (1919/1971) recognized that manic and schizophrenic (dementia praecox) patients often exhibit similar symptoms. These include disorganized speech, flight of ideas, and delusional thinking. He argued that the difference between the two disorders became apparent on examination of their long-term course. Most patients who fit Kraepelin's definition of schizophrenia showed a progressive deterioration without periods of recovery. Manic-depressive patients, on the other hand, frequently followed a remitting course. Although they might have repeated episodes of psychotic behavior, their adjustment between episodes was relatively unimpaired. This distinction has continued to be one of the most important considerations in the classification of serious mental disorders.

A less severe form of bipolar mood disorder is experienced by people who go through episodes of expansive mood and increased energy that are not sufficiently severe to be considered manic episodes. These are called *hypomanic episodes.* According to *DSM-IV,* a person who has experienced at least one major depressive episode, at least one hypomanic episode, and no full-blown manic episodes, would be assigned a diagnosis of Bipolar II Disorder. A hypomanic episode is defined in terms of the same symptoms as those that describe a manic episode. The distinction between manic and hypomanic episodes is based on duration and severity. The minimum duration of symptoms for a hypomanic episode is four days, as opposed to one week for a manic episode. In a hypomanic episode, the mood change must be noticeable to others, but it must *not* lead to impairment in social or occupational functioning or require hospitalization. If the mood change becomes that severe, it would be considered a manic episode.

Another type of mood disorder is known as cyclothymia, which is a chronic but less severe form of bipolar disorder. People who meet the criteria for cyclothymia experience several hypomanic episodes and several periods of minor depression during a period of two years. They do not, however, experience periods of disturbance that are sufficiently severe to meet the criteria for major depressive episode or manic episode during the first two years of their disturbance. After the initial two years of cyclothymia, full-blown episodes of mania or major depression would require that an additional diagnosis, such as Bipolar I Disorder or Bipolar II Disorder, be superimposed on the Cyclothymic Disorder.

Estimates of the distribution of mood disorders in the general population obviously depend on the criteria used to define depression and mania. Studies that have employed contemporary criteria for mood disorders indicate some fairly consistent patterns (Weissman, Bruce, Leaf, Florio, & Holzer, 1991). In the ECA study, lifetime prevalence was 0.8 percent for Bipolar I Disorder and 0.5 percent for Bipolar II Disorder. The lifetime prevalence for major depression was much higher: 4.9 percent overall. Gender differences are not found in the risk for bipolar mood disorders, but there are important gender differences in the rates for men and women for major depression. In the ECA study, women had a 7.0 percent lifetime prevalence for major depression, while the comparable rate for men was 2.6 percent.

There are also important differences between unipolar and bipolar disorders in terms of both the age of onset and the course of the disorder (Perris, 1992). Bipolar patients tend to be younger than unipolar patients at the time of their first episode of disturbance, usually between the ages of 20 and 30. A follow-up study reported by Angst and his colleagues indicated that bipolar patients also tend to experience a greater number of psychotic episodes during subsequent years and are more likely to experience impairment between episodes (Angst et al., 1973). Welner and his colleagues found that approximately 30 percent of their bipolar patients showed a long-term impairment either in terms of continued expression of symptoms or chronic social impairment. Another group of patients, who did not follow a chronic course, experienced a permanent decline in their social and occupational status as a consequence of their behavior during periods of acute psychosis (Welner, Welner, & Leonard, 1977).

George's case was typical of the classic picture of manic-depressive illness. He showed an early onset of symptoms and a relatively complete remission between episodes. On the other hand, his experience was also consistent with that of many patients in Welner's study. Although he did not exhibit symptoms of social impairment following a period of disturbance, his behavior was so disruptive during each manic episode that it had important long-term consequences. He had serious problems with his job, and his marriage ended in divorce.

Etiology

The fact that George's maternal uncle had also experienced manic episodes is consistent with the literature concerning genetic factors in mood disorders. Several family studies have found that the biological relatives of patients with mood disorders are more likely to develop mood disorders than are people in the general population. These data are usually reported in terms of "morbid risk," or the probability that given individuals will develop the disorder during their lifetimes. Several studies have now reported that the relatives of unipolar depressives are at increased risk for unipolar depression but that they are unlikely to exhibit bipolar mood disorder (Katz & McGuffin, 1993). The relatives of bipolar patients, on the other hand, typically demonstrate an increased risk for both unipolar and bipolar disorders. These data have generally been taken to indicate that the bipolar and unipolar subgroups are genetically distinct. George's positive family history for bipolar disorder thus may be taken as further validation of his bipolar diagnosis and was, in fact, helpful in the decision to try lithium carbonate prior to his first full manic episode.

The role of genetic factors in the etiology of mood disorders would be clearer if a specific model of genetic action could be identified. Polygenic models of transmission have not been ruled out, but many investigators are currently placing their bets on a single-locus model in order to take advantage of exciting technological advances in a procedure known as *linkage analysis.* This technique involves studying the occurrence of mood disorder across a family pedigree and simultaneously assessing some other characteristic—a genetic marker for which the mode of transmission is fully understood (e.g., red-green color blindness is known to result from mutations on the X chromosome). When the genes are linked, that is, when they are sufficiently close together on a chromosome, the family pedigree will tend to show that the two traits being examined are inherited together. Two groups of investigators have reported successful linkage analysis with regard to bipolar mood disorder. Egeland and her colleagues (1987) reported results of linkage analysis in a large composite family of the Old Order Amish. They found as association between bipolar disorder and chromosome 11. In contrast to this result, Baron and his colleagues (1987) found linkage between bipolar disorder and the X chromosome in three pedigrees studied in Israel. Other laboratories have failed to find any evidence for genetic linkage in bipolar disorder (Heberbrand, 1992; Mitchell et al., 1991). What should we make of these inconsistencies? One possible conclusion is that the mood disorders are genetically heterogeneous (i.e., they are produced by different genes in different people with similar disorders). Further evidence is needed from additional linkage studies, and the next few years will undoubtedly witness exciting reports in this area of research.

Although genetic factors play some role in the development of bipolar mood disorder, they cannot account for it completely (Ellicott et al., 1990; O'Connell, 1986). Various experiences throughout the person's life must also influence the onset or expression of psychotic symptoms as well as the course of the disorder. The generally accepted diathesis-stress model would suggest that bipolar patients inherited some unidentified form of predisposition to the disorder and that the expression of this predisposition then depends on subsequent environmental events. In George's case it would be reasonable to wonder whether the highly competitive atmosphere associated with college coaching might have triggered the onset of his manic symptoms or his depressive episodes. The weeks preceding his manic episode were busier than usual. His teams had been winning, and the athletic department's administration seemed to be putting considerable emphasis on the final meets of the season. Viewed from George's perspective, this amounted to enormous pressure. The job situation was also compounded by his family responsibilities. As he began to spend more and more time with his team, his wife became increasingly discontent and irritable. Her demands, coupled with his coaching responsibilities, placed George in a difficult position; he could reduce the amount of time spent planning and supervising workouts, thus increasing the probability that the team would lose, or he could reduce the amount of time spent with his wife and children, thus increasing the probability that she would ask for a divorce.

The notion that stressful experiences can precipitate manic episodes is intuitively appealing, but the research literature does not indicate a clear link between the two events. Consider, for example, the following investigation. Hall and her colleagues studied a group of bipolar patients who had been hospitalized at least once for manic behavior and who were receiving lithium treatment on an outpatient basis (Hall, Dunner, Zeller, & Fieve, 1977). Each patient was interviewed approximately once each month during his or her visit to the clinic. At each assessment, ratings were made of the patients' moods, and the patients were asked to describe important events that had occurred since their last visit. Twenty-one of the 38 patients remained well over the course of the one-year study, 6 became manic, 8 became depressed, and 3 experienced both mania and depression. The patients who remained well and those who experienced further episodes did *not* differ significantly in terms of either the number or the type of events that they reported prior to the onset of symptoms. There was a slight trend for the patients who had manic episodes to report more problems with superiors at work in the visit prior to the onset of symptoms, but the difference between these patients and those who remained well was not statistically significant.

George's relationship with his family illustrates the complex interactive nature of mood disorders. Although his marital problems may not have been caused by his affective symptoms, they certainly made an already difficult situation virtually impossible. The marital adjustment of bipolar patients has received considerable attention in the research literature, which indicates that bipolar patients are much more likely than unipolar patients or people in the general population to be divorced (Brodie & Leff, 1971). The emotional atmosphere within a family is also related to the patient's social functioning and the course of the disorder. Miklowitz and his colleagues (1988) examined family members' attitudes toward the problems of their relatives who had recently been hospitalized with manic disorders. The investigators also assessed patterns of interaction between the patients and their relatives. The patients' adjustment was then evaluated during a nine-month period following their discharge from the hospital. Patients who lived in a stressful family environment (as indicated by high ratings on either measure) were much more likely to relapse than patients from families that were rated low on both factors. George's situation was probably typical of the problems experienced by manic patients. Cheryl was forced by his erratic behavior to act as a buffer between George and the community. When he acted strangely at work, his colleagues called her to see if she could explain his behavior. She often found herself making up excuses for him in order to avoid the unpleasant necessity of disclosing the personal details of his problems. Her efforts were then "rewarded" by his continued excesses. Cheryl gradually came to see herself as a victim. The incident with the undergraduate student was the last straw. George's behavior was even more difficult for Cheryl to understand and accept because of his inconsistency. She argued that if he were always irrational or out of control, she could easily attribute these problems to a psychiatric disorder. However, between episodes, and most of the time, George was a very reasonable, considerate person. Cheryl found it difficult to believe that he could change so drastically over such a short period of time. Her first inclination was always to attribute his wild, manic behavior to some malicious intent on his part. When he became depressed, she often blamed herself. Eventually, the problem was simply more than she could handle.

Treatment

Lithium is the treatment of choice for bipolar mood disorders. The therapeutic effects of lithium salts were first reported in 1949 by John Cade, an Australian psychiatrist. Cade had been studying the toxic effects of uric acid in guinea pigs and the possibility that the lithium ion might reduce this toxicity. He was not initially interested in behavioral effects, but he happened to notice that guinea pigs that had been injected with lithium carbonate became lethargic and unresponsive to stimuli despite remaining fully conscious. This unexpected finding led Cade to wonder whether lithium carbonate might have beneficial effects for psychotic patients who were extremely excited. He used the drug with a sequence of 10 manic patients and obtained remarkable results. Even chronic patients who had been considered untreatable responded favorably within a period of several days. Furthermore, several schizophrenic patients who had previously been markedly restless and excited became quiet and amenable. When lithium was discontinued, the patients generally returned to their previous patterns of wild behavior.

Other clinicians soon began to experiment with the use of lithium and met with similar results. Their favorable impression of lithium's effects were later confirmed by a number of controlled double-blind studies (see Abou-Saleh, 1992; Keck & McElroy, 1993). Despite the uniformly positive results of these early investigations, American psychiatrists did not become enthusiastic about the use of lithium until the 1970s. A variety of factors may account for this delay. Perhaps most important were the dangerous side effects associated with the use of lithium. Lithium had been used as a substitute for table salt by patients with heart and kidney problems. A number of severe poisonings and some deaths were reported only a few months before the publication of Cade's report, leading the Food and Drug Administration (FDA) to restrict the use of lithium. The introduction of lithium also coincided with the discovery of antipsychotic, antidepressant, and antianxiety drugs in the 1950s. The startling effects of lithium seemed to get lost in the crowd. Nevertheless, a number of investigators continued to examine therapeutic effects of lithium carbonate, and the evidence was soon overwhelming. The FDA finally dropped its restrictions and approved lithium for the treatment of mood disorders in 1970.

In addition to his series of manic patients, Cade also tried lithium with a few depressed patients. His concern was that the apparent tranquilizing effects of lithium might lead depressed patients to become even more depressed and withdrawn. This did not happen. Subsequent studies have, in fact, demonstrated that lithium can be beneficial for patients who are depressed as well as for those who are manic. This is particularly true for bipolar patients. For example, Baron and his colleagues (Baron et al., 1975) treated 130 depressed patients; 80 percent of the bipolar patients improved significantly while they were receiving lithium, but only 40 percent of the unipolar patients showed similar gains. These data indicate that lithium is a reasonable choice in the treatment of bipolar patients who are depressed. They also indicate, once again, that bipolar and unipolar patients seem to be suffering from distinct disorders.

The ability of lithium to prevent future psychotic episodes was first demonstrated by Baastrup and Schou (1967). They compared the behavior of 88 bipolar patients before and after they were treated with lithium. Before treatment, the patients experienced relapses approximately once every 8 months. After they were stabilized on lithium, relapses occurred once every 60 to 85 months. Several subsequent studies that used double-blind procedures and placebo control groups have also concluded that lithium is effective in preventing the recurrence of manic episodes and probably effective in preventing recurrent depression in bipolar patients (Maj, 1992; Suppes et al., 1991).

George responded favorably to lithium during his brief stay in the hospital, and he returned to his job soon after discharge. It is possible that the episode might have been partially caused by his failure to take the medication regularly. This is a serious problem with all forms of psychopharmacological treatment. It is particularly severe with psychotic patients who characteristically lack insight into the severity of their problem. Every effort is usually made to educate the patient in this regard. The cooperation of family members is often enlisted to assist in the regulation of daily doses. The dangers of lithium also require that patients being treated on an outpatient basis be seen regularly to monitor levels of lithium in the blood. In spite of these precautions, many patients fail to follow medication schedules designed to prevent relapse.

DEPRESSION AND A SUICIDE ATTEMPT IN AN OLDER ADULT

Helen Kay, age 73, had been found at 4:00 A.M. by a city police officer during his routine patrol of the beach near the amusement pier. She was huddled against a wooden piling, an empty pint of whisky in her left hand. He thought at first that she was dead, but she was still breathing, faintly. Hustling her into his car, he took her to the emergency room of the county hospital.

When they arrived, Mrs. Kay was mumbling incoherently to herself, occasionally jumping up to run wildly about the examining room. The physician in charge was tempted to administer a tranquilizer just to quiet her down but wisely refrained from doing so, given her state of apparent alcohol intoxication and the ultrasensitivity many older people have to drugs.

Information gleaned later from acquaintances at the hotel in which she lived provided the following picture of the previous two days: Mrs. Kay failed to show up in the dining room of the retirement hotel for breakfast on a Monday morning. The manager, careful about such incidents among his elderly clientele, sent one of the waiters upstairs to check on her; he returned 30 minutes later to report that Mrs. Kay had pulled him into her room with a frightened look on her face and then proceeded to scream at him: "I did what I could!" The waiter managed to extricate himself to report the situation to his boss, who went to her room himself. He had known Mrs. Kay since she took up residence a few months earlier and believed he could deal with her better, which indeed turned out to be the case. She refused to come downstairs to eat, but she did agree to eat the breakfast that was brought up to her room.

This incident was not totally unexpected. Over the preceding months Mrs. Kay had occasionally acted peculiarly, her moods shifting from elation one moment to utter lethargy and despondency the next. These mood swings seemed to be related to her shopping trips to a nearby liquor store. She had, in fact, begun to drink heavily by herself in her room. The staff had come to expect verbal abuse from her within a few hours of her return from the store. On this particular morning, the manager noticed a strong odor of alcohol when he was persuading her to eat some breakfast; he concluded that she had been drinking earlier that morning.

Later that evening Mrs. Kay was herself again, sober and very depressed. Despondency was not unheard of among other residents of the hotel, but Mrs. Kay's sadness had a morbidity and oppressiveness that worried and angered the other guests. For example, at dinner the same day, Mrs. Kay went on and on about her aching back and feet, her poor eyesight, and generally about the woes that God had inflicted on her as punishment. A woman sitting beside her walked only with the aid of a four-pointed cane, was almost completely blind, and was otherwise in poorer physical health as well as more problematic financial straits than Mrs. Kay—and exclaimed that to her angrily. Mrs. Kay's reaction was to sulk and brood even more, eventually excusing herself before dessert was served and retreating to her room to drink herself into a stupor once again.

The following morning saw a repeat of her refusal to come down for breakfast, but this time she also refused to open her door to the manager. A tray was left outside her door but remained untouched the rest of the morning. In the early afternoon Mrs. Kay was seen leaving the hotel and heading in the direction of the liquor store. Just before dinnertime, a couple from the hotel saw her walking morosely by herself in the park across the street from the hotel. Occasionally stopping to gaze at the ocean, with a liquor bottle dangling from one hand, she seemed altogether miserable. Their impulse to approach was suppressed by their expectation of verbal abuse from her.

Mrs. Kay did not return to her hotel that evening. Instead, at twilight, she unsteadily negotiated the wooden stairs leading down to the beach and walked along the water's edge until it grew dark. Suddenly chilled by the night ocean breezes, she found her way to the pier and settled herself against a piling to finish her bottle. Hours later she was discovered by the police officer.

SOCIAL HISTORY

Mrs. Kay had led an interesting and rewarding life. The daughter of a well-to-do family from the Midwest, she had grown up amid the warmth and friendliness of a small town. She was popular with peers and successful in school. Influenced by an English teacher in her junior year of high school, she applied to some private colleges in the East in addition to the nearby state university, where most of her classmates would go. At the end of her senior year she elected to attend Radcliffe.

Her years in Cambridge were pivotal for her. Although subject to the sexism taken for granted in the 1920s, she nonetheless learned to value her own intelligence and drive, deciding—to her family's dismay—that she would forge a career for herself after college instead of immediately marrying the law student who had proposed to her.

But it was not just her ambitiousness that characterized her college years. She found herself subject to occasional profound depressive episodes, some of them serious enough to have her roommates take her to the university health service. She declined to see a psychiatrist, believing in spite of her growing worldliness that "shrinks" were only for crazy people. She believed that she could, and should, deal with her moodiness on her own, and she somehow managed to do this. She excelled at Radcliffe socially and academically and easily obtained a position with a prestigious literary monthly in New York City immediately after graduation. Her law school boyfriend, Harold Kay, visited her often. After his own graduation, he got a job with a good firm in New York City. Two years later they married.

The marriage was a generally happy one: three children, all of them bright and ultimately successful in their respective careers and lives; two careers, not a common occurrence at that time; considerable income from both their jobs; and reasonably good physical health. Three years after they married, they moved to Los Angeles, where Mr. Kay had received an offer from a noted law firm, and Mrs. Kay an editorial position with a leading city newspaper. After Mrs. Kay's near-death under the pier, her oldest son tried to understand how she could have come so close to drinking herself to death. He reflected on his mother's recurrent depressions and on the seemingly inordinate responsibility she took for anything bad that happened to her children or to her husband. The depressive episodes she had experienced since her husband's death a few years ago were not new; nor was the blame she heaped on herself for Harold's condition during his final years.

Mr. Kay retired from his lucrative law practice at 72 years of age. He had intended to continue working, slowing his pace only a little as he broke in a new young partner. But the morning cough and increasing forgetfulness thwarted those plans. A cancerous lung had to be removed, regrettably without halting the spread of the disease. His intellectual deterioration, diagnosed as senile dementia due to Alzheimer's disease, progressed month after month. Mr. Kay became bedridden for the remaining three years of his life. His wife, as devoted to him as ever, insisted on looking after him at home, against her children's wishes. She rearranged furniture in their house so that she was seldom more than a few feet from his bedside. Her books, typewriter, and sewing machine were nestled into a corner of the master bedroom, and there was even a hotplate on the dresser so that she could make tea for the two of them without leaving the room. Her depressions were coming upon her more often now and with frightening intensity, accompanied by sleeplessness, poor appetite, and thoughts of suicide. Still, she nursed her ever-deteriorating husband.

Mrs. Kay began to notice her husband being less responsive than usual. In one horrible moment of insight she confessed to herself that he had no idea who she was or who he was. She had been warned of this aspect of Alzheimer's disease; the brain wastes away inexorably and inevitably, and the worsening memory eventually obliterates the person's sense of identity. She was forced to realize that she was looking after a man whose resemblance to the person she had been married to for over 50 years was becoming more and more remote.

She hated herself for having these thoughts. Who knows what is going on in his mind, she would ask herself. Surely he needs and appreciates my personal care each day and night. Surely he will die if I let him go into a hospital. Family, friends, and Mr. Kay's own physician had been urging that decision on her for months, but she could not bear the image of his being lifted from bed to stretcher, and then to an ambulance, and then into a hospital corridor and, ultimately, into a strange bed in which he would be placed to die.

But that is exactly what happened. She was persuaded to allow his hospitalization on the basis of medical needs that the physician insisted, almost angrily now, could not be met at home. The dreaded scene of transfer to the hospital took place in a fashion eerily similar to her nightmare fantasy. One day later he died.

Although the death was hardly unanticipated, Mrs. Kay was devastated. At the funeral, she interrupted the minister's eulogy repeatedly with declamations of her responsibility for her husband's death. The other mourners, familiar with the actual circumstances of Mr. Kay's illness, shook their heads in sadness. At the graveside, she had to be physically restrained from falling on top of the casket as it was lowered. Even though she insisted that she wanted to return to her home that evening, she was taken by her son to his home. He arranged with his mother in the following weeks to sell his parents' house and have her live with him and his family.

Her welcome into the five-bedroom house of her son was genuine. Mrs. Kay's daughter-in-law was a caring person. Even though the routine of her household had to be altered to accommodate the presence of another person, she was sincere in her efforts to make her mother-in-law feel at home. But these efforts were largely unnoticed. The woman complained at meals every day of what a burden she was to the family, and no amount of reassurance changed her mind. Ironically, her very act of complaining was the most burdensome aspect of her living with them. She began, several months after her husband's death, to beseech her son to find her a place where she could live on her own; he reluctantly did so. Consulting with a social service agency, he was referred to several retirement hotels along a pleasant boulevard and across the street from a lush city park overlooking the ocean. There were palm trees and green grass all year round and many other older people living in the neighborhood. Mrs. Kay's good physical health and her favorable financial circumstances made entry into one of the hotels feasible. The social worker assured Mr. Kay that such a move was the best alternative for his mother. An inspection of the hotel by the entire family confirmed all of this. A week later Mrs. Kay moved some of her belongings into a spacious single room on the fourth floor of the Hotel Gregorian. A sign over the entrance read "A Retirement Hotel for the Active Retired."

At first Mrs. Kay did well in her new surroundings. The other residents were mostly widows like herself. A few couples who shared suites were the envy of the single women, even though many of the married folks scarcely seemed to speak to each other in the dining room or on the veranda that faced the ocean boulevard. A few women befriended Mrs. Kay, finding her to be an uncommonly intelligent and worldly woman, which she was. There were many stories to be told about going to college back east, working and living in New York City, traveling with her husband, and, of course, the wonders of children and grandchildren.

A few months after her arrival at the Gregorian, however, a change began to be noticed in Mrs. Kay by her new friends and acquaintances. She would sometimes come down to breakfast sullen and depressed. Deflecting inquiries about her health, she would eat quietly and then leave as soon as the meal was over, withdrawing to her room for most of the day and evening. But even more worrisome were her daily, almost furtive exits in the late afternoon, to return 30 minutes later with a small paper bag that seemed to contain a tall bottle. The strong odor of alcohol that one of the residents noted one day when she came to fetch Mrs. Kay for dinner confirmed the growing suspicion that she had begun drinking—heavily, regularly, and by herself.

Never more than a social drinker, Mrs. Kay, during the long illness of her husband, had happened on the numbing effects of alcohol in her frantic efforts to ease her mind during the long vigils at his bedside. For several months she had sampled from his well-supplied liquor cabinet, steadily working her way from the front to the back. When she took up residence in the hotel, she had to learn a new skill—finding a liquor store and buying her own liquor. Unfortunately, she mastered the task readily.

CONCEPTUALIZATION AND TREATMENT

The first therapeutic task was to keep Mrs. Kay from dying. Her bizarre behavior in the emergency room of the hospital to which the police officer had taken her suggested delirium from a reversible malfunction of the brain; it can be caused by such things as overmedication, alcohol intoxication, and malnutrition. The examining physician made this diagnosis because of Mrs. Kay's obvious state of alcohol intoxication and because of her age. Older people are particularly susceptible to delirium states. He also made the judgment that her diet might not have been adequate in recent days or weeks, given her disheveled appearance and the tendency for alcohol abuse and malnourishment to go together.

Her son's name and phone number were listed in her wallet; within a few hours he arrived at the hospital and was at his mother's bedside. Blaming himself for his mother's present state, Mr. Kay brooded over his stupidity and callousness at allowing her to leave the safety of his home some months ago. His first impulse was to take her home immediately, but the doctor cautioned him about the danger she was in and the need to restore her to a normal state of brain function through withdrawal from alcohol and a proper diet.

The hospital maintained a social service department, and the following day Mr. Kay and his wife spent an hour with a counselor to discuss the options for his mother. Mr. Kay believed that she needed close surveillance and round-the-clock care, which was not available at the retirement hotel. Surely she should move back with his family or enter a nursing home. The counselor, however, on the basis of the history Mr. Kay provided about his mother's recent and distant past, believed Mrs. Kay was capable of far more independent functioning than would be possible in either setting. She urged the son to consider not changing her living arrangement but to try to interest her in talking to a therapist on a regular basis while at the same time having a social worker visit her a few times a week to check on how she was doing. Mr. Kay reluctantly agreed to give it a try if his mother would agree to the plan.

Obtaining Mrs. Kay's agreement (in fact, talking about anything at all with her) proved impossible for the next few days. Not yet known to the family was her intent, as she left the hotel that evening with her bottle of scotch, to get as drunk as possible and then walk as far as she could into the nearby surf and drown herself. When she came to her senses several days later to find herself still alive, she experienced the kind of shame and guilt often felt by people who have made an unsuccessful suicide attempt. (This was not revealed until many weeks later, during a treatment session with her therapist.) After a week's time, however, Mrs. Kay was able to discuss things with the counselor and her son and agreed to the plan. Its appeal for her, however, was that it avoided having to burden her son and his family again by returning to their home, and it seemed to offer another opportunity to attempt to kill herself at a later date.

Mrs. Kay's return to the Gregorian two weeks later was a happy, almost rambunctious event. The manager had planned a surprise welcome, complete with colored bunting and a large sign reading "Welcome back, Helen, we all love you." Mrs. Kay's reaction to this outpouring of affection was mixed. She wanted desperately to believe that she was really wanted and loved, yet she felt unworthy to receive such affection from her hotel friends. On balance, her response was positive because, in her own mind, it meant that even though she had left the hotel a suicidal drinker, she was able to come back for another chance.

Mrs. Kay's therapist was a woman in her late forties, recently graduated from a clinical psychology program that offered specialty training in gerontology. Dr. Gardner had received the usual training of a clinical psychologist and had devoted special study to the physical and psychological problems of older people. The initial session was spent getting acquainted, since the psychologist knew of Mrs. Kay's previous aversion to mental health workers. Her warmth and empathy, however, won Mrs. Kay over, and the woman began in the next session to recount her reasons for the suicide attempt.

As the story unfolded, Mrs. Kay said that she initially liked the retirement hotel because she knew she was no longer "bothering" her son's family and, in a more positive vein, she enjoyed the privacy and increased feeling of independence. The other residents of the hotel, after all, were capable of getting around on their own; no one was blatantly senile, and they all shared some common experiences that could be discussed at meals and at odd hours in rocking chairs on the attractive veranda that looked out onto the oceanfront park. There was something satisfying about making a reference to the Great Depression without one's listener believing you were referring to the last time someone felt morose and despondent. However, after the initial positive period of a few weeks, her guilt about the death of her husband returned. It was only because he had worked so hard all his life that she could now afford to live out her life in these comfortable surroundings; she made no mention of her own contributions to the family's estate. If she had not been so selfish and weak, he would not have been hospitalized and allowed to die, alone among strangers and without the nurturance that a wife should have been there to provide. What good had she really been to him, not only after he became seriously ill but even during the earlier years of their long marriage? What good was she to anybody? Her son's family found her an unwelcome burden, an ordeal to endure because she was a pitiable old woman who had lost her husband. Finally, what kind of person was she that she could not cope with the loss of her beloved husband? Weren't the other widows at the Gregorian managing on their own without the self-blame and hopelessness that tormented her in her waking hours and also during her fitful sleep?

Mrs. Kay had suffered a great loss. Selling her home and moving in with her son's family led to further feelings that she no longer had control over her life. Reality, then, was providing some reason to feel helpless and depressed. But the conclusions Mrs. Kay drew from the facts seemed exaggerated and distorted, suggesting the viability of a cognitive intervention modeled after Beck's work on the treatment of depression (Beck et al., 1979). Of importance also was the fact that Mrs. Kay had been subject to depression all her adult life, and inquiry into these earlier episodes revealed a similar pattern of illogical self-blame and unjustified self-deprecation.

The following transcript of part of one therapy session illustrates the kinds of discussions Dr. Gardner had with her client over a period of several months:

Dr. Gardner: We were talking last week about why your husband died.

Mrs. Kay (eyes cast downward): Yes, I was to blame for it.

Dr. Gardner: I understand you feel that way, Helen, but let's talk about other aspects of his illness some more. You said he'd had an operation 6 months earlier to remove a cancerous lung?

Mrs. Kay (sobbing): Yes. . . . The only reason he got cancer was because of me.

Dr. Gardner: What do you mean?

Mrs. Kay: He smoked a lot till he was almost 60. When we first met in Cambridge, he was smoking two packs a day. Camels, no less. Of course, in those days, the 1920s, no one worried about cancer from cigarettes. Still, I never liked it and told him so.

Dr. Gardner: You did? What was his reaction?

Mrs. Kay: He'd pat me on my fanny and tell me I was cute when I got angry. I guess these days you'd call that pretty sexist. (Almost smiling.)

Dr. Gardner: Yes, I would myself. But then, that was then. Tell me, was it your fault that he had begun smoking in the first place?

Mrs. Kay: Well, not really. . . . Well, I guess not, you see, he'd already been smoking for several years before we met.

Dr. Gardner: Okay, so you were not responsible for his taking up the habit.

Mrs. Kay: I don't see how I could have been. But certainly I could have made him stop.

Dr. Gardner: Tell me.

Mrs. Kay: What do you mean?

Dr. Gardner: Can you tell me how you could have made him stop? How did you fail him in those early parts of your relationship?

Mrs. Kay: Well, I didn't mean to say I failed him or anything. I just . . . well . . . (Flustered.)

Dr. Gardner: Oh, sorry. I must have misunderstood. I thought I heard you say or at least imply that you were responsible for his smoking.

Mrs. Kay: I guess I did. I guess I have felt that way for a long time.

Dr. Gardner: Is it possible that *he* might have been the responsible one? Or is it possible that he was just addicted to the nicotine?

Mrs. Kay: Is that true? Do people get addicted?

Dr. Gardner: From what I have read, definitely. He might have been able to stop, but only with a lot of effort and pain.

Mrs. Kay: Yes, he tried many times. But it didn't work, somehow. He seemed able to do most anything he set out to do, but that smoking was something he never could handle. Or at least the price seemed too high to pay.

You know, he'd be unable to sit still those first few days after stopping, his work went to hell, I mean bad, and he became almost like another person. Mr. Hyde, I used to call him, when he was trying to stop. The children, too, they called him that, and it did break the tension a little.

Dr. Gardner: So he tried, but he didn't make it.

Mrs. Kay: No. But he was a good man.

Dr. Gardner: Of course. I agree a person can be good and still fail at things.

Mrs. Kay: Now, doctor, are you making a point about *me*?

Dr. Gardner (smiling): Well, now that you mention it, I guess I am. But I'm saying something else, Helen, I'm. . . .

Mrs. Kay: I know, my dear. You're telling me that I'm not to blame for everything that's not right with my life, with my dear ones. But I've always been that way. My daddy always told me to look out for others. Jesus did that, you know.

Dr. Gardner: Yes, it's a nice thing to strive for. But it doesn't mean you have to succeed every time.

Mrs. Kay: No, I suppose not. But listen, we were talking about his death. He didn't want to leave our home. (Crying again now.) He wanted to stay, with me at his side. I *know* it.

Dr. Gardner: Helen, how do you know that? He hadn't talked to you for weeks.

Mrs. Kay: Yes, poor man. (Crying loudly now.) He didn't know where he was. He didn't even know me.

Dr. Gardner: Helen, even if he did, do you really think he wanted you to be with him all the time?

Mrs. Kay: Well, now that you ask, we did have some discussions when he was thinking clearly, about his going into a nursing home when it became too much for me and. . . . (Falls silent.)

Dr. Gardner: And what?

Mrs. Kay (composing herself): . . . and he made me promise that when he didn't know me any more, I would do what the doctors said. And he knew they'd say he should go into a hospital, or something.

Dr. Gardner: Helen, he told you not to sacrifice yourself totally for him.

Mrs. Kay: Yes, dear man. (Crying loudly now.) He was too good for me.

Dr. Gardner: Tell me, Helen, how do you feel about what he said?

Mrs. Kay: What do you mean?

Dr. Gardner: I mean, well . . . did any of the other women at your hotel go through anything like this? You know, taking care of a sick husband at home and having to let him go after a while.

Mrs. Kay: Yes, there's Mrs. Hancock, a lovely woman. Her husband had gotten senile like my Harold, and she just couldn't take it. She put him in a nursing home, and he seemed okay there. But she had a hard time finding a good one.

Dr. Gardner: Yes, I know, there are some crummy ones around. But good ones, too, and necessary when people need the kind of total care that your husband needed. But besides, it was his cancer, wasn't it? And it was the hospital that you had him admitted to, wasn't it?

Mrs. Kay: Yes, the doctor insisted on it. He said the only way to make him comfortable was to have him in the hospital. The drugs he needed were too powerful and dangerous for me to give to him.

Dr. Gardner: So, it doesn't seem a bad decision.

Mrs. Kay: But then he died the following day, doctor! (Almost shrieking now.)

Dr. Gardner: Oh, my dear Helen, don't you think he'd have died the following day in your house? What could have happened in the hospital to make him die sooner?

Mrs. Kay: Maybe it was just moving him.

Dr. Gardner (conceding to herself that this was a good point): Yes, maybe, but you can't be sure, and besides, didn't the doctor say his death was inevitable, and that the morphine he planned to begin administering would probably have dulled the pain only a little, that his whole body . . .

Mrs. Kay: Oh, please don't say that. (Crying.)

Dr. Gardner (remaining silent for a minute): Helen, I know this is hard to talk about, but you need to face it squarely. You need to look at what happened more objectively. It doesn't seem that anything more could have been done for your husband. You had a wonderful life together, and taking care of him at home gave you time to talk about things with him. But at the end he was gravely ill, and he might have been made more comfortable in the hospital if it wasn't his time to die soon after he got there.

Mrs. Kay: Yes, I can see that now. I see it. Do you really believe what you're saying?

Dr. Gardner: Helen, I'll not lie to you. You're not a perfect individual—who is?—but you were wonderful to your husband, and you did everything, no, you did *more* than could have been expected. You didn't kill him, Helen. (Smiling.) You don't have *that* much power!

Mrs. Kay (smiling): You're quite the joker, doctor. Yes, I'm going to think about that for a while.

People do not change their minds easily, and Dr. Gardner was under no illusion of having convinced her client to stop blaming herself for her husband's death. But this discussion helped Mrs. Kay begin to consider other ways to construe what happened. Repeated examination over several sessions of her role in the course of her husband's illness did gradually lead Mrs. Kay to admit to herself that there were some things "even she" could not do, and that she could not reasonably blame herself for her husband's demise.

Because the heavy drinking seemed to be due to her depression, no specific treatment was undertaken for this aspect of her problem. Nevertheless,

Mrs. Kay was provided with some factual information on how a temporary delirium state could be produced in an older person by excessive alcohol consumption. The psychologist also warned her about drug interactions.

There was a total of 30 therapy sessions. Dr. Gardner had assumed at the outset that she would have to have a number of conjoint sessions with the son and his wife as well. She changed her mind when Mrs. Kay showed progress in reconstruing her responsibility for her husband's death and began to view some negative events as caused by factors beyond her control. With Mrs. Kay's permission, the therapist telephoned the son after therapy had been going on for one month to assure him that things were proceeding well and to confirm the suitability of Mrs. Kay's remaining in her hotel. The occasional visits by a social worker became less frequent. After six months, Mrs. Kay was reasonably comfortable and taking a more active interest than before in the many social functions available to older people in the surrounding community. She had also stopped drinking.

DISCUSSION

Older people have for some time been neglected by mental health professionals, but recently more and more training programs have begun to pay systematic attention to the particular physical and psychological challenges faced by people as they age. The growth in interest is perhaps in recognition of the fact that the proportion of the population that is 65 and older is increasing steadily; this is attributable to many factors, especially decreased infant, childhood, and maternal mortality, as well as improved sanitation and more effective control of infectious diseases. Estimated at 4 percent in 1900, the proportion of older adults in the United States was estimated at 10 percent in 1970, 11.3 percent in 1980, 12.2 percent in 1987 and may rise as high as 15 percent by 2010 and 21 percent by 2030. As the numbers of senior citizens increase, so will their need and demand for adequate medical and social services.

Old people face many real problems: medical care that is expensive and often poorly suited to their needs; economic challenges and sometimes privation; deteriorating health; and loss of friends and loved ones. They seem to have more than their share of problems, but they cope very well as a group. They also have their share of psychological problems, including depression, but depression does not appear to be more common in those aged 65 and older than in younger adults (Cappeliez, 1988); in fact, some epidemiological surveys find that it is *less* prevalent (Anthony & Aboraya, 1992; Myers et al., 1984; Regier et al., 1988). Although clinical depression, as diagnosed by the *DSM*, does not seem to increase with age, *symptoms* of depression may, with the highest scores on symptom checklists made by those over the age of 75

(Gatz & Hurwicz, 1990; Lewinsohn, Rohde, Fischer, & Seeley, 1991). It is interesting that there is some indication in recent data that younger cohorts of older adults may be more clinically depressed than older groups. That is, people joining the ranks of older adults today show more signs of clinical depression than cohorts born earlier in the twentieth century (Gatz, Kasl-Godley, & Karel, in press). Most of the depressive episodes among older people are recurrences from their earlier years, as was the case with Mrs. Kay, but some show up for the first time in old age (Gurland, 1976; Koenig & Blazer, 1992).

Life problems alone would not explain Mrs. Kay's depression; after all, most older people suffer losses *without* becoming profoundly depressed. The case material reveals a long tendency on her part to blame herself for negative events in her life and the lives of others close to her. She also insisted that she excel without help from others. In terms of Beck's theory of depression, the schema she was operating in was one of self-deprecation and self-blame (Beck, 1967). This cognitive structure led her to construe as her fault unfortunate events such as her husband's chronic cigarette smoking, his contracting lung cancer, and his dying in the hospital after her agreement to cease taking care of him at home. The therapy undertaken by the psychologist was aimed at uncovering these unspoken beliefs; examining them openly; considering their validity; and offering other, presumably more realistic, ways of regarding certain happenings in her life. This is a very intellectual therapy, relying on the ability and willingness of clients to understand the basic framework and accept it as applying to their own particular circumstances. Dr. Gardner no doubt saw Mrs. Kay as a suitable candidate, considering her keen intelligence and solid educational background. One of the unanswered questions in Beck's approach is whether it applies to people whose abilities and general attitudes toward life do not so readily accommodate a highly intellectual approach.

People at highest risk for suicide are those who are physically ill, feel hopeless, are isolated from others or have lost loved ones, are in dire financial circumstances, and are depressed. Because a combination of these factors is found often among older people, it should come as no surprise that suicide rates are higher for people over 65 than for younger individuals (see Koenig & Blazer, 1992, for review of literature on suicide among elderly persons). The rate is especially high for white males, increasing steadily into their eighties. Butler and Lewis (1977) suggest that white males are particularly susceptible to suicide because they suffer an especially great loss in status, having held the greatest power and influence in societies like ours. What about women like Mrs. Kay? Suicide rates increase for white females until the age of 60 but then decrease thereafter; rates for nonwhite men and women in the United States fluctuate throughout the life span, with marked increases for men (Manton, Blazer, & Woodbury, 1987).

One statistic is particularly noteworthy. The ratio of unsuccessful to completed suicides is seven to one for people under 65, but two to one for those who are older. When older people decide to commit suicide, they are more likely to die, perhaps because of a greater resolve, perhaps because their bodies are more vulnerable to sleeping pills or falls. Older people can also "give up" and passively kill themselves more readily than younger individuals because life-threatening illnesses are more prevalent among them. Suicide among older adults may also be the result of a rational and philosophical decision to stop living, such as when an elderly man decides that the intractable pain of his terminal illness is not worth the effort or the financial drain on his or his children's resources. A woman in the earliest stages of Alzheimer's disease decided, well before she was incapacitated, to end her life because of quality issues. She used the services of a retired pathologist who had invented a device that administered intravenously a lethal drug—controlled by a button pushed by the patient. As expected, this "suicide machine" and the fact that a physician actively assisted in a person's death generated considerable publicity and conflicting opinions about its morality (Egan, 1990; Wilkerson, 1990).

Intervention in suicide is similar to what is practiced with younger individuals: counseling to help the person consider nonlethal alternatives to desperate situations. Suicidologists hold that life itself is sacred; they are also mindful of the fact that many potential suicides are grateful afterward that they have another chance at life. Even in older people suicidal crises pass, as happened with Mrs. Kay, who did take advantage of a second chance. Cognitive therapy seemed to alleviate the depression viewed as the underlying cause of her attempted suicide.

The most obvious factor about an older person is his or her age. Physiological aging is an inexorable process, affecting all who make it through 60 or 70 years of existence. To be sure, certain cosmetic and medical measures can mitigate somewhat the biological effects of growing old, and there is many a 70-year-old in better physical condition than a 50-year-old. But gravity is everyone's worst enemy eventually. In some measure, it is the way older people react to inevitable and more serious physical changes that affects how psychologically sound they are in their later years. The heavy emphasis on youth in our culture does little to reassure most of us that life is worth living beyond one's forties; the burden may rest especially heavily on women, who are devalued more than men as they grow old. The feminist movement of the 1960s and beyond has helped reduce the stigma of a woman's growing old but, like other cultural phenomena, changes are slow in coming.

The problems of older people do not appear as a separate category in *DSM-IV*. Notice is taken here and there in the psychiatric nomenclature of the course of particular disorders, but the psychiatric profession has yet to confront aging itself as a major variable in mental and emotional disorders. The sole exception fits the prevalent stereotype that when an old person is unhappy or depressed or paranoid, it is somehow due to physical malfunctions: *DSM-IV* has a separate main section called Delirium, Dementia, and Amnestic and

Other Cognitive Disorders, and many of them are linked to diseases found among older people.

Only 5 percent of older adults have organic mental syndromes. One of these syndromes, Delirium, was noted in Mrs. Kay when she was found under the pier by the police officer. Delirium is described by the *DSM* as a rapid-onset disorder characterized by difficulties in maintaining and shifting attention; disorganized thinking; and disturbances in perception (e.g., hallucinations), orientation, and memory. The person's behavior can also be erratic, from thrashing around in bed to being lethargic and sluggish. The former pattern can be particularly dangerous in hospital settings, when the patient may be hooked up to intravenous food and medication; this often leads to the staff having to strap delirious patients down in restraints to protect them from harming themselves. Mood can also fluctuate widely, from anger to euphoria, from irritability to apathy.

In the past, other terms that have been used for delirium are *acute confusional state* and *acute brain syndrome.* Delirium is usually reversible if the underlying cause is temporary, self-limiting, or adequately treated. Brain tissue may malfunction because of a metabolic disturbance without being destroyed. Although it can happen at any age, delirium is especially frequent among older people, whose body chemistry is sensitive to drug effects, overdoses, and malnutrition. It is especially a problem during hospitalization: One estimate is that up to half of the hospitalized elderly are likely to become delirious at some time during their stay (Lipowski, 1983). It is important for those who care for older people to understand delirium; if not treated, it can worsen, brain cells can be destroyed, and the person may actually die (well over 25 percent actually do die, either from the untreated underlying condition or from exhaustion; Rabins & Folstein, 1982).The (unspoken) belief that old people do not get better may sometimes lead professionals to misdiagnose and regard a temporary delirium as the first sign of a progressive and irreversible brain disease.

Irreversible brain diseases do exist and are characterized by dementia, a steady and gradual deterioration of intellectual abilities over several years. (Some forms of dementia are reversible, however, depending on the underlying cause.) The more familiar term for dementia is *senility.* Memory problems are common, and abstract thinking suffers. The person becomes unable to attend even to the most basic human needs; becomes incontinent, sometimes unruly; and, in the most fundamental and tragic sense, is no longer the person he or she once was. Unlike delirium, there is often actual destruction of brain cells from such causes as stroke and especially Alzheimer's disease, in which there is an atrophy or wasting away of cortical cells. Death usually follows within 10 to 14 years of onset. In addition to his cancer, Mr. Kay had suffered from Alzheimer's.

Brain disease is not a trivial problem for older people, but it accounts for only a minority of the problems they have: Fewer than 10 percent of people between 65 and 80 suffer from dementia, though this percentage increases to approximately 20 in those over the age of 80 (Folstein et al., 1991; LaRue, Dessonville, & Jarvik, 1985). Attention must therefore be focused on their psychological difficulties. One set of problems arises from decisions about caring for the person with Alzheimer's disease. In the last few years of her husband's life, Mrs. Kay was faced with the challenge of nursing him at home. She persisted long after many caretakers would have given up and institutionalized the patient. Clinical depression and anxiety are widespread among those who care for their dementing relatives at home (Schulz & Williamson, 1991). Mrs. Kay certainly paid a steep emotional cost by looking after her husband on her own until the very end of his life, and she did not profit from advice and counsel that are becoming more widely available from mental health workers with training in gerontology. For example, she did not have a nurse come regularly to her home, even though she could have easily afforded it. She gave herself no time off, and her own inordinately high standards for herself continued to take their toll after her husband died. She blamed herself so severely for his death that she almost committed suicide.

Unfortunately, her concern about nursing homes was well founded; even in the better ones patients receive the kind of care that fosters unnecessary dependency and even muscular and mental deterioration (Rosenblatt & Spiegel, 1988). Geared to maximum levels of custodial care, most nursing homes take a conservative approach. If a person needs a walker to move about alone, better to wheel the patient around in a wheelchair because it is faster and poses less risk of injury; if a person spills food but does manage to eat, better to feed that person because it is more efficient and keeps the place neater. Even with the best intentions, this kind of care does not benefit all residents.

Older adults have not been the beneficiaries of political and professional decisions to deinstitutionalize, that is, if at all possible, to maintain in community settings people who are psychologically disabled. Older people are overrepresented in state mental hospitals. When they are discharged, they often find their way to nursing homes, whose populations have doubled over the past 25 years as the numbers of people in mental hospitals have declined. A large proportion of nursing home residents have mental health problems, but staff seldom are properly trained to deal with them (Gatz & Smyer, 1992). Furthermore, most nursing home residents do not require the level of custodial care provided in those settings. However, for deinstitutionalization to do any good, adequate community-based services must be provided. Zarit (1980), a psychologist specializing in clinical problems of older adults, proposed principles that can foster the development of effective noninstitutional services to the elderly. First, there must be comprehensive community-based services such as the availability of individual and family therapy, telephone hotlines, regular and routine phone checks to see if any help is needed or desired, Meals-on-

Wheels, and home visits by professionals to assess directly how things are going. The needs of the older person's family must also be considered; someone caring day and night for a bedridden individual can be expected to have mixed feelings and not the unending patience and concern that we unreasonably expect of them. In addition, intervention should be the minimum necessary; sometimes less is better, especially with an older person (Hofland, 1988; Rodin & Langer, 1977), who may perceive an inability to do things easily done before as good reason to become overly dependent on others. Real needs must be attended to, but, argues Zarit, one of those needs is to be an autonomous, responsible human being who is not gratuitously infantalized by helpers.

Mrs. Kay was lucky in many ways. Her son's family cared about her and remained willing to have her live with them. She had her physical health and was therefore not dependent on others for taking care of basic needs such as dressing herself, eating, shopping, and so forth. She also had money, unlike many older people. As a woman, she entered her senior years with a sharp and active mind and a set of interests developed during her own professional career as a journalist. This made her interesting to be around and probably contributed to her popularity in her retirement hotel; the welcome she received when she was discharged from the hospital played no small role in her recovery.

Pessimism has been the rule in caring for the aged. Because they have relatively little time to live — relative, that is, to the mental health professionals whose responsibility it is to look after them — their psychological problems have received less emphasis than those of younger adults. And yet older people suffer from the entire range of psychological disorders — paranoia, anxiety and depression, hypochondriasis, substance abuse, insomnia, psychosis, and sexual dysfunction. The last set of problems may be due as much to ignorance as to anything else. Evidence confirms that older people can have satisfying sexual lives, the major difference being that things take longer to happen and, when they do happen, there is less urgency (Masters & Johnson, 1966). For example, a man in his seventies can usually have erections and climaxes, but the ejaculate is smaller in volume and comes forth under less pressure than when he was younger. A woman's vaginal walls lubricate less when she is older; widely available jellies can ameliorate this problem, and orgasms are still possible after she has ceased ovulating, that is, when she is postmenopausal. One study revealed that even 80- to 100-year-old people, providing they are healthy, can have active sex lives, the preferred activities being caressing and masturbation and sometimes intercourse (Bretschneider & McCoy, 1988).

Older people also have a set of problems that are more or less unique. People in their eighties have usually outlived their friends and spouses, and new social contacts are often not as easy to make, as was the case with Mrs. Kay. As mentioned, physical losses can also be a heavy burden especially when the society at large is geared to people whose reflexes are sharper and whose sensorimotor capacities are speedier and more acute. Evidence is accumulating that psychological interventions can have a positive impact on older people. What is needed now is a strong social commitment to study the ways people change as they age and to develop appropriate methods to help them adapt and continue growing. Failure to change our thinking and actions about the elderly will prove disadvantageous not only to them but to the older adults of tomorrow — *us*.

9 SCHIZOPHRENIA: PARANOID TYPE

Bill McClary made his first appointment at the mental health center reluctantly. He was 25 years old, single, and unemployed. His sister, Colleen, with whom he had been living for 18 months, had repeatedly encouraged him to seek professional help. She was concerned about his peculiar behavior and social isolation. He spent most of his time daydreaming, often talked to himself, and occasionally said things that made little sense. Bill acknowledged that he ought to keep more regular hours and assume more responsibility, but he insisted that he did not need psychological treatment. The appointment was finally made in an effort to please his sister and mollify her husband, who was worried about Bill's influence on their three young children.

During the first interview, Bill spoke quietly and frequently hesitated. The therapist noted that Bill occasionally blinked and shook his head as though he was trying to clear his thoughts or return his concentration to the topic at hand. When the therapist commented on this unusual twitch, Bill apologized politely but denied that it held any significance. He was friendly yet shy and clearly ill at ease. The discussion centered on Bill's daily activities and his rather unsuccessful efforts to fit into the routine of Colleen's family. Bill assured the therapist that his problems would be solved if he could stop daydreaming. He also expressed a desire to become better organized.

Bill continued to be guarded throughout the early therapy sessions. After several weeks, he began to discuss his social contacts and mentioned a concern about sexual orientation. Despite his lack of close friends, Bill had had some limited and fleeting sexual experiences. These had been both heterosexual and homosexual in nature. He was worried about the possible meaning and consequences of his encounters with other males. This topic occupied the next several weeks of therapy.

Bill's "daydreaming" was also pursued in greater detail. It was a source of considerable concern to him, and it interfered significantly with his daily activities. This experience was difficult to define. At frequent, although irregular, intervals throughout the day, Bill found himself distracted by intrusive and repetitive thoughts. The thoughts were simple and most often alien to his own value system. For example, he might suddenly think to himself, "Damn, God." Recognizing the unacceptable nature of the thought, Bill then felt compelled to repeat a sequence of self-statements that he had designed to correct the initial intrusive thought. He called these thoughts and his corrective incantations "scruples." These self-statements accounted for the observation that Bill frequently mumbled to himself. He also admitted that his unusual blinking and head shaking were associated with the experience of intrusive thoughts.

Six months after Bill began attending the clinic regularly, the therapist received a call from Bill's brother-in-law, Roger. Roger said that he and Bill had recently talked extensively about some of Bill's unusual ideas, and Roger wanted to know how he should respond. The therapist was, in fact, unaware of any such ideas. Instead of asking Roger to betray Bill's confidence any further, the therapist decided to ask Bill about these ideas at their next therapy session. It was only at this point that the therapist finally became aware of Bill's extensive delusional belief system.

For reasons that will become obvious, Bill was initially reluctant to talk about the ideas to which his brother-in-law had referred. Nevertheless, he provided the following account of his beliefs and their development. Shortly after moving to his sister's home, Bill realized that something strange was happening. He noticed that people were taking special interest in him and often felt that they were talking about him behind his back. These puzzling circumstances persisted for several weeks during which Bill became increasingly anxious and suspicious. The pieces of the puzzle finally fell in place late one night as Bill sat in front of the television. In a flash of insight, Bill suddenly came to believe that a group of conspirators had secretly produced and distributed a documentary film about his homosexual experiences. Several of his high-school friends and a few distant relatives had presumably used hidden cameras and microphones to record each of his sexual encounters with other men. Bill believed that the film had grossed over $50 million at the box office and that this money had been sent to the Irish Republican Army to buy arms and ammunition. He therefore held himself responsible for the deaths of dozens of people who had died as the result of several recent bombings in

Ireland. This notion struck the therapist and Bill's brother-in-law as being quite preposterous, but Bill's conviction was genuine. He was visibly moved as he described his guilt concerning the bombings. He was also afraid that serious consequences would follow his confession. Bill believed that the conspirators had agreed to kill him if he ever found out about the movie. This imagined threat had prevented Bill from confiding in anyone prior to this time. It was clear that he now feared for his life.

Bill's fear was exacerbated by the voices that he had been hearing for the past several weeks. He frequently heard male voices discussing his sexual behavior and arguing about what action should be taken to punish him. They were not voices of people with whom Bill was personally familiar, but they were always males and they were always talking about Bill. For example, one night when Bill was sitting alone in his bedroom at Colleen's home, he thought he overheard a conversation in the next room. It was a heated argument in which one voice kept repeating "He's a goddamned faggot and we've got to kill him!" Two other voices seemed to be asking questions about what he had done and were arguing against the use of such violence. Bill was, of course, terrified by this experience and sat motionless in his room as the debate continued. When Roger tapped on his door to ask if he was all right, Bill was certain that they were coming to take him away. Realizing that it was Roger and that he had not been part of the conversation, Bill asked him who was in the next room. Roger pointed out that two of the children were sleeping in the next room. When Bill went to check, he found the children asleep in their beds. These voices appeared at frequent but unpredictable intervals almost every day. It was not clear whether or not they had first appeared before the development of Bill's delusional beliefs.

The details of the delusional system were quite elaborate and represented a complex web of imaginary events and reality. For example, the title of the secret film was supposedly *Honor Thy Father,* and Bill said his name in the film was Gay Talese. *Honor Thy Father* was, in fact, a popular novel that was written by Gay Talese and published several years prior to the development of Bill's delusion. The actual novel was about organized crime, but Bill denied any knowledge of this "other book with the same title." According to Bill's belief system, the film's title alluded to Bill's disrespect for his own father and his own name in the film was a reference to his reputation as a "gay tease." He also maintained that his own picture had been on the cover of *Time* magazine within the past year with the name Gay Talese printed at the bottom.

An interesting array of evidence had been marshaled in support of this delusion. For example, Bill pointed to the fact that he had happened to meet his cousin accidentally on a subway in Brooklyn two years earlier. Why, Bill asked, would his cousin have been on the same train if he were not making a secret film about Bill's private life? In Bill's mind, the cousin was clearly part of a continuous surveillance that had been carefully arranged by the conspirators. The fact that Bill came from a very large family and that such coincidences were bound to happen did not impress him as a counterargument. Bill also pointed to an incident involving the elevator operator at his mother's apartment building as further evidence for the existence of the film. He remembered stepping onto the elevator one morning and having the operator give him a puzzled, prolonged glance. The man asked him if they knew each other. Bill replied that they did not. Bill's explanation for this mundane occurrence was that the man recognized Bill because he had obviously seen the film recently; he insisted that no other explanation made sense. Once again, coincidence was absolutely impossible. His delusional system had become so pervasive and intricately woven that it was no longer open to logical refutation. He was totally preoccupied with the plot and simultaneously so frightened that he did not want to discuss it with anyone. Thus he had lived in private fear, brooding about the conspiracy and helpless to prevent the conspirators from spreading knowledge of his shameful sexual behavior.

SOCIAL HISTORY

Bill was the youngest of four children. He grew up in New York City where his father worked as a firefighter. Both of his parents were first-generation Irish Americans. Many of their relatives were still living in Ireland. Both parents came from large families. Bill's childhood memories were filled with stories about the family's Irish heritage.

Bill was always much closer to his mother than to his father, whom he remembered as being harsh and distant. Being the youngest child, he was treated protectively. His mother doted on him and did not encourage social activities with other children. When his parents fought, which they did frequently, Bill often found himself caught in the middle. Mr. McClary accused his wife of lavishing all her affection on Bill and seemed to blame Bill for their marital disharmony. Mrs. McClary, on the other hand, pointed out that her husband spent all of his time with their oldest son and excluded Bill from their activities. Neither parent seemed to make a serious effort to improve their relationship. Bill later learned that his father had carried on an extended affair with another woman. His mother depended on her own mother, who lived in the same neighborhood, for advice and support and would frequently take Bill with her to stay at her parents' apartment after particularly heated arguments. Bill grew to hate his father, but his enmity was tempered by guilt. He had learned that children were supposed to respect their parents and that, in particular, a son should emulate and revere his father. Mr. McClary became gravely ill when Bill was 12 years old, and Bill remembered wishing that his father would die. His wish came true. Years later, Bill looked back on this sequence of events with considerable ambivalence and regret.

Bill could not remember having any close friends as a child. Most of his social contacts were with cousins, nephews, and nieces. He did not enjoy their company or the games that other children played. He remembered himself as a clumsy, effeminate child who preferred to be alone or with his mother instead of with other boys.

He was a good student and finished near the top of his class in high school. His mother and the rest of the family seemed certain that he would go on to college, but Bill could not decide on a course of study. The prospect of selecting a profession struck Bill as an ominous task. How could he be sure that he wanted to do the same thing for the rest of his life? He decided that he needed more time to ponder the matter and took a job as a bank clerk after graduating from high school.

Bill moved to a small efficiency apartment and seemed to perform adequately at the bank. His superiors noted that he was reliable, although somewhat eccentric. He was described as quiet and polite—his reserved manner bordered on being socially withdrawn. He did not associate with any of the other employees and rarely spoke to them beyond the usual exchange of social pleasantries. Although he was not in danger of losing his job, Bill's chances for advancement were remote. This realization did not perturb Bill because he did not aspire to promotion in the banking profession. It was only a way of forestalling a serious career decision. After two years at the bank, Bill resigned. He had decided that the job did not afford him enough time to think about his future.

He was soon able to find a position as an elevator operator. Here, he reasoned, was a job that provided time for thought. Over the next several months, he gradually became more aloof and disorganized. He was frequently late to work and seemed unconcerned about the reprimands that he began receiving. Residents at the apartment house described him as peculiar. His appearance was always neat and clean, but he seemed preoccupied most of the time. On occasion he seemed to mumble to himself, and he often forgot floor numbers to which he had been directed. These problems continued to mount until he was fired after working for one year at this job.

During the first year after finishing high school, while working at the bank, Bill had his first sexual experience. A man in his middle forties who often did business at the bank invited Bill to his apartment for a drink, and they became intimate. The experience was moderately enjoyable but primarily anxiety provoking. Bill decided not to see this man again. Over the next two years, Bill experienced sexual relationships with a small number of other men as well as with a few women. In each case, it was Bill's partner who took the initiative. Only one relationship lasted more than a few days. He became friends with a woman named Patty who was about his own age, divorced, and the mother of a three-year-old daughter. Bill enjoyed being with Patty and her daughter and occasionally spent evenings at their apartment watching television and drinking wine. Despite their occasional sexual encounters, this relationship never developed beyond the casual stage at which it began.

After he was fired from the job as an elevator operator, Bill moved back into his mother's apartment. He later recalled that they made each other anxious. Rarely leaving the apartment, Bill sat around the apartment daydreaming in front of the television. When his mother returned from work, she would clean, cook, and coax him unsuccessfully to enroll in various kinds of job-training programs. His social isolation was a constant cause of concern for her. She was not aware of his bisexual interests and encouraged him to call women that she met at work and through friends. The tension eventually became too great for both of them, and Bill decided to move in with Colleen, her husband, and their three young children.

CONCEPTUALIZATION AND TREATMENT

Bill's adjustment problems were obviously extensive. He had experienced serious difficulties in the development of social and occupational roles. From a traditional diagnostic viewpoint, Bill's initial symptoms pointed to a schizotypal personality. In other words, before his delusional beliefs and hallucinations became manifest, he exhibited a series of peculiar characteristics in the absence of floridly psychotic symptoms. These included several of the classic signs outlined by Meehl (1964): anhedonia (the inability to experience pleasure), interpersonal aversiveness, and ambivalence. Bill seldom, if ever, had any fun. Even his sexual experiences were described in a detached, intellectual manner. He might indicate, for example, that he had performed well or that his partner seemed satisfied, but he never said things like, "It was terrific," or "I was really excited!" He strongly preferred to be alone. When Colleen and Roger had parties, Bill became anxious and withdrew to his room, explaining that he felt ill. Bill's ambivalence toward other people was evident in his relationship with his therapist. He never missed an appointment; in fact, he was always early and seemed to look forward to the visits. Despite this apparent dependence, he seemed to distrust the therapist and was often guarded in his response to questions. He seemed to want to confide in the therapist and was simultaneously fearful of the imagined consequences. Bill's pattern of cognitive distraction was somewhat difficult to interpret. His "scruples" were, in some ways, similar to obsessive thoughts, but they also bore a resemblance to one of Schneider's (1959) first-rank symptoms of schizophrenia—thought insertion. Considering this constellation of problems, it was clear that Bill was in need of treatment, but it was not immediately obvious that he was psychotic. The therapist decided to address Bill's problems from a cognitive-behavioral perspective. The ambiguity surrounding his cognitive impairment seemed to warrant a delay regarding biological interventions such as medication.

The beginning therapy sessions were among the most difficult. Bill was tense, reserved, and more than a bit suspicious. Therapy had been his sister's idea, not his own. The therapist adopted a passive, nondirective manner and concentrated on the difficult goal of establishing a trusting relationship with Bill. In the absence of such an atmosphere, it would be impossible to work toward more specific behavioral changes.

Many of the early sessions were spent discussing Bill's concerns about homosexuality. The therapist listened to Bill's thoughts and concerns and shared various bits of information about sexuality and homosexual behavior in particular. As might be expected, Bill was afraid that homosexual behavior per se was a direct manifestation of psychological disturbance. He also wondered about his motivation to perform sexual acts with other men and expressed some vague hypotheses about this being a reflection of his desire to have a closer relationship with his father. The therapist assured Bill that the gender of one's sexual partner was less important than the quality of the sexual relationship. In fact, the therapist was most concerned about Bill's apparent failure to enjoy sexual activity and his inability to establish lasting relationships. Instead of trying to eliminate the possibility of future homosexual encounters or to impose an arbitrary decision based on prevailing sexual norms, the therapist tried to (1) help Bill explore his own concerns about the topic, (2) provide him with information that he did not have, and (3) help him develop skills that would improve his social and sexual relationships, whether they involved men or women.

As their relationship became more secure, the therapist adopted a more active, directive role. Specific target problems were identified, and an attempt was made to deal with each sequentially. The first area of concern was Bill's daily schedule. The therapist enlisted Colleen's support. Together with Bill they instituted a sequence of contingencies designed to integrate his activities with those of the family. For example, Colleen called Bill once for breakfast at 7:30 A.M. If he missed eating with everyone else, Colleen went on with other activities and did not make him a late brunch as she had done prior to this arrangement. In general, the therapist taught Colleen to reinforce appropriate behavior and to ignore inappropriate behavior as much as possible. Over the initial weeks, Bill did begin to keep more regular hours.

Behavioral contingencies were also used to encourage more involvement in household chores; high-probability behaviors were made contingent on the production of low-probability behaviors in an effort to increase the frequency of the low-probability behaviors. This phase of the treatment program met with limited success, however, because of a lack of appropriate high-probability behaviors. High-probability behaviors are the things that the person prefers to do when he or she is given a free choice (when there are no explicit contingencies in effect). Whenever he had a chance, Bill spent most of his time daydreaming. There were few specific activities that he enjoyed.

Indeed, his relative inability to experience pleasure was one of the most troublesome aspects of Bill's behavior. The most appropriate activity in this regard involved Colleen's youngest daughter, Susan. Bill enjoyed helping Susan with her homework after dinner. The therapist considered making this activity available to Bill only if he had just cleared the table and loaded the dishwasher. While this contingency may have been effective, it seemed somewhat shortsighted. Bill's very low level of social contact was a major source of concern. The therapist decided against using a procedure that might further reduce this activity. Instead, he simply tried to encourage Bill to work with the children as much as possible and continued to coach Colleen and her husband to praise appropriate behavior and ignore inappropriate ones.

After several weeks of work, this home-based program began to produce positive changes. Bill was following a schedule closer to that of the rest of the family and was more helpful around the house. At this point, the therapist decided to address two problems that were somewhat more difficult: Bill's annoying habit of mumbling to himself and his lack of social contacts with peers. Careful interviews with Bill and his sister served as a base for a functional assessment of the self-talk. This behavior seemed to occur most frequently when Bill was alone or thought he was alone. He was usually able to control his scruples in the presence of others; if he was particularly disturbed by a distracting thought, he most often excused himself and retired to his room. Colleen's response was usually to remind Bill that he was mumbling and occasionally to scold him if he was talking loudly. Given the functional value of Bill's scruples in reducing his anxiety about irreverent thoughts, it seemed unlikely that the self-talk was being maintained by this social reinforcement. The therapist decided to try a stimulus control procedure. Bill was instructed to select one place in the house in which he could daydream and talk to himself. Whenever he felt the urge to daydream or repeat his scruples, he was to go to this specific spot before engaging in these behaviors. It was hoped that his procedure would severely restrict the environmental stimuli that were associated with these asocial behaviors and thereby reduce their frequency. Bill and the therapist selected the laundry room as his daydreaming room because it was relatively secluded from the rest of the house. His bedroom was ruled out because the therapist did not want it to become a stimulus for behaviors that would interfere with sleeping. Colleen was encouraged to prompt Bill whenever she noticed him engaging in self-talk outside of the laundry room. The program seemed to have modest, positive results, but it did not eliminate self-talk entirely.

Interpersonal behaviors were also addressed from a behavioral perspective. Since moving to his sister's home, Bill had not met any people his own age and had discontinued seeing his friends in New York City. Several avenues were pursued. He was encouraged to call his old friends and, in particular, to renew his friendship with Patty. The therapist spent several sessions with Bill rehearsing telephone calls and practicing conversations that might take place. Although Bill was generally aware of what things he should say, he was anxious about social contacts. This form of behavioral rehearsal was seen as a way of exposing him gradually to the anxiety-provoking stimuli. He was also given weekly homework assignments involving social contacts at home. The therapist discussed possible sources of friends, including a tavern not far from Colleen's home and occasional parties that Colleen and Roger had for their friends. This aspect of the treatment program was modestly effective. Bill called Patty several times and arranged to stay with his mother for a weekend so that he could visit with Patty and her daughter. Although he was somewhat anxious at first, the visit was successful and seemed to lift Bill's spirits. He was more animated during the following therapy session and seemed almost optimistic about changing his current situation.

It was during one of their visits to the neighborhood tavern that Bill first mentioned the imagined movie to Roger. When the therapist learned of these ideas, and the auditory hallucinations, he modified the treatment plan. He had initially rejected the idea of antipsychotic medication because there was no clear-cut evidence of schizophrenia. Now that psychotic symptoms had appeared, an appointment was arranged with a psychiatrist who agreed with the diagnosis and prescribed a moderate dosage of thioridazine (Mellaril), one of the standard antipsychotic drugs. Because Bill's behavior was not considered dangerous and his sister was able to supervise his activities closely, hospitalization was not necessary. All of the other aspects of the program were continued.

Bill's response to the medication was positive but not dramatic. The most obvious effect was on his self-talk, which was reduced considerably over a four-week period. Bill attributed this change to the virtual disappearance of the annoying, intrusive thoughts. His delusions remained intact, however, despite the therapist's attempt to encourage a rational consideration of the evidence. The following example illustrates the impregnable quality of delusional thinking as well as the naïveté of the therapist.

One of Bill's ideas was that his picture had been on the cover of *Time* magazine. This seemed like a simple idea to test, and Bill expressed a willingness to try. Together they narrowed the range of dates to the last eight months. The therapist then asked Bill to visit the public library before their next session and check all issues of *Time* during this period. Of course, Bill did not find his picture. Nevertheless, his conviction was even stronger than before. He had convinced himself that the conspirators had seen him on his way to the library, beaten him there, and switched magazine covers before he could discover the original. Undaunted, the therapist recommended two more public libraries for the next week. As might have been expected, Bill did not find his picture at either library but remained convinced that the cover had appeared. Every effort to introduce contradictory evidence was met by this same stubborn resistance.

Overall, the medication had a positive effect on Bill's behavior, but it also produced some bothersome side effects. Many of these were minor in nature, such as dry mouth and drowsiness. The latter problem was handled by adjusting the schedule for Bill's daily dosage so that he took most of the Mellaril two hours before bedtime. The most annoying side effect involved muscular rigidity. Bill said that his arms and legs felt stiff and that his hands sometimes trembled involuntarily. Colleen noted that his movement and posture appeared somewhat more awkward than usual. These motor disturbances, which are known as *extrapyramidal effects*, were counteracted by having Bill supplement his Mellaril with benztropine (Cogentin), a drug that can reverse this Parkinsonian syndrome. Despite the annoying side effects, Bill expressed satisfaction with the antipsychotic medication because it cleared his thinking and thus eliminated a major source of personal distress.

Over the next several weeks, Bill became somewhat less adamant about his beliefs. The conceded that there was a *chance* that he had imagined the whole thing. It seemed to him that the plot probably did exist and that the movie was, in all likelihood, still playing around the country, but he was willing to admit that the evidence for this belief was less than overwhelming. Although his suspicions remained, the fear of observation and the threat of death were less immediate, and he was able to concentrate more fully on the other aspects of the treatment program. Hospitalization did not become necessary, and he was able to continue living with Colleen's family. Despite important improvements, it was clear that Bill would continue to need a special supportive environment and it seemed unlikely that he would assume normal occupational and social roles, at least not in the near future.

DISCUSSION

The diagnostic hallmarks of schizophrenia are hallucinations, delusions, and disturbances in affect and thought. *DSM-IV* (p. 285) requires the following to support a diagnosis of schizophrenia:

A. *Characteristic Symptoms*: Two (or more) of the following, each present for a significant portion of time during a 1-month period (or less if successfully treated):
1. Delusions.
2. Hallucinations.
3. Disorganized speech.
4. Grossly disorganized or catatonic behavior.
5. Negative symptoms, such as affective flattening, alogia, or avolition.

Note: Only one of the symptoms listed above is required if delusions are bizarre or hallucinations consist of a voice keeping up a running commentary on the person's behavior or thoughts, or two or more voices conversing with each other.

B. *Social/Occupational Dysfunction*: For a significant portion of the time since the onset of the disturbance, one or more major areas of functioning such as work, interpersonal relations, or self-care are markedly below the level achieved prior to the onset.

C. *Duration*: Continuous signs of the disturbance persist for at least 6 months. This 6-month period must include at least 1 month of symptoms that meet Criterion A (active phase symptoms) and may include periods of prodromal or residual symptoms. During these prodromal or residual periods, the signs of the disturbance may be manifested by only negative symptoms or two or more symptoms listed in Criterion A present in an attenuated form (such as odd beliefs, unusual perceptual experiences).

Bill clearly fit the diagnostic criteria for schizophrenia. Prior to the expression of his complex, delusional belief system, he exhibited several of the characteristics of a prodromal phase. He had been socially isolated since moving to his sister's home. Although he did interact with his sister and her family, he made no effort to stay in touch with the few friends he had known in New York City, nor did he attempt to meet new friends in the neighborhood. In fact, he had never been particularly active socially, even during his childhood. His occupational performance had deteriorated long before he was fired from his job as an elevator operator. Several neighbors had complained about his peculiar behavior. For example, one of Colleen's friends once called to tell her that she had been watching Bill as he walked home from the grocery store. He was carrying a bag of groceries, clearly mumbling to himself, and moving in a strange pattern. He would take two or three steps forward, then one to the side onto the grass next to the sidewalk. At this point, Bill would hop once on his left foot, take one step forward, and then step back onto the sidewalk and continue the sequence. Thinking that this behavior seemed similar to games that children commonly play, Colleen asked Bill about his walk home. He told her that each of these movements possessed a particular meaning and that he followed this pattern to correct scruples that were being placed in his head as he returned from the store. This explanation, and his other comments about his scruples, would be considered an example of magical thinking. Overall, Bill's delusional beliefs and auditory hallucinations can be seen as an extension of the deterioration that began much earlier.

Schizophrenia is a relatively common disorder, affecting approximately 1 to 2 percent of the population (Keith, Regier, & Rae, 1991). It is found equally in men and women. Onset usually occurs during adolescence or early adulthood, but somewhat later for women than for men. The prognosis is mixed.

When Emil Kraepelin first defined the disorder (originally known as *dementia praecox*), he emphasized its chronic deteriorating course. Many patients do, in fact, show a gradual decline in social and occupational functioning and continue to exhibit psychotic symptoms either continuously or intermittently throughout their lives. However, a substantial number of patients seem to recover without signs of residual impairment. Much of the most informative data pertaining to prognosis have come from the World Health Organization's International Pilot Study of Schizophrenia (Leff, Sartorius, Jablensky, Korten, & Ernberg, 1992). Compared to people with other mental disorders, such as mood disorders, schizophrenics tended to have a worse outcome five years after being hospitalized. There was substantial overlap between the groups, however, and considerable variability within the schizophrenic patients. The results of this study and several others indicate that roughly 33 percent of schizophrenic patients recover, 33 percent continue to experience some kind of impairment, and the remaining patients follow the severe, chronic pattern initially described by Kraepelin (Carpenter & Strauss, 1991).

Although people with schizophrenia share some important common characteristics, they are also an extremely heterogeneous group. This feature was emphasized in the title of Eugen Bleuler's classic monograph, *Dementia Praecox or the Group of Schizophrenias* (1911/1950). Kraepelin and Bleuler both outlined subtypes of schizophrenia, including catatonic, paranoid, hebephrenic, and simple types. Each of these subtypes was defined in terms of a few characteristic symptoms. *Catatonic* patients were identified by their bizarre motor movements and the unusual postures they would assume. Their motor behavior might include either a rigid posture with total immobility or undirected, maniclike excitement. *Paranoid* patients were those expressed delusions of persecution and reference. The primary features of *hebephrenia* were taken to be inappropriate affect and florid symptomatology (e.g., bizarre delusions and hallucinations). *Simple* schizophrenia was a category originally proposed by Bleuler to describe patients without the more obvious symptoms such as hallucinations and delusions. The latter category has been eliminated from the schizophrenic disorders in *DSM-IV* and is now listed as Schizoid Personality Disorder. Bill would clearly be included in the paranoid subcategory of schizophrenic disorders.

Symptomatically defined subgroups possess a certain intuitive appeal, but they have not proved to be particularly useful in other respects (Gottesman, 1991). One major problem has been a lack of reliability in assigning patients to subcategories. Because of problems in identifying the general category of schizophrenia, it is not surprising that the subtypes present further difficulties. Inconsistency is another drawback; patients who exhibit a particular set of prominent symptoms at one point in time may exhibit another set of features during a later episode. The symptomatically defined subgroups have also not been shown to possess either etiological or predictive validity. For example, a specific treatment that is more or less effective with catatonic patients in comparison with hebephrenics has not been found.

Another system for subdividing schizophrenic patients is based on the distinction between positive and negative symptoms (e.g., Andreasen, Flaum, Swayze, Tyrell, & Arndt, 1990; Pogue-Geile & Zubin, 1988). This distinction can be traced to Hughlings-Jackson's (1931) classification of neurological disorders, in which negative symptoms are viewed as the manifestation of *loss* of functions due to structural brain damage. Positive symptoms, on the other hand, represent the *release* of functions that were formerly inhibited by higher cortical areas that are now dysfunctional. In the case of schizophrenia, positive symptoms include hallucinations, delusions, and disorganized speech. Negative symptoms include blunted or restricted affect, social withdrawal, and poverty of speech. The distinction between positive and negative syndromes has generated a considerable amount of interest and research.

Etiology

Various psychological and environmental events have been suggested as playing an important role in the development of schizophrenia.[1] Psychoanalytic theory provided the first psychological model of psychotic symptoms. Bill's concern about homosexuality is particularly interesting in light of Freud's view of paranoid ideas. Freud (1909/1925) argued that paranoid beliefs were the product of the ego's attempt to control anxiety associated with unconscious homosexual desires. According to this model, homosexual desires are unacceptable to the ego, which employs the defense mechanism of reaction formation and projection to convert the impulse to a more acceptable form. The logic is as follows: The notion that "I, a man, love him, another man" is converted, through reaction formation, to "I hate him." Since this is also an unacceptable idea, it is converted to "He hates me." This notion may be a source of concern, but it is supposedly less anxiety provoking than the original homosexual impulse. Concerns about homosexuality and paranoid ideas do seem to be associated in many cases of paranoid schizophrenia, but many paranoid clients are *aware* of their homosexual impulses. Bill realized that he was attracted to other men and had, in fact, engaged in sexual relations with other men. Psychoanalytic theory argues that the paranoid ideas are the result of complex efforts to avoid the conscious realization of these impulses, but Bill was openly struggling with the issue of sexual orientation. If the homosexual desires have already reached the level of conscious awareness, there should be no further need for the defense mechanisms of reaction formation and projection.

---

[1] These clearly operate in interaction with biological variables, which are reviewed in Chapter 10.

Several offshoots of psychoanalytic theory have focused on the role of the family in producing schizophrenia. Following the lead of Freud and based on their own clinical experience, many therapists argued that schizophrenics had been adversely affected during early childhood by their relationships with their mothers. These mothers were reportedly cold, overprotective, and domineering. As a result, the child's ego was not adequately developed. Subsequent stressful experiences encountered during adolescence and early adulthood were then likely to precipitate severe regression to the primitive state of primary process thinking and narcissism, which was seen as characteristic of schizophrenic behavior (Fenichel, 1945). Some empirical studies examined this view of schizophrenics' families, but serious methodological problems plagued this area of research (Fontana, 1966; Mishler & Waxler, 1968). Perhaps the most difficult issue concerns the direction of influence between parents and children. Many studies have shown that the parents of schizophrenics behave differently than do the parents of nonschizophrenics, particularly in the presence of their disturbed offspring. But can we conclude that the parents' unusual behavior *caused* the children to become schizophrenic? It is just as reasonable to suggest that the parents' behavior represents a *response* to their children's problems.

Whereas early research studies concerning the role of the family in schizophrenia were concerned with the *causes* of the disorder, more recent work has stressed the family's influence on the *course* of the disorder. Brown and his colleagues in England studied schizophrenic patients and their families from the point at which the patient was discharged from the hospital (Brown, Birley, & Wing, 1972; Vaughn & Leff, 1976). The families were separated into two groups based on the degree of expressed emotion (EE) prior to the patient's release. High EE families were those in which at least one family member was extremely critical of the patient and his or her behavior. None of the members of low EE homes expressed hostility toward the patient. The patients were followed for nine months after discharge, with the dependent variable being the percentage of patients who returned to the hospital for further treatment. Relapse rates were much higher for patients who returned to high EE homes. In the first nine months, 51 percent of the patients from high EE homes relapsed and only 13 percent of the patients in low EE homes returned to the hospital. The same pattern of results was also found in a follow-up study of patients in California (Vaughn, Snyder, Jones, Freeman, & Falloon, 1984).

Several additional studies have confirmed the robust predictive relation between expressed emotion and relapse rates, and they have also shown that this effect is not unique to schizophrenia. Depressed patients, for example, are also more likely to relapse if they are living with high EE family members (Hooley, Orley, & Teasdale, 1986). It has been shown that the critical attitudes of family members, which are reflected in high EE ratings, are often expressed during direct interactions with their depressed and schizophrenic family members. High EE relatives are more likely to direct negative verbal and nonverbal messages to the patients, and in some cases this aversive pattern may escalate rapidly (Hahlweg et al., 1989; Hooley, 1986). Many questions remain to be answered about this phenomenon, which is clearly an important factor in the course of these disorders. For example, it is not clear why some relatives develop critical attitudes in the first place, and the process that explains the association between relatives' attitudes and patients' adjustment has not been defined (Kuipers, 1992; Lefley, 1992). These issues are currently the topic of several important research projects (Mueser, Bellack, Wade, Sayers, Tierney, & Haas, 1993).

The data regarding expressed emotion are consistent with Bill's experience. Bill remembered that when he and his mother were living together, they made each other anxious. His descriptions of her behavior indicate that her emotional involvement was excessive, given that he was an adult and capable of greater independence; she was always worried about his job, or his friends, or what he was doing with his time. Her constant intrusions and coaxing finally led him to seek refuge with his sister's family. The supportive environment provided by Colleen and her family and their willingness to tolerate many of Bill's idiosyncrasies were undoubtedly helpful in allowing Bill to remain outside of a hospital during his psychotic episode.

One final area of investigation is relevant to Bill's case. A considerable body of evidence indicates that schizophrenia and social class are inversely related; a disproportionately large percentage of schizophrenics fall into the lowest social class on the basis of occupational and income ratings (Cohen, 1993). There are two competing explanations for this phenomenon. Some investigators have taken these data to indicate that the increased stresses associated with life in low-income homes are causally related to the development of schizophrenia. This is known as the social causation hypothesis. An equally reasonable explanation holds that schizophrenics drift into the lowest social classes as a result of the problems associated with the onset of the disorder. In other words, schizophrenia may lead to educational failure and unemployment, not the other way around. Both explanations have received some empirical support (e.g., Castle, Scott, Wessely, & Murray, 1993; Dohrenwend et al., 1992). Bill was clearly an example of the drift hypothesis. He was raised in a middle-income family and had been expected to go on to college in preparation for a professional career. His indecision at the end of high school led him to delay college enrollment. After his job at the bank, Bill moved to an unskilled position as a elevator operator and eventually became unemployed. His occupational decline was related to his growing preoccupation with unusual ideas and increased interference with his cognitive functions.

Treatment

Snyder (1974) has referred to the discovery of antipsychotic medication as "a story of serendipity." It is perhaps the most important advance that has been made in our knowledge of schizophrenia. In the late 1940s, Henri Laborit, a French surgeon, was experimenting with the use of an antihistamine, promethazine, to prevent surgical shock. Although the drug did not achieve the desired effect, Laborit noted that it was able to induce a state of disinterest without putting the patient to sleep. For this reason he suggested that this and similar drugs might be useful in psychiatry. Following his advice, Delay and Deniker administered chlorpromazine to various psychiatric patients and quickly noted a dramatic response among schizophrenics (see Deniker, 1970). Their success was confirmed by other clinicians. In a matter of months chlorpromazine was being used at hospitals throughout Europe and the United States.

There are several important variables to consider in selecting a treatment for acute schizophrenic disturbance. Antipsychotic drugs have become the principal form of intervention since their introduction in the 1950s. A large number of carefully controlled studies have demonstrated that these drugs have a beneficial effect for many acute schizophrenics (Marder, Ames, Wirshing, & Van Putten, 1993). There are other patients, however, who do not respond to antipsychotic medication. Unfortunately, investigators have thus far been unable to identify patient characteristics that will reliably predict response to antipsychotic drugs. Some investigators have reported that patients with positive symptoms (hallucinations, delusions, disorganized speech) are more likely than those with negative symptoms to benefit from antipsychotic drugs (e.g., Angrist, Rotrosen, & Gershon, 1980). In fact, there is some evidence that antipsychotic drugs may contribute to negative symptoms over time (see Schooler & Levine, 1983).

Although most traditional forms of psychotherapy are not useful with schizophrenic patients (e.g., Hogarty et al., 1974; May et al., 1976), there are some ways in which psychosocial programs can have beneficial effects. Perhaps most important is the use of family-based programs in conjunction with maintenance medication. Several recent studies have evaluated treatment programs designed to help patients with families that are rated high in expressed emotion (Bellack & Mueser, 1993). In addition to antipsychotic medication, treatment typically includes two principal components. First, the therapist provides family members with information about schizophrenia, on the assumption that some hostility and criticism result from failure to understand the nature of the patient's problems. Second, the therapist focuses on enhancing the family's ability to cope with stressful experiences by working on problem-solving and communication skills. Initial results with this type of family intervention have been very encouraging.

In Bill's case, his sister's family would not have been considered high in expressed emotion. Direct intervention focused on family patterns of communication was therefore unnecessary. The therapist did, however, spend time talking with Colleen and Roger about Bill's situation in an effort to help them cope with his idiosyncratic behavior. Bill's therapist also directed his attention to the development of social skills. These efforts met with mixed success. The research literature suggests that social skills programs are often useful with schizophrenics who are being treated on an outpatient basis (Liberman, DeRisi, & Mueser, 1989).

There is also some reason to be cautious about the use of direct, active psychological approaches to the treatment of patients who are socially withdrawn and exhibiting other negative symptoms. Several investigators have reported that directive programs that successfully increase the level of social interaction among chronic schizophrenic patients may also have adverse effects on other areas of the patient's adjustment (e.g., Schooler & Spohn, 1982). It may be that patients who are not on medication cannot cope with the increase in stress that is probably associated with an active, directive form of social intervention. This phenomenon may have been evident in Bill's case. He was not receiving medication until after the therapist became aware of his extensive delusional system. His response to the behavioral program seemed to be more positive after the introduction of antipsychotic medication. In fact, prior to that point, the role playing that was attempted during sessions and the homework assignments during the week actually seemed to increase his level of anxiety.

10 SCHIZOPHRENIA: UNDIFFERENTIATED TYPE

Margaret Willoughby arrived at the psychiatric hospital with her husband, Ray. She was 39 years old and the mother of a 7-year-old son, Michael, and a 4-year-old daughter, Susan. Margaret had a long history of psychological disturbance and had been hospitalized many times—including three occasions in the eight years that she and Ray had been married. For the past week, Margaret had refused to let Michael go to school, insisting that he and Susan stay at home with her and read aloud from the Bible. The children were quite upset by this unusual behavior, and Michael's teacher was beginning to question the excuses that Ray had been making for his son's absence from school. Ray had always tried to tolerate Margaret's idiosyncratic behavior. He had grown accustomed to her religious preoccupations, her occasionally odd speech and mannerisms, and her habit of locking herself alone in her room for hours, and sometimes days, at a time. But her interference with the children's behavior and Michael's education had become too much for him to handle. After a long and heated argument, in which Ray threatened to call the police if she did not cooperate, Margaret reluctantly agreed to accompany him to the hospital.

An involuntary admission procedure was necessary because Margaret did not believe that she needed psychiatric care. She told the psychiatrist that her problem was strictly between her and God. Margaret believed that because she had never been in love with Ray, she had committed a mortal sin by marrying him and bringing children into the world. Now, as punishment, God had made her and her children immortal, so that they would have to suffer in their unhappy home life forever. She had come to this realization one evening while she was washing the dishes. Looking down into the sink, she saw a fork lying across a knife in the shape of a cross; suddenly she knew that she had become immortal. There were two other pieces of evidence that Margaret used to support her belief. One was that a local television station had recently begun to rerun old episodes of *The Honeymooners,* a 1950s situation comedy in which the main characters, Ralph and Alice Cramden, often argue and shout at each other. Margaret interpreted the reappearance of this series as a sign from God indicating that her own marital conflict would go on forever, just as the Cramdens' fights were replayed time after time. The other clue to Margaret's and the children's immortality was her contention that the pupils of their eyes were now fixed in size and would neither dilate nor constrict. This was, of course, not the case, but Margaret insisted that it was true. She explained that ever since she had recognized the punishment that had been imposed, she and the children had been reading from the Book of Revelations in the Bible and praying that God would have mercy on them.

Throughout this interview, Margaret's face remained blank and expressionless. She spoke in a dull monotone that was punctuated by occasional, involuntary protrusions of her tongue and lip-smacking movements. Her posture was stiff, and her hands trembled slightly as she spoke. Her speech was, for the most part, relevant and coherent, but her answers were sometimes loosely related to the question that had been asked; she occasionally slipped from one topic to another without reason or warning. For example:

Psychiatrist: When you realized that you were immortal, were you afraid?
Margaret: No. You see, the sun to me is the sun to people, but it's God to me. When I look up to the sun, it's God, not the sun anymore. See what I mean? God took over my life because I didn't deserve to live it myself. I've got to get out of here so that I can be closer to Him.

At a later point in the interview, the psychiatrist asked:

Psychiatrist: In the past month, have you heard any voices that weren't really there?
Margaret: I don't think so. No, I haven't. . . . (Pause.) My husband sometimes sings to himself when he's in the shower, but that's not what you wanted to know. The kids also make a lot of noise in the bathroom. . . . (Pause.) I used to be jealous of women who wore bikinis.

Based on these and other signs of disorganized speech, her blunted affect, and her delusional belief about immortality in the absence of symptoms of mood disorder or organic impairment, the psychiatrist reached a diagnosis of schizophrenia.

Margaret had been taking antipsychotic medication (primarily phenothiazines such as Mellaril, Thorazine, and Stelazine) since her first psychotic episode at the age of 16. These drugs had a positive effect on several of her more dramatic symptoms, such as disorganized speech and auditory hallucinations (which she had experienced in the past), but they also made her feel lethargic and had gradually led to the development of the movement disorder that was now evident in her peculiar facial tics and the trembling of her hands. Because of these unpleasant side effects, and perhaps because of her tendency toward disorganization and erratic behavior, Margaret occasionally discontinued taking her medication. These interruptions were usually followed, within a month or two, by the reappearance of florid psychotic symptoms. This was what had happened in the present episode. After she was admitted to the hospital, Margaret was given an intramuscular injection of fluphenazine (Prolixin), a long-acting antipsychotic drug. Prolixin injections can be given once every two to four weeks and are particularly useful with patients such as Margaret, who are unreliable in taking oral doses.

Within two weeks she had stopped talking about her delusional ideas. Signs of disorganized speech were no longer present. Considering this general improvement in her condition, the physician in charge of her care arranged for her discharge from the hospital, despite the persistence of several residual problems. Her affect was still blunted, and she continued to remain aloof from the other patients. There was also little change in the neurological symptoms, such as her involuntary facial movements and the shaking of her hands and feet.

After her return home, Margaret continued to visit the hospital's outpatient clinic on a biweekly basis to receive further medication. Although she was no longer blatantly psychotic, she continued to exhibit serious occupational and social role impairment. Most of her time was spent aimlessly, watching television or sitting alone in her room. Ray was a full-time postal worker and also took care of almost all of the household and parental responsibilities. Ray seemed to assume these added responsibilities without resentment; he accepted the fact that Margaret had a mental disorder and was therefore less able to perform many tasks that would have otherwise been expected of her. Their marriage had reached a kind of impasse. Recognizing that she would have a difficult time living on her own and caring for the children, Margaret no longer asked for the divorce that she had demanded for several years. Ray no longer expected conventional behavior from Margaret, whom he considered to be "an emotional invalid." He seemed resigned to caring for her and the children as best he could.

SOCIAL HISTORY

Margaret was the youngest of three children. Her family was well off financially; during Margaret's infancy, they lived in an expensive apartment in New York City. Her father was a successful corporate lawyer. He was bright, ambitious, and worked long hours, rising quickly to the top of his firm. Margaret's mother was a talented dancer and actress who was also described by her family and friends as being high-strung, nervous, and somewhat eccentric. She worked intermittently in off-Broadway theater productions, but she was not particularly well known. She had been in long-term psychoanalysis with a private psychiatrist for many years and had been hospitalized for a brief period of time shortly after Margaret's birth. Although the details of her problems were not available, her hospital diagnosis had been emotionally unstable personality.[1]

Neither of Margaret's parents had much time for the children, who were sent to boarding schools as soon as they reached the third grade. Records obtained from Margaret's elementary school indicated that she was unusually passive and socially withdrawn. She did not enjoy the company of other children, preferring instead to spend her time in isolated play and wandering alone around the wooded campus. From an academic standpoint, her early performance was adequate, but not exceptional.

The only time that Margaret spent with her family was during holidays. They gathered at the family's summer home at the lake for Thanksgiving, Christmas, and the Fourth of July. For the most part, these were uneventful visits. They were pleasant, although not particularly joyful, occasions, marred only by her mother's usual irritability and intermittent outbursts of anger, which were usually directed at Margaret's father. Margaret did look forward to seeing her two older brothers, Jonathan and Peter, who attended an academy several hours' drive from Margaret's school. She was particularly fond of Jonathan, who was already a talented pianist and spent long hours performing for her during these visits. He was the only person with whom she talked openly and with whom she felt comfortable.

Margaret's academic performance declined steadily between the fifth and ninth grades, as did her scores on standardized achievement tests. Her teachers attributed the problem to her obvious lack of interest in her studies. Their comments on her report cards also frequently expressed concern about her introverted manner. In the seventh grade, when she was 12 years old, Margaret's teacher referred her to the school psychologist because he was worried about her lack of friends and the great amount of time that she seemed to

---

[1]This was a category included in *DSM-I* that no longer appears in *DSM-IV*. It applied roughly to individuals who would now be described as either Histrionic Personality Disorder or Borderline Personality Disorder.

spend daydreaming. Her scores on the verbal and performance scales of the Wechsler Intelligence Scale for Children (WISC) were both within normal limits (99 and 107, respectively). The psychologist interpreted her drawings on a projective test as indicating poorly developed ego boundaries and considerable hostility toward her mother. He encouraged her to attend individual counseling sessions with him, which she did for the next several weeks. Unfortunately, Margaret was extremely uncommunicative during these visits; despite the therapist's persistent efforts to establish rapport with her, she soon stopped coming for her appointments.

When Margaret was old enough to attend high school, her parents arranged for her to enroll in an exclusive New England prep school. She was accepted in spite of her undistinguished academic record because her father made substantial contributions to the school's endowment. Her well-established pattern of social isolation persisted, as did her marginal classroom performance. She also became the object of jokes and teasing by some of her peers. Her somewhat unusual appearance and idiosyncratic mannerisms had been ignored by the other children at her previous schools, but the social life at her prep school was governed by several cliques whose members were often intolerant of outsiders.

Margaret's first episode of psychotic behavior occurred when she was 16 and in her third year at the prep school. She was taking a psychology course from a young male teacher, Mr. Loftin, with whom she became preoccupied. Although she had never shown any interest in boys her own age, she began to demonstrate an unusual fascination with Mr. Loftin. He later reported that he had sometimes noticed her watching him from a distance when he was walking on the campus. He also noted that her direct, unflinching stares in class frequently made him feel uncomfortable. Despite these signs of interest, she never spoke to him directly. Shortly before the end of the spring semester, Mr. Loftin began receiving anonymous notes that he later realized were from Margaret. They were mostly concerned with metaphysical issues such as the nature of the universe and extrasensory perception. At some points, they lapsed into incoherent rambling. Two weeks after the notes began to appear, Margaret went to the school's headmaster to complain about Mr. Loftin. She believed that he was inserting obscene thoughts into her head. At unpredictable intervals throughout the day, Margaret suddenly found herself thinking about performing oral sexual acts with Mr. Loftin. She insisted that these ideas were not her own and were not under her control.

The headmaster referred Margaret to the school psychologist, who met with her to discuss this unusual report. Her initial impression was that Margaret had made a simple error in attributing her own previously inhibited sexual desires to Mr. Loftin. The psychologist spent several hours with Margaret discussing her interest in Mr. Loftin and her own sexual desires. Despite all efforts to reach a rational explanation for Margaret's subjective experience, she continued to insist that she was the unwilling recipient of alien, intrusive ideas. Her mood was becoming increasingly unpredictable during these days, and she was visibly agitated following the school officials' refusal to report Mr. Loftin to the police. Her parents were finally called; they arranged for her to be admitted to a private psychiatric hospital.

TREATMENT AND SUBSEQUENT COURSE

Upon admission to the hospital ward, Margaret was angry and argumentative. She insisted that she did not need help and that she was not mentally ill. Her problem, she insisted, was the simple product of Mr. Loftin's attempt to influence her thoughts. Her appearance was somewhat disheveled, and her posture seemed stiff and awkward. She avoided eye contact with the psychiatrist during the intake interview, directing most of her comments to her father, who had accompanied her to the hospital. She said that she had not experienced auditory hallucinations and denied the use of drugs. Her answers to questions were generally coherent, although they were sometimes vague and tangential. On more than one occasion, she shifted from one topic to another in the middle of a sentence. Based on these indications of disorganized speech and her report of thought insertion, the psychiatrist reached a diagnosis of schizophrenia.

Antipsychotic medication was prescribed. Margaret was encouraged to participate in various social and therapeutic activities that were available at the hospital. In fact, she spent most of her time sitting alone under trees and wandering around the hospital grounds. She cooperated with the ward routine and gradually stopped talking about the thoughts that Mr. Loftin had been inserting in her head. When she was asked about these phenomena, Margaret explained that Mr. Loftin must have lost interest in her after she left the school. Her condition seemed greatly improved after three weeks in the hospital, and she was discharged to return to her parents' apartment.

Margaret spent the following summer with her mother at their vacation home and returned to school in the fall. Mr. Loftin had resigned to accept a position at another school, thus eliminating one major source of stress from her environment. Margaret earned passing grades in all of her subjects during her senior year and seemed somewhat brighter emotionally and more outgoing than she had been in previous years. Some of this improvement might have been related to the development of an interest in English literature, which she pursued with ardent fervor. Another student in her English class, who shared her interest in the poetry of Shelley and who was also something of an outcast, became Margaret's companion and a possible source of social support. They ate meals together, talked about their readings, and occasionally went to movies on weekends. Unfortunately, neither girl took the initiative to maintain contact following their graduation in the spring; they subsequently lost touch with each other.

Margaret enrolled at a large state university the following fall (her grades were not adequate to permit entrance to a more prestigious school). She lived in a single room in a dormitory and continued to spend most of her time by herself. Her studies seemed to be progressing satisfactorily until shortly before the end of the first semester, when she suddenly stopped attending classes and began spending all of her time in her room. Her only ventures outside were to eat occasional meals in the cafeteria. The other women residents became extremely concerned about her bizarre appearance and unusual behavior. She had taken to wearing double layers of clothing, did not bathe, and sometimes muttered incomprehensibly to herself while she stood in line for food. After she was served, she returned to her room with her tray instead of sitting with the other people in the cafeteria. This behavior was brought to the attention of one of the resident counselors, who went to Margaret's room to find out was troubling her. She found Margaret sitting in her bed, surrounded by notebooks, volumes of poetry, rumpled clothes, and dirty dishes from the cafeteria. The counselor tried to ask Margaret how she was feeling or if she could help in any way, but Margaret was largely unresponsive. She had been writing for several days; crumpled sheets of paper were strewn over the top of the desk and about the floor of the room. When she did speak, her answers were accentuated by silly giggling that was inappropriate to the topic at hand. For example, Margaret seemed unable to restrain her laughter as she tried to explain that her classes no longer seemed meaningful. The counselor could easily recognize that Margaret was seriously disturbed and persuaded her to come along to the student health center, where she was admitted to their small inpatient unit on a temporary basis.

Her parents were contacted; within two days she was transferred to the private psychiatric hospital where she had been treated two years previously. The admitting psychiatrist noted the presence of complete auditory hallucinations and delusional thinking as well as disorganized speech. For the past three weeks, she had been hearing voices discussing her sexual interests. Sometimes the voices said that she was pregnant. She believed that these voices and her other thoughts were being monitored by the campus police. The following conversation is an excerpt from her intake interview:

Psychiatrist: Do you ever hear voices saying things about you?

Margaret: I had a dream about the television one night at school. On the news, they said John Lennon was dead. Sometimes I dream about television. I'm not a fairy, am I?

Psychiatrist: No.

Margaret: Fairies don't go to heaven, do they?

Psychiatrist: What do you mean by a fairy?

Margaret: I had a dream once that there was a small red door in our kitchen, and I walked through the door with my brother, and I said to my brother, "I'm going to the bathroom." I was going to run away from the house . . . and there was a dog barking outside, a police dog. So I suppose I was arrested.

Psychiatrist: Were you?

Margaret: Yes. They did arrest me, didn't they?

Psychiatrist: I don't know. What do you remember about it?

Margaret: I don't know. . . . (laughs) . . . My brother says he's under arrest for my dinner.

Psychiatrist: For your dinner? What does that mean? It sounds kind of silly.

Margaret: Yeah . . . I almost got mad. I'm not jealous of my brother, you know. He's very happy. I heard two voices talking one night. It sounded like two saints in my bedroom saying, "She's going to have the baby tonight." I think my counselor delivered a baby of mine. Do you think I caused John Lennon's death by committing adultery?

As in her previous episode, Margaret's speech was often difficult to follow. She answered questions tangentially and seemed to lose track of the point within even brief comments. The notes that the counselor had observed in her room and that her family later read were similarly disjointed and incomprehensible.

This time Margaret was hospitalized for 15 months. The treatment program involved the use of antipsychotic medication (Mellaril) and participation in the social milieu of her ward. Group psychotherapy sessions were held daily, but Margaret refused to participate. Despite the continued use of medication, Margaret's condition did not improve significantly during the first six months of her hospitalization. She continued to dress in an unusual fashion, wearing two and sometimes three dresses at a time. Although she was reluctant to discuss the voices that she had described hearing on admission, she often seemed to be responding to hallucinations. She would sit for hours staring out the window and mumbling to herself in a low voice. On occasion, she would suddenly stop whatever she was doing and turn to look at an empty hallway or room, as though someone had spoken to her when, in fact, no one was there. Her giggling diminished gradually, and her affect eventually became flat and blunted. When she did speak to staff members or other patients, her comments were sometimes difficult to follow. She continued to complain that her thoughts were being monitored by the police. This surveillance caused her considerable distress; she argued that it continually interfered with her ability to organize and express her own thoughts.

In the seventh month of her hospitalization, Margaret began to make noticeable improvements. The most obvious change occurred in her general physical appearance. She began dressing appropriately, bathed regularly without prompting from the staff, and combed her hair. Her facial expression seemed less dull and apathetic. She became more active physically. Although she continued to isolate herself, she did respond coherently to the comments of staff members and other patients.

Shortly after these changes began to develop, Margaret received word from her brother Jonathan that their father had told their mother that he wanted a divorce. The news had a dramatic effect on Margaret's behavior. She became agitated and restless, refused food, and, once again, began talking openly about people interfering with her thoughts. The day after she talked to her brother, she cornered one of the other female patients in the hospital's recreation room and threatened to hit her with a chair. Margaret claimed that she had heard the other woman talking about her and laughing at the way she dressed. The other woman was 67 years old, socially withdrawn, and essentially mute. The hapless, bewildered victim of this attack was rescued by two attendants, who restrained Margaret and took her to her room, where she was secluded for a few hours. Margaret's behavior stabilized within several days. She continued to make modest improvements in her adjustment and did not engage in any more violent outbursts. In her ninth month in the hospital, she entered an occupational training program in medical technology. She attended classes during the day and returned to the hospital ward at night. She also began to leave the hospital for occasional weekends, which she spent with Jonathan at his apartment in New York. At the end of the six-month training program, her level of adjustment was stable and much improved, so she was discharged from the hospital.

After her discharge, Margaret continued to take antipsychotic medication on a maintenance basis. Her prescription was renewed at weekly 20-minute visits that she made to the office of her private psychiatrist, who also checked for the development of side effects and asked a few questions about her adjustment. She no longer reported hallucinations or delusions; her speech was coherent and relevant, although somewhat lacking in spontaneity. The only obvious sign of residual impairment was a marked constriction of Margaret's emotional responses. She continued to seem apathetic and lifeless and reported that she had never been able to experience real pleasure or excitement.

Her father had remarried shortly after the divorce and moved to California. Her mother was still living in New York, but Margaret decided not to see her because their visits always seemed to lead to arguments and unpleasant scenes. Margaret stayed with Jonathan until she found a job as a medical technician at a nearby hospital. She then moved to a small studio apartment, where she lived alone and seemed to manage quite well, except that she found her work in the hospital laboratory to be stressful. Her responsibilities were, in fact, simple and routine, but Margaret complained that the medication made her drowsy and interfered with her ability to concentrate. She therefore discontinued the antipsychotic medication, against the advice of her psychiatrist and her brother. Shortly after doing so, she reported feeling less fatigued, but her ability to concentrate did not improve. Furthermore, several weeks after she stopped taking medication, Margaret started hearing the voices again. This time they sounded like the whispers of other people in the laboratory, talking about her appearance and commenting on her inadequate performance. One particularly frequent and persistent voice, which sounded to Margaret like that of an older woman, kept mumbling, "We don't want crazies like her working with us. Listen to what she's thinking. She's as nutty as they come. Stay away from her!" The stress and confusion quickly overwhelmed Margaret, and she quit her job three months after it began.

Jonathan helped her through the difficult months that followed. He eventually persuaded her to visit a private psychiatrist who once again prescribed antipsychotic drugs. After her return to medication, Margaret's adjustment restabilized. She continued to live by herself and seldom ventured far from her apartment. Jonathan, who was now an accomplished concert pianist, visited her regularly and tried to encourage her to become more active and continue taking her medication. She did, in fact, begin doing some volunteer work for the Red Cross at a clinic in her neighborhood. This pattern of marginal social and occupational adjustment continued for several months.

Margaret's third hospitalization occurred at the age of 22. Although she had continued to take the medication that was prescribed for her, her behavior had become more disorganized over a period of several weeks. She was once again experiencing auditory hallucinations, dressing strangely, and spending long hours staring out her apartment window, mumbling to herself. Jonathan called her psychiatrist; together they persuaded her to admit herself voluntarily to a state psychiatric hospital. She was treated and discharged after three months.

This pattern of brief hospitalizations separated by periods of marginal adjustment in the community repeated itself several times over the next few years. Margaret lost touch with everyone in her family except Jonathan, who continued to visit her regularly, whether she was in the hospital or living in her apartment. He also provided her with considerable financial support. She worked at various jobs as a hospital aide, a waitress, and a retail clerk, but she never held a position longer than one year.

Margaret met Ray when she was 30 years old. He was a 38-year-old bachelor. She was working as a waitress at the restaurant where he ate most of his meals. Ray was, in some ways, similar to Margaret. He was quiet, shy, and without many friends. They slowly became acquainted and eventually began meeting when Margaret was not working. They went for walks and saw movies together. Ray also took her to several concerts in which Jonathan was playing. Margaret was a passive participant throughout this courtship period. Her feelings about Ray were ambivalent. She sometimes enjoyed the change from her usual lonely routine, and she believed that Ray was a nice person, but she did not find him physically attractive and was not in love with him. His intrusion into her carefully developed, isolated existence was also anxiety provoking because she now felt some pressure to behave more appropriately.

Ray was persistent, despite Margaret's reluctance, and they gradually came to spend more and more time together. He was aware of her history of adjustment problems and managed to convince himself that he would be able to help her through his devotion and support. Jonathan liked Ray and also believed that this relationship would be beneficial for Margaret. Several months after they met, Ray suggested to Margaret that they should get married. After many weeks of gentle persuasion and persistent coaxing from both Ray and Jonathan, she agreed. Her major motivation was the recognition that her marriage would relieve much of the burden that her problems had placed on Jonathan over the years.

Contrary to Ray's initial expectations, their marriage did not have an obviously positive effect on Margaret's adjustment. If anything, she went downhill. She became pregnant shortly after they were married. The pregnancy was a difficult one; the usual nausea and fatigue were compounded by Margaret's poor physical condition and her inability to relax. Although she continued to visit a psychiatrist regularly and take her antipsychotic medication, she suffered a symptomatic relapse and had to be admitted to the hospital again. Michael was actually born in an obstetric wing of the psychiatric hospital. The baby was cared for by Ray's sister, who had several children of her own, until Margaret was discharged from the hospital, two months after the birth.

Margaret regretted her decision to get married from the beginning. When Michael was one year old, she began asking Ray for a divorce. He refused, saying that she would not be able to care for herself or the baby without him. She confessed to her brother and her therapist that she did not love Ray and that she never had. Nevertheless, Ray remained committed to the relationship, and Margaret did not press the issue further.

Three years after their marriage, when Margaret was 34, she developed a sudden fanatic devotion to religion. Her family had never been religious, and Margaret had never been a member of a formal church. She had, however, been interested in religious issues, particularly during her last year in high school and her brief college career when she was absorbed in romantic literature. Her conversion occurred after she was visited by two members of an evangelical Christian sect noted for its fundamental beliefs. They were canvassing her neighborhood door to door. Margaret let them into the apartment and listened as they spoke about the imminence of Christ's second coming. They left considerable literature with her, which she later read. She also began watching religious programs on a cable television channel. Within two or three days, she became completely preoccupied with her newly developed faith and began talking constantly to Ray about the wonders of eternal salvation. From the outset this change in Margaret was distressing to Ray, who preferred the quiet, withdrawn wife to whom he had grown accustomed. He refused to become an active participant in her religious activities; as a result, they grew even further apart.

Perhaps the most distressing aspect of Margaret's religious conversion was the fact that other members of her church group, with whom she began meeting regularly, convinced her that she should discontinue her medication. They argued that God would protect her from the devil, who had, in their view, been responsible for the voices that she had heard intermittently over the past 15 years. Margaret followed their advice; within several weeks she experienced another relapse. This time she was hospitalized for only 12 days. Her medication was resumed and she was soon discharged to Ray's care.

Margaret stopped going to church meetings after the psychotic episode. She did agree to continue taking medication, but she remained a devout believer in the teachings of her religious group. She and Ray continued living together despite Margaret's increased emotional estrangement from their relationship, and Susan was born the following year. It was after Susan's birth that Margaret once again began to worry about her inability to love Ray. She brooded about the sinfulness of their relationship and continually expressed the belief that she was going to be punished by God.

DISCUSSION

At various points, Margaret exhibited several of the classic symptoms of schizophrenia; she clearly fit the *DSM-IV* criteria for that disorder (these criteria are listed in Chapter 9). Disorganized speech and flat or inappropriate affect were among her most persistent problems. Judgments regarding disorganized speech are based on the listener's perception that the patient's speech is difficult to follow. Margaret's comments were often disjointed and elusive in meaning, as illustrated by the examples provided earlier. Her affective responses were also disturbed. During her earliest episodes, she was frequently observed giggling to herself for no apparent reason. Between periods of acute psychosis, particularly as she grew older, her emotional responses seemed flattened or totally absent. Her face was usually expressionless, even when she discussed topics that would provoke happiness, fear, or depression in other people. Both of these symptom categories — associative and affective disturbances — were among the cardinal features outlined by Bleuler (1911/ 1950) when he originally described schizophrenia.

Margaret also experienced some of the symptoms that Schneider (1959) listed as being of first-rank importance in the diagnosis of schizophrenia. Schneider's first-rank symptoms include a variety of specific forms of hallucinations and several types of disturbed thinking. These symptoms are given special emphasis in *DSM-IV* (p. 288). The manual indicates that the person needs to exhibit only one (rather than two) of the "active phase symptoms" if he or she also exhibits particular types of delusions and hallucinations (see the diagnostic criteria in Chapter 9). Examples are auditory hallucinations in which either a voice keeps up a running commentary on the person's behavior or thoughts in which two or more voices converse with each other. Margaret experienced the latter phenomenon. Her complaint about her high-school psychology teacher's interference with her thoughts was an example of a first-rank symptom known as "thought insertion"—the belief that alien thoughts are being projected into one's mind against one's will. The statement that she and her children had become immortal is an example of the first-rank symptom that Schneider called *delusional perception.* Delusional perception is defined as the attachment of abnormal, personal significance to a common and otherwise harmless perceptual experience.

Schneider's first-rank symptoms are useful diagnostically because they have been specifically defined and can therefore be identified reliably. They are also clearly distinct from more common experiences that are not indicative of schizophrenia. For example, most people have, at one time or another, heard their name being called when in actuality it was not. Minor perceptual anomalies of this sort are not psychotic in nature and do not indicate a need for treatment. Although Schneider's diagnostic system has received considerable attention in recent years, it should also be noted that not all schizophrenic patients have first-rank symptoms, and first-rank symptoms are not unique to schizophrenic patients. Furthermore, those schizophrenic patients who exhibit first-rank symptoms are generally indistinguishable from those who do not in terms of long-term outcome (Fenton, Mosher, & Matthews, 1981).

Margaret's subtype diagnosis was "undifferentiated" because she did not meet the specific criteria for the other types listed in *DSM-IV.* Her delusions were not predominantly persecutory or grandiose, so she would not fit in the paranoid type, and none of the typical features of the catatonic type (motor rigidity, posturing, excitement, and stupor) were present. In order to meet the criteria of disorganized type, the person must exhibit all of the following symptoms: (1) disorganized speech, (2) disorganized behavior, and (3) flat or inappropriate affect. In addition, the person must not meet the criteria for catatonic type. The manual also indicates that if delusions or hallucinations are present, "they are fragmentary and not organized into a coherent theme." Margaret did exhibit occasional speech disturbances (incoherence), her affect was often blunted and her behavior was sometimes disorganized. Nevertheless, because she also expressed a systematic delusion regarding immortality, her diagnosis was schizophrenic disorder, undifferentiated type.

The authors of *DSM-IV* have demonstrated a renewed interest in negative symptoms of schizophrenia, or the "defect state." Some clinicians have suggested that the positive and negative syndromes represent two distinct forms of schizophrenia. Margaret's case illustrates one problem with this notion; many patients show positive and negative symptoms simultaneously (e.g., Rosen et al., 1984). Even during the earliest phase of her disorder, Margaret's social isolation and peculiar affective responses became worse at the same time that she exhibited positive symptoms, such as auditory hallucinations and delusional beliefs.

Negative symptoms may not vary inversely with positive symptoms, but they do seem to be characteristic of a subgroup of patients with poor premorbid adjustment and relatively persistent deficits in social adjustment. Pogue-Geile and Harrow (1984) found that negative symptoms were typically preceded by poor social and educational functioning in a group of young hospitalized schizophrenics. Approximately 30 percent of these patients continued to show reduced amounts of speech, blunted affect, and psychomotor retardation when they were reevaluated 18 months after being released from the hospital. Schizophrenics were much more likely than depressed patients to continue to exhibit negative symptoms of this sort. Between episodes of acute psychosis, Margaret's problems were largely in the area of negative symptoms, including social isolation, impaired role functioning, and blunted affect. These problems were chronic and showed no sign of significant improvement over the years following her first episode. Difficulties of this sort are obviously central for some patients.

The development of Margaret's problems followed a common course. Before the onset of overt psychotic symptoms, there was clear evidence of a decline in intellectual performance, and her behavior was markedly passive and introverted. Both of these phenomena have been observed in research studies employing a follow-back methodology in which the investigator starts with adult schizophrenics and then locates archival data pertaining to their behavior during childhood (prior to onset of symptoms). In 1984, Aylward, Walker, and Bettes conducted a meta-analysis of research on the IQ of schizophrenics. They found that schizophrenia is associated with intellectual deficits both prior to and after onset of the disorder. Similar procedures have been used to study the premorbid social behavior of schizophrenics. Watt and his colleagues have analyzed information obtained from teachers' comments that were recorded in the children's school records and found that the premorbid behavior of schizophrenic males may be different from that of schizophrenic females. Watt's preschizophrenic boys were described as disagreeable and emotionally unstable more often than control subjects; preschizophrenic girls were more likely to be described as being introverted and passive (Watt, 1978; Lubensky, 1976). This general characterization fits Margaret's childhood behavior well.

Etiology

There is no longer any question about the fact that genetic factors are involved in the transmission of schizophrenia (Gottesman, 1991). The most persuasive data supporting this conclusion come from twin studies and investigations following various adoption methods. Twin studies depend on the following reasoning: Monozygotic (MZ) twins develop from a single zygote, which separates during an early stage of growth and forms two distinct but genetically identical embryos. In the case of dizygotic (DZ) twins, two separate eggs are fertilized by two sperm cells, and both develop simultaneously. Thus DZ twins share only, on average, 50 percent of their genes, the same as siblings who do not share the same prenatal period. Based on the assumption that both forms of twins share similar environments, MZ twins should manifest a higher concordance rate (i.e, more often resemble each other) for traits that are genetically determined. This is, in fact, the pattern that has now been reported for schizophrenia, over a large number of studies (Gottesman, McGuffin, & Farmer, 1987). One of the most careful and informative twin studies was reported by Fischer (1973). She found concordance rates of 0.48 in MZ twins and 0.20 in DZ twins.[2] This substantial difference between MZ and DZ concordance indicates the influence of genetic factors. On the other hand, the absence of 100 percent concordance among the MZ twins also indicates that genetic factors do not account for all of the variance. The development of the disorder must therefore depend on an interaction between a genetically determined predisposition and various environmental events.[3] This general view is known as a *diathesis-stress* model and is the most widely accepted notion regarding the etiology of schizophrenia.

The earliest twin studies were subject to a number of criticisms (Jackson, 1960). Among the most persuasive was the argument that twin studies do not adequately control the influence of environmental events; if MZ twins are more similar than DZ twins from a physical standpoint, their parents may be more likely to treat them in the same way. Therefore, their environments may, in fact, be more similar than those of DZ twins, and the higher concordance rates observed among MZ twins may reflect the influence of environmental variables and not genetic factors. Adoption studies were initiated in an attempt to rule out more completely the influence of environmental factors. The first such study was reported by Heston (1966), who began with a sample of children born to schizophrenic mothers and then adopted within days after birth. A control sample of adopted children whose biological mothers were not schizophrenic was matched to the schizophrenics' children with regard to age, sex, age at separation from mother, type of foster care placement, and so on. All of the children were then followed and interviewed many years later, at the average age of 36 years. The age-corrected risk for schizophrenia among the children of the schizophrenic mothers was 16.6 percent. In contrast, *none* of

[2]Actual concordance rates vary depending on a number of methodological factors. These are pairwise rates using "schizophreniclike psychosis" in the proband's cotwin as the criterion for concordance. All of the twins had passed through the standard age of risk so that age-correction procedures were unnecessary.

[3]Some of the more popular environmental considerations are discussed in Chapter 9.

the children in the control sample had become schizophrenic as adults. Once again, the clear influence of genetic factors was apparent.

Adoption studies such as Heston's and studies of the families of schizophrenic patients have also drawn attention to two related points of interest. First, the biological relatives of schizophrenics may be at risk for other psychological adjustment problems in addition to schizophrenia (Kendler & Diehl, 1993). In Heston's study, for example, the offspring of the schizophrenic mothers were also more likely than the control subjects to exhibit signs of mental deficiency and personality disorder, most notably Antisocial Personality Disorder.[4] It also may be the case that in the absence of behavioral disturbance, the genetic factors related to schizophrenia are linked to positively valued traits such as creativity. Heston, for example, noted that the most interesting people he interviewed were among the children of schizophrenic mothers who had not become mentally ill themselves. They were more spontaneous when interviewed, had more colorful life histories, worked at more creative jobs, and followed the most imaginative hobbies. This impression was also reported in another adoption study conducted in Iceland (Karlsson, 1966). Both of these phenomena were evident in Margaret's family. Her mother was a talented actress and dancer who also exhibited obvious signs of personality disorder, although she was not schizophrenic. Margaret's brother, who did not manifest signs of psychological disturbance, was widely recognized as a talented musician.

Progress has been made in our understanding of the etiology of schizophrenia, but much remains to be learned. One important consideration is the specific manner in which genetic factors take effect. Simple models based on dominant and recessive traits do not fit patterns seen in schizophrenics' families. Most evidence suggests that a large number of genes or loci are involved (McGue & Gottesman, 1989). Future efforts to identify a specific mode of transmission would benefit from the identification of distinct subtypes of schizophrenia, an extremely difficult problem that has hampered investigators for many years.

Some current speculation involves the notion of positive and negative syndromes, which some theorists consider to be etiologically distinct. Crow and his colleagues (1986), for example, have argued that the syndrome characterized by positive symptoms is related to a dysfunction in the dopamine system that transmits messages in the brain. Negative symptoms, on the other hand, may be more closely associated with structural (rather than biochemical) changes in the brain. Studies using sophisticated imaging procedures have

---

[4]Even though this pattern may indicate that disorders such as Antisocial Personality Disorder are genetically related to schizophrenia, it may also reflect the genetic influence of the target children's father, whose diagnostic status was unknown to Heston.

found that structural brain abnormalities are fairly common among schizophrenic patients, particularly those with negative symptoms (e.g., Andreasen, Ehrhardt, et al., 1990). Some of the available evidence suggests that these changes are more likely produced by nongenetic factors. For example, Suddath and his colleagues (1990) used magnetic resonance imaging (MRI) to study 15 sets of monozygotic twins who were discordant for the disorder (i.e., one twin was schizophrenic and the other was not). In comparison to their normal MZ cotwins, 14 of the 15 twins with schizophrenia had a smaller left hippocampus and larger left lateral ventricles. These brain abnormalities must be attributed to environmental events because each twin pair was genetically identical. This tentative pattern of evidence might be taken to support the argument that genetic factors are less important in the etiology of the negative syndrome.

Another important consideration in current research involves the manner in which genetic factors interact with environmental events to produce schizophrenia (Fowles, 1992). This problem is also enormously complex. The environmental events in question might take any of several different forms, including interpersonal relations within the family (see Chapter 9), nutrition, or viral infection (e.g., Kendell & Kemp, 1989; Mednick, Machon, Huttunen, & Bonett, 1988), to name only a few of the alternatives that are currently under consideration. The most promising research methods being used to address this issue involve prospective studies of people who are at risk for the development of schizophrenia (e.g., Parnas et al., 1993).

Treatment

Since the advent of antipsychotic medication (see Chapter 9), most other biological forms of intervention, including electroconvulsive therapy (ECT) and psychosurgery, have fallen into disfavor in the treatment of schizophrenia. Antipsychotic medication seems to have a specific effect on many psychotic symptoms, such as hallucinations and disorganized speech. Taken on a maintenance basis, it also reduces the probability of symptomatic relapse. In Margaret's case, medication did seem to have a positive effect. On many occasions, the administration of antipsychotic medication was associated with an improvement in her most dramatic symptoms. It was also clear that she often relapsed soon after discontinuing the medication that she was taking on an outpatient basis.

Despite these positive effects, there are also several limitations and some problems associated with the use of antipsychotic drugs. One problem, which was evident in Margaret's case, is that medication is only a partial solution. Once the most dramatic symptoms have improved, most patients continue to suffer from role impairments that are not the direct product of hallucinations and delusions. In short, medication can sometimes relieve perceptual aberrations, but it does not remove deficiencies in social and occupational skills.[5]

Another problem is the frequent development of long-term side effects, most notably a serious, involuntary movement disorder known as *tardive dyskinesia*. Margaret had been taking antipsychotic medication for several years and was beginning to manifest obvious signs of tardive dyskinesia, such as trembling of the extremities, lip smacking, and protrusions of the tongue. These symptoms can be disconcerting to both patients and those with whom they interact. Perhaps most disturbing is the fact that the disorder is often irreversible. As a result, the patient and clinician are often in a difficult bind: If medication is continued on a long-term basis, the probability increases that the patient will develop serious side effects such as tardive dyskinesia; if the medication is discontinued, the patient may relapse. This problem has not been resolved.

A final problem arises with treatment-refractory patients. Approximately 10 percent to 20 percent of schizophrenic patients do not seem to benefit from typical forms of neuroleptic medication. Others who respond initially will relapse repeatedly during maintenance drug treatment. It is therefore important that alternative forms of intervention be developed. Clozapine (Clozaril), an atypical neuroleptic drug that seems to have a different pharmacological mode of action than more traditional antipsychotic drugs, seems to offer significant hope for some of these patients. Controlled studies of clozapine's therapeutic effects have found significant improvement in approximately 30 percent of patients who were previously considered "treatment resistant" (Kane & Marder, 1993). Furthermore, the incidence of motor side effects appears to be quite low among patients who are being treated with clozapine. The availability of this alternative form of treatment offers new hope for some patients and their families.

---

[5]Psychosocial approaches to the treatment of these problems are discussed in Chapter 9.

11 ALCOHOL DEPENDENCE AND MARITAL CONFLICT

After giving her a complete physical examination, Cathy Henry's physician determined that many of her problems were psychological in origin. To be sure, she had reason to be concerned over her medical status because she had been having trouble sleeping for several months, suffered from almost continual diarrhea, fell very fatigued most of the time, and had allowed her once trim body to become flabby and poorly conditioned. One key question that the physician had asked during the examination, however, led him to be concerned about her personal life. "Have you been drinking much alcohol lately?" he had queried, as casually as possible. "No!" she had exclaimed a bit too loudly. She then burst into tears and recounted the following story.

Twenty-eight years of age, married for seven years to a successful business executive, and the mother of two children in elementary school, Cathy Henry had watched her drinking patterns change over the previous several years. She had been a social drinker since her college days, but her consumption increased and changed in nature during her first years of marriage. Initially it was the martinis that she would mix for her husband and herself to greet him each evening when he came home from his job in the city after traveling for one hour on the commuter railroad. It helps him unwind, she would think to herself, but soon realized that it was she who looked forward to the drinks. Then there were the parties they would go to or have in their spacious suburban home. She was not particularly fond of the people she met at these gatherings; in fact, when she was honest with herself, she had to admit that she found them aversive. Dick's friends and their wives led lives that were different from the way she thought she would be living. Yes, she did enjoy the affluence, the nice clothes, the obligatory Mercedes, the private school for the children, the vacations, and all the rest. But she longed for more.

She began to look forward to the numbing effects of that first drink. And then the further numbing of the second. Wasn't booze the social lubricant par excellence? What could be wrong with it if you saw it everywhere you turned? Dick's business lunches, after all, always included a Manhattan or martini before and usually a bottle of wine during the meal. And her lunches with one or two women she had managed to befriend usually followed the same pattern. No, that was not the problem. It was the drink she took by herself before making the early evening batch of martinis to enjoy with her husband before dinner and the drink she poured for herself downstairs in the kitchen while Dick was in the bedroom getting dressed for a party she was not looking forward to. And more and more often it was the second drink she somehow found herself pouring, now secretly, after she had gotten dressed and Dick was picking up the babysitter. Most recently it was the doubts she felt about being sober enough to be the perfect hostess as she sipped a drink while making the canapés on Saturday afternoons in preparation for the dinner party in her home that evening and her husband was at the supermarket with the children for some last-minute shopping.

Different as well was the kind of drink she found herself imbibing. If a dry martini is good, then a very dry one is better. And if there is Tanqueray in the liquor cabinet, why mask its exquisite taste with anything more than a twist of lemon? And why dilute such good liquor with ice cubes if the green bottle can be kept in the back of the refrigerator, next to the long-stemmed goblet that so nicely accommodated a jigger of gin, and later two jiggers and, finally, as much as she felt like pouring without using a measuring glass.

So she awakened one morning and realized that even before she got herself out of bed, she was thinking of that first drink. She also wondered whether she would be able to wait until her husband left for work and her children left for school. And if she had to do the driving for the carpool that day, would she have a few gulps of gin before she left with them to pick up the other children, or would she wait until her return? It seemed to her now that she wanted that first drink not so much to feel better but to avoid feeling worse for not having the drink.

One final aspect of her predicament worried the doctor. Not surprisingly, Cathy's marriage had been deteriorating as her drinking worsened. Intimacy was gone. Her secretiveness and shame about her drinking, coupled with extreme anger whenever her husband made a comment or suggested she get some help, created a distance between them. Dick Henry also resented his wife's increasing unreliability in looking after the children and their home. It was becoming the norm in recent months that he would arrive after work to find the children roaming around the neighborhood unsupervised, dinner unprepared, and the house looking as unkempt as his wife did, propped up on pillows in her room, on the night table next to her a glass filled with gin as she looked idly through magazines or watched whatever program was on television at the time. Sex was infrequent because Cathy was usually so drunk that neither she nor her husband was interested in initiating sexual activity.

Drinking had become the center of her life. She had denied this for some time, but it no longer seemed possible to continue the charade. Her life was going out of control.

SOCIAL HISTORY

Cathy Henry was raised in a lower-middle-class family in a large city in the Northeast. Her parents, both schoolteachers, indoctrinated their four children in the value of higher education; there was seldom any doubt that their daughter would go to college. And, indeed she did—not to the kind of teachers' college her parents had attended but to a private university on the West Coast, far from home. She viewed her college years as difficult but rewarding in that she was exposed to people and ideas that were new and challenging.

One of Cathy's clearest recollections of college was the fraternity parties on "The Row," a street just off campus that was the location for most of the fraternities and sororities. Somehow she had been invited to join one of the more prestigious sororities, a happenstance that opened the doors of the more highly regarded fraternities to her. A very attractive and likable young woman, her main problem was a lack of money relative to the obvious affluence of most of her "sisters." Her roommate, for example, drove a BMW and had a wardrobe that contained the latest in casual and formal wear—just the right kind of insignia pressed onto the front of each jersey, just the right kind of shoes and jeans. Cathy was able to buy clothing that helped her feel comfortable among her wealthy peers by virtue of the full-tuition scholarship she had obtained, a modeling job her roommate had helped her get downtown, and a hefty loan that her father had countersigned for her. Her parents, in fact, had been instrumental in her selecting this university; they viewed it as her ticket of admission into a higher stratum of society. They were not wrong.

It was at the frequent weekend parties that she was introduced to drinking. Back home liquor was a rare accompaniment to socializing, both with her parents and with her high-school friends. At college the situation could not have been more different. A conservative campus, the school was sometimes said to have missed the 1960s; that is, it had not been influenced by the social turmoil on college campuses during the Vietnam protests. Similarly missing on campus was the degree of illicit drug dealing common elsewhere. The favorite drug was drunk, not smoked or snorted, and nowhere with more élan and gusto than at the fraternity parties.

Cathy's first reaction to beer was indifferent at best. She barely finished her first can, which had been casually handed to her as she entered a party during the second week of her sophomore year. She felt somewhat jaded even holding it but soon relaxed when she saw a group of wholesome-looking young men and women guzzle the brew. By the end of the evening she "had a buzz on," as it had been labeled for her by Dick, the good-looking upperclassman who had flirted with her most of the evening.

Dick was a rambunctious fellow from a well-to-do family. He was majoring in political science and economics and headed for business school and, thereafter, the family firm, which had branches throughout the country. His principal goal in life seemed to be to work harder and be more successful than his father, but to do so while appearing to do little work and to care even less about grades. This created a strain in him from which he sought relief in alcohol. If anyone was Cathy's teacher in the fine art of drinking, it was Dick. They were pinned by Christmas and soon thereafter engaged.

Dick graduated two years before Cathy, and they both made the difficult decision that he should accept the offer from the high-powered business school back east while she finished college. They managed to see each other often; Dick flew to the West Coast a half-dozen times a year. Cathy meanwhile was elected to Phi Beta Kappa, finding more time now for her studies with Dick out of town. She did not go to the parties unless Dick was visiting. Consequently, she had stopped drinking as regularly as she had when Dick was still in school with her. Years later she would comment ruefully to herself that "back then I could really take it or leave it." It seemed impossible that there was ever a time she could actually leave it.

The wedding was an extravagant affair; the reception was held around the pool of Dick's parents' home. Cathy's family flew out for the occasion, and she hated herself for being a little ashamed of how unsophisticated they seemed compared to the family and friends of her new husband. She herself felt very much on display. It seemed to her that her value to Dick's parents lay less in her intelligence and academic achievements than in her looks, which by now were quite striking. Questions put to her during the reception revolved around starting a family—"When will Dick Jr. come along, do you think?"—and furnishing her new home in a fashionable suburb outside Manhattan, where Dick was slated to begin as a vice-president in the East Coast headquarters of the family business. No consideration was given to any career she herself might have in mind to pursue.

By the end of the first year of marriage, they had a baby (named Dick Jr!). Full-time help was well within their means, but Cathy insisted on caring for the boy and the house on her own. She told Dick and herself that this was what she wanted, but she knew at some level that she was deceiving herself as much as she was fooling Dick.

Her anger and resentment grew. She could not understand why she was not happier. Didn't she have it all—a handsome and successful husband, not a hint of financial worry, a lovely home with a summer cottage farther east on the bay and, before long, a second child? The other women in the neighborhood were pleasant enough and certainly cordial to "Dick's wife," and the many parties they attended were as lively as those fraternity and sorority affairs. They were similar as well in the lavish availability of alcohol—only the best brands and vintages. Thus it was that alcohol entered her life again, this time in a more serious way.

As already mentioned, Cathy disliked most the people at the parties she "had to" attend with Dick. She came to realize that it might not be the people themselves she found objectionable, but the lack of choice she experienced in attending parties. Their social life revolved around Dick's position. Certainly most of the people she entertained in their home were connected in one way or another with Dick's many business dealings.

CONCEPTUALIZATION AND TREATMENT

"I'm Joe, and I'm an alcoholic." "I'm Nancy, and I'm an alcoholic." Cathy looked uneasily around her at the group of strangers in the basement meeting room of the church. She had decided to attend a meeting of Alcoholics Anonymous after seeing a television commercial earlier that week. The first step, it was said, was to admit to oneself that one was an alcoholic. Like many problem drinkers, Cathy had avoided that frightening confrontation for several years, fooling herself with intellectual games such as the proper definition of alcoholism, the scientific status of alcohol as an addicting drug, and other academic questions that protected her from facing the fact that her drinking was out of control and threatening to ruin her life, whether she was actually addicted or not. She recalled from a psychology course in college that AA helped many people stop drinking, so why not her?

"I'm Cathy, and I'm a . . . a . . . " She stopped in midsentence, looked beseechingly at the unturned face of an older woman sitting in the row in front of her as if to ask this woman what to say next. The stranger smiled and nodded, somehow helping Cathy take what might be her first step to helping herself: ". . . I'm an alcoholic." She marveled to herself how relieved she felt just saying these words aloud, words reflecting a thought she had believed would itself spell ruination. But nothing terrible happened. No one in the room laughed, no one cried. They just greeted her by name, and the meeting went on as it had been proceeding before she spoke.

She was told by other members of the group that alcoholism is a disease and that an alcoholic has to learn to abstain entirely. A buddy was assigned to her, a woman whom she could telephone day or night for encouragement not to take a drink. She was pleased and grateful to have someone she could talk to anytime she felt the need, someone who she believed would understand the craving, the almost painful need for a drink.

She drove home that evening feeling more optimistic than she had for years. As she got out of the car, however, she realized that she was already thinking about a drink. Would Dick see her pouring it? Would one of the children? Should she phone her buddy right away? She had been warned that the first few days would be the worst, so perhaps she should call.

She intended to do just that, but, as she dialed the number, Dick came into the kitchen and angrily asked her where she had been. Regrettably, Cathy had told him she was going shopping with Ethel, one of her friends, but Ethel had phoned an hour earlier to ask her to have lunch later that week. Cathy knew she should have told Dick where she was going, but she was so ashamed of her drinking that she did not feel she could even tell him of her resolve to do something about it. As she had learned at the AA meeting, to take that first step meant to admit to others as well as to oneself that one was an alcoholic.

An ugly scene followed. At first Dick did not believe she had gone to AA. He regarded it as "unseemly," as a quasi-religious group for lower-class people — self-help groups were for those who could not afford professional help. Surely she was having an affair. Cathy could scarcely believe what she was hearing. Things became violent. She punched at Dick, grabbed at his hair. He restrained her as best he could without hurting her and then left the room in a rage. The telephone call to her buddy now forgotten, Cathy downed several ounces of gin from the refrigerator within a few minutes and then collapsed.

She awoke the next day in the hospital. She had hit her head on the edge of a kitchen counter as she fell, opening a deep gash in her scalp. Torn by remorse, guilt, and anger, Dick rushed her to the emergency room and had her admitted. The X-rays were negative for skull fracture, and her EEG was normal, so she was discharged the following day.

Cathy did not go back to AA, and she wondered years later what course her life might have taken had she returned. She thought many times that the best outcome would have been abstention and a return to her nondrinking days, accompanied by some improvement in her marital relationship. She was not prepared for what did happen, and she was never certain, even years later, about how good the outcome was.

The scene the evening of her return from the AA meeting had frightened both Cathy and Dick. The gentility of their lives had no room for shouting and hitting, nor did it allow for open admission of the loss of control that Cathy had confronted at the AA meeting. Dick would not or could not believe it. He pleaded with her not to return to AA. But what was to be done, she pleaded in return. He would do anything to help her with her drinking; he had not known how serious it was (he had unwittingly collaborated with Cathy in hiding the facts both from her and from himself). He would find a therapist for her. No, she said, it was not just her problem. She had begun drinking during the beginnings of their relationship at college; she had stopped when he was away at business school; and she had begun again in earnest soon after their marriage and move to the East Coast. No, she said, she could not stop drinking unless there were some fundamental changes in the marriage.

To say that Dick did not want to hear this is an understatement. For him life had been perfect until now—terrific position in the family business, gorgeous wife and children, lovely expensive home. A bad marriage was not part of his version of the American dream. So he resisted for weeks until, drunk, Cathy wrecked the station wagon and almost herself with it.

So it was that the two of them sat next to each other on a sofa in Dr. Seymour's large office, a 30-minute drive from their home. Dr. Seymour had a good reputation for dealing with seriously troubled marriages, including those in which alcohol abuse was involved. Neither Cathy nor Dick had even seen a therapist, although she had thought of it often enough. The first session began as follows:

Dr. Seymour: How can I be of help?

Dick: Well, my wife has this drinking problem. She tried AA but that didn't work. Then she . . .

Cathy: Wait a minute, Dick. I went to one meeting, and your crummy reaction to it landed me in the hospital with a laceration in my head.

Dr. Seymour: Hold on a minute, please. Cathy, let's hear from Dick and then we'll hear from you. Okay?

Cathy (suspiciously): Okay.

Dr. Seymour: Dick, you were telling me of Cathy's drinking problem.

Dick spoke for several minutes about his wife's problems, not only her drinking but her grouchiness, her unresponsiveness in bed, and her neglect of household tasks. Dr. Seymour listened attentively, watching both of them closely.

Dr. Seymour: Okay, Dick, now tell both Cathy and me what *your* problems are.

Dick (taken aback): What do you mean, *my* problems?

Dr. Seymour: I'd like to know how *you* feel about your marriage, about your life. We'll spend some time on Cathy's drinking and all the rest, but right now I'd be interested in what you might get out of therapy here.

Dick continued as he had begun, this time emphasizing how much easier his life would be if Cathy stopped drinking, started preparing meals regularly, and the like.

Dr. Seymour (sensing he had to do something to get Dick away from concentrating entirely on how Cathy would have to change): Dick, what's happening?

Dick (puzzled, a little nervous): What do you mean, what's happening? I'm telling you what you want to know.

Dr. Seymour: No, I mean, your leg. What's happening to your leg?

Dick's leg had been shaking for several minutes, unnoticed by him but not by Dr. Seymour.

Dick: I don't know. I guess it's moving around a little.

Dr. Seymour: Can you say, "*I'm* moving around a little?"

Dick: What?!? What is this bullshit? (Turning to Cathy.) I told you this therapy business was a crock. He tells me I'm doing something when it's my leg that's moving a little.

Dr. Seymour: Dick, you talk about your leg as if it belongs to someone else. Just tell me that *you* (pointing at Dick's chest) are moving around, that *you* are moving away from the issue.

Dick (eyes suddenly filled with tears, confused about what was happening inside him, feeling himself on the edge of some sort of emotional release): This whole business is driving me crazy. I'm really angry at Cathy. She's screwing up my life. She . . .

Dr. Seymour (interrupts): Dick, say anything you want, but begin with the words "I feel . . ."

Long pause, Dr. Seymour and Dick looking unflinchingly at each other.

Dick (suddenly bursts into tears): I feel scared. I feel I am losing it all. I feel like I'm dying. I feel . . . (Sobs.)

In the meantime Cathy has been looking alternately at the two men as if watching a tennis match, one moment puzzled, the next hurt, the next expectant, now experiencing a rush of affection and protectiveness for Dick that she has not felt since their engagement 10 years ago.

Dr. Seymour: Yes, you feel scared. And what do you need?

Dick: I need . . . I need . . . I need Cathy.

Dr. Seymour: Say it again.

Dick: I need Cathy.

By this point Cathy and Dick are in tears, but there is some distance between them on the sofa. Dr. Seymour sees Dick's hand inch toward Cathy, then withdraw.

Dr. Seymour: Dick, what's happening? To your hand?

Dick: It wants to touch Cathy.

Dr. Seymour: Can you take responsibility for that feeling, Dick? What do *you* want? What do *you* need?

Dick (grabbing her hand but still looking at Dr. Seymour): I need *her*!

Dr. Seymour: Tell her. Don't tell me. *Tell her!*

Dick (turning to Cathy): I need you, Cathy!

Dr. Seymour had taken some chances in this first session, but his clinical intuition had told him that this take-charge business executive was terrified at what was happening to his marriage, that he felt that he was losing his wife, that he needed her, and that he was unlikely to admit to these fears without prodding and confrontation. Dr. Seymour was less sure why Dick needed Cathy or whether that need could form the basis for a good marriage, but, for now, he deemed it necessary to get Dick to acknowledge his own emotional stake and to show Cathy how scared he was about losing her.

Cathy's drinking was not ignored, but it did take some time to attend to it directly. Cathy had been managing to come to the twice-weekly sessions sober, which told Dr. Seymour that her drinking was not as much out of her control as she believed. An agreement had been reached that she be sober during each therapy meeting, and it turned out that Dick was able to help her achieve this subgoal by spending time with her every Saturday and Tuesday morning before their noon sessions. Formal attention to Cathy's drinking began with an exercise that had her and Dick talking to an empty chair.

Dr. Seymour: Okay, we were going to talk about the alcohol today.

Dick: Yes, let me tell you what I think's going on.

Dr. Seymour: Hold on, Dick, let's try it this way. I want you to look at that empty chair and imagine that Cathy's bottle of chilled Tanqueray is in it.

Dick (laughing nervously): Doctor, does you mother know what you do for a living?

Dr. Seymour (smiling): Not a chance. The chair, Dick. Cathy's liquor bottle is in that chair. Talk to it.

Dick (by now accustomed to Dr. Seymour's unorthodox techniques and style): Okay. Let's see. I'd say . . .

Dr. Seymour: No, don't tell me what you *would* say. Just say it.

Dick: Okay. . . . Listen, you're causing us a lot of problems. . . . You're . . . (Eyes fill with tears; Dr. Seymour leans forward and whispers encouragingly for him to express the emergent feeling.) You're getting in the way, bottle. You're like an intruder, a home-wrecker. I'm angry at you. No, that's not it. I'm afraid of you. I'm not as strong as you. I'm not as attractive to Cathy as you are. Yes, that's it. I'm afraid Cathy cares for you more than she cares for me. I'm feeling displaced. I almost feel like Cathy's having an affair, right under my nose, right in our own home. She can't wait to get to you when she comes home. She spends more time with you than she does with me. She touches you more. (Begins to cry.)

Dr. Seymour: Cathy, what do you have to say to the liquor in that chair?

Cathy (sobbing): Dick's right. You *are* an intruder. You're my gigolo. You're reliable. I know just what you'll do for me. I know just how to treat you, how much of you to pour, how much of you to take into my body. I've turned to you for help instead of asking Dick for help. I can't love both of you at the same time. But you're always there. I know you won't reject me. I know you so well. And I always know where to find you.

Dr. Seymour developed the clinical hypothesis that Cathy's liquor was like a lover, a threat to their marriage in almost a human sense. Cause and effect were impossible to isolate, but it was clear that the growing distance between the two partners was correlated with Cathy's increasing dependence on the alcohol. Any possible addiction Dr. Seymour conceptualized as the kind of power that a forceful and compelling lover can have over another person. He cared less about whether she was truly addicted than about her inability to turn to her husband for the solace she seemed to find in drink. The fanciful scenario with the empty chair made a profound impression on the couple; they both realized that alcohol was interfering with intimacy in their marriage. And Dick got in touch with his great need for and love of Cathy and of the threat posed by the alcohol. Cathy became more aware of how she turned to the bottle for what she wanted and needed from her husband — not the anesthetizing effects of the drug, but a reliable source of companionship and solace.

Therapy had been progressing well until now, all three parties believing that they were on the right track to improving the marriage and reducing Cathy's reliance on alcohol. But things took an unexpected turn. Dick's fantasy of a favorable outcome to the treatment was a contented Cathy raising their children, tending to the home, and being eager to meet him on his (triumphant) return each day from work. Cathy's ideas were different. The Gestalt therapy approach was helping Cathy discover many of her deepest wants and concerns. She was coming to realize that some of her happiest times had been her last two years of college, when she was engaged to Dick and yet separate from him, functioning independently. She had no need for liquor at that time, and she also excelled in her classes, as noted earlier. She abhorred the idea of living like a china doll in her lovely home, her life revolving around ferrying the children and their friends in the station wagon, shopping for clothes, chatting over lunch with her "girl friends." In short, although she loved Dick, the traditional marriage was suffocating her.

She expressed these "radical feminist" (Dick's terms) ideas during one of the therapy sessions. Dick's reaction was predictable to her, and it seemed that no amount of discussion with the psychologist or at home was going to help him see things her way. For Dick it was a gross violation of the marriage contract; more than that, it was unnatural. On the positive side, he was able to express his fear of being emasculated and humiliated by the fact of his wife working outside the home and having a real say in major family decisions. At least he had some clarification of the issues, and things were being brought out into the open. But change was another matter.

This crisis took place several months after they had begun seeing Dr. Seymour, and it almost drove Cathy back to alcohol. But she realized that to succumb would be tantamount to not taking responsibility for her feelings and for the need to make a choice if she was to continue growing. So she asked that regular sessions be suspended for a month; she needed some time to think by herself. Dick agreed that she would spend a few weeks at her parents' home; the children would be looked after by a family friend. During this time away from her home, her decision to ask Dick for a separation solidified. Paradoxically, this decision was both the most sensible, inevitable one for her and the most unpredicted, rash one. All sorts of issues had to be faced now—change in financial circumstances, the reactions of the children and of the two families, a possible move to another house or even another city. She and Dick had a few more sessions with Dr. Seymour, who respected the decision Cathy had made and agreed to do what he could to help them both adjust to it, even though deep down he believed that marriage itself was too sacred to give up on if there was any hope of accommodation at all.

DISCUSSION

When *DSM-III* (1980) was published, it drew a distinction between substance abuse and substance dependence. In the former a person is so involved in drug use that his or her work and other responsibilities suffer. With some drugs, abuse develops into dependence, or addiction; when addicting drugs such as heroin or alcohol are ingested for long periods of time, the body chemistry changes so that the person desperately craves more and more of the substance. The symptoms of dependence include tolerance and withdrawal. *Tolerance* refers to the need to take increasing dosages to achieve a desired state of intoxication; *withdrawal* refers to the very unpleasant reactions that accompany an attempt to stop taking the addicting drug. Both kinds of disorders, abuse and dependence, can be serious, and no drug causes more widespread pain and suffering than alcohol.

The definition of substance dependence and substance abuse were completely revised in *DSM-III-R* (1987) and in *DSM-IV* (1994). The definition of substance dependence was broadened by placing less emphasis on physical aspects of dependence, such as tolerance and withdrawal symptoms. Substance dependence is now defined in terms of a list of seven problems that indicate a substantial degree of involvement with a psychoactive substance. At least three of these criteria must be present to justify a diagnosis of dependence. Examples of the criteria including taking the substance in larger amounts or over longer periods than the person intended; unsuccessful efforts to cut down; spending a great deal of time in activities necessary to get the substance; and frequent intoxication when the person is expected to fulfill major role obligations at work, school, or home. Tolerance and withdrawal symptoms are included in this list, but they are no longer necessary criteria (as they had been in *DSM-III*). Substance abuse is a residual category. It is defined as a maladaptive pattern of substance use that does not meet the criteria for dependence—for example, failure to meet major social or occupational obligations or legal problems such as arrests for disorderly conduct.

The use of wine, beer, and other alcoholic beverages dates back thousands of years; their presence is a veritable institution in the United States and other Western countries. In moderation, alcohol has pleasant effects for most people and is widely regarded as a "social lubricant" because of its disinhibiting properties. Conversation seems easier, one's everyday woes recede in importance, and life seems generally more pleasant for most individuals who drink occasionally. To be sure, many traffic accidents are caused by people who drive when their reflexes, motor coordination, and judgment have been impaired by alcohol, as happened in the case study. But by and large the moderate use of these beverages has some positive effects for the majority of adults.

Problems arise when people drink on a regular basis, even if they have not become addicted. Cathy Henry was not truly physically addicted to alcohol (although she may have been very close to it). Nevertheless, her life was being seriously affected by her reliance on alcohol to deaden her senses and somehow help the time pass in an otherwise meaningless and aversive existence. It is difficult to meet responsibilities to others and even to oneself when our thinking is slowed, our senses dulled, and our memory impaired by the intoxicating effects of a drug such as alcohol. So, even if one's reliance on a drug is "only" psychological, the impairment can be profound.

Addiction is even more serious, of course, because the body so craves the substance that even a resolve to desist from its use is often insufficient. Dependence upon the drug increases as one's life revolves around obtaining and ingesting it. There are many physiological effects of long-term drug use. In the case of alcohol, there can be damage to the heart, endocrine glands, and circulatory system, generally through hypertension, or high blood pressure. Cirrhosis of the liver is another consequence of heavy drinking; in this disease active liver cells are replaced by fibrous connective tissue, thereby interfering with blood circulation. Cirrhosis ranks ninth among the causes of death (USDHHS, 1990).

For women there is an additional risk: the harm that can be inflicted on a fetus in the womb. Fetal alcohol syndrome has been linked to heavy consumption of alcohol during pregnancy, causing many abnormalities in the developing infant, including mental retardation. So concerned are medical experts that almost two decades ago, the National Institute on Alcohol Abuse and Alcoholism counseled pregnant women not to drink at all (*Alcohol, Drug Abuse and Mental Health Administration News,* May 2, 1980). Furthermore, in 1988 several states began to pass laws requiring explicit warnings in liquor stores and restaurants that drinking during pregnancy can cause birth defects.

Etiology

Research indicates that genetic factors play a role in the transmission of alcohol abuse and dependence (Saunders & Williams, 1983). Evidence suggests that the importance of genetic factors and the way in which they interact with environmental events to produce alcoholism may vary across different forms of the disorder. An extensive adoption study conducted in Sweden (Bohman, Sigvardsson, & Cloninger, 1981; Cloninger, Bohman, & Sigvardsson, 1981; Cloninger et al., 1988) identified two subtypes of alcoholism that seemed to be etiologically distinct. The more severe, and less common, form of the disorder was seen only in men and was associated with a family history of criminal behavior. This type of alcohol abuse was highly heritable. The other type of alcoholism was more common and less severe and was seen in both men and women. Genetic factors were less influential in the development of this form of alcohol abuse; its expression was largely dependent on the presence of certain predisposing environmental events. Similarly, a study of twins by McGue, Pickens, and Suikis (1992) showed that genetic factors were much more important in men than in women and in early rather than late onset alcoholism. Other research does point to a role for genetic factors in women when alcoholism begins early in life (Hill & Smith, 1991). Molecular researchers have been pursuing the specific gene or genes that might confer increased vulnerability, focusing on a gene for the neurotransmitter dopamine (Uhl, Perscio, & Smith, 1992).

If a predisposition to the development of alcohol abuse is inherited, it would be useful to know how to identify individuals who are genetically predisposed or vulnerable. It would also be interesting to know why they are more likely than other people to drink alcohol excessively. One interesting possibility was suggested by Sher and Levenson (1982), who compared two groups of nonalcoholic males: those who were considered to be at risk for the future development of alcohol abuse and another group of subjects who were not at risk. After consuming alcohol, subjects who were at risk showed more pronounced reduction of their physiological responses to stress. These data indicate that alcohol consumption can provide a powerful form of negative reinforcement—escape from the effects of stress. This effect is much more salient for some people than for others. Those who experience clear-cut stress-response-dampening after the consumption of alcohol may be more likely to become alcohol abusers.

Support for a tension-reduction hypothesis is inconsistent, however (e.g., Thyer & Curtis, 1984). In an effort to explain these conflicting findings, Steele and Josephs (1988) analyzed more closely the situations in which alcohol is consumed. They have shown that alcohol apparently produces its tension-reducing effect by altering cognition and perception. Specifically, their research suggests that alcohol impairs cognitive processing, narrowing attention to the most immediately available cues. This results in what they call *alcohol myopia*, whereby the intoxicated person has less attentional capacity than when sober to distribute between worry and an ongoing activity. If an available activity can command all or most of the drinker's limited attentional capacity, his or her attention will wander less to worrisome thoughts, the result being tension or anxiety reduction. However, if the drinking person has no such distractions, his or her limited attention can more likely dwell on worries, leading to even more depression. Such findings, arising from analogue experiments with subjects who are *not* alcoholic, may help us understand why people have sometimes unpleasant and sometimes pleasant experiences when drinking, and they may cast light on what leads some nonalcoholics to rely more and more on drinking to deal with life stress.

Over time, people can develop expectations about the effects of alcohol; whether or not they turn to alcohol under stress may well have a good deal to do with whether or not they *expect* alcohol to reduce their discomfort (Rather, Goldman, Roehrich, & Brannick, 1992; Sher, Walitzer, Wood, & Brent, 1991). Clearly, Cathy had learned that alcohol alleviated her negative moods and helped her shift attention away from serious dissatisfactions with her married life.

Treatment

Although answers continue to be sought for why people drink, other research concentrates on how to help people stop drinking altogether, or at least to achieve better control over their consumption. Millions of dollars are spent each year by the government, private industry, and individuals themselves in efforts to discover effective ways for people to stop their abuse of alcohol. Careful hospital supervision is advised for people who are addicted. Then psychological treatment programs can be undertaken, encompassing many of the following procedures that are also available in noninstitutional settings.

Probably the best-known approach to problem drinking is Alcoholics

Anonymous, a self-help group formed in 1935 by two former alcoholics. AA now has more than 30,000 chapters in more than 100 countries; membership totals more than one million people. They run regular meetings, like the one Cathy Henry attended. Members provide each other with emotional support and constant encouragement to lead a life without the drug. AA's central assumption is that alcoholism is an incurable disease marked by a permanent susceptibility to that first drink. Total abstinence, then, is the goal of AA. It will be recalled that one of the features of AA that offended Cathy's husband was its religious tone. Indeed, there is a strong spiritual or religious atmosphere in AA, as can be seen from its 12 suggested steps for recovery (e.g., having made a decision that we are powerless to stop drinking on our own and therefore must turn for help to God or a "higher power"). Defects of character must also be admitted; resolves must be made to make amends to those we have wronged and to make an ongoing moral inventory of ourselves. There are many who regard AA as the most effective treatment for alcoholism. Although many alcoholics drop out of AA, there is some evidence that AA helps most of those who stay with the program to remain abstinent (Hoffman & Miller, 1992).

Behavior therapists have paid a good deal of attention to alcoholism and have devised a number of procedures and approaches. Conceptualizing problem drinking as inappropriate attraction to a set of stimulus conditions, workers have designed a variety of aversion therapies to instill in the drinker a distaste for drinking. In fact, one of the earliest articles in behavior therapy concerned aversion therapy with alcoholics (Kantorovich, 1930). In the most general terms, the drinker is shocked on the fingertips or made nauseous by ingesting a drug such as apomorphine or by imagining a disgusting scene—all the while confronted by an actual or imagined drinking situation. The assumption is that people can be classically conditioned to fear or otherwise find unpleasant a previously attractive stimulus if that stimulus is repeatedly paired with a negative emotional state. The research is hard to interpret or summarize, but it is fair to say that many drinkers have been helped in this fashion, even though it is far from clear how the techniques work (Cannon, Baker, Gino, & Nathan, 1986; Davison & Neale, 1994; Smith, Frawley, & Polissar, 1991). If used at all, aversion therapy, like the controlled drinking approach to be described next, is best implemented in the context of broadly based programs that attend to the patient's life circumstances, for example, marital conflict, social fears, and other factors often associated with problem drinking (Tucker, Vuchinich, & Downey, 1992). Certainly Cathy Henry's drinking problems illustrate this complexity.

A controversial direction in therapy is to encourage controlled drinking. Research has brought into question whether alcoholics really have no control over their behavior once they take a drink; instead, it has been suggested that their beliefs about themselves and what they are drinking play a central role, maybe as important as any physiological addiction (Marlatt, Demming, & Reid, 1973). Add to these findings the realization that it is virtually impossible to avoid alcohol in our society and you come up with the idea that alcoholics might be taught to drink in moderation. A controlled drinking program has the person drink some alcohol and then be informed, by a special monitoring apparatus, what his or her blood alcohol level is. Alcoholics seem to have inordinate difficulty knowing how intoxicated they actually are, so one such treatment program shocked them when they drank more than a moderate amount and taught them how to cope with problematic situations in a less destructive fashion than retreating into the numbing effects of alcohol. Results were encouraging (Sobell & Sobell, 1976), although some people, including those involved in AA, decry the idea that an alcoholic can ever become a social drinker. Still, controlled drinking therapy programs are becoming more prevalent, especially in Canada, and they may be particularly well suited to younger alcoholics whose life circumstances have not yet deteriorated (Sobell, Toneatto, & Sobell, 1990).

The therapy for Cathy Henry's problem drinking took a different course from what we have just reviewed. After her husband rejected the idea of her going to AA, she ultimately insisted that they go together to a therapist who would deal with the marital problems Cathy believed were instrumental in her abuse of alcohol. The therapist tacitly agreed with this general conceptualization and, within his Gestalt therapy framework (Perls, Hefferline, & Goodman, 1951), saw the drinking as a block or intruder between two people who basically loved each other. Gestalt therapy has an overall goal of enabling people to understand what their needs and wants and fears are, to take responsibility for them, and to find ways to incorporate these factors into their whole personality, thereby making themselves whole again (hence the term *Gestalt,* the German term for shape). Gestalt therapists are very imaginative in devising unusual techniques to make more vivid to clients what they are doing and how they are avoiding feelings. The empty chair technique employed with Cathy and her husband is designed to help people confront their innermost feelings directly. It seemed to have had a profound effect on the Henrys, and research lends support to the efficacy of the procedure in uncovering emotions that people may not be aware of (e.g., Davison & Binkoff, 1978; Greenberg & Rice, 1981). This therapy is representative of a more clinical and individualized approach to problem drinking, since it appreciates that different people can drink for different reasons. Not only Gestalt therapists but behavior therapists and analytically oriented therapists in practice attempt to tailor their interventions to what they believe are the particular needs of the people they are treating. All therapists work within a given theoretical framework, but considerable ingenuity and inventiveness are required to apply the general viewpoint to each client (Davison & Lazarus, in press).

The Henrys, then, found themselves in a Gestalt-oriented, conjoint marital treatment. Therapists who see couples differ in theoretical orientation, but they do share the basic assumption that a problem apparently in one of the partners is best dealt with by making changes in the relationship. Even if one of the partners brings a particular individual problem into the marriage, anxiety or depression, for example, that problem becomes intertwined in the relationship and, it is assumed, must be worked with in the context of that relationship. Another theme common in marital therapy is communication. Distressed couples are frequently unaware of how their actions affect the other person, and they are often unaware as well of the motivations of their partner. A variety of techniques are employed by marital therapists; illustrated in this case study are some Gestalt techniques designed to help the partners understand themselves and each other better so that their needs could be expressed and satisfied.

This case also highlights a burning issue in the field: the way therapeutic goals are set and the manner by which we evaluate the success of an intervention. Cathy and her husband began seeing the psychologist because of her drinking. Dick had not initially wanted to join Cathy in any therapeutic attempt to control her drinking, but she more or less gave him no choice; her implicit message was "Go see a therapist with me or else. . . ." The choice of Dr. Seymour from all the therapists they might have contacted influenced the direction of treatment because he was known to specialize in marital problems. Thus it was not surprising that the relationship became the principal focus of therapy. Cathy's drinking was not ignored, but it was dealt with as a by-product of a poor relationship. From our earlier discussion it should be obvious that there are many other ways to deal with problem drinking.

How should we think about the outcome of the therapy? It was successful to the extent that Cathy stopped drinking and was abstaining even in the face of tremendous stress—the dissolution of her marriage. But at what cost? Should the separation be viewed as a minor price to pay for reducing her use of alcohol? What about Dick's state of mind? He was devastated by the outcome. The children were also put under stress, although it can be argued that they were being compromised earlier by their mother's alcohol abuse. The answers are not clear.

The selection of Dr. Seymour might have had an additional biasing effect on the outcome of treatment. In outpatient therapy, the goals are presumably set by the client(s). Consider how valid this argument is in the present case. Dr. Seymour's Gestalt orientation had him train his clients to dig deep into their psyches to uncover feelings of which they were unaware. This was a first step toward owning up to these feelings and taking responsibility for them. Cathy did have some prior awareness of how unfulfilling her suburban mother/housewife life was, but the training she received in therapy opened up these issues for her in a way that might not have happened if she had stayed in AA and concentrated on her drinking. The Gestalt therapy also taught Dick how he truly felt about things; it made him more vulnerable, less macho, and thereby brought him closer to his wife. *But*, from his point of view, what did it get him? He lost his home, his family and, at least in the short run, emerged from therapy in worse shape than before. To be sure, things might have been better for him if he could have met Cathy's needs for greater autonomy, but he did not. Should Dr. Seymour have applied more pressure on him to do so? Perhaps the psychologist's own personal biases discouraged him; he was sad to see the marriage dissolve, but he did agree with the feminist direction Cathy was taking. Perhaps it was unwise, even unethical, for him to expose Cathy and Dick to fears and wants so long denied without being more certain of the possible outcome. And yet his humanistic orientation has him trust the goodness and "wisdom of the psyche" of his clients, if only the distortions and inhibitions imposed by negative learning can be removed. The implicit tenet of insight therapy, after all, is that knowledge will set you free. It seemed to do so for Cathy, but what about Dick?

12

SEXUAL DYSFUNCTION: FEMALE ORGASMIC DISORDER

Barbara Garrison was concerned about a number of problems when she arrived for her first appointment at the mental health center. Her principal complaint was an inability to achieve orgasm during sexual intercourse with her husband, Frank. They were both 33 years old and had been married for 15 years. Frank was a police detective, and Barbara had recently resumed her college education. Their children, Bonnie and Dennis, were 15 and 12, respectively.

Barbara's orgasmic problem was situational in nature. She had experienced orgasms through masturbation, and she masturbated an average of once or twice a week; however, she had never reached orgasm during sexual activity with Frank. The problem did not involve sexual desire or arousal. She found Frank sexually attractive, wanted to enjoy a more satisfying sexual relationship with him, and did become aroused during their sexual encounters. They had intercourse two or three times each month, usually late at night after the children had gone to sleep and always at Frank's initiative. Their foreplay was primarily limited to genital manipulation and seldom lasted more than five minutes. Frank always reached orgasm within a minute or two after penetration and often fell asleep shortly thereafter, leaving Barbara in a frustrating state of unfulfilled sexual arousal. On many occasions she resolved this dilemma by slipping quietly out of the bedroom to the TV room, where she would secretly masturbate to orgasm. Frank realized that Barbara did not experience orgasms during intercourse but chose not to discuss the problem. He did not know that she masturbated.

This situation was distressing to Barbara. She felt considerable guilt over her frequent masturbation, particularly after sexual intercourse, because she believed that masturbation was a deviant practice. She was also concerned about the sexual fantasies she had during masturbation. She often imagined herself in a luxurious hotel room having sexual intercourse with a sequence of 8 or 10 men. They were usually men she did not know, but she would sometimes include men to whom she had been attracted, such as classmates from the university and friends of her husband. Barbara believed that these promiscuous fantasies proved that she was a latent nymphomaniac. She feared that she could easily lose control of her own desires and worried that she might someday get on a train, leave her family, and become a prostitute in a large city. Her anxiety regarding sexual interests and arousal was also a problem during intercourse with Frank. He had, in fact, made numerous efforts to find out what she found arousing, but she remained uncommunicative. She was afraid to tell him what she liked because she thought that he would then realize that she was "oversexed." She was self-conscious during sexual activity with Frank. She worried about what he would think of her and whether she was performing adequately. Questions were continually running through her mind, such as "Am I paying attention to the right sensations?" or "Will it happen this time?" The combination of fear of loss of control of her sexual impulses and continual worry about her inadequacy as a sexual partner finally persuaded Barbara to seek professional help.

In addition to Barbara's inability to reach orgasm during intercourse, Barbara and Frank were not getting along as well as they had in the past. Several factors were contributing to the increased strain in their relationship. One involved Barbara's decision to resume her education. Frank had not completed his college education, and the possibility that Barbara might finish her degree was threatening to him. He was also uncomfortable around the friends Barbara met at the university. His job as a detective seemed to increase this tension because relations between students and the police had been strained by several years of demonstrations on the campus. Frank believed that Barbara's younger classmates saw him as a fascist, or an agent of the establishment. He resented changes in the way she dressed (she often wore blue jeans) and also attributed their increasingly frequent political disagreements to the subversive influence of the university environment.

They also had more financial concerns than in previous years. Barbara's tuition and other fees amounted to a considerable amount of money each semester and, within three years, their daughter, Bonnie, would be old enough to go to college. They had also taken out a substantial loan to build an addition onto their home. In order to make more money, Frank had been working many more overtime hours. Considering that he was away from home so often, Barbara resented the fact that he spent most of his spare time working on the new rooms in their house.

Bonnie and her friends were another major problem. She was a freshman in high school, and her boyfriend, John, was a senior. Barbara did not like most of Bonnie's friends. She wanted Bonnie to be one of the leaders of the school—a good student, popular, active in school organizations—but Bonnie did not fit in that mold. She was a marginal student, did not care for sports or group activities, and spent most of her time with John and her other friends at a local video arcade. John was not a good student either. He worked part-time at a service station and planned to become a mechanic after graduation. Barbara and Bonnie argued continuously, mostly about Bonnie's relationship with John. Barbara was preoccupied with the possibility that Bonnie might get pregnant. They did not talk about sex openly because the topic was too anxiety provoking for Barbara. She made every effort to prevent Bonnie and John from being by themselves. Bonnie had asked on several occasions whether John could come over to their house to watch television and listen to music. Barbara would allow John to be in the house only if she or Frank were in the same room with them. The net effect of this rule was to ensure that Bonnie and John spent most of their time away from the Garrisons' home. It also led to arguments between Barbara and Frank because he believed that Barbara was being too severe. Frank thought that the problem was mostly in Barbara's imagination. These problems were, in most ways, typical of the conflict that parents experience with teenage children. In the Garrisons' case the tension was compounded by Barbara's sexual difficulty and their financial and educational worries.

Despite their frequent arguments and differences of opinion, Barbara and Frank were both seriously committed to their marriage. Neither of them was particularly happy, but they were not considering a divorce. Barbara believed that their relationship would be markedly improved if she could overcome her orgasmic dysfunction. Frank was less concerned about that particular issue but agreed that Barbara might feel better if a therapist could "help her understand *her* problem." He also hoped that a psychologist might be able to improve the relationship between Barbara and Bonnie.

SOCIAL HISTORY

Barbara's parents were both in their middle forties when she was born. They had one other child, a boy, who was five years older than Barbara. Her father was a police officer, and her mother was a homemaker. They were conservative, devoutly religious people. In addition to taking care of the children and her other household responsibilities, Barbara's mother spent a considerable amount of time in volunteer work at their church. She was a Sunday school teacher for many years and always took Barbara with her to her classes. Barbara's parents clearly cared for each other and for the children, but they were not openly affectionate. She could not remember seeing them embrace or kiss each other except for frequent pecks on the cheek or top of the head; nor, on the other hand, could she remember hearing them argue. It was a quiet, peaceful household in which emotional displays of any kind were generally discouraged.

Barbara's parents and her older brother were unusually protective of her. She was "the baby of the family" and was always closely supervised. It seemed to Barbara that she was not allowed to do many of the things that her friends' parents permitted. When she was young, she was not allowed to leave their yard. When she was older and in high school, she was not allowed to go out on school nights and had to be home by 10 P.M. on weekends. Her parents insisted on meeting all of her friends and, in some cases, forbade her to associate with certain other children. Until she was 16 years old, Barbara was not allowed to go to parties if boys were also invited. She remembered her first date as an awkward experience that occurred during her junior year in high school. A boy whom she had admired for several months had finally asked her to go to a movie. Her parents agreed to allow her to go after her father asked several of his friends about the boy and his parents. When he picked her up before the movie, Barbara's parents asked so many questions that they were finally late for the show. Later, as they were leaving the theater, Barbara realized that her brother and his girlfriend, who both attended a local junior college, had been sitting several rows behind them. Their parents had called him and asked if he would keep an eye on her "to be sure everything was okay." He did not intend to be secretive and, in fact, asked Barbara if she and her friend would like to go out for hamburgers and Cokes after the show. This carefully arranged supervision did not ruin the experience. Everyone had a good time, and Barbara went out with this same boy several times in the next year. Nevertheless, the protective manner in which Barbara was treated by her family prevented her from developing close relationships with boys her own age and later left her feeling uncomfortable when she was alone with men.

Barbara's knowledge about and experiences with sexual activity were extremely limited during childhood and adolescence. Neither of her parents made an effort to provide her with information about her own body or reproductive functions. Her mother did discuss general issues such as romance and marriage with Barbara, but only at the most abstract level. All of the books and magazines in their home were carefully screened to avoid exposing the children to suggestive literature or photographs. Barbara was not able to learn much about these matters from her friends because she was so closely supervised. After she began menstruating at the age of 11, her mother gave her a book that explained the basic organs and physiology associated with the human reproductive system and, once again, avoided any personal discussion of Barbara's concerns about sexuality. The implicit message conveyed by her parents' behavior and attitudes was that sex was a mysterious and dangerous phenomenon.

After she graduated from high school, Barbara began taking classes at the local junior college. She continued to live at home with her parents and maintained several of the same friends she had had in high school. During her first semester, Barbara met Frank, who was then a student at the police academy. After several weeks, they began to see each other regularly. Her parents liked Frank, perhaps because her father was also a policeman, and they gradually began to allow her greater freedom than they had when she dated in high school. Frank and Barbara were both 18 years old, but he was much more mature and experienced. He had been dating regularly since he was 15 and had had sexual intercourse for the first time when he was 17. Their sexual relationship progressed rapidly. Although she was initially apprehensive and shy, Barbara found that she enjoyed heavy petting. She refused to have intercourse with Frank for several months; finally she gave in one evening after they had both been drinking at a party. She later remembered being disappointed by the experience. Frank had climaxed almost immediately after penetration, but she had not reached orgasm. Her guilt was replaced by utter shock when she realized several weeks later that she was pregnant. They did not discuss the pregnancy with her parents and agreed they should be married as soon as possible. Bonnie was born less than six months after their marriage. Despite the obvious "prematurity" of the birth, Barbara's parents never mentioned the issue of premarital intercourse or pregnancy. Barbara dropped out of college before Bonnie was born and did not return to school for many years.

Barbara and Frank's sexual relationship did not change much over the next few years, although their frequency of intercourse declined markedly during their second year of marriage. Intercourse continued to be a pleasurable experience for both of them, even though Barbara was not able to experience orgasm. Her first orgasm occurred after they had been married for more than three years and both of their children had been born. Following their typical pattern, Frank had fallen asleep after intercourse and Barbara was lying in bed, half awake and very much aroused. She was lying on her stomach and some of the blankets happened to be bunched up under her pelvis and between her legs. Without recognizing what she was doing, Barbara began rocking rhythmically from side to side. She was relaxed and noticed that this motion created a pleasurable sensation. Several minutes after she began rocking, she experienced an intense, unmistakable orgasm. It was an extremely pleasurable phenomenon restrained only by her fear of waking Frank. After her accidental discovery of masturbation, Barbara experimented further with various styles of self-manipulation and was soon masturbating regularly. She was afraid to describe these experiences to Frank, however, because she believed that masturbation was an immoral and selfish act, and her ability to reach orgasm by self-stimulation did not generalize to intercourse with Frank. Barbara also avoided conversations about sex when she was talking to other women. She believed that masturbation and sexual fantasies were sinful behaviors and was convinced that none of her friends had ever had such experiences.

CONCEPTUALIZATION AND TREATMENT

In approaching the sexual problem described by Barbara, the therapist focused on Barbara and Frank as a couple, not on Barbara as an individual. He was principally concerned with the things they did and said when they were together. It was clear from Barbara's description of the problem that she knew very little about sexual behavior. Her reports also indicated that she and Frank were not communicating effectively during sexual activity and were not engaging in effective sexual behaviors. Because of the focus on the relationship and not on Barbara alone, the therapist asked Barbara to bring Frank with her to the second treatment session.

Frank was initially reluctant to join Barbara in treatment because he had always believed that the problem was primarily hers. Nevertheless, he agreed to talk to the therapist at least once, and, during this interview, he indicated that he was also dissatisfied with their sexual relationship. On further questioning, he even admitted that he had secretly worried that he was to blame for Barbara's orgasmic difficulty. This thought had caused him considerable anxiety from time to time, particularly when he was also worried about his performance in other roles such as work and his relationship with the children. The therapist asked Frank to describe their sexual activity from his perspective and noted, as Barbara had previously indicated, that little emphasis was placed on foreplay. Two considerations seemed to be particularly important in this regard. First, Frank said that he did not know what sorts of activity might be more pleasurable for Barbara, since she had never expressed any feelings in this regard. Second, Frank indicated that he generally felt unsure of his own ability to delay ejaculation and therefore preferred to insert his penis in Barbara's vagina before he "lost control." This concern was related to his belief that intercourse was the most mature form of sexual activity and his fear that Barbara would begin to question his virility if he were unable to accomplish intercourse. Although he realized that Barbara was not entirely happy with their sexual relationship, Frank privately conceded that he would rather not draw attention to his own difficulty. The therapist responded in a reassuring manner emphasizing that he did not want to ascribe responsibility to either partner. The primary concern of treatment, he said, would be to increase both partners' satisfaction with their sexual relationship. He also noted that most forms of sexual dysfunction, particularly premature ejaculation, are amenable to brief, behavioral forms of therapy. Given this explanation of the problem and considering the optimistic prognosis, Frank agreed to work together with Barbara toward a solution of their problems.

During his initial interviews with both Barbara and Frank, the therapist made an effort to consider various factors that might contribute to sexual dysfunction, such as depression, fatigue, and marital disharmony. None of these seemed to account for the problem. Both partners were somewhat unhappy, but neither was clinically depressed. Although their relationship had been strained by the sexual problem, they were both committed to the marriage. Neither was involved in an extramarital relationship, which might detract from their involvement in treatment or their interest in change, and both Barbara and Frank expressed affection for one another. It was interesting to note that they were more willing to express their positive feelings for the other person when they were talking with the therapist than when they were interacting directly. Overall, the sexual dysfunction did not seem to be secondary to other adjustment problems.

Before beginning a psychological approach to their sexual problem, Barbara and Frank were also asked to obtain complete physical examinations. This assessment was recommended in an effort to rule out the possibility that their difficulty could be traced to a physical disorder. Various diseases that affect the central nervous system, hormone levels, and vascular functions can influence sexual arousal and performance. Abnormalities in the musculature and tissue structure of the genital area can also be problematic. None of these factors was evident in this particular case.

During the third session, the therapist explored many of Barbara's and Frank's attitudes and beliefs about sexual behavior. His purpose was to improve their communication with each other about sexual matters and to open a discussion in which they could acquire additional knowledge and correct mistaken beliefs. Several issues were particularly important and seemed to be related to their failure to engage in more satisfying sexual behavior. For example, both Barbara and Frank believed that vaginal stimulation should be the principal source of sexual pleasure for women and that orgasm during coitus is dependent solely on such stimulation. The therapist explained that the clitoris is, in fact, more sensitive than the vagina. Female orgasm seems to depend on both direct and indirect stimulation of the clitoris during both masturbation and intercourse.

Considerable time was also spent discussing the Garrisons' attitudes toward and use of sexual fantasies. The topic was broached cautiously by the therapist. He commented in a matter-of-fact tone that most normal adults engage in sexual fantasies; he then asked Frank to describe one of his favorite fantasies. Despite some initial embarrassment, and much to Barbara's surprise, Frank told Barbara and the therapist that he often pictured himself working late at night and being seduced in the detectives' lounge by an attractive female colleague. This was the first time that Barbara and Frank had discussed sexual fantasies. While Barbara expressed some mild jealousy that Frank would think about another woman, she was relieved to learn that he also used sexual fantasies. His self-disclosure lowered her anxiety on the topic. She then shared a description of one of her own fantasies—admittedly one that was less provocative than her thoughts of having intercourse with several men in a row. Having explored these and other issues at some length, the therapist recommended a few books that the Garrisons should read in order to learn more about human sexuality. One of the books was *Becoming Orgasmic: A Sexual Growth Program for Women* (Heiman, LoPiccolo, & LoPiccolo, 1988). It was hoped that this information would reduce their anxiety about their own interests and practices and, at the same time, suggest new activities that they had not yet tried.

The next step in treatment was to eliminate some of the obstacles that were interfering with Barbara's ability to become totally aroused and to teach her and Frank to engage in more enjoyable sexual behavior. This could be accomplished only in a totally nondemanding atmosphere. Because of their history of sexual difficulty and dissatisfaction, Barbara and Frank had become self-conscious about their sexual behavior. Barbara felt considerable pressure, which was mostly self-imposed, to reach orgasm; Frank was secretly concerned about whether he could delay ejaculation long enough for Barbara to become more aroused. From the point at which Frank initiated sexual activity, both of them tended to assume a detached perspective as they observed what they were doing and how they were feeling. The therapist attempted to eliminate pressure to perform by telling Barbara and Frank that they were *not* to attempt sexual intercourse under any circumstances during the next few weeks. He told them that he was going to ask them to practice an exercise known as "sensate focus" in which their only goal would be to practice giving and receiving pleasurable sensations.

Sensate focus is a touching exercise in which the partners simply take turns gently massaging each other's body. The therapist instructed them to begin by finding a quiet time when they would not be disturbed or distracted and they were not overly tired. Having removed their clothes, Barbara was to lie on her stomach across the bed while Frank massaged her back and legs. She was encouraged to abandon herself to whatever pleasures she experienced. Barbara's instructions were to concentrate on the simplest sensations—warm and cold, smooth and rough, hard and soft—and to let Frank know what she enjoyed and what she wanted to change. Stimulation of Barbara's breasts and genital area was expressly prohibited to avoid demand for increased sexual arousal. They were asked to practice sensate focus at least four times before their next session.

Barbara and Frank both responded positively to this initial exercise. They described these extended periods of touching and caressing as relaxing and pleasurable; they both said that they had felt a sense of warmth and closeness that had disappeared from their relationship years ago. Barbara also expressed some relief that she was able to focus on the pleasure of Frank's touch without worrying about whether she would have an orgasm or whether he would ejaculate quickly and leave her stranded in a state of unfulfilled arousal. With this positive beginning, the therapist suggested that they move on to the next step. They were to change positions for the next week. Frank would sit on the bed with his back against the headboard and his legs spread apart. Barbara would sit in front of him, facing in the same direction, with her back resting against his chest and her legs resting over his. In this position, Frank would be able to touch and massage the front of her body; the restriction against touching her breasts and genitals were removed. He was told, however, to avoid direct stimulation of the clitoris because it can be irritating and in some cases painful. She was instructed to rest her hand gently on his and to guide his touch to convey the sensations that were most pleasurable to her, including location, pressure, and rhythm of movement. The therapist emphasized that Barbara was to control the interaction. As before, they were asked to practice at least four times in the following week.

At the beginning of the next session, minor problems were noted in the progress of treatment. Barbara reported that she had become somewhat self-conscious with the new exercise. She found the experience pleasant and arousing, but her mind wandered and she was unable to achieve a state of total abandon. Frank had also encountered some difficulty with ejaculatory control. On the third evening of practice, he had become totally absorbed in the process and, without completely realizing what he was doing, he had rubbed his erect penis against Barbara's back and reached orgasm. The therapist reassured Frank that this experience was not unexpected and could, in fact, be seen as the predictable outcome of his immersion in the sensate focus exercise. It was also clear, however, that some additional changes should be made in the process to help Frank gain more control and to reduce Barbara's tendency toward detachment.

The therapist decided to address the issue of ejaculatory control by recommending that Barbara and Frank practice the "start–stop" procedure. Frank was instructed to lie on his back so that Barbara could stimulate his erect penis manually. His task would be to concentrate on his own level of arousal and signal Barbara when he experienced the sensation that immediately precedes ejaculation. At this point, Barbara would discontinue stimulation. When Frank no longer felt that ejaculation was imminent, she would resume stimulation until he again signaled that he was experiencing the urge to ejaculate. They were asked to repeat this cycle four or five times initially and to work toward achieving 15 to 20 minutes of continuous repetitions.

The sensate focus exercise was also continued with additional instruction. Barbara was specifically encouraged to engage in her favorite sexual fantasies while guiding Frank's hands over her body. Frank's acceptance and support were particularly helpful in this regard because of Barbara's guilt about the use of sexual fantasies. By concentrating on these images, she would be able to avoid other mental distractions that had impaired her ability to become completely involved in the sensate focus exercise.

The next two weeks of practice were very successful. Frank was able to control his ejaculatory urges within four or five days; Barbara found that the start–stop exercise was also quite pleasurable for her. In the past Frank had always discouraged her from stroking or playing with his erect penis because he was afraid that he would ejaculate prematurely. It was becoming clear that their improved communication about what they enjoyed and when to start and stop various activities resulted in considerably greater freedom and pleasure than their previously constricted interactions had allowed. Barbara was now able to reach orgasm through Frank's manual stimulation of her breasts and clitoris. She was much less inhibited about directing his touch, and he noted he had learned a lot about Barbara's erotic zones. Much of the tension and inhibition had been reduced.

The final step was to help Barbara experience orgasm during intercourse. The prohibition against intercourse was lifted, and a new procedure was introduced. As before, they were instructed to begin their exercises by alternating in sensate focus. When they were both moderately aroused, Frank would lie on his back and Barbara would sit on top of him with her knees drawn toward his chest and insert his penis into her vagina. She would then control the speed and rhythm of their movements. Emphasis was placed on moving slowly and concentrating on the pleasurable sensations associated with vaginal containment. If Frank experienced the urge to ejaculate, Barbara was instructed to withdraw his penis until the sensation had passed. If she became less aroused during intercourse, they would also separate, and Frank would once again employ clitoral stimulation until Barbara reached a stage of more intense arousal, at which point they would resume coitus.

Barbara and Frank practiced this procedure many times over the next few weeks. It was an extremely pleasurable experience, and they noticed that they had made considerable progress, most notably Frank's ability to delay ejaculation throughout 20 to 30 minutes of intercourse with Barbara in the superior position. Nevertheless, Barbara was not able to reach orgasm through penile stimulation alone. They continued to alternate periods of insertion with manual stimulation of the clitoris, but Barbara's orgasms were limited to the latter intervals. The therapist noted that this was not uncommon and encouraged them to begin experimenting with other positions for intercourse that would also allow manual stimulation of her clitoris during coitus. The Garrisons were perfectly satisfied with this solution.

Fifteen weeks after their initial visit, Barbara and Frank had made significant changes in their sexual adjustment. Both of them were pleased with these developments, which included Frank's confidence in his ability to control ejaculation and Barbara's ability to reach orgasm during intercourse. Perhaps most important, these changes were not specifically limited to their sexual interactions. They reported that they also talked more frequently and openly about other areas of their lives and felt closer to each other than they had at the beginning of treatment. Thus the new lines of communication that had been developed in sexual activities did generalize, or transfer, to some other situations.

Even though some of the Garrisons' peripheral problems were resolved spontaneously after the successful treatment of Barbara's orgasmic inhibition, other difficulties remained. Several were addressed directly in further treatment sessions. Their relationship with Bonnie, for example, continued to be a source of frequent irritation. They argued with her individually and as a couple and sometimes fought with each other when she was not present. Most of these arguments centered on the issues of freedom and responsibility. Could Bonnie stay out past 10 P.M. on weekdays? Should she and her boyfriend be alone in the house when Barbara and Frank were out? What chores was she expected to do, and how often should she do them? All of these questions were addressed in conjoint family sessions in which the therapist served as a mediator. Bonnie and her parents negotiated a mutually acceptable contract that specified what she could expect from them and, in turn, what they could expect from her. The agreement also included contingencies that would go into effect when and if anyone failed to fulfill his or her commitments. The level of conflict in the Garrison home was substantially reduced after the negotiation of this contract.

DISCUSSION

Sexual dysfunctions are defined in terms of interference with any phase of the human sexual response cycle. This cycle may be thought of as a continuous sequence of events or sensations, beginning with sexual desire and ending with the decrease in tension following orgasm. This cycle can be roughly divided into four phases that are characteristic of both men and women. The *sexual desire phase* reflects the person's willingness to approach or engage in those experiences that will lead to sexual arousal. During the *excitement phase,* the person begins to respond to sexual stimulation with increased flow of blood to the genital area. This engorgement leads to erection in the male and vaginal lubrication in the female. Various physiological changes, including more rapid breathing and an increase in heart rate and blood pressure, occur throughout the excitement phase. These changes reach their maximum intensity during the *orgasmic phase,* a very brief period of involuntary response. In males the orgasmic phase occurs in two stages, beginning with the collection of sperm and seminal fluid in the urethra (creating a sensation of inevitability, or "point of no return") and ending with ejaculation. In females the orgasmic phase involves rhythmic contractions in the outer third of the vagina. From a subjective point of view, the orgasmic phase is the point of peak physical pleasure. It is followed by a rapid dissipation of tension. The period following orgasm, known as the *resolution phase,* encompasses the return of bodily functions to a normal resting state.

Interference with sexual response may occur at any point and may take the form of subjective distress (such as the fear of losing ejaculatory control) or disrupted performance (such as the inability to maintain an erection sufficient for intercourse). *DSM-IV* (pp. 496–515) provides the following definitions of problems experienced by men and women:

Hypoactive Sexual Desire Disorder: Persistently or recurrently deficient (or absent) sexual fantasies and desire for sexual activity.

Sexual Aversion Disorder: Persistent or recurrent extreme aversion to, and avoidance of, all (or almost all) genital sexual contact with a sexual partner.

Female Sexual Arousal Disorder: Persistent or recurrent inability to attain, or to maintain until completion of the sexual activity, an adequate lubrication-swelling response of sexual excitement.

Male Erectile Disorder: Persistent or recurrent inability to attain or maintain until completion of the sexual activity, an adequate erection.

Female Orgasmic Disorder (Inhibited Female Orgasm): Persistent or recurrent delay in, or absence of, orgasm following a normal sexual excitement phase.

Male Orgasmic Disorder: Persistent or recurrent delay in, or absence of, orgasm following a normal sexual excitement phase during sexual activity.

Premature Ejaculation: Persistent or recurrent ejaculation with minimal sexual stimulation before, on, or shortly after penetration and before the person wishes it.

Dyspareunia: Recurrent or persistent genital pain in either a male or a female before, during, or after sexual intercourse.

Vaginismus: Recurrent or persistent involuntary spasm of the musculature of the outer third of the vagina that interferes with sexual intercourse.

All of these problems may be general or situational in nature. In the case of male erectile disorder, for example, the person may never have been able to attain or maintain an erection until completion of the sex act. On the other hand, he may have been able to do so in the past, or with a different partner, but cannot do so presently.

Most people with hypoactive sexual desire retain the capacity for physical sexual response, but they are generally unwilling to participate and are unreceptive to their partner's attempts to initiate sexual relations. Lack of interest in sexual activity may be an important source of distress, particularly for the spouse or partner of such an individual, but it is also a difficult problem to define. What is a normal sexual appetite? Instead of establishing an arbitrary standard, *DSM-IV* has opted for a flexible judgment in this area that depends on a consideration of factors that affect sexual desire such as age, sex, health, intensity and frequency of sexual desire, and the context of the individual's life.

Diagnostic judgments in the area of sexual dysfunction often depend on subtle considerations. Is the problem sufficiently persistent and pervasive to warrant treatment? And, if it is, does the problem center on one partner or the other? These may be difficult questions. In the Garrisons' case, for example, it was not clear whether Barbara's inability to reach orgasm during intercourse could be attributed to Frank's difficulty in delaying or controlling his ejaculatory response. On the other hand, if she had been able to reach orgasm quickly, he might not have worried about the question of control. Two conclusions can be drawn from these considerations. First, sexual dysfunction is most easily defined in the context of a particular interpersonal relationship. The couple, not either individual, is the focus for assessment and treatment. Second, the identification of sexual dysfunction rests largely with the couple's subjective satisfaction with their sexual relationship and not with absolute judgments about typical, or normal, levels of performance.

Surveys conducted among the general population indicate that various forms of sexual dysfunction are relatively common (Nathan, 1986; Spector & Carey, 1990). Premature ejaculation may be the most frequent form of sexual dysfunction, affecting at least one in every five adult men. Relatively few of these men seek treatment for their problems. Erectile dysfunction (that is, difficulty maintaining sexual arousal until completion of sexual activity) may be experienced by another 10 percent to 20 percent of the male population.

Inhibited female orgasm may also be a relatively common problem. The definition of the disorder has been the topic of some controversy, however, which casts doubt on the actual prevalence of the problem. One fact is relatively clear; approximately 10 percent of adult women report a total lack of previous orgasmic response (Anderson, 1983). Does this failure to experience orgasm automatically indicate a dysfunction or the absence of the capacity to reach orgasm? Some women voluntarily refrain from sexual activity. Others may not have engaged in activities, such as masturbation, that are likely to result in orgasmic response. The *DSM-IV* definition of female orgasmic disorder stipulates that the delay or absence of orgasm *must follow a normal sexual excitement phase*. The diagnosis is to be made only if the clinician decides that the woman's orgasmic capacity is "less than would be reasonable for her age, sexual experience, and the adequacy of sexual stimulation she receives" (*DSM-IV*, p. 507). Using this more restrictive definition, many fewer women would meet the criteria for this disorder. Wakefield (1988) has argued that true orgasmic dysfunction is relatively rare when the *DSM* definition is employed (cf. Morokoff, 1989).

Etiology

Some cases of sexual dysfunction may be the result of other forms of physical or mental disturbance. Human sexual response involves a complicated and delicate system that may be disrupted by any number of factors. Various physical conditions, including diseases of the central nervous system, drug ingestion, and fatigue, can impair the person's interest in sexual activity or the ability to perform sexual responses. Other psychological adjustment problems can also lead to disturbances in sexual activity. Depression, for example, is commonly associated with a drastic decline in a person's interest in sex. These factors should be considered before a direct treatment approach is attempted, but most instances of sexual dysfunctions are not simple by-products of physical or mental disorders. Based on their extensive clinical experience, Masters and Johnson estimate that fewer than 5 percent of the cases of inhibited female orgasm that they have treated could be traced to organic factors. In males, erectile failure can be caused by a number of organic conditions, but premature ejaculation is rarely the product of physical illness or neurological impairment (Masters, Johnson, & Kolodny, 1985).

Various psychological explanations have been proposed to account for the development and maintenance of sexual dysfunction. Psychoanalytic theory traces sexual problems to an inadequate resolution of the Oedipal conflict. In Barbara's case, for example, a psychoanalyst might have argued that her inability to reach orgasm during intercourse was associated with fear of success in the sense that being successful in her adult sexual relationship might be analogous to succeeding in the Oedipal situation. According to this notion, Barbara wanted to have intercourse with her father and was thus in competition with her mother. But she was also afraid that if she succeeded her mother would punish her severely. To the extent that her husband was symbolic of her father and reaching orgasm during intercourse with him was equivalent to "winning" the struggle with her mother. Barbara's orgasmic inhibition could be determined by this unconscious mental conflict. The treatment approach that follows from this theoretical position would involve long-term, individual psychotherapy with Barbara in which the goal would be to help her achieve insight into her frustrated sexual desire for her father, her consequent fear of her mother, and the relationship between this conflict and her current relationship with her husband.

Certain aspects of this theory are consistent with the present case. Most notable might be the resemblance between her father and her husband, Frank. They were both police officers and shared various interpersonal characteristics, such as conservative social and political beliefs. On the other hand, they did not resemble each other physically, and Frank's behavior toward Barbara and their children was much less stern and protective than her father's had been. Barbara's current relationship with her mother might also be raised as evidence in support of a psychoanalytic approach to the case. Her father had died shortly after Barbara and Frank were married. Barbara's mother moved into an apartment near the Garrisons' home, and she and Barbara continued to see each other often. Barbara admitted privately that her mother was usually more of an annoyance than a help, meddling in their daily activities and criticizing the manner in which Barbara and Frank handled the children. Barbara was markedly unassertive with her mother and usually acquiesced to her demands. A psychoanalyst might have argued that this close, ongoing interaction exacerbated and maintained Barbara's rivalry with her mother and that her submissive yet covertly hostile attitude was mostly motivated by her fear of retaliation. Barbara's problems with her teenage daughter, Bonnie, could also be explained in psychoanalytic terms. Without much difficulty, Barbara's exaggerated concerns about Bonnie's sexual behavior could be seen as the projection of her fear that she would lose control of her own sexual desires (as was evident in her discussion of her sexual fantasies and the fear that she might flee to Los Angeles to become a prostitute). There are, however, more parsimonious explanations for these phenomena. Her parental behavior may have a simple reflection of the pattern modeled by her parents; they were overly protective of her when she was young, and she was now protective of Bonnie.

Learning theorists (e.g., Tollison & Adams, 1979) have also stressed the importance of past events in determining present sexual adjustment, but they have emphasized the importance of conditioning procedures, not unconscious mental conflict and sexual desire for one's parents. From a behavioral perspective, many forms of sexual dysfunction can be seen as the product of learned inhibitions that are acquired as a result of unsuccessful, early sexual experiences. In some cases, these may have been traumatic events such as being raped or molested. They may also include other situations. Consider, for example, an adolescent boy who is discovered masturbating by his mother, particularly if she responds with anger or disgust. The boy may develop, through classical conditioning, an association between the stimuli that lead to sexual arousal (say he was looking at pictures of nude women at the time) and shame or anxiety. Subsequent anticipatory anxiety may interfere with his ability to maintain an erection during sexual intercourse. Operant learning principles may also play a similar role. For example, some teenagers have their first sexual experience in the backseat of a parked automobile, a situation in which they run the risk of being discovered and possibly humiliated. In this situation, the male may be reinforced for ejaculating quickly after penetration by escape from the anxiety-provoking situation of being partially exposed to any curious passerby who happened to peer in the window. In general, behavioral models of sexual dysfunction emphasize the importance of learned, anticipatory anxiety that is associated with sexual stimulation and the development of avoidance responses that serve to reduce this anxiety. They also stress the importance of knowing how to engage in effective sexual behaviors; they focus on what the people do during sexual activity instead of on the symbolic meaning of the act.

The cognitive-behavioral perspective is also compatible with several elements of Barbara's case. Her parents' inability to display physical affection (at least in front of the children), their failure to provide her with any information about sexual behavior, and the implicit message that sexual activity was somehow shameful or disgusting were all important factors that contributed to both her anxiety regarding sexual activity and her lack of appropriate heterosexual social skills. Prior to her relationship with Frank, Barbara had no sexual experience other than brief kisses and hugs after dates. She and Frank, at his insistence, progressed rapidly in their own sexual relationship without giving Barbara sufficient time to extinguish gradually her fear of physical intimacy. Furthermore, their first experience with intercourse was generally unpleasant. This unfortunate event, coupled with their subsequent realization that Barbara had become pregnant, contributed to furthering her discomfort in sexual activity. Instead of addressing the problem directly and learning more enjoyable ways of interacting sexually, Barbara and Frank tried to ignore the problem. They had intercourse infrequently and shortened the occasions when they did have sex to the briefest possible intervals.

Although it is difficult to determine whether certain conditions or experiences *cause* sexual dysfunction, it is somewhat easier to identify conditions that serve to *maintain* problems that have already developed. Perhaps the most important consequence of the general behavioral approach to sexual dysfunction has been the emphasis that is placed on the current, situational determinants of the problem. Kaplan (1974) summarized these factors under four general headings. The first is "failure to engage in effective sexual behavior." This category includes practices such as rushing to the point of penetration before the woman is sufficiently aroused, as was the Garrisons' habit. Kaplan points out that this sort of error is almost always the result of ignorance about human sexual responses and not the product of deeply ingrained neuroses or personality disorders. Frank and Barbara did not know that most women take longer than men to reach an advanced stage of sexual arousal and, as a result, neither of them had made a serious effort to improve or prolong their activity during foreplay.

The second category is "sexual anxiety," which includes problems associated with subjective factors such as the pressure to perform adequately and fear of failure. This type of interference was clearly present in the Garrisons' case. Frank has been concerned for a number of years about losing control of his ejaculatory response. Because of this fear, he continued to rush through the initial stages of sexual activity and resisted any subtle efforts that Barbara made to slow things down. She, on the other hand, was troubled by a double-edged concern. Although she always *tried* very hard to have an orgasm (and was, in fact, quite self-conscious about her failure to reach a climax), she was simultaneously worried about getting carried away. Barbara was convinced that if she really abandoned herself completely and followed her "raw sexual instinct," she would lose control of herself. In so doing, she feared that she would risk losing Frank completely because he would be repulsed by her behavior. This was truly a vicious dilemma. If she did not relax and let herself go, she would not have an orgasm, thus perpetuating her own unhappiness as well as Frank's conviction (as she imagined it) that she was an inadequate lover. On the other hand, if she did relax and let herself go, she would lose control and run the risk of alienating him completely.

The third set of factors that maintain sexual dysfunctions include "perceptual and intellectual defenses against erotic feelings." Sexual responses are not under voluntary control. The surest way to lose an erection, for example, is to think about the erection instead of the erotic stimuli. Nevertheless, some people engage in a kind of obsessive self-observation during sexual activity and, as a result, become spectators, not participants, in their own love making. Laboratory studies have provided further insight regarding this phenomenon, and they have suggested some interesting distinctions between sexually functional and dysfunctional people (Barlow, 1986). The arousal levels of sexually functional subjects are typically enhanced by performance-related erotic cues, such as the presence of a highly aroused partner. The same kind of stimulation can distract people who are sexually dysfunctional. The cognitive interference that they experience in response to these stimuli leads to a decrease in their sexual arousal. This problem was particularly characteristic of Barbara's behavior. She often found herself ruminating during sexual activity and asking herself questions about her own performance and desires (Will I come this time? What would happen if Frank knew what I have been thinking about?).

"Failure to communicate" is the final category of immediate causes of sexual dysfunction. Women suffering from orgasmic disorder report that in addition to holding negative attitudes toward masturbation and feeling guilty about sex, they are uncomfortable talking to their partner about sexual activities, especially those involving direct clitoral stimulation (Kelly, Strassberg, & Kircher, 1990). The Garrisons' failure in this regard was painfully obvious. Both were unwilling to talk to the other person about their desires and pleasures. In Barbara's case, her inhibitions could be traced to the environment in which she was raised. Her parents explicitly conveyed the message that decent people did not talk about sex. If she could not talk to her own mother about basic matters such as menstruation and pregnancy, how could she expect to discuss erotic fantasies with her husband? Consequently, Barbara and Frank knew little about the kinds of stimulation and fantasies that were most pleasing to their partner.

Treatment

The widely publicized work of Masters and Johnson (1970) had an important impact on the development and use of direct psychological approaches to the treatment of sexual dysfunction. Although questions have been raised about the way in which they evaluated and reported the results of their treatment program (e.g., Zilbergeld & Evans, 1980), their apparent success created an optimistic and enthusiastic environment in which further research and training could be accomplished. Instead of treating the problem as a symbol of unconscious turmoil, sex therapists are primarily concerned with the problem itself and the current, situational determinants that serve to maintain it. This approach is clearly behavioral. Therapists seek to eliminate sexual anxiety by temporarily removing distracting expectations (intercourse is typically forbidden during the first several days of treatment) and substituting competing responses. The sensate focus exercise, for example, is employed to create an erotic atmosphere, devoid of performance demands, in which couples can learn to communicate more freely. In later sessions couples are instructed in the use of specific exercises designed to foster skills related to their specific sexual problem (Wincze & Carey, 1991).

The "start–stop" procedure, which was originally introduced by Semans (1956), is a good example of this approach. The male partner is taught to attend to important sensations that signal the imminence of ejaculation and to interrupt further stimulation until the urge passes. Frank's experience indicates that there are important cognitive changes that accompany the physiological and behavioral components of this technique. As he became more successful in controlling his ejaculatory responses, Frank experienced less apprehension during extended periods of foreplay. His increased confidence and willingness to communicate were, in turn, important assets in addressing Barbara's orgasmic difficulty. Considerable success has been achieved with this approach. Masters and Johnson[1] treated 186 men for premature ejaculation and found that 182 were able to learn to control ejaculation so that their partners could achieve orgasm during coitus at least 50 percent of the time. Furthermore, in a five-year follow-up of 74 of these men, Masters and Johnson identified only one instance of relapse. Similarly high rates of improvement have been reported by other investigators (O'Donohue, Letourneau &

---

[1] Masters and Johnson used a variant of Seman's procedure known as the "squeeze technique," in which the wife also squeezes the end of the penis between her thumb and forefinger during interruptions of sexual stimulation.

Geer, 1993). These data suggest that patients treated with the start – stop and squeeze techniques are likely to show positive improvement.

The prognosis for orgasmic dysfunction in women is also quite good. LoPiccolo and Stock (1986) reported a 95 percent rate of success for directed masturbation training with 150 women who had never had an orgasm prior to treatment. Approximately 85 percent of the women were also able to reach orgasm if they were stimulated directly by their partners. It is also interesting to note, however, that only 40 percent of these women were able to reach orgasm during intercourse. The goals of treatment and the criterion of success for this form of therapy are therefore somewhat difficult to establish.

With few exceptions, all women can learn to experience orgasm, but a substantial percentage cannot reach climax through the stimulation afforded by intercourse alone. As in Barbara's case, many women require additional stimulation beyond that associated with the motion of the erect penis in the vagina. Kaplan (1974) has argued that in the absence of information to the contrary, these women should not be considered treatment failures, and they should not be encouraged to believe that they are settling for "second best." Research studies have tended to focus on certain aspects of sexual performance, such as ability to delay ejaculation and orgasmic responsiveness. It must be remembered, however, that performance variables represent only one aspect of sexual adjustment. Factors such as subjective arousal, personal satisfaction, and feelings of intimacy and closeness with one's partner are also important considerations. Barbara and Frank were happy with their sexual relationship despite the fact that she could not achieve orgasm through intercourse alone. They had made remarkable changes in their ability to communicate and share sexual pleasure and were content to utilize positions that allowed either Frank or Barbara to stimulate Barbara's clitoral area manually while they were having intercourse. With this limitation in mind, direct approaches to orgasmic dysfunction have been very successful.

The literature concerned with evaluating treatment programs for sexual dysfunction made significant strides during the decade of the 1980s. The enthusiasm that had been generated by Masters and Johnson's initial reports was tempered by the publication of several critical reviews (e.g., Cole, 1985; Warner & Bancroft, 1986). There are many difficulties associated with evaluating sex therapy. Some studies have failed to include appropriate control groups. Others did not assign patients randomly to treatment groups. Many studies can be questioned because their outcome measures were based on the therapists' subjective evaluations, which could easily be biased by knowledge of the treatment program and expectations for success. In spite of these difficulties, there is still considerable reason for optimism in the treatment of sexual dysfunction (Kolodny, 1981; LoPiccolo & Stock, 1986). Most investigators recognize a need for more rigorous evaluation studies to determine exactly which intervention procedures are useful for different types of sexual problems.

13 PARAPHILIA: EXHIBITIONISM

Pete Wilson began therapy in November with a clinical psychologist. During the initial interview, Pete, a 34-year-old white male, explained that he was coming for therapy concerning a sexual problem that he had had for years. The immediate precipitant of entering therapy was that he had been arrested in September for a sexual assault. He had been driving home, taking a shortcut along some back roads, when he saw a car with its hood up and a woman looking at the engine. He stopped to offer assistance. In response to his questions about what was wrong, the woman told him that she had stopped because her alternator light had come on. Pete was able to correct the problem by adjusting the fan belt. When the woman thanked him, he pulled her close to him, trying to fondle her buttocks. As she pushed him away, he exposed himself and started masturbating. The woman ran to her car and drove off. Pete made no attempt to follow. Later that night, the police came to his home and arrested him. An initial hearing was held the next day and bail was set. Pete's wife attended the hearing and paid the bail. At his subsequent trial, Pete was allowed to plead guilty to a reduced charge of attempted assault and was put on probation for two years. Part of the probation agreement was that Pete seek professional help.

This was not the first time that Pete had done something sexual that could get him into trouble. He had a long history of sexual deviance, dating back to early adolescence, but he had never actually attacked a woman before. His deviant sexual practices took two forms. One was getting himself into crowded places—shopping centers, subway trains, and the like—moving up close behind a woman, and rubbing his pelvis against her buttocks. This type of activity is called *frottage*; the disorder is called *frotteurism*. Pete's other deviant sexual practice was exhibitionism. Sometimes he would park his car in a place where many women would be walking, remain seated behind the wheel, and masturbate as he watched them. He did not expose himself directly but hoped that the passing woman would look into his car and see him. Other times he would masturbate under a raincoat while in a place frequented by women. Teenagers with "cute, little behinds" were the preferred target for both activities.

Pete had engaged in both of these activities since adolescence. The first time he clearly remembered doing either was as a 16-year-old high-school student. He was at a football game on a drizzly Saturday afternoon and had on a raincoat, one in which the pockets allow a hand to go from the outside all the way through the coat to the body. Sitting next to a female acquaintance, he found himself sexually aroused and masturbated to orgasm, apparently undetected by anyone.

When he got his driver's license later that year, he began his practice of openly masturbating in his car. Since then he had engaged in either frottage or exhibitionism fairly regularly—an average of 15 to 20 times per year. Pete reported that the urge to do either usually increased when he was under stress, such as during exams in high school, or while under work pressures in adulthood. His sexual behavior had worried him for some time. He had been in therapy for brief periods on three previous occasions. Each time he dropped out after several sessions because it seemed to him that little progress was being made.

This time, other important facets of Pete's problem were explored over several sessions. One of these was his sexual fantasies, which were a mirror of his deviant sexual practices. During the day, he often imagined rubbing against or masturbating in front of young women. His masturbatory fantasies also had the same content. He reported that the frequency of his sexual fantasies had been increasing lately, stimulated by advertisements for designer jeans in magazines and on television. But there was an important difference between his fantasies and his actual sexual experiences. In real life he had never succeeded in arousing a woman by rubbing against her or publicly masturbating. Women he rubbed against moved away from him or, less frequently, threatened to call for help if he persisted. When women saw him masturbating in his car, their reaction was shock or disgust. In his fantasies, however, Pete's frottage or masturbation usually served as a prelude to intercourse. The young women of his dreams became aroused as he rubbed against them or when they saw his erect penis. His fantasy would then expand to include a more conventional sexual encounter. Fantasies limited only to conventional intercourse, however, were not stimulating to Pete.

Pete also had problems in other areas of his life. Although a college graduate, he had never been able to find a job that he found satisfying. His interests in painting and music had never turned into anything economically viable. He had held a long series of jobs he regarded as dull. The longest period for which he had the same job was 18 months. He was currently working the day shift in a 24-hour topless bar, hardly a sensible job choice given his problems.

Pete had married Helen when he was 24 and she was 22. They had dated for about six months before the marriage. Their son, Steve, was now five years old. Helen was a high-school graduate who had gone to secretarial school and now worked as an executive secretary for the vice-president of an engineering firm. She held this relatively high-paying and responsible job for the past four years. Pete reported that their marriage had gradually gone downhill. It was not so much that they were fighting or arguing a lot but that Helen had become less affectionate and less interested in sex and did not seem to care as much for him as she once had. Currently, he said, she found excuses to avoid most of his sexual advances. The frequency of intercourse had dropped to about twice per month. He reported that he did enjoy sex with his wife. Foreplay usually involved rubbing his penis on her bare buttocks, and intercourse was in the rear entry position. As with his fantasies, however, frottage was a necessary prelude to arousal and subsequent intercourse. According to Pete, the birth of their son seemed to coincide with the beginning of Helen's decline in interest in him. Pete was initially openly resentful of his son and refused to be involved in feedings, diaper changes, and the like. More recently, his feelings were changing; he was beginning to feel and act more like a father.

SOCIAL HISTORY

The origins of Pete's current problems seemed to lie in his childhood. He reported he had been "emotionally deprived" as a child. His father never held jobs for very long; consequently, the Wilsons moved a great deal. For this reason, Pete felt that he never had a chance to develop close childhood friendships. Furthermore, he felt rejected by his father. He reported that they never played or went on outings together and that his father always seemed cold and distant. Pete's father died when he was 12.

His relationship with his mother was better, but also deviant. Although Pete felt that he and his mother had a warm relationship, he also thought that she was overprotective and somewhat smothering. After the death of Pete's father, his mother never dated and seemed to invest all of her emotional needs in her children, especially Pete. For example, she continued to bathe him until he was 15. During these baths in Pete's early adolescence, she took great care in cleaning his penis, stroking it with the wet bar of soap and seeming to enjoy the erections that were often produced.

When Pete was 13, he and his mother were living in an apartment complex. His principal playmates were three young women, slightly older than himself. The four of them often engaged in rough and tumble play, including wrestling. During one of these play sessions, Pete had his first orgasm. He was wrestling with one of the women and was on top of her, his genitals against her buttocks. While moving, he became erect and continued thrusting until he climaxed.

After this initial pleasurable experience, Pete repeated it with his 8-year-old sister. At night, whenever the opportunity presented itself, he would go to her bed and rub his penis against her bare buttocks until he reached orgasm. He continued this practice regularly for the next couple years and stopped only after his sister finally threatened to tell their mother. When he stopped the frottage with his sister, he turned to regular masturbation with fantasies of both rubbing and conventional intercourse during his self-stimulation. At 15, an opportunity for conventional intercourse presented itself. Pete had heard stories for some time about the sexual exploits of a 17-year-old girl who lived in the same apartment building as he did. He went out of his way to get to know her, did errands and favors for her, and, finally, was invited to have sex with her one night in a nearby park. Although he became aroused as they kissed and petted, he lost his erection when he attempted intercourse. Thereafter Pete reported that he became afraid to approach women. The first instance of public masturbation occurred the next year.

On a social level, adolescence was not much better for Pete than childhood had been. He did hang around with a group, but he did not develop any really close relationships. He did not date much and reported that even being around popular and attractive women made him anxious. He also indicated that it was difficult for him to participate in conversations. He felt that most often people talked only about trivialities and that he was just not interested in that.

After graduating from high school, Pete went to a local community college and then to a university, where he graduated with a bachelor's degree in psychology. He then drifted through a series of jobs and casual affairs until meeting his wife. She was the first woman with whom he had ever had a lasting relationship.

Another perspective on Pete, and particularly on his marriage, was gained through a marital assessment conducted in separate sessions with Pete and Helen. Pete's main complaints about Helen centered on her lack of affection and their poor sexual relationship. He also reported that they did argue somewhat about how to spend their leisure time. Helen liked to socialize with friends, but Pete found most of them boring. Helen did not know about Pete's long history of deviant sexuality. She thought that Pete's trouble with the law was the only time he had ever engaged in such activity.

She could not understand why he had done it. She was extremely upset and repulsed by the entire incident, but she had stood by him. She also made it clear that another such incident would end their marriage. Helen's description of the problems in their marriage were similar to Pete's. She recognized that infrequent sex, absence of affection, and disagreements about socializing with friends were serious problems. Helen also complained about Pete as a father and husband. She resented the fact that he was less than a full partner in the marriage, sharing only minimally in parenting and other household duties. Her resentment was increased because she worked all day and then had to come home to cook, clean, and take care of their son while Pete did little but watch television. Even when Pete was not working, which had occurred often, he made little attempt to help out. She had lost respect for him because of his failure to share in the marriage and because of his job history and consequent inability to make much of a financial contribution. She was currently somewhat ashamed and suspicious about Pete's job as a bartender in a topless bar. Indeed, she attributed most of her inability to be affectionate and her declining interest in sex to this loss of respect. She added that she wished Pete would not always follow the same routine in their sexual encounters. Helen and Pete both completed the Locke–Wallace (1959) marital adjustment test. Each of their scores was in the maritally maladjusted range; Helen indicated substantially more marital dissatisfaction than did Pete.

CONCEPTUALIZATION AND TREATMENT

Initially, Pete's therapist needed to implement some procedures to increase the likelihood that Pete would be able to stop both the public masturbation and the frottage. He had not engaged in either activity for almost two months, the longest period for which he had ever refrained since adolescence. But Pete reported that the urges were still there and that they would pop up unexpectedly. Because the frottage and public masturbation were linked to particular situations—parking lots, shopping centers, and subways—Pete was instructed to avoid these situations as much as possible. In addition, Pete was taught how to handle an urge if it arose. He was told to distract himself by imagining that he was on a beach, feeling drowsy, and enjoying the warm sun and then to leave the situation. Pete practiced imagining this scene several times during the session and reported that he was able to visualize it clearly and that he found it calming and relaxing. Neither procedure was viewed as a "cure" for Pete's problems, but the hope was that they would serve as stopgap measures while more lasting changes were produced by other means.

The plan for therapy involved two components. First, an attempt was made to try to change Pete's sexual fantasies, both when masturbating and when he felt attraction to or arousal by any woman. Second, marital therapy seemed necessary, both for the marriage itself and more specifically, for the sexual relationship between Pete and Helen. Both aspects of the therapy were directed toward increasing the frequency and attractiveness of intercourse.

The first step in trying to make conventional intercourse more attractive to Pete was to have him masturbate while fantasizing only about intercourse. Initially, Pete reported that he was unable to develop a full erection unless he imagined frottage or public masturbation. He was first instructed to arouse himself with any fantasy—for him this was most often frottage or public masturbation—to begin masturbating and, when he was close to orgasm, to switch to an intercourse scene. He was able to do this easily. After a week of practice, he was told to switch to the intercourse fantasy closer to the start of masturbation. He was able to do so with no loss of arousal. By the fourth week, he was able to initiate and complete masturbation with no fantasies of frottage or public masturbation.

As this part of the therapy was progressing, Pete also began to work on altering fantasies elicited by women. His usual response to seeing a young woman, particularly one in tight jeans, was to begin imagining rubbing against her buttocks. A treatment was devised to help Pete change these fantasies. Initially, during a therapy session, Pete was shown a series of pictures of young women in tight jeans. For each stimulus he was asked to generate a nonsexual fantasy, such as trying to guess the woman's occupation. He was encouraged to focus on the woman's face instead of her buttocks as he thought about the picture. Over a series of trials in which Pete verbalized his thoughts, a number of distracting thoughts and fantasies were developed with the therapist guiding Pete and providing feedback. Over the next several weeks, Pete continued to practice his new fantasies, both in session and at home. As this skill became better established, Pete was also encouraged to use it in his day-to-day life.

At this point Pete was able to masturbate with no thoughts of frottage or public masturbation. He reported that he was beginning to have fewer and fewer thoughts of frottage when he encountered attractive young women. Marital therapy was then initiated.

At first the focus was on the nonsexual problems in the marriage. With the therapist functioning as a mediator and facilitator, the couple was instructed to talk about the various difficulties they were experiencing. The first problem they discussed was Pete's failure to help out with household chores. He acknowledged that he had not helped out very much but added also that when he did try to do something, Helen usually found fault with his efforts. Helen agreed, in part, with Pete's analysis. For example, when Pete did the laundry he would leave the clothes in the dryer so they became very wrinkled and would need ironing. From Helen's perspective, she was therefore not really saved from any work; if she had done the laundry herself, she would have quickly folded the clothes and not had to iron them. From Pete's viewpoint, his efforts had gone unappreciated. With the therapist's guidance, Helen and Pete were led to realize the aspects of the situation that were creating the problem. Neither of them was feeling good about what the other person had done. To solve the problem, Pete agreed to do the laundry and fold it immediately after it was dry, and Helen agreed to be sure to let Pete know that she appreciated his efforts. A similar system was instituted for several other household chores (cooking, vacuuming, general cleaning) in which Pete had tried to be helpful, but his efforts had failed to elicit Helen's approval.

Next the therapist tried to move the couple into a consideration of Pete's feelings that Helen was not affectionate toward him. But he was not able to limit the discussion to this problem; Helen was soon talking about her general lack of respect for Pete. The session became highly emotional. Pete, understandably somewhat defensive, argued that he had always done the best he could to be a provider for the family. This issue was not even close to resolution by the end of the session; the therapist instructed Pete and Helen not to talk about it further over the coming week but to think about it and be ready to discuss it the next week.

Two days later, Pete called the therapist to request an extra session. Pete was visibly tense when they met the next day. He said that he had really been shaken by the last session, that he had no idea that Helen had come to see him so negatively. This realization, he said, had a profound effect on him, and he felt compelled to let the therapist know something that he had previously not told anyone. Over the past several years he had had a series of casual sexual experiences with young women. During most of them, he had not been able to complete intercourse satisfactorily. The pattern was similar to his initial attempt at intercourse. He would first become aroused and fully erect but later would lose his erection. He said that he wanted to start over now, to stop the affairs, and do more to please Helen.

At the next session with Pete and Helen, Pete quickly announced that he had decided to change jobs, was job hunting, and had several promising leads. Helen was obviously delighted and also reported that Pete was helping out more around the house and that she felt good about expressing her appreciation toward him. The next week, Pete landed a job as a camera salesperson in a department store. Helen was very pleased. The two of them stated that they were ready to deal with sex.

Before beginning this phase of therapy, the therapist met individually with Pete to check on his progress in dealing with the urge to masturbate publicly or engage in frottage. Pete had continued to masturbate successfully to fantasies of conventional intercourse. Furthermore, he reported that seeing an attractive young woman no longer led automatically to thoughts of frottage and that he had not really experienced any of his old urges.

From this point on, the therapy progressed quickly. Because Helen was beginning to feel better about Pete, she said that she would not resist his sexual advances. They discussed with the therapist their sexual likes and dislikes and agreed to plan several sexual experiences over the next week. Pete was told to refrain from his usual foreplay (rubbing his penis against Helen's buttocks). The couple agreed on manual and oral stimulation to take its place. They had intercourse four times the next week. Over the next few sessions, the couple continued working on their marital problems. Progress was excellent. They reported that their sexual interactions were both frequent and pleasurable. Occasional sessions with Pete alone revealed that he no longer felt the urge to masturbate publicly or engage in frottage.

DISCUSSION

Pete's problems fall within the *DSM-IV* category of paraphilias, frequently occurring sexual urges, fantasies, or behaviors that involve unusual objects and activities. The diagnosis is made only if the person is distressed by their urges or behavior or if social or occupational functioning is impaired. *DSM-IV* lists nine paraphilias. These include:

1. Fetishism: the repeated use of nonliving objects to produce sexual excitement.
2. Transvestic fetishism: recurrent cross-dressing to produce sexual arousal.
3. Pedophilia: sexual activity with prepubescent children.
4. Voyeurism: repetitive looking at unsuspecting people, either while they are undressing or engaging in sexual activity.
5. Sexual masochism: the production of sexual arousal by being made to suffer.
6. Sexual sadism: the production of sexual arousal by inflicting physical or psychological suffering on someone else.
7. Paraphilia not otherwise specified: a heterogenous group of unconventional activities with impressive and mysterious names (e.g., coprophilia—obtaining sexual gratification from handling feces; necrophilia—being sexually intimate with a corpse).

The remaining two paraphilias, exhibitionism and frotteurism, were Pete's specific problems. In exhibitionism, the person repeatedly exposes his genitals to a stranger for the purpose of achieving sexual excitement. Like the other paraphilias, exhibitionism is practiced almost exclusively by men and is the most common sexual offense for which people are arrested. Exhibitionism can involve either the exposure of a flaccid penis or an erect one, accompanied by masturbation, as in Pete's case. At the time of the act, the exhibitionist may feel both cognitive and physiological signs of anxiety—nervousness, palpitations, perspiring, and trembling. Many report that the urge becomes so powerful that they lose control and even some awareness of what they are doing. No further sexual contact is typically sought.

The penile plethysmograph was used in a study of male exhibitionists in an effort to determine whether they are sexually aroused by stimuli that do not arouse nonexhibitionists (Fedora, Reddon, & Yeudall, 1986). Compared with normals and with sex offenders who had committed violent assaults, the exhibitionists showed significantly greater arousal to slides of fully clothed women in nonsexual situations, such as riding on an escalator or sitting in a park, while showing similar levels of sexual interest in erotic and sexually explicit slides. These results are consistent with the hypothesis that exhibitionists misread cues in "the courtship" phase of sexual contact, in the sense that they construe certain situations to be sexual that are judged to be nonerotic by nonexhibitionists.

They may also show an erotic preference for people with whom they are unfamiliar (Freund & Watson, 1990). Clinical lore suggests that the exhibitionist derives much gratification from the reaction of the victim, which is generally shock, fear, or disgust. In a laboratory study of sexual arousal in exhibitionists, however, they were not particularly aroused by filmed depictions of female anger or fear (Kolarsky & Madlafousek, 1983). According to data from court referrals, exhibitionism usually begins in adolescence, continues into the twenties, and declines thereafter. Whether the frequency truly declines or whether older exhibitionists are arrested less frequently is unknown. Educationally and intellectually, exhibitionists seem to be normal (Mohr, Turner, & Jerry, 1964). About 75 percent of exhibitionists over the age of 21 are married. Forgac and Michaels (1982) have compared the personality characteristics of exhibitionists who do and do not participate in other criminal activities. Consistent with expectation, the criminal exhibitionists were more psychopathic and had higher levels of psychopathology.

Comparing Pete to the usual descriptions of exhibitionists, we can see that he is atypical in some respects. Instead of exposing himself openly, as is usually the case. Pete stayed in his car, hoping that he might be seen. He also indicated that he hoped his exposure would lead to a sexual contact; this is atypical, because most authors regard exhibitionists as actually fearing sexual contact with their victims.

Some features of Pete's background, however, are quite similar to characteristics of exhibitionists in general. Mohr et al. (1964) report that many exhibitionists felt that they were distant from their fathers. Furthermore, their marriages tended to be poor, with special difficulties in sexual adjustment. Interpersonally, exhibitionists tended to be socially isolated, with few close friends. And, like Pete, exhibitionists tend to be more active during periods of stress (Witzig, 1968).

Frotteurism involves intense sexual urges and sexually arousing fantasies involving touching and rubbing against a nonconsenting person. It is the touching, not the coercive nature of the act, that is sexually exciting. Little is known about frotteurism although clinical reports indicate that it does not often occur in isolation and more commonly appears in conjunction with paraphilias such as exhibitionism (Allen, 1969).

Theories

In psychoanalytic theory the various paraphilias are viewed as defenses against the anxiety aroused by conventional sexual intercourse. Fenichel (1945), for example, sees the exhibitionist as a person who did not successfully resolve the oedipal conflict. Instead of giving up his mother as his love object, getting over his fear of castration by the father, and identifying with him, the exhibitionist continues to fear castration, which is associated with conventional intercourse. According to Karpman (1954), the mother is the villain of the piece. Motivated by unconscious penis envy, she identifies fully with her son and even may be sexually provocative toward him.

The act of exposing is thought to confirm to the exhibitionist that he does have a penis and has not been castrated. Furthermore, Fenichel believes that the exhibitionist unconsciously hopes that the women to whom he exhibits will expose themselves to him. Seeing that they have no penis is supposed to reduce his own castration anxiety. Other psychoanalytic explanations propose that exhibitionism is a substitute for the true wish to exhibit to mother, an expression of repressed homosexuality, and a substitute for incestuous urges (Karpman, 1954). Similarly, psychoanalytic theory would regard Pete's frotteurism as a substitute way of expressing sexual impulses. Although some of these speculations ring true for certain aspects of Pete's case (his seductive mother, his early sexual experiences with his younger sister), there are few data that would allow us to evaluate them better. Furthermore, the fact that Pete had been able to complete intercourse successfully is not easily handled by the psychoanalytic position.

The learning-based conceptualization of Pete's case, which guided the therapy that was developed, involved the following considerations: First, during early adolescence Pete experienced a chance conditioning trial in which orgasm was linked to rubbing. Although a single experience like this one would not likely produce a durable effect, the link between rubbing and orgasm may have been strengthened through the many similar experiences he arranged between himself and his sister. His initial failure in conventional intercourse, coupled with his lack of social skills and infrequent dates, maintained his interest in frottage and set the stage for the development of exhibitionism. Finally, his unsatisfactory sexual relationship with his wife did not provide him with an opportunity to give up his old behavior patterns.

This account is still incomplete in many respects. Why did Pete reinforce his habit of frottage with his younger sister? What led him to exhibit instead of trying to develop skills that might have enabled him to date and to enjoy more conventional sexual pleasures? It also appears that early sexual experiences need not have life-long effects. The point has been clearly made in a study of the Sambia tribe in New Guinea (Stoller & Herdt, 1985). All male members of the tribe are exclusively homosexual from age seven to marriage. During a first stage, from seven to puberty, the boys perform fellatio on older boys as often as possible because it is their belief that they have to drink a lifetime's supply of semen. From puberty to marriage, women are taboo, and the young men are fellated often by the younger boys. After marriage, in the late teens or early twenties, the tribesmen become completely heterosexual. Their early homosexual experiences apparently have had little effect on their capacity for heterosexual arousal.

Treating Paraphilias

There are very few controlled studies of the effectiveness of particular therapies in treating exhibitionism, frotteurism, and the other paraphilias. Psychoanalytic therapy follows from the etiological model discussed previously. Using the standard techniques of psychoanalysis—free association, dream analysis, and interpretation—the exhibitionist is encouraged to explore the unconscious impulses (e.g., castration fears or incestuous impulses) that are assumed to be causing the problem. In addition, analysts (e.g., Karpman, 1954) recommend making changes in the patient's life situation, such as moving out of his mother's home or improving the sexual relationship between the exhibitionist and his wife.

Several case reports of behavioral approaches to exhibitionism have also appeared. Wickramsekara (1977), for example, reported on the successful use of systematic desensitization coupled with shaping more appropriate sexual responses. The desensitization aspect of the treatment was oriented toward reducing the young man's anxiety concerning sexual contact. He was first taught deep muscle relaxation and then, while relaxed, imagined a hierarchy of scenes ranging from social contact with a woman to sexual intercourse. As the desensitization progressed, the client was instructed to read erotic material, beginning with lightly sexual material and progressing to *Fanny Hill*. Although he had previously avoided such material for religious reasons, he became more and more involved in this task. Finally, the client was given direct instruction in initiating a sexual relationship with his fiancée. As their sexual relationship progressed, he reported that his desire to exhibit decreased. The case was successfully terminated after the eighteenth session.

Aversion therapies, in which an attempt is made to attach negative properties to exhibiting, have also been employed. MacCullouch, Williams, and Birtles (1977), for example, reported on a case of a 12-year-old exhibitionist whose acts of exposing were limited to older women with well-developed breasts and large buttocks. The procedure involved showing him pictures of women — either of the type linked to his problem or of girls his own age. Slides of the older women were followed by an electric shock that could be avoided if the client pressed a button, turning on a picture of a girl, before eight seconds had elapsed. The goal of the procedure was to associate fear and anxiety with the stimulus of an older woman and simultaneously to make pictures of young girls a cue for anxiety relief, thereby increasing their attractiveness. After 18 therapy sessions using this procedure, the patient reported that he no longer had urges to exhibit.

In a better controlled study with groups of treated and untreated exhibitionists, Marshall, Eccles, and Barbaree (1991), however, did not find that aversive and reconditioning methods were successful. Instead, a multifaceted treatment including cognitive restructuring, stress management, and improving interpersonal skills lowered recidivism.

Biological interventions have also been employed. Case studies suggesting positive outcomes have been reported for clomipramine and fluoxetine (Perilstein, Lipper & Friedman, 1991; Wawrose & Sisto, 1992). Several studies have also been conducted with medroxyprogesterone acetate, a drug that reduces testosterone levels and thereby lowers sexual arousal. Although effective in reducing recidivism when taken regularly, the disorders recur when the treatment is discontinued (Meyer, Cole, & Emory, 1992). This is especially problematic because the drug produces a number of unpleasant side effects that are likely to lead to discontinuation.

The therapy used with Pete was similar to a procedure originally developed by Davison (1968) in treating a case of a young man who required sadistic fantasies to produce sexual arousal. As in the present case, Davison had the client initiate sexual arousal with a sadistic fantasy and then masturbate while looking at a picture of a nude woman. If arousal began to wane, he could return to his sadistic images, but he was told to ensure that orgasm was associated only with the picture. As therapy progressed, the sadistic fantasies were relied on less and less until the client could masturbate to orgasm relying only on the stimulation produced by the nudes. Like Davison's client, Pete learned to become fully aroused and reach orgasm by changing his masturbatory fantasies from exhibiting and frottage to conventional intercourse. In addition, Pete came to change the fantasies that attractive women elicited by practicing new ones, first with pictures and then with women he encountered in the natural environment. Finally, a reduction in marital conflict and an improved sexual relationship between him and his wife were likely contributors to the overall success of the therapy.

14 GENDER IDENTITY DISORDER: TRANSSEXUALISM

Chris Morton was a 21-year-old senior in college. In most respects, she was an exceptionally well-adjusted student, successful academically and active socially. Her problem involved a conflict in gender identity—a problem so fundamental that it is difficult to decide whether to refer to Chris as he or she, although Chris used the masculine pronoun. We have somewhat arbitrarily decided to use the feminine pronoun in relating this case because it may be less confusing to the reader. And in many respects this is a confusing case. It calls into question one of the most fundamental, and seemingly irrefutable, distinctions that most of us make—the distinction between men and women.

Chris's physical anatomy was that of a woman. But this distinction was not made easily on the basis of overt, physical appearance. She was tall and slender: 5'8" inches and about 130 pounds. Her hips were narrow and her breasts, which she wrapped with an Ace   bandage under her clothes, were small. Chris's face was similarly androgynous; her skin had a soft, smooth appearance, but her features were not particularly delicate or feminine. Her hair was cut short, and she wore men's clothes. A typical outfit included Levi's and a man's shirt with a knit tie and a sweater vest. She wore men's underwear and men's shoes, often Oxfords or penny loafers. She also wore a man's ring on her right hand and a man's wrist watch. Her appearance was generally neat and preppy. At first glance, it was not clear whether Chris was a man or a woman. Listening to Chris's voice did not provide any more useful clues

228

because it was neither deep nor high pitched. Many people assumed that she was a man; others were left wondering.

On the basis of her own attitudes and behaviors, Chris considered herself to be like men. Like other transsexuals, she described herself as being a man trapped in a woman's body. She did not consider herself to be confused about her gender identity. From a biological point of view, Chris recognized that she was not a man. She knew that she had breasts and a vagina. She menstruated. But there was more to it than physical anatomy. In every other way possible, and for as long as she could remember, Chris had always felt more male than female. When she tried to explain this feeling to others, she would say, "You can think what you want—and I know that most people don't want to believe this—but if you spend time with me, talk to me, just be with me, you will see what I mean. You'll know that I am not a woman." The details of this subjective perception, the experiences that served as support for Chris's belief, lie at the core of our notions of what is feminine and what is masculine.

Chris felt a sense of camaraderie in the presence of men. She wasn't sexually attracted to them, and it never would have occurred to her to flirt with them. She wanted to be buddies with them—to swap stories about adventures and compare notes on sexual exploits with women. They were her friends. In her behavior toward women, Chris was often characteristically masculine and excessively polite; she liked to hold doors for women, to pull out their chairs when they sat down to eat, to stand up when they entered a room. If she went for a ride in a car with a woman, she felt that she should drive. This is, of course, not to say that these behaviors are innately masculine, for they are learned as part of our upbringing. Chris felt more comfortable behaving this way because it made her feel masculine, and she said it seemed natural.

People responded in a variety of ways when meeting Chris for the first time. Most assumed that she was a man, but others took her to be a woman. Chris usually corrected people if they happened to address her as a woman. For example, if an instructor used a feminine pronoun when addressing or describing Chris during an initial meeting, she would quickly say "he" or "his." In situations that might arouse curiosity or attract attention, Chris tried to adopt exaggerated male postures or vocal patterns to overcome the observer's sense of ambiguity. One example occurred when she walked into a small seminar for the first time. Chris sauntered across the room, sat down so her legs crossed with one heel on the other knee, and then slouched down in the chair, adopting a characteristically masculine posture. When answering the phone, she usually tried to lower the pitch of her voice.

Chris was sexually attracted to women and, consistent with her male gender identity (her conviction that she was more like men than women), she considered herself to be heterosexual. In fact, she had had two long-term, intimate relationships, and both were with other women. Her present lover,

Lynn, was a 26-year-old bisexual who treated Chris as a man and considered their relationship to be heterosexual. Lynn said that when they first met, she thought that Chris was a woman and she was attracted to her as a woman. But as their relationship developed, Lynn came to think of Chris as a man. Part of this impression could be traced to physical behaviors. Lynn agreed that making love with Chris was more like making love with a man than a woman. Although this impression was difficult to describe in words, it seemed to revolve around the way Chris held her and touched her. Perhaps more important were the emotional and intellectual qualities that Lynn noticed. Chris cried about different things than Lynn cried about and seemed unable to empathize with many of Lynn's experiences — experiences that seemed characteristically feminine. She was surprised, for example, at Chris's apparent inability to empathize with her discomfort during menstruation. And Lynn was often surprised by Chris's questions. Once when they were making love, Chris asked Lynn what it felt like to have something inside her vagina. It was a sensation Chris had never experienced (and never wanted to experience).

Chris's parents had known about her gender identity conflict since her senior year in high school. This was a difficult issue for them to address, but they both assured Chris that their love for her was more important than their concern about the problems she would face as a transsexual. Their reactions were also very different. Chris's mother accepted the problem and made every effort to provide emotional support for Chris. Her father, on the other hand, seemed to deal with the issue at a more intellectual level and continued to believe that it was merely a phase that she was going through. Both were opposed to her interest in physical treatment procedures that might permanently alter her appearance.

Although Chris's life was going well in most respects, she wanted to do something about her body to make it more compatible with her masculine gender identity. Several options seemed reasonable. First, she wanted to have her breasts removed. She also wanted to begin taking male hormones so that her voice would deepen and she would grow facial hair. Finally, she wanted to have surgery to remove her uterus and ovaries, primarily because their continued presence might conflict with the consumption of testosterone. Although she would also have preferred to have a penis, she did not want to go through genital surgery because it would not leave her with a functional male organ. Furthermore, the possibility of "mutilating" her existing organs and losing her capacity for orgasm through clitoral stimulation frightened her.

One interesting feature of Chris's masculine identity was revealed in her discussion of the advantages and disadvantages of the physical procedures involved in changing her body. Lynn mentioned, for example, the possible traumatic consequences of losing the capacity to bear children. What if Chris decided in a few years that she had been mistaken and now wanted to raise a family? The idea was totally foreign to Chris! It was a concern that never would have occurred to her. For Chris, the justification for the change was primarily cosmetic. Her concern involved plans for the future. Right now I can pass for a young man. That's okay when I'm 21, but what happens when I'm 40 and still look like I'm 20 because I don't have facial hair? I can't date 20-year-old women all my life. I wouldn't be happy." Her reluctance centered on physical-health consequences. It was hard to imagine that she could have been less concerned about her reproductive capacity. There was no doubt that she would not miss her breasts, because since adolescence she had gone to great lengths to conceal their appearance.

During her senior year in college, Chris made an appointment to see a psychologist at the student health center on campus. She wanted to talk about her desire to take male hormones and alter her body surgically. Although she had thought about the decision for a long time and discussed it with several other people, she wanted to get the opinion of a mental health professional. Were these procedures the most reasonable course of action, or was her desire to change really the product of some deeply ingrained psychological disturbance?

SOCIAL HISTORY

Chris was the oldest of four children. She had one brother, Rick, who was one year younger than she, and two younger sisters, Debbie, who was 16, and Susan, who was 12.

Chris said that she had always felt like a boy. Other people viewed her as a typical "tomboy," but Chris recognized the difference. When she was very young, she and Rick and their father played together all the time. Sports were a central activity in the family, especially basketball. Mr. Morton spent numerous hours teaching Chris and Rick to dribble and shoot baskets on their driveway. These were pleasant memories for Chris, but she also remembered feeling excluded from this group as she and her brother grew older. For example, at that time, Little League rules prohibited girls from participating, and Chris found that she was generally discouraged from playing with boys in the organized games that became more common when they were 9 or 10 years old. She and Rick both played on organized youth teams, and their father served as a coach for both of them. But Chris had to play on girls' teams and she didn't think that was fair, either for her or to the other girls. She remembered thinking to herself that, although she way always the best player on the girls' team, she would have been only an average player on a boys' team, and that was where she felt she belonged. When she got to high school, she finally quit the team, in spite of the fact that she was one of the best players, because she didn't want her name or picture to appear in the paper as being part of a girls' team.

Although Chris spent a great deal of time with her father and brother, she also had a good relationship with her mother, whom she remembers as being a source of emotional support and sympathy in difficult times. Her mother was not athletically inclined, so she didn't participate in the activities of Mr. Morton and the children, but she and Chris did spend time talking and shopping together. On the other hand, Chris was never interested in many of the other activities that some girls share with their mothers, like cooking.

She also wasn't interested in playing with toys that many other girls preferred. She and Rick shared most of their favorite toys, including slot cars, toy soldiers, and baseball cards. She and a friend did play with Barbie dolls for a while, but they only did so when combining them with G.I. Joes and weaving them into mock wars and sexual adventures.

When she started school and began meeting other children in public situations, Chris began to confront and think about issues that are taken for granted by virtually everyone else. How many children, for example, ever think twice about which bathroom to use? As early as the first and second grade, Chris could remember feeling uncomfortable about using the girls' room. In the first grade, she attended a parochial school in which the girls were required to wear uniforms. She wore the dress and had her hair long and in a pony tail, but that changed as soon as she reached the second grade. After their parents arranged for Chris and Rick to transfer to a public school, Christ cut her hair very short and began wearing slacks and shirts that made her indistinguishable from the boys.

Similar issues centered around locker rooms. When Chris was nine years old, her mother arranged for her and Rick to take swimming lessons at a public pool. Chris developed a crush on a cute girl in her class. She remembered feeling ashamed and embarrassed at being in the same locker room with the other girls and being seen in a girl's swimming suit.

She was a Brownie for one year when she was in the second grade. She remembered liking the merit patches and the uniform, except for the fact that it was a dress. During the summer between the second and third grade, she went to camp with the other Brownies. It was the first time that she was away from home overnight. She felt awkward because it was also the first time that she was forced to spend all of her time with other girls. The week was spoiled quickly when the counselor announced on the first day that everyone was going swimming. Chris liked swimming but didn't like to wear a girl's swimming suit, so she pretended to be sick for the rest of the week. She also dropped out of Brownies the next fall because she didn't like always doing "girls' stuff."

Chris's sex play as a child involved little girls rather than little boys. When she was 9 years old, Chris spent long hours "making out" with an 11-year-old neighbor girl named Patti, who also experimented sexually with many of the young boys in their neighborhood. Thus, even at this fairly young age, Chris was sexually attracted to girls rather than boys. She had numerous opportunities to play sex games with young boys, including Patti's brother, who occasionally asked Chris to "mess around," but she wasn't interested. Girls were more attractive and interesting.

By the time she reached junior high school, Chris had begun to systematically avoid using her given name, Christine. She also came to dislike Chris, because although it is a name that is used by both men and women, she thought of it as being more feminine. She came instead to be known by her nickname, "Morty," which sounded more masculine to her.

Adolescence presented a difficult turning point for Chris. The separation of the sexes became more obvious. All of the girls wanted to wear dresses and date boys. Chris wanted to wear pants and date girls. The situation became even more frustrating in high school as her body began to change in obvious ways. The onset of menstruation was awkward, and the development of her breasts presented an even more difficult situation because their presence could be noticed by other people. As soon as her breasts began to enlarge, Chris began binding them tightly with a skin-colored belt that would not show through her shirt. The belt often left bruises on her chest. When she had to change clothes for gym class, she always had to find an isolated locker, away from the other girls, so that no one would see her taking off the belt. Nevertheless, the discomfort and pain associated with this procedure were preferable to the embarrassment of having other people realize that she was developing a woman's body.

When Chris was 17, she finally decided to have a talk with her mother about her discomfort with femininity. She told her mother that she wanted to be a boy. Her mother's reply was, "I know you do. I was also a tomboy when I was your age, but you'll grow out of it." Her mother tolerated her masculine dress but didn't seem to comprehend the depth of Chris's feelings.

Chris continued to have a lot of friends and to be active in academic and extracurricular activities in spite of her discomfort with gender-specific roles and behaviors. In fact, she was so popular and well respected by the other students that she was elected president of her freshman class in high school. Although she dressed in masculine clothes, everyone knew that she was a girl because she was forced to take the girls' gym class at school. Many of the social activities in which Chris and her friends engaged centered on roller skating in the evening and on weekends. Large numbers of teenagers from their own school and several others in the city gathered there to skate to rock music, eat pizza, and have a good time. Because she was a good athlete and enjoyed physical activity, these were pleasant times for Chris. There were awkward moments, however, such as when the disc jockey would announce "girls only" or "boys only." In either case, Chris would leave the rink; she didn't want to be seen with the girls and wasn't allowed to be with the boys.

Chris's parents separated and were eventually divorced when she was a sophomore in high school. Because their parents had concealed the fact that they were not getting along, the news came as a shock to all of the children. In retrospect, Chris said that she should have known that something was going on because her parents had been spending so much time together talking quietly in their room; her parents had usually been content to go their separate ways. There were, of course, hard feelings on both sides, but the arrangements for the separation were made to minimize the children's involvement in the dispute. They continued to live with their mother and visited their father on weekends.

Chris's best friends in high school were three boys who spent most of their time together. They were the liberal intellectuals of the class. These boys accepted Chris as one of their group without being concerned about her gender. One of her friends later told her, "I never really thought of you as a girl. I guess it wasn't important. You were just Morty." She did attract some attention, however, from other children and teachers. She wore men's pants and shirts, and sometimes ties and sport coats. Chris and her friends were also good dancers and spent a lot of time on weekends at a local club. They were the life of the party. When they arrived, everyone else started dancing and having fun.

The club also gave Chris a chance to meet kids from other schools who did not know her as a girl, so she was able to dance with other girls. On at least one occasion, this situation led to problems. Chris met two sisters with whom she became friends. They all liked each other, danced together at the club, and talked to each other on the phone during the week. In an awkward moment, she gave the sisters her phone number (which she usually refused to do). They called one night when she wasn't home, and Chris's mother said, "*She's* not here." This was the first hint the sisters had that Chris was not a boy. They checked with some other friends who knew people at Chris's school and were surprised to learn that Chris was a girl. They were shocked and angry. When they subsequently told some of their male friends about the situation, the boys made a point of finding Chris at the club one night and pushed her around to teach her a lesson.

Sex presented an extremely frustrating dilemma for Chris. She was attracted to girls, as were all of her male friends. When the boys talked — in the usual crude adolescent way — about girls they knew, Chris wanted to join in. But all of her friends knew that she was a girl. She was particularly attracted to one girl, Jennifer, who had moved to their school the previous year. Jennifer was bright, attractive, and engaging. Her appearance and manners were quite feminine. She spent a lot of time with Chris and her friends, but she was going with a boy who was the captain of the basketball team. Chris and Jennifer began to spend more and more time together as the school year wore on. They talked on the phone every night for at least an hour and were virtually inseparable on weekends.

During their junior year, Jennifer's boyfriend moved away to go to college. The relationship began to deteriorate, but Jennifer didn't know how to break things off. Chris became her principal source of emotional support during these difficult months. Chris became very fond of Jennifer and recognized that she was sexually attracted to her but feared that she might destroy their relationship if she mentioned these feelings to Jennifer.

This all changed rather abruptly one Saturday evening. They went to see a movie together, and, as they were sitting next to each other in the darkened theater, Jennifer became conscious of the strong emotional attraction that she felt toward Chris. She sat wishing that Chris would put her hand on her leg or put her arm around her. Jennifer explained these feelings to Chris as they drove home after the film was over, and Chris, in turn, made an effort to explain her feelings for Jennifer. They continued the discussion inside Jennifer's house, and eventually retired to Jennifer's bedroom where they spent the rest of the night talking and making love.

Their physical relationship—which both Chris and Jennifer considered to be heterosexual in nature—was an exceptionally pleasant experience for both of them. It was not without its awkward moments, however. For example, Chris would not let Jennifer touch her breasts or genitals for the first six months after they began having sex. She touched Jennifer with her mouth and hands, but did not let Jennifer reciprocate beyond holding and kissing. In fact, Chris always kept her pants on throughout their love making. This hesitation or resistance was primarily due to Chris's sense that she was in the wrong body. If she allowed Jennifer to touch her, they would both be reminded that she had a woman's body. This was frustrating for both of them, but especially for Jennifer, who by this point was not concerned about whether Chris was a man or a woman. She was simply in love with Chris as a person and wanted a complete, reciprocal relationship. Chris was also frustrated because she continued to feel—in spite of Jennifer's frequent protests to the contrary—that she could not satisfy Jennifer in the way that Jennifer most wanted because she did not have a penis. Their relationship gradually extended to allow more open physical reciprocity, primarily as a result of Jennifer's gentle insistence. Chris found that she enjoyed being stimulated manually and orally by Jennifer and had no trouble reaching orgasm.

Chris and Jennifer were able to continue their intimate relationship without interference from their parents because their parents viewed Chris as a girl and never considered the possibility that she and Jennifer were lovers. They frequently spent nights together at Jennifer's house without arousing any serious suspicion. Jennifer's mother occasionally made comments and asked questions about Chris's masculine wardrobe and manners, but she was totally oblivious to the complexities of Chris's behavior and to the nature of her daughter's involvement.

Despite Jennifer's obvious affection for Chris, their relationship created problems as Jennifer became increasingly sensitive to the reactions of other people. Part of the problem centered on gossip that spread quickly through their school, despite attempts by Chris and Jennifer to conceal the fact that they were dating. Other students had always been reasonably tolerant of Chris's masculine behavior, but their criticism became more overt when a close friend, in whom they had confided, let it become known that Chris and Jennifer were dating each other. That seemed to step beyond most other students' limit for acceptable behavior. Jennifer also began to feel that other people, whom they did not know, would look at her and Chris when they were out in public together. Although Chris was convinced that everyone saw her as a man, Jennifer believed that other people were sometimes confused by Chris's appearance. She also thought that Chris's excessively polite behavior, such as opening doors for her or standing up if Jennifer left a table, attracted further attention. She gradually came to feel so awkward in public that she was comfortable only when they were alone at one of their homes.

Their sexual relationship ended during Chris's freshman year at college. Jennifer's mother discovered some intimate love letters that Chris had written to Jennifer, who was also in college. She was furious! She threatened to discontinue any financial support for Jennifer's education and refused to let her be in their home as long as Jennifer continued to see Chris. The pressure was simply too much. Chris and Jennifer continued to be good friends, but the romantic side of their relationship had to be abandoned. Jennifer dated two or three men afterwards and was eventually married.

After breaking up with Jennifer, Chris met and dated a few other women before starting her relationship with Lynn. One of these encounters is particularly interesting, because it also provides some insight into Chris's sexual orientation and gender identity. One of her male friends from high school, Robert, was also a freshman at the university. They continued to spend a lot of time together and eventually talked openly about Chris's "story" and the fact that Robert was gay. Both admitted considerable interest regarding sexual response in bodies of the opposite sex — responses that neither had had the opportunity to observe. In order to satisfy their curiosity, they decided to have sex with each other. Chris later described it as a pleasant experience, but one that felt uncomfortable. They engaged in mutual masturbation, but Chris did not allow him to penetrate her vagina with his penis. Chris had never experienced a sexual encounter with a male before, and her principal interest was in observing Robert's behavior. She wanted to watch him become aroused and reach orgasm. She had always sensed that her own sexual behavior was more like that of a man than a woman, and this would give her a chance to decide. She ended the evening convinced more than ever that her own behavior was masculine and that she was not sexually attracted to men.

Chris strongly preferred monogamous relationships. This was in part a matter of convenience, because it was obviously very difficult for her to get to know someone with sufficient intimacy to begin a sexual relationship. It was also a matter of choice. She did not understand, for example, how some people—particularly males—could be so promiscuous.

During her sophomore year in college, Chris stumbled across some literature on transsexualism. This was the first time that she realized that other people experienced the same feelings that she had, and that the condition had a formal label. In addition to the comfort that she was not alone in this dilemma, she also obtained some useful information. For example, she learned that many transsexual females use Ace bandages, rather than belts, to bind their breasts. She felt much more comfortable after the change. She also learned about the possibilities of hormonal treatments and various surgical procedures that might be used to alter the appearance of her body. Recognition of these alternatives led Chris to pursue extensive reading at the university library. Having decided that she would like to change the appearance of her body, she made an appointment at the student health center.

CONCEPTUALIZATION AND TREATMENT

When Chris came to see a psychologist at the student health center, she did not indicate that she wanted to change her behavior. Extended consultation with a mental health professional is generally considered to be a prerequisite for the other procedures that might be used to alter her appearance. Chris sincerely wanted to learn as much as possible about her feelings and motivations for change before embarking upon a difficult set of procedures that carried some possibility for health hazards. She knew, for example, that the hormone treatments might lead to the development of acne, and that the hair on the top of her head might begin to thin out. Although she felt strongly about her masculine gender identity, she was willing to consider the possibility that she needed psychological treatment rather than the sex change procedure.

Chris's exceptional social adjustment was an important consideration in the evaluation of her condition. She was clearly functioning at a high level; her grades were good, and she had lots of friends—many of whom knew her only as a man—and she was satisfied with her current sexual relationship, which was based on her masculine identity. Even if procedures were available to alter her gender identity and convince Chris to act and feel like a woman, it did not seem likely that she could be any better adjusted. And, in all probability, she would have been miserable. Therefore, the psychologist decided that she would not try to persuade her that her problem regarding gender identity was the manifestation of more deeply ingrained psychopathology. She played a supportive role as Chris made her own decision about the pending medical procedures.

DISCUSSION

Because the discussion of this case involves a number of subtle and frequently controversial issues, it may be helpful to begin with the definition of several elementary terms. *Gender identity* involves a person's belief or conviction that he or she is a male or a female. The public expression of this belief involves role-specific behaviors associated with masculinity and femininity. *Sexual orientation,* on the other hand, represents the person's preference for male or female sexual partners. In the infinite variety of human behavior, there can be endless combinations of gender identity, gender-role behaviors, and sexual orientations.

People with gender identity disorders vary considerably with regard to the severity and persistence of their problems. Relatively few children who exhibit gender identity problems continue to experience similar problems as adults (Green, 1987). In *DSM-IV*, the term *transsexualism* is used to describe severe gender identity disorder in adults.

Why is gender identity disorder a controversial topic? Perhaps because it raises such difficult questions about the way in which we view ourselves and our world. Perhaps because the attitudes of many transsexuals, as well as the surgical procedures that have been used to help them attain their goals, are inconsistent with popularly held notions about men and women.

> Transsexuals raise a larger issue, in an era of wholesale efforts to relax rigid sex roles and give men and women more freedom to behave in ways that have traditionally been labeled "masculine" or "feminine." For, by their insistence on surgery — which gives them the form if not always the function of the sexual apparatus they desire — transsexuals seem to reassert the primacy of genital forms in defining sex and gender. (Restak, 1979, p. 20)

The following discussion is focused on clinical and scientific issues involved in the study of transsexualism rather than its political and social implications.

Descriptions of individuals whose gender identity is inconsistent with their anatomical sex can be traced to antiquity, but the term *transsexualism* was not introduced until 1949 by Caldwell. The disorder began to attract attention in the professional literature through the writings of Benjamin (1953, 1966) and descriptions of famous cases — such as Christine Jorgensen — that appeared in the popular press during the 1950s. The term first appeared in APA's official nomenclature with the publication of *DSM-III* (1980), in which transsexualism was listed with adult forms of sexual disorder under the heading Gender Identity Disorders.

In *DSM-IV*, Gender Identity Disorder is listed in a general section with sexual dysfunctions and paraphilias. There is, of course, an important difference between Gender Identity Disorders and Sexual Disorders. The latter are defined primarily in terms of problems that interfere with the capacity for reciprocal, affectionate sexual activity. Chris's situation illustrates why Gender Identity Disorders are not considered sexual disorders. Although she was uncomfortable with her anatomic sex and wanted to live as a man, she was sexually functional and actively involved in a mutually satisfying relationship with Lynn.

The *DSM-IV* (pp. 537–538) description of Gender Identity Disorder can apply to children, adolescents, or adults. In fact, most transsexuals report that their discomfort with their anatomic sex began during childhood. The disorder is defined by the following criteria:

A. A strong and persistent cross-gender identification (not merely a desire for any perceived cultural advantages of being the other sex).

In children, the disturbance is manifested by four (or more) of the following:
1. Repeatedly stated desire to be, or insistence that he or she is, the other sex.
2. In boys, preference for cross-dressing or simulating female attire; in girls, insistence on wearing only stereotypical masculine clothing.
3. Strong and persistent preferences for cross-sex roles in make-believe play or persistent fantasies of being the other sex.
4. Intense desire to participate in the stereotypical games and pastimes of the other sex.
5. Strong preference for playmates of the other sex.

In adolescents and adults, the disturbance is manifested by symptoms such as a stated desire to be the other sex, frequent passing as the other sex, desire to live or be treated as the other sex, or the conviction that he or she has the typical feelings and reactions of the other sex.

B. Persistent discomfort with his or her sex or sense of inappropriateness in the gender role of that sex.
C. The disturbance is not concurrent with a physical intersex condition.
D. The disturbance causes clinically significant distress or impairment in social, occupational, or other important areas of functioning.

Because discomfort with one's anatomic sex and the desire to be rid of one's own genitals form a central part of this definition, it is important to point out that transsexuals are not the only people who seek sexual reassignment surgery. Meyer (1974) described a number of subtypes among those individuals seeking sex change surgery at the Johns Hopkins Sexual Behaviors Consultation Unit. These include self-stigmatized homosexuals who believe that they should be punished, schizoid and psychotic individuals, and sadomasochists who derive sexual pleasure from inflicting and experiencing physical pain.

Disturbances in gender identity should also be distinguished from two related but generally distinct conditions. First, it would be misleading to say that transsexuals are, by definition, delusional. There are, of course, a few transsexuals who are psychotic, but the vast majority are not. They acknowledge the inconsistency between their anatomy and their gender identity. A delusional man might argue, for example, that he *is* a woman; a transsexual would be more likely to say, "I am not a woman *anatomically,* but I am a woman in almost every other way." Furthermore, unlike delusional patients whose beliefs are completely idiosyncratic, transsexuals are frequently able to convince other people that they are right. In Chris's case, for example, Jennifer and Lynn concurred with the belief that Chris was more like a man than a woman.

Second there is an important difference between transsexualism and transvestic fetishism, but the two conditions are not mutually exclusive (Bradley et al., 1991). Transvestic fetishism is a disorder in which heterosexual (or bisexual) men dress in women's clothing for the purpose of sexual excitement. The gender identity of transvestic fetishists is typically not inconsistent with their anatomic sex, and many transsexuals do not become sexually excited by cross-dressing. Nevertheless, a substantial proportion of male-to-female transsexuals do become sexually aroused at least occasionally when they dress in women's clothing (Blanchard & Clemmensen, 1988), and some transvestic fetishists do seek sex reassignment surgery (Wise & Meyer, 1980). According to *DSM-IV,* males who meet the criteria for both gender identity disorder and transvestic fetishism should be assigned both diagnoses.

Precise epidemiological data regarding transsexualism are difficult to obtain. Estimates of the prevalence of the disorder are based on the number of people who apply for treatment rather than comprehensive surveys of the general population. We do know that transsexualism is a relatively infrequent problem and that it is more common among men than women. Most early studies reported a male-to-female ratio of approximately 3:1, although the proportion of females has increased in more recent estimates. One study computed prevalence estimates on the basis of the number of patients seeking treatment at the only gender treatment center in the Netherlands. The investigators reported a prevalence of 1 transsexual in every 12,000 males and 1 in 30,000 females (Bakker, van Kesteren, Gooren, & Bezemer, 1993).

There also appears to be some fairly consistent differences between male and female transsexuals in terms of psychological characteristics. For example, female transsexuals tend to report better relationships with their parents, more stable relationships with sexual partners, and greater satisfaction with their sexual experiences prior to treatment (e.g., Kockott & Fahrner, 1988; Verschoor & Poortinga, 1988).

Many male transsexuals, perhaps as many as half of those seeking treatment, experience additional psychological problems. The most common symptoms are depression, anxiety, and social alienation (Bradley & Zucker, 1990; Zucker & Green, 1992). Some exhibit severe personality disorders, but very few are considered psychotic. The level of psychopathology observed in female transsexuals, on the other hand, does not seem to be different from that seen in the general population. Chris may therefore be similar to other female transsexuals. Aside from the issue of gender identity, she was well adjusted in terms of her mood, her schoolwork, and her extensive network of friends.

The sexual partners of transsexuals are also interesting in a number of ways. Jennifer and Lynn, for example, considered their relationship with Chris to be heterosexual, despite the fact that she was anatomically a woman. Green (1974) has interviewed a number of girlfriends and wives of female-to-male transsexuals and noted that most of their prior experiences with male partners had been unsatisfactory. Many of these women reported that they had not reached orgasm during intercourse prior to the relationship with their transsexual partner. This description is consistent with Jennifer's situation, because the sexual relationship she had with her boyfriend prior to that with Chris was not particularly enjoyable. She was, however, able to develop and enjoy a satisfactory heterosexual relationship with another man after she and Chris stopped going together.

Green (1974) also suggested that it would be overly simplistic to think of the partners of female transsexuals as being homosexual. "They want a relationship with all the trappings of a conventional heterosexual union. They want it, however, with a 'man' who lacks a penis" (p. 117). Jennifer's description of Chris's behavior and her willingness to think of Chris as a man might usefully be seen as an index of the extent of Chris's masculinity rather than an indication that Jennifer was herself irrational or psychologically disturbed.

The relationship between transsexualism and homosexuality has been the source of some controversy, as suggested by Chris's experience. Some people have argued that transsexuals are simply homosexuals who use their cross-gender identity as a convenient way of escaping cultural and moral sanctions against engaging in sexual behavior with members of their own sex (cf. Leitenberg & Slavin, 1983). There are a number of problems with this hypothesis. First, unlike transsexuals, homosexual men and women are not uncomfortable with their own gender identities. Lesbians, for example, are typically proud of their status as women and would be horrified at the suggestion that they want to be men. Second, many transsexuals, like Chris, are not obviously uncomfortable with homosexuals. The suggestion that transsexuals are denying their homosexual inclinations is sometimes supported by the observation that some transsexuals go out of their way to avoid any contact or association with homosexual men or women. However, some of Chris's friends were homosexual men and women. In fact, her current lover, Lynn, was bisexual and was living with another woman when they met. Third, comparisons involving developmental histories and patterns of sexual arousal indicate that transsexualism and homosexuality are clearly distinct types of behavior (Blanchard, 1989).

Etiology

It is not clear why some people develop gender identity disorders. In fact, the process by which anyone develops a sense of masculine or feminine identity is a matter of considerable interest and dispute (Ashmore, 1990; Ehrhardt, 1984). As in other areas of human behavior, alternative explanations invoke the ubiquitous nature/nurture controversy. Is gender identity determined genetically prior to the infant's birth, or is it largely determined by biological or social factors that the individual encounters in his or her environment? Explanations for the development of transsexualism have taken both sides of this argument, but various versions of the environmental perspective seem to have been favored in the clinical literature.

Some investigators and clinicians have emphasized the importance of the parents and family in the etiology of the disorder. Stoller (1985), for example, placed principal emphasis in male transsexualism on the absence (either physical or psychological) of the father and the presence of a close-binding, dominant mother. A different family pattern was identified in cases of female transsexualism. In these families, according to Stoller, the mothers are prone to depression. Rather than providing support and care for their spouses, the fathers are presumably aloof and uninvolved. Thus, the daughter is forced to fill the supportive, masculine role vacated by her father. Other masculine behaviors are also reinforced by the father, but femininity is discouraged.

Chris's experience was not consistent with Stoller's observations. Her mother was not depressed while Chris was a child, and she was not expected to take the place of her father. Chris's parents were not close to each other, but they did not involve the children in their disagreements, and her masculine gender identity was clearly fixed several years before her parents' conflict became known to the children. Although she did not spend a great deal of time with her mother, they did have a good relationship; they spoke to each other openly — including several talks about the fact that Chris felt more like a boy than a girl — and cared very much for each other.

Green (1974; 1987) has proposed a multifaceted model for the development of feminine behavior in boys and masculine behavior in girls. His view places considerable emphasis on learning principles such as modeling and social reinforcement. According to Green, gender identity disturbances are likely to develop when the parent of the opposite sex is dominant and provides the most salient model for the child's social behavior. The same-sexed parent is presumably retiring or unavailable. When the child begins to imitate cross-role behaviors, rather than objecting, the parents provide attention and praise. Peer relations also play a role in Green's model; feminine boys prefer and spend more time with girls while masculine girls spend more time with boys. This combination of parental and peer support enhances the process of identification with the opposite sex. Eventually, this process of socialization becomes an obstacle to any attempts to change the pattern and integrate the child with members of his or her own sex.

In Chris's case, her father certainly provided reinforcement for playing masculine games. Chris spent a great deal of time in rough, competitive play with boys. Her father also discouraged open displays of emotion, such as crying. It is difficult to say, however, that the social reinforcement he provided was definitely responsible for her gender identity disorder, particularly since so many other girls are treated in similar ways without becoming transsexual.

Relatively little empirical evidence is available regarding the influence of environmental events in the development of transsexualism. A few research studies have compared people with gender identity disorders and control subjects in terms of their recollections of their parents' behavior. One study found that male-to-female transsexuals remembered their fathers as having been less warm and more rejecting in comparison to the way in which control subjects remembered their fathers (Cohen-Kettenis & Arrindell, 1990). It is important to note, however, that these data were collected after the people with gender identity disorder were adults and had sought treatment for their condition. It is not clear that the interactional styles that were reported by the subjects preceded or contributed to the original development of their problems in gender identity. Interactions between the parents and their transsexual sons and daughters may have been determined, at least in part, by a *reaction to* the gender identity problems of the children. Prospective data, collected prior to the onset of gender identity problems, have not been reported on this issue.

Case studies provide the basis for much speculation regarding the possible influence of environmental and biological factors in the etiology of transsexualism. For example, Garden and Rothery (1992) described one pair of 13-year-old female monozygotic (MZ) twins who were discordant for gender identity disorder. The authors hypothesized that differences between the girls in terms of their social upbringing were responsible for the discrepancy in their gender identities. Their father had problems with alcohol dependence and played little, if any, role in the family. Their anxious and depressed mother seemed to treat the transsexual twin as a confidante. This pattern is consistent with Stoller's hypothesis. The fact that these genetically identical individuals were discordant for the condition indicates that genetic factors do not account for all of the variance in its etiology. That is, of course, not a particularly surprising result because concordance rates in MZ twins do not approach 100 percent for any form of mental disorder.

There is, in fact, good reason to believe that certain aspects of gender identity are influenced by biological as well as environmental factors (Gooren, 1990; Zucker & Green, 1992). Speculation regarding biological considerations has also been fueled by case studies. One example involves the extraordinary experiences of several members of a single extended family in the Dominican Republic (Imperato-McGinley, Guerrero, Gautier, & Peterson, 1974). These individuals are unable to produce dihydrotestosterone, a hormone that is responsible, in the male fetus, for shaping the penis and scrotum. In the absence of this hormone, the children are born with external genitalia that are ambiguous in appearance, including a very small, clitoral-like penis, a scrotum that looks like labial folds, and a blind vaginal pouch. Of the 24 cases described in the initial report, 18 were raised as girls. Then, when they reached puberty, everything changed in response to an increase in testosterone. Each child's "clitoris" enlarged and became a penis—just as it would have in utero if the appropriate hormone had been present—and testicles descended into a scrotum. Their voices deepened and the muscle mass of their bodies increased to produce a masculine appearance. Quite remarkably, they all quickly adjusted to their newly developed bodies. They now consider themselves to be men and are sexually attracted to women.

The cases of the Dominican children suggest that the effects of the postnatal environment may not be as salient as many investigators concerned with transsexualism have suggested. The children were raised as girls, but they were able to alter their gender identities quickly and with considerable success when their anatomy changed. If their interactions with parents, siblings, and peers during childhood were of primary importance, how could this transformation have been accomplished? Strictly environmental views of gender identity have obvious difficulty dealing with this problem. An alternative account, favored by more biologically minded investigators (e.g., Diamond, 1979), holds that gender identity is one characteristic that may be shaped very early, during the development of the human embryo, by exposure to male hormones.

The latter possibility suggests that Chris's masculine gender identity is the product of a fundamental, biological process rather than the influence of her parents during childhood. Viewed from a subtle neurological perspective, and regardless of the shape of her external sexual characteristics, this argument would hold that her brain is essentially masculine. Unfortunately, although there is considerable reason to believe that there are reliable group differences between men and women in terms of brain structure and function, there are not valid tests that would be useful in this regard at an individual level. The issue is, therefore, unresolved.

Treatment

There are two obvious solutions to problems that involve gender identity conflict: change the person's gender identity to match his or her anatomy, or change the anatomy to match the person's gender identity. Various forms of psychotherapy have been used in an attempt to alter the gender identity of transsexual patients, but the success of these interventions has been limited (Pauly, 1965). More positive results were reported by Barlow, Abel, and Blanchard (1979), who used behavioral procedures to shape and maintain masculine sex role behaviors in three male transsexual patients. Uncontrolled follow-up reports indicate that behavior therapy can be beneficial for prepubescent boys who exhibit symptoms of gender identity disorder. Rekers, Kilgus, and Rosen (1990) studied a group of 29 boys approximately four years after the end of treatment. Greatest improvement was found among those boys who had been treated at younger ages.

As an alternative to trying to change the transsexual's gender identity, some physicians have used surgical procedures to transform transsexual's bodies so that they will conform with their gender identities. Surgical procedures can be used to alter and construct both male and female genitalia. Some of these methods were initially developed for the treatment of problems such as traumatic loss, or congenital abnormalities. An artificial penis can be constructed from abdominal tissue that is transplanted and formed into a tube (see Noe, Sato, Coleman, & Laub, 1978). The goals of such surgery may include cosmetic considerations (i.e., the construction of an organ that resembles a penis) as well as physiological criteria (e.g., passing urine in a standing position, accomplishing intercourse, and sensing stimulation). Although it is not possible to construct a completely functional penis that will become erect in response to sexual stimulation, erection can be achieved through the use of removable implants made of bone, cartilage, or silicone. In the case of female-to-male transsexuals, the labia are fused, but the clitoris is left intact and remains the primary receptor for sexual stimulation. Prostheses can be inserted to resemble testicles in a scrotum.

The sporadic use of surgical procedures for the treatment of patients with gender identity disorders can be traced back at least as far as 1922, when Hirschfeld reported the use of sex reassignment surgery in a case of female-to-male transsexualism (see Pauly, 1974). They did not, however, become widely used or attract the attention of the general public until 1953, when Hamburger, Sturup, and Dahl-Iverson reported the case of Christine Jorgensen, a male-to-female transsexual who had received surgery in Copenhagen in 1951. This case differed from many of the previous reports in that the patient was treated with large doses of female sex hormones for several months prior to the surgical removal of his penis and the construction of female genitalia. Subsequent to this report, a number of gender identity clinics were established at medical schools in Europe and the United States. One of the best known was begun at the Johns Hopkins University in 1965. Sex reassignment surgery was performed frequently throughout the 1960s and 1970s. Exact figures are not available regarding the numbers of men and women who have received this radical treatment, but reports suggest that they must number in the thousands.

Initial impressions regarding the relative success of these procedures were rather positive. Case studies suggested that most patients were pleased with the results of the surgery and relieved to finally have the body they desired. Many found that they were able to adjust to life as a member of the opposite sex, and some reported adequate sexual functioning and marriage. Almost no one reported postsurgical grief over the loss of his sexual organ, although isolated cases have occurred. The most frequent complaints centered on requests for further medical and surgical procedures. In the case of male-to-female trans-sexuals, these requests include improvements in genital appearance and functioning, increased breast size, and inhibition of beard growth. Follow-up reports suggested that 80 percent were considered generally satisfied by their surgeons (Blanchard & Sheridan, 1990). Interviews with patients who have gone through sex reassignment surgery indicate that most are satisfied with the results and the vast majority believe that they do not have any trouble passing as a member of their newly assumed gender (Kuiper & Cohen-Kettenis, 1988). Psychological tests obtained from patients who have completed surgery indicate reduced levels of anxiety and depression (Mate-Kole, Freschi, & Robin, 1990).

Although these results seem rather encouraging, there are some limitations associated with the data that have been used to evaluate the outcome of sex reassignment surgery. Postsurgical adjustment was often assessed in terms of the surgeon's global, subjective impression of the patient's adjustment rather than specific measures of occupational and social functioning made by people who did not know that the patient had received surgery. Appropriate control groups were almost never employed, and follow-up periods were often rather short. It should not be surprising, therefore, that some reports have provided a more pessimistic picture of surgical outcome (Meyer & Reter, 1979; Sorensen, 1981). These studies demonstrate, for example, that the social and occupational functioning of many transsexuals does not improve following surgery in spite of the fact that the patients are subjectively satisfied with the results of the operation. Partially in response to data of this sort and questions that were raised about the value of surgery, the Gender Identity Clinic at Johns Hopkins stopped providing sex reassignment surgery for transsexuals in 1979. There are, however, many other centers that continue to perform these procedures.

In a case such as Chris's, should a psychologist support her desire to live as a man? Or should Chris be encouraged to explore possible reasons for her gender identity disorder in an effort to help her accept a feminine identity? Results with surgical procedures are obviously mixed; some transsexuals respond more positively than others to sexual reassignment. Those who are most likely to benefit from the procedure fall into a core group that is characterized by "stable ego strength and intact reality testing" (Sorensen, 1981). Chris fit this description and would therefore seem to be among the more likely patients to respond positively to surgery. On the other hand, she was already well adjusted in her role without surgery. There is little reason to believe that there would be beneficial effects associated with attempts to help Chris become more feminine in either her overt behavior or the way she thought about herself. It also seems unlikely that the surgical alteration of her body would lead to an even better adjustment.

EATING
DISORDER:
ANOREXIA
NERVOSA

Joan was a 38-year-old woman with a good job and family life. She lived with her second husband, Mike; Charlie, her 16-year-old son from her first marriage; and 18-year-old Cindy, her husband's daughter from a previous marriage. Joan was employed as a secretary at a university, and Mike was a temporary federal employee. Joan, who was 5'3", and weighed approximately 125 pounds. Although she was concerned about her weight, her current attitudes and behaviors were much more reasonable than they had been a few years earlier, when she was anorexic.

Joan had struggled with a serious eating disorder from the ages of 29 to 34. She was eventually hospitalized for a period of 30 days. The treatment that she received during that hospital stay had finally helped her overcome her eating problems. Four years later, her condition remained much improved. In the following pages, we trace the history of Joan's problems from her childhood and adolescence through their eventual resolution in adulthood.

SOCIAL HISTORY

Joan was born in a suburb on the outskirts of a large northeastern city. She had one brother who was two years younger. She remembered her father holding various jobs, including that of a supervisor for an aircraft subcontractor. Joan's mother stayed at home when the children were young and then worked

248

part-time for a number of years as a waitress and bookkeeper. Eventually she took a full-time bookkeeping job. Both parents were of average weight.

Joan's early childhood was quite ordinary. She was an above-average student and enjoyed school. She and her brother bickered, but their disagreements did not extend beyond the usual sibling rivalry. Her family lived in a large neighborhood development, filled with lots of children. Joan remembered herself as being somewhat heavy during elementary school. She had high personal standards and strove to be a perfect child. She always did what was right and listened to her parents as well as the parents of her friends with utmost respect.

When Joan was 14 and entering the ninth grade, tragedy struck her family and forever changed her home life. She and her 12-year-old brother had been left home alone while her parents went to work. Although her brother was too old to require baby-sitting, she was supposed to keep an eye on him. Joan had a friend over, and the two girls were upstairs in her room. Joan heard some loud noise outside and looked out the window. She saw her brother lying dead in the road. He had been run over by a car. Although the feeling became less intense, Joan would feel guilty about her brother's death for years.

After the accident, Joan's parents changed. They became extremely overprotective, and Joan remembered feeling as if she "had a leash on all of the time." From age 14 on, she no longer had a normal childhood. She could not hang out with friends, be away from the house for long periods of time, or go out in cars. Her parents wanted to know where she was and what she was doing, and they set a strict curfew. Joan knew that if she were late her parents would worry, so she always tried to be home early. She made a special effort to do exactly as she was told. Joan did not go out much because she felt the need to stay near her parents so that they would know that she was alive and well.

The rest of high school was unremarkable. Joan received reasonably good grades and got along well with the other students. During the summer after her brother's death, when Joan was 15, she met and began to date a boy who was two years older than she. Joan's parents were initially unhappy with this relationship, in part because Randy owned a car, and they didn't want her to ride around with him. Joan had to meet Randy secretly for the first few months. As her parents got to know him better, they grew to like him, and the young couple no longer had to sneak around. During this time, Joan continued to feel guilty when she was in cars because she was reminded of her brother's death. If anything happened to her, she knew that her parents would suffer horribly. As a result, Joan frequently stayed home.

After high school, Joan attended a one-year business school and became engaged to Randy. The couple was married after Joan graduated. She was 19 years old as she began her marriage and her first full-time job, as a secretary in a medical office. Prior to this time, Joan's father had never allowed her to hold even a part-time job. He insisted on providing for all of her needs.

Although this marriage lasted legally for six years, it became clear within nine months that the relationship was in trouble. Joan cared for her husband, but she did not love him. She soon realized that she had used Randy as an escape route from her parents' home. She felt as if she had simply jumped from one dependent relationship into another. When she had been at home, her parents provided everything. Now Randy was taking care of her. Joan worried that she did not know how to take care of herself. In spite of these negative feelings, Joan and Randy tried to make the marriage work. They bought a home one year after their wedding. Two years later, Joan accidentally became pregnant.

Joan gained 80 pounds during the course of her pregnancy. When Charlie was born, she weighed 200 pounds. Over the next few months, Joan found it difficult to lose weight but eventually got down to 140 pounds. Although it was hard for her to adjust to this weight gain, she did not try to change her weight because it felt "safe" to her. Joan and Randy were legally separated two years after Charlie was born. They continued to see each other occasionally and sought marital counseling at various times during the next couple of years. They could not reconcile their differences, however, and Randy eventually moved to another state. The divorce was finalized when Joan was 25 years old.

Joan stopped working and went on welfare shortly after she and Randy were separated. With financial help from her father, she managed to keep up the mortgage payments on her house for several months. She and Charlie continued to live on their own, but Joan fell further into debt while she and Randy tried to work things out. She was forced to sell her home when the divorce became final. Although she came to regret the decision, she moved back into her parents' home. Living at home was stressful for Joan. Although she was 25 years old, she felt like a child. Her parents once again took care of Joan, and now they also provided for her son. In this submissive role, Joan started to feel more like Charlie's older sister than his mother.

Joan lost some weight after she and Charlie were involved in a serious car accident, six months after moving back to live with her parents. Charlie was not hurt, but Joan's left hip and leg were broken. She spent a month in the hospital. She was immobile when she came home, and her mother had to take even greater care of her and Charlie. Joan needed repeated surgery on her knee, as well as extensive physical therapy, and she had to relearn how to walk. During her recovery she had little appetite, was nauseous, and did not eat much, but she was not consciously dieting. Joan's weight went down to about 110 pounds, which she considered to be a reasonable weight.

While she was recovering from her injuries, Joan became involved with a man named Jack, whom she met in one of the hospital's rehabilitation programs. She was now 27 years old. In order to escape her parents' overly protective home, she decided to take Charlie and move in with Jack. But this move actually created more problems than it solved, in large part because Jack had a serious problem with alcohol. Joan had never been a heavy drinker. In the beginning of their relationship, Joan drank alcohol only during the weekend. After she started living with Jack, drinking became a daily activity. Much of their relationship and socializing revolved around alcohol. On the average weekday, Joan consumed a couple of beers and some wine, or perhaps a glass or two of bourbon. On weekends she drank considerably more. Charlie was increasingly left at day-care centers and with baby-sitters. Joan eventually recognized the destructive nature of this relationship and ended it after a few months. She reluctantly moved back into her parents' home. After leaving Jack, Joan stopped drinking, except occasionally when she was out socializing.

ONSET OF THE EATING DISORDER

After breaking up with Jack, Joan lived with her parents for two more years. When she was 29 years old, almost three years after her accident, Joan returned to the hospital for more surgery on her leg. After being discharged, she began the diet that set the stage for five years of serious eating problems and nearly destroyed her life. Joan had gained a few pounds while she was drinking heavily and now weight 125 pounds. She was concerned that she would start to gain more weight while she was inactive, recovering from surgery.

Joan's diet was strict from the beginning; she measured and weighed all of her food. Within a year, she weighed less than 100 pounds. Her food intake was severely restricted. During the day she consumed only coffee with skim milk and an artificial sweetener. Occasionally, she ate a piece of fruit or a bran muffin. When she and Charlie ate dinner with her parents, Joan took a normal amount of food on her plate but played with it rather than eating it. After dinner, she usually excused herself to go to the bathroom where she took laxatives in an effort to get rid of what little food she had eaten. Joan hardly ate any meats, breads, or starches. She preferred fruits and vegetables because they consist mainly of water and fiber. Although she did not allow herself to eat, Joan still felt hungry; in fact she was starving most of the time. She thought about food constantly, spent all of her time reading recipe and health books, and cooked elaborate meals for the family.

Although she weighed less than 100 pounds, Joan still felt overweight and believed that she would look better if she lost more weight. She had an overwhelming fear of getting fat, because she believed that gaining weight would mean that she was not perfect. She tried to be a model young adult and struggled to be what she imagined everybody else wanted. She gave little thought to what she would want for herself. It seemed to Joan that everything in her life was out of control and that her weight and body were the only things over which she could be in charge. The demonstration of strict self-control with regard to eating was a source of pride and accomplishment to Joan.

As she lost weight, Joan experienced several of the physical effects that accompany starvation. Her period stopped; she had problems with her liver; her skin became dry and lost its elasticity; her hair was no longer healthy; and she would often get dizzy when she stood up. At this time, Joan was working as a secretary in a university medical school. Some of her co-workers noticed the drastic change in her appearance and became concerned. An internist in her department recognized her symptoms as those of anorexia nervosa and tried to get Joan to seek help. Joan did attend an eating disorders support group and even went to some outpatient therapy sessions. She also consulted a dietician at the university hospital and worked on an eating plan. Joan realized that her behavior was not normal, but she was unsuccessful in fighting it. When she was transferred to a different department within the university, she left therapy and returned to her restrictive dieting.

Joan's parents were also acutely aware of their daughter's abnormal patterns of eating and her excessive weight loss. They were extremely worried about her health. The more they tried to talk to Joan about this issue, the more resistant she became to their pleadings. Arguments about eating became frequent, and the level of tension in the home escalated dramatically.

A year and a half after the onset of her eating disorder, Joan moved with Charlie into a place of their own. Her decision was prompted in large part by the aversive nature of her interactions with her parents. She continued to diet and now weighed about 90 pounds. Charlie's diet had also become restricted, in part because there was very little food in the house. Joan could hardly bring herself to go to the grocery store. Once there, she made an effort to behave normally and went through the store putting food into her shopping cart. When it came time to pay, however, she would not actually buy anything. She believed that food was bad and that it was a waste of money. Instead of purchasing anything, she would wander up and down the aisles, eating much of what was in her shopping cart. Her reasoning was that it made no sense to pay for food that could be eaten while you were in the store.

This type of binge eating also happened whenever she did manage to buy something. In one afternoon, she would occasionally eat two dozen donuts, a five-pound box of candy, and some ice cream. After this, Joan took 20 to 30 laxatives to rid herself of the food. At times she tried to make herself vomit by sticking a toothbrush down her throat, but she preferred to take laxatives. Some weeks she did not binge at all, others once or twice. On the days in between binges she ate only a little fruit and drank some liquids.

Joan's eating problems persisted for the next five years. Her weight fluctuated between 90 and 105 pounds during this period. At times she ate more normally, but then she would eat practically nothing for months. She tried therapy and read many books, realizing that she had the symptoms of anorexia nervosa. Her life seemed like a roller coaster, as she cycled back and forth between relatively healthy patterns of eating, severe restricting, and binging and purging. Most of her diet consisted of liquids such as diet sodas, water, and coffee. Occasionally she drank beer, seeking the numbing effect it had on her appetite. She was pleased with her weight, especially when it was very low, but she felt horrible physically. She was weak most of the time, and other people constantly told her that she was too thin. In Joan's mind, however, she was still too heavy.

When she was 32 years old, almost three years after the onset of her eating problems, Joan met Mike at a church group she was attending. They began to date on a regular basis. Mike was different from all of the other men in Joan's past. He genuinely cared about her, and he also liked her son. Her weight was at one of its peaks when they met, somewhere between 100 and 105 pounds, so her eating problems were not immediately obvious to him.

Unfortunately, soon after they began dating, Joan once again began to restrict her eating, and her weight quickly dropped to another low point. Mike noticed the obvious change in her behavior and appearance. His reaction was sympathetic. As their relationship grew stronger, Mike seemed to help Joan feel differently about herself. They talked frequently about her weight and how little she ate. Mike expressed great concern about her health, pleading gently with her to gain weight, but her restrictive patterns of eating persisted in spite of the other psychological benefits that accompanied the development of this relationship.

One year after she started dating Mike, Joan needed major abdominal surgery to remove two cysts from her small intestine. During the operation, the surgeon saw that she had other problems and reconstructed her entire bowel system. When she left the hospital, Joan's weight had fallen to 85 pounds. She ate reasonably well at first, trying to regain her strength. After two months she was feeling better, returned to work, and went back on a restrictive diet. This time, however, Mike and her friends would not let her continue this prolonged pattern of self-imposed starvation.

TREATMENT

Mike and one of Joan's friends from the medical school sought help for her. Realizing that she would never be free of her problems unless she faced them, Joan agreed to contact an eating disorder specialist. Though it was one of the hardest decisions she ever made, Joan had herself committed to a 30-day stay in a psychiatric ward. She was now 34 years old.

Joan's diet was completely controlled in the hospital. She was started on a 1500-calorie-a-day diet and was required to eat three meals a day in the presence of a staff member. Privileges such as use of the phone, visitors, and outings were made contingent upon eating. Specific goals were set for weight gain, and caloric intake was increased gradually. There were also daily individual therapy sessions in which a staff psychologist explored with Joan how she felt about herself.

At first, hospitalization was difficult for Joan. The amount of food that she was required to eat for breakfast (two pancakes, a bowl of cereal, a glass of milk, one piece of fruit, and a piece of toast) would previously have lasted her for a whole week. She was initially rebellious, refusing to eat or giving her food away to other patients. She didn't earn any privileges in the first ten days of her hospital stay. Unaccustomed to eating, she experienced severe constipation, bloating, and indigestion. At times she tried to vomit to get rid of the food, but she was not successful. She eventually accepted the fact that she had no choice and allowed herself to gain 30 pounds. She felt stronger physically but was still troubled. Joan convinced herself that she would lose those extra pounds as soon as she was released from the hospital.

An important turning point in her attitude came during the third week of treatment when Joan received a pass to go home. Outside the hospital, she felt out of control, as if she were too weak to take care of herself. She asked Mike to take her back to the hospital immediately. Safely back in her hospital room, she cried and felt as though she would never get better. This wrenching experience helped Joan recognize that she would, indeed, need to change her eating behavior as well as her attitudes regarding weight control and physical appearance. She had suddenly developed a clear insight into the nature of her disorder. Somehow, at the end of 30 days, Joan found the strength to leave the hospital. She was frightened at first, but with support from Mike and her family, she was able to maintain a normal pattern of eating. Joan remained in therapy for a short time, but treatment was discontinued after six months.

While she was in the hospital, Joan learned her own attitudes about eating and her body were the principal problem, and she had become her own worst enemy. She learned that she could control her weight without becoming extremely restrictive in her eating. She began to feel differently about herself and food. With the support of Mike and her improved health due to weight gain, her attitudes changed. Joan could not pinpoint exactly what had happened, but she has become a different person who was no longer preoccupied with dieting and weight control.

DISCUSSION

Anorexia nervosa is a condition characterized by extreme weight loss. It tends to occur most commonly in female adolescents who come from a higher social class background. Although 90 percent to 95 percent of anorexics are female, males sometimes develop this condition. Current estimates of prevalence vary, but approximately 1 in 100 adolescent girls is affected by this disorder. The course of the disorder can be chronic, and 5 percent of anorexics starve to death (Hoek, 1993). The *DSM-IV* (pp. 544–545) diagnostic criteria are as follows:

A. Refusal to maintain body weight at or above a minimally normal weight for age and height (e.g., weight loss leading to maintenance of body weight less than 85% of that expected; or failure to make expected weight gain during period of growth, leading to body weight less than 85% of that expected).

B. Intense fear of gaining weight or becoming fat, even though underweight.

C. Disturbance in the way in which one's body weight or shape is experienced, undue influence of body weight or shape on self-evaluation, or denial of the seriousness of the current low body tion, or denial of the seriousness of the current low body weight.

D. In postmenarcheal females, amenorrhea, i.e., the absence of at least three consecutive menstrual cycles.

The *DSM-IV* specifies two types of anorexia nervosa. Individuals are considered to be the *restricting type* if during the episode of anorexia nervosa they do not regularly binge or purge (whether through vomiting or laxative misuse). The *binge-eating/purging type,* which is consistent with Joan's behavior, involves the regular occurrence of binge eating or purging behavior during the episode of anorexia. This approach to subclassification of eating disorders recognizes the frequent appearance of overlapping symptoms. Approximately one-half of anorexics also have bulimic symptoms, and roughly one-third of bulimics have a history of anorexia.

Research has revealed some important differences between the two subtypes of anorexia nervosa. Anorexics who also binge and purge tend to have weighed more before their illness, are more sexually experienced, and are more outgoing, tend to have reduced impulse control, and are more likely to abuse drugs or steal, and have more variable moods than restrictors (Coovert, Kinder, & Thompson, 1989; DaCosta & Halmi, 1992; Garfinkel & Garner, 1982). The presence of binging and purging is also thought to be a sign of greater psychological disturbance and an indication of a poorer prognosis (Garfinkel & Garner, 1982).

One interesting diagnostic issue is whether anorexia nervosa is, in fact, a distinct type of disorder or whether it represents a variation on mood disorders (Garfinkel & Garner, 1982). This controversy is fueled by the considerable comorbidity that has been observed between anorexia and depression, as well as studies that have shown an increased prevalence of mood disorders in the relatives of patients with anorexia. These two conditions actually share many of the same symptoms such as insomnia, disturbed sleep, weight loss, constipation, loss of interest in sex, indecisiveness, poor concentration, loss of interests, and social withdrawal. To examine this relationship, Strober and Katz (1987) conducted a prospective study of adolescents with mood disorders. At the time of follow-up (range of 8 to 48 months), none of the female teens had developed anorexia nervosa. These data suggest that despite similarity of symptoms and diagnostic overlap, anorexia is a separate disorder. It is distinguished from depression by the relentless pursuit of thinness and a more chronic course (Strober, 1986; Strober & Katz, 1987).

Joan met the diagnostic criteria for anorexia nervosa, binge eating/purging type. She experienced a drastic, self-induced loss of weight, was intensely afraid of becoming fat, could not recognize the true size of her body or the seriousness of her condition, and was no longer menstruating. In addition to her severe restriction of food intake, Joan would also periodically eat large amounts of food and then try to rid herself of the unwanted calories through vomiting and laxatives.

Joan also experienced many of the physical and psychological side effects that accompany starvation. These include constipation, hypotension, skin changes, bloating, abdominal pains, dehydration, and lanugo (downy hair growth). It is important to recognize that some of the psychological symptoms of anorexia nervosa are produced by the lack of food and are not necessarily inherent aspects of the anorexic's personality. For example, people who are starving become preoccupied with food and eating. Like Joan, they will often cook for others, read recipe books, and may even develop peculiar food rituals. Obsessive behaviors, such as hoarding, may also appear. There is often an exaggeration of previous personality traits, such as increased irritability, social withdrawal, and a narrowing of interests (Garfinkel & Garner, 1982). Although anorexics are often characterized as being extremely compliant, emotionally reserved, compulsive, and dependent, there does not seem to be one single type of personality in those who suffer from anorexia (Strober, 1986).

Etiological Considerations

Various biological factors have been considered in the search for the causes of anorexia nervosa. For example, in the early 1900s, many clinicians believed that anorexia was the product of a primary pituitary disorder. It is now recognized that the hallmark signs of anorexia — such as unending drive for thinness, denial of the illness, body image disturbances, and cyclic dieting — are not present in pituitary disorders. More recent speculation has focused on the possible influence of a dysfunctional hypothalamus, a part of the brain that plays a crucial role in the regulation of feeding behavior (Logue, 1991). Hypothalamic irregularities have been observed among anorexic patients, but it is likely that these problems are the product, rather than the cause, of the eating disorder (Leibowitz, 1987). Anorexia nervosa does not seem to be produced solely by biological factors (Garfinkel & Kaplan, 1986).

Because the onset of anorexia nervosa typically occurs during adolescence, many theories discuss anorexia in terms of maturational problems that are sparked by the physical, emotional, and cognitive changes that occur at this time. Some clinicians view anorexia as the product of resistance to sexual and psychological maturity, or more broadly as trouble with individuation and separation from the family (Garfinkel & Garner, 1982). The family often plays a role to the extent that parents may set high performance demands and may actively resist attempts by their children to gain independence. Families of anorexic adolescents have been characterized as being enmeshed, overprotective, rigid, and unable to solve problems (Minuchin, Rosman, & Baker, 1978; Yates, 1989). Although it is far from clear what role this pattern plays, it may contribute to the development of anorexia in vulnerable adolescents who have other predisposing factors (Strober, 1986).

Joan's case was atypical, in the sense that her eating problems appeared when she was 29 years old. Nevertheless, her family situation did fit the "anorexic profile." After the death of her brother, her parents became overly protective. When she returned to their home after her divorce, she felt as if she were a child again. She seemed to lose her sense of being an independent adult. Joan's parents conscientiously provided for her needs, but by not allowing her to work, they may have contributed to her feelings of ineffectiveness and inadequacy. These aspects of Joan's situation fit the theoretical perspective outlined by Hilde Bruch (1973, 1981), who described anorexia nervosa as the product of fundamental deficits in ego functioning. According to this theory, the anorexic presumably suffers from low self-esteem, a sense of personal ineffectiveness, and a lack of trust in her internal states and emotions. Mastery over her body becomes a means of achieving a sense of control.

Cultural attitudes and standards are also thought to play an important role in the development of anorexia nervosa (Garfinkel & Garner, 1982). Culture has a strong influence on the appearance of women. In Western society, for example, the feminine ideal has shifted from the buxom figure of the early 1900s, to the thin flapper of the 1920s, to the hourglass shape of the 1950s, and more recently, back to a thin body shape. This ideal shape is more than a "look." It takes on additional meaning and comes to symbolize other attributes such as success, beauty, and self-control.

At the same time that contemporary cultural standards have emphasized thinness, women's body weight has been increasing as a result of improved health and nutrition. These circumstances create a conflict between the ideal shape and a woman's actual shape. The conflict typically leads to dieting. Of course, all dieting does not develop into anorexia nervosa. It is hypothesized that sociocultural pressures are part of a larger model of development, which includes other predisposing factors such as problems with autonomy, rapid physical change at puberty, premorbid obesity, personality traits, cognitive style, perceptual disturbances, and interpersonal and familial difficulties.

Another important consideration is the lower frequency of eating disorders among nonwhite and non-Western women. Until recently it was thought that black women were rarely affected by anorexia. There is still some debate over the extent to which this difference is real or simply a reflection of the biases of the medical profession. Nonwhite women may have reduced access to health services, may utilize these services less, or may not be given the diagnosis of anorexia due to the ethnocentric assumptions of health care providers. With these factors in mind, Dolan (1991) has argued that speculation about the incidence or form of eating disorders in nonwhite women may be premature. Nevertheless, research has found that the incidence of anorexia nervosa in nonwhite women is eight times lower than that for white women (Dolan, 1991). By 1987, only 18 cases of black anorexic women in either North America or Western Europe had been reported in the literature. Anorexia affects non-Western women in more developed countries such as Japan, but it is relatively rare elsewhere (Hsu, 1987).

Researchers have been interested in factors that may help to protect some women from developing anorexia. For example, some evidence suggests that white teenage girls diet more than black teenage girls, regardless of socioeconomic status. White adolescent females tend to be more focused on weight and shape, have a poorer self-image and lower self-esteem, and are actually heavier than black adolescents (Hsu, 1987). On the other hand, it seems that anorexia has recently become more common among black women in the United States (Hsu, 1987). Increased adherence to middle-class values and the influence of the media may be responsible for this change.

The role of sexuality in the development of anorexia is not clear (Coovert, Kinder, & Thompson, 1989). Although the disorder has been characterized as a retreat from maturity, psychosexual issues are not necessarily the central problem. Rather, the anorexic may be more focused on achieving mastery through control of her body and diet (Yates, 1989). No consistent relation has been found between eating disorders and a history of sexual abuse (Connors & Morse, 1993). It has been estimated that 30 percent of women with eating disorders were sexually abused as children. This figure is comparable to that found in the general female population and is actually lower than that of some psychiatric groups (Connors & Morse, 1993). Therefore, sexual abuse does not explain the development of most cases of anorexia nervosa. It is best seen as one of many risk factors.

Treatment

A recent survey of physicians and psychologists at the International Conference on Eating Disorders showed that less than 50 percent believed that there is a consensus on the treatment of eating disorders. This may be due, in part, to the fact that research on anorexia has not identified one form of treatment that is consistently more effective than others (Herzog, Keller, Strober, Yeh, & Pai, 1992). Talking therapy was endorsed by many clinicians, with most using cognitive-behavioral therapy or a combination of cognitive-behavioral and psychodynamic techniques. In order to maximize the long-term health of the anorexic, both behavioral and emotional issues must be addressed (Herzog, Hamburg, & Brotman, 1987).

A number of steps are typically followed in treatment. The first step is often hospitalization. This may be necessary in cases in which weight loss is extreme, suicidal thoughts are present, the anorexic is still denying her illness, or previous outpatient therapy has been ineffective (Yates, 1990). Weight restoration must occur before any psychological treatment can begin. This is necessary to alleviate the psychological symptoms of starvation and also to confront the anorexic with the body size that she fears. Although there is no single best way to restore weight, the key is to elicit as much cooperation as possible and to be sensitive to the anorexic's concerns. It is important to work with the client to set a target weight, usually 90 percent of the average weight for a particular age and height. Behavioral techniques, such as those used with Joan, are popular for immediate weight gain.

Even after the person's weight is restored to a normal level, dysfunctional attitudes toward food and body shape will remain. Most clinicians advocate psychotherapy as essential for long-term management. Although the particular orientation of the therapist may vary, the crucial aspect of psychotherapy is believed to be the therapeutic relationship. Anorexic clients are usually not self-referred and most are resistant to treatment. The therapist's goal is to build a trusting relationship within which other interventions can be employed. Cognitive distortions, superstitious thinking, trouble with expressing emotion, body-image misperceptions, self-esteem, and autonomy are some of the issues that often need to be addressed. When the patient is under the age of 16 and is still living at home, family therapy is recommended. Joan's treatment followed parts of this approach. During her hospitalization, various behavioral techniques were used to restore her weight to a healthy level. Because Joan was older and living on her own, she was treated individually, rather than in family therapy.

Consistent with a cognitive approach, Joan's ways of viewing the world and herself were challenged directly. Cognitive therapy procedures that were originally developed by Beck for the treatment of depression can also be applied in the treatment of anorexia nervosa. This process involves several steps: (1) learning to be more aware of thoughts and beliefs; (2) exploration and clarification of the connection between the dysfunctional beliefs and maladaptive behaviors; (3) examination of the truth of those beliefs; (4) learning to replace the dysfunctional beliefs with more realistic ones; and (5) eventually changing the underlying assumptions that are creating the dysfunctional beliefs (Garner, 1986).

The prognosis for patients with anorexia nervosa is mixed. Approximately 50 percent relapse after hospitalization. Five percent die as a direct result of the biological effects of self-imposed starvation. Those who have a relatively good outcome often continue to have difficulties with attitudes toward weight and eating (Yates, 1990). One long-term follow-up study of women who had recovered from anorexia investigated the subjective experience of this process. The women were interviewed 20 years after the onset of their disorder. They reported that "personality strength," "self-confidence," and "being understood" were the most important factors in their sustained health (Hsu, Crisp, & Callender, 1992). Joan had some of these factors working in her favor. She was fortunate to have her husband and close friends as sources of support. She may have also had the advantage of psychological maturity because she was already an adult when she developed her eating disorder. Although she was initially resistant to treatment, she decided to admit herself to the hospital on a voluntary basis and was determined to change her behavior. These factors may have played an important role in her eventual recovery.

16 EATING DISORDER: BULIMIA NERVOSA

Gary Robbins, a 27-year-old white male, came to the county clinic in late October. He was somewhat sloppily dressed, but he spoke well and quickly launched into a vivid description of his current problems. At the time Gary entered therapy, his life seemed to be coming apart at the seams. He was moderately depressed and low in self-esteem and had even thought of suicide. During the first session, he explained that his most pressing problem was staying out of jail, a real enough threat considering the 20 or so bad checks he had written in the last few weeks. To cover these checks, Gary explained that he had taken several advances on his salary, had borrowed money from close family and friends, and had furthered his indebtedness by borrowing from high-interest, short-term lending institutions. All of this resulted in outstanding debts totaling $12,000. The possibility of borrowing additional funds to cover the checks was bleak.

Supermarket, restaurant, and fast-food purchases were responsible for Gary's financial predicament. During the course of a weekday, he would spend between $20 and $50 on groceries and prepared foods. On weekends the figure would rise to upward of $100 in a single day. Gary explained that these vast quantities of foodstuffs were quickly consumed, usually at home, but sometimes at restaurants or in his automobile. He was able to eat all of this food only by regurgitating several times during a "meal."

Further details concerning these gastronomical binges were discussed in later therapy sessions. On weekdays, trying to conserve money Gary would not eat anything until lunchtime. Lunch might consist of a dozen McDonald's hamburgers, five jumbo orders of french fries, four chocolate shakes, and several single-portion apple pies. If time permitted, more enjoyable lunches were leisurely ones at "all you can eat" restaurants offering spreads of unlimited pastas, salad, fried fish, or chicken. These meals could easily last for two hours during which several whole pizza pies, many orders of fish or chicken, or plate upon plate of pasta were consumed. Several trips to the bathroom, during which he would vomit, allowed him to consume these vast quantities of food. Perhaps fortunately for Gary, although to his dismay, these "all you can eat" establishments recognized his voracious appetite; many banned him from partaking of their specials.

Gary usually left work about 6:00 P.M. On his way home, he would stop at a supermarket to buy his groceries for the evening. Ten pounds of potatoes, two quart jars of mayonnaise, several quarts of club soda, four heads of lettuce, bags of potato chips and pretzels, and bottles of salad dressing to accompany them made up a routine shopping list for dinner. Once home at his one-bedroom apartment, located only a few miles from his office, Gary would spend as little time as possible transforming his raw groceries into edible fare. With the ingredients just described, the meal would consist of about 10 pounds of potato salad and many large bowls of green salad, accompanied by glasses of club soda to, as Gary explained, facilitate eating and vomiting. If potatoes were not purchased, several large boxes of rice or many loaves of bread might replace them. The volume of food was Gary's overriding concern.

With the television turned to his favorite programs and surrounded by several of the day's newspapers, Gary would settle down to dinner in his living room. He reported that he ate rapidly and that satisfaction was not derived from the food's taste, but, instead, from a sensation that was related to filling himself up. When too full to continue eating, he retired to his bathroom and regurgitated. The soda water and judicious selection of foods enabled him to do this easily; by the time Gary came to the clinic, he could vomit voluntarily without putting his finger down his throat. This binging and purging combination was repeated as often as necessary until all of the food was consumed. Occasionally, he would finish "too early" and would have to go out to buy more food. During the evening, Gary required from 5 to 15 trips to the bathroom, depending on the amount and type of food consumed.

This pattern of behavior was very distressing to Gary, not only because of the financial problems it was creating but also because it was associated with a sense of helplessness. Often, he would resolve to eat normally during the day, but, when evening came, he would be unable to resist. His thoughts would turn more and more to food, and his desire to binge strengthened and became irresistible. Hunger did not seem to play a significant role in his binging. The urge to fill himself simply increased as evening approached.

As for his financial condition, Gary reported that weekends and paydays were especially costly periods for him. With a pocketful of money, he would forego preparing all his own meals and eat some of them at diners and restaurants instead. He would eat at several restaurants during a single evening and, although the tab was moderate at each place (about $10), stopping at five or six restaurants quickly ate into his paycheck. Weekends were also problematic because he had more time available. Binging could start before noon and continue well into the night. Gary said that on these all-day eating and purging sprees he would be left physically exhausted, to the point of falling asleep in front of the television with half-empty bowls and plates surrounding him.

Gary was employed as an electronics engineer in a large manufacturing firm specializing in aerospace navigation equipment. During his six years of employment, he had received two promotions, each with substantial salary increases, for his innovations in design and his devotion to the job. In later sessions Gary reported that he often worked long hours on the job, coming in early and staying until quite late in the evening, to avoid eating. The engineering work that Gary did was on the solitary side; he was given an assignment and returned a finished design to his supervisor. Gary indicated that working alone was to his liking and that on occasions when a project required the collaboration of several design specialists, animosities between him and the group inevitably developed. Dr. Black, Gary's supervisor, had nonetheless taken a liking to Gary and had supported Gary's salary advances without question.

Gary's social life was almost nonexistent. There were very few single women working in his section at the firm, and he did not care to frequent bars as a way of meeting people. He did not enjoy either loud music or alcohol. Although he did say he had a few casual male friends, he saw them infrequently. Besides working and eating, the only other waking activity that Gary engaged in regularly was swimming at a local YMCA. He swam with the same intensity that he applied to his job. His early morning swims consisted of 85 laps in the Olympic-size pool while he raced against the clock. He reported feeling deprived and angry with himself whenever he had an off day at the pool. Such disappointments usually led to an even longer and more intense eating binge later in the day.

Swimming was also a means of keeping fit and trim. Gary mentioned in several of the early therapy sessions that he had an intense fear of becoming overweight and flabby, although he was actually somewhat underweight for his height. He attributed his regurgitation to this fear and recognized that it created a serious threat to his health. Because meals were rarely eaten without subsequent regurgitation, Gary was satisfying very few of his body's nutritional needs. He occasionally ate a sandwich and kept it down, but this was not done on a regular basis. Frequent exposure of his upper digestive system to stomach acids was also a problem; he had stomachaches often. Because of embarrassment about his binging, he had not consulted a physician recently.

SOCIAL HISTORY

Gary was raised in an affluent suburb of Chicago where his father was vice-president of a large investment firm. His childhood was unremarkable. Gary said he got along well with his two older sisters and had an "okay" time growing up. Gary's mother was described as overprotective and stern. His father was rarely present due to frequent business trips and long hours at the office. Gary reported that his mother was obese and that she dieted frequently, lost weight, and then regained it. He recalled how his mother would often complain about her weight problem and warn her children about never becoming fat. All of the children in the Robbins family attended a prestigious private school; like his father, who had attended the school, Gary excelled academically.

Gary's history of vomiting and purging dated back to his high-school days. He was not able to remember specific events that triggered unusual eating behavior, but he clearly recalled an instance of overeating that occurred during the summer between his junior and senior high-school years. It happened the first time that Gary was away from home for an extended period at a summer camp for teenagers gifted in science. Camp activities included morning classes, followed by nature hikes in the early afternoon, more traditional recreational activities later in the afternoon, and movies or stargazing at night. It was hardly a fun-filled summer, but a highly competitive, intellectual atmosphere — one that he did not enjoy. In August, he recalled sneaking off to a small grocery store in town and buying 9 to 10 candy bars, finding a secluded spot in the woods, and consuming all of the candy. When asked why he did this, Gary admitted that it had puzzled him somewhat at the time, but, since it did not do anyone harm and seemed to lift his spirits, he thought little of it.

Several months later, in his senior year, Gary recalled stuffing himself with pizza at a party held by one of his classmates. Because he was watching his weight for the swimming team and realized how fattening the pizza was, he reasoned that the simplest way to prevent weight gain was to induce vomiting. As soon as he returned home, he went to the bathroom, stuck his fingers down this throat, and regurgitated the food. He said he felt a bit disgusted with himself, but, after all, he had prevented weight gain. Gary found himself in the same situation several weeks later. Feeling stressed by college applications and all of the choices that entailed, he purchased five jumbo bags of potato chips one afternoon and ate them in his bedroom. Regurgitation was easier the second time, and Gary had few second thoughts about the episode. Soon he found himself regularly eating larger dinners to the point that his mother remarked about his "healthy" appetite, attributing it to her son's vigorous athletics. Gary now had a way of enjoying as much food as he liked without concern for his weight.

Gary was accepted to the engineering college of a prestigious midwestern university several hundred miles from his home. Adjusting to college life presented some problems for him. Making new friends was somewhat difficult. For the first time he felt challenged by his course work. Initially, he binged very infrequently—most often when stressed in some way. However, during his first two years in college, his frequency of binging began to increase.

Two years later, when Gary was home from college during a midsemester break, Mrs. Robbins no longer felt that her son's appetite was healthy. During that two-week period, Gary's mother noticed that her refrigerator was emptying out at a distressingly rapid rate. At first she thought it was friends whom Gary had over late in the evenings; by the end of his vacation, she suspected that something was wrong. When she asked him about the food, he denied overeating and tried to pass the blame off to his sisters and their boy friends. Back at school, Gary was forced to limit his binging to weekends for financial reasons. He continued to have a few buddies from the swimming team, but he saw less of them on weekends because the binging was beginning to occupy all of his time. Although he limited his binging to several times per week, each binge involved the consumption of vast quantities of food. Between binges he watched his diet very carefully.

When he graduated *summa cum laude,* several engineering firms offered him responsible, high-paying jobs. He accepted one and began to work for a large engineering firm in Indianapolis. For the previous nine months he had been dating a young woman, Glenda. In late May they decided to live together. With a new job to contend with and a lifestyle that did not afford him much privacy, Gary's eating habits were normal for several months. Indeed, he reported that he was hardly troubled by the desire to binge. However, as Glenda and Gary's situation became more routine, his binging and vomiting slowly returned. He tried to eat when he was out of the house or when Glenda was not at home or asleep. But, like Gary's mother, Glenda soon noticed that after the weekly shopping the cupboard was bare in a matter of a few days.

Inevitably, Glenda discovered Gary's secret. He reported that at first she was disgusted and angry. But a few days later she became more sympathetic, and they both decided that he should seek help. Gary's visit to a psychiatrist that year was the first of many such professional consultations. Ten sessions with a dynamically oriented psychiatrist who probed Gary's childhood did not relieve the problem; in fact, it seemed to get out of hand during those months. Unable to accept Gary's "bizarre eating," Glenda left him.

Feeling depressed by Glenda's absence, Gary took solace in eating. His savings account was quickly depleted by his dietary excesses, and soon he was requesting advances from his employer. At first, these were forthcoming without question. After several months of advances, sensing his employer's suspicions, Gary sought help to stall what seemed to be impending financial ruin and embarrassment. He went to his physician and told him the entire story. A three-week stay at a nearby private hospital was the result. To Gary's surprise, the hospital stay relieved many of the pressures resulting from his excessive spending. Going into the hospital with a "medical" problem seemed, in his mind, to provide an excuse for his borrowing; he was isolated from creditors, and his company-supplied insurance paid the bills. While in the hospital Gary was permitted to eat only three meals a day. Opportunities to acquire extra food (e.g., by visiting the hospital cafeteria and shops) were limited. His behavior after meals was carefully monitored to ensure that no vomiting was induced. Gary found that he could eat normally in the hospital, and that lifted his spirits. Life seemed considerably brighter when Gary left the hospital; he had high hopes of maintaining a regular eating routine. Within 15 days of discharge, however, Gary was back to binging and purging. This pattern of economic distress arising from bad checks at grocery stores, brief hospitalization to relieve pressure, and a temporary normalization of his eating occurred three more times in the next five years.

CONCEPTUALIZATION AND TREATMENT

The first problem dealt with in therapy was eliminating the threat of imprisonment, which was imminent if Gary continued to write bad checks. Several supermarket chains had already hired collection agencies, and they were hounding Gary. Furthermore, all possibilities of borrowing money had been exhausted several months ago; so it was, Gary believed, a desperate situation. His therapist agreed than an immediate step should be taken to prevent further excessive spending and binging. An unusual primary intervention was implemented: Gary was to destroy his checkbook and to deposit his payroll check into an account that required both his and his therapist's signatures for withdrawals. The intent of this move was obvious. If Gary had no checks or cash readily available to him, he would not be able to incur further indebtedness, thus reducing his likelihood of imprisonment.

The therapist did not view this intervention as a cure, but only as a means of creating an atmosphere in which more traditional psychotherapeutic techniques could be effective. With some relief of the financial pressure, Gary's eating patterns might be modified to the point at which he could manage his own finances. Within two weeks, Gary's daily spending was cut by approximately two-thirds, and he was able to make substantial payments to creditors and friends from whom he had borrowed money. These payments lifted Gary's spirits considerably, and the therapist believed that more basic causes of the binging and purging pattern could be addressed.

There were several areas for possible intervention. Gary believed that even small amounts of food would make him fat. It was difficult for him to eat regular meals without vomiting because of his intense fear of becoming obese. Socially, Gary had withdrawn from all interpersonal contacts with the exception of on-the-job contact with co-workers. Eating had become his main source of reinforcement. Because he was almost always eating and purging in his apartment, it was also likely that those surroundings had acquired stimulus control properties that would make it difficult for him to avoid eating in that environment. Finally, over the past several years, Gary's self-esteem had waned markedly, and he had become more and more depressed. The therapist believed these problems could hinder progress in the other areas of intervention.

The therapist decided to begin by addressing Gary's irrational belief that if he ate regular meals he would become obese. Playing the "devil's advocate," the therapist agreed with Gary that eating regular meals would indeed lead to his being overweight; moreover, the therapist contended that eating only two regular meals a day could lead to overweight. Gary also agreed with this argument, thus confirming the presence of an irrational belief. The therapist went one step further. He suggested that eating a very small lunch and dinner would also lead to obesity. "Even if you ate a half grapefruit and small salad for lunch and a small piece of broiled fish and another small salad for dinner, you'd probably gain weight." Gary admitted that no one could possibly gain much weight on such a diet. With a foothold achieved, the therapist further cajoled Gary with extreme examples. Ultimately, he seemed to convince Gary that with reasonable eating one could maintain a trim figure.

To encourage participation in social activities, Gary was given a specific plan that involved meeting people. Community meetings, including town hearings and local political committees, religious groups, and organizations for the improvement of the environment were all discussed, with particular emphasis on how to make initial contact. During the session when these plans were discussed, the therapist and Gary role-played possible approaches to strangers at these meetings. Specifically, Gary played the part of a man or woman while the therapist demonstrated how to begin a conversation with a stranger. After several demonstrations, the roles were reversed, and Gary played himself attempting to start a conversation with a stranger, played by the therapist. After he adjusted to the initial anxiety of the situation, Gary quickly learned how to approach people. These social activities would not only encourage more social contacts and perhaps lessen his depression, but they would also keep Gary out of his apartment and cut down on his binging.

In order to break the almost automatic chain of events leading to binging, the therapist carefully examined Gary's actions during his free time: lunchtimes and evenings after work. He discovered that Gary had tremendous difficulty passing a grocery store or a fast-food restaurant without going in and buying something. New routes for coming home from work that did not have any markets or fast-food chains along the way were devised. Gary used them instead of his normal routes. The idea was, simply, to eliminate the temptation to stop.

Over the last few years, Gary's self-esteem had suffered markedly. He regretted harassing his family and friends for money. They in turn had come to treat him as an outcast. Gary also reported that he sometimes despised himself because his eating habits were disgusting and he felt out of control. After weekends of especially excessive binging, the therapist observed temporary changes in Gary's mood. He was much more subdued than usual, and his affect was depressed. During the previous financial crises, Gary mentioned that he had contemplated taking his life as a way out, but he had never made any concrete plans or attempted to do so. Considering the lack of positive, encouraging feedback that Gary's environment provided, it was not surprising that the therapist's genuine concern about Gary, expressed in his willingness to see Gary frequently and his warmth during sessions, had increased Gary's self-esteem.

Considerable progress in reducing Gary's eating was made in the first two months of therapy. His average daily expense was down to about $7, and the amount of time spent binging and purging had been reduced by about 75 percent. Additionally, at least twice a week, Gary was attending a group concerned with preventing the opening of a local nuclear power station and had met several interesting people. He felt much better about himself because he no longer was borrowing money and because he was not binging as much.

Despite these positive changes, virtually all progress was eradicated in one weekend. Gary had been working for 17 months on the design of a component that was the heart of the navigational system for a new commercial airliner. On the Friday morning prior to the weekend, the company was notified that production of the airliner had been scrapped. All of Gary's efforts for the past $1\frac{1}{2}$ years had been wasted. Gary left work at 1 P.M. and began a three-day binge; during that time he wrote nearly $350 in bad checks. At his session with the therapist the following week, Gary said he wanted to stop therapy for an indefinite period while he "got himself together." The therapist's phone call to Gary several months later revealed that he had declared bankruptcy and was continuing to binge.

DISCUSSION

Gary's disorder, bulimia nervosa, is one of two eating disorders described in *DSM-IV*. The other eating disorder is anorexia nervosa: an intense fear of becoming obese resulting in reduced intake of food and severe weight loss. The key to the diagnosis of bulimia nervosa is recurrent episodes of binge eating couple with compensatory behavior, such as vomiting, to prevent weight gain. Literally, bulimia means "ox hunger," or voracious appetite, but it now refers to binging. The binges typically involve eating high-calorie, easily ingested food, usually in secret. The binges end when abdominal pains become severe or when the person is interrupted or falls asleep. Vomiting frequently follows the binge, either terminating it or allowing further eating to take place. Bulimics are usually intensely concerned about their weight, which may show fairly dramatic fluctuations. They realize that their eating is abnormal but report that they cannot control themselves. Their inability to control their eating often leads to feelings of depression, guilt, and low self-esteem. The prevalence of bulimia is not known precisely, principally because it is a secretive problem. Probably about 2 percent of a college-aged population has the disorder (Fairburn & Beglin, 1990). The disorder typically begins in the late teens (Fairburn & Cooper, 1982) and is much more common in women than men. Parents and other first-degree relatives of bulimics are frequently described as alcoholic or depressed (Herzog, 1982; Kassett et al., 1987) and more frequently than usual have bulimia themselves (Kassett et al., 1987).

Bulimia can occur either by itself, as in Gary's case, or as an accompanying symptom of anorexia nervosa. In anorexia nervosa, which begins in adolescence and is much more common in women than men, the person severely restricts his or her food intake and loses a significant proportion of his or her body weight. In addition, anorexics show distorted attitudes toward eating, food, and weight. They may, for example, deny that anything is wrong, even when their emaciated state is obvious to everyone else. A distorted body image is common. Anorexics think that they are too fat, even though objective data indicate otherwise.

Some anorexics report they have no appetite, but among anorexics with episodes of binge eating, 69 percent report strong urges to eat. Somewhat more than 50 percent of anorexics also have episodes of binge eating. The frequency of binges and vomiting in these patients, however, is less than was true for Gary. Anorexics who binge differ in several ways from those without this feature. Before the onset of the disorder, anorexic patients who binge are more likely to be overweight, and many of them report that their mothers were obese. They are also more likely to be depressed and anxious, to use alcohol and drugs, and to display impulsive behavior such as stealing (Casper et al., 1980; Garfinkel, Moldofsky, & Garner, 1980). They are also likely to have anxiety disorders, especially social phobia (Schwalberg et al., 1992).

Russell (1979) reported on the characteristics of a group of 30 patients with bulimia nervosa, collected over a 6½-year span. All patients were currently bulimic but *not* anorexic. Twenty-eight were women. Seventeen had previously had definite anorexia and another seven may have had a mild form of anorexia (e.g., moderate weight loss). Comparing Gary to Russell's figures clearly shows how unusual his problems were. First, he was male; second, he did not have anorexia before the onset of bulimia. Schneider and Agras (1987) have published the first detailed comparison of male and female bulimics. Males' weight fluctuated more over time and they had a more realistic perception of their ideal body weight. They used laxatives less than the women but had more problems with drugs and alcohol. Unfortunately, these data are not especially revealing about Gary's case.

Among Russell's patients vomiting was typically induced by sticking fingers or a toothbrush down the throat, although six patients had acquired the ability to vomit voluntarily. Thirteen patients were heavy laxative users (e.g., 12 to 20 tablets per day). The patients reported that they continually thought about food, even to the extent that their eating fantasies interfered with completing daily activities. Their dreams were often of food and eating! The patients reported that they did not eat to satisfy hunger. "It is not hunger. Hunger is a feeling of a gap inside of you. You eat something small to stop that feeling. I go on eating after I've satisfied that hunger. I want to keep eating till I feel full—it's the final limit—you can then eat no more" (Russell, 1979, pp. 434–435). The frequency of binging varied greatly in Russell's sample. Some patients would only do so every week or so, but others were more like Gary, with daily binging, particularly in the evening. Depressive symptoms were very common. Thirteen patients had moderate depression and another thirteen were so severely depressed that, in addition to their symptoms, they were unable to work or cope with daily activities, had made a serious suicide attempt, or had had a course of electroconvulsive therapy.

Several serious physical complications may result from bulimia. The repeated vomiting can lead to potassium depletion, which, in turn, can produce epilepsy. Urinary infections and kidney failure also occur in some patients. Menstrual irregularity is common (Pyle et al., 1981). Sore throat (Fairburn, 1981) and destruction of dental enamel (Herzog, 1982) occur due to frequent acid in these areas.

On a theoretical level, two aspects of bulimia need to be understood—the binging itself and the behaviors that follow the binging (such as vomiting and laxative use). A variety of factors could cause binging—an intense fear of becoming fat, an overestimation of one's actual body size, and societal pressures toward thinness (Powers et al., 1987) coupled with high sensitivity to how the bulimics are perceived by others (Striegel-Moore, Silberstein, & Rodin, 1993). In one study, for example, women with bulimia or anorexia were shown silhouettes of very thin to obese women. They were asked to select the one closest to their own body size and the one they would most like to be. Both the bulimic and anorexic women overestimated their current body size and chose thinner ideals than control women (Williamson, Cubic, & Gleaves, 1993). In Gary's case, his mother's obesity may have triggered his extreme concerns about weight.

It is more difficult to account for the binging itself. Some psychoanalytic writers have proposed that eating disorders generally occur in people who fear sex and symbolically equate sex with eating. Anorexia then is a symbolic means of avoiding pregnancy, and binging occurs when the repressed sexual urges can no longer be held in check. This account does not fit Gary well. The theory is meant to apply to women, who are much more likely than men to have eating disorders. Furthermore, Gary's relationship with Glenda did not indicate any serious conflicts over sex.

Alternatively, binging may result from a chain of events beginning with an intense fear of becoming fat. The fear leads to dietary restraint, which then, paradoxically, *increases* the likelihood of binging when the person is stressed. The onset of bulimia is indeed associated with major life stressors such as the end of a significant relationship. Supporting this formulation are data showing that emotional arousal does increase eating among people who are engaging in dietary restraint (Cools, Schotte, & McNally, 1992). What function did binging serve for Gary? Several processes could be involved. First, Gary was afraid of becoming fat and did often restrain his eating, for example, by skipping breakfast. Second, Gary's early binges seemed, at least in part, to be stress related. Binging could have been established as a way of coping with stress. His binging may have filled up a life that was devoid of many other pleasurable activities.

Both biological and psychological treatments have yielded some success for bulimics. The tricyclic antidepressants are somewhat effective, but their unpleasant side effects often lead to discontinuation. More promising is another antidepressant, fluoxetine, which has fewer side effects (Fluoxetine Bulimia Nervosa Collaborative Study Group, 1993). As to psychological interventions, success has been achieved by group therapy (Gordon & Ahmed, 1988), cognitive behavior therapy (Agras et al., 1989; Freeman et al., 1985) and the interpersonal therapy developed for treating depression (Fairburn et al., 1993). As in Gary's case, an attempt to change the bulimic's irrational beliefs about eating and weight gain may be a valuable area for intervention. Of even greater potential, however, would be a therapy based on an understanding of the functional significance of binging. Unfortunately, we do not understand exactly what the binge eating does for the bulimic.

Little information is available on the prognosis for bulimia. Anorexics with bulimia, however, have poorer prognoses than anorexics without this feature, suggesting that successful management of the disorder is difficult. Furthermore, in studies of bulimic patients the average duration of the disorder is five to six years, again suggesting a chronic course (Fairburn & Cooper, 1982). Indeed, Gary's relapse seems similar to what often happens in the treatment of addictions. Marlatt and Gordon (1978) have noted that about 67 percent of alcoholics, smokers, and heroin addicts relapse within 90 days following the end of treatment. These relapses are precipitated by life stresses or social pressure to resume the old habit. A single violation of abstinence is usually sufficient to wipe out totally the treatment gains that had occurred. Marlatt and Gordon refer to this as the *abstinence violation effect*. They argue that when a person violates his or her commitment to abstinence, a state of dissonance is created between the behavior and the self-image of the person. This dissonance motivates attempts to reduce it, for example, by changing the self-image: "I guess I haven't really recovered." Furthermore, the transgression is attributed to personal weakness and thus the person is likely to expect future failures.

This analysis seems highly relevant to Gary, who relapsed in a situation of stress and whose first binge reinstituted the full-blown pattern. Treatment, then, should include components to deal with relapse. Gary might have first been trained to recognize situations that could create pressure for him. Furthermore, he could have been given specific training in coping, either skills to handle problematic life situations or to deal with negative emotional states. Finally, he might have been told that relapse is likely and that it does not indicate that the treatment has failed or that he is a weak person. Within this framework, he could also have been instructed on how to cope with a single binge to reduce the likelihood that one abstinence violation would lead to a complete resumption of his old pattern.

17 PARANOID PERSONALITY DISORDER

This case study is based on personal, rather than clinical, experience. Joe Fuller was in treatment for a brief period of time, but he terminated the relationship well before a therapy plan was formulated. This pattern is, in fact, characteristic of this type of person; they seldom seek professional services and, when they do, are difficult to work with. One of the authors was well acquainted with Joe during high school and college and has stayed in contact with him throughout subsequent years.

SOCIAL HISTORY

Joe was the third of four children. He had two older brothers and a younger sister. His father was a steamfitter and his mother was a homemaker. The family lived in a lower-middle-class neighborhood in a large, northeastern city. Joe's grandmother also lived with them, beginning when Joe was 11 years old. She was an invalid and could not care for herself after Joe's grandfather died.

Our first information about Joe comes from his high-school years. Unlike his older brothers, Joe was an exceptionally bright student. On the basis of his performance in elementary school and entrance examinations, he was admitted to a prestigious public high school. The school was widely recognized for academic excellence. More than 90 percent of the graduating seniors went on to college; most went to Ivy League schools. The school was also known as a "pressure cooker." All of the students were expected to meet very high standards; those who failed were denigrated by their peers. Joe thrived in this intellectually competitive environment. He usually received the highest test scores in his classes, particularly in science. These achievements were based on a combination of intelligence and hard work. Joe was clearly very bright, but so were most of the other students in this school. Joe was a serious student who worked hard and seemed to be driven by a desire to succeed. While many of the other students worried about examinations and talked to each other about their fear of failure, Joe exuded self-confidence. He knew that the teachers and other students viewed him as one of the best students; he often made jokes about people who "couldn't make the grade." This critical attitude was not reserved for other students alone. Whenever a teacher made a mistake in class, Joe was always the first to laugh and make a snide comment. His classmates usually laughed along with him, but they also noticed a sneering, condescending quality in Joe's humor that set him apart from themselves.

Joe was a classic example of the critic who could "dish it out but couldn't take it." He was extremely sensitive to criticism. It did not seem to matter whether the criticism was accurate or justified; Joe was ready to retaliate at the slightest provocation. He argued endlessly about examinations, particularly in mathematics and science classes. If he lost points on any of his answers, even if he had gotten an "A" on the exam, he would insist that his answer was correct, the question was poorly written, or the topic had not been explained adequately by the teacher prior to the exam. He never admitted that he was wrong. His sensitivity was also evident in interpersonal relationships. Most people are able to laugh at themselves, but Joe could not. His family background was a particular sore spot. Many of the other students in his school were from wealthy homes. Their parents were mostly professionals with advanced degrees. Joe seemed to be self-conscious about his father's lack of formal education and the fact that his family did not live in a large, modern house. He never admitted it openly, but the topic led to frequent arguments. The following example was a typical instance of this sort. Joe had been arguing in class about his grade on a chemistry examination. After class, he overheard another student say to one of his friends, "I don't know why some people have to work so hard for everything." The other boy's father happened to be a successful businessman. Joe took his comment to mean that Joe was trying to compensate for the fact that his family did not have a lot of money. This implied insult, which may or may not have been a simple comment about Joe's aggressive behavior, infuriated him. Two nights later, while everyone else was watching a school basketball game, Joe sneaked out into the parking lot and poured sugar into the gas tank of the other boy's car so that the engine would be ruined.

Joe did not participate in organized sports or student organizations, and he tended to avoid group activities. He did have a small circle of friends and was particularly close to two other boys. They were people whom he had judged to be his intellectual equals and they were the only people in whom he could confide. He was interested in women, but his attitude toward them and his interactions with them struck his friends as being somewhat odd. The issues of dependence and control seemed to be of central importance to Joe. Whenever one of his friends spent a lot of time with a girlfriend or went out with a her instead of a group of guys, Joe accused him of being "henpecked." Joe seldom dated the same woman twice. He usually insisted that she was "weird" or "a drag" but, if the truth were known, most of them would not have gone out on another date with him if he had asked. They found Joe to be rude and arrogant. Conversations with him were one-sided, with Joe trying to impress his date with his intelligence and simultaneously implying that she was barely worthy of his company. He was not interested in being friends; his sole purpose was to make a sexual conquest. He often bragged about having sex with many women, but his closest friends suspected that he was still a virgin.

In most respects, Joe's relationship with his family was unremarkable. They were not a tightly knit family, but he respected his parents and got along well with his older brothers and his sister. His principal problem at home centered on his grandmother, whom he hated. He complained about her continuously to his friends, saying that she was old and crippled, and he wished that his parents would ship her off to an old folks' home. Her inability to care for herself and her dependence on Joe's parents seemed to be particularly annoying to him. He noted on several occasions that if he was ever in a similar situation, he hoped that someone would put him out of his misery.

After graduating from high school, Joe enrolled at Columbia University, where he majored in chemistry and maintained a "straight A" average throughout his first two years. He seemed to study all the time; his friends described him as a "workaholic." Everything he did became an obsession. If he was studying for a particular course, he concentrated on that topic day and night, seven days a week. If he was involved in a laboratory project, he practically lived in the laboratory. Relaxation and recreation were not included in his schedule. Even if he had the time, there were few leisure activities that Joe enjoyed. He had never been particularly athletic and was, in fact, clumsy. He hated to lose at anything and was also afraid of being ridiculed for looking awkward, so he avoided sports altogether. He was also uninterested in art and films. Joe argued that these activities were a waste of time and a sign of weakness and effeminacy.

Joe's first steady relationship with a woman began during his sophomore year. Carla was a student at a small liberal arts college in upstate New York. They happened to meet at a small party while she was visiting friends in New

York City. Several weeks later, Joe drove to spend the weekend with her. They continued to see each other once or twice a month throughout the spring semester. From Joe's point of view, this was an ideal relationship. He liked Carla; she shared his sarcastic, almost bitter sense of humor, and they got along well sexually. Perhaps most important, the fact that she was not in the same city meant that she could not demand a great deal of his time and could not try to control his schedule or activities. Unfortunately, the relationship ended after a few months when Carla told Joe that she had another boyfriend. Although he was shocked and furious, he made every effort to seem calm and rational. He had always taken pride in his ability to avoid emotional reactions, particularly if they were expected. In discussing the situation with friends, Joe maintained that he had never really cared for Carla and said that he was interested only in her body. Nevertheless, he was clearly interested in revenge. His first plan was to win her back so that he could then turn the tables and drop her. Presumably this process would demonstrate to everyone that he, not Carla, had been in control of the relationship. When this effort failed, he settled for spreading rumors about Carla's promiscuous sexual behavior.

After his breakup with Carla, Joe became more deeply involved in his laboratory work. He would disappear for days at a time and seldom saw any of his friends. The experiments he was running were apparently based on his own ideas. His assigned work and routine studying were largely ignored; consequently his academic performance began to deteriorate somewhat.

The experience with Carla also contributed to a decline in Joe's already cynical attitude toward women. He described her behavior as treacherous and deceitful and took the rejection as one more piece of evidence proving that he could not trust anyone, particularly a woman. He continued to go out on dates, but he was extremely suspicious of women's intentions and obviously jealous of their attention to other men. On one occasion, he went to a party with a woman he met in one of his classes. They arrived together, but Joe chose to ignore her while he chatted with some male friends in the kitchen. When he later discovered his date talking with another man in the living room, he became rude and offensive. He insulted the woman, made jokes about her clothes and the makeup she was wearing, and suggested that her friend was a homosexual. As might be expected, they never saw each other again. Another time, after he had dated a woman once, he sat in his parked car outside her apartment and watched the entrance for two nights to determine whether one of his friends was also seeing her.

LATER ADJUSTMENT

After receiving his B.S. degree, Joe stayed on at Columbia to do graduate work in biochemistry. He continued to work very hard and was considered one of the best students in the department. His best work was done in the laboratory, where he was allowed to pursue independent research. Classroom work was more of a problem. Joe resented being told what to do and what to read. He believed that most faculty members were envious of his intellect. Highly structured reading lists and laboratory assignments, which were often time consuming, were taken by Joe to be efforts to interfere with his professional advancement. In one case, he became convinced that a professor had cheated him on a final examination. The professor had, in fact, gone out of her way to avoid bias in scoring the examinations; every answer had been typewritten and identified only by social security number. When Joe received a "B+" instead of an "A," he argued that the entire process had been designed to cover up the professor's effort to cheat him. He said that the examination booklets had been decoded *prior* to being read! When his friends asked him why the system was used, he pointed out that the professor was not stupid and, knowing that Joe would discover the plot, had devised a means to make it look as though she had been fair. The chemistry faculty was concerned by this incident but decided to tolerate Joe's eccentricity because he was doing creative work and did not present any other problems.

In his second year of graduate school, Joe began dating an undergraduate woman in one of his study sections. Ruth was unremarkable in every regard. His friends described her as plain, bland, and mousy. They were surprised that Joe was even interested in her, but in retrospect, she had one general feature that made her perfect for Joe—she was not at all threatening. He made all of the decisions in the relationship, and she acquiesced to his every whim and fancy. Other men were not interested in her. In fact, they seldom noticed her, so Joe did not have to remain constantly alert to the possibility of desertion. They were perfect complements to each other and were married within a year.

Joe's first job after getting his Ph.D. was as a research chemist for a major drug company. At the beginning, it seemed like an ideal position. He was expected to work somewhat independently doing basic biochemical research. There was no question that he was intellectually capable of the work, and his willingness to work long hours would be beneficial to his advancement, which was closely tied to productivity. Joe expected to be promoted rapidly and was confident that he would be the head of a division within five years.

When Joe began working in the company laboratory, he quickly evaluated all of the employees and their relationship to his own position. There were several young Ph.D.s like himself, three supervisors, and the head of the laboratory, Dr. Daniels, a distinguished senior investigator. Joe admired Dr. Daniels and wanted to impress him. He did not think much of his young colleagues and particularly resented the supervisors, whom he considered to be his intellectual inferiors. He believed that they had been promoted because they were "yes-men," not because they were competent scientists. He often complained about them to his peers and occasionally laughed openly about their mistakes. When they asked him to perform a specific experiment, particularly if the task was tedious, he was arrogant and resentful, but he usually complied with the request. He hoped that the quality of his work would be noticed by Dr. Daniels, who would then allow him to work more independently. He also worried, however, that the others would notice that he was being subservient in an effort to gain Dr. Daniel's favor. He became more and more self-conscious and was constantly alert to signs of disdain and rejection from the others in the laboratory. The others gradually came to see him as rigid and defensive, and he eventually became isolated from the rest of the group. He interpreted their rejection as evidence of professional jealousy.

Joe's initial work did gain some recognition, and he was given greater independence in his choice of projects. He was interested in the neurochemical basis of depression and spent several months pursuing a series of animal experiments aimed at specific details of his personal theory. Very few people knew what he was doing. He refused to discuss the research with anyone other than Dr. Daniels; even then he was careful to avoid the description of procedural details. His principal concern was that other people might get credit for his ideas. He wanted to impress Dr. Daniels, but he also wanted to take over Dr. Daniels's job. The quickest way to do that was to make a major breakthrough in the laboratory, one for which he alone would receive credit.

Dr. Daniels and the other supervisors recognized that Joe was exceptionally bright and a talented, dedicated scientist. They liked his early work at the company but were dissatisfied with the independent work that he was pursuing. It seemed overly ambitious and, more important, highly esoteric. There were no immediate, practical implications to this line of research, and it did not promise to lead to any commercial results in the near future. Consequently, Joe was told that his work was not acceptable and that he would have to return to doing work that was more closely supervised.

Joe's response to this criticism was openly hostile. He complained bitterly about the imbeciles in company management and swore that he would no longer tolerate their jealousy and stupidity. He was certain that someone had learned about his ideas and that Dr. Daniels and the others were trying to force him out of the company so that they could then publish the theory without giving him credit. Their insistence that he discontinue his work and return to more menial tasks was clear proof, from Joe's point of view, that they wanted to slow down his progress so that they could complete the most important experiments themselves. His paranoid ideas attracted considerable attention. Other people began to avoid him, and he sometimes noticed that they gave him apprehensive glances. It did not occur to him that these responses were provoked by his own hostile behavior; he took their behavior as further evidence that the whole laboratory was plotting against him. As the tension mounted, Joe began to fear for his life.

The situation soon became intolerable. After three years with the firm, Joe was told that he would have to resign. Dr. Daniels agreed to write him a letter of reference so that he could obtain another position as long as he did not contest his termination. Joe considered hiring a lawyer to help him fight for his job, but he became convinced that the plot against him was too pervasive for him to win. He also had serious doubts about being able to find a lawyer he could trust. He therefore decided to apply for other positions and eventually took a job as a research associate working with a faculty member at a large state university.

In many ways the new position was a serious demotion. His salary was considerably less than it had been at the drug company, and the position carried much less prestige. Someone with Joe's academic credentials and experience should have been able to do better, but he had not published any of his research. He was convinced that this lack of professional success could be attributed to inference from jealous, incompetent administrators at the drug company. A more plausible explanation was that his work had never achieved publishable form. Although the ideas were interesting and his laboratory techniques were technically skillful, Joe was not able to connect the two facets of his work to produce conclusive results. He was also a perfectionist. Never satisfied with the results of an experiment, he insisted on doing follow-up after follow-up and could not bring himself to consider a piece of work finished. The thought of submitting an article and having it rejected by a professional journal was extremely anxiety provoking. Thus, despite his recognized brilliance and several years of careful research, Joe was not able to land anything better than this job as a research associate.

Joe did not like the new job, partly because he thought it was beneath him and also because his activity was even more highly structured than it had been at the drug company. He was working on a research grant in which all of the experiments had been planned in advance. Although he complained a good deal about the people who had ruined his career and expressed a lack of interest in the new line of work, he did high-quality work and was tolerated by the others in the laboratory. The salary was extremely important to Joe and Ruth because they now had a young daughter, Janice, who was two years old. There were also some other features about the job that were attractive to Joe. Much of his work was planned, but he was allowed to use the laboratory in his spare time to pursue his own ideas. It was an active research program, and the department included a number of well-known faculty members. Joe believed that these people, particularly his boss, Dr. Willner, would soon recognize his talent and that he would eventually be able to move to a faculty position.

Things did not work out the way Joe had planned. After he had been working at the university for one year, Dr. Willner asked him to curtail his independent research. He explained that these outside experiments were becoming too expensive and that the main research funded by the grant would require more of the laboratory's time. Joe did not accept this explanation, which he considered to be an obvious excuse to interfere with his personal work. He believed that Dr. Willner had pretended to be disinterested in Joe's work while he actually kept careful tabs on his progress. In fact, he took this interference to indicate that Dr. Willner believed Joe's research was on the verge of a breakthrough. Joe continued to work independently when he had the opportunity and became even more secretive about his ideas. Several weeks after these developments, Dr. Willner hired another research associate and asked Joe to share his office with the new person. Joe, of course, believed that the new person was hired and placed in his office solely to spy on his research.

As the tension mounted at work, Joe's relationship with Ruth became severely strained. They had never had a close or affectionate relationship and now seemed on the verge of open conflict. Ruth recognized that Joe was overreacting to minor events; she did not want him to lose another job. She often tried to talk rationally with him in an effort to help him view these events from a more objective perspective. These talks led to arguments, and Joe finally accused her of collaborating with his enemies. He suggested that the people from the drug company and from the university had persuaded her to help them steal his ideas and then get rid of him. As Joe became more paranoid and belligerent, Ruth became fearful for her own safety and that of her daughter. She eventually took Janice with her to live with her parents and began divorce proceedings. Her desertion, as Joe viewed it, provided more evidence that she had been part of the plot all along.

Two weeks after Ruth left, Joe began to experience panic attacks. The first one occurred while he was driving home from work. He was alone in the car, the road was familiar, and the traffic pattern was not particularly congested. Although the temperature was cool, Joe noticed that he was perspiring profusely. His hands and feet began to tingle, and his heart seemed to be beating irregularly. When he began to feel dizzy and faint, he had to pull the car off the road and stop. His shirt was now completely soaked with perspiration, and his breathing was rapid and labored. At the time, he thought that he was going to smother. All in all, it was a terrifying experience. The symptoms disappeared as quickly as they had appeared; within 10 minutes he was able to get back on the road and drive home. He experienced three such incidents within a two-week period and became so concerned about his health that he overcame his distrust of physicians and made an appointment for a physical examination.

The physician was unable to discover any medical disorder and recommended that Joe consult a psychiatrist about his anxiety. Joe reluctantly agreed that a psychiatrist might be of help and arranged an appointment with Dr. Fein. The issue of Joe's paranoid thinking did not come up during his conversations with Dr. Fein because Joe did not consider it to be a problem. Furthermore, he knew that other people thought that he was overly suspicious and that some people would consider him to be mentally ill. He therefore carefully avoided talking about the efforts to steal his ideas and did not mention the plot involving his wife and former colleagues. He simply wanted to know what was causing the panic attacks and how he could control them. At the end of his second session, Dr. Fein suggested that Joe begin taking phenelzine (Nardil), an antidepressant drug that has also been effective in treating panic anxiety. This suggestion precipitated an extended conversation about the physiological action of mood-stabilizing drugs that escalated into a heated argument.

Joe had been disappointed with Dr. Fein; he did not believe that Dr. Fein understood his problem (i.e., the panic attacks) and resented the many open-ended, probing questions that he asked about Joe's personal life. Dr. Fein believed that he was trying to complete a thorough assessment that would allow him to place this specific problem in an appropriate context, but Joe considered this line of inquiry an invasion of privacy regarding matters for which he had not sought advice. The prospect of taking antidepressant drugs further aroused Joe's suspicions. He began asking Dr. Fein about the neurological mechanisms affected by this drug—a topic with which he was intimately familiar because of his own research at the drug company. He was obviously better versed on this subject than Dr. Fein and concluded that Dr. Fein was therefore incompetent because he recommended a treatment that he could not explain completely. Joe finally ended the conversation by telling Dr. Fein that he thought he was a quack. He stormed out of the office and did not return.

The panic attacks continued at the approximate rate of one a week for the next three months. Joe also noticed that he frequently felt physically ill and nauseous, even on days when he did not experience a panic attack. Searching for an explanation for these escalating problems, and considering his conviction that other people were trying to harm him, he finally borrowed some equipment from another department and checked the radiation levels in his laboratory. He claimed that he found an unusually high level of radiation coming from a new balance that Dr. Willner had recently purchased. That was the final piece of evidence he needed. He believed that the people who were conspiring against him, including Dr. Willner, the people from the drug company, and his wife, had planted the radioactive balance in his laboratory so that he would eventually die from radiation poisoning. It struck him as a clever plot. He spent much more time in the laboratory than anyone else and would therefore receive very high doses of radiation. The others were presumably wearing special clothing to screen them from the radiation, thus further reducing their own risk.

Joe confronted Dr. Willner with this discovery; as expected, he denied any knowledge of radioactivity emanating from the balance. Dr. Willner suggested that Joe should take some time away from the laboratory. He had obviously been under a lot of strain lately, considering the divorce proceedings, and could benefit from the rest. Joe was certain that this was a ruse to allow the conspirators to remove the evidence of what he now called the assassination attempt. He refused to take time off and insisted that he would not let the others steal his ideas. The following day he went to the office of the president of the university to demand a formal investigation. An informal series of meetings was eventually arranged involving various members of the laboratory and representatives of the university administration. Joe also contacted the governmental agency that funded Dr. Willner's research, which conducted its own investigation. The result of this time-consuming process was that Joe lost his job. No one was able to find any evidence of a conspiracy to harm Joe or steal his ideas. Both investigations concluded that Joe should seek professional help to deal with his unwarranted suspicions.

When he left the university, Joe took a job driving a cab. This final fiasco had ruined his chances of obtaining another research position. No one would write him letters of recommendation. He was, of course, convinced that he had been blacklisted and did not consider the possibility that his problems were created by his own antagonistic behavior. In many ways the change in occupations led to positive changes in Joe's adjustment. He seemed to love driving a cab. He worked late at night, when most other cabbies were sleeping, and was thus in a noncompetitive situation. The people with whom he interacted were not threatening to his sense of intellectual superiority; in fact, he derived considerable enjoyment from telling his friends stories about the derelicts and imbeciles that rode in his cab. At last contact, Joe was quite content with the situation. He lived by himself in a small apartment, maintained a small circle of friends, and planned to continue working as a cab driver. He was still arrogant and resented his past treatment but seemed resigned to his status as a martyr in the world of chemistry. The need for constant vigilance was greatly reduced because he no longer had access to a laboratory and could not continue to work on his ideas.

DISCUSSION

Personality disorders are defined in terms of stable, cross-situational patterns of behavior that lead to impairment in social and occupational functioning or subjective distress. These response patterns are exhibited in a rigid and inflexible manner, despite their maladaptive consequences. The principal features of a paranoid personality are unwarranted suspicion and mistrust of other people. People with this personality disorder are often seen by others as cold, guarded, and defensive; they refuse to accept blame, even if it is justified, and they tend to retaliate at the slightest provocation. *DSM-IV* (pp. 637–639) lists the following criteria for paranoid personality disorder:

A. A pervasive distrust and suspiciousness of others such that their motives are interpreted as malevolent, beginning by early adulthood and present in a variety of contexts, as indicated by four (or more) or the following:

1. Suspects, without sufficient basis, that others are exploiting, harming, or deceiving him or her.
2. Is preoccupied with unjustified doubts about the loyalty or trustworthiness of friends or associates.
3. Is reluctant to confide in others because of unwarranted fear that the information will be used maliciously against him or her.
4. Reads hidden demeaning or threatening meanings into benign remarks or events.
5. Persistently bears grudges (for example, is unforgiving of insults, injuries, or slights).
6. Perceives attacks on his or her character or reputation that are not apparent to others and is quick to react angrily or to counterattack.
7. Has recurrent suspicions, without justification, regarding fidelity of spouse or sexual partner.

B. Does not occur exclusively during the course of schizophrenia, a mood disorder with psychotic features, or another psychotic disorder and is not due to the direct physiological effects of a general medical condition.

These characteristics are not limited to periods of acute disturbance; they are typical of the person's behavior over a long period of time.

Personality disorders are among the most controversial categories included in *DSM-IV* (Widiger & Costa, 1994). Part of the controversy derives from the debate regarding personality traits and situational specificity of behavior. Social learning theorists have argued that human behavior is largely determined by the situation or context in which it occurs and not by internal personality characteristics (e.g., Mischel & Peake, 1982). This position has been supported by studies reporting considerable inconsistency in individuals' behavior measured across different situations. There are, however, other data indicating that ratings of personality traits can be useful predictors of behavior, especially when the ratings are made by several observers, the observers are thoroughly familiar with the people who are being rated, observations are made on a number of occasions, and the ratings are made on dimensions that are publicly observable (Funder & Colvin, 1991). It is possible to recognize the importance of situational variables while also taking into account individual differences in the probability of making a particular response in a given situation. As Epstein (1979, pp. 1122–1123) has argued:

> The fact that people read in a library and swim in a swimming pool does not establish that there is no generality, or "cross-situational stability," in either swimming or in reading behavior. More to the point is that some people are more prone to swim than others when there is a reasonable opportunity to do so, and this may include swimming in pools, in lakes, and in oceans. Furthermore, one cannot test such a cross-situational proclivity to swim by observing a person once

in the vicinity of a swimming pool and once in the vicinity of a lake, as there may be many reasons for that person to forego swimming on a particular occasion. Behavior is obviously determined by more than response dispositions. Given an adequate sample of occasions, however, response dispositions will out.

The definition of Paranoid Personality Disorder does not assume that people so diagnosed will always be suspicious, guarded, or tense, regardless of the specific circumstances or people with whom they are interacting, but it does assume that they often behave in this manner and that, given a particular situation, they are more likely than nonparanoid people to behave in this manner.

Two other issues also contribute to the controversial status of the personality disorders. One involves reliability. During the field trials for the development of *DSM-III*, interrater reliability for personality disorders was considerably lower than it was for many other disorders. This situation has improved in subsequent years, partly because of the introduction of structured interview schedules that are aimed specifically at personality disorders. For example, Pfohl and his colleagues (1986) interviewed 131 psychiatric patients and rated each patient for the presence or absence of each personality disorder. The reliability for the diagnosis of some specific categories was good (e.g., 0.90[1] for dependent personality disorder and 0.85 for borderline personality disorder). Reliability was rather low for other categories (e.g., 0.49 for avoidant personality disorder and 0.30 for compulsive personality disorder). This study indicated that some personality disorders can be diagnosed reliably by trained clinicians who use structured diagnostic interviews. But the results also suggest that skepticism is still warranted with regard to the reliability of diagnosing personality disorders (Merson, Tyrer, Duke, & Henderson, 1994).

Another issue that must be mentioned with regard to the personality disorders is the overlap between diagnostic categories (Widiger & Rogers, 1989). Many patients meet the criteria for more than one form of personality disorder. Pfohl et al. (1986) found that among patients who met the criteria for at least one type of personality disorder, *54 percent met the criteria for more than one form of personality disorder.* Overlap has been shown to be particularly striking for certain categories. In the study reported by Pfohl et al., two-thirds of the patients who met the diagnostic criteria for borderline personality disorder also met the criteria for histrionic personality disorder. Another study found that 71 percent of patients who met diagnostic criteria for avoidant personality disorder also met criteria for dependent personality disorder (Trull, Widiger, & Frances, 1987). This extensive overlap indicates that

[1]In this case, reliability was measured using a statistic known as *kappa*, which takes into account the probability of agreement by chance. A kappa value of zero indicates agreement that is no better than chance. A kappa of $+1.0$ would indicate perfect agreement between raters. Although there is no single criterion for interpreting this statistic, kappa values greater than 0.70 are often considered to indicate a good level of agreement.

the specific personality disorder categories listed in *DSM-IV* may not be the most efficient or meaningful way to describe this particular type of abnormal behavior.

Joe's case illustrates the overlap among different types of personality disorders. In addition to Paranoid Personality Disorder, Joe also met the *DSM-IV* (p. 661) criteria for Narcissistic Personality Disorder, which require that the person exhibit five (or more) of the following features:

1. Has a grandiose sense of self-importance (for example, exaggerates achievements and talents, expects to be recognized as superior without commensurate achievements).
2. Is preoccupied with fantasies of unlimited success, power, brilliance, beauty, or ideal love.
3. Believes that he or she is "special" and unique and can only be understood by, or should associate with, other special or high-status people (or institutions).
4. Requires excessive admiration.
5. Has a sense of entitlement (that is, unreasonable expectations of especially favorable treatment or automatic compliance with his or her expectations).
6. Is interpersonally exploitative (that is, takes advantage of others to achieve his or her own ends).
7. Lacks empathy: is unwilling to recognize or identify with the feelings and needs of others.
8. Is often envious of others or believes that others are envious of him or her.
9. Shows arrogant, haughty behaviors or attitudes.

Joe's inflated sense of his own intellectual abilities and scientific accomplishments clearly fit the pattern for Narcissistic Personality Disorder. He also exhibited the lack of empathy and feelings of entitlement that are described in these criteria. In addition to these characteristics, his behavior was arrogant and occasionally exploitative.

The principal issue regarding differential diagnosis and paranoid personality disorders concerns the distinction between this category and delusional disorder, in which the patients exhibit persistent persecutory delusions or delusional jealousy. Delusional Disorder is listed on Axis I, while paranoid personality is listed on Axis II. The paranoid ideas in paranoid personality disorders are presumably not of sufficient severity to be considered delusional, but the criteria to be used in making this distinction are not entirely clear. The two categories may be etiologically distinct, but it has not been demonstrated that they carry different treatment implications. *DSM-IV* lists the categories separately, but the reliability and validity of the two categories remain open questions (Bernstein, Useda, & Siever, 1993).

Personality disorders seem to be among the most common forms of abnormal behavior. It is difficult to provide empirical support for that claim, however, because the existing epidemiological data are inconsistent. The overall lifetime prevalence of Axis II disorders varies between 10 percent and 14 percent in samples of adults who are not in treatment for a mental disorder (Weissman, 1993). Rates for specific disorders vary from one study to the next, depending on the type of assessment procedure that was used and the way in which the sample of subjects was identified. One study that used structured interviews with community residents in Germany found a lifetime prevalence of 1.8 percent for paranoid personality disorder (Maier, Lichtermann, Klingler, Heun, & Hallmayer, 1992). A similar study conducted in the United States found a lifetime prevalence of only 0.4 percent for Paranoid Personality Disorder (Zimmerman & Coryell, 1990).

Psychological Theories

Despite the lack of information about the distribution of Paranoid Personality Disorder within the general population, and the fact that large samples of these patients are not available for research purposes, several theories have been proposed that attempt to account for the development of paranoid ideas (Akhtar, 1990). Perhaps the earliest hypothesis regarding paranoia was suggested by Freud (1909/1925) in his analysis of the memoirs of Daniel Paul Schreber, an accomplished lawyer who had spent close to 14 years of his life in mental hospitals. Schreber's problems centered on an elaborate set of persecutory and grandiose delusions, including the notion that he would be transformed into a woman. Following this transformation, Schreber believed that he would become God's mate and that they would produce a better and healthier race of people. Freud argued that the content of Schreber's delusions revealed the presence of an unconscious homosexual wish-fantasy. This hidden desire was taken to be the core of the conflict motivating paranoid ideas. The process presumably begins with the unacceptable thought that "I (a man) love him (a man)." To avoid the anxiety associated with the conscious realization of this idea, the thought is transformed to its opposite: I *do not* love him — I *hate* him.

> This contradiction, which could be expressed in no other way in the unconscious, cannot, however, become conscious to a paranoiac in this form. The mechanism of symptom-formation in paranoia requires that internal perceptions, or feelings, will be replaced by external perceptions. Consequently, the proposition "I hate him" becomes transformed by *projection* into another one: "He hates (persecutes) me, which will justify me in hating him." And thus the unconscious feeling, which is, in fact, the motive force, makes its appearance as though it were the consequences of an external perception: "I do not *love* him — I *hate* him, because HE PERSECUTES ME." (Freud 1909/1925, pp. 448–449)

There are at least two aspects of Joe's case that might be consistent with this psychodynamic model. He occasionally made comments about other men's sexual orientation, particularly when he was trying to embarrass them. We might infer from these remarks that he was concerned about his own sexual desires, but we do not have any direct evidence to validate this conclusion. His only sexual experiences had been with women, and he did not express any ambivalence about his interest in women. Joe's panic attacks might also fit into Freud's model, which suggests that Joe was using the defense mechanism of projection to avoid the anxiety associated with unconscious homosexual impulses. It could be argued that the panic attacks represented a spilling over of excess anxiety that was not being handled efficiently by projection and other secondary defense mechanisms such as repression. Once again, the model seems plausible, but it cannot be tested directly.

An alternative explanation for the development of paranoid delusions was proposed by Cameron (1959). He argued that predelusional patients are anxious, fearful, socially withdrawn, and reluctant to confide in other people. Cameron went on to point out that social isolation leads to a deficiency in social skills. In particular, he argued that predelusional patients are less adept than others in understanding the motivations of other people. They are therefore more likely to misinterpret other people's behavior and, having done so, are also less able to elicit disconfirming evidence from their peers. From time to time most of us have thought that someone else was angry with us or trying to do us harm when, in fact, they were not. We usually come to realize our mistake by talking to our friends about what happened. Cameron's argument was that predelusional patients are even more likely to misinterpret other people's behavior and, given an instance of misinterpretation, are also less able to correct the mistake through interaction with other people. According to Cameron's hypothesis, this cycle is perpetuated by the paranoid person's subsequent behavior. For example, someone who believes that his relatives are plotting against him is likely to behave in a hostile, defensive manner when his relatives are present. They, in turn, may become angry and irritable in response to his apparently unprovoked hostility, thus confirming the paranoid's original suspicion that they are out to get him. Thus Cameron's formulation allows for a complex interaction of personality traits, social skills, and environmental events.

Several elements of Cameron's theory seem applicable in Joe's case. He was not withdrawn and fearful, but he was reluctant to confide in other people. He tended to be a "loner" and felt awkward in social situations such as parties. His habit of laughing at people and provoking arguments would indicate that he was not sensitive to their feelings and point of view, as suggested by Cameron. Perhaps most important is the effect that Joe's behavior had on other people. He was completely unable to consider the possibility that other people talked about him and avoided him because he was initially hostile and belligerent.

Colby (1975, 1977) proposed an information-processing view of paranoid thinking in which the principal feature is sensitivity to shame and humiliation. The model focuses exclusively on verbal interactions. In the "paranoid mode" of processing, people presumably scan linguistic input for comments or questions that might lead to the experience of shame (defined as "a rise in the truth value of a belief that the self is inadequate"). Faced with the threat of humiliation, the person in the paranoid mode responds by denying personal inadequacy and blaming others. The theory implies that paranoia is associated with low self-esteem and that episodes of paranoid behavior may be triggered by environmental circumstances that increase the threat of shame (e.g., failure, ridicule). Other negative emotions, most notably fear and anger, are presumably not likely to elicit paranoid responses. Some indirect support for this hypothesis comes from the observation that the family members of patients with paranoid disorders are more likely than people in the general population to exhibit feelings of inferiority (Kendler & Hays, 1981).

Colby's model provides a plausible explanation for Joe's problems at the drug company and the university laboratory; his paranoid comments provided a rationale for his own failure to succeed. Joe was a brilliant chemist, but he had not developed a successful, independent line of research. The limitations of his work were particularly evident after he had been allowed some independence at the drug company. Joe's supervisors finally became so disappointed with his progress that he was reassigned to more structured projects. Shortly after this demotion his suspicions began to reach delusional proportions. Colby would probably argue that Joe chose to blame his colleagues' interference for failures that would otherwise indicate his own professional inadequacy. The shame-humiliation model also accounts for Joe's later improvement following his change of occupations. As a cab driver, Joe was removed from the field of professional competition in which he was continually exposed to threatening messages. He was reasonably successful as a cab driver, and his self-esteem did not suffer in comparison to the people with whom he usually interacted. There was therefore little need for him to behave in a hostile or defensive manner.

TREATMENT

Psychotherapy is generally of limited value with paranoid patients because it is so difficult to establish a trusting therapeutic relationship with them. Joe's case is a good example. He expected the therapist to help him cope with his anxiety but was unwilling to discuss his problems at anything other than a superficial level. This defensive attitude would hamper most attempts to engage in traditional, insight-oriented psychotherapy. The client-centered approach developed by Carl Rogers might be more effective with paranoid clients because it fosters a nonthreatening environment. The therapist must also be careful to avoid the display of excessive friendliness or sympathy, however, because it might be interpreted as an attempt to deceive the patient (Akhtar, 1992; Millon, 1981). From Colby's point of view, Rogers's emphasis on the provision of accurate empathy and unconditional positive regard would also be likely to bolster the paranoid's fragile self-esteem and thereby reduce his or her sensitivity to potential embarrassment. Unfortunately, there are no data available to support this type of speculation.

Cameron's model might lead to a more directive form of intervention focused on the development of specific social skills. For example, various situations might be constructed in order to demonstrate to the client the manner in which his or her behavior affects other people. Similarly, the therapist might practice various social interactions with the client in an effort to improve his or her ability to discuss initial social impressions. It might also be possible to improve the client's ability to read social cues. This behavioral approach would be used in an effort to expand the client's repertoire of appropriate social behaviors so that the client could respond more flexibly to specific situational demands.

When paranoid ideas reach delusional proportions, the use of antipsychotic medication may also be considered. These drugs are effective in the treatment of schizophrenia, but their effect has usually been measured in terms of global improvement ratings; it is not clear if they have an equally positive effect on all of the symptoms of schizophrenia. In fact, a few studies have examined changes in specific symptoms and concluded that antipsychotic drugs are most likely to have a positive effect on auditory hallucinations and incoherent speech. Paranoid delusions are among the *least* responsive symptoms (Manschreck, 1992). Thus, in the absence of other schizophrenic symptoms, patients with paranoid delusions are not likely to benefit from drug treatment.

18 BORDERLINE PERSONALITY DISORDER

Alice Siegel was 22 years old when she reluctantly agreed to interrupt her college education in midsemester and admit herself for the eighth time to a psychiatric hospital. Her psychologist, Dr. Swenson, and her psychiatrist, Dr. Smythe, believed that neither psychotherapy nor medication was currently effective in helping her control her symptoms and that continued outpatient treatment would be too risky. Of most concern was that Alice was experiencing brief episodes in which she felt that her body was not real and, terrified, would secretly cut herself with a knife in order to feel pain, thereby feeling real. During the first part of the admission interview at the hospital, Alice angrily denied that she had done anything self-destructive. She did not sustain this anger, however, and was soon in tears as she recounted her fears that she would fail her midterm examinations and be expelled from college. The admitting psychiatrist also noted that, at times, Alice behaved in a flirtatious manner, asking inappropriately personal questions such as whether any of the psychiatrist's girlfriends were in the hospital.

Upon arrival at the inpatient psychiatric unit, Alice once again became quite angry. She protested loudly, using obscene and abusive language when the nurse-in-charge searched her luggage for illegal drugs and sharp objects (a routine procedure with which Alice was well acquainted). These impulsive outbursts of anger had become quite characteristic for Alice over the past several years. She would often express anger at an intensity level that was out of proportion to the situation. When she became this angry, she would actually

290

do or say something that she later regretted, such as extreme verbal abuse of a close friend or breaking a prized possession. In spite of the negative consequences of these actions and the ensuing guilt and regret on Alice's part, she seemed unable to stop herself from periodically losing control of her anger.

That same day, Alice filed a "3-Day Notice," a written statement expressing an intention to leave the hospital within 72 hours. Dr. Swenson told Alice that if she did not agree to remain in the hospital voluntarily, he would initiate legal proceedings for her involuntary commitment on the ground that she was a threat to herself. Two days later, Alice retracted the 3-Day Notice, and her anger seemed to subside.

Over the next two weeks, Alice seemed to be getting along rather well. Despite some complaints of feeling depressed, she was always very well dressed and groomed, in contrast to the more psychotic patients. Except for occasional episodes when she became verbally abusive and slammed doors, Alice appeared and acted like a staff member. Indeed, Alice began taking on a "therapist" role with the other patients, listening intently to their problems and suggesting solutions. She would often serve as a spokesperson for the more disgruntled patients, expressing their concerns and complaints to the administrators of the treatment unit. With the help of her therapist, Alice also wrote a contract stating that she did not feel like hurting herself, and that she would notify staff members if that situation changed. Given that her safety was no longer an issue, she was allowed a number of passes off the unit with other patients and friends.

Alice became particularly attached to several staff members and arranged one-to-one talks with them as often as possible. Alice used these talks to complain about alleged inadequacies and unprofessionalism of other staff members. She would also point out to whomever she was talking that he or she was one of the few who knew her well enough to be of any help to her. These talks usually ended with flattering compliments from Alice as to how understanding and helpful she found that particular staff person. These overtures made it difficult for certain of these selected staff members to confront Alice on issues such as violations of rules of the treatment unit. For instance, when Alice returned late from a pass off grounds, it was often overlooked. If she was confronted, especially by someone with whom she felt she had a special relationship, she would feel betrayed and angrily accuse that person of being "just like the rest of them."

By the end of the third week of hospitalization, Alice no longer appeared to be in acute distress, and discussions were begun concerning her discharge from the hospital. At about this time Alice began to drop hints in her therapy sessions with Dr. Swenson that she had been withholding some kind of secret. Dr. Swenson confronted this issue in therapy and encouraged her to be more open and direct if there was something about which she was especially concerned. Alice then revealed that since her second day in the hospital, she had been receiving illegal street drugs from two friends who visited her. Besides occasionally using the drugs herself, Alice had been giving them to other patients on the unit. This situation was quickly brought to the attention of all the other patients on the unit in a meeting called by Dr. Swenson; during the meeting Alice protested that the other patients had "forced" her to bring them drugs and that she actually had no choice in the matter. Dr. Swenson interpreted this as meaning that Alice had found it intolerable to be rejected by other people and was willing to go to any lengths to avoid such rejection.

Soon after this incident came to light, Alice experienced another episode of feeling as if she were unreal and cut herself a number of times across her wrists with a soda can she had broken in half. The cuts were deep enough to draw blood but were not life threatening. In contrast to previous incidents, she did not try to keep this hidden and several staff members, therefore, concluded that Alice was malingering—that is, exaggerating the severity of her problems so she could remain in the hospital longer. The members of Alice's treatment team then met to decide the best course of action with regard to the dilemma. Not everyone agreed that Alice was malingering. Although Alice was undoubtedly self-destructive and possibly suicidal and, therefore, in need of further hospitalization, she had been sabotaging the treatment of other patients and could not be trusted to refrain from doing so again. With the members of her treatment team split on the question of whether or not Alice should be allowed to remain in the hospital, designing a coherent treatment program would prove difficult at best.

SOCIAL HISTORY

Alice was the older of two daughters born to a suburban middle-class family. She was two years old at the time her sister Jane was born. Alice's mother and father divorced four years later, leaving the children in the custody of the mother. Financial problems were paramount at that time, as Alice's father provided little in the way of subsequent child support. He remarried soon afterwards and was generally unavailable to his original family. He never remembered the children on birthdays or holidays. When Alice was seven years old, her mother began working as a waitress in a neighborhood restaurant. Neighbors would check in on Alice and Jane after school, but the children were left largely unattended until their mother returned home from work in the evening. Thus, at a very early age Alice was in a caretaker role for her younger sister Jane. Over the next few years Alice took on a number of household responsibilities that were more appropriate for an adult or much older child (e.g., babysitting, regular meal preparation, shopping). Alice voiced no complaints about the situation and did not present any behavioral problems at home or in school. Her most significant concern was the absence of her father. Had she somehow had something to do with the divorce? How much better would her life have been if only her father was with her?

When Alice was 13 years old, her mother married a man she had been dating for about three months. The man, Arthur Siegel, had a 16-year-old son named Michael who joined the household on a somewhat sporadic basis. Michael had been moving back and forth between his mother's and father's houses since their divorce four years earlier. His mother had legal custody but was unable to manage his more abusive and aggressive behaviors, so she frequently sent him to live with his father for several weeks or months. Because she still entertained the fantasy that her mother and father would remarry, Alice resented the intrusion of these new people into her house. Alice was quite upset when her mother changed her and her children's last name to Siegel. She also resented the loss of some of her caretaking responsibilities, which were now shared with her mother and stepfather.

The first indications of any behavioral or emotional problems with Alice occurred shortly after the marriage. She was doing very well academically in the seventh grade when she began to skip class. Her grades fell precipitously over the course of a semester, and she began spending time with peers who were experimenting with alcohol and street drugs. Alice became a frequent user of these drugs, even though she experienced some frightening symptoms after taking them (e.g., vivid visual hallucinations, strong feelings of paranoia). By the end of the eighth grade, Alice's grades were so poor and her school attendance so erratic that it was recommended that she be evaluated by a psychologist and possibly held back for a year. The family arranged for such an assessment, and Alice was given a fairly extensive battery of intelligence, achievement, and projective tests. She was found to be extremely intelligent, with an IQ of 130 (Wechsler Intelligence Scale for Children — Revised). Projective test results (Rorschach, Thematic Apperception Test) were interpreted as reflecting a significant degree of underlying anger, which was believed to be contributing to Alice's behavioral problems. Of more concern was that Alice gave a number of bizarre and confused responses on the projective tests. For example, when people report what they "see" in the famous Rorschach inkblots, it is usually easy for the tester to also share the client's perception. Several of Alice's responses, however, just didn't match any discernible features of the inkblots. This type of response is usually seen in more serious disorders such as schizophrenia. The psychologist, although having no knowledge of Alice's home life, suspected that her problems may have been a reflection of her difficulties at home and recommended family therapy at a local community mental health center.

Several months later Alice and her mother and sister had their first appointment with a social worker at the mental health center. Mr. Siegel was distrustful of the prospect of therapy and refused to attend, stating "no shrink is going to mess with my head!" In the ensuing therapy, the social worker first took a detailed family history. She noticed that Alice appeared very guarded and was reluctant to share any feelings about or perceptions of the events of her life. The next phase of family therapy was more educational in nature, consisting of teaching Mrs. Siegel more effective methods of discipline and helping Alice to see the importance of attending school on a regular basis.

Family therapy ended after three months with only marginal success. Although Mrs. Siegel had been a highly motivated client and diligently followed the therapist's suggestions, Alice had remained a reluctant participant in the therapy and was unwilling to open up. One very serious problem Alice had been experiencing had not even been brought to light; she was being sexually abused by her older stepbrother Michael. The abuse had started soon after her mother's marriage to Mr. Siegel. Michael had told Alice that it was important for her to learn about sex and, after having sexual intercourse with her, threatened that if she ever told anyone he would tell all her friends that she was a "slut." This pattern of abuse continued on numerous occasions whenever Michael was living with his father. Even though Alice found these encounters aversive, she felt unable to refuse participation or to let anyone know what was occurring. At the time Mr. and Mrs. Siegel divorced, when Alice was 15 years old, these instances of sexual abuse were the extent of Alice's sexual experience. She was left feeling depressed and guilty.

When Alice began high school, she continued her association with the same peer group she had known in junior high. As a group, they regularly abused drugs. It was under the influence of drugs that Alice began to have her first experiences of feeling unreal and dissociated from her surroundings. She felt as though she were ghostlike, that she was transparent and could pass through objects or people.

Alice also began a pattern of promiscuous sexual activity within the peer group. As happened when she was being abused by her stepbrother, she felt guilty for engaging in sex but unable to turn down sexual advances, from either men or women. She was particularly vulnerable when under the influence of drugs and would, under some circumstances, participate in various sadomasochistic sexual activities. For example, Alice was sometimes physically abused (e.g., struck in the face with a fist) by her sexual partners while having sex. She didn't protest and, after a while, came to expect such violence. On some occasions, Alice's sexual partners would ask her to inflict some kind of pain on them during sexual activity, for example, biting during fellatio or digging her nails into her partner's buttocks. Even though these activities left Alice with a sense of shame and guilt, she felt unable either to set limits on her peers, to leave her particular peer group, or to avoid those whose sexual activities were particularly troubling to her.

By the time Alice was 16 years old, she found that she rarely, if ever, wanted to spend time alone. She was often bored and depressed, particularly if she had no plans for spending time with anyone else. One night while cruising in a car with friends, a siren and flashing lights appeared. The police stopped the car because it had been stolen by one of her friends. A quantity of street drugs was also found in the car. Alice claimed that she had not known that the car was stolen.

The judge who subsequently heard the case was provided with information concerning Alice's recent history at home and school. He was quite concerned with what appeared to be a progressive deterioration in Alice's academic and appropriate social functioning. Because previous outpatient treatment had failed, he recommended inpatient psychiatric treatment as a means of helping her gain some control over her impulses and preventing future legal and psychological problems. In some sense, Alice was being offered a choice between being prosecuted as an accessory to car theft and possession of illegal substances or signing into a mental hospital. Reluctantly, she chose the latter.

During the first hospitalization, Alice's emotional experiences seemed to intensify. She vacillated between outbursts of anger and feelings of emptiness and depression. She showed some vegetative signs of depression such as lack of appetite and insomnia. Antidepressant medication was tried for several weeks and found to be ineffective. Alice spent most of her time with a male patient in the hospital. To any observer, their relationship would not have seemed to have a romantic component. They watched TV together, ate together, and played various games that were available on the ward. There was no physical contact or romantic talk. Nonetheless, Alice idealized the man and had fantasies of marrying him. When he was discharged from the hospital and severed the relationship, Alice had her first non-drug-induced episode of feeling unreal (derealization) and subsequently cut herself with a kitchen knife in order to feel real. She began making suicide threats over the telephone to the former patient, saying that if he did not take her back she would kill herself. She was given a short trial of antipsychotic medication, which proved ineffective.

During this first hospitalization, Alice started individual psychotherapy, which was continued after discharge from the hospital. The therapy was psychodynamically oriented and focused on helping Alice to establish a trusting relationship with a stable adult (her therapist). The therapist also attempted to help Alice work through the intrapsychic conflicts that had started very early in her life. For example, the therapist hypothesized that Alice's mother had been critical of Alice's appropriate autonomous behavior during early childhood. It was believed that the mother offered support and comfort to Alice only if Alice behaved in a childish, dependent, and regressive manner. This was presumed to have led to Alice's fear of being abandoned by people who were important to her, should she act in an independent or self-assertive manner. One of the therapist's goals was to show Alice that he would still be available (i.e., not leave her) when she acted in a mature, adult fashion. It was hoped that this would help Alice to feel more secure in her interpersonal relationships.

Despite these therapy sessions, Alice continued to exhibit the symptoms that had developed over the past several years, including drug abuse, promiscuity, depression, feelings of boredom, episodes of intense anger, suicide threats, derealization, and self-mutilation (cutting herself). A number of hospitalizations were required when Alice's threats and/or self-mutilation became particularly intense or frequent. These were usually precipitated by stressful interpersonal events, such as breaking up with a boyfriend or discussing emotionally charged issues in psychotherapy (e.g., her past sexual abuse). Most of the hospitalizations were relatively brief (two to four weeks), and Alice was able to leave after the precipitating crisis had been resolved. She received a number of diagnoses during these hospitalizations, including brief reactive psychosis, major depressive episode, atypical anxiety disorder, adjustment disorder with mixed emotional features, substance use disorder, mixed personality disorder, and borderline personality disorder. During one of these hospitalizations, Alice decided that she wanted to change therapists, and, after careful consideration, her treatment team decided to grant her request. When Alice was 19 years old, she was introduced to Dr. Swenson, a psychologist, and she began individual behaviorally oriented psychotherapy with him.

CONCEPTUALIZATION AND TREATMENT

Dr. Swenson's approach was somewhat different from that of Alice's previous therapist. Together, Alice and Dr. Swenson identified several problem areas: (1) lack of direction or goals, (2) feelings of depression, (3) poor impulse control, and (4) excessive anger. Specific interventions were designed for each of these areas. Concerning the first problem, Alice had done so poorly in her schoolwork and was so far behind that going back to high school to graduate was not realistic. Alice therefore decided to study to take an examination for a General Equivalency Diploma, which would then allow her to pursue further education or job training. Alice was able to pass the exam after studying for approximately four months. This success enhanced her self-esteem, because she had never before maintained the self-discipline necessary to accomplish any but the most short-term goals.

Two approaches were used with regard to Alice's depression. Dr. Swenson referred her to a psychiatrist, Dr. Smythe, for a medication evaluation. Dr. Smythe decided that her depression did not warrant the use of antidepressant medicine at that time, but the option would be kept open for the future. The second approach used was cognitive therapy along the lines elaborated by Beck and his colleagues (see Beck, 1967; Beck et al., 1979). The therapy is based on the assumption that a person's thoughts can affect her mood. In order to help Alice become more aware of the thoughts that might make her more vulnerable to depression, she was asked to keep a written record of her mood three times daily. Next to her mood, she wrote down what she was thinking, particularly those thoughts that involved predictions about how a given situation might turn out. Through this exercise, Alice came to realize that she often made negative predictions about how events would turn out and subsequently felt sad and depressed. In order to learn to restructure or "talk back" to these negative thoughts, Alice was given another exercise. When faced with an anxiety-provoking situation, Alice was asked to write three different scenarios for the situation: (1) a worst-case scenario in which everything that could go wrong did go wrong; (2) a best-case scenario in which events turned out just as she wanted; and (3) a scenario that she believed, after appropriate reflection, was most likely to occur. The actual outcome was then compared with the three different predicted outcomes. More often than not, the actual events were markedly different from either the best- or worst-case predictions. With time, this exercise helped Alice control some of her more negative thoughts and replace them with more adaptive and realistic ways of thinking that were based on her own experiences.

An example of the use of cognitive therapy had to do with Alice's difficulties establishing a stable occupational record. She held numerous part-time jobs that usually lasted for one or two months before she quit or was fired for not showing up to work. Alice typically believed that other people at work (particularly her supervisors) did not like her to begin with and were looking for excuses to fire her. After the smallest of negative interactions with someone at work, Alice assumed that being fired was imminent. She then stopped showing up to work and created a self-fulfilling prophecy. Through monitoring her mood, Alice came to see that the predominant emotion she experienced in these situations was fear — fear that she would be rejected by either her co-workers or supervisors. In order to prevent that, she typically rejected them first. After Alice obtained a part-time job in a supermarket, her therapist had her write out the three scenarios mentioned, prior to her actually starting work. The scenarios Alice produced were as follows:

[worst case] I'll show up to work and nobody will like me. Nobody will show me how to do my job, and they will probably make fun of me because I'm new there. I'll probably quit after one day.

[best case] This will be a job that I can finally do well. It will be the kind of work I have always wanted, and I'll be promoted quickly and earn a high salary. Everyone at work will like me.

[most likely] I'm new at work, but everyone else was new at one time too. Some people may like me, and some may not — but that's the way it is with everyone. Some conflict with other people is inevitable. I can still do my job even if everyone does not like me. One bad day at work does not mean I have to quit.

Alice was instructed to rehearse the "most likely" scenario daily, especially when she felt like quitting. This helped her to keep the part-time job in the supermarket for $1\frac{1}{2}$ years, which was substantially longer than she had kept previous jobs.

Alice had a number of problems with impulsivity, chiefly drug abuse, self-mutilation, promiscuity, and anger. Swenson convinced Alice to join Narcotics Anonymous (NA), a nonprofessional self-help group for drug addicts based on the same principles as Alcoholics Anonymous. Whenever Alice had an impulse to use drugs, she was to use a technique called *time delay*. This involves a commitment not to use drugs for at least 15 minutes and during that time to engage in an alternative activity. This alternative activity could be telephoning another member of NA and asking for help in controlling the impulse to use drugs. A similar approach was taken with Alice's self-mutilation behaviors, in that she was instructed to telephone Dr. Swenson or go to a hospital emergency room if she could not control the impulse. Since Alice's problems with anger concerned the impulsive manner in which she acted it out, this too was handled with similar procedures. Dr. Swenson attempted to help Alice see anger not as a negative emotion, but as a positive emotion that becomes destructive only when it is too intense. He then taught Alice time-delay procedures with which she would wait before expressing anger. During the waiting period, the intensity of the emotion declined, and she had an opportunity to think over different ways of dealing with the situation, possibly resulting in a more appropriate expression of anger.

Alice made noticeable progress over the first few months of therapy with Dr. Swenson, showing a marked decline in her symptoms. She felt optimistic for the first time in a long while. However, this optimism soon deteriorated in the face of conflicts at home. For example, Alice did not want to help maintain the household, either financially or by doing work around the house. She insisted that it was her mother's responsibility to take care of her. She also wanted her boyfriends to be able to spend the night with her, which her mother would not allow. Alice's mother then asked her to move out of the house, but Alice refused. Instead, she threatened suicide, superficially cut her wrists with a razor blade, and had to be rehospitalized. Alice followed this same pattern over the next few years, making apparent gains in therapy for a month or so and then falling back in the face of interpersonal conflict. Each regression and subsequent rehospitalization seemed more difficult for Alice, because she usually came to believe during her periods of relative stability that her problems had been "cured."

When Alice was 22 years old, she decided to attend college on a full-time basis while living at home. Dr. Swenson was opposed to this because Alice had not shown enough psychological stability to complete even a semester of college, let alone a degree program. Alice went to college anyway and soon became sexually involved with another student. As with previous relationships, Alice idealized this boyfriend and became quite dependent upon him. After an argument in which Alice smashed plates and glasses on the floor, her boyfriend left her. Alice once again became suicidal and self-destructive. This episode led to the hospitalization described at the beginning of this chapter.

Alice's treatment team at the hospital noted that none of the therapeutic interventions attempted with Alice (e.g., psychotropic medication, insight-oriented psychotherapy, behavior therapy) had had any lasting impact. Alice had a mediocre employment history and showed little evidence that she would be able to support herself independently in the foreseeable future. It was also feared that she might continue to deteriorate, perhaps winding up in a state hospital on a long-term basis. It was decided that Dr. Swenson needed help in managing Alice's symptoms, especially because those symptoms tended to worsen after dealing with difficult issues in therapy. She was referred to a day-treatment program at a local hospital, where she would have regular access to staff members who could provide therapy and support, while living outside the hospital and possibly working part-time at an entry-level unskilled job. The treatment team realized that it would require a great deal of work to convince Alice to accept these recommendations, because accepting them would be an admission that she was more seriously disturbed than she cared to admit. Even if she did follow the recommendations, Alice's prognosis was guarded.

DISCUSSION

Personality disorders are a heterogeneous group of long-standing, inflexible patterns of behavior or inner experiences. They typically begin in adolescence and cause impairment and distress. According to *DSM-IV*, personality disorders are to be indicated on Axis II, which means that their presence or absence is to be considered whenever a diagnosis is made.

Personality disorders had little diagnostic reliability as they were defined in previous editions of the *DSM* (e.g., Beck et al., 1962). Although *DSM-III* changed a number of the names given to specific personality disorders and attempted to improve the clarity of the definitions, in the field trials of *DSM-III* the reliability of diagnoses of personality disorders was lower than that of most other categories. This rather low reliability figure was for personality disorders *as a class* rather than for the specific disorders. Even though personality disorders were diagnosed in over 50 percent of the patients in field trials of *DSM-III*, the reliabilities of some of the individual personality disorders were totally inadequate. These low reliabilities, however, may have been caused by the lack of a good assessment device in the *DSM-III* field trials. More recent work with structured interviews specially designed for assessing personality disorders indicates that good reliabilities can be achieved (Loranger et al., 1987; Widiger et al., 1988).

Problems still remain with this diagnostic category, however. It is often difficult to diagnose someone with a single, specific personality disorder. The reason is that many disordered people exhibit a wide range of traits that make several diagnoses applicable. For example, Widiger, Frances, and Trull (1987) found that 55 percent of patients with borderline personality disorder also met the diagnostic criteria for schizotypal personality disorder, 47 percent for antisocial personality disorder, and 57 percent for histrionic personality disorder. Data such as these are particularly discouraging when we try to interpret the results of research comparing patients with a specific personality disorder to some other group. If, for example, we find that the borderlines differ from normals, have we learned anything specific to borderline personality disorder or do the findings relate to personality disorders in general or perhaps even to another diagnosis?

These data suggest that the categorical diagnostic system of the *DSM* may not be ideal for classifying personality disorders. The personality traits that comprise the data for classification form a continuum; that is, most of the relevant characteristics are present in varying degrees and in most people. The diagnostic categories are in fact defined by the extremes. This suggests that a dimensional approach to classification may be more appropriate. In a dimensional classification system, patients would simply be assessed on a number of traits, and their diagnoses would be their position on each trait assessment. Indeed, a dimensional system was considered for inclusion in the *DSM,* but consensus could not be reached on which dimensions to include. A promising effort in the direction of dimensional classification has been reported by Widiger et al. (1987). A larger sample of patients was assessed on all symptoms relevant to a diagnosis of personality disorder. The correlations among the symptoms were then analyzed to determine if a smaller number of dimensions could explain the relationships. Three dimensions were found to do so:

1. Social Involvement; positive and friendly versus not involved with other people.
2. Assertion/Dominance versus Passive Submission.
3. Anxious Rumination versus Behavioral Acting Out.

Using a dimensional approach to classification, each patient would then be assessed, described, and scored on each dimension. For example, a person diagnosed by *DSM-IV* as an avoidant personality would score below average on the first and second dimensions, and above average on the third.

According to *DSM-IV,* the borderline personality reveals instability in relationships, mood, and self-image. For example, attitudes and feelings toward other people may vary considerably and inexplicably over short periods of time. Emotions are also erratic and can shift abruptly, particularly to anger. Borderline personalities are argumentative, irritable, and sarcastic. Their unpredictable and impulsive behavior, such as gambling, spending, sex, and eating sprees, is potentially self-damaging. These individuals have not developed a clear and coherent sense of self and remain uncertain about their values, loyalties, and choice of career. They cannot bear to be alone and have fears of abandonment. They tend to have a series of intense one-on-one relationships that are usually stormy and transient, alternating between idealization and devaluation. Subject to chronic feelings of depression and emptiness, they may make manipulative attempts at suicide. Paranoid ideation and dissociative symptoms may appear during periods of high stress. Of all these varied symptoms, unstable and intense interpersonal relationships appear as a critical feature (Modestin, 1987). Alice's interpersonal relationships were both intense and unstable. She was very impulsive, couldn't control her anger, and had an unstable self-image. She clearly met the diagnostic criteria.

A voluminous literature on patients diagnosed as borderlines has been published over the last few decades. Although this category was not included in the first or second edition of *DSM*, it was still widely used in certain areas of the country. Its description and inclusion in *DSM-III* and *DSM-IV* refueled long-standing discussions that make borderline personality disorder one of the more controversial diagnostic categories in use today. Before discussing particular aspects of Alice's case, a brief mention of the development of the borderline concept is in order (for a more thorough historical review, see Mack, 1975).

In the late 1940s and throughout the 1950s, patients were observed who were thought of as presenting façades of neurotic functioning, but who were capable of "regressing" to more primitive levels of functioning, especially in relatively unstructured treatment situations such as psychoanalysis. This was somewhat of a problem for traditional psychoanalytic thought, since neurosis and psychosis generally were not thought to coexist within the same individual. A variety of terms were used to describe these patients, such as *pseudoneurotic schizophrenia* (Hoch & Polatin, 1949) and *subclinical schizophrenia* (Peterson, 1954). Knight's (1953) work was instrumental in the eventual widespread use of the term *borderline*. The clear gist of this early work was that some individuals exist on the "border" between neurotic and schizophrenic-like psychopathology. More recent work has raised the possibility that borderline personality may reflect a border with affective disorders as opposed to schizophrenic disorders (e.g., Akiskal, 1981), although this issue is far from settled.

As interest in reliable diagnostic descriptions increased, so did studies aimed at delineating the borderline concept (e.g., Grinker, Werble, & Drye, 1968; Gunderson & Kolb, 1978; Gunderson & Singer, 1975; Perry & Klerman, 1980). The criteria for borderline personality disorder that appeared in *DSM-III* were derived from a 1979 study by Spitzer, Endicott, and Gibbon. These authors, in collaboration with a number of other researchers in the field, decided that the term *borderline* had been used in two different ways. The first described enduring personality characteristics that reflect the instability observed in patients such as Alice. The second described schizophrenic-like characteristics sometimes seen in relatives of schizophrenics (see Kety et al., 1971). Two sets of items describing clinical symptoms were developed for each of these clinical entities, and some members of the American Psychiatric Association were asked to rate one of their borderline patients and a nonborderline control patient on the descriptive items. The two sets indeed described two different dimensions within the domain of what psychiatrists had considered "borderline." The first set of items became the *DSM-III* criteria for borderline personality disorder, and the second set became the criteria for schizotypal personality (described in this book in the chapter on paranoid schizophrenia). The *DSM-IV* criteria for borderline and schizotypal personality are very similar to the *DSM-III* criteria.

As an Axis II diagnosis, borderline personality disorder is used to describe a set of inflexible and maladaptive traits that characterize an individual's long-term functioning. This diagnosis may be used alone or in conjunction with other Axis I diagnoses. On several occasions, Alice met criteria for an Axis I diagnosis of major depressive episode (e.g., depressed mood, suicidal thoughts, insomnia, poor appetite, feelings of self-reproach and guilt).

Borderline personality disorder has a prevalence of 2 percent and is more common in women than in men (Maier et al., 1992; Swartz et al., 1990). High frequencies of childhood physical and sexual abuse are reported by borderline personalities (Ogata et al., 1990). The disorder begins in adolescence (McGlashan, 1983). Furthermore, it runs in families, with high rates in first-degree relatives of index cases (Loranger, Oldham, & Tulis, 1983).

Borderline personalities are very likely to have an Axis I mood disorder (Manos, Vasilopoulou, & Sotiriou, 1987), and even their relatives are more likely than average to have mood disorders (Zanarini et al., 1988). There is a high rate of completed suicide (Paris, 1990). The depression of borderlines is somewhat different from that of patients who suffer only depression. Borderlines are higher in dependency (e.g., "I urgently need things that only other people can provide.") and self-criticism (e.g., "I often find that I don't live up to my own standards and ideals.") (Westen et al., 1992). About half of those with borderline personality disorder also meet the diagnostic criteria for Posttraumatic Stress Disorder (Gunderson & Sabo, 1993).

Pope et al. (1993) also found that most of their borderline patients met diagnostic criteria for other personality disorders—histrionic, narcissistic, or antisocial. Other researchers have also found that many borderline patients psychoanalysis is consistent with a long-term study conducted at the world-famous analytically oriented Menninger Clinic (Stone, 1987).

Therapy for the Borderline Personality

A number of drugs have been tried in the pharmacotherapy of borderline personality disorder, most notably antidepressants and neuroleptics. However, until recently, most of the available data came from uncontrolled clinical trials. The results from better controlled studies are inconsistent. One researcher group first found that neuroleptics were useful but later failed to replicate this finding and instead determined that an antidepressant (a monoamine oxidase inhibitor) was of some benefit (Soloff et al., 1993).

Object Relations Psychotherapy. Object relations theory, a branch of psychoanalytic theory, deals with the nature and development of mental representations of the self and others (the object relations). It includes not only the representations themselves but also the fantasies and emotions attached to these representations and how these variables mediate interpersonal functioning. The object relations of borderlines are often described as malevolent. Analyses of borderlines' responses to projective tests indicate that they view other people as capricious and destructive for no reason (e.g., Nigg et al., 1992). This theory has been particularly important in the field of personality disorders. The leading contemporary object relations theorist is Otto Kernberg, who has written extensively about the borderline personality.

Kernberg (1985) operates from the basic assumption that borderline personalities have weak egos and therefore inordinate difficulty tolerating the regression (probing of childhood conflicts) that occurs in psychoanalytic treatment. The weak ego fears being flooded by primitive primary process thinking of the id. Kernberg's modified analytic treatment has the overall goal of strengthening the patient's weak ego. Therapy involves analysis of a principal defense of the borderline person, namely, splitting, or dichotomizing into all good or all bad and not integrating positive and negative aspects of a person into a whole. Splitting is the result of an inability to form complex object representations that do not fit a simple good–bad dichotomy. It causes extreme difficulty in regulating emotions because the person sees the world in black-and-white terms.

The borderline patient must also be helped to reality-test (although it is not clear in what way this is different from the overall psychoanalytic goal of helping patients discriminate between irrational childhood-based fears and adult reality). Kernberg's approach is more directive than that of most analysts: He gives the patient concrete suggestions for behaving more adaptively and will hospitalize a patient whose behavior becomes dangerous to either the

self or others. His opinion that such patients are inappropriate for classical
meet the diagnostic criteria for schizotypal personality disorder (Serban,
Conte, & Plutchik, 1987; Spitzer et al., 1979).

Dialectical Behavior Therapy.   An approach that combines client-centered
empathy with behavioral problem solving is suggested by Marsha Linehan.
What she calls *dialectical behavior therapy (DBT)* centers on the therapist's
full acceptance of borderline personalities with all their contradictions and
acting out, empathically validating their (distorted) beliefs with a matter-of-
fact attitude toward their suicidal and other dysfunctional behavior. The
behavioral aspect of the treatment involves helping patients learn to solve
problems, that is, to acquire more effective and socially acceptable ways of
handling their daily living problems and controlling their emotions. Work is
also done on improving their interpersonal skills and in controlling their
anxieties. After many months of intensive treatment, limits are set on their
behavior, consistent with what Kernberg advocates.

Linehan and her associates have recently published the results of the first
randomized, controlled study of a psychological intervention of borderline
personality disorder (Linehan et al., 1991). Patients were randomly assigned
either to dialectical behavior therapy or to treatment-as-usual, meaning any
therapy available in the community (Seattle, Washington). At the end of one
year of treatment and again six and twelve months later, patients in the two
groups were compared on a variety of measures (Linehan, Heard, & Armstrong, 1992). The findings immediately after treatment revealed highly significant superiority of DBT on the following measures: intentional self-injurious
behavior including suicide attempts, fewer dropouts from treatment, and
fewer inpatient hospital days. At the follow-ups, superiority was maintained
and, additionally, DBT patients had better work histories, reported less anger,
and were judged as overall better adjusted than the comparison therapy patients. As a result of this study, increasing interest can be expected in this
approach to borderline personality disorder.

Alice's therapists faced a common dilemma encountered with borderline
patients: Should treatment be aimed at structural intrapsychic change or
simply better adaptation to the environment (see Gordon & Beresin, 1983)?
Waldinger and Gunderson (1984) found in a retrospective study that relatively
few borderline patients complete the process of intensive psychotherapy, often
terminating when an impasse in therapy occurs. When Alice decided to
change therapists, a decision had to be made as to whether or not she was
seeking change in order to avoid working through a difficult impasse in
therapy. It was determined that this may have been the case, but that she was
unlikely to remain in therapy if her request was not granted.

Although Alice's treatment seemed largely unsuccessful, it should not be
assumed that all borderlines are equally impaired. Indeed, there is a great deal

of heterogeneity within the domain of borderline personality disorder. Many patients are able to be maintained in outpatient psychotherapy without ever being admitted to a hospital, and the outcome of therapy is not invariably negative. One of the major differences between hospitalized and nonhospitalized borderlines is that the latter group is involved in significantly fewer incidents of self-mutilation (Koenigsberg, 1982). Clearly, not all borderline patients are as self-destructive as Alice. Nevertheless, they present a daunting challenge to anyone who treats them.

PSYCHOPATHY

This case differs from most of the others in this book because Bill was never in therapy. One of the authors was acquainted with Bill during his childhood and adolescence. The following case history is based on this personal experience.

Bill was the third child in the Wallace family. His parents, originally from Europe, had emigrated when Bill was nine years old. They rented an apartment on the upper floor of a house in a middle-class neighborhood, and Bill's father got a job in a local factory. His mother worked part-time in a supermarket. No information is available concerning the family's history when they lived in Europe.

Bill and his older brother, Jack, quickly became part of the neighborhood group and participated in the usual run of activities, including baseball, football, and outings to the beach. Jack became a leading figure in the group and Bill, although not as well regarded as his brother, was always included in its activities.

It was at this time that I began to get to know Bill well. We were the same age; most of the other boys were older. Although we became friends, our relationship was also characterized by a good deal of conflict. When things did not go Bill's way, his response was single and direct—a fight. My first fight with Bill took place during a baseball game at a local park. We were on opposing teams and were involved in a close play at second base. He slid into the base; I tagged and called "out," and Bill jumped up swinging his fists.

Although he lost these fights as often as he won them, fighting became a consistent pattern in his relationships, both with me and with other neighborhood children. Not even an older and obviously stronger opponent could get Bill to back down.

Bill's aggressiveness was not really what led me to regard him as "different" as we grew up together. His escalating daredevil and antisocial behavior seemed more peculiar. One of the first of these episodes occurred when Bill organized a window-breaking competition. He explained to me and three other boys that he had recently been walking neighborhood streets at night, throwing rocks through windows. With great enthusiasm he described the excitement this created and how he had easily eluded the few residents who had come out to try to catch him. Bill wanted the four of us to compete in a window-breaking contest. He had worked out a detailed point system—the larger the window, the more points—and wanted to start that night. We all agreed to meet at 7:30 P.M. in front of his house.

We met as planned and first filled our pockets with stones. The competition soon began, with Bill clearly in the role of leader, encouraging the rest of us and pointing out windows that would yield many points. My own reaction, as all this began, was extreme fear. All I could think of was "What if we get caught?" Bill, in contrast, showed no signs of apprehension. Indeed, he seemed ecstatic and was virtually bubbling over with enthusiasm. His only negative reaction of the evening was directed toward me when, after "missing" several windows, I emptied my pockets and withdrew from the competition. The other two boys went along with Bill. They also seemed frightened, but they looked up to Bill and may have been more concerned about eliciting his disapproval. Although I was excluded from subsequent nights of competition, Bill eagerly kept me informed of the results. After several months, he was declared the winner when he broke all the large windows of the supermarket in which his mother worked.

At age 10, petty theft replaced window breaking as Bill's major source of excitement. It seemed to me that I was never in a store with him when he did not steal something. He would steal anything—candy, fruit, clothing, toys—not just things he wanted. In fact, he often threw away the things he had stolen. He seemed more interested in the excitement than in any actual material gain. He had discovered several ways of getting money. The first was a Roman Catholic church that had two easy sources of cash—a poor box and a container for donations left by worshipers who had lit a candle. Bill cleaned both out on a regular basis. His second source was a restaurant that had a wishing well, located in a rear garden, whose proceeds were to go to the Salvation Army. Although the wishing well was covered with a metal grate, Bill found that there was one opening that was just large enough to get his hand through. Every couple of weeks, armed with a flashlight and a long stick, he would sneak into the garden at night, move the coins to the right spot, and collect them. Finally, he regularly stole milk money from various neighborhood homes.[1] Bill even stole the milk money from my home. The first time our money was missing, I went directly after him and accused him of the theft. He denied it. The second time, he admitted the theft and offered to cut me in if I would keep quiet!

A final incident, which occurred when Bill and I were both 12, crystallized for me how Bill was somehow different. About a 15-minute walk from our homes was a river that had many expensive houses along its banks. A tremendous rainstorm caused a flood and, tragically, more than one hundred people were killed. Early the next morning, with the news of the disaster in the papers and on the radio, Bill set out for the scene, not just to see the devastation but with a plan. Because the victims were wealthy, Bill reasoned, he might strike it rich if he could be the first one to find some bodies and take their wallets, watches, and jewelry. He went alone, returned later in the day, and proudly displayed his loot—six watches and several hundred dollars. He returned to the river several more times over the next few days and, although he returned empty handed, he would enthusiastically relate his experiences to anyone who would listen. The excitement and danger seemed more important than the valuables he found.

During these three years, most of the neighborhood youngsters had also received more than a glimpse of the Wallaces' family life. Bill's father was frequently out of work and seemed to have trouble holding a job for more than several months at a stretch. He drank heavily. While we played street ball, we often saw him returning home, obviously drunk. At a first glimpse of their drunken father, Bill and Jack would get out of his sight as quickly as possible. Both boys reported frequent beatings, particularly when their father had been drinking. At the same time, Bill's father allowed him to get away with things, such as staying out late at night, that none of the other neighborhood children were allowed to do. Bill and Jack both reported that their father was unpredictable in his punishments. Their father and mother also fought often. On many occasions, our play was interrupted by yelling and the sound of loud crashes from their apartment.

The Wallaces eventually moved to an apartment in a lower-middle-class area of the city, about a 30-minute bus ride from their first home. Bill and I were no longer close friends, but I kept track of him through Jack, his older brother. According to Jack, Bill's pattern of antisocial behavior began to escalate. He continued to steal regularly, even from members of his family. He was frequently truant from school and got into even more serious trouble for hitting a teacher who had tried to break up a fight between him and another boy. Jack was very concerned about Bill and attempted to talk to him several

---

[1] At the time, most homes got daily milk deliveries and people simply left money and empty bottles in a place where the milkman could collect them.

times. Jack reported that during these talks, Bill would genuinely seem to agree that he had to change and would express shame and regret about whatever he had done most recently. However, within a few days, the old pattern would be back in full force. Jack eventually came to see Bill's contrition as a con.

We were both 15 the next time I met Bill. Through my continued contacts with Jack, I had learned that Bill had been sent to reform school. I did not know any of the details because Jack had been so ashamed of his brother's behavior that he would not talk about it. One evening, shortly after dinner, the doorbell rang. I answered, and Bill motioned me outside. He had escaped from reform school and wanted me to buy him a meal and loan him some money. Off we went to a local restaurant where I bought him a hamburger and Cokes for both of us. He told me that he had been convicted of car theft and rape the previous year. He had been stealing cars regularly and taking them on joyrides. He was caught when he decided to hold on to a stolen car, one that had particularly caught his fancy. The third day that he had the car, he had parked in a deserted place with a 12-year-old girl he knew from school. He raped her, and she reported him.

As Bill related the story, he became visibly disgusted, not at himself, but at the girl. As he explained it, he was only trying to have some fun and had picked this particular girl because she was only 12 years old and not likely to get pregnant. From his perspective, it was an ideal situation. With pregnancy impossible, she should have just lain back and enjoyed it.

I never saw Bill again but, through Jack, learned what happened to him over the next several years. Several weeks after our meeting, he was apprehended by the police. He had again stolen a car; while driving drunk, he had smashed into a telephone pole. After a short stay in a hospital, he was returned to the reformatory, where he spent two years. When he was released, Bill had changed greatly. It seemed to Jack that he had now become a real criminal. Car thefts were no longer for joyrides but for profit. Bill became involved in selling stolen cars to others who stripped them to sell their parts. He briefly returned to high school but, with no friends there and little real interest, he soon dropped out. He became a regular at the racetrack and lost money there and with several bookmakers. As had happened before, Jack tried to talk to his younger brother about the trouble for which he seemed headed. But now even the charade of shame and guilt was gone. Bill expressed an "I'll take what I want when I want it" attitude. When Jack tried to point out the likely negative consequences of his behavior, Bill simply shrugged it off, saying that he was too smart ever to end up in jail.

Shortly after his eighteenth birthday, Bill attempted a bank robbery, armed with a .38-caliber automatic pistol. It must have been an incredible scene. Bill was driving a stolen car. On seeing what he thought was a bank, he impulsively decided to rob it. In his rush he had actually undertaken to rob an office of the electric company. Seeing the people lined up at tellers' windows to pay their bills had made him think it was a bank. Once inside, although recognizing his mistake, he decided to go through with the holdup anyway and had several tellers empty their cash drawers into a sack. A patrol car passed by the office as the holdup was in progress and, seeing what was happening, the policemen stopped to investigate. Bill ran out of the office directly into the police and was easily arrested. He was tried, convicted, and sentenced to ten years in the penitentiary.

DISCUSSION

In current usage the terms *antisocial personality disorder* and *psychopathy* (and sometimes *sociopathy* as well) are often used interchangeably, although we will soon see that there are important differences between the two. The current *DSM-IV* concept of *antisocial personality disorder* involves two major components. The first refers to the presence of a conduct disorder before the age of 15. Criteria include truancy, running away from home, frequent lying, theft, arson, and deliberate destruction of property. The second part of the *DSM-IV* definition refers to the continuation of this pattern of antisocial behavior in adulthood. The adult antisocial personality shows irresponsible and antisocial behavior by not working consistently, breaking laws, being irritable, and physically aggressive, defaulting on debts, and being reckless. He or she is impulsive and fails to plan ahead. In addition, he or she shows no regard for truth or remorse for misdeeds.

It is estimated that about 4 percent of adult American men and 1 percent of women are antisocial personalities (Robins et al., 1984). Pimps, confidence artists, murderers, and drug dealers are by no means the only antisocial personalities. Business executives, professors, politicians, physicians, plumbers, salespeople, carpenters, and bartenders have their share of antisocial personalities as well.

The concept of *psychopathy* is closely liked to the writings of Hervey Cleckley and his classic book *The Mask of Sanity* (1976). On the basis of his vast clinical experience, Cleckley formulated a set of criteria by which to recognize the disorder. Unlike the *DSM* criteria for antisocial personality disorder, Cleckley's criteria for psychopathy refer less to antisocial behavior per se and more to the psychopath's psychology. For example, one of the key characteristics of the psychopath is poverty of emotions, both positive and negative. Psychopaths have no sense of shame and even their seemingly positive feelings for others are merely an act. The psychopath is superficially charming and manipulates others for personal gain. The lack of some negative emotions may make it impossible for psychopaths to learn from their mistakes, and the lack of positive emotions leads them to behave irresponsibly toward others. Another key point is that Cleckley describes the antisocial behavior of the psychopath as inadequately motivated; it is not due, for example, to a need for something like money but is performed impulsively, as much for thrills as anything else.

Currently, most researchers identify psychopaths using a checklist developed by Hare and his associates (Hare et al., 1990). The checklist identifies two major clusters of psychopathic behaviors. The first describes a selfish, remorseless individual who exploits others. The second characterizes an antisocial lifestyle. Psychopathy is often associated with abuse of alcohol and other drugs (Smith & Newman, 1990).

We have, then, two related but not identical diagnoses—antisocial personality disorder and psychopathy. Hare, Hart, and Harpur (1991) have criticized the antisocial personality diagnosis because it requires accurate reports of events that took place many years ago by people who are habitual liars. In addition, it is important that the diagnostic concept here not be synonymous with criminality. But 75 to 80 percent of convicted felons meet the criteria for antisocial personality disorder. In contrast, the corresponding figure for psychopaths is 15 to 25 percent (Hart & Hare, 1989). Therefore, the concept of *psychopathy* seems to have some distinct advantages. As we review the research in this area, it will be important to keep in mind that it has been conducted on individuals diagnosed in different ways—some as antisocial personalities and some as psychopaths. Integrating these findings may therefore be somewhat difficult.

Bill's behavior during childhood and adolescence clearly meets many of Cleckley's criteria. He was unreliable, untruthful, lacking in any feelings of shame about his misconduct, and totally without anxiety. His antisocial behavior (such as stealing) was not motivated by any genuine desire to possess the stolen objects, and he often displayed poor judgment, particularly in his escapades of late adolescence. His poverty of emotion was amply demonstrated by his thefts from homes of his friends and by his completely cavalier attitude toward the victim of his rape.

Etiology of Psychopathy

What causes behavior like Bill's? As with most disorders, the search for the causes of psychopathy had considered both physiological and psychological variables. We will describe research efforts in several areas—the role of the family, genetics, and on psychopath's inability to avoid some noxious stimuli.

The Role of the Family.   Because the family is presumed to play a strong role in teaching children standards of acceptable conduct, it is not surprising that researchers have looked to possible family problems as the causes of the psychopath's failure to abide by society's rules. McCord and McCord (1964) concluded, on the basis of a review of the literature, that lack of affection and severe parental rejection were the primary causes of psychopathic behavior. Several other studies have related psychopathic behavior to the parent's inconsistency in discipline and a failure of parents to teach children their responsibilities to others (Bennet, 1960).

Such data on early rearing must be interpreted with extreme caution because they were gathered by means of retrospective reports. Information about early family experiences and about how the child was taught to behave socially was obtained either from an adult psychopath or from parents, relatives, and friends at a time very much later than when the events actually occurred. The reliability of information obtained in this way is often poor.

One way to avoid the problems of retrospective data is to follow up in adulthood individuals who as children were seen at a child guidance clinic. In one such study very detailed records had been kept on the children, including the type of problem that had brought them to the clinic and information on numerous variables related to the family (Robins, 1966). By interviewing the now-adult individuals, the investigators were able to assign diagnoses and describe their adjustment as adults. Adult problems were then related back to the characteristics that these people had had as children in order to determine which of them predicted psychopathic behavior in adulthood. Robins (p. 157) summarized her results as follows:

> If one wishes to choose the most likely candidate for a later diagnosis of [psychopathic personality] from among children appearing in a child guidance clinic, the best choice appears to be a boy referred for theft or aggression who has shown a diversity of antisocial behavior in many episodes, at least one of which could be grounds for Juvenile Court appearance, and whose antisocial behavior involves him with strangers and organizations as well as with teachers and parents . . . more than half of the boys appearing at the clinic [with these characteristics were later] diagnosed sociopathic personality. Such boys had a history of truancy, theft, staying out late, and refusing to obey parents. They lied gratuitously, and showed little guilt over their behavior. They were generally irresponsible about being where they were supposed to be or taking care of money.

In addition to these characteristics, variables related to family life that were mentioned earlier were again found to be important. Both inconsistent discipline and no discipline at all predicted psychopathic behavior in adulthood, as did antisocial behavior of the father.

Note the excellent match between Robins's description of the childhood characteristics of psychopaths and Bill's behavior during childhood. The harsh yet inconsistent disciplinary practices of Bill's father also mesh well with Robins's findings. Both the case history and research findings suggest that child-rearing practices play an important role in the etiology of psychopathy. It is also clear, however, that parental characteristics cannot provide a complete explanation of the development of psychopathy. Bill's brother, although exposed to a very similar home environment, had no psychopathic traits at all.

Avoidance Learning and Punishment. In defining psychopathy, Cleckley pointed out the inability of these persons to learn from experience. In particular, they seemingly feel no need to avoid the negative consequences of social misbehavior. Cleckley also remarked that they were not neurotic and seldom anxious. From these clinical descriptions, Lykken (1957) deduced that psychopaths may have few inhibitions about committing antisocial acts because they experience no anxiety. One of his tests of this hypothesis involved avoidance learning.

A group of male psychopaths was selected from a penitentiary population. Their performance on an avoidance-learning task was compared to that of nonpsychopathic penitentiary inmates and of college students. It was critical that only avoidance learning and not learning mediated by other possible rewards be tested. If subjects perceive that their task is to learn to avoid pain, they may be motivated not only by the desire to avoid pain but also by a desire to demonstrate their cleverness to the investigator. To ensure that no other motives would become manifest, Lykken made the avoidance-learning task incidental. He used the following apparatus: On a panel in front of the subject there were four red lights in a horizontal array, four green lights (one below each of the red ones), and a lever below each pair of lights. The subject's task was to learn a sequence of 20 correct lever presses, but, for each, he first had to determine by trial and error which of the four alternatives was correct. The correct lever turned on a green light. Two of the remaining three incorrect levers turned on red lights, indicating an error. The third incorrect lever delivered an electric shock to the subject. The location of the correct lever was not always the same. The subject was simply told to figure out and to learn the series of 20 correct lever presses. He was not informed that avoiding shock was desirable or possible, only that shock was randomly administered as a stimulant to make him do well. Thus the task yielded two measures of learning: the total number of errors made before the subject learned the correct sequence of 20 presses and the number of errors that produced shock. Avoidance learning was measured by this second index.

In terms of the overall number of errors made, there were no significant differences among any of the groups in Lykken's study. The college students, however, were apparently best able to remember the sequence of presses that produced shock and thus sharply decreased their proportion of shocked errors. The psychopaths made the most shocked errors, but the differences between their shocked errors and those of the other penitentiary inmates only approached statistical significance. The results of Lykken's investigation, therefore, tentatively supported the hypothesis that psychopaths have lower levels of anxiety than do normal individuals.

The hypothesis was subsequently given stronger support in a study by Schachter and Latané (1964). The study was much like Lykken's except that all participants were tested twice—once after an injection of a placebo and once after an injection of adrenalin, a drug that mimics the activity of the sympathetic nervous system and thus should increase anxiety. When tested in the placebo condition, the psychopaths avoided the shocks less well than did other subjects. When aroused by the adrenalin injection, however, the psychopaths quickly learned to avoid the shocks, thus supporting the theory.

An avoidance-learning study by Schmauk (1970) qualifies the findings of Lykken and of Schachter and Latané. Schmauk showed that a particular kind of punishment, losing money, can have an effect on psychopaths. He tested three groups: psychopathic prisoners, nonpsychopathic prisoners, and a control group consisting of farm workers and hospital attendants. As in the previous studies, an avoidance-learning task was devised, but this time three different aversive stimuli could be avoided: a physical punishment—electric shock; a tangible punishment—losing a quarter from an initial pile of forty; and a social punishment—the experimenter's saying "wrong" to the subject. There were again no differences among the groups in the total number of errors made before the task was mastered. The major finding of this study was that the psychopath's avoidance performance varied with the nature of punishment. When the punishments confronting them were physical and social, the members of the control group were vastly superior to the psychopaths in learning to avoid punishment. But the psychopaths outdid the controls in learning to avoid the tangible punishment of losing a quarter. The nonpsychopathic prisoners did better than the psychopaths in learning to avoid physical punishment but less well in avoiding social punishment.

It appears then that psychopaths *can* learn to avoid punishment. The difference found between psychopaths and nonpsychopaths in previous investigations may reflect not a general deficit in avoidance-learning ability but rather the fact that some punishments have no meaning for the psychopath. Evidently, psychopaths will learn to avoid punishment that is relevant to their system of values, and money may very well be particularly motivating to them.

An alternative explanation of these results has been suggested by Newman and Kosson (1986). They pointed out that Schmauk's tangible punishment condition differed from shock avoidance in several respects. Most important to Newman and Kosson was the fact that in the tangible punishment condition the punishment was salient. Subjects saw the stack of quarters in front of them and could keep their winnings. In contrast, the shock avoidance condition, subjects were not even told that the shock could be avoided.

On the basis of this reasoning, Newman and Kosson hypothesized that salience of the punishment was the critical variable and tested their hypothesis by studying psychopaths and controls on two versions of a discrimination learning task. In one condition subjects were rewarded when they responded correctly and punished when they made an error. In the second condition subjects were not rewarded for a correct response; they were only punished for errors. The punishment should be more salient in the second condition because it is the only consequence to which a subject had to attend.

Comparison of the number of punished errors in each condition supported the hypothesis. Psychopaths did not differ from controls in the punishment-only condition, but in the reward and punishment condition they showed their usual performance deficit, making more punished errors than did controls. Similarly, psychopaths are unable to delay gratification only in situations where both reward and punishments are present (Newman, Kosson, & Patterson, 1993). Getting the psychopath's attention may be what's needed for a punishment to be effective. Indeed, in situations in which both rewards and punishments are present, psychopaths focus on the rewards rather than balancing their attention between both the rewards and punishments (Raine et al., 1990).

Gorenstein (1991) noted that although the avoidance-learning theory of psychopathy is promising, it is also incomplete. It assumes, for example, that fear of punishment (going to prison) is what motivates us all to refrain from criminal activity. Lacking this fear, the psychopath commits frequent crimes. But it is likely that the reasons people don't commit crimes are much more complex. Most people are socialized into a value system that teaches them standards and moral values that they use to make decisions about acceptable conduct. Fear of punishment may play little role in the decisions most of us make about what's right and wrong. Furthermore, the avoidance-learning model fails to account for other important aspects of psychopathy, such as gratuitous lying, insensitivity to others, and failure to follow a life plan.

The research findings we have just reviewed seem particularly applicable to Bill. The fear that might prevent stealing, breaking windows, and looting seemed totally absent in him. From his own statement we can conclude that they felt little shame or remorse about his transgressions. Finally, Bill also displayed characteristics similar to those revealed in Newman and Kosson's study, not reflecting on the negative consequences of his antisocial behavior.

Biological Research.   Schachter and Latané's work suggests that the avoidance-learning deficits of psychopaths may be mediated by some problem in the autonomic nervous system. Because the autonomic nervous system is assumed to play a central role in states of emotion, several investigators have examined psychopaths for both their resting levels of autonomic activity and their patterns of autonomic reactivity to various classes of stimuli. Hare (1978) has summarized the results of many of these investigations. In resting situations, most studies show that psychopaths have lower than normal levels of skin conductance. They are also less reactive when intense or aversive stimuli are presented. Both of these results are consistent with clinical descriptions (see Ellis, 1987) of psychopaths as being nonanxious and with research that shows that psychopaths are generally less emotionally reactive than normals (Patrick, Bradley, & Lang, 1993). A different picture emerges, however, when heart rate is examined. The heart rate of psychopaths is like that of normals under resting conditions. Their heart-rate reactivity to stimuli is also unremarkable but, in situations where a stressful stimulus is anticipated, psychopaths show greater than normal increases in heart rate.

These data indicate that we cannot simply speak of the psychopath as being underaroused. To do so we would have needed a pattern of data that showed consistency in both electrodermal and heart-rate measures. Hare (1978) focuses on the *pattern* of psychophysiological differences found in psychopaths. Increased heart rate is viewed as a concomitant of lowered cortical arousal and a gating out of sensory input. Thus the increased heart rate of psychopaths who are anticipating an aversive stimulus would indicate that they are "tuning it out." The lowered levels of skin conductance are then hypothesized to result from the psychopaths' successful coping with the impending aversive stimulus. That is, with skin conductance considered as an index of anxiety, the data indicate that psychopaths are less anxious, perhaps because they have successfully coped with the aversive stimulus by gating it out. Further research with both behavioral (Raine & Venables, 1987) and physiological data (Jutai & Hare, 1983; Ogloff & Wong, 1990) confirms that psychopaths are particularly adept at ignoring stimuli, and focusing their attention on what interests them (Forth & Hare, 1989). This is a plausible interpretation of the data and is consistent with the studies reviewed earlier on avoidance learning.

How do psychopaths acquire this pattern of autonomic responding? One possibility is that it is genetically transmitted. Adoptee studies suggest that heredity may play a role in psychopathy. Schulsinger (1972) examined the rate of psychopathy in both the biological and adoptive relatives of psychopaths. He found more psychopathy in the biological relatives than in the adoptive ones. Results favoring this genetic theory have also been found in studies of the adopted children whose biological parents were antisocial personalities (Cadoret et al., 1986; Crowe, 1974). Bohman et al. (1982) and Cloninger et al. (1982) have reported more complicated data in which both criminality and alcoholism were studied. A large sample of adopted individuals were classified according to whether or not they had criminal records, histories of alcoholism, both, or neither. Risk for criminality among alcoholic individuals was linked to their own alcoholism but not to criminal behavior in their biological parents. Among nonalcoholic criminals risk for criminality was associated with a history of petty crime in their biological parents as well as instability in their placements prior to adoption. Thus the evidence suggests that a disposition to become psychopathic, possibly involving the autonomic nervous system, may be inherited. Gene-environment interaction may also be important in the development of antisocial behavior. In Cadoret et al.'s (1983) study, the increase in the number of antisocial behaviors due to both genetic and environmental factors acting together was greater than the predicted increase from either factor acting alone.

Treatment

There is general agreement that treatment is unsuccessful for psychopaths. Cleckley (1976, pp. 438–439) summarized his clinical impressions as follows:

> Over a period of many years I have remained discouraged about the effect of treatment on the psychopath. Having regularly failed in my own efforts to help such patients . . . I hoped for a while that treatment by others would be more successful. I have had the opportunity to see patients of this sort who were treated by psychoanalysis, by psychoanalytically oriented psychotherapy, by group and by milieu therapy. . . . None of these measures impressed me as achieving successful results. . . . I have now, after more than three decades, had the opportunity to observe a considerable number of patients who, through commitment or the threat of losing their probation status or by other means, were kept under treatment . . . for years. The therapeutic failure in all such patients leads me to feel that we do not at present have any kind of psychotherapy that can be relied on to change the psychopath fundamentally.

Empirical evaluations of the many treatments that have been employed with psychopaths—psychoanalysis, milieu therapy, group therapy, amphetamines, aversive conditioning, psychosurgery—reach conclusions quite similar to Cleckley's (McCord & McCord, 1964; Suedfeld & Landon, 1978).

Indeed, therapy may even have negative effects on psychopaths. Rice, Harris, and Cormier (1992) compared the results of a therapeutic community to standard institutionalization in a sample of prison inmates. While the special program reduced recidivism in nonpsychopaths, it actually increased it among psychopaths. The inability of sociopaths to form an honest, trusting relationship with a therapist may be a major reason for the ineffectiveness of psychotherapy. A person who lies, cares little for the feelings of others, and has few regrets about personal misconduct is certainly a poor candidate for most forms of psychotherapy. One clinician (Lion, 1978, p. 286), experienced in working with psychopaths, has suggested the following guidelines:

> First, the therapist must be continually vigilant with regard to manipulation on the part of the patient. Second, he must assume, until proved otherwise, that information given to him by the patient contains distortions and fabrications. Third, he must recognize that a working alliance develops, if ever, exceedingly late in any therapeutic relationship. . . .

Somatic treatments for psychopathy—psychosurgery, electroconvulsive therapy, and various drugs—have fared no better than psychotherapy. Even the use of stimulants, which Schachter and Latané's data would suggest to be of possible benefit, has not produced long-lasting success.

Because many psychopaths spend time in prison, the discouraging results of imprisonment and the efforts at rehabilitation of convicts are relevant to the treatment of psychopathy. As criminologists have stated repeatedly, prisons operate more as schools for crime (as happened for Bill) than places of rehabilitation. An interesting argument in favor of the incarceration of psychopaths, however, is that psychopaths tend to settle down in middle age (Hare et al., 1988). Prisons, then, may protect society from the antisocial behavior of "active" psychopaths.

20 AUTISTIC DISORDER

Sam Williams was born in 1974, the second child of John and Carol Williams. The couple had been married for five years; he was a lawyer, and she a homemaker. Sam weighed 7 pounds, 11 ounces at birth, which had followed an uncomplicated full-term pregnancy. Delivered by Caesarean section, he came home six days after the delivery.

His parents reported that Sam's early development seemed quite normal. He was not colicky, and he slept and ate well. During his first two years, there were no childhood illnesses except for a mild cold at age 14 months. After Sam's second birthday, however, his parents began to become concerned. He has been somewhat slower than his older sister in achieving some developmental milestones (such as sitting up alone and crawling). Furthermore, his motor development seemed uneven. He would crawl normally for a few days and then not crawl at all for awhile. Although he made babbling sounds, he had not developed any speech and did not even seem to understand anything his parents said to him. Simple commands such as "Get the ball," "Come," or "Do you want a cookie?" elicited no response. Initially, the Williamses thought that Sam might be deaf. Later they vacillated between this belief and the idea that Sam was being stubborn. They reported many frustrating experiences in which they tried to force him to obey a command or say "Mama" or "Dada." Sometimes Sam would go into a tantrum during one of these situations, yelling, screaming, and throwing himself to the floor. That same year, the Williamses' pediatrician told them that Sam might be mentally retarded.

Toward his third birthday, Sam's parents began to notice him engaging in more and more strange and puzzling behavior. Most obvious were his repetitive hand movements. Many times each day he would suddenly flap his hands for several minutes. Other times he rolled his eyes around in their sockets. He still did not speak, but he made smacking sounds and sometimes he would burst out laughing for no apparent reason. He was walking now and often walked on his toes. Sam had not been toilet trained, although his parents had tried to do so. Sam's social development was also beginning to concern his parents. Although he would let them hug and touch him, he would not look at them and generally seemed indifferent to their attention. He also did not play at all with his older sister, seeming to prefer being left alone. Even his solitary play was deviant. He did not really play with his toys—for example, pretending to drive a toy car into a service station. Instead, he was more likely to just manipulate a toy, such as a car, holding it and repetitively spinning its wheels. The only thing that really seemed to interest him was the family stereo. He was content to sit for as long as permitted, watching intently as a record spun on the turntable. Temper tantrums often ensued when the stereo was turned off.

At the age of three, the family's pediatrician recommended a complete physical and neurological examination. Sam was found to be in good health, and the neurological examination revealed nothing remarkable. A psychiatric evaluation was performed several months later. Sam was brought to a treatment facility specializing in behavior disturbances of childhood and was observed for a day. During that time, the psychiatrist was able to see firsthand most of the behaviors that Sam's parents had described—hand flapping, toe walking, smacking sounds, and preference for being left alone. When the psychiatrist evaluated Sam, she observed that a loud slapping noise did not elicit a startle response as it does in most children. The only vocalization she could elicit that approximated speech was a repetitive "nah, nah." Sam did, however, obey some simple commands such as "Come" and "Go get a potato chip." The psychiatrist diagnosed Sam as having autistic disorder and recommended placement in a day-treatment setting.

CONCEPTUALIZATION AND TREATMENT

Sam was four years old by the time there was an opening for him at the treatment center. He was bused to and from a special school five days a week, spending the remainder of his time at home with his parents and sister. The school provided a comprehensive educational program conducted by specially trained teachers. The program was organized mainly along operant conditioning principles. In addition, Sam's parents attended classes once a week to learn operant conditioning so they could continue the school program at home. The school's personnel conducted another evaluation of Sam, observing him in the school and later at home. Interviews with the parents established that they were both well adjusted and that their marriage was happy.

One of the first targets of the training program was eye contact. When working with Sam, his teacher provided small food rewards when Sam spontaneously looked at him. The teacher also began requesting eye contact and again rewarded Sam when he complied. Along with this training, the teacher worked on having Sam obey other simple commands. The teacher would try to select a time when Sam seemed attentive and would then, establishing eye contact, say the command and at the same time show him what was meant (i.e., model the desired behavior). For example, the teacher would say, "Sam, stretch your arms up like this," and then the teacher would lift Sam's arms up and reward him with praise and a small amount of food, such as a grape. This procedure was repeated several times. Once Same began to become more skilled at following the command, the teacher stopped raising Sam's arms for him and let him do it entirely for himself. These training trials were conducted daily. As the response to a particular command became well established, the command would be made in other situations and by other people. Sam's progress was slow. It often took weeks of training to establish his response to a simple command. After his first year in the school, he did respond reliably to several simple requests such as "Come," "Give it to me," and "Put on your coat."

At the same time that Sam was learning to respond to commands, other aspects of the training program were also being implemented. While Sam was in the classroom, his teacher worked with him on trying to develop skills that would be important in learning, for example, sitting in his seat, maintaining eye contact, and listening and working for longer periods of time. Each activity was rewarded in much the same way as his performance of simple behaviors had been. As these skills became better established, the teacher also began working on expanding Sam's vocabulary by teaching him the meaning of pictures of common objects. A picture of one object, such as an orange, was placed on a table in front of Sam. Once Sam had looked at the object, the teacher said, "This is an orange. Point to the orange." When Sam pointed to the orange, he was rewarded. If necessary, the teacher would move his hand for him at first. Next another picture, such as a cat, was selected and the same procedure followed again. Then the two pictures were placed in front of Sam and the teacher asked him to point to one of them: "Point to the orange." If Sam pointed correctly, he was rewarded. If he did not, the teacher moved his hand to the correct object. After Sam had correctly pointed to the orange several times in a row, the teacher asked him to point to the cat. With that response established, the teacher switched the position of the pictures and repeated the process. When Sam had begun to point correctly to the orange and the cat, a third picture was introduced and the training procedure was started anew. During one year of training, Sam learned the names of 38 common objects with this procedure.

Sam's speech therapist, whom he saw daily, was also working with him on language skills. Initially they worked on getting Sam to imitate simple sounds. Sitting across a table from Sam and waiting until Sam was looking (or prompting him to look by holding a piece of food near his mouth), the teacher would say "Say this, ah," taking care to accentuate the movements required for this sound. At first Sam was rewarded for making any sound. Subsequently, rewards were only forthcoming as Sam's productions approximated more and more closely the required sound. As sounds were mastered, Sam was trained to say simple words in a similar fashion. Over the course of a year, Sam learned a few words — "bye-bye," "no more," and "mine"; however, overall, his verbal imitation remained poor.

Having Sam learn to dress and undress himself was another target during the first year. Initially, his teacher helped him through the entire sequence, describing each step as they did it. Next, they would go through the sequence again, but now Sam had to do the last step himself (taking off his shoes, putting on his shoes). More difficult steps (tying shoes) were worked on individually to give Sam more practice on them. Once some progress was being made, this aspect of the treatment was carried out by the parents. They first observed the teacher working with Sam and then discussed the procedure and were shown how to make a chart to record Sam's progress. Over a period of weeks, the number of steps that Sam had to complete by himself was gradually increased, moving from the last toward the first. Sam was rewarded each time he dressed or undressed, usually with a special treat (e.g., a favorite breakfast food). In this case, the training was quite successful. By midyear Sam had mastered dressing and undressing.

Toilet training was another area that Sam's parents and teachers worked on. At home and at school, Sam was rewarded for using the toilet. He was checked every hour to see if his pants were dry. If they were, he was praised and reminded that when he went to the toilet he would get a reward. Shortly thereafter, Same would be taken to the toilet, where would remove his pants and sit. If he urinated or defecated, he was given a large reward. If not, he was given a small reward just for sitting. As this training was progressing, Sam was also taught to associate the word "potty" with going to the toilet. Progress was slow at first, and there were many "accidents," which both teachers and parents were instructed to ignore. But Sam soon caught on and began urinating or defecating more and more often when he was taken to the bathroom. Then the parents and teachers began working on having Sam tell them when he had to go. When they checked to see if his pants were dry, they would tell him to let them know, by saying "potty" when he had to go to the toilet. Although there were many ups and downs in Sam's progress, by the end of the year he was having an average of less than two accidents per week.

One reason for Sam's relatively slow progress during his first year in the special school was his temper tantrums. These occurred sometimes when he was given a command or when a teacher interrupted something he was doing. Not getting a reward during a training session was another common cause. Sam would scream loudly, at the top of his voice, throw himself to the ground, and flail away with his arms and legs. Several interventions were tried. It had been observed that Sam's tantrums usually led to getting his own way, particularly at home. For example, a tantrum had often been a successful device for having his parents keep a record spinning on the turntable even when they did not want to listen. Thus, ignoring the tantrum was the first approach. Sam's teachers simply let the tantrum play itself out, acting as if it had not happened. The procedure had no apparent effect. Next, time-out was tried. Every time a tantrum started, Sam was picked up, carried to a special room, and left there for 10 minutes or until the screaming stopped. This procedure also failed to have an effect on the tantrums and screaming, even with several modifications such as lengthening the time-out period.

During the second year of Sam's treatment, many of the first year's programs were continued. The range of commands to which Sam responded was expanded, and his ability to recognize and point to simple objects increased. In his speech therapy he learned to imitate more sounds and some new words ("hello," "cookie," and "book"). His progress in speech therapy, however, remained slow and uneven. He would seem to master some sound or word and then somehow lose it. He was, however, still dressing and undressing himself and going to the toilet reliably.

Feeding skills were one of the first targets for the second-year program. Although his parents had tried to get him to use a knife, fork, and spoon, Sam resisted these attempts and ate with his fingers or by licking the food from his plate. Drinking from a cup was also a problem. Sam still used a baby cup with only a small opening at the top. As in some of the previous programs, this one was implemented by both Sam's teachers and parents and involved a combination of modeling and operant conditioning. Training sessions conducted at mealtime first involved getting Sam to use a spoon. Sam was shown how to hold the spoon; then the teacher picked up the spoon, saying "Watch me. You push the spoon in like this and then lift it up to your mouth." Sam did not initially imitate, so the teacher had to guide him through the necessary steps: moving his hand and spoon to pick up food, raising his arm until the spoon was at his mouth, telling him to open his mouth, and guiding the spoon in. Praise was provided as each step in the chain was completed. After many repetitions, Sam was required to do the last step by himself. Gradually, more and more of the steps were done by Sam himself. Successes were followed by praise and failures by saying no or removing his meal for a short time. When eating with a spoon was well established, the training was expanded to using a fork and drinking from a cup. In several months, Sam was eating and drinking well.

Sam's failure to play with other children was also a major focus during the second year. The first step was to get Sam to play near other children. Most of his playtime was spent alone, even when other children were in the playroom with him. So his teacher watched Sam carefully and rewarded him with small bits of food whenever he was near another child. A procedure was also used to force Sam to interact with another child. Sam and another child would be seated next to one another and given the task of stacking some blocks. Each child was, in turn, given a block and prompted to place it on the stack. In addition to praising them individually as they stacked each block, both children were rewarded with praise and food when they had completed their block tower. After repeating this process several times, the program was expanded to include the cooperative completion of simple puzzles. "Sam, put the dog in here. Okay, now Nancy, put the cat here." Gradually, the prompts were faded out and the children were simply rewarded for their cooperative play. Although this aspect of therapy progressed well, transferring these skills to the natural play environment proved difficult. Attempts were made to have Sam and another child play together with toys such as a farm set or a small train. The teacher encouraged them to move the objects around, talking to them about what they were doing and rewarding them for following simple commands. Although Sam would usually follow these commands, his play remained solitary, with little eye contact or cooperation with the other child.

Sam's self-stimulatory behavior was a final target worked on during the second year. Sam's hand flapping and eye rolling had already decreased somewhat over the past year, perhaps because more of his day was being filled with constructive activities. Now a specific intervention, to be used by Sam's teachers and his parents, was planned. Whenever Sam began hand flapping, he was stopped and told to hold his hands still, except when told to move them, for 5 minutes. During the 5-minute period he was told to hold his hands in several different positions for periods of 30 seconds. If he did not follow the command, the teacher or parent moved his hands into the desired position; if he did not maintain the position for 30 seconds, the teacher or parent held his hands still. Food rewards were provided for successful completion of each 30-second period. Gradually, the teachers and parents were able to get Sam to comply without moving his hands for him or holding him. Then they turned to the eye rolling and implemented a similar program, having Sam fix his gaze on certain objects around his environment whenever he began to roll his eyes. Over a period of several months of training, Sam's self-stimulatory behavior decreased by about 50 percent.

At the beginning of his third year in school, Sam, now seven years old, was tested with the Stanford-Binet and achieved an IQ of 30. The language and speech training continued, as did the attempt to reduce the frequency of his self-stimulatory behavior. His tantrums, which had not responded to previous interventions, were becoming worse. In addition to screaming and throwing himself on the floor, he now became violent at times. On several occasions he had either punched, bitten, or kicked his sister. His parents reported that during these tantrums he became so out of control that they feared he might seriously injure someone. Similar episodes occurred in school, usually when an ongoing activity was interrupted or he failed at some task. Trouble had also emerged on the bus that brought him to and from school. All the children were required to keep their seat belts on, but Sam would not do so and was often out of his seat. Twice in one week the bus driver stopped the bus and tried to get Sam buckled back into his seat. She was bitten once the first time and five times the second. The bus company acted quickly and suspended service for Sam. In an initial attempt to resolve the problem, Sam was put on Thorazine, a drug widely used in the treatment of schizophrenia. But after a month of the drug and no apparent effect, it was stopped. In the meantime, Sam's mother had to drive him to and from school. He was beginning to miss days or be late when his mother's schedule conflicted with the school's.

Because of the seriousness of the problem and the fact that other treatments had not worked, a punishment system was implemented. Because Sam's tantrums and violent outbursts were almost invariably preceded by loud screaming, it was decided to try to break up the usual behavior sequence and punish the screaming. Whenever Sam began to scream, a mixture of water and Tabasco sauce was squirted into his mouth. The effect of this procedure, which was used by both his teachers and parents, was dramatic. The first day of the treatment, Sam began screaming six times. His response to the Tabasco mixture was one of shock and some crying, which stopped quickly after he was allowed to rinse out his mouth. For the next three days, he experienced the Tabasco twice each day, went two days with no screams, and then had one screaming episode; thereafter, he neither screamed nor had a severe temper tantrum again for the rest of the year.

Sam's progress in other areas was not so dramatic. He continued to expand his vocabulary slowly, learning to say more words and recognize more and more objects. But his performance remained highly variable from day to day. His self-stimulatory behavior continued, although at a level below that which had been present earlier. He still remained isolated, preferring to be alone rather than with other children.

DISCUSSION

From the time it was first identified, autistic disorder seemed to have a mystical aura about it. The syndrome was first described in 1943 by a psychiatrist at Harvard, Leo Kanner, who noticed that 11 disturbed children behaved in ways that were not common in children with mental retardation or with schizophrenia. He named the syndrome *early infantile autism* because he observed that there is an extreme autistic aloneness that shuts out anything that comes to the child from the outside. Kanner considered autistic aloneness the most fundamental symptom, but he also found that these 11 children had been unable from the beginning of life to relate to people in the ordinary way, were severely limited in language, and had a great obsessive desire that every-thing about them remain exactly the same. Despite its early description by Kanner and others (e.g., Rimland, 1964), the disorder was not accepted into official diagnostic nomenclature until the publication of *DSM-III* in 1980. In *DSM-IV*, autistic disorder is classified as one of the "Pervasive Developmental Disorders."

A major feature of autism is "extreme autistic aloneness," an inability to relate to people, or to any situation other than being alone in a crib, that is found from the very beginning of life. Autistic infants are often reported to be "good babies," apparently because they do not place any demands on their parents. They do not coo or fret or demand attention, nor do they reach out or smile or look at their mothers when being fed. When they are picked up or cuddled, they often arch their bodies away from their caretakers instead of molding themselves against the adult as other babies do. Autistic infants are content to sit quietly in their playpens for hours, never even noticing other people. After infancy they do not form attachments with people but, instead, may become extremely attached to mechanical objects such as refrigerators or vacuum cleaners. Because they avoid all social interaction, they rapidly fall behind their peers in development. Clearly, this feature was very characteristic of Sam. Although he did not actively avoid human contact or develop an attachment with a mechanical object, he was almost totally asocial.

Communication deficits are a second major feature of autism. Even before the period when language is usually acquired, autistic children show deficits in communication. *Babbling,* a term used to describe the utterances of children before they actually begin to use words, is less frequent in autistic children and conveys less information than it does with other children (Ricks, 1972). Even on a nonvocal level, autistic children manifest a communication deficit. They do not, for example, use gesture as a substitute for speech (Bartak, Rutter, & Cox, 1975).

The difficulties that older autistic children have with language are even more pronounced. Mutism, complete absence of speech, is prevalent, as was true with Sam. About 50 percent of all autistic children never learn to speak (Rutter, 1966). When they do speak, peculiarities are often found, including echolalia. The child echoes, usually with remarkable fidelity, what he or she has heard another person say. In delayed echolalia the child may not repeat the sentence or phrase until hours or weeks after hearing it.

Another abnormality common in the speech of autistic children is pro-noun reversal. The children refer to themselves as "he," "you," or by their own proper names; the pronouns "I" or "me" are seldom used and then only when referring to others. Pronoun reversal is closely linked to echolalia. Since autistic children often use echolalic speech, they will refer to themselves as they have heard others speak of them; pronouns are, of course, misapplied.

Communication deficiencies are clearly one of the most serious problems of autistic children. The fact that about 75 percent of autistic children score in the mentally retarded range on IQ tests is undoubtedly a reflection of these deficiencies. They may also leave a lasting mark of social retardation on the child. The link between social skills and language is made evident by the often spontaneous appearance of affectional and dependent behavior in these children after they have been trained to speak (Churchill, 1969; Hewett, 1965).

An autistic child's ability or inability to speak is often an effective means of predicting later adjustment, an additional indication of the central role of language. Rutter (1967) found that of 32 autistic children without useful speech at five years of age, only seven had acquired speech when followed up about nine years later. Eisenberg and Kanner (1956) had earlier followed up a sample of 80 autistic children classified according to whether or not they had learned to speak by age five. Fifty percent of the children who had been able to speak at this age were later rated as showing fair or good adjustment, but only 3 percent of the nonspeaking children were so rated. Other studies have also shown a close link between the acquisition of language and later adjustment (Lotter, 1974; Treffert, McAndrew, & Driefuerst, 1973). Based on these findings, we would predict a relatively poor outcome for Sam.

A third major feature of autism is compulsive and ritualistic activity, such as a fascination with spinning objects, as shown by Sam. Furthermore, autistic children often become extremely upset over changes in daily routine and their surroundings. An offer of milk in a different drinking cup or a rearrangement of furniture may make them cry or bring on a temper tantrum. Even common greetings must not vary. Sam did not exhibit this symptom.

In addition to the three major signs just described, many autistic children have problems in eating, often refusing food or eating only one or a few kinds of food. They may also have difficulty walking but be quite proficient at twirling and spinning objects and in performing ritualistic hand movements. Other rhythmic movements, such as endless body rocking, seem to please autistic children. They may also become preoccupied with manipulating a mechanical object and be very upset when interrupted. Often the children have sensory problems. Like Sam, some autistic children are first diagnosed as being deaf because they never respond to any sound; some even seem to be insensitive to sound or light. Bowel training is frequently delayed, and head banging and other self-injurious behaviors are common (Rutter, 1974). Autistic children have been shown to be negativistic, turning their backs on others and actively resisting whatever is expected of them (Cowan, Hoddinott, & Wright, 1965). Finally, other features of autistic children's behavior also have an "obsessional" quality, similar to the preservation of sameness. In their play, they may continually line up toys or construct intricate patterns out of house-hold objects. They engage in much less symbolic play (e.g., driving a toy car to a gas station) than either normal or mentally retarded children of the same mental age (Sigman et al., 1987). They may become preoccupied with train schedules, subway routes, or number sequences. Clearly, Sam displayed many of these behaviors.

What happens to such severely disturbed children when they reach adult-hood? Kanner (1973) has reported on the adult status of 9 of the 11 children whom he had described in his original paper on autism. Two developed epileptic seizures; by 1966 one of them had died and the other was in a state mental hospital. Four others had spent most of their lives in institutions. Of the remaining three, one had remained mute but was working on a farm and as an orderly in a nursing home. The last two have made at least somewhat satisfactory recoveries. Although both still live with their parents and have little social life, they are gainfully employed and have some recreational interests. From his review of all published follow-up studies, Lotter (1978) concluded that 5 to 17 percent of autistic children had a relatively good outcome in adulthood. Most of the remaining children had a poor outcome, and 50 percent were institutionalized.

Biological Theories

Several considerations make physiological accounts of autism plausible. First, the age of onset is very early. If a psychological stress were to precipitate such disorders, it would indeed have to be a particularly noxious event. Yet the available evidence does not indicate that autistic children are reared in espe-cially unpleasant environments or that they have suffered some severe trauma. This point was certainly true in Sam's case. Second, a syndrome quite similar to autism may develop in the aftermath of brain diseases such as encephalitis. Third, mental subnormality is often associated with some kind of brain dysfunction; about 80 percent of children with autism have low levels of intelligence.

Early EEG studies of autistic children indicated that many had abnormal brain wave patterns (e.g., Hutt et al., 1964). Other types of neurological examination have also revealed signs of damage in a large percentage of autistic children (Gillberg & Svendson, 1983; Steffunburg, 1991). Further evidence supporting the possibility of neurological dysfunction includes a study using magnetic resonance scans of the brain, which found that portions of the cerebellum were underdeveloped in autistic children (Courchesne et al., 1988). This abnormality was present in 14 out of 18 autistic subjects. The degree of neurological abnormality or central nervous system dysfunction seems to be related to the severity of the autistic symptoms. In adolescence 30 percent of those who had severe autistic symptoms as children begin having epileptic seizures. Furthermore, the prevalence of autism in children whose mothers had rubella during the prenatal period is approximately 10 times higher than in the general population of children. A syndrome similar to autism may follow in the aftermath of meningitis, encephalitis, and tuberous sclerosis, all of which may affect central nervous system functioning. These findings, plus the degree of mental retardation, would seem to link autism and brain damage.

Genetic studies of autism are difficult to conduct because the disorder is so rare. Indeed, the family method presents special problems because autistic persons almost never marry. In cases where autistic children have siblings, the rate of autism in their brothers and sisters is about 2 percent (Rutter, 1967). Although this is a small percentage, it represents a fiftyfold increase in risk as compared to the morbidity risk in the general population. Further evidence of the importance of genetic factors in autism is provided by a methodologically sound study conducted by Folstein and Rutter (1978). In 10 pairs of fraternal twins, one of whom had autism, there was no concordance of the cotwins. But in the 11 pairs of identical twins, one of whom had autism, the concordance rate was 36 percent: Four of the cotwins had autism. Even more striking results have been reported by Steffunberg et al. (1989); concordance for autism was 91 percent in MZ pairs and 0 percent in DZ pairs.

Folstein and Rutter also looked for cognitive disabilities, such as delayed speech, problems in saying words properly, and low IQ, in the cotwins. Concordance for cognitive impairment was 82 percent for the MZ twins and 10 percent for the DZ. Thus the identical twin of an autistic child is very likely to have difficulties of speech and intellect, but the fraternal twin of an autistic child is not. Autism is apparently linked genetically to a broader deficit in cognitive ability. Further support for this position comes from finding a higher incidence of a spectrum of learning disabilities in the families of autistic children (August, Stewart, & Tsai, 1981). Taken together, the evidence from family and twin studies supports a genetic basis for autistic disorder.

In Sam's case there was no evidence of any neurological abnormality, nor was there any family history of autism. Consistent with Folstein and Rutter's findings, however, Sam's older sister did have a learning disability.

Psychological Theories

As might be expected, theorists of a psychogenic bent attribute autism to early experiences, especially those shared by the mother and child. Perhaps the best known of the psychological theories was formulated by Bruno Bettelheim (1967). The basic supposition of Bettelheim's theory is that autism closely resembles the apathy and hopelessness found among inmates of German concentration camps during World War II. Bettelheim hypothesizes that the young infant is able to perceive negative feelings from his rejecting parents.

The mother, on the one hand, may expect too much of the infant and be easily disappointed. Or the mother may expect too little, treating the child as a passive object. In either case the child comes to believe "that one's own efforts have no power to influence the world, because of the earlier conviction that the world is insensitive to one's reactions" (p. 46).

This experience of helplessness is viewed as extremely frustrating for the children. But they are unwilling to communicate their frustration because they believe that nothing good can come from it. They continue to withdraw from the world, their only activities—ritualistic hand movements and echolalic speech—being more a means of shutting out the world than truly meeting it. An elaborate fantasy life is created, and insistence on sameness is the rule that brings permanence and order to the world. Autistic children remain safe only if everything about them stays put. Since the essential purpose of activity is to bring about change, autistic children avoid any sort of action; their universe centers on a static environment, beyond which they will not move.

Bettelheim's theory rests primarily on the hypothesis that at early critical periods, when the effect on children is profound, the parents reject them. In his early papers Kanner had described the parents of autistic children as cold, insensitive, meticulous, introverted, distant, and highly intellectual (Kanner & Eisenberg, 1955). He concluded that the children are reared in "emotional refrigeration." Others (e.g., Rimland, 1964; Singer & Wynne, 1963) have also noted the detachment of parents of autistic children, although in less pejorative terms.

Social learning theorists have also postulated that certain childhood learning experiences cause psychotic childhood disorders. Ferster (1961), in an extremely influential article, suggested that the inattention of the parents, especially of the mother, prevents establishment of the associations that make human beings reinforcers. Because the parents have not become reinforcers, they cannot control the child's behavior.

Both Bettelheim and Ferster imply that parents play the crucial role in the etiology of autism. Thus many investigators have studied the characteristics of these parents. Most investigations (e.g., Cox et al., 1975) have failed to confirm the earlier clinical impressions. When the parents of autistic children were compared to those of children with receptive aphasia (a disorder in understanding speech), the two groups did not differ in warmth, emotional demonstrativeness, responsiveness, and sociability. Similarly, DeMyer et al. (1973) did not find that parents of autistic children were rejecting, and Cantwell, Baker, and Rutter (1978) and McAdoo and DeMyer (1978) did not observe parental deviance using standard measures such as the MMPI. The weight of the evidence is overwhelming: The parents of autistic children are unremarkable, as was the case with the Williamses.

Even if we were to ignore these findings, the direction of a possible correlation between parental characteristics and autism is not easily determined. The deviant parental behavior that has been reported could easily be a reaction of the child's abnormality rather than the other way around. And if parental behavior causes autism, why is the incidence of similar difficulties so low in siblings? Moreover, although autism is a severe disorder, the parental behavior that has been discussed does not seem likely to be more than mildly damaging. It would seem that only very gross mistreatment, such as keeping the child in a locked closet, could precipitate such severe problems so early in life.

Treatment

Numerous biological therapeutic approaches have been tried with autism. Autistic children have been treated similarly to adult psychotic patients. Common procedures include electroconvulsive therapy, psychosurgery, vitamins, and various drugs, particularly the phenothiazines. None has proved to be highly effective. Reports on the effects of fenfluramine, an amphetamine derivative, are somewhat more positive (Ritvo et al., 1983). Consistent with the somewhat encouraging results of fenfluramine, which acts on the neurotransmitter serotonin, are data suggesting decreased serotonin responsiveness in autism (McBride et al., 1989). Furthermore, a number of recent studies have shown clinical improvements in autistic children with other drugs that stimulate this neurotransmitter (Gordon et al., 1993; McDougle et al., 1992). However, concerns have been raised about the negative side effects of fenfluramine, and there have also been failures to replicate the cognitive and behavioral improvements (Campbell, 1988). Another newly researched medication is naltrexone, a drug that blocks the brain's opiate receptors (Campbell et al., 1990). Data on its effectiveness are inconclusive at this time.

A number of different psychological approaches have been proposed. One of the most famous is Chicago's Orthogenic School, founded by Bruno Bettelheim (1967). Based on this theory of autism, he developed a residential treatment center in which the autistic child could overcome the fear and mistrust of the environment and begin the process of development anew. The child, isolated from his or her parents, is provided with a person who satisfies all needs and reduces environmental pressures. The therapy, conducted by paraprofessionals, is meant to encompass the child totally.

Somewhat similar is Mahler's (1965) program, which is also based on the notion that autism develops from an inadequate mother–child relationship. In Mahler's procedure, an attempt is made, in some sense, to have the mother and child relive the period during which development went astray. The child is encouraged to regress (e.g., by eating and acting in a babylike fashion or through more symbolic representations of regression); the mother, with instruction from the therapist, tries to meet the child's emotional needs.

Unfortunately, the effectiveness of the treatments we have just discussed (and many other procedures as well) is difficult to evaluate. Many studies have examined the effects of psychotherapy in poorly defined groups of psychotic children, thus precluding definitive statements about autism. Furthermore, a basic requirement for statements concerning therapeutic effectiveness—an untreated control group—is lacking in almost all studies. Finally, the reported rates of success are difficult to evaluate because objective criteria for improvement are usually not specified.

Like the psychotherapeutic approaches, behavior therapy with autistic children requires a great expenditure of time and effort. Furthermore, autistic children have several problems that make teaching them difficult. They have difficulty adjusting to changes in routine, such as substitute teachers. Their self-stimulatory behavior interferes with effective teaching, and finding reinforcers that motivate autistic children can be difficult. The problems and effort involved are well illustrated by our description of the therapy program that was developed for Sam. Results of behavior therapy studies, however, are much easier to evaluate because the researchers have typically paid attention to the basic rudiments of experimental design. In general, behavior therapists focus on reliably assessed, observable behaviors and manipulate the consequences these behaviors elicit from the environment. As in Sam's case, desirable behaviors (e.g., speech, playing with other children) are rewarded, and undesirable ones (e.g., hand flapping, screaming) are either ignored or punished. The desired behaviors are broken down into smaller elements that are learned first and then assembled into a whole. A good example of this procedure was seen in the procedures used to try to get Sam to speak. Modeling is a frequent adjunct in these operant behavior therapy programs.

Many aspects of autism can be changed with behavioral programs. Self-care skills, social behavior, and language have all shown improvements in controlled studies (e.g., Koegel et al., 1982). Undesirable behaviors such as self-stimulation and self-injurious behavior have been decreased (Ross & Nelson, 1979).

Ivar Lovaas, a leading clinical researcher at the University of California at Los Angeles, describes an intensive operant program with very young (under four years) autistic children (Lovaas, 1987). Therapy encompassed all aspects of the children's lives for more than 40 hours a week for more than two years. Parents were trained extensively so that treatment could continue during almost all waking hours of the children's lives. Nineteen youngsters receiving this intensive treatment were compared to 40 controls who received a similar treatment for less than 10 hours per week. All children were rewarded for being less aggressive, more compliant, and more socially appropriate, including talking and playing with other children. The goal of the program was to mainstream the children, the assumption being that autistic children, as they improve, benefit more from being with normal peers rather than remaining by themselves or with other severely disturbed children.

The results were quite dramatic and encouraging for the intensive therapy group. Their measured IQs averaged 83 in first grade (after about two years in the intensive therapy) compared to about 55 for the controls; 12 of the 19 reached the normal range as compared to only 2 (of 40) in the control group. Furthermore, 9 out of the 19 intensives were promoted to second grade in a normal public school, whereas only one of the much larger control group achieved this level of normal functioning. This ambitious study confirms the need for heavy involvement of both professionals and parents in dealing with the extreme challenge of autistic disorder. Although such intensive treatment is expensive and time-consuming, the long-term dependence and loss of productive work in less intensively treated autistic children represent a far greater cost to society than a treatment that enables some of these children to achieve a normal level of functioning.

21 ATTENTION DEFICIT HYPERACTIVITY DISORDER

Ken's mother telephoned the clinic in the middle of November. Ken was seven years old and in the first grade at the time. His mother explained that he was having trouble at school, both academically and socially. The school psychologist had said that Ken was either brain damaged or hyperactive. An initial appointment was scheduled for the following week for Ken and both parents.

SOCIAL HISTORY

The case was assigned to an intern in clinical psychology who met the family in the clinic's waiting room. After a brief chat with all of them, he explained that he would first like to see the parents alone and later spend some time with Ken. Mr. and Mrs. Wilson, a white, middle-class couple, had been married for 12 years. He was 37, she 36. Ken was the middle of three children; an older sister was 9 and a younger brother 4. There were no apparent problems with either sibling. Mrs. Wilson experienced a full-term pregnancy with Ken. The actual delivery was without complication, although labor was fairly long (14 hours). After collecting this background information, the therapist explained that he would like to get an overview of the problem as it existed now.

According to the parents, Ken's problem began in kindergarten. His teacher frequently sent notes home about disciplinary problems in the classroom. In fact, there had been considerable question about promoting Ken to the first grade. The final result was a "trial promotion." Everyone hoped that Ken would mature and do much better in first grade, but his behavior became even more disruptive. Ken's mother reported that she had heard from his teacher several times over the first two months of school. Ken's teacher complained about his failure to get work done, classroom disruption, and aggressiveness.

Finally, Ken was evaluated by the school psychologist, who administered the Children's Apperception Test, a series of pictures to which the child is to make up stories, and the Bender-Gestalt, a test in which the child copies a standard series of geometric designs. According to the school psychologist, Ken's stories indicated a good deal of emotional turmoil and a lack of "impulse control." His drawings on the Bender-Gestalt were "immature." This was the basis for the diagnosis of possible brain damage.

The therapist then turned to an evaluation of the parents' perception of Ken at home and his developmental history. They described him as a difficult infant, much more so than his older sister. He cried frequently and was described as a colicky baby by their pediatrician. He did not eat well, and his sleep was often fitful and restless. As Ken grew, his mother reported even more difficulties with him. He was into everything. Verbal reprimands, which had been effective in controlling his sister's behavior, seemed to have no effect on him. When either parent tried to stop him from doing something (e.g, playing with an expensive vase, turning the stove off and one), he would often have a temper tantrum, which included throwing things, breaking toys, and screaming. His relationship with his sister was poor. He bit her on several occasions and seemed to take delight in trying to get her into trouble.

A similar pattern emerged with neighborhood children. Many of the parents no longer allowed their children to play with Ken. During this period, Ken's parents also reported that he had low frustration tolerance and a short attention span. When the therapist asked what they meant, they were able to provide concrete examples: Ken could not stay with puzzles and games for more than a few minutes and often reacted angrily when his brief efforts did not produce success. Going out for dinner had become impossible because of Ken's misbehavior in restaurants. Even mealtimes at home had become unpleasant. Indeed, Ken's parents had begun to argue frequently about how to deal with him.

Toward the end of the first session, the therapist brought Ken to his office while his parents remained in the clinic waiting room. Ken initially maintained that he did not understand why he was at the clinic, but later he allowed that he was getting into a lot of trouble at school. He agreed that it would probably be a good idea to try to do something about his misbehavior.

Ken and his parents were brought together for the final minutes of the first session. The therapist explained that the next several sessions would be devoted to conducting a more thorough assessment, including visits to the Wilsons' home and Ken's school. The parents signed release forms so the therapist could obtain information from their pediatrician and the school. The following information was gathered through these sources and from further interviews with the parents.

THE CURRENT PROBLEM

School records generally corroborated Ken's parents' description of his behavior in kindergarten. His teacher described him as being "distractible, moody, aggressive," and a "discipline problem." Toward the end of kindergarten, he had been given the Peabody Picture Vocabulary Test (PPVT) and the California Achievement Test (CAT). Although his IQ (as estimated from the PPVT) was 120, he did not perform very well on the reading and mathematics subsections of the CAT.

An interview with Ken's first-grade teacher revealed information that agreed with other reports. Ken's teacher complained that he was frequently out of his seat, was unable to sit still, did not complete assignments, and had poor peer relations. Ken seemed indifferent to efforts at disciplining him. Ken's teacher also completed a short form of the Conners Rating Scale (Sprague, Cohen, & Werry, 1974) on Ken. The instrument corroborated the hyperactive picture that had already emerged (see Table 21.1).

The therapist also arranged to spend a morning in Ken's classroom. During the morning, Ken was out of his seat inappropriately six times. On one occasion, he jumped up to look out the window when a noise, probably a car backfiring, was heard. He went to talk to other children three times. Twice he got up and just began walking quickly around the classroom. Even when he stayed seated, he was often not working and instead was fidgeting or bothering other children. Any noise, even another child coughing or dropping a pencil, distracted him from his work. When his teacher spoke to him, he did not seem to hear; it was not until the teacher had begun yelling at him that he paid any attention.

Subsequent sessions with Ken's parents focused on his current behavior at home. The pattern that had begun earlier in Ken's childhood had continued. He still got along poorly with his sister, had difficulty sitting still at mealtimes, and reacted with temper tantrums when demands were made of him. His behavior had also taken on a daredevil quality, as illustrated by his climbing out of his second-story bedroom window and racing his bicycle down the hill of a heavily trafficked local street. Indeed, his daring acts seemed to be the only way he could get any positive attention from his neighborhood peers, who seemed to be generally afraid of him. He had no really close friends.

Mr. Wilson missed two of these sessions because of his business schedule.

Table 21.1   Teacher's Ratings of Ken's Behavior on the Short Form of the Conners Rating Scale

Observation: Classroom Behavior	Degree of Activity			
	(0) Not At All	(1) Just a Little	(2) Pretty Much	(3) Very Much
Constantly fidgeting			X	
Demands must be met immediately—easily frustrated				X
Restless or overactive				X
Excitable, impulsive			X	
Inattentive, easily distracted				X
Fails to finish things he starts—short attention span				X
Cries often and easily		X		
Disturbs other children				X
Mood changes quickly and drastically		X		
Temper outbursts, explosive and unpredictable behavior				X

Source: Sprague, Cohen, and Werry (1974).

Most days he had to commute to work, a two-hour train trip each way. During one of the sessions with just Mrs. Wilson, a hint of marital discord emerged. When this was brought up directly, Mrs. Wilson agreed that their marriage was not as good now as it once had been. A major source of their arguments centered around how to handle Ken. Mrs. Wilson had come to believe that severe physical punishment was the only answer. She described an active, growing dislike of Ken and feared that he might never change. The next time Mr. Wilson was present, he was asked about his child-rearing philosophy. He admitted that he took more of a "boys will be boys" approach. In fact, he reported that as a youngster he was rather like Ken. He had "grown out of it," and he expected that Ken would too. As a result, he let Ken get away with things for which Mrs. Wilson would have punished him. The couple's arguments, which had recently become more heated and frequent, usually occurred after Mr. Wilson had arrived home from his two-hour commute. Mrs. Wilson, after a particularly exasperating day with Ken, would try to get Mr. Wilson to discipline Ken. He would refuse and accuse his wife of overreacting, and the battle would begin.

The therapist's visit to the Wilson home began at 3 P.M. just before Ken and his sister got home from school. The first part of the visit was uneventful, but, at about 4:30 P.M., Ken and his sister got into a fight over who was winning a game. Ken broke the game, and his sister came crying to her mother, who began shouting at Ken. Ken tried to explain his behavior by saying that his sister had been cheating. His mother ordered him to his room; shortly thereafter, when she heard him crying, she went up and told him he could come out. The children were served their dinner at 5:30; Mrs. Wilson planned to wait until her husband came home later to have hers. The meal began with Ken complaining that he did not like anything on this plate. He picked at his food for a few minutes and then started making faces at his sister. Mrs. Wilson yelled at him to stop making the faces and eat his dinner. When she turned her back, he began shoving food from his plate onto his sister's. As she resisted, Ken knocked over his glass of milk, which broke on the floor. Ken's mother was enraged at this point. She looked as if she was ready to hit Ken, but she calmed herself, perhaps because of the therapist's presence. Although she told Ken that he would be in big trouble when his father got home, nothing happened. When Mr. Wilson came home, he made light of the incident and refused to punish Ken. Even though Mrs. Wilson's exasperation was obvious, she said nothing.

In subsequent direct evaluations of Ken, the therapist administered the Wechsler Intelligence Scale for Children-Revised (WISC-R) and the Lincoln-Ozeretsky Test of motor development, which is thought to provide information relevant to the possible presence of a neurological dysfunction. Ken's full-scale IQ was slightly above average (106), and he performed at age level on the various subtests of the Lincoln-Ozeretsky.

CONCEPTUALIZATION AND TREATMENT

The therapist conceptualized Ken's problem in an operant conditioning framework. Although open to possible biological causes of Ken's behavior, the therapist believed that a structured program of rewards and punishments would help. Treatment would then involve trying to increase the frequency of positive behaviors (complying with parental requests, interacting positively with his sister, staying in his seat in the classroom) by providing positive consequences for them. Similarly, undesirable behaviors should be followed by negative consequences. It was explained to Ken's parents that many of these undesirable behaviors actually produced positive results for him. His tantrums, for example, frequently allowed him to have his own way. The complicating feature was the attitude of Ken's parents. Would either of them be willing to engage in the considerable effort that is required to make a contingency management system work? To try to counter this potential problem, the therapist, after explaining the results of his overall assessment and the broad outlines of his treatment plan, asked both parents to try to put aside their existing attitudes for a brief period while they implemented a simple, scaled-down version of the overall plan. The hope was that a simple intervention, directed at only a couple of problem areas, would produce visible, quick results. This small change might be sufficient to increase the parents' enthusiasm and allow a complete therapeutic package to be instituted later.

Two target behaviors were selected — out of seat in the classroom and inappropriate behavior at mealtimes at home. The latter category was further defined as meaning no complaining about the food served; no kicking his sister under the table; staying in his chair; and no laughing, giggling, or making faces. During the next week, the parents were instructed to record the frequency of disruptive behavior at mealtimes as well as several other target behaviors (temper tantrums, fights with siblings, and noncompliance with parental requests) that could be targets for later interventions. The next day, Ken's teacher was contacted. He agreed to keep a record of the number of times Ken was out of his seat each day.

During the next session, an intervention was planned. The records of the past week indicated that every meal had been problematic. Ken had also been out of his seat when he was supposed to be working at his desk an average of nine times per day. The therapist explained to Ken and his parents that in the next week daily rewards would be made available if Ken was not disruptive at mealtimes and if he reduced the number of times he was out of his seat at school. After discussion with all parties, it was agreed that Ken would be allowed to select an extra half-hour of television watching, a favorite dessert, or a game to be played with one of his parents if his behavior met an agreed-on criterion. The initial criterion was being out of his seat less than five times per day at school and being nondisruptive for at least one of the two meals eaten at home. (On weekends, only the mealtime criterion was in effect.) Ken's parents were shown how to make a chart that was to be posted on the refrigerator. Ken's teacher would send a daily note home indicating how many times he was out of his seat and that number, along with checks for a "good" meal, would be entered on the chart. Ken's teacher was telephoned after the session, and the program was explained. He agreed to keep sending home a daily record of the number of times Ken was out of his seat.

Ken's parents were obviously excited as they met the therapist at the beginning of the next session. They had brought their chart with them; some changes had obviously occurred. Ken met criterion on six of the seven days. The average number of times he was out of his seat went from 9 to 3.6, and he had been unpleasant at mealtimes only five times (two of these occurred on Saturday, resulting in his single failure to obtain a reward).

During the next several sessions, the parents and the therapist worked on expanding the program. Temper tantrums, fighting with his siblings, and noncompliance with parental requests had all been frequent the previous week. Ken's parents now seemed eager to attempt to deal with them. Of the three targets, noncompliance proved to be the most difficult to deal with. It presented such a large array of possibilities that a specific description of a criterion was problematic. The program that was developed involved the following components: Temper tantrums were to lead to a time-out procedure in which Ken would have to go to his room and remain there quietly for 10 minutes. Fighting was handled first by a simple request to stop. If that was ineffective, the time-out procedure would be employed. To try to get Ken to comply with parental requests (e.g., to go to bed, to stop teasing his sister), the parents were instructed to make the requests calmly and clearly to be sure Ken had heard them. If he did not comply, they were to give him one reminder, again in a calm fashion; if that failed, he would be sent to his room. The therapist stressed to the parents that their requests to stop or do something had to be made calmly and that time-out should also be administered calmly. Finally, the parents were instructed to provide social reinforcement for cooperative play and being pleasant at meals (e.g., by simply telling Ken how pleased they were when they saw him playing nicely with his siblings). Based on the records from the previous weeks, it look as though Ken would have experienced about 20 time-outs if the new system had been in effect. It was therefore decided that if Ken was sent to his room fewer than 10 times, he would receive a special end-of-week reward, a trip to the theater to see a film. The mealtime procedure was kept in effect and, as before, a chart was to be completed showing school behavior, mealtimes, and frequency of time-outs. This time the parents were also asked to keep a log of the number of times they praised Ken and of the specific details of instances of noncompliance. The latter feature was included so the therapist could be assured that the parental requests were not unreasonable.

In the interim, the therapist contacted Ken's teacher and increased the scope of the school program. The teacher was told to maintain his record keeping of Ken's being out of his seat, but he was also instructed to try to praise Ken as often as possible when Ken was working appropriately. The daily report card was expanded to include number of assignments completed and aggressive interactions with peers, defined broadly to include both physical and verbal aggression. Other instances of disruptive behavior (being noisy, making faces) were also to be recorded in this manner. The records from this week were to be used in planning another intervention during the next session with the parents.

At the session following the implementation of the time-out procedure, the parents were decidedly less enthusiastic than they had been the previous week. Although the improvement in mealtime behavior had been maintained, Ken had been sent to his room 17 times over the course of the week and thus did not get his Sunday trip to the movie. It seemed that time-out was not an effective consequence for Ken. The therapist asked the parents for more details on how they were using the procedure. It turned out that Ken had lots of toys in his room, so the therapist decided to change the system. In an effort to increase the effectiveness of time-out, Ken's toys were put away so that time-out consisted of sitting on his bed with no toys to play with or books to look at. Furthermore, all the at-home targets were linked to a daily reward (one of the three described earlier). Specifically, Ken was to get 2 points for each pleasant meal, 2 points if he had only one time-out before dinner, and 2 points for none after dinner. The expanded school program was also converted to a point system. The teacher's records for the previous week indicated that Ken had been out of his seat an average of three times per day, had completed 55 percent of his assignments, and was either aggressive or disruptive five times during the average day. A set of new criteria was adopted for school and linked to points: 2 points for out of seat less than three times per day, 2 points for completing 70 percent or more of his assignments, and 2 points for reducing the frequency of aggressive behavior or disruptiveness to less than three times per day. Thus, overall Ken could earn 12 points on each school day and 6 on weekends. The criterion for one of the daily rewards was set at 8 points on a school day and 4 points on weekends. In addition, a weekly total of 54 points would result in Ken's being taken to see a movie.

The system now appeared to be working well. During one typical week, Ken earned 58 points and thus got his trip to the movie. In addition, he met the criterion for a daily reward each day. At home, he averaged only one time-out per day, and 12 of 14 meals had been without incident. At school, he was out of his seat slightly less than twice per day, completed an average of 70 percent of his assignments, and was either aggressive or disruptive less than three times per day.

For the following week, the criteria were increased again. At school, points could be earned for being out of seat less than twice per day, completing 80 percent of his assignments, and being aggressive or disruptive less than twice per day. At home, the point system was left unchanged. The criterion for a daily reward was raised to 10 for school days and 6 on weekends; the criterion for the end-of-week reward was raised to 66. In addition, a new daily reward was added to the program—a bedtime story from Ken's father. The parents were also encouraged to continue providing praise for good behavior. Ken's teacher was telephoned to discuss a similar tactic for the classroom.

The program continued to evolve over the next few weeks, and Ken made steady progress. By the fourteenth week, it was clear that Ken's behavior had changed greatly and his academic performance was improving. At this point, sessions were held only once every two weeks, and the family was followed for three more months. Increased emphasis was placed on teaching Ken's parents the general principles that they had been following—that when problems arose they would be able to handle them on their own by making the necessary modifications in the system. Both Ken's parents and his teacher were also reporting changes in Ken that had not been targets of the intervention. He was described as being less moody, more pleasant, and more able to deal with frustration. He had also begun to form some friendships and was being invited to other children's homes to play. Although Ken was still reported to be somewhat difficult to handle, his parents now believed that they had some skills they could use. Ken's mother reported that she now felt much more positively toward him. The couple also indicated that their arguments had become much less frequent. Two steps remained. First, the daily rewards were phased out. Instead, the parents were to provide social reinforcement for good behavior during the day. The rewards were still provided, but in a less formal manner in which they were not linked explicitly to the number of points earned during the day. Finally, the formal contingency aspect of the weekend reward was dropped. A "good week" still led to a special treat or activity but was not linked specifically to a particular criterion. Ken's behavior remained stable; the family terminated treatment.

DISCUSSION

Problems such as Ken's have been described by a number of different diagnostic terms over the past two decades. *Minimal brain dysfunction, hyperkinesis,* and *hyperactivity* have been the most commonly applied terms. According to *DSM-IV,* Ken's diagnosis would be attention deficit hyperactivity disorder (ADHD), one of the subcategories in the manual's section headed "Disorders Usually First Diagnosed in Infancy, Childhood or Adolescence." This large section encompasses disorders of the intellect (e.g., mental retardation), overt behavior (e.g., attention deficit hyperactivity disorder), and pervasive disorders of development (e.g., autistic disorder).

The current diagnostic term, *attention deficit hyperactivity disorder,* reflects the prevailing view that problems in attention are the principal aspect of the disorder. These difficulties include failure to finish tasks, not listening, being easily distracted, and having problems concentrating and maintaining attention. This description fits Ken well. Overactivity and restlessness are reflected in problems staying seated in school, fidgeting when seated, and being described as "always on the go." Hyperactivity is especially evident in any situation that requires controlling activity level, such as school and mealtimes. Ken's behavior in the classroom and at home was consistent with the *DSM-IV* description of the features of hyperactivity. Ken's formal diagnosis was ADHD, combined type, because he met the *DSM* criteria for both the inattention and hyperactivity components. The ADHD diagnosis would also be given to children who are primarily inattentive or primarily hyperactive.

In addition to their core problems, children with attention deficit hyperactivity disorder have a number of other difficulties. As evidenced by poor academic and test performance (Barkley, DuPaul, & McMurray, 1990), between 20 and 25 percent have learning problems. Misconduct at school is found in about 80 percent (Satterfield et al., 1972). They are commonly described by adults as immature and choosing to play with children younger than themselves and with toys inappropriate to their age. They also persist in baby talk (Weiss et al., 1971), are often described as stubborn, have low frustration tolerance, low self-esteem, and throw temper tantrums frequently. As many as 50 percent also meet the diagnostic criteria for conduct disorder or oppositional defiant disorder.

The problems of these children begin in early infancy. They are more likely than their peers to develop colic (Stewart et al., 1966), and they fail to reach developmental milestones at the expected ages (Denhoff, 1973). Furthermore, even during infancy there are deviations in activity level. Some children are overactive; others are too passive (Werry, Weiss, & Douglas, 1964). By the preschool years, their overactivity and inattentiveness are evident. At this stage in their lives, they are often considered temperamental and emotional children (Schain & Reynard, 1975). But their problems continue into the elementary school years; eventually most of them come to the attention of mental health professionals.

It is estimated that 8 to 9 percent of elementary school boys and 2 to 3 percent of girls have the disorder (Miller, Palkes, & Stewart, 1973; Szatmari, Offord, & Boyle, 1989). At one time it was though that the problem simply went away by adolescence. However, longitudinal studies begun in the 1980s have shown that ADHD children continue to have adjustment problems throughout adolescence and into young adulthood. In one study, over 70 percent of children with ADHD still met diagnostic criteria for the disorder in adolescence (Barkley et al., 1990). In adulthood some of these ADHD people, mostly men, are more likely to abuse alcohol, display antisocial behavior, and have deficits in social and occupational behavior (Gittelman et al., 1985; Mannuzza et al., 1993). Unfavorable outcomes are found both among those who were treated as youngsters and those who were not.

In a series of important studies, Loney and her associates have identified some of the predictors of adolescent outcome in a large sample of hyperactive children. By factor analyzing the symptoms, Loney, Langhorne, and Paternite (1978) identified two principal clusters. The first was called the *hyperactivity factor* and included hyperactivity, inattention, and deficits in judgment. The second, called the *aggression factor,* included aggression as well as problems of control and negative emotion. The better predictor of both hyperactivity and aggressive behavior at follow-up in adolescence was the aggression factor (Paternite & Loney, 1980). The aggressive aspect of ADHD, then, can extend beyond childhood and may even be a lifelong problem.

Biological Theories

A predisposition toward the disorder may be inherited. For example, Siederman et al. (1992) have found that the first-degree relatives of ADHD children were more likely than controls to also have ADHD. Similarly, Goodman and Stevenson (1989) found concordance for clinically diagnosed hyperactivity in 51 percent of identical twins and 33 percent of fraternal twins. Reports from Ken's father indicate that he may have had attention deficit hyperactivity disorder as a child, but the information is too sketchy to be sure.

What is it that ADHD children inherit? Preliminary studies of brain *functioning* (as opposed to anatomical structures) suggest that neurological differences between ADHD and normal children, specifically involving the frontal-limbic system, may be the biological basis for the disorder. Zametkin and his colleagues (1990) used PET scans of the brain to demonstrate that adults with childhood-onset ADHD have reduced cerebral glucose metabolism; that is, their brains are less active than the brains of normal adults during an auditory-attention task. The difference was most striking in those regions of the brain involved in self-regulation of motor functions and attentional systems. Evidence of the poorer performance of ADHD children on neuropsychological tests of frontal lobe functioning (such as inhibiting behavioral responses) provides further support for the theory that a basic deficit in this part of the brain may be related to the symptoms of the disorder (Chelune et al., 1986).

A biochemical theory of hyperactivity, proposed by Feingold (1973), has enjoyed much attention in the popular press. Based on one of his earlier clinical cases, Feingold concluded that attention deficit hyperactivity disorder might be caused by food additives. He embarked on a study in which children were kept on a diet free of such additives. Many children responded favorably. Feingold's work was subsequently replicated (Hawley & Buckley, 1974). Thus it is possible that the central nervous systems of some hyperactive children, perhaps through a genetically transmitted predisposition, are upset in some way by food additives. It is unlikely, however, that many cases of attention deficit hyperactivity disorder are caused by sensitivity to food additives. Well-controlled studies of the Feingold diet have found that very few such children respond positively (Goyette & Conners, 1977).

Psychological Theories

Bettelheim (1973) suggests that hyperactivity develops when a predisposition to the disorder is coupled with unfortunate rearing by parents. A child with a disposition toward overactivity and moodiness is stressed further by a mother who easily becomes impatient and resentful. The child is unable to cope with the mother's demands for obedience; the mother becomes more and more negative and disapproving, and the mother–child relationship becomes a battleground. With a disruptive and disobedient pattern already established, the demands of school cannot be handled, and the behavior of the child is often in conflict with the rules of the classroom.

The Fels Research Institute's longitudinal study of child development supplies some evidence that is consistent with Bettelheim's position (Battle & Lacey, 1972). Mothers of children with attention deficit hyperactivity disorder were found to be critical of them and relatively unaffectionate, even during the children's infancy. These mothers continued to be disapproving of their children and dispensed severe penalties for disobedience. The parent-child relationship, however, is bidirectional; the behavior of each is determined by the actions and reactions of the other. While parents of hyperactive children give them more commands and have negative interactions with them, hyperactive children have also been found to be less compliant and more negative in their interactions with their parents (Barkley, Karlsson, & Pollard, 1985; Tallmadge & Barkley, 1983). As indicated later in the section on treatment, stimulant medication has been shown to reduce hyperactivity and increase compliance in ADHD children. Significantly, when such medication is used, the parent's commands and negative behavior also decrease (see Barkley, 1990). In Ken's case it seemed that his mother's negative attitude toward him was principally a response to his disruptive behavior. Nevertheless, her negative attitude, coupled with the inconsistent disciplinary practices of the parents, may have exacerbated Ken's disorder.

Finally, although no comprehensive theory has been proposed (O'Leary, 1980), two ways in which learning might be involved in hyperactivity should be mentioned. First, some of the child's undesirable behavior could be directly reinforced. In Ken's case, his daredevil acts and classroom clowning did elicit attention from his parents, peers, and teachers. Ken's temper tantrums also allowed him to get his own way. Second, as Ross and Ross (1976) suggest, hyperactivity may be modeled in the behavior of parents and siblings. This did not seem to be the case in the Wilson family.

Treatment

One of the major therapies used for children with attention deficit hyperactivity disorder is the administration of central nervous system stimulants such as dextroamphetamine (Dexedrine) and methylphenidate (Ritalin). Although it may at first seem strange to stimulate further a child who may already be having problems with overactivity, research indicates that these drugs improve attention and lower activity level in both normal and ADHD children (Rapoport et al., 1980). The main therapeutic effect may be to improve attention or to increase their sensitivity to rewards (Barkley, 1990); activity level then decreases because the child is able to stay with various activities for longer periods of time and is more strongly reinforced by them.

The available research clearly indicates that stimulants, particularly methylphenidate, are partially effective in treating attention deficit hyperactivity disorder. From 33 to 50 percent of treated children show an immediate positive response to stimulants. Another 10 to 20 percent show moderate improvement. One ingenious study even demonstrated that Ritalin helped children playing softball to assume the ready position in the outfield and keep track of the status of the game. Children given placebos, in contrast, frequently threw or kicked their gloves while the pitch was in progress (Pelham et al., 1990). Short-term side effects of stimulant treatment, principally insomnia and loss of appetite, usually disappear quickly. However, possible long-term risks of treatment with stimulants have not been well researched, so the decision to use them should be weighed carefully (Ross & Ross, 1976). Furthermore, although the drugs cause improvement, they do not lead to fully normal functioning. For example, Whalen et al. (1989) found significantly better peer appraisals during treatment, but the ADHD boys were still liked less than average. Finally, the effects of drugs on academic performance remain controversial, with some studies revealing positive changes and others none (see Henker & Whalen, 1989, for a review).

A variety of psychological therapies have also been employed for attention deficit hyperactivity disorder, but the one that has been most thoroughly studied is an operant-learning approach such as that used in Ken's case. Positive reinforcement is used to increase on-task behavior; remaining in one's seat; and positive interaction with peers, teachers, and parents; negative consequences follow undesirable behaviors such as being disruptive in the classroom. Such programs have been used successfully to treat outpatients on an individual basis as well as with children in special classrooms (O'Leary, 1980). Although hyperactive children have proven very responsive to these programs, the optimal treatment for the disorder may require the use of both stimulants and behavior therapy (Barkley, 1990; Gittelman et al., 1980).

22 SCHOOL PHOBIA

Mr. and Mrs. Berg had taken Robert to doctors and clinics repeatedly. One Sunday night they even took him to the emergency room of the city hospital after they found him panic-stricken, writhing in bed with pain. An attractive, curly haired, underweight eight-year-old, Robert, now in second grade, had always been very much afraid of school. Recently, his fears were becoming tinged with a morbid depression that had begun to alarm his parents.

The child sat in an overstuffed chair in the office of the family doctor, someone who did not take an especially psychological approach to her patients. Had the warm Ovaltine she had suggested helped?, she asked the skeptical Robert, who shook his head sheepishly, looking all the while to his mother. She was sitting nearby with an expression of desperation and love that only made the boy feel even more guilty about the pain he was causing his family. If only he could stop being a baby, Robert thought to himself, as the doctor and his mother discussed the latest pattern of school morning and evening "shenanigans."

Without fail, Sunday through Thursday evenings found the boy eating little at dinner, staring morosely at his plate, picking idly at his food, and wondering whether it was really worth eating, since he would probably be vomiting it all up one to two hours later. His skinny little body was beset with a host of twitches and rituals that simply became more pronounced if someone commented on them. Robert felt as ill equipped to resist them as he felt helpless to control the anxiety that mounted as the evening wore on.

Bedtime offered little solace. Robert found it necessary to observe whether or not he would fall asleep before 9 P.M.; if he was still awake after 9:30 P.M.; he would sometimes break into tears that brought his mother into bed with him. In a fruitless effort to distract his worrying mind and ease him into sleep, she told Robert fanciful stories and promised him rewards if he would manage to go to school the following day without the usual somatic complaints and pitiful entreaties that he be allowed to stay home "just for today."

But it was the morning that really threw the household into total chaos. Rising by 6:00 A.M., Robert would pace the floor of the small apartment, causing the boards to creak and usually waking up his older brother. By 7:00 A.M., everyone was awake. While preparations for the day occupied everyone else, Robert spent the time groaning in a corner of the kitchen, rubbing his stomach, and occasionally dashing into the bathroom to throw up in the toilet. His mother would plead, cajole, insist that he at least drink a glass of milk for breakfast, but Robert would generally refuse, whining that it would only make him vomit more.

When it was time to set out to school, Robert had to be pushed out of the apartment. His tearful pleading and complaints of stomach upset and all manner of body ills led many times to relenting on his mother's part, and she would allow him to remain at home. (The fact was that Robert, an unusually bright child, did not get much out of school scholastically, a fact that his mother had come to use to justify her frequent decision to let Robert stay with her instead of insisting he go to school.) Much of the time, however, Robert's entreaties were rebuffed, especially when his stern father had not yet left for work. Robert would make his way miserably to school, trying to hide his tears from schoolmates.

Once at school, Robert usually settled down by lunchtime, but not without a visit from his mother, who would come to the school yard at recess with encouraging and loving words to her little boy and a container of milk and some cookies. This midmorning contact with mother was an implicit part of the "deal" Robert had struck with her for his going off to school. She continued these visits even though she admitted to herself that it was probably not in her son's best interests. It was, she knew, in her own interests; she would otherwise be nervous and upset about Robert's well-being in her absence.

Robert's peer relationships were surprisingly good. He was well liked by his schoolmates and by neighborhood friends, in spite of the fact (it seemed to Robert) that he acted like a baby as far as school was concerned. Although thin and almost emaciated in appearance from all the vomiting and his generally lackluster appetite, Robert was healthy and possessed an above-average athletic prowess. If he could not get to school without crying and vomiting, he could at least play stickball with enthusiasm and distinction.

But he had no way to express adequately to another human being, even to his mother, how terrified school made him. It was not just the separation from home that frightened him—although, to be sure, he did not ever stray far from his neighborhood or even spend much time at friends' houses. There was something particular about *school*. Yes, his present teacher in second grade was not an especially warm person, but she was always nice to Robert, both out of concern and out of appreciation for how good a student he was. The building itself seemed to him as cheery and attractive as a haunted house, and the authoritarian atmosphere did little to make the boy feel better. It is not an exaggeration to say that Robert's sorrowful walk to school in the morning resembled that of a convicted murderer as he was led from his death cell to the room being readied for him with cyanide gas.

SOCIAL HISTORY

Robert was the younger of two sons; his brother was six years his senior. The mother and father were third-generation Jews, and Mr. Berg was a self-employed insurance broker. He had graduated from a business school and worked for several years in a large agency downtown before striking out on his own. Mrs. Berg did not attend college; she married soon after her graduation from high school and became pregnant three months after. Years later Mr. Berg angrily told her that he would have gone into another line of work if he had not been saddled so quickly with family responsibilities. For some time Mrs. Berg blamed herself for having prevented her husband from pursuing a vocation he might have been better suited for than selling insurance.

Money was a constant worry for the household. Suppertime conversation revolved around things the family needed but (apparently) could not afford, and particularly around the importance of higher education for the two boys. It was never a question of *whether* Robert and his brother would go to college and to some professional school afterward but of *which* college and *which* type of postgraduate training. For many lower-middle-class Jewish families, education was viewed as *the* golden opportunity for advancement. Even though it had been 90 years since Robert's great-grandparents fled from Russia to the United States to escape tsarist pogroms, the youngster had already incorporated these values and anxiety-laden goals.

Robert and his older brother were very different from each other—Robert tense and nervous much of the time, his older brother jovial and optimistic, at least outwardly. They were alike, however, in that they were both intelligent and serious about their schooling. Indeed Robert's recollections years later were that he viewed kindergarten as the first difficult and challenging step to making his way in life.

Robert's home life was hardly an unmitigated disaster, even if he sometimes acted as if it were. Both boys were the recipients of a seemingly boundless outpouring of love and approbation from grandparents and parents alike, none more effusive than their mother. She constantly hugged and kissed her two boys, showering praise and food on them whenever they were near her, which was often. Robert's brother seemed to respond positively to this affection (and his rotund, cherubic appearance attested to his enjoyment of the food), but somehow Robert experienced it as yet another source of tension. In his worrying mind, every display of love and every word of approval only reminded him of the possibility of *not* having the love and approval. Even though praise and affection seemed to be constantly available, Robert began, even in earliest childhood, to worry if his mother would still love him if he was not "good." When he began school, there suddenly seemed to be countless hoops to be jumped through in an unending effort to retain the closeness and approbation that, already by age five, he had developed a strong need for, especially from his mother.

Another aspect of Robert's home life that assumed significance for him was the comparison he made between the modest, lower-middle-class surroundings in which he was growing up and the relative affluence of his cousins. His uncle was an extroverted lawyer who had built a lucrative general practice. As far back as Robert could remember, the visits to his cousins' home (in the "better" section of town) were a mixture of gleeful enjoyment of expensive and elaborate toys and a spacious house and a brooding envy and resentment that these "nice things" were not his. The return to the small, crowded apartment on a Sunday evening, after an afternoon of temporary immersion in the material things that only money could buy, oppressed Robert for reasons his young mind could not grasp. All he knew was that he felt tense, angry, and hurt.

Robert was afraid of school from the very outset. His extreme fear and avoidance, however, were almost less remarkable than something else, an attitude that was apparent on the days he managed to get to school. His kindergarten teacher noted to herself the first few days of school that this little boy was unusually serious. While the other children would act like the five-year-olds they were. Robert behaved more like a goal-oriented first-year medical student. He always sat with his hands tightly folded on the table in front of him looking attentively at the teacher, eager to do her bidding, even trying to anticipate her wishes—anything to be patted on the head, assured that he was a good boy, a smart boy, not prone to make mistakes or to give cause for a cross word or rebuke. So sensitive had he become by then to criticism and disapproval that it would wound him deeply even when some other child was spoken to sternly. So he was on edge continuously, lest he himself fall short in the teacher's eyes or lest a classmate be victim of such a disaster.

This pattern persisted until the middle of second grade, when a visit to the family doctor—who by now was at her wits' end with Robert—resulted in a promising referral. At the nearby university, a professor visiting from another country was teaching a seminar on child psychotherapy. Word was disseminated in the professional community that children with psychological problems were being sought for practicum work for the graduate students under the professor's supervision. This referral led to the following intervention.

CONCEPTUALIZATION AND TREATMENT

The way therapy was planned and implemented was unusual in that Robert's case was discussed intensively in the clinical seminar of Professor Long. The more behavioral members of the group argued that Robert's school phobia be handled straightforwardly, as a fear and avoidance of school and therefore amenable to a graduated exposure therapy regimen, modeled on a case report by Lazarus, Davison, and Polefka (1965). According to these authors, a counterconditioning approach is appropriate in the earliest stages of treatment, when fear and avoidance are so high that virtually no approach responses are being performed. The strategy is to expose the child gradually to school, all the while trying to induce states antagonistic to anxiety by comforting him, hugging him, and the like, even if it means reinforcing avoidance. Later on, as the child is more and more able to attend school, rewards can be made contingent on varying degrees of school attendance.

But other, less behaviorally oriented students suggested a more complex and less strictly behavioral intervention. First, it was noted that Robert was subject to anxieties other than those surrounding school, although his school phobia was obviously a dominating force in his life and that of his family. He showed anxiety and extreme reluctance about venturing far from home for *any* reason unless in the company of a family member, especially his mother. Notice was also taken of the mother's apparent need to have the boy overly dependent on her. She seemed to accede too readily to his demands to stay home; if he made it to school, she would visit during recess and lovingly hand milk and cookies to Robert through the bars of the school fence (even though he could have brought the snack with him). In addition, Robert's unusual seriousness and concern about doing perfect work in school were believed to play a part in the phobia; school seemed to represent a grave and weighty affair at an age when most children have fun and enjoy the simple pleasures of childhood. Robert's resentment and envy of his wealthy uncle also seemed relevant, perhaps highlighting the material benefits that awaited those who would work instead of play. Finally, since the household had been organized around Robert's timorousness, it was thought that adjustments would be necessary in order to support whatever improvement Robert might show in going to school regularly and without duress.

Therapy proceeded along several fronts, often simultaneously—an intensive approach made feasible by virtue of Robert's becoming a teaching case for the graduate students. Professor Long and one of his students conducted office sessions with Robert alone, with Robert accompanied by his parents, and with the parents by themselves; another student worked with the boy directly on the school phobia every weekday.

The latter, as the most straightforward and behavioral aspect of the treatment program, can be described first. The overall goal was to expose Robert gradually and steadily to more and more of the school situation. For the first few mornings, the student-therapist would come to the apartment about 30 minutes before Robert's scheduled departure, talk soothingly with him, trying to point out the fun aspects of school. Robert knew, in other words, that he would not attend school the first few days but would just practice walking in the company of the therapist (whom he grew quickly to like). By the end of the week, Robert felt he was ready to enter the school yard with the therapist and decide only then whether to proceed to the classroom. By this point the school administration and Robert's teacher had been apprised of the graduated exposure program and that, for a while, Robert would not be attending regularly (not much of a change, to be sure); when present, he would be accompanied by an adult. It was also explained to the other children in his class that Robert's "friend" was someone who was trying to make him more at ease in school. The children showed understanding and support; they liked Robert, even with his occasional vomiting and erratic attendance, and hoped that the man with him would succeed in making him more comfortable in school.

After two weeks, Robert was able to leave his house by himself, walk to school, and enter the school yard to see the therapist waiting for him. A few days later he was able to make it into the classroom, with the therapist waiting for him there; two weeks after that, he could remain at school all day, meeting the graduate student as he left the building for the walk home. During these weeks, the emphasis was on rewarding approximations to school attendance; it was necessary to caution his mother against coming to school at recess or being (overly?) willing to allow the boy to remain home if he expressed a desire to do so. Dealing with the mother's reluctance to stay away from school at recess was something that occupied the other therapist team, as will be seen shortly.

What was regarded as a breakthrough occurred seven weeks after the beginning of therapy. The therapist was waiting for the boy to come out of the school building and then accompany him home when Robert appeared with several classmates who lived in his neighborhood. In a serious manner, more appropriate for a child several years older, Robert asked the therapist if he would mind not walking him home because he would rather be in the company of his friends.

The preceding exposure regimen was sufficient for eliminating the phobia of the child reported by Lazarus et al. However, it can never be known whether or not this alone would have sufficed as well for Robert; as indicated,

Professor Long's seminar elected to have different therapists work simultaneously with Robert and his parents.

Without necessarily implicating the mother as the cause of the boy's dependency and school avoidance, Professor Long and his student cotherapists decided that her attitudes and needs should be examined. Perhaps Mrs. Berg derived something positive from Robert's fearfulness; at the very least, she put up with monumental disruption in her own life just to cater to Robert's wishes and anxieties.

The first few sessions in Professor Long's office were with Robert and his parents. The therapists asked each of them for their perspectives on what was going on and what might help the situation. Robert was fairly uncommunicative, looking frequently at his parents for help in answering even the simplest and most mundane questions, such as what his teacher's name was and how many students were in his class. The mother sighed a great deal during the sessions, occasionally weeping and declaring that she would lay her life down for Robert, would do anything "just to make my little boy happy." The father was distant in the sessions, seeming acutely uncomfortable about discussing things of an emotional nature. His was a very traditional marriage, and the raising of the children was entirely the mother's responsibility. In the case of Mrs. Berg, it became more and more clear that this was a responsibility she treasured and was reluctant to share with her husband, even though she complained now and then that he did not take enough of an interest in the children.

Two sessions were spent with Robert alone, and the therapists were pleasantly surprised at how loquacious and insightful he was when his parents were absent. He was able to express that he dreaded making a mistake at school, that he desperately needed the approval of his teacher even as he needed that of his mother, that "perfect" performance at school seemed to him the best and most reliable way to obtain this approbation, without which existence itself seemed doubtful. In Robert's eyes, entrance into college also depended very much on his work in second grade. The pressure this created made going to school a dreaded duty, an awesome task. At the same time, Robert expressed, albeit vaguely and unclearly, a sense that his mother was almost as anxious about his leaving her side as he was. Even when she pleaded with him to set out for school or to play in a friend's house on a Saturday morning, he somehow felt that she would rather he not do so. At the very least, he felt confused about what his mother actually wanted. Not wishing to disappoint her, the boy was made even more nervous by this ambiguity. He also wondered how she could be so accepting of his frequent vomiting and complaining. He experienced himself as a burdensome individual and found it hard to believe that she did not occasionally resent his "antics." (Several weeks into therapy Robert got his mother to admit that, indeed, she had often been angry at him for his dependency and angry at herself as well for needing it.)

The student-therapist who saw Robert alone considered the boy intelligent enough to attempt some rational-emotive therapy (RET) with him (Ellis, 1962), so he engaged him in the following dialogue:

Therapist: Okay, Robert, can you tell me what makes you nervous when Ms. Zeiss returns the test papers?

Robert: I dunno . . . maybe it's because my grade won't be good.

Therapist: How good is good?

Robert (smiling sheepishly): Well . . . kind of like . . . uh . . . having everything right.

Therapist: That must be hard to do all the time.

Robert: Naw, not that hard, not if I think real well on the test.

Therapist: But can't it happen that you make a mistake?

Robert: Yup, I once did.

Therapist (restraining himself from laughing): Well, what happened?

Robert: I felt really awful when I saw my paper.

Therapist: What did the teacher say? Did she say anything to you as she handed it to you?

Robert: No, she kind of smiled. But I just knew she was disappointed in me. That's why she smiled.

Therapist: Is that the only reason she could have smiled?

Robert: Well . . . , yah, I think so.

Therapist: Okay, I'm going to play a little game with you about things we say to ourselves. Will you do it with me?

Robert (unenthusiastically): I guess so, if we have to.

Therapist: Well, I think it might help you. So let's give it a try. Let's pretend I'm your teacher, and I am smiling at you while I hand you a test that you made a mistake on. What I want you to do is talk out loud about whatever comes into your mind. You know, tell me what you are saying to yourself.

Robert: Isn't it nutty to talk to yourself?

Therapist: Nope, I do it all the time. Don't you?

Robert: Hmm, yah. But I didn't know if it was normal.

Therapist: Sure it is. Everyone does it. And the kind of stuff I'm learning from Professor Long shows me that what people talk about with themselves has a lot to do with how they feel. Does that make any sense to you, Robert?

Robert: Yah, I guess so.

Therapist (not wanting to push the issue): Okay, let's just see what comes up. (Pretends to hand Robert his test that has an error on it.)

Robert (forehead furrowed): Oy, I made a mistake. She thinks I'm a jerk, a dope. She doesn't like me anymore. I can't stand this.

Therapist: Hmm, that's heavy stuff, little friend. Is that what you'd really think to yourself?

Robert: Well, I think so. I give myself a hard time when I make a mistake, and I'm sure other people think I'm a jerk.

Therapist: Do *you* think other people are jerks when they make mistakes?

Robert: Well, sometimes I do. I mean, if you're careful about what you do, won't you always be right?

Therapist: I don't think so. I make lots of mistakes, but I don't think I'm a jerk for doing that. That's part of being a human being. Aren't you one of those? (Pokes Robert playfully in the ribs.)

Robert (laughs in spite of himself): Yah, I guess so. I'm sure no angel!

Therapist: That would be kind of boring, don't you think?

Robert: I guess so.

Therapist: Listen, Robert. I think that the kind of hard time you give yourself when you make a mistake is what makes you feel bad. Ms. Zeiss's smile can't make you feel bad, can it?

Robert: No, I guess not.

Therapist: And even if she frowned at you, would that make you a total jerk? Wouldn't there be good things about you, like all the other things you do nicely? And how nice you are to other kids? And other stuff?

Robert: Well, I guess so.

Therapist: Let's try this. I'm going to pretend I'm your teacher again, giving you back that same test. This time instead of telling me what you'd usually think, I want you to try to tell yourself something that might make you not feel so bad. Can you try?

Robert: Okay. (Takes imaginary test paper from T.) Oy—I mean, oh. A mistake. Poo. I don't like making mistakes. Hmm. She's smiling at me. Maybe she likes me even though I made a mistake. Come to think of it, she always tells us kids that as long as we do our best, she isn't going to be disappointed or mad.

Therapist: How do you feel?

Robert: A little better, I guess. But I don't think I can do that at school.

Therapist: Well, we'll do lots of practice here, and you can try these new things out at school, and at home, and anywhere you like. And we can see how it works for you.

Such dialogues were repeated many times in the six sessions the graduate student-therapist had alone with Robert; they were also discussed in the conjoint family sessions with Robert's parents. It required a fair amount of explaining and "selling" for the parents to accept the viability of the approach. To no one's surprise, Mr. and Mrs. Berg found that their own self-talk bore similarities to that of their son.

In the family sessions the mother's needs and fears also came up for discussion. The professor and his cotherapist encouraged her to talk about how she felt on mornings that Robert left the house for school. At first insisting that she was grateful and delighted to have him out of the house, she slowly came to admit that her own anxieties would mount within minutes of Robert's departure. "What if he falls down? What if some bully picks on my little Robert? What if Robert begins to vomit—will he be okay? What if he gets upset by something the teacher says?" She began to muse about how she was getting herself worked up by dwelling on these remote negative possibilities. She also came to realize that there was an emptiness in her life at home. An intelligent woman, she had not attended college but, instead, married right out of high school and quickly became pregnant with Robert's older brother. Her home life was not terribly exciting; her husband worked long hours and played a very small role in household activities, including the rearing of his two sons. The marital relationship was impoverished, and Mrs. Berg lavished her considerable affection on her boys, especially little Robert who, "after all," needed extra love and affection.

After several sessions that included Robert, therefore, it was decided that the parents come without him to work in improving their communication. There turned out to be a number of unresolved issues in their marriage, among them Mr. Berg's feelings of having let his family down by not earning as much money as he felt he should, Mrs. Berg's guilt about having (in her eyes) deprived Mr. Berg of a more satisfying career by getting married early and beginning a family right away, and other problems that had developed over the years and underlay the remoteness each felt from the other.

These marital therapy sessions took place at the same time Robert began to show some significant improvement in school attendance. His mother was thus able to support Robert's leaving the house in the morning and endure not seeing him again until he returned home. The midmorning visits to the school yard seemed less necessary to Mrs. Berg as her relationship with her husband improved. She even began to go to his office several mornings a week to help out with some clerical chores, something that brought the two people together in a way that was new to each of them and rekindled some of the personal interest they used to have in each other.

An interesting development took place regarding Robert's love–hate attitudes toward his wealthy uncle. Prior to treatment, Mrs. Berg would complain periodically at dinner about the family's marginal financial picture. Mr. Berg's reaction would be to withdraw into sullen silence. Robert's anxieties would mount, fearing in some inchoate way that a disaster was about to befall the household. His reaction would quickly turn to anger at what was viewed to be an unfair attack on his father—anger, however, of which he was barely aware, so quickly was it avoided or repressed by his love for his mother. Yet, how could his beloved mother do anything so wrong as attack her husband? Somehow in Robert's young mind these feelings took the form of violent envy of his uncle's affluence tinged with resentment at the uncle and at his father as well. These revelations emerged at one of the closing individual sessions the boy had with the therapist in which his fears of failing at school were linked to the belief that he had to do well at this early stage of his education if he were to succeed financially later in life. Nondirective discussions helped the child elaborate on these concerns and see their origins more clearly. At the last therapy session, a conjoint one with Robert and his parents, each family member used the opportunity to talk openly about the financial worries each had been harboring for several years. Ironically, it turned out that Robert's father was doing a good deal better in his insurance business than the mother or Robert believed. Robert himself was becoming less anxious about his need to succeed in elementary school; the rational-emotive treatment seemed to have helped him view things in general as less serious and forbidding.

Two months after the initial contact with Professor Long, Robert was managing to attend school regularly, with only an occasional bout of nervousness in the morning. When he did report reluctance to leave for school, his mother matter-of-factly informed him that she would not be able to look after him at home because of a prior commitment, usually to go to Mr. Berg's office. Robert's father, on his part, made it a point not to leave for work until Robert had left for school, enabling him to support his wife in the firm decision that weekday mornings were a time for children to go to school and parents to begin their own activities. There was overall much less tension in the household as the parents' relationship improved; this improvement in emotional tone apparently lessened Robert's general anxiety level and helped him regard school as less threatening, even as inviting. Robert's brother, who had played little role in the treatment, proved to be helpful in providing rewards to his younger brother, such as taking him to a nearby park on Friday afternoons after a week of regular school attendance.

DISCUSSION

Even though Robert sometimes felt that he was the only little boy with the kind of problem from which he had been suffering, school phobia is not uncommon. Unlike other childhood fears, school phobia does not have a good prognosis without intervention; it does not seem to be a problem that children outgrow. But the intervention itself does not have to be professional; many school phobic children get over the problem if they are somehow forced to attend school, regardless of their misery. Repeated exposures to school, as is the case with most fears, tend to extinguish the fear if nothing traumatic occurs during an exposure.

School phobia does not appear as a separate category in *DSM-IV*; it is discussed as one facet of the separation anxiety disorders which, in turn, are among the disorders of childhood or adolescence. The essential feature of separation anxiety disorder is excessive anxiety lasting more than four weeks and associated with being away from home and loved ones. Such children often fear for the well-being of their parents when separated from them, become extremely homesick, are afraid of becoming lost and never reunited with their parents or other attachment figures, *and may refuse to go to school.* Sometimes their anxieties are expressed as anger and even depression. The *DSM* indicates that as the person grows into adulthood, separation anxiety disorder can take the form of having great difficulties handling new situations, like getting married or moving, and being overly preoccupied with the safety of his or her own children. The *DSM* description clearly characterizes Robert, who manifested reluctance to be away from his mother under various circumstances. School itself becomes a serious issue because (1) it is a regular event, and (2) it is expected that children go. Unlike staying overnight at a friend's house or going to a neighborhood party without one's mother, going to school is something that is to take place most weekdays, rain or shine.

The principal theories of the etiology of phobias come from psychoanalytic writers and from workers in the behavioral camp. Still accepted by psychoanalytically oriented clinicians is Freud's view that phobias are a defense against the anxiety produced by repressed id impulses. The anxiety linked to a particular id impulse is said to be displaced to an object or situation that has some symbolic connection to the impulse. By avoiding the phobic object, the person avoids dealing with repressed conflicts. Another way to state this is to say that neurotic anxiety—of which the fear of school is one example—is the fear of the disastrous consequences that are expected to follow if a previously punished and repressed id impulse is allowed expression. The therapeutic implication of this theory is that a direct approach to alleviating the fear should not be undertaken; that would leave the person defenseless against a terrifying confrontation with repressed id impulses. Instead, psychoanalytic treatment of phobias attempts to uncover the repressed conflicts gradually, helping the person examine them in the light of present-day reality. The person has to be taught not to fear his or her impulses.

A wide range of techniques, such as free association, dream analysis, and interpretation, is used by analysts. For most young children, a clinician would probably employ play therapy. Children are usually less able and willing to express their concerns verbally to adults. The work of Klein (1932) and Anna Freud (1946) provides a vehicle to delve into the child's unconscious. A play therapy room is equipped with toys such as puppets, puzzles, sand and water, and rubber clowns. The child might be asked to arrange little dolls to represent dinnertime at home. The way the youngster does this is interpreted by the analytic clinician in an effort to understand what is really bothering the child. Therapists from other theoretical orientations also employ play therapy. In nondirective play therapy, for example, instead of interpreting the child's play as symbolic expressions of unconscious conflicts and concerns, the client-centered therapist responds to the child's words and actions in an empathic manner, demonstrating unconditional acceptance (Axline, 1964). Behavior therapists also use the play therapy setting, but their focus is different: One report used short-term puppet play as a modeling procedure to help reduce anxiety in children about to undergo surgery (Cassell, 1965). Therapists of varying persuasions, then, often use the playroom at least to establish a relationship with a child client and to determine from what the child says and does with toys the youngster's perspective on the problem. Evidence on the effectiveness of play therapy in general is spotty (Barret, Hampe, & Miller, 1978; Phillips, 1985).

A particular treatment can be effective even if the etiological theory from which it arises lacks supporting evidence. That is, analytic play therapy could one day be found effective for some children's fears even if the analytic theory of the development of fears is found wanting. This distinction between etiology and treatment is important when we examine behavioral viewpoints on phobias because there is far more evidence supporting behavior therapy for eliminating phobias than there is evidence supporting the etiological views favored by behavioral workers.

It is wisely assumed by behavioral theorists that phobias are acquired by classical conditioning, as seems to have happened in a well-known case by Watson and Rayner (1920). A young child, little Albert, was shown a white rat, to which he evidenced no signs of fear. Then a loud noise was created during several presentations of the animal. After five such associations between the rat and the frightening noise, Albert came to fear the creature. In classical conditioning terms, the child acquired a conditioned response to a previously harmless stimulus, the conditioned stimulus, by virtue of its being paired with an intrinsically noxious event, the loud tone, or the unconditioned stimulus. Subsequent attempts (e.g., English, 1929) to replicate this notorious demonstration have not been successful, however, warranting considerable caution in believing that phobias usually develop in this manner.[1]

A variation of straightforward classical conditioning might provide a better account of how phobias develop. Perhaps certain kinds of neutral stimuli are more likely than others to be conditioned to fear. That is, it may be that people are physiologically predisposed to acquire classically conditioned fear responses to certain types of events. This notion of preparedness was originally proposed by Garcia (Garcia, McGowan, & Green, 1972) to explain experimental findings that rats more readily associate visual stimuli with fear produced by electric shock and taste stimuli with nausea produced by radiation. In fact, the rats learned to avoid the taste of a particular food even if they

---

[1]See Harris (1979) and Samelson (1980) for discussions of the limitations of this study and the curious role it has played in the development of learning models of phobias.

became nauseated several hours after eating; by contrast, pairing food taste with pain from electric shock did not lead to a conditioned fear and avoidance of the food. Based on this research, Seligman (1971) hypothesized that human beings may be "prepared" to acquire classically conditioned fear and avoidance to certain types of objects and situations. Consonant with this view is the finding that people tend to have phobias for animals such as cats and dogs, but not lambs. Moreover, few people are phobic about electrical outlets, even though they present greater dangers than do most domesticated animals. Some human experimental evidence lends support to this preparedness ides (McNally, 1987; Öhman, Erixon, & Löfberg, 1975). Perhaps this extension of learning theory will provide a fruitful link with the emphasis psychoanalytic theory places on the symbolic significance of phobias.

Another behavioral view hypothesizes that phobic reactions can be learned by imitating others. Laboratory research does confirm that a wide range of behaviors and emotions can be acquired through modeling (see Bandura, 1986) but, as with the classical conditioning view, there is a dearth of evidence that modeling accounts for the origins of most phobias. In Robert's case, for example, the therapists did not find instances of other school phobic children whom Robert knew; the youngster with whom he had the closest relationship, his older brother, seemed to be an unusually happy child, not one who could provide a model for fearfulness. On the other hand, Robert's mother seemed to be an overly anxious person, and there is evidence that anxiety problems are often found in the families of school phobic children (Bernstein & Garfinckel, 1988). Indeed, one study found that 75 percent of children with school phobia had mothers who had this problem in childhood (Last & Strauss, 1990). It may be that a mother can communicate to her child her own separation anxieties, which would implicate modeling, and she may also unwittingly reinforce her child's dependent and avoidant behavior, a factor that we turn to next.

A third behavioral hypothesis concerns operant conditioning. Perhaps phobic avoidance is directly rewarded. For whatever reason, the child begins to shy away from school; this behavior is reinforced by the parents. There is suggestive evidence for this in Robert's case; his mother seemed to give in readily to Robert's pleas to remain by her side instead of setting out for school and, even when he made it to school, she would visit during recess, perhaps communicating to the boy that leaving the situation would be okay. But such an account does not explain the initial avoidance of school, nor does it help us understand the great fear that accompanies the avoidance of a school phobic child.

Despite the questions raised about these behavioral views on the development of phobia, behavior therapies based on these ideas have been found to be successful in reducing or eliminating groundless fears (Davison & Neale, 1994). The treatment described for Robert contains a number of elements that were combined to provide a broad-spectrum approach to the several facets of his problem.

School phobics often have other fears as well. Robert fit this description, too, although the concerns uncovered by the therapists focused on his extreme need for approval and perfection. Indeed, the judgment of the therapy team and clinical seminar was that Robert's fear of school had a great deal to do with his extreme sensitivity to criticism and his inordinate desire to do well and not to make mistakes in a setting that he had learned to construe as vital for his ultimate ability to be a success in life. Thus, while Robert experienced anxiety whenever he had to be away from a family figure, especially his mother, the therapists nonetheless attended to his fears of making mistakes in the belief that improvement here would complement other efforts to get him to attend school in a normal fashion.

The treatment undertaken individually with Robert was consistent with the need to expose him to what he feared (Thyer, 1991) and with the desirability of dealing with particular sensitivities that could be seen as contributing to the phobia—in Robert's case, the demands he placed on himself never to err. Following the treatment model proposed by Lazarus et al. (1965), exposure to school was accomplished by gradually bringing the boy into more and more contact with the school situation, initially while trying to reduce his anxiety (through the comforting presence of the therapist); in the later stages of treatment, when he seemed capable of actually approaching the school and remaining there on his own, attendance was treated more as an operant, reinforced by praise at home and from the therapist.

Robert's perfectionism was conceptualized as the result of self-statements that informed him of how catastrophic it was to make a mistake. Following Ellis (1962), the therapist taught Robert to say different things to himself, along the lines of it not being so essential to perform flawlessly. Though usually employed with adults, rational emotive therapy (RET) has more recently been applied with children as well (Bernard, 1990; Ellis & Bernard, 1983; Haaga & Davison, 1989). Coupled with the graduated *in vivo* exposure regimen, Robert's fear and avoidance of school diminished over the two months of intensive therapy.

The separation anxiety component of the phobia was not overlooked by the therapy team. Robert's extreme dependency on his mother seemed to be a major contributing factor to the avoidance of school and other "away-from-mother" situations. The initial interviews with Robert and his parents suggested that Mrs. Berg was, as it were, conspiring to keep Robert near her, both because of her own morbid fears of something dreadful befalling him and because he had become the center of her existence. Her relationship with her husband was found wanting, especially in honesty and depth of communication. Several sessions of training the two people to express their concerns and feelings to the other helped reestablish the intimacy that was once there and shifted the mother's attentions to someone other than Robert: to her husband and to herself. This seemed to help the boy in another way. He found it hard to believe that his mother did not resent his fearfulness at least a little, and her protestations that she would do "anything" for Robert's well-being were as suspicious to Robert as they were false to the mother herself. Her increased honesty with the boy helped solidify the gains in his attending school because she was better able to resist his pleas to stay at home with her; she now had other things to turn to and felt more justified than before in asserting her own needs. Fortunately for Robert, the satisfaction of those needs was inconsistent with his remaining at home any weekday he did not feel like going to school. Mrs. Berg's constant availability had, it seemed, undermined attempts by Robert to get himself to school.

A caution is in order vis-à-vis Mrs. Berg's role in her son's school phobia. For many years Mom has been the "villain" in theories of psychopathology (Davison & Neale, 1994). Either her overprotectiveness, as in the present case, or her neglect, as in the case of autistic children (Ferster, 1961), has been designated a major pathogenic factor, that is, a variable causing the disorder in question. In most instances the validity of the claim is impossible to evaluate; in some cases it is almost certainly untrue. Schizophrenia, in particular, is linked much more to a genetic predisposition than to any harm inflicted on the child by a parent.

And yet the way parents or primary caretakers deal with children is likely to be important, if not in the genesis of a disorder then at least in its course. In Robert's case the therapists hypothesized that Mrs. Berg's own dependency on Robert and the exclusive focus he provided in her otherwise uninteresting life were reducing still further whatever inclination and capacity the boy had to make it to school. The reinforcement she provided for avoidance would be expected to help maintain the problem by diminishing Robert's opportunities to be exposed to the school situation. And whatever their theoretical differences, the therapists and parents have long recognized the need for people to face up to their fears if they hope to conquer them.

So the therapists realized that Mrs. Berg would have to change her reactions to Robert's early morning activities if therapy was to proceed. She would have to stop relenting when Robert pleaded with her to stay at home, and she would have to allow the student-therapist to apply some pressure as well as encouragement in getting the youngster out of the apartment and at least partway to school.

On the surface this seems to be a straightforward matter, but it is not. The graduated exposure regimen, as benign and gentle as it was, nonetheless required the child to urge himself on to do things that he would have preferred not to do; it would have been easier for him to fall back and stay at home. On some mornings the therapist did not easily get him to leave the house; the conduct of treatment seldom is as smooth as it sometimes seems in case reports. On one morning in particular Robert's mother tugged at the therapist's sleeve, her eyes moist, and whispered to him that Robert be allowed to remain at home "just this one more time." The therapist empathized with her pain but saw it as his professional responsibility to apply more pressure than the mother would. Not being as emotionally involved with the boy as the mother was, he was able to overlook the boy's pathetic and pained entreaties and nudge him out of the door. (It is not without good reason that most professionals avoid treating their own kin—there is such a thing as caring too much.)

There is a further moral to this story. Mental health workers, especially if they themselves have never raised children, must appreciate the torment a parent goes through when a child suffers, whether psychologically or physically. Children have fewer emotional resources than adults to cope with pain and difficulty. This vulnerability elicits protectiveness from adults, especially from parents, and considerable empathy and mature judgment are called for by therapists in deciding when to break those strong ties of dependency to urge the child to move forward even when that means he or she moves away from the parent.

When a child is referred for treatment, the impetus usually comes from an adult. This is natural; one can hardly expect a youngster to understand as well as an adult can that he or she needs professional assistance for a psychological problem. But this points out an issue for those working with childhood problems: the tendency for the child to be designated as the one having the problem and as the only family member in need of change. If the therapists in our case study had employed only a graduated exposure regime with Robert without involving the parents at all, Robert might have been rid of his school phobia. But, for reasons already stated, it seemed unlikely that attending only to Robert would have had a positive outcome because the child was inevitably enmeshed in the parents' relationship. The therapists therefore wisely considered how Mrs. Berg's marital problems might be influencing her dealings with Robert. On the assumption that she was unwittingly reinforcing the boy's school avoidance and that her doing so arose from her own excessive dependency on Robert for life satisfaction, Professor Long and his cotherapist helped her make beneficial changes in her marital relationship, the result being that she could focus on things other than her total absorption in and devotion to her younger son. It is conceivable that treatment could have been initiated by the parents for their marital problems, with Robert's phobia of school regarded as a secondary problem that would have been remedied by improving the relationship between mother and father. Here, too, however, some special attention to Robert, perhaps along the lines reported here, would probably have been needed.

In general terms, any therapy for a child must usually involve the child's caretakers, who are most often the parents. To be sure, an adult's life is bound up with other people, but children are particularly intertwined with others; they are under more constant surveillance and are subject to more control by others than are most adults. To intervene only with a child, keeping the parents uninvolved in and even ignorant of the treatment, is not seen by most contemporary child clinicians as a prudent or productive course.

A case study, as has been mentioned, cannot provide scientifically acceptable evidence. Robert's school phobia was indeed eliminated during the two months of treatment, but it is not possible to know which aspect of the multifaceted therapy was most important or which was even superfluous. For example, the case reported by Lazarus et al. (1965) emphasized the importance of graduated exposure to school, with little if any explicit attention paid to familial or marital factors or to the boy's self-talk as something in need of change. Would Robert have fared as well without the conjoint sessions? Like all clinicians, the professor and his students made the conservative judgment that family factors should be considered. Robert's mother seemed so very dependent on the boy—in some ways even more than Robert was dependent on her—that the concern was that she would undermine the attempts to help the boy leave home each morning. As much as she sincerely wished for Robert to attend school normally, his presence with her at home seemed so reinforcing to her that denying her that without helping her find some adequate substitute might have been poor clinical practice.

This was not a wealthy family, it should be remembered, and it was fortunate for them that Robert's problem was used as a teaching case for the graduate students in Professor Long's seminar. Over the two months of treatment, it was estimated that 25 hours of professional time were devoted to the Berg family; in many communities in the early 1990s, this could cost upward of $2500. Even with some assistance from health insurance, this expenditure might have been beyond the family's means.

REFERENCES

Abou-Saleh, M.T. (1992). Lithium. In E.S. Paykel (Ed.), *Handbook of affective disorders* (2nd ed., pp. 369–386). New York: Guilford.

Abrams, R., & Fink, M. (1984). The present status of unilateral ECT: Some recommendations. *Journal of Affective Disorders, 7,* 245–247.

Abramson, L.Y., Metalsky, G.I., & Alloy, L.B. (1989). Hopelessness depression: A theory-based subtype of depression. *Psychological Review, 96,* 358–372.

Abramson, L.Y., Seligman, M.E.P., & Teasdale, J. (1978). Learned helplessness in humans: Critique and reformulation. *Journal of Abnormal Psychology, 87,* 49–74.

Adams, W.A. (1950). The Negro patient in psychiatric treatment. *American Journal of Orthopsychiatry, 20,* 305–310.

Agras, W.S. (1993). The diagnosis and treatment of panic disorder. *Annual Review of Medicine, 44,* 39–51.

Agras, W.S., Schneider, J.A., Arnow, B., Raeburm, S.D., & Telch, C.F. (1989). Cognitive-behavioral and response prevention treatments for bulimia nervosa. *Journal of Consulting and Clinical Psychology, 57,* 215–221.

Akhtar, S. (1990). Paranoid personality disorder: A synthesis of developmental, dynamic and descriptive features. *American Journal of Psychotherapy, 44,* 5–25.

Akhtar, S. (1992). *Broken Structures: Severe personality disorders and their treatment.* Northvale, NJ: Jason Aronson.

Akhtar, S., Wig, N.N., Varma, V.K., Pershad, D., & Varma, S.K. (1975). A phenomenological analysis of symptoms in obsessive-compulsive neurosis. *British Journal of Psychiatry, 127,* 342–348.

Akiskal, H.S. (1981). Subaffective disorders: Dysthymic, Cyclothymic, and Bipolar II Disorders in the "borderline" realm. *Psychiatric Clinics of North America, 4,* 25–46.

Alexander, F. (1950). *Psychosomatic medicine.* New York: Norton.

Allen, C. (1969). *A textbook of psychosexual disorders.* New York: Oxford University Press.

American Psychiatric Association (1968). *Diagnostic and statistical manual of mental disorders: Second edition (DSM-II).* Washington, DC: American Psychiatric Association.

American Psychiatric Association (1980). *Diagnostic and statistical manual of mental disorders: Third edition (DSM-III).* Washington, DC: American Psychiatric Association.

American Psychiatric Association (1987). *Diagnostic and statistical manual of mental disorders: Third edition revised (DSM-III-R).* Washington, DC: American Psychiatric Association

American Psychiatric Association (1994). *Diagnostic and statistical manual of mental disorders: Fourth edition (DSM-IV).* Washington DC: American Psychiatric Association.

Anderson, B.L. (1983). Primary orgasmic dysfunction: Diagnostic considerations and review of treatment. *Psychological Bulletin, 93,* 105–136.

365

Andreasen, N.C., Ehrhardt, J.C., Swayze, V.W., Alliger, R.J., Yuh, W.T.C., Cohen, G., & Ziebell, S. (1990). Magnetic resonance imaging of the brain in schizophrenia: The pathophysiologic significance of structural abnormalities. *Archives of General Psychiatry, 47,* 35–44.

Andreasen, N.C., Flaum, M., Swayze, V.M., Tyrell, G., & Arndt, S. (1990). Positive and negative symptoms in schizophrenia: A critical appraisal. *Archives of General Psychiatry, 47,* 615–621.

Angrist, B., Rotrosen, J., & Gershon, S. (1980). Differential effects of amphetamine and neuroleptics on negative vs. positive symptoms of schizophrenia. *Psychopharmacology, 72,* 17–19.

Angst, J., Baastrup, P., Grof, P., Hippius, H., Poldinger, W., & Weis, P. (1973). The course of monopolar depression and bipolar psychoses. *Psychiatrica, Neurologica et Neurochirurgia, 76,* 489–500.

Anthony, J.C., & Aboraya, A. (1992). The epidemiology of selected mental disorders in later life. In J.E. Birren, R.B. Sloane, & G.D. Cohen (Eds.), *Handbook of mental health and aging* (2nd ed., pp. 27–73). San Diego: Academic Press.

Ashmore, R.D. (1990). Sex, gender, and the individual. In L.A. Pervin (Ed.), *Handbook of personality: Theory and research* (pp. 486–526). New York: Guilford.

August, G.J., Stewart, M.A., Tsai, L. (1981). The incidence of cognitive disabilities in the siblings of autistic children. *British Journal of Psychiatry, 138,* 416–422.

Axline, V.M. (1964). *Dibs: In search of self.* New York: Ballantine.

Aylward, E., Walker, E., & Bettes, B. (1984). Intelligence in schizophrenia. *Schizophrenia Bulletin, 10,* 430–459.

Baastrup, P.D., & Schou, M. (1967). Lithium as a prophylactic agent against recurrent depressions and manic-depressive psychosis. *Archives of General Psychiatry, 16,* 162–172.

Baer, L., & Jenike, M.A. (1992). Personality disorders in obsessive compulsive disorder. *Psychiatric Clinics of North America, 15,* 803–812.

Bakker, A., van Kesteren, P.J.M., Gooren, L.J.G., & Bezemer, P.D. (1993). The prevalence of transsexualism in the Netherlands. *Acta Psychiatrica Scandinavica, 87,* 237–238.

Ballenger, J.C., Burrows, G.D., DuPont, R.L., Lesser, I.M., Noyes, R., et al. (1988). Alprazolam in panic disorder and agoraphobia: Results from a multicenter trial: I. Efficacy in short-term treatment. *Archives of General Psychiatry, 45,* 413–422.

Bandura, A. (1986). *Social foundations of thought and action: A social cognitive theory.* Englewood Cliffs, NJ: Prentice-Hall.

Barkley, R.A. (1990). *Attention-deficit hyperactivity disorder: A handbook for diagnosis and treatment.* New York: Guilford.

Barkley, R.A., DuPaul, G.J., & McMurray, M.B. (1990). A comprehensive evaluation of attention deficit disorder with and without hyperactivity defined by research criteria. *Journal of Consulting and Clinical Psychology, 58,* 775–789.

Barkley, R.A., Fischer, M., Edelbrock, C.S., & Smallish, L. (1990). The adolescent outcome of hyperactive children diagnosed by research criteria: I. An 8-year prospective follow-up. *Journal of the American Academy of Child and Adolescent Psychiatry, 29,* 546–557.

Barkley, R.A., Karlsson, J., & Pollard, S. (1985). Effects of age on the mother–child interactions of hyperactive children. *Journal of Abnormal Child Psychology, 13,* 631–638.

Barlow, D.H. (1986). Causes of sexual dysfunction: The role of anxiety and cognitive interference. *Journal of Consulting and Clinical Psychology, 54,* 140–148.

Barlow, D.H. (1988). *Anxiety and its disorders: The nature and treatment of anxiety and panic.* New York: Guilford.

Barlow, D.H., Abel, G.G., & Blanchard, E.B. (1979). Gender identity change in transsexuals: Follow-up and replications. *Archives of General Psychiatry, 36,* 1001–1007.

Barlow, D.H., Craske, M.G., Cerny, J.A., & Klosko, J.S. (1989). Behavioral treatment of panic disorder. *Behavior Therapy, 20,* 261–282.

Baron, M., Gershon, E.S., Rudy, V., Jonas, W.Z., & Buchsbaum, M. (1975). Lithium carbonate response in depression. *Archives of General Psychiatry, 32,* 1107–1111.

Baron, M., Risch, N., Hamburger, R., et al. (1987). Genetic linkage between X chromosome markers and manic depression. *Nature, 326,* 806–808.

Barrett, C.L., Hampe, E., & Miller, L. (1978). Research on psychotherapy with children. In S.L. Garfield & A.E. Bergin (Eds.), *Handbook of psychotherapy and behavior change: An empirical analysis* (2nd ed.). New York: Wiley.

Bartak, L., Rutter, M., & Cox, A. (1975). A comparative study of infantile autism and specific developmental language disorders: I. The children. *British Journal of Psychiatry, 126,* 127–145.

Battle, E.S., & Lacey, B. (1972). A context for hyperactivity in children, over time. *Child Development, 43,* 757–773.

Bebbington, P.E., Brugha, T., MacCarthy, B., Potter, J., et al. (1988). The Camberwell Collaborative Depression Study: I. Depressed probands: Adversity and the form of depression. *British Journal of Psychiatry, 152,* 754–765.

Beck, A.T. (1967). *Depression: Causes and treatment.* Philadelphia: University of Pennsylvania Press.

Beck, A.T. (1987). Cognitive models of depression. *Journal of Cognitive Psychotherapy, 1,* 5–37.

Beck, A.T., & Emery, G. (1985). *Anxiety disorders and phobias: A cognitive perspective.* New York: Basic Books.

Beck, A.T., Rush, A.J., Shaw, B.F., & Emery, G. (1979). *Cognitive therapy of depression.* New York: Guilford.

Beck, A.T., Ward, C.H., Mendelson, M., Mock, J.E., & Erbaugh, J.K. (1962). Reliability of psychiatric diagnosis: II. A study of consistency of clinical judgements and ratings. *American Journal of Psychiatry, 119,* 351–357.

Bellack, A.S., & Mueser, K.T. (1993). Psychosocial treatment for schizophrenia. *Schizophrenia Bulletin, 19,* 317–336.

Benjamin, H. (1953). Transvestism and transsexualism. *International Journal of Sexology, 7,* 12–14.

Benjamin, H. (1966). *The transsexual phenomenon.* New York: Julian Press.

Bennet, I. (1960). *Delinquent and neurotic children.* London: Tavistock Publications.

Benson, H. (1975). *The relaxation response.* New York: Morrow.

Bernard, M.E. (1990). Rational-emotive therapy with children and adolescents. *School Psychology Review, 19,* 294–303.

Bernstein, D.P., Useda, D., & Siever, L.J. (1993). Paranoid personality disorder: Review of the literature and recommendations for DSM-IV. *Journal of Personality Disorders, 7,* 53–62.

Bernstein, G.A., & Garfinckel, B.D. (1988). Pedigrees, functioning, and psychopathology in families of school phobic children. *American Journal of Psychiatry, 145,* 70–74.

Berrios, G.E., & Chiu, H. (1989). Obsessive-compulsive disorders in Cambridgeshire: A follow-up study of up to 20 years. *British Journal of Psychiatry, 154 (Suppl.* 4), 17–20.

Bettelheim, B. (1967). *The empty fortress.* New York: Free Press.

Bettelheim, B. (1973). Bringing up children. *Ladies Home Journal, 90,* 28.

Biederman, J., Faraone, S.V., Keenan, K., et al. (1992). Further evidence for family-genetic risk factors in attention deficit hyperactivity disorder: Patterns of comorbodity in probands and relatives in psychiatrically and pediatrically referred samples. *Archives of General Psychiatry, 49,* 728–738.

Black, D.W., Noyes, R., Goldstein, R.B., & Blum, N. (1992). A family study of obsessive-compulsive disorder. *Archives of General Psychiatry, 49,* 362–368.

Black, D.W., Noyes, R., Pfohl, B., Goldstein, R.B., et al. (1993). Personality disorder in obsessive-compulsive volunteers, well comparison subjects, and their first-degree relatives. *American Journal of Psychiatry, 150,* 1226–1232.

Blanchard, E. (1990). Biofeedback treatments of essential hypertension. *Biofeedback and Self-Regulation 15,* 209–228.

Blanchard, R. (1989). The classification and labeling of nonhomosexual gender dysphoria. *Archives of Sexual Behavior, 18,* 315–334.

Blanchard, R., & Sheridan, P.M. (1990). Gender reorientation and psychosocial adjustment. In R. Blanchard & B.W. Steiner (Eds.), *Clinical management of gender identity disorders in children and adults* (pp. 161–189). Washington, DC: American Psychiatric Press.

Bleuler, E. (1950). *Dementia praecox or the groups of schizophrenias.* New York: International Universities Press. (Originally published 1911)

Bliss, E.L. (1986). *Multiple personality, allied disorders and hypnosis.* Oxford: Oxford University Press.

Bohman, M., Cloninger, R., Sigvardsson, S., & Knorring, A. von (1982). Predisposition to criminality in Swedish adoptees: I. Genetic and environmental heterogeneity. *Archives of General Psychiatry, 39,* 1233–1241.

Bohman, M., Sigvardsson, S., & Cloninger, C.R. (1981). Maternal inheritance of alcohol abuse: Cross-fostering analysis of adopted women. *Archives of General Psychiatry, 38,* 965–969.

Boon, S., & Draijer, N. (1993). Multiple personality disorder in the Netherlands: A clinical investigation of 71 patients. *American Journal of Psychiatry, 150,* 489–494.

Borkovec, T.D., & Costello, E. (1993). Efficacy of applied relaxation and cognitive-behavioral therapy in the treatment of generalized anxiety disorder. *Journal of Consulting and Clinical Psychology, 61,* 611–619.

Bownes, I.T., O'Gorman, E.C., & Sayers, A. (1991). Assault characteristics and post-traumatic stress disorder in rape victims. *Acta Psychiatrica Scandinavica, 83,* 27–30.

Boyd, J.H., Rae, D.S., Thompson, J.W., Burns, B.J., et al. (1990). Phobia: Prevalence and risk factors. *Social Psychiatry and Psychiatric Epidemiology, 25,* 314–323.

Bradley, S.J., Blanchard, R., Coates, S., Green, R., Levine, S.B., Meyer-Bahlburg, H.F.L., Pauly, I.B., & Zucker, K.J. (1991). Interim report of the DSM-IV subcommittee on gender identity disorders. *Archives of Sexual Behavior, 20,* 333–343.

Bradley, S.J., & Zucker, K.J. (1990). Gender identity disorder and psychosexual problems in children and adolescents. *Canadian Journal of Psychiatry, 35*, 477–486.

Bretschneider, J.G., & McCoy, N.L. (1988). Sexual interest and behavior in healthy 80- to 102-year-olds. *Archives of Sexual Behavior, 17*, 109–129.

Brewin, C.R., Andrews, B., & Gotlib, I.H. (1993). Psychopathology and early experience: A reappraisal of retrospective reports. *Psychological Bulletin, 113*, 82–98.

Brodie, H., & Leff, M. (1971). Bipolar depression: A comparative study of patient characteristics. *American Journal of Psychiatry, 127*, 1086–1090.

Brown, G.W., Bifulco, A., & Harris, T.O. (1987). Life events, vulnerability and onset of depression: Some refinements. *British Journal of Psychiatry, 150*, 30–42.

Brown, G.W., Birley, J.L.T., & Wing, J.K. (1972). Influence of family life on the course of schizophrenic disorders: A replication. *British Journal of Psychiatry, 121*, 241–258.

Brown, G.W., & Harris, T. (1978). *Social origins of depression: A study of psychiatric disorder in women.* New York: Free Press.

Brown, T.A., & Barlow, D.H. (1992). Comorbidity among anxiety disorders: Implications for treatment and DSM-IV. *Journal of Consulting and Clinical Psychology, 60*, 835–844.

Bruch, H. (1973). *Eating disorders: Obesity, anorexia nervosa, and the person within.* New York: Basic Books.

Bruch, H. (1981). Developmental considerations of anorexia nervosa and obesity. *Canadian Journal of Psychiatry, 26*, 212–217.

Butler, R.N., & Lewis, M. (1977). *Aging and mental health* (2nd ed.). St. Louis: Mosby.

Cade, J.F.J. (1949). Lithium salts in the treatment of psychotic excitement. *Medical Journal of Australia, 36*, 349–352.

Cadoret, R.J., Cain, C.A., & Crowe, R.R. (1983). Evidence for gene–environment interaction in the development of adolescent antisocial behavior. *Psychological Medicine, 12*, 235–239.

Cadoret, R.J., Troughton, E., O'Gorman, T.W., & Heywood, E. (1986). An adoption study of genetic and environmental factors in drug abuse. *Archives of General Psychiatry, 43*, 1131–1136.

Caldwell, D. (1949). Psychopathia transsexualis. *Sexology, 16*, 274–280.

Cameron, N. (1959). The paranoid pseudo-community revisited. *American Journal of Sociology, 65*, 52–58.

Campbell, M. (1988). Fenfluramine treatment of autism. *Journal of Child Psychology and Psychiatry, 29*, 1–10.

Campbell, M., Anderson, L.T., Small, A.M., Locascio, L.L., Lynch, N.S., & Choroco, M.C. (1990). Naltrexone in autistic children: A double-blind and placebo controlled study. *Psychopharmacology Bulletin, 26*, 130–135.

Cannon, D.S., Baker, T.B., Gino, A., & Nathan, P.E. (1986). Alcohol-aversion therapy: Relation between strength of aversion and abstinence. *Journal of Consulting and Clinical Psychology, 54*, 825–830.

Cantwell, D.P., Baker, L, & Rutter, M. (1978). Family factors. In M. Rutter & E. Schopler (Eds.), *Autism: A reappraisal of concepts and treatment.* New York: Plenum.

Cappeliez, P. (1988). Some thoughts on the prevalence and etiology of depressive conditions in the elderly. Special Issue: Francophone research in gerontology in Canada. *Canadian Journal on Aging, 7*, 431–440.

Carey, G., & Gottesman, I.I. (1981). Twin and family studies of anxiety, phobic, and obsessive disorders. In D.F. Klein & J.G. Rabkin (Eds.), *Anxiety: New research and changing concepts.* New York: Raven Press.

Carpenter, W.T., & Strauss, J.S. (1991). The prediction of outcome in schizophrenia: IV. Eleven-year follow-up of the Washington IPSS cohort. *Journal of Nervous and Mental Disease, 179,* 517–525.

Casper, R.C., Eckert, H.A., Halmi, S.C., Goldberg, S.C., & Davis, J.M. (1980). Bulimia. *Archives of General Psychiatry, 37,* 1030–1035.

Cassell, S. (1965). Effect of brief puppet therapy upon the emotional responses of children undergoing cardiac catheterization. *Journal of Consulting Psychology, 29,* 1–8.

Castle, D.J., Scott, K., Wessely, S., & Murray, R.M. (1993). Does social deprivation during gestation and early life predispose to later schizophrenia? *Social Psychiatry and Psychiatric Epidemiology, 28,* 1–4.

Chambless, D.L., Cherney, J., Caputo, G.C., & Rheinstein, B.J. (1987). Anxiety disorders and alcoholism: A study with inpatient alcoholics. *Journal of Anxiety Disorders, 1,* 29–40.

Chambless, D.L., & Gillis, M.M. (1993). Cognitive therapy of anxiety disorders. *Journal of Consulting and Clinical Psychology, 61,* 248–260.

Chelune, G.J., Ferguson, W., Koon, R., & Dickey, T.O. (1986). Frontal lobe disinhibition in attention deficit disorder. *Child Psychiatry and Human Development, 16,* 264–281.

Churchill, D.W. (1969). Psychotic children and behavior modification. *American Journal of Psychiatry, 125,* 1585–1590.

Clark, D.M. (1986). A cognitive approach to panic. *Behaviour Research and Therapy, 24,* 461–470.

Cleckley, H.E. (1976). *The mask of sanity.* St. Louis: Mosby.

Cloninger, C.R., Bohman, M., & Sigvardsson, S. (1981). Inheritance of alcohol abuse: Cross-fostering analysis of adopted men. *Archives of General Psychiatry, 38,* 861–868.

Cloninger, C.R., Sigvardsson, S., Bohman, M., & von Knorring, A. (1982). Predisposition to petty criminality in Swedish adoptees: II. Cross-fostering analysis of gene–environment interaction. *Archives of General Psychiatry, 39,* 1242–1247.

Cloninger, C.R., Sigvardsson, S., Gilligan, S.B., von Knorring, A., et al. (1988). Genetic heterogeneity and the classification of alcoholism. *Advances in Alcohol and Substance Abuse, 7,* 3–16.

Cohen, C.I. (1993). Poverty and the course of schizophrenia: Implications for research and policy. *Hospital and Community Psychiatry, 44,* 951–958.

Cohen-Kettenis, P.T., & Arrindell, W.A. (1990). Perceived parental rearing style, parental divorce and transsexualism: A controlled study. *Psychological Medicine, 20,* 613–620.

Colby, K.M. (1975). *Artificial paranoia: A computer simulation of paranoid processes.* New York: Pergamon.

Colby, K.M. (1977). Appraisal of four psychological theories of paranoid phenomena. *Journal of Abnormal Psychology, 86,* 54–59.

Cole, J.O., & Davis, J.M. (1969). Antipsychotic drugs. In L. Bellak & L. Loeb (Eds.), *The schizophrenic syndrome.* New York: Grune and Stratton.

Cole, M. (1985). Sex therapy—A critical appraisal. *British Journal of Psychiatry, 147,* 337–351.

Comas-Diaz, L. (1992). The future of psychotherapy with ethnic minorities. *Psychotherapy, 29*, 88–94.

Compton, A. (1992). The psychoanalytic view of phobias: III. Agoraphobia and other phobias of adults. *Psychoanalytic Quarterly, 61*, 400–425.

Connors, M.E., & Morse, W. (1993). Sexual abuse and eating disorders: A review. *International Journal of Eating Disorders, 13*, 1–11.

Cooks, J., Schotte, D.E., & McNally, R.J. (1992). Emotional arousal and overeating in restrained eaters. *Journal of Abnormal Psychology, 101*, 348–351.

Coons, P.M., Bowman, E.S., & Milstein, V. (1988). Multiple personality disorder: A clinical investigation of 50 cases. *Journal of Nervous and Mental Disease, 176*, 519–527.

Coovert, D., Kinder, B., & Thompson, J. (1989). The psychosexual aspects of anorexia nervosa and bulimia nervosa: A review of the literature. *Clinical Psychology Review, 9*, 169–180.

Costello, C.G. (1970). Dissimilarities between conditioned avoidance responses and phobias. *Psychological Review, 77*, 250–254.

Courchesne, E., Yeung-Courchesne, R., Press, G.A., Hesselink, J.R., & Jernigan, T.L. (1988). Hypoplasia of cerebellar vermal lobules VI and VII in autism. *New England Journal of Medicine, 318*, 1349–1354.

Cowan, P.A., Hoddinott, G.A., & Wright, B.A. (1965). Compliance and resistance in the conditioning of autistic children: An exploratory study. *Child Development, 36*, 913–923.

Cox, A., Rutter, M., Newman, S., & Bartak, L. (1975). A comparative study of autism and specific developmental language disorders: II. Parental characteristics. *British Journal of Psychiatry, 126*, 145–159.

Coyne, J.C. (1976). Toward an interactional description of depression. *Psychiatry, 39*, 14–27.

Coyne, J.C., & Gotlib, I.H. (1983). The role of cognition in depression: A critical appraisal. *Psychological Bulletin, 94*, 472–505.

Coyne, J.C. (1992). Cognition in depression: A paradigm in crisis. *Psychological Inquiry, 3*, 232–235.

Coyne, J.C., Downey, G., & Boergers, J. (1993). Depression in families: A systems perspective. In D. Cichetti & S.L. Toth (Eds.), *Rochester symposium on developmental psychopathology: Vol. 4. Developmental approaches to the affective disorders.* Rochester, NY: University of Rochester.

Crow, T.J., Ferrier, I.N., & Johnstone, E.C. (1986). The two-syndrome concept and neuroendocrinology of schizophrenia. *Psychiatric Clinics of North America, 9*, 99–113.

Crowe, R.R. (1974). An adoption study of antisocial personality. *Archives of General Psychiatry, 31*, 785–791.

Crowe, R.R. (1984). Current concepts: Electroconvulsive therapy—a current perspective. *New England Journal of Medicine, 311*, 163–167.

DaCosta, M., & Halmi, K.A. (1992). Classifications of anorexia nervosa: Question of subtypes. *International Journal of Eating Disorders, 11*, 305–313.

Davidson, J.R.T., & Foa, E.B. (1991). Diagnostic issues in posttraumatic stress disorder: Considerations for DSM-IV. *Journal of Abnormal Psychology, 100*, 346–355.

Davison, G.C. (1968). Elimination of a sadistic fantasy by a client-controlled counterconditioning technique. *Journal of Abnormal Psychology, 73*, 84–90.

Davison, G.C., & Binkoff, J. (1978). [Unpublished data.]

Davison, G.C., & Lazarus, A.A. (in press). Clinical innovation and evaluation: Integrating practice with inquiry. *Clinical psychology: Science and Practice.*

Davison, G.C., & Nealer, J.M. (1994). *Abnormal psychology* (6th ed.). New York: Wiley.

Davison, G.C., Robins, C., & Johnson, M.K. (1983). Articulated thoughts during simulated situations: A paradigm for studying cognition in emotion and behavior. *Cognitive Therapy and Research, 7,* 17–40.

Davison, G.C., Williams, M.E., Nezami, E., Bice, T.L., & DeQuattro, V. (1991). Relaxation, reduction in angry articulated thoughts, and improvements in borderline essential hypertension and heart rate. *Journal of Behavioral Medicine, 14,* 453–468.

DeMyer, M.K., Pontius, W., Norton, J.A., Barton, S., Allen, J., & Denhoff, E. (1973). The natural history of children with minimal brain dysfunction. *Annals of the New York Academy of Sciences, 205,* 188–205.

Denhoff, E. (1973). The natural history of children with minimal brain dysfunction. *Annals of the New York Academy of Sciences, 205,* 188–205.

Deniker, P. (1970). Introduction of neuroleptic chemotherapy into psychiatry. In F.J. Ayd & B. Blackwell (Eds.), *Discoveries in biological psychiatry.* Philadelphia: Lippincott.

Diamond, M. (1979). Sexual identity and sex roles. In V. Bullough (Ed.), *The frontiers of sex research.* Buffalo: Prometheus.

Dimsdale, J.E., Pierce, C., Schoefeld, D., Brown, A., Zusmann R., & Graham, R. (1986). Suppressed anger and blood pressure: The effects of race, sex, social class, and age. *Psychosomatic Medicine, 48,* 430–436.

DiTomasso, R.A. (1987). Essential hypertension: A methodological review. In L. Michelson & L. M. Ascher (Eds.), *Anxiety and stress disorders: Cognitive-behavioral assessment and treatment* (pp. 520–582). New York. Guilford.

Dohrenwend, B.P., Levav, I., Shrout, P.E., Schwartz, S., Naveh, G., Link, B.G., Skodol, A.E., & Stueve, A. (1992). Socioeconomic status and psychiatric disorders: The causation-selection issue. *Science, 255,* 946–952.

Dolan, B. (1991). Cross-cultural aspects of anorexia and bulimia: A review. *International Journal of Eating Disorders, 10,* 67–78.

Egan, G. (1975). *The skilled helper.* Monterey, CA: Brooks/Cole.

Egan, T. (1990, June 7). As memory of music faded, Alzheimer patient met death. *New York Times,* pp. A1, A1b.

Egeland, J.A., Gerhard, D.S., Pauls, D.L., Sussex, J.N. et al. (1987). Bipolar affective disorders linked to DNA markers on chromosome 11. *Nature, 325,* 783–787.

Ehrhardt, A.A. (1984). Gender differences: A biosocial perspective. *Nebraska Symposium on Motivation, 32,* 37–57.

Eisenberg, L., & Kanner, L. (1956). Early infantile autism. *American Journal of Orthopsychiatry, 26,* 556–566.

Elkin, I., Shea, M.T., Watkins, J.T., Imber, S.D., Sotsky, S.M., Colins, J.F., Glass, D.R., Pilkonis, P.A., Leber, W.R., Docherty, J.P., Fiester, S.J., & Parloff, M.B. (1989). NIMH Treatment of Depression Collaborative Research Program: I. General effectiveness of treatments. *Archives of General Psychiatry, 46,* 971–982.

Ellicott, A., Hammen, C., Gitlin, M., Brown, G. et al. (1990). Life events and the course of bipolar disorder. *American Journal of Psychiatry, 147,* 1194–1198.

Ellis, A. (1962). *Reason and emotion in psychotherapy.* New York: Lyle Stuart.

Ellis, A., & Bernard, M.E. (Eds.). (1983). *Rational-emotive approaches to the problems of childhood.* New York: Plenum.

Ellis, L. (1987). Relationships of criminality and psychopathy with eight other apparent behavioral manifestations of sub-optimal arousal. *Personality and Individual Differences, 8,* 905–925.

English, H.B. (1929). Three cases of the "conditioned fear response." *Journal of Abnormal and Social Psychology, 34,* 221–225.

Epstein, S. (1979). The stability of behavior: I. On predicting most of the people much of the time. *Journal of Personality and Social Psychology, 37,* 1097–1126.

Esler, J., Julius, S., Sweifler, A., Randall, O., Harburg, E., Gardiner, H., & DeQuattro, V. (1977). Mild high-renin essential hypertension: A neurogenic human hypertension. *New England Journal of Medicine, 296,* 405–411.

Fahy, T.A., Abas, M., & Brown, J.C. (1989). Multiple personality: A symptom of psychiatric disorder. *British Journal of Psychiatry, 154,* 99–101.

Fahy, T.A. (1988). The diagnosis of multiple personality disorder: A critical review. *British Journal of Psychiatry, 153,* 597–606.

Fairburn, C. (1981). A cognitive-behavioral approach to the treatment of bulimia. *Psychological Medicine, 11,* 707–711.

Fairburn, C., & Cooper, P.J. (1982). Self-induced vomiting and bulimia nervosa: An undetected problem. *British Medical Journal, 284,* 193–197.

Fairburn, C.G., & Beglin, S.J. (1990). Studies of the epidemiology of bulimia nervosa. *American Journal of Psychiatry, 147,* 401–498.

Fairburn, C.G., Jones, R., Peveler, R.C., Hope, R.A., & O'Connor, M. (1993). Psychotherapy and bulimia nervosa: Longer term effects of interpersonal psychotherapy, behavior therapy, and cognitive therapy. *Archives of General Psychiatry, 50,* 419–428.

Fedora, O., Reddon, J.R., & Yeudall, L.T. (1986). Stimuli eliciting sexual arousal in genital exhibitionists: A possible clinical application. *Archives of Sexual Behavior, 15,* 417–427.

Feingold, B.F. (1973). *Introduction to clinical allergy.* Springfield, IL: Charles C Thomas.

Fenichel, O. (1945). *The psychoanalytic theory of neuroses.* New York: Norton.

Fenton, W.S., Mosher, L.R., & Matthews, S.W. (1981). Diagnosis of schizophrenia: A critical review of current diagnostic systems. *Schizophrenia Bulletin, 7,* 452–476.

Ferster, C.B. (1961). Positive reinforcement and behavior deficits in autistic children. *Child Development, 32,* 437–456.

Fink, M. (1977). Myths of "shock therapy." *American Journal of Psychiatry, 134,* 991–996.

Fischer, M. (1973). Genetic and environmental factors in schizophrenia: A study of schizophrenic twins and their families. *Acta Psychiatrica Scandinavica, Suppl. 238.*

Fluoxetine Bulimia Nervosa Collaborative Study Group. (1992). Fluoxetine in the treatment of bulimia nervosa: A multicenter, placebo-controlled, double-blind trial. *Archives of General Psychiatry, 49,* 139–147.

Foa, E.B., Feske, U., Murdock, T.B., Kozak, M.J., & McCarthy, P.R. (1991). Processing of threat-related information in rape victims. *Journal of Abnormal Psychology, 100,* 156–162.

Foa, E.B., Kozak, M.J., Steketee, G.S., & McCarthy, P.R. (1992). Treatment of depressive and obsessive-compulsive symptoms in OCD by imipramine and behaviour therapy. *British Journal of Clinical Psychology, 31,* 279–292.

Foa, E.B., & Rothbaum, B.O. (1990). Rape: Can victims be helped by cognitive behavior therapy? In K. Hawton & P. Cowen (Eds.), *Dilemmas and difficulties in the management of psychiatric patients* (pp. 197–204). Oxford: Oxford University Press.

Foa, E.B., Rothbaum, B.O., Riggs, D.S., & Murdock, T.B. (1991). Treatment of posttraumatic stress disorder in rape victims: A comparison between cognitive-behavioral procedures and counseling. *Journal of Consulting and Clinical Psychology, 59,* 715–723.

Foa, E.B., & Steketee, G. (1989). Behavioral/cognitive conceptualization of post-traumatic stress disorder. *Behavior Therapy, 20,* 155–176.

Foa, E.B., Steketee, G.S., & Ozarow, B.J. (1985). Behavior therapy with obsessive-compulsives: From theory to treatment. In M. Mavissakalian, S.M. Turner, & L. Michelson (Eds.), *Obsessive-compulsive disorders: Psychological and pharmacological treatment.* New York: Plenum.

Folstein, S., & Rutter, M. (1978). A twin study of individuals with infantile autism. In M. Rutter & E. Schopler (Eds.), *Autism: A reappraisal of concepts and treatment.* New York: Plenum.

Fontana, A.F. (1966). Familial etiology of schizophrenia: Is a scientific methodology possible? *Psychological Bulletin, 66,* 214–227.

Forgac, G.E., & Michaels, E.J. (1982). Personality characteristics of two types of male exhibitionists. *Journal of Abnormal Psychology, 91,* 287–293.

Forth, A.E., & Hare, R.D. (1989). The contingent negative variation in psychopaths. *Psychophysiology, 26,* 676–682.

Fowles, D.C. (1992). Schizophrenia: Diathesis-stress revisited. *Annual Review of Psychology, 43,* 303–336.

Freeland, A., Manchanda, R., Chiu, S., Sharma, V., et al. (1993). Four cases of supposed multiple personality disorder: Evidence of unjustified diagnoses. *Canadian Journal of Psychiatry, 38,* 245–247.

Freeman, C., Sinclair, F., Turnbull, J., & Annandale, A. (1985). Psychotherapy for bulimia: A controlled study. Conference on Anorexia Nervosa and Related Disorders. *Journal of Psychiatric Research, 19,* 473–478.

Freud, A. (1946). *The psychoanalytic treatment of children: Lectures and essays.* London: Imago.

Freud, S. (1925). Mourning and melancholia. In *Sigmund Freud, Collected Papers, Volume IV* (Alix and James Strachey, trans.). London: Hogarth Press. (Originally published in Zeitschrift, 1917)

Freud, S. (1925). Psycho-analytic notes upon an autobiographical account of a case of paranoia (dementia Paranoides). In *Sigmund Freud, Collected Papers, Volume III* (Alix and James Strachey, trans.). London: Hogarth Press. (Originally published in Jahrbuch für psychoanalytische und psychopathologischen Forschungen, 1909)

Freund, K., & Watson, R. (1990). Mapping the boundaries of courtship disorder. *Journal of Sex Research, 27,* 589–606.

Friedberg, J. (1977). Shock treatment, brain damage, and memory loss: A neurological perspective. *American Journal of Psychiatry, 134,* 1010–1014.

Frost, R.O., Steketee, G., Cohn, L., & Griess, K. (1994). Personality traits in subclinical and non-obsessive-compulsive volunteers and their parents. *Behaviour Research and Therapy, 32,* 47–56.

Funder, D.C., & Colvin, C.R. (1991). Explorations in behavioral consistency: Properties of persons, situations, and behaviors. *Journal of Personality and Social Psychology, 60,* 773–794.

Garcia, J., McGowan, B.K., & Green, K.F. (1972). Biological constraints on conditioning. In A.H. Black & W.F. Prokasy (Eds.), *Classical conditioning: II. Current research and theory.* New York: Appleton-Century-Crofts.

Garden, G.M., & Rothery, D.J. (1992). A female monozygotic twin pair discordant for transsexualism: Some theoretical implications. *British Journal of Psychiatry, 161,* 852–854.

Garfinkel, P.E., & Garner, D.M. (1982). *Anorexia nervosa: A multidimensional perspective.* New York: Brunner/Mazel.

Garfinkel, P.E., & Kaplan, A.S. (1986). Anorexia nervosa: Diagnostic conceptualizations. In K.D. Brownell & J.P. Foreyt (Eds.), *Handbook of eating disorders.* New York: Basic Books.

Garfinkel, P.E., Moldofsky, H., & Garner, D.M. (1980). The heterogeneity of anorexia nervosa. *Archives of General Psychiatry, 37,* 1036–1040.

Garner, D.M. (1986). Cognitive therapy for anorexia nervosa. In K.D. Brownell & J.P. Foreyt (Eds.), *Handbook of eating disorders.* New York: Basic Books.

Gatz, M., Kasl-Godley, J., & Karel, M. (in press). Aging and mental disorders. In J.E. Birren & K.W. Schaie (Eds.), *Handbook of the psychology of aging,* 4th ed. San Diego, CA: Academic Press.

Gatz, M., & Hurwicz, M.L. (1990). Are old people more depressed? Cross-sectional data on CES-D factors. *Psychology and Aging, 5,* 284–290.

Gatz, M., & Smyer, M.A. (1992). The mental health system and older adults in the 1990s. *American Psychologist, 47,* 741–751.

Gentry, W.D., Chesney, A.P., Gary, H.G., Hall, R.P., & Harburg, E. (1982). Habitual anger-coping styles: I. Effect on mean blood pressure and risk for essential hypertension. *Psychosomatic Medicine, 44,* 195–202.

Gentry, W.D., Chesney, A.P., Hall, R.P., & Harburg, E. (1981). Effect of habitual anger-coping pattern on blood pressure in black/white, high/low stress area respondents. *Psychosomatic Medicine, 43,* 88.

Gillberg, C., & Svendsen, P. (1983). Childhood psychosis and computed tomographic brain scan findings. *Journal of Autism and Developmental Disorders, 13,* 19–32.

Gittelman, R., Abikoff, H., Pollack, E., Klein, D., Katz, F., & Mattes, J. (1980). A controlled trial of behavior modification and methylphenidate in hyperactive children. In C. Whalen & B. Henker (Eds.), *Hyperactive children: The social ecology of identification and treatment.* New York: Academic Press.

Gittelman, R., Mannuzza, S., Shenker, R., & Bonagura, N. (1985). Hyperactive boys almost grown up: I. Psychiatric status. *Archives of General Psychiatry, 42,* 937–947.

Goodman, R., & Stevenson, J. (1989). A twin study of hyperactivity: II. The aetiological role of genes, family relationships, and perinatal adversity. *Journal of Child Psychology and Psychiatry, 30,* 691–709.

Goodman, W.K., McDougle, C.J., & Price, L.H. (1992). Pharmacotherapy of obsessive compulsive disorder. *Journal of Clinical Psychiatry, 53 (Suppl.* 4), 29–37.

Gooren, L. (1990). The endocrinology of transsexualism: A review and commentary. *Psychoneuroendocrinology, 15*, 3–14.

Gordon, C., & Beresin, E. (1983). Conflicting treatment models for the inpatient management of borderline patients. *American Journal of Psychiatry, 140*, 979–983.

Gordon, C.T., State, R.C., Nelson, J.E., Hamburger, S.D., & Rapoport, J.L. (1993). A double-blind comparison of clomipramine, desipramine, and placebo in the treatment of autistic disorder. *Archives of General Psychiatry, 50*, 441–447.

Gordon, P., & Ahmed, W. (1988). A comparison of two group therapies for bulimia. *British Review of Bulimia and Anorexia Nervosa, 3*, 17–31.

Gorenstein, E.E. (1991). A cognitive perspective on antisocial personality. In P.A. Magaro (Ed.), *Cognitive bases of mental disorders*. Newbury Park, CA: Sage.

Gotlib, I.H., & Hammen, C. (1992). *Psychological aspects of depression: Toward a cognitive-interpersonal integration*. New York: Wiley.

Gottesman, I.I. (1991). *Schizophrenia genesis: The origins of madness*. New York: Freeman.

Gottesman, I.I., McGuffin, P., & Farmer, A.E. (1987). Clinical genetics as clues to the "real" genetics of schizophrenia: A decade of modest gains while playing for time. *Schizophrenia Bulletin, 13*, 23–47.

Goyette, C.H., & Conners, C.K. (1977). *Food additives and hyperactivity*. Paper presented at the 85th annual convention of the American Psychological Association.

Greaves, G.B. (1980). Multiple personality: 165 years after Mary Reynolds. *Journal of Nervous and Mental Disease, 168*, 577–596.

Green, R. (1974). *Sexual identity conflict in children and adults*. New York: Basic Books.

Green, R. (1987). *The "sissy boy syndrome" and the development of homosexuality*. New Haven, CT: Yale University Press.

Greenberg, L.S., & Rice, L.N. (1981). The specific effects of a gestalt intervention. *Psychotherapy: Theory, Research, and Practice, 18*, 31–37.

Greene, B.A. (1985). Considerations in the treatment of black patients by white therapists. *Psychotherapy, 22*, 115–122.

Grinker, R.R., Werble, B., & Drye, R. (1968). *The borderline syndrome: A behavioral study of ego functions*. New York: Jason Aronson.

Gruenewald, D. (1984). On the nature of multiple personality. Comparisons with hypnosis. *International Journal of Clinical and Experimental Hypnosis, 32*, 170–190.

Gunderson, J.G., & Kolb, J.E. (1978). Discriminating features of borderline patients. *American Journal of Psychiatry, 135*, 792–795.

Gunderson, J.G., & Sabo, A.N. (1993). The phenomenological and conceptual interface between borderline personality disorder and PTSD. *American Journal of Psychiatry, 150*, 19–27.

Gunderson, J.G., & Singer, M.T. (1975). Defining borderline patients: An overview. *American Journal of Psychiatry, 132*, 1–10.

Gurland, B.J. (1976). The comparative frequency of depression in various adult age groups. *Journal of Gerontology, 31*, 283–292.

Haaga, D.A., & Davison, G.C. (1989). Outcome studies of rational-emotive therapy. In M.E. Bernard & R. DiGiuseppe (Eds.), *Inside rational-emotive therapy*. New York: Academic Press.

Hahlweg, K., Goldstein, M.J., Nuechterlein, K.H., Magana, A.B., Mintz, J., Doane, J.A., Miklowitz, D.J., & Snyder, K.S. (1989). Expressed emotion and patient–relative interaction in families of recent onset schizophrenics. *Journal of Consulting and Clinical Psychology, 57,* 11–18.

Hall, K.S., Dunner, D.L., Zeller, G., & Fieve, R.R. (1977). Bipolar illness: A prospective study of life events. *Comprehensive Psychiatry, 18,* 497–502.

Hamburger, C., Sturup, G.K., & Dahl-Iverson, E. (1953). Transvestism: Hormonal, psychiatric and surgical treatment. *Journal of the American Medical Association, 152,* 391–396.

Hammen, C. (1991). The generation of stress in the course of unipolar depression. *Journal of Abnormal Psychology, 100,* 555–561.

Harburg, E., Erfurt, J.C., Hauenstein, L.S., Chape, C., Schull, W.J., & Schork, M.A. (1973). Socioecological stress, suppressed hostility, skin color and black–white male blood pressure: Detroit. *Psychosomatic Medicine, 35,* 276–296.

Hare, R.D. (1978). Electrodermal and cardiovascular correlates of sociopathy. In R.D. Hare & D. Schalling (Eds.), *Psychopathic behaviour: Approaches to research.* New York: Wiley.

Hare, R.D., Harpur, T.J., Hakstian, R.A., et al. (1990). The revised Psychopathy Checklist: Reliability and factor structure. *Psychological Assessment, 2,* 338–341.

Hare, R.D., Hart, S.D., & Harpur, T.J. (1991). Psychopathy and the DSM-IV criteria for antisocial personality disorder. *Journal of Abnormal Psychology, 100,* 391–398.

Hare, R.D., McPherson, L.M., & Forth, A.E. (1988). Male psychopaths and their criminal careers. *Journal of Consulting and Clinical Psychology, 56,* 710–714.

Harris, B. (1979). Whatever happened to Little Albert? *American Psychologist, 34,* 151–160.

Hart, S.D., & Hare, R.D. (1989). Discriminant validity of the Psychopathy Checklist in a forensic psychiatric population. *Psychological Assessment, 1,* 211–218.

Hastrup, J.L., Light, K.C., & Obrist, P.A. (1982). Parental hypertension and cardiovascular response to stress in healthy young adults. *Psychophysiology, 19,* 615–622.

Hawley, C., & Buckley, R. (1974). Food dyes and the hyperkinetic child. *Academic Therapy, 10,* 27–32.

Hay, P.J., Sachdev, P.S., Cumming, S., Smith, J.S., et al.: (1993). Treatment of obsessive-compulsive disorder by psychosurgery. *Acta Psychiatrica Scandinavica, 87,* 197–207.

Heberbrand, J. (1992). A critical appraisal of X-linked bipolar illness. Evidence for the assumed mode of transmission is lacking. *British Journal of Psychiatry, 160,* 7–11.

Heiman, J., LoPiccolo, L., & LoPiccolo, J. (1988). *Becoming orgasmic: A sexual growth program for women.* Englewood Cliffs, NJ: Prentice-Hall.

Helzer, J.E., Robins, L., & McEvoy, L. (1987). Post-traumatic stress disorder in the general population: Findings of the Epidemiological Catchment Area Survey. *New England Journal of Medicine, 317,* 1630–1634.

Henker, B., & Whalen, C.K. (1989). Hyperactivity and attention deficits. Special Issue: Children and their development: Knowledge base, research agenda, and social policy application. *American Psychologist, 44,* 216–223.

Herzog, D.B. (1982). Bulimia: The secretive syndrome. *Psychosomatics, 23,* 481–483.

Herzog, D.B., Hamburg, P., & Brotman, A.N. (1987). Psychopathology and eating disorders: An affirmative view. *International Journal of Eating Disorders, 6*, 545–550.

Herzog, D.B., Keller, M.B., Strober, M., Yeh, C., & Pai, S.Y. (1992). The current status of treatment for anorexia nervosa and bulimia nervosa. *International Journal of Eating Disorders, 12*, 215–220.

Heston, L.L. (1966). Psychiatric disorders in foster home reared children of schizophrenic mothers. *British Journal of Psychiatry, 112*, 819–825.

Hewett, F.M. (1965). Teaching speech to an autistic child through operant conditioning. *American Journal of Orthopsychiatry, 33*, 927–936.

Hill, S.Y., & Smith, T.R. (1991). Evidence for genetic mediation of alcoholism in women. *Journal of Substance Abuse, 3*, 159–174.

Hoch, P., & Polatin, P. (1949). Pseudoneurotic forms of schizophrenia. *Psychiatric Quarterly, 23*, 248–276.

Hodapp, V., Weyer, G., & Becker, J. (1976). Situational stereotypy in essential hypertension patients. *Journal of Psychosomatic Research, 19*, 113–121.

Hoek, H.W. (1993). Review of the epidemiological studies of eating disorders. *International Review of Psychiatry, 5*, 61–74.

Hoffman, N.G., & Miller, N.S. (1992). Treatment outcomes for abstinence-based programs. *Psychiatric Annals, 22*, 402–408.

Hofland, B.F. (1988). Autonomy in long term care: Background issues and a programmatic response. *The Gerontologist, 28* (Suppl.), 3–9.

Hogarty, G.E., Goldberg, S.C., Schooler, N.R., & the Collaborative Study Group (1974). Drug and sociotherapy in the aftercare of schizophrenic patients: III. Adjustment of nonrelapsed patients. *Archives of General Psychiatry, 31*, 609–618.

Hokanson, J.E., & Burgess, M. (1962). The effects of three types of aggression on vascular processes. *Journal of Abnormal and Social Psychology, 65*, 446–449.

Hokanson, J.E., Rubert, M.P., Welker, R.A., Hollander, G.R., & Hedeen, C. (1989). Interpersonal concomitants and antecedents of depression among college students. *Journal of Abnormal Psychology, 98*, 209–217.

Hooley, J.M. (1985). Expressed emotion: A review of the critical literature. *Clinical Psychology Review, 5*, 119–139.

Hooley, J.M. (1986). Expressed emotion and depression: Interactions between patients and high- versus low-expressed emotion spouses. *Journal of Abnormal Psychology, 95*, 237–246.

Hooley, J.M., Orley, J., & Teasdale, J.D. (1986). Levels of expressed emotion and relapse in depressed patients. *British Journal of Psychiatry, 148*, 642–647.

Hoover, C.F., & Insel, T.R. (1984). Families of origin in obsessive-compulsive disorder. *Journal of Nervous and Mental Disease, 172*, 207–215.

Hsu, L.K. (1987). Are eating disorders becoming more common in blacks? *International Journal of Eating Disorders, 6*, 113–124.

Hsu, L.K., Crisp, A.H., & Callender, J.S. (1992). Recovery in anorexia nervosa: The patient's perspective. *International Journal of Eating Disorders, 11*, 341–350.

Hughlings-Jackson, J. (1931). In J. Taylor (Ed.), *Selected writings*. London: Hodder & Stoughton.

Hutt, C., Hutt, S.J., Lee, D., & Ounsted, C. (1964). Arousal and childhood autism. *Nature, 204*, 908–909.

Imperato-McGinley, J., Guerrero, L., Gautier, T., & Peterson, R.E. (1974). Steroid 5a-reductase deficiency in man: An inherited form of male pseudohermaphroditism. *Science, 186*, 1213–1215.

Jackson, D.D. (1960). A critique of the literature of the genetics of schizophrenia. In D.D. Jackson (Ed.), *The etiology of schizophrenia*. New York: Basic Books.

Jacobson, E. (1938). *Progressive relaxation*. Chicago: University of Chicago Press.

Jenike, M.A., Baer, L., & Minichiello, W.E. (Eds.) (1986). *Obsessive-compulsive disorders: Theory and management*. Littleton, MA: PSG.

Jutai, J.W., & Hare, R.D. (1983). Psychopathy and selective attention during performance of a complex perceptual-motor task. *Psychophysiology, 20,* 140–151.

Kane, J.M., & Marder, S.R. (1993). Psychopharmacologic treatment of schizophrenia. *Schizophrenia Bulletin, 19,* 287–302.

Kanner, L. (1943). Autistic disturbances of affective contact. *Nervous Child, 2,* 217–250.

Kanner, L. (1973). Follow-up of eleven autistic children originally reported in 1943. In L. Kanner (Ed.), *Childhood psychosis: Initial studies and new insights*. Washington, DC: Winston/Wiley.

Kanner, L., & Eisenberg, L. (1955). Notes on the follow-up studies of autistic children. In P. Hoch & J. Zubin (Eds.), *Psychopathology of childhood*. New York: Grune and Stratton.

Kantorovich, N.V. (1930). An attempt at associative-reflex therapy in alcoholism. *Psychological Abstracts, 4,* 493.

Kaplan, H.S. (1974). *The new sex therapy: Active treatment of sexual dysfunctions*. New York: Brunner/Mazel.

Karlsson, J.L. (1966). *The biologic basis of schizophrenia*. Springfield, IL: Charles C Thomas.

Karno, M., & Golding, J.M. (1991). Obsessive compulsive disorder. In L.N. Robins & D.A. Regier (Eds.), *Psychiatric disorders in America: The Epidemiologic Catchment Area Study* (pp. 204–219). New York: Free Press.

Karpman, B. (1954). *The sexual offender and his offenses*. New York: Julian Press.

Kasl, S.V., & Cobb, S. (1970). Blood pressure changes in men undergoing job loss: A preliminary report. *Psychosomatic Medicine, 6,* 95–106.

Kassett, J.A., Gershon, E.S., Maxwell, M.E., & Guroff, J.J. (1989). Psychiatric disorders in the first-degree relatives of probands with bulimia nervosa. *American Journal of Psychiatry, 146,* 1468–1471.

Katz, R., & McGuffin, P. (1993). The genetics of affective disorders. In D. Fowles (Ed.), *Progress in experimental personality and psychopathology research*.

Keane, T.M. (1985). Defining traumatic stress: Some comments on the current terminological confusion [Letter to the editor]. *Behavior Therapy, 16,* 419–423.

Keane, T.M., Zimering, R.T., & Caddell, J.M. (1985). A behavioral formulation of posttraumatic stress disorder in Vietnam veterans. *The Behavior Therapist, 8,* 9–12.

Keck, P.E., & McElroy, S.L. (1993). Current perspectives on treatment of bipolar disorder with lithium. *Psychiatric Annals, 23,* 64–69.

Keith, S.J., Regier, D.A., & Rae, D.S. (1991). Schizophrenic disorders. In L.N. Robins & D.A. Regier (Eds.), *Psychiatric disorders in America: The Epidemiologic Catchment Area Study* (pp. 33–52). New York: Free Press.

Kelly, M.P., Strassberg, D.S., & Kircher, J.R. (1990). Attitudinal and experiential correlates of anorgasmia. *Archives of Sexual Behavior, 19,* 165–177.

Kendler, K.S., & Diehl, S.R. (1993). The genetics of schizophrenia: A current, genetic-epidemiologic perspective. *Schizophrenia Bulletin, 19,* 261–285.

Kendell, R.E., & Kemp, I.W. (1989). Maternal influenza in the etiology of schizophrenia. *Archives of General Psychiatry, 46,* 878–882.

Kendler, K.S., & Hays, P. (1981). Paranoid psychosis (delusional disorder) and schizophrenia: A family history study. *Archives of General Psychiatry, 38,* 547–551.

Kendler, K.S., Neale, M.C., Kessler, R.C., Heath, A.C., & Eaves, L.J. (1992a). Generalized anxiety disorder in women: A population-based twin study. *Archives of General Psychiatry, 49,* 267–272.

Kendler, K.S., Neale, M.C., Kessler, R.C., Heath, A.C., & Eaves, L.J. (1992b). The genetic epidemiology of phobias in women: The interrelationship of agoraphobia, social phobia, situational phobia, and simple phobia. *Archives of General Psychiatry, 49,* 273–281.

Kelly, M.P., Strassberg, D.S., & Kircher, J.R. (1990). Attitudinal and experiential correlates of anorgasmia. *Archives of Sexual Behavior, 19,* 165–177.

Kennedy, J.A. (1952). Problems posed in the analysis of Negro patients. *Psychiatry, 15,* 313–327.

Kernberg, O.F. (1985). *Borderline conditions and pathological narcissism.* Northvale, NJ: Jason Aronson.

Kessler, R.C., McGonagle, K.A., Zhao, S., Nelson, C.B., Hughes, M., Eshleman, S., Wittchen, H., & Kendler, K.S. (1994). Lifetime and 12-month prevalence of DSM-III-R psychiatric disorders in the United States. *Archives of General Psychiatry, 51,* 8–19.

Kety, S.S., Rosenthal, D., Wender, P.H., & Schulsinger, F. (1971). Mental illness in the biological and adoptive families of adopted schizophrenics. *American Journal of Psychiatry, 128,* 82–86.

Keyes, D. (1981). *The minds of Billy Milligan.* New York: Bantam.

Kilpatrick, D.G., Saunders, B.E., Amick-McMullan, A., Best, C.L., Veronen, L.J., & Resnick, H.S. (1989). Victim and crime factors associated with the development of crime-related post-traumatic stress disorder. *Behavior Therapy, 20,* 199–214.

Kilpatrick, D.G., Saunders, B.E., Veronen, L.J., Best, C.L., & Von, J.M. (1987). Criminal victimization: Lifetime prevalence, reporting to police, and psychological impact. *Crime and Delinquency, 33,* 479–489.

Kilpatrick, D.G., Veronen, L.J., & Resick, P.A. (1979). Assessment of the aftermath of rape: Changing patterns of fear. *Journal of Behavioral Assessment, 1,* 133–148.

Kinzie, J.D. (1989). Post-traumatic stress disorder. In H.I. Kaplan & B.J. Sadock (Eds.), *Comprehensive textbook of psychiatry* (Vol. 1, 5th ed., pp. 1000–1008). Baltimore, MD: Williams & Wilkins.

Klein, D.F. (1981). Anxiety reconceptualized. In D.F. Klein & J. Rabkin (Eds.), *Anxiety: New directions and changing concepts.* New York: Raven Press.

Klein, D.F. (1993). False suffocation alarms, spontaneous panics, and related conditions: An integrative hypothesis. *Archives of General Psychiatry, 50,* 306–317.

Klein, D.F., & Ross, D.C. (1993). Reanalysis of the National Institute of Mental Health Treatment of Depression Collaborative Research Program general effectiveness report. *Neuropsychopharmacology, 8,* 241–251.

Klein, M. (1932). *The psychoanalysis of children.* London: Hogarth Press.

Klerman, G.L., Weissman, M.M., Rounsaville, B.J., & Chevron, E.S. (1984). *Interpersonal psychotherapy of depression.* New York: Basic Books.

Kluft, R.P. (1987). An update on multiple personality disorder. *Hospital and Community Psychiatry, 38,* 363–374.

Kluft, R.P. (1991). Clinical presentations of multiple personality disorder. *Psychiatric Clinics of North America, 14*, 605–629.

Knight, R. (1953). Borderline states. *Bulletin of the Menninger Clinic, 17*, 1–12.

Kockott, G., & Fahrner, E.M. (1988). Male-to-female and female-to-male transsexuals: A comparison. *Archives of Sexual Behavior, 17*, 539–545.

Koegel, R.L., Schreibman, L., Britten, K.R., Burke, J.C., & O'Neill, R.E. (1982). A comparison of parent training to direct child treatment. In R.L. Koegel, A. Rincover, & A.L. Egel (Eds.), *Educating and understanding autistic children*. San Diego, CA: College-Hill.

Koenig, H.G., & Blazer, D.G. (1992). Mood disorders and suicide. In J.E. Birren, R.B. Sloane, & G.D. Cohen (Eds.), *Handbook of mental health and aging* (2nd ed., pp. 379–407). San Diego: Academic Press.

Koenigsberg, H.W. (1982). A comparison of hospitalized and nonhospitalized borderline patients. *American Journal of Psychiatry, 139*, 1292–1297.

Kohn, M.L. (1968). Social class and schizophrenia: A critical review. In D. Rosenthal & S.S. Kety (Eds.), *The transmission of schizophrenia*. New York: Pergamon.

Kolarsky, A., & Madlafousek, J. (1983). The inverse role of preparatory erotic stimulation in exhibitionists: Phallometric studies. *Archives of Sexual Behavior, 12*, 123–148.

Kolodny, R.C. (1981). Evaluating sex therapy: Process and outcome at the Masters & Johnson Institute. *Journal of Sex Research, 17*, 301–317.

Koss, M.P., & Burkhart, B.R. (1989). A conceptual analysis of rape victimization. *Psychology of Women Quarterly, 13*, 27–40.

Koss, M.P., Gidycz, C.A., & Wisniewski, N. (1987). The scope of rape: Incidence and prevalence of sexual aggression and victimization in a national sample of higher education students. *Journal of Consulting and Clinical Psychology, 55*, 162–170.

Kraepelin, E. (1971). *Dementia praecox and paraphrenia* (R.M. Barclay, trans.). Huntington, NY: Krieger. (Originally published 1919)

Kringlen, E. (1970). Natural history of obsessional neurosis. *Seminars in Psychiatry, 2*, 403–419.

Kuiper, B., & Cohen-Kettenis, P. (1988). Sex reassignment surgery: A study of 141 Dutch transsexuals. *Archives of Sexual Behavior, 17*, 439–457.

Kuipers, L. (1992). Expressed emotion research in Europe. *British Journal of Clinical Psychology, 31*, 429–443.

Kuipers, L., & Bebbington, P. (1988). Expressed emotion research in schizophrenia: Theoretical and clinical implications. *Psychological Medicine, 18*, 893–909.

Kushner, M.G., Riggs, D.S., Foa, E.B., & Miller, S.M. (1992). Perceived controllability and the development of posttraumatic stress disorder (PTSD) in crime victims. *Behavioral Research and Therapy, 31*, 105–110.

LaRue, A., Dessonville, C., & Jarvik, L.F. (1985). Aging and mental disorders. In J.E. Birren & K.W. Schaie (Eds.), *Handbook of psychology of aging* (2nd ed.). New York: Van Nostrand Reinhold.

Last C.G., & Strauss, C.C. (1990). School refusal in anxiety-disordered children and adolescents. *Journal of the American Academy of Child and Adolescent Psychiatry, 29*, 31–35.

Lauer, J., Black, D.W., & Keen, P. (1993). Multiple personality disorder and borderline personality disorder: Distinct entities or variations on a common theme? *Annals of Clinical Psychiatry, 5*, 129–134.

Lazarus, A.A., Davison, G.C., & Polefka, D. (1965). Classical and operant factors in the treatment of a school phobia. *Journal of Abnormal Psychology, 70,* 225–229.

Lee, D., DeQuattro, V., Cox, T., Pyter, L., Foti, A., Allen, J., Barndt, R., Azen, S., & Davison, G.C. (1987). Neurohormonal mechanisms and left ventricular hypertrophy: Effects of hygienic therapy. *Journal of Human Hypertension, 1,* 147–151.

Leff, J., Sartorius, N., Jablensky, A., Korten, A., & Ernberg, G. (1992). The International Pilot Study of Schizophrenia: Five-year follow-up findings. *Psychological Medicine, 22,* 131–145.

Lefley, H.P. (1992). Expressed emotion: Conceptual, clinical, and social policy issues. *Hospital and Community Psychiatry, 43,* 591–598.

Leibowitz, S.F. (1987). Hypothalamic neurotransmitters in relation to normal and disturbed eating patterns. In R.J. Wurtman & J.J. Wurtman (Eds.), *Human obesity.* New York: New York Academy of Sciences.

Leitenberg, H., & Slavin, L. (1983). Comparison of attitudes toward transsexuality and homosexuality. *Archives of Sexual Behavior, 12,* 337–346.

Leonard, H.L., Swedo, S.E., Rapoport, J.L., Koby, E.V., Lenane, M.C., Cheslow, D.L., & Hamburger, S.D. (1989). Treatment of obsessive-compulsive disorder with clomipramine and desipramine in children and adolescents: A double-blind crossover comparison. *Archives of General Psychiatry, 46,* 1088–1092.

Lewinsohn, P.M., Hoberman, H.M., & Rosenbaum, M. (1988). A prospective study of risk factors for unipolar depression. *Journal of Abnormal Psychology, 97,* 251–264.

Lewinsohn, P.M., Hoberman, H.M., Teri, L., & Hautzinger, M. (1985). An integrative theory of depression. In S. Reiss & R.R. Bootzin (Eds.), *Theoretical issues in behavior therapy* (pp. 331–359). San Diego: Academic Press.

Lewinsohn, P.M., Rohde, P., Fischer, S.A., & Seeley, J.R. (1991). Age and depression. Unique and shared effects. *Psychology and Aging, 6,* 247–260.

Liberman, R.P., DeRisi, W.J., & Mueser, K.T. (1989). *Social skills training for psychiatric patients.* New York: Pergamon.

Linehan, M.M., Armstrong, H.E., Suarez, R.A., Allmon, D., & Heard, H.L. (1991). Cognitive-behavioral treatment of chronically parasuicidal borderline patients. *Archives of General Psychiatry, 48,* 1060–1064.

Linehan, M.M., Heard, H.L., & Armstrong, H.E. (1992). *Naturalistic follow-up of a behavioral treatment for chronically parasuicidal borderline patients.* Unpublished manuscript, University of Washington.

Lion, J.R. (1978). Outpatient treatment of psychopaths. In W.H. Reid (Ed.), *The psychopath: A comprehensive study of antisocial disorders and behaviors.* New York: Brunner/Mazel.

Lipowski, Z.J. (1983). Transient cognitive disorders (delirium and acute confusional states) in the elderly. *American Journal of Psychiatry, 140,* 1426–1436.

Locke, H.J., & Wallace, K.M. (1959). Short marital adjustment and prediction tests: Their reliability and validity. *Marriage and Family Living, 21,* 251–255.

Logue, A.W. (1991). *The psychology of eating and drinking* (2nd ed.). New York: Freeman.

Loney, J., Langhorne, J.E., Jr., & Paternite, C.E. (1978). An empirical basis for subgrouping the hyperkinetic/minimal brain dysfunction syndrome. *Journal of Abnormal Psychology, 87,* 431–441.

LoPiccolo, J., & Stock, W.E. (1986). Treatment of sexual dysfunction. *Journal of Consulting and Clinical Psychology, 54,* 158–167.

Loranger, A.W., Oldham, J.M., & Tulis, E.H. (1983). Familial transmission of DSM-III borderline personality disorder. *Archives of General Psychiatry, 40,* 795–799.

Loranger, A., Oldham, J.M., & Tulis, E.H. (1987). Structured interviews and borderline personality disorder. *Archives of General Psychiatry, 41,* 565–568.

Lotter, V. (1974). Factors related to outcome in autistic children. *Journal of Autism and Childhood Schizophrenia, 4,* 263–277.

Lotter, V. (1978). Follow-up studies. In M. Rutter & E. Schopler (Eds.), *Autism: A reappraisal of concepts and treatment.* New York: Plenum.

Lovaas, O.I. (1987). Behavioral treatment and normal educational and intellectual functioning in young autistic children. *Journal of Consulting and Clinical Psychology, 55,* 3–9.

Lykken, D.T. (1957). A study of anxiety in the sociopathic personality. *Journal of Abnormal and Social Psychology, 55,* 6–10.

McAdoo, W.G., & DeMyer, M.K. (1978). Personality characteristics of parents. In M. Rutter & E. Schopler (Eds.), *Autism: A reappraisal of concepts and treatment.* New York: Plenum.

McBride, P.A., Anderson, G.M., Hertzig, M.E., Sweeney, J.A., et al. (1989). Serotonergic responsivity in male young adults with autistic disorder: Results of a pilot study. *Archives of General Psychiatry, 46,* 213–221.

McCord, W., & McCord, J. (1964). *The psychopath: An essay on the criminal mind.* New York: Van Nostrand Reinhold.

McDougle, C.J., Price, L.H., Volkmar, F.R., Goodman, W.K., et al. (1992). Clomipramine in autism: Preliminary of efficacy. *Journal of the American Academy of Child and Adolescent Psychiatry, 31,* 746–750.

MacCullouch, M.J., Williams, C., & Birtles, C.J. (1977). Successful application of aversion therapy to an adolescent exhibitionist. In C. Fischer & H.L. Gochros (Eds.), *Handbook of behavior therapy with sexual problems.* New York: Pergamon.

McGlashan, T.M. (1983). The borderline syndrome: I. Testing three diagnostic systems. *Archives of General Psychiatry, 40,* 1311–1318.

McGrady, A., Nadsady, P.A., & Schumann-Brzezinski, C. (1991). Sustained effects of biofeedback-assisted relaxation in essential hypertension. *Biofeedback and Self-Regulation, 16,* 399–411.

McGue, M., & Gottesman, I.I. (1989). A single dominant gene still cannot account for the transmission of schizophrenia. *Archives of General Psychiatry, 46,* 478–480.

McGue, M., Pickens, R.W., & Suikis, D.S. (1992). Sex and age effects on the inheritance of alcohol problems: A twin study. *Journal of Abnormal Psychology, 101,* 3–17.

McNally, R.J. (1987). Preparedness and phobias: A review. *Psychological Bulletin, 101,* 283–303.

McNally, R.J. (1990). Psychological approaches to panic disorder: A review. *Psychological Bulletin, 108,* 403–419.

Mack, J.E. (1975). Borderline states: An historical perspective. In J.E. Mack (Ed.), *Borderline states in psychiatry.* New York: Grune and Stratton.

Mahler, M. (1965). On early infantile psychosis. The symbiotic and autistic syndromes. *Journal of the American Academy of Psychiatry, 4,* 554–568.

Maier, W., Lichtermann, D., Klingler, T., Heun, R., & Hallmayer, J. (1992). Prevalences of personality disorders (DSM-III-R) in the community. *Journal of Personality Disorders, 6*, 187–196.

Maj, J. (1992). Clinical prediction of response to lithium prophylaxis in bipolar patients: A critical update. *Lithium, 3*, 15–21.

Mandler, G. (1975). *Mind and emotion.* New York: Wiley.

Mannuzza, S., Klein, R.G., Bessler, A., Malloy, P., & LaPadula, M. (1993). Adult outcome of hyperactive boys: Educational achievement, occupational rank, and psychiatric status. *Archives of General Psychiatry, 50*, 563–551.

Manos, N., Vasilopoulou, E., & Sotiriou, M. (1987). DSM-III diagnoses borderline disorder and depression. *Journal of Personality Disorders, 1*, 263–268.

Manschreck, T.C. (1992). Delusional disorders: Clinical concepts and diagnostic strategies. *Psychiatric Annals, 22*, 241–251.

Manton, K.G., Blazer, D.G., & Woodbury, M.A. (1987). Suicide in middle age and later life: Sex and race specific life table and cohort analyses. *Journal of Gerontology, 42*, 219–227.

Marder, S.R., Ames, D., Wirshing, W.C., & Van Putten, T. (1993). Schizophrenia. *Psychiatric Clinics of North America, 16*, 567–587.

Marks, I.M. (1970). The classification of phobic disorders. *British Journal of Psychiatry, 116*, 377–386.

Marks, I.M. (1986). Epidemiology of anxiety. *Social Psychiatry, 21*, 167–171.

Marks, I.M. (1987). *Fears, phobias, and rituals: Panic, anxiety, and their disorders.* New York: Oxford University Press.

Marks, I.M., Hodgson, R., & Rachman, S. (1975). Treatment of chronic obsessive-compulsive neurosis by in-vivo exposure. *British Journal of Psychiatry, 127*, 349–364.

Marlatt, G.A., Demming, B., & Reid, J.B. (1973). Loss of control drinking in alcoholics: An experimental analogue. *Journal of Abnormal Psychology, 81*, 233–241.

Marlatt, G.A., & Gordon, J.R. (1978). *Determinants of relapse: Implications for the maintenance of behavior change.* Paper presented at the Tenth International Conference on Behavior Modification, Banff, Alberta, Canada.

Marshall, W.L., Eccles, A., & Barbaree, H.E. (1991). The treatment of exhibitionism: A focus on sexual deviance versus cognitive and relationship factors. *Behaviour Research and Therapy, 29*, 129–135.

Masters, W.H., & Johnson, V.E. (1966). *Human sexual response.* Boston: Little, Brown.

Masters, W.H., & Johnson, V.E. (1970). *Human sexual inadequacy.* Boston: Little, Brown.

Masters, W.H., Johnson, V.E., & Kolodny, R.C. (1985). *Human sexuality* (2nd ed.). Boston: Little, Brown.

Mate-Kole, C., Freschi, M., & Robin, A. (1990). A controlled study of psychological and social change after surgical gender reassignment in selected male transsexuals. *British Journal of Psychiatry, 157*, 261–264.

Matthews, K.A., & Rakaczky, C.J. (1987). Familial aspects of Type A behavior and physiologic reactivity to stress. In T. Dembroski & T. Schmidt (Eds.), *Behavioral factors in coronary heart disease.* Heidelberg: Springer-Verlag.

May, P.R.A., Tuma, A.H., Yale, C., Potepan, P., & Dixon, W.J. (1976). Schizophrenia—A follow-up study of results of treatment: II. Hospital stay over two to five years. *Archives of General Psychiatry, 33*, 481–486.

May, P.R.A., Van Putten, T., Yale, C., Potepan, P., Jenden, D.J., Fairchild, M.D., Goldstein, M.J., & Dixon, W.J. (1976). Predicting individual responses to drug treatment in schizophrenia: A test dose model. *Journal of Nervous and Mental Disease, 162*, 177–183.

Mednick, S.A., Machon, R.A., Huttunen, M.O., & Bonett, D. (1988). Adult schizophrenia following prenatal exposure to an influenza epidemic. *Archives of General Psychiatry, 45*, 189–192.

Meehl, P.E. (1964). *Manual for use with checklist of schizotypic signs.* Unpublished manuscript, University of Minnesota Medical School, Minneapolis.

Merskey, H. (1992). The manufacture of personalities: The production of multiple personality disorder. *British Journal of Psychiatry, 160*, 327–340.

Merson, S., Tyrer, P., Duke, P., & Henderson, F. (1994). Interrater reliability of ICD-10 guidelines for the diagnosis of personality disorders. *Journal of Personality Disorders, 8*, 89–95.

Meyer, J.K. (1974). Clinical variants among sex reassignment applicants. *Archives of Sexual Behavior, 3*, 527–558.

Meyer, J.K., & Reter, D.J. (1979). Sex reassignment: Follow-up. *Archives of General Psychiatry, 36*, 1010–1015.

Meyer, W.J., Cole, C., & Emory, E. (1992). Depo provera treatment for sex offending behavior: An evaluation of outcome. *Bulletin of the American Academy of Psychiatry and the Law, 20*, 249–259.

Minuchin, S., Rosman, B.L., & Baker, L. (1978). *Psychosomatic families: Anorexia nervosa in context.* Cambridge, MA: Harvard University Press.

Miklowitz, D.J., Goldstein, J.J., Nuechterlein, K.H., Snyder, K.S., & Mintz, J. (1988). Family factors and the course of bipolar affective disorder. *Archives of General Psychiatry, 45*, 225–231.

Miller, N.E. (1948). Studies of fear as an acquirable drive: I. Fear as motivation and fear-reduction as reinforcement in the learning of new responses. *Journal of Experimental Psychology, 38*, 89–101.

Miller, R.G., Palkes, H.S., & Stewart, M.A. (1973). Hyperactive children in suburban elementary schools. *Child Psychiatry and Human Development, 4*, 121–127.

Millon, T. (1981). *Disorders of personality: DSM-III, Axis II.* New York: Wiley.

Mischel, W., & Peake, P.K. (1982). Beyond déjà vu in the search for cross-situational consistency. *Psychological Review, 89*, 730–735.

Mishler, E.G., & Waxler, N.E. (1968). *Interaction in families: An experimental study of family processes and schizophrenia.* New York: Wiley.

Mitchell, P., Waters, B., Morrison, N., et al. (1991). Close linkage of bipolar disorder to chromosome 11 markers is excluded in two large Australian pedigrees. *Journal of Affective Disorders, 21*, 23–32.

Mitchell-Heggs, N., Kelly, D., & Richardson, A. (1976). Stereotactic limbic leucotomy—A follow-up at 16 months. *British Journal of Psychiatry, 128*, 226–240.

Modestin, J. (1987). Quality of interpersonal relationships: The most characteristic DSM-III BPD criterion. *Comprehensive Psychiatry, 28*, 397–402.

Modestin, J. (1992). Multiple personality disorder in Switzerland. *American Journal of Psychiatry, 149*, 88–92.

Mohr, J.W., Turner, R.E., & Jerry, M.B. (1964). *Pedophilia and exhibitionism.* Toronto: University of Toronto Press.

Monroe, S.M., & Simons, A.D. (1991). Diathesis-stress theories in the context of life stress research: Implications for the depressive disorders. *Psychological Bulletin, 110,* 406–425.

Morokoff, P.J. (1989). Sex bias and primary orgasmic dysfunction. *American Psychologist, 44,* 73–75.

Mowrer, O.H. (1947). On the dual nature of learning—A reinterpretation of "conditioning" and "problem-solving." *Harvard Educational Review, 17,* 102–148.

Mueser, K.T., Bellack, A.S., Wade, J.H., Sayers, S.L., Tierney, A., & Haas, G. (1993). Expressed emotion, social skills, and response to negative affect in schizophrenia. *Journal of Abnormal Psychology, 102,* 339–351.

Myers, J.K., Weissman, M.M., Tishler, G.L., Holzer, C.E., Leaf, P.J., Orvaschel, J., Anthony, J.C., Boyd, J.H., Burke, J.D., Kramer, M., & Stoltzman, R. (1984). Six-month prevalence of psychiatric disorders in three communities. *Archives of General Psychiatry, 41,* 959–970.

Nathan, S.C. (1986). The epidemiology of the DSM-III psychosexual dysfunctions. *Journal of Sex and Marital Therapy, 12,* 267–281.

Netter, P., & Neuhauser-Metternich, S. (1991). Types of aggressiveness and catecholamine response in essential hypertensives and healthy controls. *Journal of Psychosomatic Research, 35,* 409–419.

Newman, J.P., & Kosson, D.S. (1986). Passive avoidance learning in psychopathic and nonpsychopathic offenders. *Journal of Abnormal Psychology, 95,* 257–263.

Newman, J.P., Kosson, D.S., & Patterson, D.S. (1992). Delay of gratification in psychopathic and nonpsychopathic offenders. *Journal of Abnormal Psychology, 101,* 630–636.

Nigg, J.T., Lohr, N.E., Westen, D., Gold, L.J., & Silk, K.R. (1992). Malevolent object representations in borderline personality and major depression. *Journal of Abnormal Psychology, 101,* 61–67.

Noe, J.M., Sato, R., Coleman, C., & Laub, D.R. (1978). Construction of male genitalia: The Stanford experience. *Archives of Sexual Behavior, 7,* 297–303.

Noyes, R., Jr. (1991). Treatments of choice for anxiety disorders. In W. Coryell & G. Winokur (Eds.), *The clinical management of anxiety disorders* (pp. 140–153). New York: Oxford University Press.

O'Connell, R.A. (1986). Psychosocial factors in a model of manic-depressive disease. *Integrative Psychiatry, 4,* 150–154.

O'Donohue, W., & Elliott, A. (1992). The current status of post-traumatic stress disorder as a diagnostic category: Problems and proposals. *Journal of Traumatic Stress, 5,* 421–439.

O'Donohue, W., & Geer, J.H. (1993). *Handbook of sexual dysfunctions: Assessment and treatment.* Boston: Allyn & Bacon.

O'Donohue, W., Letourneau, E., & Geer, J.H. (1993). Premature ejaculation. In W. O'Donohue & James H. Geer (Eds.), *Handbook of sexual dysfunctions: Assessment and treatment* (pp. 303–334). Boston: Allyn & Bacon.

Ogata, S.N., Silk, K.R., Goodrich, S., et al. (1990). Childhood sexual and physical abuse in adult patients with borderline personality disorder. *American Journal of Psychiatry, 147,* 1008–1013.

Ogloff, J.R., & Wong, S. (1990). Electrodermal and cardiovascular evidence of a coping response in psychopaths. *Criminal Justice and Behavior, 17*, 231–245.

Öhman, A., Erixon, G., & Löfberg, I. (1975). Phobias and preparedness: Phobic versus neutral pictures as conditioned stimuli for human autonomic responses. *Journal of Abnormal Psychology, 84*, 41–45.

O'Leary, K.D. (1980). Pills or skills for hyperactive children? *Journal of Applied Behavior Analysis, 13*, 193–204.

Orne, M.T., Dinges, D.F., & Orne, E.C. (1984). On the differential diagnosis of multiple personality in the forensic case. *International Journal of Clinical and Experimental Hypnosis, 32*, 118–169.

Paris, J. (1990). Completed suicide in borderline personality disorder. *Psychiatric Annals, 20*, 19–21.

Parnas, J., Cannon, T.D., Jacobsen, B., Schulsinger, H., Schulsinger, F., & Mednick, S.A. (1993). Lifetime DSM-III-R diagnostic outcomes in the offspring of schizophrenic mothers: Results from the Copenhagen high-risk study. *Archives of General Psychiatry, 50*, 707–714.

Patel, C., Marmot, M.G., Terry, D.J., Carruthers, M., Hunt, B., & Patel, M. (1985). Trial of relaxation in reducing coronary risk: Four-year follow-up. *British Medical Journal, 290*, 1103–1106.

Paternite, C.E., & Loney, J. (1980). Childhood hyperkinesis: Relationships between symptomatology and home environment. In C.K. Whalen & B. Henker (Eds.), *Hyperactive children*. New York: Academic Press.

Patrick, C.J., Bradley, M.M., & Lang, P.J. (1993). Emotion in the criminal psychopath: Startle reflex modulation. *Journal of Abnormal Psychology, 102*, 82–92.

Pauly, I.B. (1965). Male psychosexual inversion: Transsexualism. *Archives of General Psychiatry, 13*, 172–191.

Pauly, I.B. (1974). Female transsexualism: Part I. *Archives of Sexual Behavior, 3*, 487–507.

Pauls, D.L. (1992). The genetics of obsessive compulsive disorder and Gilles de la Tourette's syndrome. *Psychiatric Clinics of North America, 15*, 759–766.

Paykel, E.S. (1988). Antidepressants: Their efficacy and place in therapy. *Journal of Psychopharmacology, 2*, 105–118.

Pelham, W.E., McBurnett, K., Harper, G.W., Milich, R., Murphy, D.A., Clinton, J., & Thiele, C. (1990). Methylphenidate and baseball playing in ADHD children: Who's on first? *Journal of Consulting and Clinical Psychology, 58*, 130–133.

Penk, W., Keane, T., Robinowitz, R., Fowler, D.R., Bell, W.E., & Finkelstein, A. (1988). Post-traumatic stress disorder. In R.L. Green (Ed.), *The MMPI: Use with specific populations* (pp. 198–213). Philadelphia: Grune & Stratton.

Perilstein, R.D., Lipper, S., & Friedman, L.J. (1991). Three cases of exhibitionism responsive to fluoxetine treatment. *Journal of Clinical Psychiatry, 52*, 169–170.

Perls, F.S., Hefferline, R.F., & Goodman, P. (1951). *Gestalt therapy: Excitement and growth in the human personality*. New York: Julian Press.

Perris, C. (1992). Bipolar–unipolar distinction. In E.S. Paykel (Ed.), *Handbook of affective disorders* (2nd ed., pp. 57–75). New York: Guilford.

Perry, C.J., & Klerman, G.L. (1980). Clinical features of the borderline personality disorder. *American Journal of Psychiatry, 13*, 165–173.

Perse, T. (1988). Obsessive-compulsive disorder: A treatment review. *Journal of Clinical Psychiatry, 49*, 48–55.

Persson, G., & Nordlund, C.L. (1985). Agoraphobics and social phobics: Differences in background factors, syndrome profiles, and therapeutic response. *Acta Psychiatrica Scandinavica, 71*, 148–159.

Peterson, C., & Seligman, M.E.P. (1984). Causal explanations as a risk factor for depression: Theory and evidence. *Psychological Review, 91*, 347–374.

Peterson, D.R. (1954). The diagnosis of subclinical schizophrenia. *Journal of Consulting Psychology, 18*, 198–200.

Pfohl, B., Coryell, W., Zimmerman, M., & Stangl, D. (1986). DSM-III personality disorder: Diagnostic overlap and internal consistency of individual DSM-III criteria. *Comprehensive Psychiatry, 27*, 21–34.

Phillips, R.D. (1985). Whistling in the dark? A review of play therapy research. *Psychotherapy, 22*, 752–760.

Pogue-Geile, M.F., & Harrow, M. (1984). Negative and positive symptoms in schizophrenia and depression: A follow-up. *Schizophrenia Bulletin, 10*, 371–387.

Pogue-Geile, M.F., & Zubin, J. (1988). Negative symptomatology and schizophrenia: A conceptual and empirical review. *International Journal of Mental Health, 16*, 3–45.

Pope, H.G., Jonas, J.M., Hudson, J.I., Cohen, B.M., & Gunderson, J.G. (1983). The validity of the DSM-III borderline personality disorder. *Archives of General Psychiatry, 40*, 23–30.

Popiel, D.A., & Susskind, E.C. (1985). The impact of rape. *American Journal of Community Psychology, 13*, 645–676.

Powers, P.S., Schulman, R.G., Gleghorn, A.A., & Prange, M.E. (1987). Perceptual and cognitive abnormalities in bulimia. *American Journal of Psychiatry, 144*, 1456–1460.

Putnam, F.W. (1991). Recent research on multiple personality disorder. *Psychiatric Clinics of North America, 14*, 489–502.

Putnam, F.W., Guroff, J.J., Silberman, E.K., Barban, L., & Post, R.M. (1986). The clinical phenomenology of multiple personality disorder: Review of 100 recent cases. *Journal of Clinical Psychiatry, 47*, 285–293.

Pyle, R.L., Mitchell, J.E., & Eckert, E.D. (1981). Bulimia: A report of 34 cases. *Journal of Clinical Psychology, 42*, 60–64.

Rabins, P.V., & Folstein, M.F. (1982). Delirium and dementia: Diagnostic criteria and fatality rates. *British Journal of Psychiatry, 140*, 149–153.

Rachman, S.J. (1976). The modification of obsessions: A new formulation. *Behavior Research and Therapy, 14*, 437–443.

Rachman, S.J. (1979). Obsessional compulsive disorders. In E.S. Valenstein (Ed.), *The psychosurgery debate: Scientific, legal, and ethical perspectives.* San Francisco: Freeman.

Rachman, S.J., & Hodgson, R.J. (1980). *Obsessions and compulsions.* Englewood, Cliffs, NJ: Prentice-Hall.

Raine, A., O'Brien, M., Chan, C.J. et al. (1990). Reward learning in adolescent psychopaths. *Journal of Abnormal Child Psychology, 18*, 451–463.

Raine, A., & Venables, P.H. (1987). Contingent negative variation, P3 evoked potentials, and antisocial behavior. *Psychophysiology, 24*, 191–199.

Rapee, R.M. (1991). Generalized anxiety disorder: A review of clinical features and theoretical concepts. *Clinical Psychology Review, 11*, 419–440.

Rapee, R.M., & Barlow, D.H. (1988). Cognitive-behavioral treatment of panic disorder. *Psychiatric Annals, 18*, 473–477.

Rapoport, J.L., Buchsbaum, M.S., Weingartner, H., Zahn, T.P., Ludlow, C. & Mikkelsen, E.J. (1980). Dextroamphetamine: Its cognitive and behavioral effects in normal and hyperactive boys and normal men. *Archives of General Psychiatry, 37*, 933–943.

Rasmussen, S.A., & Eisen, J.L. (1992). The epidemiology and clinical features of obsessive compulsive disorder. *Psychiatric Clinics of North America, 15*, 743–758.

Rather, B.C., Goldman, M.S., Roehrich, L., & Brannick, M. (1992). Empirical modelling of an alcohol expectancy memory network using multidimensional scaling. *Journal of Abnormal Psychology, 101*, 174–183.

Regier, D.A., Boyd, J.H., Burke, J.D., Rae, D.S., et al. (1988). One-month prevalence of mental disorders in the United States: Based on five epidemiologic catchment area sites. *Archives of General Psychiatry, 45*, 977–986.

Rekers, G.A., Kilgus, M., & Rosen, A.C. (1990). Long-term effects of treatment for gender identity disorder of childhood. *Journal of Psychology and Human Sexuality, 3*, 121–153.

Resick, P.A., & Schnicke, M.K. (1992). Cognitive processing therapy for sexual assault victims. *Journal of Consulting and Clinical Psychology, 60*, 748–756.

Resnick, H.S., Kilpatrick, D.G., Best, C.L., & Kramer, T.L. (1992). Vulnerability-stress factors in development of posttraumatic stress disorder. *Journal of Nervous and Mental Disease, 180*, 424–430.

Restak, R.M. (1979). The sex-change conspiracy. *Psychology Today, 13*, 20–24.

Rice, M.E., Harris, G.T., & Cormier, C.A. (1992). An evaluation of a maximum security therapeutic community for psychopaths and other mentally disordered offenders. *Law and Human Behavior, 16*, 399–412.

Ricks, D.M. (1972). *The beginning of vocal communication in infants and autistic children.* Unpublished dissertation, University of London.

Ridley, C.R. (1984). Clinical treatment of the nondisclosing black client. *American Psychologist, 39*, 1234–1244.

Riggs, D.S., Dancu, C.V., Gershuny, B.S., Greenberg, D., & Foa, E.B. (1992). Anger and post-traumatic stress disorder in female crime victims. *Journal of Traumatic Stress, 5*, 613–625.

Rimland, B. (1964). *Infantile autism.* New York: Appleton-Century-Crofts.

Ritvo, E.R., Freeman, B.J., Geller, E., & Yuwiler, A. (1983). Effects of fenfluramine on 14 outpatients with the syndrome of autism. *Journal of the American Academy of Child Psychiatry, 22*, 549–558.

Robins, L.N. (1966). *Deviant children grown up.* Baltimore: Williams and Wilkins.

Robins, L.N., Helzer, J.E., Weissman, M.M., et al. (1984). Lifetime prevalence of specific psychiatric disorders in three sites. *Archives of General Psychiatry, 41*, 942–949.

Robins, L.N., & Regier, D.A. (Eds.). (1991). *Psychiatric disorders in America: The Epidemiologic Catchment Area Study.* New York: Free Press.

Rodin, J., & Langer, E.J. (1977). Long-term effects of a control-relevant intervention with the institutionalized aged. *Journal of Personality and Social Psychology, 35,* 897–902.

Rosen, W.G., Mohns, R.C., Johns, C.A., Small, N.S., Kendler, K.S., Horvath, T.B., & Davis, K.L. (1984). Positive and negative symptoms in schizophrenia. *Psychiatry Research, 13,* 277–284.

Rosenblatt, R.A., & Spiegel, C. (1988, December 2). Half of state's nursing homes fall short in federal study. *Los Angeles Times,* Part I, pp. 3–34.

Ross, A.O., & Nelson, R. (1979). Behavior therapy. In H.S. Quay & J.S. Werry (Eds.), *Psychopathological disorders of childhood.* New York: Wiley.

Ross, C.A. (1991). Epidemiology of multiple personality disorder and dissociation. *Psychiatric Clinics of North America, 14,* 503–517.

Ross, D.M., & Ross, S.A. (1976). *Hyperactivity: Research, theory and action.* New York: Wiley.

Rothbaum, B.O., Foa, E.B., Riggs, D.S., Murdock, T., & Walsh, W. (1992). A prospective examination of post-traumatic stress disorder in rape victims. *Journal of Traumatic Stress, 5,* 455–475.

Royal College of Psychiatrists (1989). *The practical administration of electroconvulsive therapy (EDT).* London: Gaskell.

Russell, G. (1979). Bulimia nervosa: An ominous variant of anorexia nervosa. *Psychological Medicine, 9,* 429–448.

Rutter, M. (1966). Prognosis: Psychotic children in adolescence and early adult life. In J.K. Wing (Ed.), *Childhood autism: Clinical, educational, and social aspects.* New York: Pergamon.

Rutter, M. (1967). Psychotic disorders in early childhood. In A.J. Cooper (Ed.), Recent developments in schizophrenia. *British Journal of Psychiatry, 1,* Special Publication.

Rutter, M. (1974). The development of infantile autism. *Psychological Medicine, 4,* 147–163.

St. Clair, H.R. (1951). Psychiatric interview experience with Negroes. *American Journal of Psychiatry, 108,* 113–119.

Samelson, F. (1980). J.B. Watson's Little Albert, Cyril Burt's twins, and the need for a critical science. *American Psychologist, 35,* 619–625.

Satterfield, J.H., Cantwell, D.P., Lesser, L.I., & Podosin, R.L. (1972). Psychophysiological studies of the hyperactive child. *American Journal of Psychiatry, 128,* 1418–1424.

Saunders, J.B., & Williams, R. (1983). The genetics of alcoholism: Is there an inherited susceptibility to alcohol-related problems? *Alcohol and Alcoholism, 18,* 189–217.

Schachter, S., & Latané, B. (1964). Crime, cognition and the autonomic nervous system. In D. Levine (Ed.), *Nebraska symposium on motivation* (Vol. 12). Lincoln: University of Nebraska Press.

Schain, R.J., & Reynard, C.L. (1975). Effects of a central stimulant drug (methylphenidate) in children with hyperactive behavior. *Pediatrics, 55,* 709–716.

Schmauk, F.J. (1970). Punishment, arousal, and avoidance learning in sociopaths. *Journal of Abnormal Psychology, 76,* 443–453.

Shneider, J.A., & Agras, W.S. (1987). Bulimia in males: A matched comparison with females. *International Journal of Eating Disorders, 6,* 235–242.

Schneider, K. (1959). *Clinical psychopathology.* New York: Grune and Stratton.

Schooler, N.R., & Levine, J. (1983). Strategies for enhancing drug therapy of schizophrenia. *American Journal of Psychotherapy, 37*, 521–532.

Schooler, C., & Spohn, H.E. (1982). Social dysfunction and treatment failure in schizophrenia. *Schizophrenia Bulletin, 8*, 85–98.

Schreiber, F. (1973). *Sybil.* Chicago: Henry Regnery (reprinted by Warner Paperback Library, New York, 1974).

Schulsinger, F. (1972). Psychopathy: Heredity and environment. *International Journal of Mental Health, 1*, 190–206.

Schulz, R., & Williamson, G.M. (1991). A 2-year longitudinal study of depression among Alzheimer's caregivers. *Psychology and Aging, 6*, 569–578.

Schwab, J.J., Fennell, E.B., & Warheit, G.J. (1974). The epidemiology of psychosomatic disorders. *Psychosomatics, 15*, 88–93.

Schwalberg, M.D., Barlow, D.H., Alger, S.A., & Howard, L.J. (1992). Comparison of bulimics, obese binge eaters, social phobics, and individuals with panic disorder on comorbidity across DSM-III anxiety disorders. *Journal of Abnormal Psychology, 101*, 675–682.

Seligman, M.E.P. (1971). Phobias and preparedness. *Behavior Therapy, 2*, 307–320.

Seligman, M.E.P. (1975). *Helplessness: On depression, development, and death.* San Francisco: Freeman.

Semans, J.H. (1956). Premature ejaculation: A new approach. *Southern Medical Journal, 49*, 353–357.

Serban, G., Conte, H.R., & Plutchik, R. (1987). Borderline and schizotypal personality disorders: Mutually exclusive or over-lapping? *Journal of Personality Assessment, 5*, 15–22.

Sher, K.J., & Levenson, R.W. (1982). Risk for alcoholism and individual differences in the stress-response-dampening effect of alcohol. *Journal of Abnormal Psychology, 91*, 350–367.

Sher, K.J., Walitzer, K.S., Wood, P.K., & Brent, E.F. (1991). Characteristics of children of alcoholics: Putative risk factors, substance use and abuse, and psychopathology. *Journal of Abnormal Psychology, 100*, 427–448.

Sigman, M., Ungerer, J.A., Mundy, P., & Sherman, T. (1987). Cognition in autistic children. In D.J. Cohen, A.M. Donellan, & R. Paul (Eds.), *Handbook of autism and pervasive developmental disorders.* New York: Wiley.

Silverstone, T. (1992). New aspects in the treatment of depression. *International Clinical Psychopharmacology, 6, (Suppl. 5)*, 41–44.

Singer, M., & Wynne, L.C. (1963). Differentiating characteristics of the parents of childhood schizophrenics, childhood neurotics, and young adult schizophrenics. *American Journal of Psychiatry, 120*, 234–243.

Smith, J.W., Frawley, P.J., & Polissar, L. (1991). Six- and twelve-month abstinence rates in inpatient alcoholics treated with aversion therapy compared with matched inpatients from a treatment registry. *Alcoholism: Clinical and Experimental Research, 15*, 862–870.

Smith, S.S., & Newman, J.P. (1990). Alcohol and drug dependence in psychopathic and nonpsychopathic criminal offenders. *Journal of Abnormal Psychology, 99*, 430–439.

Smith, W.H. (1993). Incorporating hypnosis into the psychotherapy of patients with multiple personality disorder. *Bulletin of the Menninger Clinic, 57*, 344–354.

Snyder, S.H. (1974). *Madness and the brain.* New York: McGraw-Hill.

Sobell, L.C., Toneatto, A., & Sobell, M.B. (1990). Behavior therapy. In A.S. Bellack & M. Hersen (Eds.), *Handbook of comparative treatments for adult disorders* (pp. 479–505). New York: Wiley.

Sobell, M.B., & Sobell, L.C. (1976). Second-year treatment outcome of alcoholics treated by individualized behavior therapy: Results. *Behavior Research and Therapy, 14,* 195–215.

Soloff, P.H., Cornelius, J., George, A., Nathan, S., Perel, J.M., & Ulrich, R.F. (1993). Efficacy of phenelzine and haloperidol in borderline personality disorder. *Archives of General Psychiatry, 50,* 377–386.

Spector, I.P., & Carey, M.P. (1990). Incidence and prevalence of the sexual dysfunctions: A critical review of the empirical literature. *Archives of Sexual Behavior, 19,* 389–408.

Solyom, L., Beck, P., Solyom, C., & Hugel, R. (1974). Some etiological factors in phobic neurosis. *Canadian Psychiatric Association Journal, 19,* 69–78.

Sorensen, T. (1981). A follow-up study of operated transsexual males. *Acta Psychiatrica Scandinavica, 63,* 486–503.

Spanos, N.P., Weekes, J.R., & Bertrand, L.D. (1985). Multiple personality: A social psychological perspective. *Journal of Abnormal Psychology, 94,* 362–376.

Speilberger, C.D., Johnson, E.H., Russell, S.F., Crane, F.J., & Worden, T.J. (1985). The experience and expression of anger. In M.A. Chesney & R.H. Rosenman (Eds.), *Anger and hostility in cardiovascular and behavioral disorders.* New York: Hemisphere.

Spitzer, R.L., Endicott, J., & Gibbons, M. (1979). Crossing the border into borderline personality and borderline schizophrenia: The development of criteria. *Archives of General Psychiatry, 36,* 17–24.

Sprague, R.L., Cohen, M., & Werry, J.S. (1974). *Normative data on the Conners Teacher Rating Sale and abbreviated scale.* Technical Report. Children's Research Center, University of Illinois, Urbana.

Steele, C.M., & Josephs, R.A. (1988). Drinking your troubles away: II. An attention-allocation model of alcohol's effects on psychological stress. *Journal of Abnormal Psychology, 97,* 196–205.

Steffenburg, S. (1991). Neuropsychological assessment of children with autism: A population-based study. *Developmental Medicine and Child Neurology, 33,* 495–511.

Steffenburg, S., Gillberg, C., Hellgren, L., Andersson, L. et al. (1989). A twin study of autism in Denmark, Finland, Iceland, Norway and Sweden. *Journal of Child Psychology and Psychiatry and Allied Disciplines, 30,* 405–416.

Stewart, M.A., Pitts, F.N., Craig, A.G., & Dieruf, W. (1966). The hyperactive child syndrome. *American Journal of Orthopsychiatry, 36,* 861–867.

Stokes, P. (1993). Fluoxetine: A five-year review. *Clinical Therapeutics, 15,* 216–243.

Stoller, R.J. (1985). *Presentations of gender.* New Haven: Yale University Press.

Stoller, R.J., & Herdt, G.H. (1985). Theories of the origin of male homosexuality: A cross-cultural look. *Archives of General Psychiatry, 42,* 399–404.

Stone, H.H. (1987). Psychotherapy of borderline patients in light of long-term follow-up. *Bulletin of the Menninger Clinic, 51,* 231–247.

Stone, L.J., & Hokanson, J.E. (1969). Arousal reduction via self-punitive behavior. *Journal of Personality and Social Psychology, 12,* 72–79.

Striegel-Moore, R.H., Silberstein, L.R., & Rodin, J. (1993). The social self in bulimia nervosa: Public self-consciousness, social anxiety, and perceived fraudulence. *Journal of Abnormal Psychology, 102,* 297–304.

Strober, M. (1986). Anorexia nervosa: History and psychological concepts. In K.D. Brownell & J.P. Foreyt (Eds.), *Handbook of eating disorders.* New York: Basic Books.

Strober, M., & Katz, J.L. (1987). Do eating disorders and affective disorders share a common etiology? A dissenting opinion. *International Journal of Eating Disorders, 6,* 171–180.

Suddath, R.L., Christison, G.W., Torrey, E.F., Casanova, M.R., & Weinberger, D.R. (1990). Anatomical abnormalities in the brains of monozygotic twins discordant for schizophrenia. *New England Journal of Medicine, 322,* 789–794.

Suedfeld, P., & Landon, P.B. (1978). Approaches to treatment. In R.D. Hare & D. Schalling (Eds.), *Psychopathic behavior: Approaches to research.* New York: Wiley.

Sullivan, P.A., Procci, W.R., DeQuattro, V., Schoentgen, S., Levine, D., Van der Meulen, J., & Bornheimer, J.F. (1981). Anger, anxiety, guilt and increased basal and stress-induced neurogenic tone: Causes or effects in primary hypertension? *Clinical Science, 61,* 389–392.

Sullivan, P.A., Schoentgen, S., DeQuattro, V., Procci, W., Levine, D., Van der Meulen, J., & Bornheimer, J.F. (1981). Anxiety, anger, and neurogenic tone at rest and in stress, in patients with primary hypertension. *Hypertension, 3,* 119–123.

Suppes, T., Baldessarini, R.J., Faedda, G.L., & Tohen, M. (1991). Risk of recurrence following discontinuation of lithium treatment in bipolar disorder. *Archives of General Psychiatry, 48,* 1082–1088.

Sussman, N., & Chou, J.C.Y. (1988). Current issues in benzodiazepine use for anxiety disorders. *Psychiatric Annals, 18,* 139–145.

Swartz, M., Blazer, D., George, L., & Winfield, I. (1990). Estimating the prevalence of borderline personality in the community. *Journal of Personality Disorders,* 257–272.

Szatmari, P., Offord, D.R., & Boyle, M.H. (1989). Ontario Child Health Study: Prevalence of attention deficit disorder with hyperactivity. *Journal of Child Psychology and Psychiatry and Allied Disciplines, 30,* 219–230.

Tallmadge, J., & Barkley, R.A. (1983). The interactions of hyperactive and normal boys with their mothers and fathers. *Journal of Abnormal Child Psychology, 11,* 565–579.

Teasdale, J.D. (1974). Learning models of obsessional-compulsive disorder. In H.R. Beech (Ed.), *Obsessional states.* London: Methuen.

Tennant, C. (1988). Parental loss in childhood: Its effect in adult life. *Archives of General Psychiatry, 45,* 1045–1050.

Thigpen, C.H., & Cleckley, H.M. (1957). *The three faces of Eve.* New York: McGraw-Hill.

Thigpen, C.H., & Cleckley, H.M. (1984). On the incidence of multiple personality disorder. *International Journal of Clinical and Experimental Hypnosis, 32,* 63–66.

Thomas, J.A., & Dobbins, J.E. (1986). The color line and social distance in the genesis of essential hypertension. *Journal of the National Medical Association, 78,* 532–536.

Thompson, T. (1993, November 21). The wizard of Prozac: A pilgrimage to the center of a medical debate. *Washington Post*, pp. F1–F5.

Thorpe, G.L., & Burns, L.E. (1983). *The agoraphobic syndrome.* New York: Wiley.

Thyer, B.A. (1991). Diagnosis and treatment of child and adolescent anxiety disorders. *Behavior Modification, 15,* 310–325.

Thyer, B.A., & Curtis, G.C. (1984). The effects of ethanol on phobic anxiety. *Behaviour Research and Therapy, 22,* 599–610.

Tollison, C.D., & Adams, H.E. (1979). *Sexual disorders: Treatment, theory, research.* New York: Gardner.

Torgersen, S. (1983). Genetic factors in anxiety disorders. *Archives of General Psychiatry, 40,* 1085–1089.

Treffert, D.A., McAndrew, J.B., & Dreifuerst, P. (1973). An inpatient treatment program and outcome for 57 autistic and schizophrenic children. *Journal of Autism and Childhood Schizophrenia, 3,* 138–153.

Trull, T.J., Widiger, T.A., & Francis, A. (1987). Covariation of criteria for avoidant, schizoid, and dependent personality disorders. *American Journal of Psychiatry, 144,* 767–771.

Tucker, J.A., Vuchinich, R.E., Downey, K.K. (1992). In K.S. Calhoun & H.E. Adams (Eds.), *Handbook of clinical behavior therapy* (pp. 203–223). New York: Wiley.

Tynes, L.L., White, K., & Steketee, G.S. (1990). Toward a new nosology of obsessive compulsive disorder. *Comprehensive Psychiatry, 31,* 465–480.

Uhl, G.R., Perscio, A.M., & Smith, S.S. (1992). Current excitement with D2 dopamine receptor alleles in substance abuse. *Archives of General Psychiatry, 49,* 157–160.

U.S. Department of Health and Human Services, National Center for Health Statistics (1990, August 30). *Monthly vital statistics.* Washington, DC: U.S. Government Printing Office.

Vaughn, C.E., & Leff, J.P. (1976). The influence of family and social factors on the course of psychiatric illness: A comparison of schizophrenic and depressed neurotic patients. *British Journal of Psychiatry, 129,* 125–137.

Vaughn, C.E., Snyder, K.S., Jones, S., Freeman, W.B., & Falloon, I.R.H. (1984). Family factors in schizophrenic relapse: Replication in California of British research on expressed emotion. *Archives of General Psychiatry, 41,* 1169–1177.

Verschoor, A.M., & Poortinga, J. (1988). Psychosocial differences between Dutch male and female transsexuals. *Archives of Sexual Behavior, 17,* 173–178.

Wakefield, J. (1988). Female primary orgasmic dysfunction: Masters and Johnson versus DSM-III-R on diagnosis and incidence. *Journal of Sex Research, 24,* 363–377.

Waldinger, R.J., & Gunderson, J.G. (1984). Completed psychotherapies with borderline patients. *American Journal of Psychotherapy, 38,* 190–202.

Warner, P., & Bancroft, J. (1986). Sex therapy outcome research: A reappraisal of methodology. 2. Methodological considerations. *Psychological Medicine, 16,* 855–863.

Warshaw, R. (1988). *I never called it rape: The Ms. report on recognizing, fighting, and surviving acquaintance rape.* New York: Harper & Row.

Watson, J.B., & Rayner, R. (1920). Conditioned emotional reactions. *Journal of Experimental Psychology, 3,* 1–14.

Watt, N.F. (1978). Patterns of childhood social development in adult schizophrenics. *Archives of General Psychiatry, 35,* 160–170.

Watt, N.F., & Lubensky, A. (1976). Childhood roots of schizophrenia. *Journal of Consulting and Clinical Psychology, 44,* 363–375.

Wawrose, F.E., & Sisto, T.M. (1992). Clomipramine and a case of exhibitionism. *American Journal of Psychiatry, 149,* 843.

Wegner, D.M. (1989). *White bears and other unwanted thoughts: Suppression, obsession, and the psychology of mental control.* New York: Viking Penguin.

Weiner, H. (1977). *Psychobiology and human disease.* New York: Elsevier.

Weiss, G., Minde, K., Werry, J.S., Douglas, V., & Nemeth, E. (1971). Studies on the hyperactive child: VII. Five-year follow-up. *Archives of General Psychiatry, 24,* 409–414.

Weissberg, M. (1993). Multiple personality disorder and iatrogenesis: The cautionary tale of Anna O. *International Journal of Clinical and Experimental Hypnosis, 41,* 15–34.

Weissman, M.M. (1985). The epidemiology of anxiety disorders: Rates, risks, and familial patterns. In A.H. Tuma & J.D. Maser (Eds.), *Anxiety and the anxiety disorders.* Hillsdale, NJ: Erlbaum.

Weissman, M.M. (1990). The hidden patient: Unrecognized panic disorder. *Journal of Clinical Psychiatry, 51 (Suppl.),* 5–8.

Weissman, M.M. (1993). The epidemiology of personality disorders: A 1990 update. *Journal of Personality Disorders (Suppl.),* 44–62.

Weissman, M.M., Bruce, M.L., Leaf, P.J., Florio, L.P., & Holzer, C. (1991). Affective disorders. In L.N. Robins & D.A. Regier (Eds.), *Psychiatric disorders in America: The Epidemiologic Catchment Area Study* (pp. 53–80). New York: Free Press.

Weissman, M.M., & Markowitz, J.C. (1994). Interpersonal psychotherapy: Current status. *Archives of General Psychiatry, 51,* 599–606.

Welner, A.W., Welner, Z., & Leonard, M.A. (1977). Bipolar and manic-depressive disorder: A reassessment of course and outcome. *Comprehensive Psychiatry, 18,* 327–332.

Werry, J.S., Weiss, G., & Douglas, V. (1964). Studies on the hyperactive child: I. Some preliminary findings. *Canadian Psychiatric Association Journal, 9,* 120–130.

Westen, D., Moses, J., Silk, K.R., Lohr, N., Cohen, R., & Segal, H. (1992). Quality of depressive experience in borderline personality disorder and major depression: When depression is not just depression. *Journal of Personality Disorders, 6,* 382–393.

Whalen, C.K., Henker, B., Buhrmester, D., Hinshaw, S.P., Huber, A., & Laski, K. (1989). Does stimulant medication improve the peer status of hyperactive children? *Journal of Consulting and Clinical Psychology, 57,* 545–549.

Wickramsekara, I. (1977). The application of learning theory to the treatment of a case of exhibitionism. In J. Fischer & H. Gochros (Eds.), *Handbook of behavior therapy with sexual problems.* New York: Pergamon.

Widiger, T.A., & Costa, P.T., Jr. (1994). Personality and personality disorders. *Journal of Abnormal Psychology, 103,* 78–91.

Widiger, T.A., Frances, A., Spitzer, R., & Williams, J. (1988). The DSM-III-R personality disorders: An overview. *American Journal of Psychiatry, 145,* 786–795.

Widiger, T.A., Frances, A., & Trull, T.J. (1987). A psychometric analysis of the social-interpersonal and cognitive-perceptual items for the schizotypal personality disorder. *Archives of General Psychiatry, 44,* 741–745.

Widiger, T.A., & Rogers, J.H. (1989). Prevalence and comorbidity of personality disorders. *Psychiatric Annals, 19,* 132–136.

Widiger, T.A., Trull, T.J., Hurt, S., Clarkin, J., & Francis, A. (1987). A multidimensional scaling of the DSM-III personality disorders. *Archives of General Psychiatry, 44,* 557–566.

Wilkerson, I. (1990, June 7). Physician fulfills a goal: Aiding a person in suicide. *New York Times,* p. A16.

Williamson, D.A., Cubic, B.A., & Gleaves, D.H. (1993). Equivalence of body image disturbance in anorexia and bulimia nervosa. *Journal of Abnormal Psychology, 102,* 173–176.

Wincze, J.P., & Carey, M.P. (1991). *Sexual dysfunction: A guide for assessment and treatment.* New York: Guilford.

Wise, T.N., & Meyer, J.K. (1980). The border area between transvestism and gender dysphoria: Transvestitic applicants for sex reassignment. *Archives of Sexual Behavior, 9,* 327–342.

Witzig, J.S. (1968). The group treatment of male exhibitionists. *American Journal of Psychiatry, 125,* 75–81.

Wolpe, J. & Rowan, V.C. (1988). Panic disorder: A product of classical conditioning: *Behavior Research and Therapy, 26,* 441–450.

Wood, A., Tollefson, G.D., & Birkett, M. (1993). Pharmacotherapy of obsessive-compulsive disorder: Experience with fluoxetine. *International Clinical Psychopharmacology, 8,* 301–306.

Wood, D.L., Sheps, S.G., et al. (1984). Cold pressor test as a predictor of hypertension. *Hypertension, 6,* 301–306.

World Almanac and Book of Facts 1993. (1992). New York: Pharos Books.

World Health Organization. (1990). International classification of diseases and related health care problems (10th ed.). Geneva.

Yalom, I.D., & Lieberman, M.A. (1971). A study of encounter group casualties. *Archives of General Psychiatry, 25,* 16–30.

Yates, A. (1989). Current perspectives on the eating disorders: I. History, psychological and biological aspects. *Journal of the American Academy of Child and Adolescent Psychiatry, 28,* 813–828.

Yates, A. (1990). Current perspectives on the eating disorders: II. Treatment, outcome, and research directions. *Journal of the American Academy of Child and Adolescent Psychiatry, 29,* 1–9.

Zametkin, A.J., Nordahl, T.E., Gross, M., King, A.C., Semple, W.E., Rumsey, J., Hamburger, S., & Cohen R.M. (1990). Cerebral glucose metabolism in adults with hyperactivity of childhood onset. *New England Journal of Medicine, 20,* 1361–1366.

Zanarini, M.C., Gunderson, J.G., Marino, M.F., et al. (1988). DSM-III disorders in the families of borderline outpatients. *Journal of Personality Disorders, 2,* 292–302.

Zarit, S.H. (1980). *Aging and mental disorders: Psychological approaches to assessment and treatment.* New York: Free Press.

Zilbergeld, B., & Evans, M. (1980). The inadequacy of Masters and Johnson. *Psychology Today, 14,* 29–43.

Zimmerman, M., & Coryell, W.H. (1990). Diagnosing personality disorders in the community: A comparison of self-report and interview measures. *Archives of General Psychiatry, 47,* 527–531.

Zucker, K.J., & Green, R. (1992). Psychosexual disorders in children and adolescents. *Journal of Child Psychology and Psychiatry, 33,* 107–151.

INDEX

397